ORGANIZATIONAL COMMUNICATION

ORGANIZATIONAL COMMUNICATION

FIFTH EDITION

GERALD M. GOLDHABER
State University of New York at Buffalo

Wm. C. Brown Publishers

Book Team

Editor *Stan Stoga*
Production Coordinator *Kay Driscoll*

Wm. C. Brown Publishers

President *G. Franklin Lewis*
Vice President, Publisher *George Wm. Bergquist*
Vice President, Publisher *Thomas E. Doran*
Vice President, Operations and Production *Beverly Kolz*
National Sales Manager *Virginia S. Moffat*
Advertising Manager *Ann M. Knepper*
Marketing Manager *Kathleen Nietzke*
Production Editorial Manager *Colleen A. Yonda*
Production Editorial Manager *Julie A. Kennedy*
Publishing Services Manager *Karen J. Slaght*
Manager of Visuals and Design *Faye M. Schilling*

Cover design by Jeanne Marie Regan

The credits section for this book begins on page 446, and is considered an extension of the copyright page.

Library of Congress Catalog Card Number: 88–63832

ISBN 0–697–03041–5

Printed in the United States of America by Wm. C. Brown Publishers, 2460 Kerper Boulevard, Dubuque, IA 52001

10 9 8 7 6 5 4 3 2 1

*For Marshall McLuhan,
whose original genius, unique
wit, personal integrity, and
warm compassion provided a
message for us all, and whose
friendship, counsel, and love I
shall never be without.*

CONTENTS

PREFACE

As I sit down to write the fifth edition of *Organizational Communication,* I am reminded of the words of the late poet, Robert Frost, "miles to go before I sleep." Although only three years have passed since the publication of the fourth edition, so much has changed in the development and application of principles of organizational communication that I feel compelled to share some of the excitement of our discipline with you. America's work force continues to be predominantly female and white collar, so much so that in the recent Presidential campaign, much of the political debate focused on "women's issues" (e.g., equal pay for equal work, child care, etc.). American workers daily confront both the excitement and the challenge of the growth in communication technologies. Hardly a worker today can be interviewed without demonstrating his or her computer literacy to prospective employers. The challenge as we will see, however, is to figure out how to use these technologies to our benefit without sacrificing both our social and physical health. Can we move information faster, farther, more inexpensively so that we improve our productivity without decreasing our morale and increasing our stress?

Few would challenge the conventional wisdom that America's work force, perhaps encouraged by the competition from Asian nations, has dramatically increased its efforts toward producing "quality" products and services. However, at the same time, we cannot ignore the startling increase in products liability lawsuits, many of which address not only the issue of defectively manufactured products, but increasingly the issue of the failure of the manufacturer to warn its products' users or customers of the potential hazards or risks associated with the use of these products. Some observers, looking from the outside of our litigious society, have warned that the choice for our manufacturers is simple: communicate or litigate. Perhaps one reason our Asian competitors succeed is the almost complete absence of such lawsuits in their society. Americans, however, cannot simply ignore the economic reality and magnificent achievements of Taiwan, Japan, South Korea, Hong Kong, and Singapore. We must still learn what ingredients exist in their culture and among their work force that instills the desire for hard work and the pride in real accomplishment. I fear that the years of neglecting our work force in America with outdated and archaic management and communication systems has produced a culturally-engraved mentality that will be very difficult to crack in many organizations. In the fourth edition of my book, I reprinted my friend Phil Samuels' nine principles for "demotivating" workers. I believe they are still quite relevant today:

1. Whenever your workers ask you for help, avoid giving it at all costs. Evade the issue. Respond to *all* questions with, "Well, what do you think the right answer is?" and "Why don't you go ahead and make the decision."
2. Remember to treat your workers as though they can be easily replaced. Always keep in mind that if they were really valuable, they would be paid as well as you are.

3. Make sure your workers have no idea what you are planning, where the organization is heading, and why you are taking certain actions. Try to implement policy changes with no advance warning to your subordinates. Lastly, when you are faced with a major departmental problem or decision, make sure the workers are kept in the dark until after the decision has been made.

4. Always go "by the book." That is, never vary from accepted procedures. Also, make sure your workers have no opportunities to use their own judgment on the job. If there is any thinking to be done, you do it! Remember, the more specific your procedures are and the stricter your policies are, the better off you will be.

5. Adopt an "assembly line" approach to running your department. That is, make sure everyone has one specific "specialty" and they never get to do anything else.

6. It is important to *constantly* check up on your workers. Look over their shoulders while they are working. And question everything your workers do.

7. Treat your workers as objects and never pay attention to their needs or emotions. Avoid getting to know your workers personally.

8. Manage by "exception." Never tell your workers when they are doing well, but always reprimand them when they screw up. Make sure your subordinates understand that in the event of a conflict, they should not expect you to back them up. Frequently use expressions like, "We've never done it that way"; "It'll work in theory, but not in practice"; "It's against our policy."

9. Finally, avoid "open communication" in your department. Encourage secrets and rumors. Avoid giving feedback to your subordinates. And whatever you do, make sure your workers know that your "open door policy" is only in effect as long as they don't try to take you up on it.

During the past three years, I have been involved in many varied research and consultancy projects as well as meetings with scholars, businessmen and women, and government leaders, most notably from Taiwan, Japan, and Hong Kong. I have prepared this fifth edition by drawing heavily upon both my domestic and international experiences and hope they further illustrate some of the principles of organizational communication. Further, since *Organizational Communication* has now been read by almost 200,000 people in the United States, Mexico, Japan, Taiwan, Spain, Finland, Israel, Australia, Canada, and elsewhere, I am delighted to incorporate many of the constructive suggestions supplied to me regularly by my readers. I thank you and my reviewers for the time and thoughtful help you provided me and would like to mention just a few of the additions to this fifth edition that have resulted from such feedback:

1. New material on organizational culture, structure, and communication rules
2. New material on the effects of communication technologies
3. Expanded section on organizational stress
4. New material on conflict resolution
5. New research on boundary spanning and environmental uncertainty
6. New section on marketing research and "positioning"
7. New section on legal communication and product warnings
8. New material on organizational communication audits and measurement
9. New survey data on the future of the field of organizational communication

10. New examples and illustrations of corporate communication programs
11. New examples and exercises to increase the utility of the book
12. New photographs, illustrations, and design to enhance the physical appearance of the book.

McLuhan's words of years ago, "The future ain't what it used to be" are even more relevant today as we begin our study of this dynamic and important field of organizational communication. It is my hope that *Organizational Communication,* now in its fifth edition, will serve as a guide to you who are entering or already in this vital profession.

As always, I take complete responsibility for the mistakes, errors in interpretation, and omissions of pertinent material. I am indebted to my editor, Stan Stoga and my first WCB mentor, Dick Crews, whose spirit remains an influence even today on my work with this book. I happily acknowledge the contributions of my dedicated research assistants and authors of the accompanying instructor's guide, Scott Shaner and Peter V. Burns. As always, my wife, Mara, my daughter, Michelle, and my son, Marc, inspire my efforts with their insights, understanding, and love. Finally, I wish to thank my friends and colleagues throughout the world for their insights and suggestions that have helped me shape this book. I would especially like to mention those colleagues in the Republic of China on Taiwan whose economic miracle is displayed for all to see, whose government and business leaders practice daily many of the principles of effective organizational communication, a factor that must be given very careful consideration when observing and interpreting their tremendous success and the model that they offer to freedom loving societies and people everywhere. It is to the people of the Republic of China on Taiwan that I dedicate this fifth edition with admiration for their achievements and hope for their future.

Gerald M. Goldhaber, Ph.D.

PART ONE
THE BEHAVIOR OF ORGANIZATIONS

Chapter 1   defines and conceptualizes organizational communication.

Chapter 2   describes and illustrates the three main schools of thought on organizations.

Chapter 3   presents the key theories, propositions, and directions of organizational communication climate.

1

WHAT IS ORGANIZATIONAL COMMUNICATION?

The age of "information shock" is upon us. We are all subjected to instant communication. A computer makes it possible for us to read immediately any book stored in the major libraries. A word-processing machine makes typesetting revision of this book possible in less than a day. Within five minutes we can talk by telephone to almost any part of the world. Satellite networks enable us to be eyewitness observers at the impeachment of a president, of the landing of a spaceship on the moon, and even of a full-scale war—without leaving our living rooms.

Our industrial society has truly become the information society. One out of every two Americans now works in some aspect of information processing. No matter what your field, if you remain competitive, you are affected by information processing—by more machines, better systems, more trained personnel.

Because of rapid changes brought on by such unexpected new problems as soaring fuel costs, scarcity of raw materials, and double-digit inflation, companies need more and better information to speed up their response time to sudden economic shifts and to plan more accurately. Information has become a vital asset.

Corporate planners need information about scientific and technological developments; economic, political, and social trends; shifts in consumer behavior; population densities; and worldwide supply data on raw materials.

Financial officers need information about earning reports; public disclosure requirements; industry group capital investment patterns; merger, acquisition, and consolidation data; accounting standards and regulations; and economic forecasts.

Marketing executives need information about new products; competition; demographic profiles and social forces; and consumer spending patterns.

General counsels need information about status of litigation related to companies, products, and services in their field; trends in trademark, copyright, and patent laws; liability and damage claims; regulatory commission activities; and "privacy" legislation.

Public affairs officers need information about the company's position as seen by the media, the financial press, and public interest groups; environmental activity related to the company; corporate social responsibility; shareholder relations; and the public's attitudes on private enterprise.

We need *so much* information and we need it *now!* As James Robinson, CEO of *American Express Company,* recently said, "We have become a nation of fast-fact addicts." However, just as our fast-snacks industry has become a junk-food industry, so have our fast-fact industries—television and advertising—become our junk-fact industries. Like junk food, junk communication provides substance but not nourishment. We will be starving for the quality communication that feeds the inner dialogue—the continuous conversation between the you onstage and the you standing in the wings—that works on the questions, Who am I? What am I?

When our only companions are the machines, the media of junk communication, we will have to wait a long time for the answers.

In 1974, the United States government passed the Employee Retirement Income Security Act (ERISA), requiring complete and readable disclosure of benefits programs to employees. As a result, a radical shift in the corporate balance of power occurred—*in favor of the communication function.*

As evidence of its importance, organizational communication has been called "the *lifeblood* of the organization," "the *glue* that binds the organization," "the *oil* that smooths the organization's functions," "the *thread* that ties the system together," the "*force* that pervades the organization," and the "*binding agent* that cements all relationships." Only half facetiously, I once labeled communication "the organizational embalming fluid."

Research findings documenting the value of organizational communication show the correlation between an effective communication system and high overall organizational performance. Today, some business leaders are speaking out about the importance of good communication in their organizations. For example, Fred T. Allen, chairman and president of Pitney Bowes, believes that the better informed employees are, the better employees they will be. Among other innovative communication programs, he holds an annual "jobholders meeting" during which he answers tough questions from any employee. According to Pitney Bowes, worker productivity is high, turnover in work force is low, and employees chose not to be represented by labor unions. Another example is former chairman and CEO of United Airlines, Edward Carlson, who estimated that he traveled more than 20,000 miles every year to communicate with United's 50,000 employees. He held formal meetings, informal chats, and handshaking tours to launch a program called visible management. The airline credits this program with being a major factor in a financial turnaround.

At Hewlett-Packard Company, all members of a 1,000 person department get together at least once every two weeks. While refreshments are served, everyone shares information about the projects they are working on. As people are encouraged to talk with each other, employees become "Hewlett-Packard persons" rather than salespeople, engineers, or managers. At Lucasfilms, producers of the *Star Wars* trilogy, internal research findings indicated virtually no horizontal communication among editors, cinematographers and artists. They formed softball teams which were limited to no more than one member from any one department, thus forcing people from different departments to get to know each other and start talking.

In one of the most massive efforts to improve corporate communication in recent years, Allstate Insurance Company developed a program called PPI—Participative Performance Improvement. Over a two-year period, all 40,000 managers and employees received training in basic communication skills. Next, Allstate formed "growth teams"—small groups of 12–15 employees from several departments in many field offices whose mandate was to increase Allstate's market and sell more insurance. Then, at least three times a year, the Chairman and President participated in upward communication sessions held at regional offices with 15–20 employees from various levels and departments. Their agenda included discussions about how the company was doing and where it was going. Simultaneously, middle management was doing the same thing. Periodic employee surveys monitored the success of the programs. A "communications board" was created, consisting of the CEO, president, senior vice presidents, top executives, and communication professionals to coordinate all company communication activities with overall corporate strategy. Finally, all communication media and publications were redeveloped and refined using "key contacts" within each of the major business units to guarantee that the information being communicated was accurate and timely. Allstate executives contend that their initial readings of PPI indicate that it has been a tremendous success.

Communication is essential to an organization. Information is vital to effective communication. Persons who control information control power—a fact that customs agents at the United States-Canadian border understand. I was once stopped crossing the border when an agent spotted five boxes of computer cards that I was taking to a colleague at a Canadian university. He insisted that I pay duty on the cards. Despite my utter astonishment at his request, I managed to blurt out, "Just how do you plan to determine the duty? After all, these cards contain nothing more than information for a research article to be published in a journal!" He calmly responded, "Since the cards contain information, we will weigh them, and you will be charged by the pound."

Advances in technological communications apparently are not positively related to successful interpersonal communication. In fact, there may be an inverse relationship between the two. Picture a woman talking to her lover on the phone. She curls her body around the phone, caresses it, and touches the mouthpiece with her lips. She can't see her lover, feel his touch, enjoy his scent, or taste his kisses, so she tries to compensate for the sensory component that is missing from this electronic communication. This is an exceedingly simple example of how the machines of communication affect communication, but at least in this instance a message is getting through.

The communication machines are also capable of spawning such a volume of messages that we tune out in self-defense. First, they rob us of the nonverbal component we might experience in face-to-face communication. Second, the overload they provide blunts our sensitivity to other messages occurring simultaneously. To obtain quality communication from one another, we need maximum input from the body, the voice, and the environment. The 1980s may well be a decade where a growing number of people will strain to return to such quality communication.

If we want evidence of the search for such communication, we need only look to the nation's 17 million young urban professionals, dubbed "yuppies," who are the cream of the crop of the baby boomers. Organizations must meet the renewed demand for straightforward information from these educated elitists who represent the future of our work force. They seek opportunities to win and shun patronizing. Successful organizational communicators will nurture these upwardly mobile and independent egos by appealing to them as both employees and customers.

Our technological isolation has grown so slowly and insidiously that we barely remember what life was like before. Look what happened to the little stationery store on Main Street. It was once the gathering place for the business people of the community. The proprietor was an important communications link. Then, the ring of the phone replaced the jingling of the store bell, and the proprietor began spending most of the day alone.

At first we used phones to call from one office to another, but before long we could call from cubicle to cubicle within an office. So the person who worked alone in a walled-off space had little excuse to leave it and enjoy human contact once in a while.

Today, society has many people, such as transients and singles, who have lost human communications networks and have not yet established new links. They depend upon their communications machines—the telephone to disembody them and the computer terminal to take away their voices.

Electronics has isolated us not only in the business area. Look what happened to Grandmother when she got wired into the phone system. Great, you thought. Now she won't be lonely, and I won't have to run over there every other day. Indeed, Grandmother talked to you more, but she saw you less. Even her neighbor phoned sometimes instead of running over to visit. Days passed when Grandmother saw no one.

Computers now allow homemakers to do comparison shopping, order tickets for the theater, make plane reservations, and bank—all at the touch of a button. Wonderful. People can stay home all day, alone, or with only children for company.

CB radio, Qube, and video-conferencing are other examples of communication that isolates us. CB radio, except as it is used in business and for emergencies, is simply fantasy communication. We project a personal image we would like to match. Think of the handles: Tall Texan, Sexy Sue, Range Rider. Ever hear of Square Claire, Fat Francis, or Dopey Dan? We use CB just as we sometimes use the radio, to escape communicating with people directly. We might get some road information and avoid lurking smokies, but the conversations are superficial communication.

Qube, the two-way cable television being demonstrated in Columbus, Ohio, has been exploring the potential of the cathode-ray tube. Qube is more than ordinary TV, but it is not, as its producers claim, truly two-way TV. Our only input involves responses to canned questions. We cannot ask questions; we cannot give qualified replies. Besides, our input leads to a privacy problem. Our answers are fed into a computer. Do we really *want* a record of how we responded to the questions? Think of the implications. Each new cathode-ray-tube service will demand another chunk of our privacy.

In 1987, Nielsen announced plans to install "people meters" for the fall season to elicit more accurate ratings. Biagi (1988) cited that people meters combine the data gathered by Audimeters and Nielsen diaries into one data-gathering system based on a four-inch by ten-inch people meter box that sits on the television set in the metered homes. Family members punch in an assigned button on top of the set when they begin to watch TV. The system's central computer, linked to the home by telephone lines, correlates each viewers number with information about that person stored in its memory. Biagi went on to state that in early trials, people meters recorded lower ratings for the networks, especially among certain important groups, such as adult women. This could mean lower prices for network advertising.

TV has also given us the videoconference, which seems like an excellent substitute for long-distance travel in order to have a meeting. However, the small group dynamics just do not work. The concessions that must be made to the camera put the communicators in poor positions. They cannot all see one another. If the camera concentrates on a face, it misses a tapping foot, a clenched hand. The International Communication Association's audits have consistently indicated that employees want more contact with managers, but managers rely more and more on machines instead of human contacts.

It may sound simplistic, but people need people. We need other people to compare notes with, to affirm our worth, to anchor us to reality. We need the quality of communication that allows us to ask, "What answers have you found?"

If we hole up with machines, we will exchange only facts—machines do a superior job of that. However, we will suffer from the junk-communication phenomenon mentioned earlier.

Marriage counselors tell us that the divorce rate has never been higher and that a leading cause of divorce is failure of husbands and wives to achieve effective communication. A youth poll indicates that half the teenagers in the United States think communication between themselves and their parents is poor and the causes are mostly lack of time, lack of input into family decisions, and poor listening behavior. Political scientists tell us that 45 percent of Americans believe that the leaders of our most important institutions and professions are out of touch with the people—the very ones they are supposed to lead or help. A presidential commission points out that the cost of federal paperwork exceeds $100 billion per year—about $500 for every American citizen—just to fill out the more than 4,500 different forms the federal bureaucracy requires. Is it any wonder that the Oklahoma State Regents for Higher Education in 1981 turned down $950,000 in federal funds for collegiate programs in technical and occupational education? The federal reporting requirements and the associated paperwork would have cost participating Oklahoma institutions an estimated $3 in administrative expenses for every $1 received in federal aid.

More than a century ago Alex de Tocqueville, French statesman and philosopher, observed that regulation "blankets society with a network of small complicated rules, minute and uniform, through which the most original minds and the most energetic characters cannot penetrate." De Tocqueville later said, "America is the only nation to go directly from barbarism to decadence without any intervening civilization." Perhaps he was thinking about America's regulatory and paperwork mess.

In the ten minutes or so that it takes you to read this page, the federal government will spend $47 million of your money, much of it due to wasteful inefficiencies. Recognizing this waste, in 1981 President Reagan set up the Grace Commission whose charge was to examine the federal system and identify simple ways for the government to save money through better management. As a consultant to the Grace Commission, I noticed such frivolities as the existence of more than 12,000 U.S. post offices that serve fewer than 100 customers apiece and that the Army spends $4 to process a payroll check compared with the $1 spent in private business and, due to the absence of competition, that the military spends $100 for 25-cent compressor caps, $114 for 9-cent batteries, and $511 for 60-cent lamps.

Reliance Insurance Company of Philadelphia did a study in 1980 which showed that 25 percent of its workers' time was spent creating, storing, and shepherding paper. The study also showed that *80 percent of that paper was never referred to again!* In response, Reliance declared a "paper-free" day during which all employees were forbidden to use the photocopy machine or to exchange memos, reports, and papers.

Management and communication consultants say that more than 10 percent of U.S. business enterprises fail every year primarily because of bad management and ineffective employee communication.

This is the most unfortunate since several studies link communication effectiveness to improved productivity in organizations. Tubbs and Hain (1979), in combining the results from eight studies, found "consistent and strong support for the assumption that management commmunication behaviors do play a significant part in contributing to or detracting from total organizational effectiveness." Tubbs and Widgery (1978) designed a communication training program for a manufacturing plant that, after its implementation, saved $7 million in productivity costs and decreased absenteeism. Another group of studies done in the military by O'Reilly and Roberts (1977) found the following results:

1. Individuals who passed information freely were rated as higher performers.
2. Individuals who were rated as having lower performance levels tended to be seen in terms of information overload, redundancy, and gatekeeping functions.
3. Individuals who were active participants in communication networks were seen as more productive than isolates.

Finally, Clampitt and Downs in research reported in 1983 found that feedback significantly improved productivity.

In the 1950s, the presidents of the top 100 corporations identified their major communication problems as follows: inadequate use of communication media; lack of communicative ability in management personnel; withholding of information from subordinates by management; and little opportunity for upward communication. The following are the results of my major study of sixteen organizations, released in 1980:

1. Employees receive insufficient information about their jobs and organizations.
2. Management doesn't follow up on employee messages.
3. Messages are sent too early or too late to be of use.
4. The grapevine supplements the void filled by the lack of openness, candor, and visibility of top management.
5. Impersonal channels substitute for face-to-face contact.
6. Lack of employee input into decisions that affect them is common.

What is alarming about these findings is not so much their indication of faulty communication systems as their striking similarity to the problems identified by corporate presidents *over thirty years ago!* Our research apparently confirms and quantifies what corporate leaders have known in their gut and heart for years. These research findings also bear close resemblance to the answers from the teenagers surveyed in the youth poll. Perhaps the parents who have difficulty communicating with their children at home are also the bosses who have difficulty communicating with their employees at work. Thomas Jefferson said, "If the people know all the facts, the people won't make a mistake." Much later, industrialist Bernard Baruch proclaimed, "The American people can do anything if you tell them *why,* but you must tell them." My research findings indicate that in the corporate world we have not done a good job of telling them why.

Our organizational leaders today must confront the reality of inadequately informed and uninvolved employees, distant and aloof management teams, poor-quality messages, and an overall poor state of organizational communication systems.

Is it fair to blame the problems of our families, governments, and businesses on "ineffective communication?" Maybe we oversimplify complex problems by analyzing them as "failure to communicate" or "communication breakdown." Perhaps we are all guilty of abusing and misusing the term *communication*. One of the purposes of this book is to help clear away the clichés and destroy some of the popular myths surrounding communication. The specific subject of this book is communication within large, complex organizations: hospitals, banks, industries, schools, universities, labor unions, and government agencies.

An increasingly important area of study in these types of organizations is organization development (OD). OD is a method of changing an organization and its beliefs, values, attitudes, and structures so that it can better adapt to the changing and turbulent environment of coming decades. Neilsen (1984) describes the importance of OD: "Organizational processes such as decision making, problem solving, planning, communication, and teamwork can be identified as important targets of OD efforts because they are likely to change in ways that reflect and reinforce changes in values regarding candidness and personal responsibility." OD will be covered in more depth in part four of this text.

Osmo Wiio, a colleague from Finland, has developed six "laws" of communication based on his years of teaching and writing about organizational communication.[1] I believe his laws summarize many of my findings. Wiio's first law states:

> *Communication usually fails—except by chance.* If we begin a communication with this assumption, the result may then be better than if we start with the opposite assumption that a communication usually succeeds. There is a wealth of research data showing that the general efficiency of the communication process is very low, often under 5 percent—a figure approaching statistical randomness.

Wiio's first law of communication has four corollaries:

1. *If communication can fail, it will.* This corollary means that if you give communication a chance to fail, it will fail. If you as a communicator are careless, indifferent, unskillful, or just plain lazy, you usually fail in communication.
2. *If communication cannot fail, it nevertheless usually does fail.* Even with the best of intentions, your communication is bound to fail because nature is against you and will use hidden flaws, deficiencies, misprints, and misunderstandings to defeat you.
3. *If communication seems to succeed in the way intended, it must be in a way which was not intended.* If everything seems to go fine, be careful; success may be illusory. Receivers may think they understand your message. In reality, they misunderstand it or just want to humor you or do not want to admit misunderstanding.
4. *If you are satisfied that your communication is bound to succeed, it is then bound to fail.* To be content with your own communication usually means that you designed the communication process according to your own taste and did not consider the receiver. The message should be designed for the receiver, not for the sender.

Wiio's second law is this:

> *If a message can be understood in different ways, it will be understood in just that way which does the most harm.* If there is a misunderstanding, the maximum damage will then result. Again, nature is against you: misprints, misunderstandings, and noise all have a multiplier effect instead of canceling each other out.

---

1. Wiio's laws are adapted from Osmo Wiio, *Wiio's Laws—and Some Others* (Espoo, Finland: Welin-Göös, 1978).

The more communication there is, the more difficult it is for communication to succeed.

Wiio's third law is as follows:

There is always somebody who knows better than you what you meant by your message. Many people think they can read our thoughts better than we can ourselves. If only we were half as smart as we would have to be to say the things these people think we are saying! We are, unfortunately, stupid enough to try to say only what we mean.

Wiio's fourth law is the following:

The more communication there is, the more difficult it is for communication to succeed. First of all, our information-processing capacity is limited. In modern industrial societies, we are subjected to an increasing amount of information. The amount of information increases so rapidly in many professions that it is impossible to keep up with it. The result is overload, and channels become blocked. Further, it is naïve to believe that increased communication is always for the better—that organizations function better the more communication they generate; that human relations are better and people trust each other more the more they communicate; and that conflicts and even wars can be avoided if we just communicate more. Wiio's organizational studies indicate that the correlation between the amount of communication and satisfactory social relationships is not linear. Too much information may be as bad as too little information. It may be better not to know what some people think and thus be able, perhaps, to avoid conflict.

Wiio's fifth law states:

In mass communication, it is not important how things are, the important thing is how things seem to be. Mass media—press, radio, television, etc.—often create a world of their own which has few, if any, links with observable reality. They create happenings that never took place, plots never plotted, words never said, and deeds never done. To the general public this, then, is reality. We may even have two parallel worlds: the imaginary world of mass media and the real world of everyday life. Very seldom do they meet.

The sixth and last of Wiio's laws is the following:

The importance of a news item is inversely correlated with the square of distance. This law is included mainly to impress Wiio's learned colleagues—professors and otherwise—because it shows them that he is not talking nonsense. He is stating a mathematical law of causal relationships, and who can argue with such wisdom? In plain language, the law means that a fist fight in my neighbor's family is to me a more important news item than 10,000 persons killed in a flood 10,000 miles away.

The specific subject of this book is communication within large, complex organizations.

In 1956, William Whyte labeled most men organization men because of the large amount of time they spent within organizations. Recently, Harry Levinson claimed that this is still true, that 90 percent of all working people work in organizations. When the time we spend in civic and social clubs, religious and educational institutions, hospitals, and banks is added, it is relatively simple to conclude that all of us today are organization men and women.

Since we spend most of our waking time in organizations, it is obvious that the problems of our governments, universities, and businesses are organizational problems. We might hypothesize that, given the technology to conquer outer space, we should be able to master the daily people problems that face complex organizations. We might also hypothesize that, given our current sociopsychological and clinical-medical models of handling people, we should be able to minimize intragroup and intergroup conflict and the morale and motivation problems associated with managing complex organizations.

Yet, despite the research reported by the nation's leading organizational experts who advocate new approaches to structuring organizations and managing people, most organizations today rigidly adhere to the military model of structuring the organization with control directed from the top of the hierarchy. Despite the findings of behavioral scientists, most organizations maintain detailed job descriptions and specific goal-oriented objectives, with an absolute minimum of flexibility. To compound the problem, many managers, fresh from a sensitivity training session or a group dynamics workshop or an organization development seminar, claim to be new people with a changed outlook on life and their job. Only a few weeks or even days are needed for them to return to their old ways of management based upon carrot-and-stick philosophies of dealing with people. Levinson calls this the "jackass fallacy" and predicts organizational crises will continue as long as managers, superiors, and leaders maintain their basic attitudes of "the powerful treating the powerless as objects as they maintain anachronistic organizational structures that destroy the individual's sense of worth and accomplishment." The evidence ("increased inefficiency, lowered productivity, heightened absenteeism, theft, and sometimes outright sabotage") seems to support Levinson's conclusion that organizations are still in a state of crisis that will ultimately result in both destruction of the organization and alienation of youth.

Since 1938 when Chester Barnard defined the main task of an executive as that of communication, it has been demonstrated continuously that organization members are communicating men and women. Our focus in later chapters will be to examine the key variables influencing the communication behavior of people in organizations and those variables most affected by that behavior. Our frame of reference will be the organization as a living, open system connected by the flow of information between and among people who occupy various roles and positions.

Each chapter in the book begins by stating its instructional objectives, that is, defining the behavior you should be able to perform after reading the chapter. They are "informational objectives." For example, after reading the chapter on planning communication diagnosis (chapter 9), you should be able to do the following: describe and illustrate the factors affecting the establishment of the consultant-client relationship; list and exemplify problems encountered by the communication consultant during intervention activities; describe and illustrate the factors affecting the termination of the consultant-client relationship, etc. Note that you are not expected to be able to perform the duties of a communication consultant after reading the chapter. The instructional objectives throughout this book are cognitive and informational; that is, they are limited to presenting factual data and do not include the teaching of skills. A more complete discussion of the nature of informational objectives is given in chapter 11 on implementing communication changes.

The specific objectives of this first chapter follow:

1. To describe several authors' perceptions of the field of organizational communication
2. To present a paradigm of the field of organizational communication and illustrate the limits of the field discussed in this book
3. To define organizational communication as the term is used in this book
4. To define and illustrate the following concepts as they are used in this book:
   a. process
   b. message
   c. network
   d. interdependence
   e. relationship
   f. environment
   g. uncertainty

Perceptions of Organizational Communication

In 1981, Pace and Ross released the results of a national survey of introductory organizational communication courses. Among their findings were the following:

1. Communication and speech communication departments are the ones most likely to offer a basic organizational communication course.
2. The course is required by one-third of the departments for its majors and minors.
3. Typical enrollment in the course is between twenty-five and fifty students per section.
4. The primary and secondary books used in the course were most often published after 1976.
5. Content of most courses includes: communication networks; informal/grapevine communication; communication climate; communication theory/models; organization theory; leadership; management styles; theory of organizational communication; motivation theory; and conflict/conflict management.

It is apparent from the results of this survey that the field of organizational communication has grown remarkably in just a few years. All indications are that this growth will continue. Students who enter the field of communication demand that their education lead directly to a future occupation or profession rather than more education. Organizational communication as a field appears to answer these demands. What is organizational communication? What does it include and what does it exclude?

Several authors have attempted to offer their perceptions of the limits of this relatively new discipline. Redding and Sanborn define organizational communication as the sending and receiving of information within a complex organization. Their perception of the field includes the following: internal communication; human relations; management-union relations; downward, upward, and horizontal communication; communication skills of speaking, listening, and writing; and communication program evaluation. Katz and Kahn perceive organizational communication as the flow of information—the exchange of information and the transmission of meaning—within an organization. Using the general systems model developed for the physical sciences by von Bertalanffy (1956, 1962) and others, Katz and Kahn define organizations as open systems and discuss such properties as the importing of energy from the environment; the transformation of this energy into a product or service characteristic of the system; the exporting of that product or service into the environment; and the reenergizing of the system from energy sources found once again in the environment. Zelko and Dance primarily discuss the "skills" of communicating in businesses and professions (speech making, listening, interviewing, counseling, conferences, selling, persuading). They perceive organizational communication as an interdependent system that includes both internal (upward, downward, and horizontal) and external (public relations, sales, advertising) communications. Lesikar shares Zelko and Dance's perceptions of internal-external communication and adds a third dimension, personal communication (the informal exchange of information and feelings among organizational members).

Thayer, also using the general systems approach to communication, refers to organizational communication as those data flows that subserve the organization's communication and intercommunication processes in some way. He identifies three communication systems within the organization: operational (task- or operations-related data), regulatory (orders, rules, instructions), and maintenance and development (public and employee relations, advertising, training). Bormann and others limit their study of organizational communication to "speech communication" (as opposed to written communication) within a system of overlapping and interdependent groups. They emphasize the communication skills of listening, meeting in small groups, and speaking to persuade. Huseman and others (1969) limit the field of organizational communication to organizational structure, motivation, and such communicative skills as listening, speaking, writing, interviewing, and discussing. Several writers emphasize the written media of communication: reports, letters, memos, bulletins, proposals, and the like.

Greenbaum (1971, 1972) perceives the field of organizational communication as including the formal and informal communication flows *within* the organization. He separates internal from external organizational communication and views the role of communication primarily as *coordination* of personal and organizational objectives and problem-generating activities. Witkin and Stephens define an organizational communication system as "those interdependencies and interactions among and within subsystems, through the act of communication, which serve the purposes of the organization." Haney, using a general semantics approach to communication, defines organizational communication as the coordination by communication of a number of people who are interdependently related.

This conceptual disparity is further illustrated by the finding of Downs and Larimer that the following twenty-one areas of subject matter are currently being taught in organizational communication courses: downward communication; upward communication; organizational theory; horizontal communication; decision making; small group communication; leadership; research techniques; motivation; interviewing; change and innovation; conflict management; organizational development; organizational culture; conference techniques; management theory; consultation training; listening; job satisfaction; public speaking; writing; and sensitivity training.

Several writers have developed their own taxonomies to, supposedly, bring clarity out of the confusion. Voos divides the field into decision making; upward, downward, and horizontal communication; persuasion; cognitive dissonance; networks; and feedback. Knapp writes about interpersonal and intergroup communication in organizations; individual-organizational interaction; organizational communication as a field; training and research in organizational communication; characteristics of communicators and receivers; channels of information flow; communication media; and the total system of communication within an organization. Carter (1972) speaks of theories and systems of organizational communication; barriers to organizational communication; vertical and horizontal communication; media and informal channels; organizational change; and evaluation of the effectiveness of organizational communication.

Bernstein (1976), summarizing findings of an Industrial Communication Council survey, identifies the most important concern of organizational communicators to be interaction between management and the organization, employees, and external publics.

Falcione and Greenbaum (1976) developed a taxonomy for the following series of organizational communication abstracts: interpersonal, intragroup, and intergroup communication in organizations; communication factors and organization goals; skills improvement and training; communication media; communication system analysis and research methodology; and general review of the field. Finally, in 1981, Foltz defined organizational communication as "the exchange of information, ideas, feelings down, up and across organizational lines."

If these different perceptions and viewpoints seem confusing, consider the survey by my colleague, Don Rogers, of twenty-six organizational communication textbooks. He identified thirty-nine major topic areas in these books, 80 percent of which were published after 1972. His conclusion is *no topic is covered in every textbook, and the majority of topics are covered in less than one-half the textbooks.*

Most of the above perceptions, however, seem to share an empirical logical-positivist view of organizational communication, a paradigm often referred to as "functionalist." The functionalist perspective views organizational life as mechanistic, using systems theory to posit that organizations control and coordinate people and resources through communication (Farace, Taylor, Stewart, 1978). According to Putnam and Cheney (1983), the functionalist paradigm's assumptions include the following:

1. Work as purposeful-rational action dominates social existence.
2. Social reality is objective, materialistic, and subject to prediction and technical control.
3. The goals of research are understanding and prediction for the purpose of exerting technical control.

While the functionalist relies upon an empirical tradition and orientation, a perspective that relies more upon an anecdotalist's mode of thinking is growing in popularity among some organizational communication scholars and researchers. This paradigm, called "interpretive," presumes that social reality is intersubjectively created (Sotirin, 1984) and that organizing and communicating are interdependent processes of organizational life (Putnam, 1982). Further, if organizational life is identified as culture, then (according to Sotirin) organizing and communicating become the focal activities of organizational culture. In fact, Pacanowsky and O'Donnell-Trujillo have stated (1982):

> Organizational culture is not just another piece of the puzzle, it *is* the puzzle. From our point of view, a culture is not something an organization has; a culture is something an organization *is*.

Those who subscribe to the interpretive approach tend to conduct naturalistic research using participant-observation techniques to collect the "talking and writing," the primary data that reflects the social reality of the organization's participants (Hawes, 1976).

Paradigm and Definition of Organizational Communication

It is apparent that approaches to and definitions and perceptions of organizational communication are legion. Organizational communication can mean and refer to whatever an author wants. Despite such a variety of viewpoints, a few common strands can be detected in many of these perceptions. (1) Organizational communication occurs within a complex open system which is influenced by and influences its environments, both internal (called culture) and external. (2) Organizational communication involves messages and their flow, purpose, direction, and media. (3) Organizational communication involves people and their attitudes, feelings, relationships, and skills.

These propositions are illustrated in figure 1.1. This functionalist paradigm leads to the definition of organizational communication used in this book: *Organizational communication is the process of creating and exchanging messages within a network of interdependent relationships to cope with environmental uncertainty.* This perception of the field of organizational communication includes seven key concepts: process, message, network, interdependence, relationship, environment, and uncertainty. Each concept is defined and illustrated briefly in the following sections of this chapter and in more detail in later chapters.

Process

An organization is a dynamic open system that creates and exchanges messages among its members and between its members and its environment. We talk about "process" because the phenomenon of creating and exchanging messages is *ongoing, ever changing, and continuous.* To illustrate the notion of process, let us build a banking organization. As we construct our bank, note the relationship between environmental interactions and internal exchanges.

Figure 1.1 Paradigm of organizational communication.

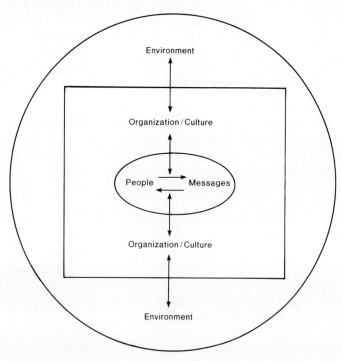

Eleven people in a small town gathered one evening in the home of Jasper Smith, a leading citizen of the town, to discuss the need for a bank. The town's population had grown from 200 to 1,500, and community members needed a place both to store excess funds and to seek additional funds in the form of loans. Jasper proposed to his ten guests that collectively they form a bank, name Jasper president, sell stock at $5 per share, seek a loan from an upstate bank to finance a building, and attempt to service both the savings and borrowing needs of the town's population. One of Jasper's guests mentioned the federal and state banking regulations that would govern both the interest rates and methods of operation of the bank. Another guest suggested that the new bank would need a computer, an automatic teller, and a drive-in window to run the bank efficiently and provide fast service for its customers. Another mentioned the poor state of the economy and its effect on the bank's ability to provide housing loans. Finally, someone else said that the group would need to tell the rest of the town about their decision and explain the beginning operations of the bank.

Toward the end of the meeting, all agreed to do as Jasper requested. They produced a written document outlining exactly what the bank's goals would be; how the goals would be achieved; who would assume what role in reaching the goals; and how much of their own resources they would expend toward helping the bank become effective.

The group had formed an organization, the Smith Bank, in response to environmental needs. They had organized and assigned various roles to their members, again in response to their environment. Each member would have to interact with certain parts of the environment and with the other members, whatever their roles. Notice the steps that they followed:

1. Environmental needs in the town changed.
   a. Population changes (social factor) occurred, resulting in people's desire for a bank.
   b. Recession (economic factor) was underway, forcing the bank to sell stock and borrow money to start its business.
   c. Banking technologies (technological factor) required computers, drive-in windows, and automatic banking.
   d. Federal and local regulations (legal factor) limited the amount of interest the bank could charge and pay.
2. People interacted to discuss environmental changes.
   a. Environmental changes produced uncertainty among residents.
   b. Alternatives for coping with this uncertainty were discussed.
3. People initiated and exchanged messages among themselves, defining roles and functions needed in the bank to cope with environmental uncertainty.
   a. The goals for the bank were decided: to provide fast and reliable savings and lending services to the town's residents.
   b. The kinds of roles and functions needed to meet the goals were determined: customer services, legal services, research and development, financial services, and advertising and communications.
   c. Division of responsibility and roles or functions were assigned people within the organization.
   d. Allocation of resources of members of the bank was made.
   e. A written charter and corporate plan outlining the bank's goals, objectives, and methods of operating were developed.

One year later the eleven people who had assembled in Jasper Smith's house opened the doors of the Smith Bank, a small bank with legal, finance, customer service, communications, and research development departments. Jasper Smith was president and chief executive officer, and the other ten members were treated equally, two in each of the five departments.

During the first few months of the bank's operation, the recession began to ease somewhat, and more money became available for the town's economy. These factors prompted the finance department to propose to Jasper that the Smith Bank consider forming a trust department. Jasper asked the communication department to interview a sample of the town's residents to confirm the need for the new program. The legal department studied the implications of state banking codes for the trust department and reported its findings to the finance department and to Jasper. While this research was underway, an employee of the bank asked the communications department to indicate when the bank's first dividend would be paid. Before an answer could be provided, the legal department told the communications department to consider the Security and Exchange Commission guidelines on giving an insider information without making it available simultaneously to all stockholders.

In all of these interactions or environmental shifts, organizational uncertainty was reduced by the creation and exchange of messages among the members of the organization and between organizational members and members of various publics. Thus, *an organization is an open system in which messages are created and exchanged within a network of interdependent relationships to cope with environmental uncertainty.*

Message

A symbol is something that stands for something else. A word, for example, is a symbol when it refers to an object. To communicate, a person must be able to evolve a mental picture of something (create a concept), give it a name, and develop a feeling about it. Effective communication with another person implies that the concept, the name, and the feeling are similar to those of the other person. In other words, effective communication means that you and I refer to the same things when we talk. We share understanding.

A *message* is one or more symbols that we perceive and to which we attach meaning. We may be simultaneously sending and receiving the same symbols. The symbols may be verbal or nonverbal. The creation of meaning is what changes the symbols into messages. Thus, messages are composed of meaningful symbols about people, objects, and events and are generated by the interaction of people.

In organizational communication, we study the creation and exchange of messages throughout organizations. Organizational message behavior can be examined according to several taxonomies: language modality, intended receivers, method of diffusion, and purpose flow. *Language modality* differentiates *verbal* (linguistic) from *nonverbal* (nonlinguistic) messages. Examples of verbal messages in organizations are letters, speeches, and conversations. With verbal messages, we are most interested in studying the exact word choice used in the speech, letter, or conversation. Nonverbal messages are primarily unspoken or unwritten. Examples of nonverbal messages are body language (eye movement, gesturing); physical characteristics (height, weight, hair length); touching behavior (handshaking, stroking, hitting); vocal cues (tone, pitch, rhythm); personal space (spatial arrangements, territoriality); objects (glasses, wigs, clothing); and environment (room size, furniture, music).

Intended receivers include people either within or outside the organization. Messages in the first instance are intended for *internal* use, and those in the second instance, for *external* use. Examples of internal message systems include memos, bulletins, and meetings. External message behavior is illustrated by advertising campaigns, public relations efforts, sales efforts, and civic duties. Internal messages are intended for consumption by the employees of the organization. In this book we will study primarily internal messages. However, within the systems framework, it is important to realize that external messages satisfy the needs of an open system by linking the organization to its public and its environment.

Method of diffusion identifies the particular communication activity employed during the sending of the messages to other people. Diffusion implies that messages are spread throughout the organization, either widely or narrowly. Here we are interested in *how* messages are spread. Most organizational communication diffusion methods can be divided into two general categories: those using software, and those using hardware for dissemination. Hardware methods depend upon electrical or mechanical *power* to make them function.

Software methods depend upon our individual abilities and skills—particularly thinking, writing, speaking, and listening—to communicate to and with others. Included in the software methods are such *oral* face-to-face communication activities as conversations, meetings, interviews, and discussions and such *written* activities as memos, letters, bulletins, reports, proposals, policies, and manuals. Hardware methods use such *technological* processes as the telephone, teletype, word-processing machines, microfilm, radio, walkie-talkie, videotape, and computers. In this book, we will be concerned most with *oral software* methods of message diffusion. (Many current books deal exclusively with written and technological communication activities.)

Purpose of flow refers to *why* messages are sent and received in organizations and *what* specific functions they serve. Redding suggests three general reasons for message flow within an organization: task, maintenance, and human. *Task* messages relate to those products, services, and activities of specific concern to the organization, for example, messages about improving sales, markets, quality of service, and quality of products. *Maintenance* messages, such as policy or regulation messages, help the organization to remain alive and perpetuate itself. *Human* messages are directed at people within the organization—their attitudes, morale, satisfaction, and fulfillment.

Thayer presents four specific functions of message flow within an organization: to inform, to regulate, to persuade, and to integrate. Informative and persuasive messages most likely fall within Redding's category of task messages. Regulatory functions, approximate maintenance messages, and integrative messages serve functions similar to human messages. In this book, we will examine these three types of message behavior plus *innovative* messages—those messages that enable the organization to adapt to its changing environment. For example, new plans, new activities, and new programs or directions generated in problem-solving and planning sessions are typical of innovative messages.

In sum, we recognize the different modalities, audiences, diffusion methods, and purposes of messages. Since we are primarily concerned with *speech communication* phenomena within organizations, our discussion of message behavior emphasizes the following kinds of messages: *verbal and nonverbal messages orally diffused to internal audiences for task, maintenance, human, and innovative purposes.*

Network

The colonel communicated the following message[2] to the major: "At nine o'clock tomorrow there will be an eclipse of the sun, something which does not occur every day. Get the men to fall out in the company street in their fatigues so that they will see this rare phenomenon, and I will then explain it to them. Now, in case of rain, we will not be able to see anything, of course, so then take the men to the gym."

The major passed on the message to the captain: "By order of the colonel tomorrow at nine o'clock there will be an eclipse of the sun. If it rains, you will not be able to see it from the company street, so then, in fatigues, the eclipse of the sun will take place in the gym, something which does not occur every day."

---

2. I first heard this story in a speech delivered by W. C. Redding at the University of New Mexico, March 6, 1973. The source is believed to be the United States Military Academy, West Point, New York.

The captain then said to the lieutenant: "By order of the colonel in fatigues tomorrow at nine o'clock in the morning the inauguration of the eclipse of the sun will take place in the gym. The colonel will give the order if it should rain, something which does occur every day."

The lieutenant then told the sergeant: "Tomorrow at nine the colonel in fatigues will eclipse the sun in the gym, as it occurs every day if it's a nice day. If it rains, then this occurs in the company street."

The sergeant then assured the corporal: "Tomorrow at nine the eclipse of the colonel in fatigues will take place because of the sun. If it rains in the gym, something which does not take place every day, you will fall out in the company street."

Finally, one private said to another private: "Tomorrow, if it rains, it looks as if the sun will eclipse the colonel in the gym. It's a shame that this does not occur every day."

This story illustrates the most common written-about pattern of communication within an organization: the downward pattern that progresses from superior to subordinate until the message is diffused throughout the organization. This is not the only pattern, or even the major pattern, used in most organizations. Organizations are composed of a series of people, each of whom occupies a specific position or role. Creation and exchange of messages among these people takes place over a set of pathways called a *communication network*. A communication network may include two people only, a few people, or an entire organization. Many factors influence the nature and scope of the network such as, role relationships, direction of the message flow, serial nature of message flow, and content of the message. Since message content was considered previously, we will now briefly discuss the role of a person in the network, the direction of the message, and the serial process that influences the effectiveness of the network.

Role behavior in an organization dictates who occupies what specific position or job, either formally or informally prescribed. For example, an employee may be hired as a secretary and be told that the job duties include such behaviors as typing, taking shorthand, running errands, and setting appointments. These duties constitute the *formal* role of a secretary. This formal role influences to whom the employee communicates in the course of the job. The secretary may ask the boss a question about a filing error, may have lunch with other secretaries, or may supervise other secretaries or clerical personnel. Besides communicating with people through normal channels in the course of the job, the secretary may also talk with certain employees in other departments or divisions within the organization, may communicate with other secretaries about nonjob-related events or activities, and may discuss rumors about the boss or certain recent unofficial reports. In all cases, the secretary is communicating unofficially via a network of *informal* relationships. This basic difference between formal and informal networks of communication explains why much, perhaps most, communication within an organization does *not* follow a prescribed pattern dictated by such management bibles as the organization chart. We will study extensively the relationship between formal and informal networks in subsequent chapters of this book.

We will examine the various network roles people may assume as they create and exchange messages. Specifically, we will compare the behavior of network participants (members of communication groups, group members who link with members of other groups, and liaisons who connect groups without belonging to any one group) with the behavior of nonparticipants (that is, isolates who exchange very few messages). We will see the degree to

Organization chart

which network members are integrated into the entire system as well as the degree to which groups are connected to each other and to the system.

Direction of the network has been traditionally trichotomized into downward, upward, and horizontal communication—depending upon who initiates the message and who receives it or is supposed to receive it. *Downward communication* refers to messages that flow from superiors to subordinates, as in the military example given earlier. Most downward communication concerns task or maintenance messages related to directions, goals, discipline, orders, or questions. *Upward communication* refers to messages that flow from subordinates to superiors, usually for such purposes as asking questions, providing feedback, and making suggestions. Upward communication has the effect of improving morale and employee attitude. Therefore, upwardly directed messages usually are classified as integrative or humanly related. *Horizontal communication* is the lateral exchange of messages among people on the same organizational level of authority. Messages communicated horizontally usually relate to problem solving, coordination, conflict resolution, and rumors. Each of these three network directions is examined more closely in a later chapter.

Serial process is a term meaning step-by-step and implies that the communication process in organizations goes from person-to-person-to-person. Imagine five small children playing the telephone game where one youngster whispers a secret to another, and so on, until the last child repeats aloud the secret. Comparisons with the initial secret usually reveal marked differences. When messages are passed up, down, or across the organization, they are being reproduced serially as they flow over the various networks. When rumors spread via the organization's grapevine, they are being spread serially.

Usually several things happen to a message as it travels in an organization. Details are omitted (leveling), added (adding), highlighted (sharpening), or modified (assimilating) to conform to the interests, needs, and feelings of the reproducer. Members of organizations soon find that as the number of links in a human message transmission system increases, so also does the probability for error, distortion, and omission. March and Simon call this phenomenon "uncertainty absorption." Pace and others have proposed that errors tend to develop in the serial reproduction process when messages from more than one channel are mixed, when too many messages are processed at the same time, and when messages come too fast. Applying the concept of uncertainty absorption to decision making along the organizational hierarchy, Redding (1967) concludes: *"The higher one goes in the hierarchy, the more must decisions be based upon less and less detailed information of the 'life-facts.' "*

Before you claim that the world is ruled by "Peter-Principled managers," be advised that if the top of an organization were to receive all available information, the organization would probably collapse from information overload. Other variables to study in order to understand the effects of the serial process on message flow are type of network, rate of message flow, redundancy in messages, efficiency of network pathway, and function of network.

In sum, we will examine both formal and informal upward, downward, and horizontal messages as they travel serially through organizational networks.

Interdependence

Earlier, we defined an organization as an open system whose parts are all related to its whole and to its environment. We say that the nature of this relationship is *interdependent* or interlocking because all parts within the system, called subsystems, affect and are affected by each other. This means that a change in any part of the system will affect all other parts of the system. This also means that, in a sense, communication networks within an organization *overlap*.

Implications for the concept of interdependence center on the relationships between the people who occupy the various organizational roles. For example, when managers make a decision, they would be wise to account for the implications of their decision on the entire organization. Of course, one way to compensate for the interdependent relationships affected by and affecting a decision is to communicate all possible messages to all possible people within the organization. Naturally, so much information would cause the organization to collapse from information overload. On the other hand, too little information communicated may affect other variables, such as morale, attitude, production, and turnover. Somewhere there is a formula for determining the appropriate number of messages for effectively maintaining the organization's existence without overloading it. One purpose of this book is to provide answers to this dilemma.

Relationship

The fifth key concept inherent in our definition of organizational communication is relationship. Exactly what relationships are important for study in an organization? Since an organization is an open, living, social system, its connecting parts function in the hands of people. In other words, the network through which messages travel in an organization is connected by people. Thus, one of our interests is to study the human relationships within the organization by focusing on the communication behavior of the people involved in a relationship. We will study the effects of these behaviors upon specific relationships within the organization's subparts as they interact with each other. We will study employee attitudes, skills, and overall morale as they affect and are affected by organizational relationships.

One way to look at the various relationships possible within an organization is to examine the degree of aggregation of the individuals being studied, ranging from the simplest system, the dyad, to the most complex, the entire organization. Thayer lists three levels of communication within the organization: individual, group, and organizational. Pace and Boren use the term *interpersonal* to refer to situations in which communication occurs in a face-to-face relationship and go on to identify four specific face-to-face relationships according to the number of people involved: dyadic communication, serial communication, small group communication, and audience communication. All four exist within an organization. In a *dyad* two people interact. In *serial communication* (just discussed) the dyad is expanded, so a message is relayed from A to B to C to D to E by a series of interactions in which everyone interprets and transmits the message along the chain. In *small group communication* three to approximately twelve individuals are concerned in the interaction. Last, in *audience communication,* a gathering of thirteen to many more people is involved. Subsequent chapters examine ways to strengthen interpersonal relationships within the organization.

Environment

Duncan (1972) has defined the environment as "the totality of physical and social factors that are taken into account in the decision-making behaviors of individuals in the system." He further breaks down and analyzes the environment in terms of its internal and external components. The former refers to the personnel component, the functional and staff component, and the organizational level component (e.g., objectives/goals, products/services, integration). The external component refers to customers, suppliers, competitors, technology, etc.

In our paradigm of organizational communication, we are equally concerned with transactions occurring within the internal environment, comprised of an organization and its culture, and those between an organization and its external environment, often referred to as boundary-spannning activities. Recently, the study of an organization's culture has grown in both prominence and popularity. Schwartz and Davis (1981) have defined culture as the "pattern of beliefs and expectations shared by the organization's members—which produce

Organizational communication is the process of creating and exchanging messages within a network of interdependent relationships to cope with environmental uncertainty.

norms that shape the behavior of individuals and groups in the organization." Culture typically refers to the beliefs, rituals, values, myths, mores, and stories that differentiate one organization from another. In short, by examining the symbols, language, and ideology of an organization's culture, we can typically describe how it behaves. We will examine culture in more detail in chapter 3 and see how it contrasts with an organization's climate.

An organization is defined as an open system because it interacts with its external environment. In the earlier example, we listed several environmental contingencies outside organization, such as technology, economy, law, and social factors. Present-day organizations must constantly monitor these and other factors, such as government regulations, stockholder concerns, community issues, political controversies, cultural differences, and even energy shortages. As the environment changes, new information demands are placed upon the organization. It must cope with these changes in environment by creating and exchanging messages both internally among relevant units and externally to important publics. Organizations that do will live and probably be effective. Those that do not will die. In a later chapter, we will examine in detail the various environmental contingencies affecting organizations and the kinds of communicative behaviors called for in coping with these contingencies.

Uncertainty

An organization creates and exchanges messages among its members to reduce the uncertainty they face from environmental factors. Some organizations, such as research and development organizations, faced with highly complex tasks, require a high degree of integration among members in order to cope with environmental uncertainty. Other organizations involved in more routine behaviors, such as producing automobiles by assembly line, may require more differentiation among their members, less integration, and thus, fewer message exchanges to confront uncertainty in the environment. We define *uncertainty* as the difference between information available and information needed. Members of an organization who need and have a lot of information—for example, about new government regulations affecting their product line—are more certain in their ability to manufacture products that conform to the regulations. If, however, the members do not have the information they need, they are more uncertain and may produce substandard products.

Uncertainty can also occur when members of an organization receive *too much* information or more than they really need to confront the demands of their environment. If he is given fourteen books to review, a staff attorney researching the impact of a new state regulation will be just as ineffective as an attorney who is given no books. One of the major concerns of organizational communication is to determine exactly how much information people need to reduce their uncertainty without being overloaded. Unfortunately, such decisions rarely include the input of the persons most directly affected by the decisions, namely, the employees themselves.

This view of uncertainty presumes that an organization *reacts* to its external environment by receiving and diffusing information from it to reduce uncertainty. Another view, promoted by Karl Weick (1969), argues that, while organizations are information-processing units that interact with their environments to remove as much uncertainty from their informational inputs as possible, the organizations will process *only* those information inputs relevant to them. They will attend to only those relevant inputs, thus creating and constituting the environment to which they react. According to Weick, they *enact* their own environment. Organizations interpret the information and assimilate it according to their own needs. Weick's position leads to a process view of the organization as it interacts with its external environment.

SUMMARY

We live in an age of organizations. We are all affected by organizations every day. Organizations as communication systems are in a state of crisis mainly due to archaic structure and faulty communication. Several authors and researchers have offered explanations and solutions to the organizational communication problems inherent in our systems. Common to many of their perceptions is the proposition that an organization operates as a complex, open social system through which energy flows to and from the environment via the interaction of people and messages within the system. Organizational communication is discussed from a functionalist perspective as a dynamic process by which the organization interacts with the environment and by means of which the organization's subparts interact with each other. Thus, organizational communication can be seen as the *creation and exchange of messages within a network of interdependent relationships to cope with environmental uncertainty.*

Seven key concepts in organizational communication were reviewed: process, messages, network, interdependence, relationship, environment, and uncertainty. Process was emphasized since organizations exchange messages in a dynamic, continuous, ongoing manner. Message behavior was considered through examination of language modality (verbal and nonverbal), intended receivers (internal and external audiences), method of diffusion (oral and written software and hardware), and purpose of flow (task, maintenance, human, and innovative). In the discussion of message behavior, we emphasized verbal and nonverbal messages orally diffused to internal audiences for task, maintenance, human, and innovative purposes. Networks were discussed with focus on role relationships, direction of message flow, and the serial nature of message flow. We considered both formal and informal messages as they travel serially upward, downward, and horizontally through organizational networks. We defined the concept of interdependence, discussing its implications for human relationships in organizations. We also mentioned relationships, identifying four possible interpersonal relationships according to the number of people involved: dyadic, serial, small group, and audience communication relationships. Internal environmental transactions of an organization were shown to be linked to its culture, or way an organization behaves. The external environmental factors that directly impact on an organization were identified as economic, legal, technological, political, cultural, and social. Finally, uncertainty—the difference between the amount of information an organization has and the amount it needs—was shown to involve both message underload and overload.

EXERCISES

1. List all the organizations to which you belong (work, school, social, family, civic). Compare your list with those of your classmates. Discuss both the differences and the similarities of the lists.
2. Calculate the approximate amount of time you spend each day in organizational activity.
3. Think of an organization (which you may belong to) in terms of the separate roles and functions perceived (as defined by an organizational chart). For each role, develop a list of the types of information that need to be "processed" daily.
4. Ask three people what they perceive the words "organizational communication" to mean. Select the three people from the following categories: a friend in another class; an employee of an organization who is classified as a manager executive, staff member, or officer; and a communication expert from the fields of consulting, training, or teaching.
5. Based upon information in exercise 4, make up your own definition of organizational communication. How does it differ from that in the text?

6. Based upon the paradigm of organizational communication presented in the text, list those aspects of an organization's external social environment that must be considered for the organization to operate efficiently. Think in terms of an organization to which you currently belong or have belonged.
7. List three differences between verbal and nonverbal messages you have observed in an organization. Give specific examples.
8. Interview a communication director (or an employee relations, labor relations, or personnel director) in an organization. Ask that person to provide examples of both internal and external messages used in the organization. Also ask for examples of diffusion methods.
9. Construct a message (approximately one paragraph long). Assemble a group of five people. Place all but one of the people outside of hearing range. Read your message to the remaining person. Ask the person to repeat the message as closely as possible to one of the other people while the rest remain out of hearing. Repeat this process until all five people have had a chance to say aloud the message they heard. Tape record this process and listen to the tape afterward. Look for changes in the message due to additions, omissions, modifications, and highlights. Discuss these changes among the group.
10. Design a message to be presented orally face-to-face to 2, 11, and 85 people at three separate times. Discuss the changes in the message for each presentation. Did you change the method of diffusion? the content of the message? the direction of the network?
11. List all technological "improvements" that have become part of the organizational structure and have fostered a climate of impersonal communicative behavior.
12. Share Wiio's Laws with someone you know in an organization. Does this person agree with them? Can he or she provide you with situations in which some or all of the laws applied to the organization?
13. Consider the seven concepts that make up organizational communication. Can you develop (in one to three pages) a short description of an organization or an outline that includes these seven concepts?

BIBLIOGRAPHY AND REFERENCES

Barnard, Chester. *The Functions of the Executive.* Cambridge: Harvard University Press, 1938.
Bernstein, Belle. "Organizational Communication Theories: Issues Analysis." Paper presented at a meeting of the International Communication Association, Portland, Oregon, 1976.
Bertalanffy, L. von. "General Systems Theory." *General Systems* 1 (1956):1.
————. "General Systems Theory." *General Systems* 7 (1962):1–12.
Biagi, S. *Media/Impact: An Introduction to Mass Media.* Belmont, CA: Wadsworth Publishing Company, 1988, p. 144.
Bormann, Ernest, William Howell, Ralph Nichols, and George Shapiro. *Interpersonal Communication in the Modern Organization.* Englewood Cliffs, N.J.: Prentice-Hall, 1969.
Carter, Robert. *Communication in Organizations.* Detroit: Gale Research Co., 1972.
Clampitt, Phillip, and Cal Downs. "Communication and Productivity." Paper presented at a meeting of the Speech Communication Association, Washington, November 1983.

Duncan, Robert. "Characteristics of Organizational Environments and Perceived Environmental Uncertainty." *Administrative Science Quarterly* 17 (1972):313–27.

Falcione, Raymond, and Howard Greenbaum. *Organizational Communication Abstracts* 1975. Urbana, Ill.; American Business Communication Association, Austin, Texas; International Communication Association, 1976.

Farace, Richard, and Donald MacDonald. "New Directions in the Study of Organizational Communication." Unpublished mimeographed manuscript, 1971.

Farace, Richard, and Hamish Russell. "Beyond Bureaucracy—Message Diffusion as a Communication Audit Tool." Paper presented at a meeting of the International Communication Association, Atlanta, April 1971.

Farace, Richard, James Taylor, and John Stewart. "Review and Synthesis: Criteria for the Evaluation of Organizational Communication Effectiveness." Paper presented at a meeting of the International Communication Association, Chicago, April 1978.

Foltz, Roy. *Inside Organizational Communication*. New York: Longman, 1981.

Greenbaum, Howard. "Organizational Communication Systems: Identification and Appraisal." Paper presented at a meeting of the International Communication Association, Phoenix, April 1971.

———. "The Appraisal of Organizational Communication Systems." Paper presented at a meeting of the International Communication Association, Atlanta, April 1972.

Haney, William. *Communication and Organizational Behavior*. Homewood, Ill.: Richard D. Irwin, 1973.

Hawes, Leonard. "How Writing Is Used in Talk: A Study of Communicative Logic-In-Use." *Quarterly Journal of Speech* 62 (1976):350–60.

Huseman, Richard, Cal Logue, and Dwight Freshley. *Readings in Interpersonal and Organizational Communication*. Boston: Holbrook Press, 1969.

Katz, Daniel, and Robert Kahn. *The Social Psychology of Organizations*. New York: John Wiley & Sons, 1966.

Knapp, Mark L. "A Taxonomic Approach to Organizational Communication." *Journal of Business Communication* 7 (1969):37–46.

Lesikar, Raymond. *Business Communication*. Homewood, Ill.: Richard D. Irwin, 1972.

Levinson, Harry. "Asinine Attitudes toward Motivation." *Harvard Business Review* 51 (1973):70–76.

March, James, and Herbert Simon. *Organizations*. New York: John Wiley & Sons, 1958.

Massie, J. L. "Automatic Horizontal Communication in Management." *Academy of Management Journal* 2–3 (1960):87–91.

Miller, J. G. "Toward a General Theory for the Behavioral Sciences." *American Psychologist* 10 (1955):513–31.

Neilson, E. C. *Becoming An OD Practitioner*. Englewood Cliffs, NJ., Prentice-Hall, 1984.

O'Reilly, Charles, and Karlene Roberts. "Communication and Performance in Organizations." Paper presented at a meeting of the Academy of Management, Orlando, August 1977.

Pacanowsky, Michael, and Nick O'Donnell-Trujillo. "Organizational Communication as Cultural Performance." *Communication Monographs* 50 (1983):126–47.

Pace, R. W., and R. Boren. *The Human Transaction*. Glenview, Ill.: Scott, Foresman, 1973.

Pace, R. Wayne, R. Boren, and B. Peterson. *A Scientific Introduction to Speech Communication*. Belmont, Calif.: Wadsworth Publishing Co., 1974.

Pace, R. Wayne, and R. Ross. "The Basic Course in Organizational Communication." Unpublished manuscript, Brigham Young University, January 1981.

Putnam, Linda. "Paradigms for Organizational Communication Research: An Overview and Synthesis." *Western Journal of Speech Communication* 46 (1982):192–206.

Putnam, Linda, and George Cheney. "A Critical Review of Research Traditions in Organizational Communication." Paper presented at a meeting of the International Comunication Association, Dallas, 1983.

Putnam, Linda, and Michael Pacanowsky, eds. *Communication and Organizations: An Interpretive Approach.* Beverly Hills: Sage Publications, 1983.

Redding, W. C. "Position Paper: A Response to Discussions at the Ad Hoc Conference on Organizational Communication." Paper presented at a meeting of the Ad Hoc Conference on Organizational Communication, University of Missouri at Kansas City, February 1967.

———. *Communication Within the Organization.* New York: Industrial Communication Council, 1972; and Lafayette, Ind.: Purdue Research Foundation.

———. "The Organization Man Communicates or to Paradise Via Paradox." Paper presented at the University of New Mexico, March 1973.

Redding, W. C., and George Sanborn. *Business and Industrial Communication.* New York: Harper & Row, 1964.

Rogers, Donald. "The Content of Organizational Communication Texts." *Journal of Business Communication* 16 (Fall 1978):56–62.

Schutte, William, and Erwin Steinberg. *Communication in Business and Industry.* New York: Holt, Rinehart & Winston, 1960.

Schwartz, Howard, and Stanley Davis. "Matching Corporate Culture and Business Strategy." *Organizational Dynamics* 10 (Summer 1981):30–48.

Shannon, Claude, and Warren Weaver. *The Mathematical Theory of Communication.* Urbana, Ill.: University of Illinois Press, 1949.

Sotirin, Patty. "Organizational Culture—A Focus on Contemporary Theory/Research in Organizational Communication." Paper presented at a meeting of the Speech Communication Association, Chicago, 1984.

Thayer, Lee. *Communication and Communication Systems.* Homewood, Ill.: Richard D. Irwin, 1968.

Toffler, Alvin. *Future Shock.* New York: Random House, 1970.

Tubbs, Stewart, and Tony Hain. "Managerial Communication and its Relationship to Total Organizational Effectiveness." Paper presented at a meeting of the Academy of Management, Atlanta, 1979.

Tubbs, Stewart, and Robin Widgery. "When Productivity Lags, Are Key Managers Really Communicating?" *Management Review* 67 (1978):20–25.

Vardaman, Gordon, and Patricia Black Vardaman. *Communication in Modern Organizations.* New York: John Wiley & Sons, 1973.

Voos, Henry. *Organizational Communication: A Bibliography.* New Brunswick, N.J.: Rutgers University Press, 1967.

Weick, Karl. *The Social Psychology of Organizing.* Reading, Mass.: Addison-Wesley Publishing Co., 1969.

Whyte, William. *The Organization Man.* New York: Doubleday & Co., 1956.

Wiio, Osmo. *Wiio's Laws—and Some Others*. Espoo, Finland: Welin-Göös, 1978.

Wiio, Osmo, Gerald Goldhaber, and Michael Yates. "Organizational Communication Research: Time for Reflection." In *Communication Yearbook* 4, ed. Dan Nimmo, 83–97. New Brunswick, N.J.: Transaction-International Communication Association, 1980.

Witkin, Belle Ruth, and Kent Stephens. "A Fault Tree Approach to Analysis of Organizational Communication Systems." Paper presented at a meeting of the Western Speech Communication Association, Honolulu, November 1972.

Zelko, Harold, and Frank Dance. *Business and Professional Speech Communication*. New York: Holt, Rinehart & Winston, 1965.

2
THE THEORY OF ORGANIZATION

A team of research anthropologists once described a large, complex business composed of twenty-four divisions evenly distributed through the United States and linked together by a nine-member central governing body. Members of this business are drawn primarily from one ethnic group. Each of the twenty-four divisions has a hierarchical structure of positions and roles that regulates the power in the total business. As evidence of the importance of this business to the United States economy, its annual profits approach $15 billion, and its liaison network extends into labor unions, state and federal legislatures and judiciary, and several large corporations. The research team described this business as a "formal organization," a social unit deliberately designed and constructed to achieve specific goals. They were *not* describing General Motors, the Roman Catholic Church, the U.S. Army, or the Teamsters Union. However, they did state that this business is similar to many business and government bureaucracies: "rationally designed and constructed formal organizations with personnel arranged in a hierarchy which can be diagrammed and then changed by recasting the organization charts."

Perhaps it will be easier to guess the particular business Ianni was discussing with another quotation from her book:

> Their officials paint a compelling portrait of a carefully organized and powerful nationwide confederation of Italian-Americans which, they claim, is also a portrait of organized crime. They picture a secret organization of ruthless and violent men bound by a common interest in illicit gain, ordered by a rigid code of rules, rights, and obligations, and maintained by the constant threat of death to informers or defectors. They describe an intricate national and even international network ruled by a council of overlords which maintains exacting discipline. Members of this vast criminal conspiracy are alleged to have influence in all levels of government and to control numbers of politicians at all levels. With the money gained from illicit enterprises the syndicate members are now reputedly moving into and corrupting legitimate business.

Without the references to crime, corruption, and other illicit goals and methods, the description could very easily apply to a national woman's club, an international social fraternity, a large clothing manufacturer, a political party, or any other complex organization with a specific purpose, large profits, and national communication network.

In chapter 1, we defined an organization as a network of interdependent relationships. In this chapter, we present an overview of three schools of thought on the term *organization*. Our specific objectives are these:

1. To define and illustrate the term *organization*
2. To describe, illustrate, and list the key concepts of the following schools of thought on business organizations:
   a. classical school
   b. human relations school
   c. social systems school
3. To list the key questions that each of the three schools asks about organizations
4. To discuss the important theorists and their contributions to each school of thought
5. To examine the communication implications in the three schools of thought

Overview and Definition

When we view an organization as a network of interdependent relationships, we can focus on the underlying structure that generates and guides the relationships; we can focus on the people who actually do the relating; or we can focus on how the various relationships contribute to the organization as a whole. These three ways of examining organizational relationships represent the essence of the three major schools of organizational thought and theory.

The classical theory of organization asks such questions as the following: How is the work divided? How is the labor force divided? How many levels of authority and control are there? How many people are there at each level? What are the specific job functions of each person?

The human relations school of thought studies work groups of people and asks such questions as the following: What roles do people assume in the organization? What status relationships result from the various roles? What are the morale and attitudes of the people? What social and psychological needs do the people have? What informal groups are there within the organization?

The third school of thought is concerned with social systems and emphasizes the relationship of the parts to the whole organization. Questions commonly asked by this approach are these: What are the key parts of the organization? How do they relate interdependently to each other? What processes in the organization facilitate these interdependent relationships? What are the main goals of the organization? What is the relationship between the organization and its environment?

The following example should clarify these three ways of viewing organizations. In its investigation of the possible involvement of the White House in the Watergate scandal, the Senate used the principles of each of these three approaches at different times.

Using the classical approach, the Senate examined the existing hierarchical structure in the White House, the specific job duties of White House aides, the authority certain aides had over other aides, and the number of employees who worked for each aide. Several aides admitted their guilt in the episode by stating, "It would have been out of place for me to question orders." This statement illustrates the importance of role and status in an organizational hierarchy. It is also evidence of the structure of the organization and the authority that structure imposed on people.

Questions of motivation, status, role, morale, and attitude underlie the human relations view of organizations. The Senate used the human relations approach in its examination of the social and psychological needs of the persons concerned. Throughout the Senate hearings, the question of motivation was raised. Witnesses were asked why they did what they did. One answered, "Out of loyalty to the president." Another witness explained, "I hoped that if I performed well here, I would be considered for a better job in the White House itself." Both answers illustrate the types of psychological and social needs that could have motivated the convicted Watergate burglars.

The Senate used the social systems approach in its constant reference to the relationship between the actual burglary and other issues in such questions as: Who financed the Watergate burglary? Who designed the plans? Who attempted to cover up the burglary? What information did the burglars hope to gain? These questions illustrate how impossible it was to isolate the burglary (as some people attempted to do) and not look into the implications it had for many greater issues. The action of the Senate in sifting through thousands of pages of testimony to answer such questions demonstrated the interdependent and interlocking relationships between the burglary and other acts. It was trying to demonstrate the relationship between parts (the burglary, the cover-up, motivation) and whole (the overall plan). Interdependence is the basic principle of the social systems view of organizations.

The remainder of this chapter describes in detail each of the three schools of organization theory. The important theorists and their contributions to each school are discussed, the concepts of each theory are examined.

The Classical School

Robert Townsend's advice about organization charts in *Up the Organization* demonstrates the existence of the classical school:

> Don't print and circulate organization charts. They mislead you and everybody else into wasting time conning one another. Anyway, you probably spend a major fraction of your time dealing directly with people who aren't really above or below you on the chart. Don't let yourself be conned into thinking you relate only up or down and sideways to peers. If people are off to one side but *below* you on the chart, you may be tempted to ignore them, summon them to your office, or at least assume they'll do whatever you want. In your own self-interest, to avoid their attack, or to enlist their required support in advance, you should go to *them* at *their* convenience to explain and persuade.

> The head of the mail room or the chief telephone operator may hold your destiny someday. Figure out who's important to your effectiveness and then *treat him (or her) that way.*

> It wouldn't hurt to assume, in short, that every man—and woman—is a human being, not a rectangle.

The classical theory of organization is concerned almost entirely with the structure of the formal organization.

The classical theory of organization is concerned almost entirely with the design and structure of organizations, not with people. The chief tool is the organization chart. Around World War I, classical theory evolved from the scientific management movement in which man was described as a rational, economic being who can best be motivated to work by such carrot-and-stick techniques as piecework systems, bonus systems, time-and-motion studies, and cost-figuring systems. Scientific managers believed that workers will produce at peak efficiency if they are motivated sufficiently *by money*. Given the nature of the times, it was easy to motivate workers by appealing to their most basic human needs—needs heavily dependent upon money for fulfillment.

Here are two examples that illustrate key principles of scientific management and the fact that many managers still practice the technique. A large clothing manufacturer in the Southwest requires each employee to produce a certain amount of work each day. How each worker maintains, exceeds, or fails to meet the expected standard is recorded and communicated to all workers in the following way. Both a graph and a flag are placed at the right upper corner of each worker's desk or station. The graph charts the worker's production efforts for the month (in bright red pencil). All employees, supervisors, and visitors can observe an individual's production efforts by simply examining the graph. The colored flag also communicates this message. When the expected standard is not met, a red flag is raised at the worker's desk; when the standard is met, a green flag is hoisted; when the worker exceeds the expectation, the reward is a golden flag raised high above the work station. Needless to say, this organization also has a piecework bonus system.

The other example of scientific management in practice concerns the manager of an agency who requires all employees to time their interviews with clients, record the number of minutes involved in clerical work, and calculate the average length of an interview and the average time involved in written work. Norms are calculated for all employees and regularly reported at weekly meetings. Employees deviating downward from the norms are constantly reminded of the relationship between time and money. Continued deviation downward is rewarded by eventual termination.

These examples illustrate the main techniques employed by scientific managers. In later chapters, we will discuss differences in values and psychological needs limiting the effectiveness of such techniques in a postindustrial society. What is important to consider now, however, is that the classical theory of organizing workers developed to meet the needs of scientific managers. Two foremost scholars of the classical school were Henri Fayol and Max Weber. Others were James Mooney and Alan Reiley, Luther Gulick, and Lyndall Urwick, and Chester Barnard.

Among the recommended principles of management, Fayol included the following:

1. Division of work (specialization)
2. Authority and responsibility (power)
3. Discipline (obedience)
4. Unity of command (one boss)
5. Unity of direction (one plan)
6. Subordination of individual interest to general interest (concern for the organization first)
7. Remuneration of personnel (fair pay)
8. Centralization (consolidation)

9. Scalar chain (chain of command)
10. Order (everyone has a unique position)
11. Equity (firm but fair)
12. Stability of tenure of personnel (low turnover)
13. Initiative (thinking out a plan)
14. Esprit de corps (high morale)

Max Weber took issue with Fayol's view of classical organization theory, distinguishing between inherent authority (traditional power, which may have been illegitimate) and legitimate authority (earned, respected, established by norms, rational and legal). Legitimate authority provided the foundation for what Weber called "bureaucracy." According to him, a bureaucracy is an organization having the following characteristics:

1. Continuity dependent upon adherence to rules
2. Areas of competence in which workers share the work and work toward specific goals under predetermined leaders
3. Scalar (hierarchical) principals
4. Rules that are either norms or technical principles
5. Separation of administrative staff and ownership of production devices
6. Separation of private belongings and the organization's equipment
7. Resources free from outside control
8. Structure in which no administrator can monopolize personnel positions
9. All administrative acts, rules, policies, etc., stated in writing

Keith Davis has advised that members of a bureaucracy will probably maintain job security as long as they follow rules and do not rock the boat. Remember the earlier statement of one of the Watergate conspirators, "It would have been out of place for me to question orders." Davis summarized the four key ingredients in a bureaucracy as high specialization, rigid hierarchy of authority, elaborate rules and controls, and impersonality. One of the best examples of bureaucracy is the federal government.

Some of the problems associated with the federal bureaucracy were publicized recently by a presidential commission that investigated paperwork in government. According to the commission, veteran bureaucrats are skilled at evading issues, shifting responsibility, and diverting work to someone else. Proliferation of committees and subcommittees ensures that people share both the burden of decision making and the blame for bad decisions. When Ernest Boyer was U.S. Commissioner of Education in 1979, he would get particularly incensed at memos that contained language designed to protect or "hide" the bureaucrats who wrote them—such as, "Before prioritizing this project, the cost-benefit ratio should be finalized by the agency"; *or* "It has come to the attention of this office . . . ." "Such cold and distant messages only deepen the conviction that Federal agencies are indeed nameless, faceless institutions," wrote a saddened Boyer. The best bureaucrats are those who can move problems through channels without making decisions of their own. One senior official advises newcomers, "Look important, act busy, call conferences, lots of them. But don't make any decisions. If you are forced to do so, make sure they are made in someone else's name."

The commission estimated that the federal government has more than 4,500 different forms that the public can be required to fill out. The champion department appears to be the Internal Revenue Service, which recently had only 1,611 different forms, a 31 percent reduction from a high in 1976 of 2,335 forms. A congressman who once purchased $4.91

Figure 2.1 Division of labor.

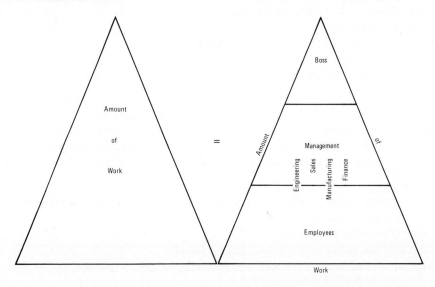

worth of government stationery was billed for it by the General Services Administration with eight copies of a form, six copies of a computer printout, and two computer punch cards. The congressman concluded that the government's cost for billing was more than the stationery was worth.

Former President Ronald Reagan pledged to eliminate the bureaucratic deadwood, but without a clear performance standard to apply, it was not easy to achieve. The standard of competence of private business is furnished inexorably by the profit factor. There is no sure way to determine either excessive cost or concrete achievement in the federal bureaucracy. Even the Russian czars or Mao Tse-tung, who reduced whole populations to serfdom, were not able to subjugate their bureaucracies once they were established.

Much of the management literature is summarized in Scott's definition of a formal organization: "a system of coordinated activities of a group of people working cooperatively toward a common goal under authority and leadership." Scott identifies four key components of classical organization theory: division of labor, scalar and functional processes, structure, and span of control.

Division of labor refers to how a given amount of work is divided among the available human resources. The division can be according to the nature of the various jobs or according to the amount of responsibility and authority each person assumes. The first is a *functional* division of labor, the second is *scalar*. Figure 2.1 illustrates division of labor according to both functional and scalar processes.

Scalar and functional processes express, respectively, the vertical and the horizontal growth and structure of the organization. *Scalar* refers to the levels of the hierarchy (the chain of command) in the organization. *Functional* refers to the specific job duties of each employee in the organization. The scalar process at a university refers to how authority is allocated among the board of regents, the university president, the vice presidents, the deans, the department chairmen, the faculty members, the administration staff, and the students.

Figure 2.2 Scalar processes in a university.

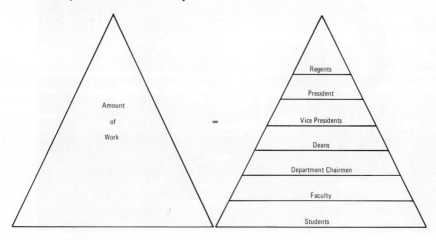

Figure 2.3 Functional processes in a university.

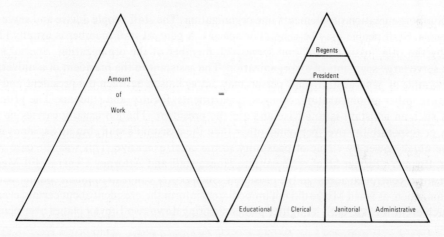

The functional process at a university refers to how job responsibilities are assigned to faculty, clerical, maintenance, and administrative personnel. Figures 2.2 and 2.3 illustrate these two concepts.

Structure refers to the network of relationships and roles throughout the organization. Structure enables the organization to meet its objectives effectively and in an orderly manner. Classical theory usually distinguishes two kinds of structure: line and staff. Line organization includes the chain of command and the primary functions of the formal organization. It can be readily described by an organization chart. A university's primary functions are to educate students, generate research, and serve the public's needs. Line organization is devoted to these ends. The line functions of a clothing manufacturer are to produce and distribute clothes. A supermarket's line functions are to buy and sell food.

The job of assistants usually carries no authority or responsibility, but assistants may receive much power by virtue of their proximity to the executive chief.

Staff organization supplements line organization. The staff people advise and serve the line people. Staff people may be general or special. A general staff member is usually identified by the title "assistant to" and serves one member of the organization. Special staff people serve large segments of an organization. The assistant to the president of a university is an example of general staff. This person may act as liaison between the president and the legislature, other administrators, colleges, departments, faculty, and students. The primary role of such an assistant is to advise and aid the president. The job usually carries no authority or responsibility over personnel other than the assistant's staff, but an assistant may achieve much power by virtue of proximity to the chief executive. This was the case with Ronald Reagan's former chief of the White House staff and Attorney General, Ed Meese, who in effect controlled access to the president. Such power can lead to much conflict within an organization, as when Meese did not immediately inform the president about certain events. One such event was the U.S. jet fighter planes shooting down two Libyan planes over neutral waters.

A common example of special staff is the personnel department that services many departments in the organization. Other examples are the public relations, employee relations, and communication departments, in which specialized staff serve and advise other units in the organization. As we will soon see, *formal* structure does not define the only network of relationships. There are also *informal* contacts that lead to the creation and exchange of messages.

In his review of the literature on formal organization structure, Jablin (1987) describes four key structural dimensions that predominate in most theoretical analysis: (1) configuration (e.g., span of control, organizational size), (2) complexity (vertical and horizontal), (3) formalization, and (4) centralization.

Figure 2.4 Comparison of a tall organization with a flat organization.

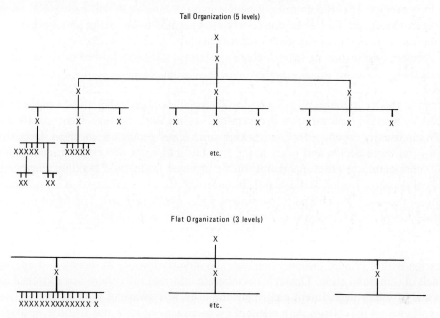

Span of control

Span of control refers to the number of employees a manager can effectively supervise. Graicunas (1933, 1937) explained the mathematics of the total number of possible relationships between a manager and employees. As the number of supervised employees increases, the number of possible relationships increases *geometrically*. According to Graicunas's formula, a manager with four subordinates had forty-four possible interrelationships. The interrelationships increase to a hundred with the addition of just one employee. Obviously, there are implications for the limits of effective management. The greater the number of possible interrelationships, the greater is the possibility for human conflict. The typical span of control is between five and fifteen subordinates.

Healey reported that 94 percent of 409 plants in Ohio had spans no greater than eight employees. Many factors (e.g., management skill, managerial style, employee skill, morale and attitude, type of organization) influence the desirable span of control for an individual manager.

Span of control influences the shape of an organization. If most managers throughout the organization have a small span, the overall shape of the organization will then be tall. If the typical span is great, then the overall shape of the organization will be flat. Figure 2.4 illustrates this point.

It is easy to see that the multiple levels of a tall organization increase the number of channels of communication and the possibility for distortion. Flat organizations have fewer levels through which messages travel, but, the number of face-to-face contacts is reduced, and a communication overload may be created at the manager's office. Further implications for communication of a tall versus a flat organization will be explored later.

Sometimes it may not be possible to control the growth of the span of control. Parkinson's Law predicts that the number of people in an organization will increase at an annual rate regardless of the work to be done. Parkinson seemed to be joking about organizational growth, but there is some evidence to support his law.

Another implication of span of control relates to how centralized or decentralized an organization is. In centralized organizations, power and decision points are few. In decentralized organizations, authority and decision making are spread throughout the organization, and authority is generally delegated to the smallest practicable units. Centralization is more likely in a tall structure and decentralization in a flat structure. Centralization of authority can usually expedite decision making since fewer people are involved. Decentralization involves more people and takes more time but may improve organizational morale by giving more employees the opportunity to be involved in decision making. Further implications of decentralization and centralization are discussed in chapter 3 as a function of the climate of the organization and the prevalent style of management. The following example illustrates some of the strengths and weaknesses of both approaches.

A college was once managed by a dean who adhered to the classical principles of chain of command, strict functionalization of job duties, unity of command, and a strong line organization with a printed organization chart to identify lines of authority and appropriate channels of communication. Through an elaborate informal spy system and a kitchen cabinet composed of senior department chairmen, the dean was aware of most of the activities of the faculty within the college. As a result of his management style and attitude, he assembled a relatively tall structure with a highly centralized decision center—his office. The impact of this approach on the college was that while decisions were made quickly, with authority and responsibility, very few people were involved or informed until after the decisions were made. The ultimate result was an efficient operation with highly specific goals and directions *but* with low morale and even apathy among those not fortunate enough to be in the kitchen cabinet.

Shortly after this dean was promoted to the vice presidency, a new dean arrived whose style was radically different. He believed in spreading authority and decision making to as many faculty and students as possible. He believed that goals and directions for the college should be generated from within the college by all faculty and students. In short, he rigidly followed the principles of a decentralized organization. He assembled several collegewide committees whose responsibility was advisory, and decision making was in the form of recommendations to the faculty at large. He rarely made any decisions himself. He assembled a relatively large staff of assistants who further advised and serviced the committees and departments. The result of the new dean's decentralized style was a high sense of morale and good spirit among the majority of the faculty. Many students and faculty were involved in decision making, which was slow and methodical, and at times a sluggish preliminary to action. At the same time, however, departments and some committees grew more autonomous and powerful, and some were freely labeled "empires." Horizontal communication among the departments was almost nonexistent. College goals appeared to be vague, and the general direction of the college appeared to be inconsistent. Ultimately, a group of senior faculty members developed into a clique that successfully sought the resignation of the new dean.

This elaborate example illustrates that both centralized and decentralized approaches to organizing people and making decisions have strengths and weaknesses. Ideally, a combination of centralized and decentralized authority may be required. The actual amounts of both should vary according to the specific goals, directions, personnel, and environment of the organization. For example, a dean who assumed final decision-making authority and based decisions upon recommendations from the general faculty and the committees might have satisfied both factions. Another example is General Motors, which decentralized its automobile manufacturing into several independent plants, each responsible for the production and sales of a particular model. At the same time, General Motors maintained a corporatewide, highly centralized labor relations department to handle all labor mediation throughout the organization.

The example of the college also highlights the main axiom of the classical theory of organization: adherence to structure and function as the sole basis for the organization of people. The greatest criticism of this approach is the rigidity of strict adherence to structure. The president of a certain university retained for years a highly efficient secretary who, because of her personality and her perception of her power as the president's secretary, had had numerous conflicts with other members of the president's staff. Despite constant warning and criticism from his staff, the president retained her as his secretary "because she was so efficient." Finally, after the president had received significant amounts of data demonstrating the harm the secretary was doing to the university, both internally and externally, she was discharged. This president had for many years strictly followed the precept of organizational structure that people are employed and retained according to their ability to master a particular job function. Interpersonal ability, attitude, and relations are minimized as values. A more pleasant solution, which might have worked earlier, would have been to transfer this secretary to a job where she could perform efficiently *without* contact and interaction with many people. In this way her strength would have been utilized, and her liability as a communicator would have been minimized, to her own benefit and that of the organization. The second school of thought, the human relations school, uses more solutions like this.

The Human Relations School

Approximately ten years after the scientific managers began to publish their recommendations for organizing workers, a group of researchers from the National Academy of Sciences began to study the relationship between production and lighting intensity at Western Electric Company. Their study did not find a relationship. Soon afterward another group of researchers, from the Harvard Business School, under the leadership of Elton Mayo, began a series of projects at the same plant. Their research also tested the relationship between worker output and working conditions. They also found no relationship, but they did notice one interesting phenomenon. During their study of lighting intensity they noticed that, even when the lights were practically turned off, *worker production increased.* They attributed this effect (called the Hawthorne effect, after the Hawthorne plant of Western Electric) to the fact that the workers were receiving attention, even though worsened working conditions resulted from the attention.

These studies marked the beginning of the human relations movement in industry. For the first time, evidence on such variables as worker attitude, morale, informal work groups,

The human relations theory of organization states that people-oriented management is more effective than production-oriented management.

and social relations was collected. No longer was it satisfactory to claim that production is totally a function of the structure and design of formal organizations. No longer could workers and their feelings, attitudes, capabilities, and perceptions be ignored. After the Hawthorne studies were reported, other researchers designed studies that tested people-oriented variables and their effect within the organization.

Representative of this research were the studies by Fleishman, Harris, and Burtt which asserted that people-oriented management is more effective than production-oriented management. The basic logic of the human relations approach was to increase concern for workers by allowing them to participate in decision making, by being more friendly, and by calling them by their first names, which improved worker satisfaction and morale. The net outcome would be lower resistance to and improved compliance with management's authority. In short, "If I'm nice to you, you'll feel happy and do what I want." Unfortunately, many managers saw this approach as an opportunity to *manipulate* their employees. Huse and Bowditch warned that the outspoken criticism of the movement may have caused some of the important findings of the early human relations research to be overlooked:

> In some circles human relations has been described as "warm feeling" training and consists primarily of company picnics, getting the wives together, and company-sponsored athletics. But this is a distortion of the research findings provided by the original human relations studies.

Rush summarized much of the thinking and criticism of the human relations approach as follows:

> Here the emphasis was on creating a work force with high morale. It represented an attempt to break down formal or arbitrary boundaries that are part of the fabric of a stratified and bureaucratic organizational structure. Managers trained in human relations learned to be "friendly"

toward their subordinates, to call them by their first names, and generally to try to keep people content as a part of "one big happy family." The attempt to democratize the organization found expression in company-sponsored recreational activities, and in increased emphasis on fringe benefits.

The human relations movement . . . has been criticized widely as manipulative, insincere, and, most importantly, as ignoring the reality of economic variables. It is accused of equating high morale with high productivity. To some organization theorists, this represents a naive and simplistic view of the nature of man. They hold that, on the contrary, "there are a lot of happy but unproductive workers."

Herzberg spoofed the entire human relations movement in his classic article in the *Harvard Business Review:*

Over thirty years of teaching and, in many instances, of practicing psychological approaches to handling people have resulted in costly human relations programs and, in the end, the same question: How do you motivate workers? Here, too, escalations have taken place. Thirty years ago it was necessary to request, "Please don't spit on the floor." Today the same admonition requires three "please's" before the employee feels that his superior has demonstrated the psychologically proper attitudes toward him.

A contemporary example of the human relations approach to organizing people is the management of a major league baseball team. The owner of this team paid his players higher salaries than any other team in baseball. Curfews were relaxed and almost never enforced. Star players were practically their own boss, and if a conflict between a star and an average player arose, the latter was usually traded quickly, with no attempt made to resolve the conflict. As a result of this human relations approach, the members of the team reported to the press that they were extremely satisfied with the management. Word spread around the league, and this team was soon labeled "the country club of baseball." The team hardly ever finished out of the second division (which in baseball is very unimpressive).

Another example of the strict human relations approach to management is offered by the manager in a small organization who practiced the following behaviors. He frequently joked and laughed with his employees; he often patted them on the back; he scheduled and hosted frequent and expensive parties; he supplemented the incomes of certain favored employees with paid-for trips and vacations; he resolved conflict by avoiding issues, attempting to "laugh it off"; he rewarded even the incompetent employees with token and merit salary increases. The net result of his behavior was a relatively happy but stagnant organization.

Before you condemn the entire human relations movement as a disastrous, insincere, and manipulative approach to management, remember that this approach became the foundation for successful present-day management theories. In the next chapter, we make an important distinction between *human relations* (which concerns only people-oriented variables) and *human resources* (which concerns both production and human variables). One very important outgrowth of the human relations movement was the identification of *the informal organization* not shown on management charts. Since the Hawthorne studies first demonstrated that certain relationships arise that are not linked to formal authority and job functions, the study of personal and informal relationships has continued. Davis described an informal organization as based on people and their relationships rather than on positions and their functions. He distinguished informal power as personal and formal power as institutional:

> Power in informal organization is earned or given permissively by group members, rather than delegated; therefore, it does not follow the official chain of command. It is more likely to come from peers than from superiors in the formal hierarchy; and it may cut across organizational lines into other departments. It is usually more unstable than formal authority, since it is subject to the sentiments of people. Because of its subjective nature, informal organization is not subject to management control in the way that formal organization is.

For Davis, the main criteria of an informal leader are age, seniority, technical competence, work location, freedom to move around the work area, and a responsive personality. It would be wise for the manager in an organization to identify and have rapport with the informal leaders; such rapport may minimize potential conflict. An example of an informal organization concerns an assistant professor in a university department of fifteen members. Despite his lack of tenure and relatively low seniority in the department and at the university, this faculty member achieved prominence within his department as a competent researcher, an excellent teacher, and an active member in his professional organizations. As a result, he was highly respected by his colleagues and gained much influence and prominence in the university and the community. When decisions regarding promotion, tenure, and staffing were to be made, the department chairman frequently sought the advice of this faculty member. The chairman reasoned that the assistant professor wielded much influence within the department and had the potential to generate much negative opinion toward him as chairman. In short, the chairman recognized this faculty member's informal power and decided to use it to his advantage.

One communication-related phenomenon that arises from the informal organization is the grapevine and the spread of rumors. In chapter 4, we will study the grapevine, its roots in the informal organization, and ways to control the spread of rumors.

As we conclude this section on the human relations school, it should be apparent that just as the classical school is narrow and rigid in its emphasis on structure and function, so is the human relations school rigid in its concern for people. As the next section on the social systems school will show, there is no one best way to organize and manage people. It all depends!

The Social Systems School

I was once scheduled to depart on a plane to the West Coast at 9:30 A.M. When the plane was thirty minutes late arriving (and still not in sight), I asked the airline supervisor about the delay and was informed that the plane "was late getting into St. Louis and would arrive in fifteen minutes." I asked why it was late getting into St. Louis, and he replied, "Because it was late getting into Chicago." Finally, in anger I asked, "Why was it late getting into Chicago," and he answered, "Because of a snowstorm in Boston."

This example illustrates the underlying logic inherent in the social systems school of organization: all parts affect the whole; every action has repercussions throughout the organization. In this case, a snowstorm in one city affected airplane timetables, airport operations, and passenger nerves in three other cities thousands of miles apart. A baseball player may make an error in fielding a ball, which allows a runner to reach first oase, the runner on first base to go to second base, the runner on second base to reach third base, and the runner on third to get home with the winning run. A student may fail a test and by that failure lower the curve for the rest of the students, which may help raise the grade of a lucky friend. A faculty member may publish an article that establishes her as a national expert in her field, which influences positively her application for a large grant, which provides overhead funds to the university, a percentage of which ultimately reaches her department, which uses some of the funds to send another faculty member to a meeting in another city.

In all these cases, what affected one part of the organization affected all parts of the organization. Nothing exists without eventual impact on something else. In chapter 1, we defined an organization as an open system whose parts all related to its whole and its environment. We stated that all parts of an organization are interdependent or interlocking because all parts within the system, called subsystems, affect and are affected by each other. This means simply that a change in any part of the system will affect all other parts of the system.

When the organization is viewed as a social system, questions of structural and human variables assume new importance. No longer can the job function of a machine riveter be divorced from the successful functioning of the entire organization; nor can the morale of one employee be a minor point of concern. No longer can a single message sent via the grapevine be ignored; nor can the orders of one supervisor to her staff be minimized. The organization must be considered from a large point of view that acknowledges that both functional and human issues influence an organization. Questions of job duty, chain of command, span of control, and decision making are *equal* in importance to questions of attitude, morale, behavior, role, and personality. Managers who focus upon their own department and overlook the effect of their employees on other departments or on the organization as a whole may face the loss of production efficiency. Longenecker has supported this point of view:

> The systems concept is useful because of its strong emphasis upon these interrelationships. These interrelationships are stressed as being of primary importance. The role of management is seen as the management of interrelationships. This emphasis avoids some of the pitfalls of a "components" mentality in which departments work out their own relationships in a haphazard manner.

Because of the importance of interrelationships, some organizations employ the "fast-track" system for determining immediately the likely success of new executives. New employees are asked to produce within one month a list of the major job objectives they consider to be included in their responsibilities. Next, they must identify *who* in the organization (people, department, units) both influence and are influenced by these objectives. Finally, they must list the resources and information they will need from these other people and units and what the other people and units will need from them. The fast-track system can help organizations both teach and screen system thinking as they orient their leaders. One organization that uses the fast-track system gave this assignment to a new manager: "Look at your new department and at all other departments in the company whose operations could impinge on your department and upon whose operations your department could impinge. Uncover all problems and look for impediments to the success of both your department and the company. Within twenty days compile a list of the problems and prepare a plan of action for solving the problems and moving the company forward. List the steps in your plan in order of priority and provide a timetable for accomplishing each step."

Among researchers who have made the major contributions to the development of both general systems theory and the use of systems theory in organizations are Ludwig von Bertalanffy, Kenneth Boulding, James March and Herbert Simon, Daniel Katz and Robert Kahn, and Paul Lawrence and Jay W. Lorsch.

Scott likened organization theory to general systems theory because both study the following factors:

1. Parts (individuals) in aggregates and movement of individuals into and out of the system
2. Interaction of individuals with the environment of the system

Interactions among individuals in the system

3. General growth and stability problems of systems

Huse and Bowditch summarized the main characteristics that define an organization as a system:

1. Composed of a number of subsystems, all of which are interdependent and interrelated
2. Open and dynamic, having inputs, outputs, operations, feedback, and boundaries.
3. Striving for balance through both positive and negative feedback
4. With a multiplicity of purposes, functions, and objectives, some of which are in conflict, which the administrator strives to balance

Some of the key concepts necessary to the understanding of an organization as an open social system are feedback, balance, input, transformation, output, and interdependence. We agree with Katz and Kahn's (1966) theoretical model for the understanding of an organization:

> . . . [it is] an energic input-output system in which the energic return from the output reactivates the system. Social organizations are flagrantly open systems in that the input of energies and the conversion of output into further energic input consist of transactions between the organization and its environment.

Figure 2.5 presents our model for viewing an organization as an open system. We will now define each of the concepts just listed and provide organizational examples that illustrate their use.

The Organization as an Open System

A system may be labeled either open or closed, depending upon the nature of its boundaries. Fisher and Hawes distinguish the two as follows:

> A closed system has fixed boundaries which permit no interaction with the environment. The result is that the structure, function, and behavior of the system are relatively stable and predictable if the initial arrangement of components is known. An open system, on the other hand, has permeable boundaries which allow for environment-system interaction. The result is that the structure, function, and behavior of the open system is changing perpetually.

Figure 2.5 Diagram showing that an organization is an open system.

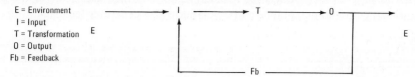

An open system is dynamic, changing constantly; a closed system is static and stable. An organization is an open system because of its constant interaction with its environment. Organizations receive inputs from their environment (workers, raw materials, information) and send outputs into their environment (products, services, pollution, information). Few organizations can survive if they are not cognizant of their potential markets, suppliers, users, publics, and government regulations.

For many years universities, especially public universities, appeared to ignore their public. Courses without apparent relevance to the immediate needs of the students and their future employment were offered. Research programs whose goals were not communicated and which offered no benefit to the immediate community proliferated. The public considered student unrest and demonstrations to be regular occurrences. The cumulative effect of these and other events was that the voting, taxpaying public developed a negative attitude toward universities. The ultimate impact of this attitude is now felt by universities dependent upon legislative budgets, private donations, and foundation grants for their very survival. Today, we see many universities engaging in extensive public relations programs, using such techniques as speakers' bureaus, rap sessions, visitors' day, and television and radio commercials as they attempt to interact positively with their environment.

An example of an organization that failed to monitor and respond to the signals of its consumer environment—the marketplace—was Chrysler Corporation. Only under the threat of bankruptcy did it finally shift manufacturing and engineering strategies to produce cars more in tune with energy-conscious consumers' demands.

Key Concepts of the Organization as an Open System

Feedback

The cyclic nature of systems is reflected in feedback. In other words, some of the system's outputs are sent back into the system as new inputs. Huse and Bowditch explained this concept thus:

> Since open systems are never completely closed off from the outside world, they are affected by the environment and, in turn, have an effect on the environment through output information which, in turn, is fed back into the system as an input to guide and control the operation of the system.

For example, students who receive an education from a university regenerate the university by getting jobs and paying taxes, some of which are returned to the university. Alumni who contribute directly to the university development fund or persuade younger brothers or sisters to attend the same university or communicate favorably or unfavorably with the board of regents all provide feedback to the system by regenerating its inputs. A clothing manufacturer who sells cotton products for monetary gain and then uses some of the money to buy additional cotton to manufacture more clothing also generates feedback.

Balance

Systems ensure their survival by importing more energy than they export. When the ratio is reversed, the system dies. A steady balance between energy input and product output, if maintained, produces a state of homeostasis. A balanced state within the system should *not* be confused with a static, nonchanging system. The constant flow of inputs which are transformed into outputs provides the dynamism characteristic of open systems. When we talk, therefore, about a balanced, homeostatic system, we mean a system that is surviving because it is able to generate sufficient input from its environment. Today, we are faced with an energy crisis because the oil cannot be produced and imported indefinitely.

Another example of the impact of the environment upon the functioning of an organization is the electric company of a southwestern state which is now engaged in an extensive campaign to win public understanding of its building a new plant with a relatively high air pollution potential. In this example, the pollution from the plant *and* the campaign of the speakers' bureau both represent system-environment interaction patterns.

Input

The energy from the environment that is imported into the organization is input. Just as human systems require oxygen, computers need data cards, and automobiles use gasoline, so do organizations require energy, people, resources, and information. By definition, an organization as an open system needs natural and human resources from its environment in order to maintain itself. These resources are called system input. A university requires such inputs as students, faculty, money, buildings, books, roads, support services, and personnel. An automobile plant is sustained by such inputs as steel, plastics, rubber, workers, high temperatures, and large assembly-line buildings.

Transformation

The process by which the inputs are changed into outputs is transformation. Katz and Kahn referred to this process as throughput. Here we are talking about the actual process of computation, manufacturing, engine movement, photosynthesis, and digestion. In an organization, transformation occurs as products are designed and built, people are educated and trained, and services are provided or sold. At a university, students are transformed from new, young learners into knowledgeable, educated citizens. In a clothing manufacturing plant, cotton is transformed into a pair of pants. At a police department, untrained individuals are transformed into powerful forces that protect and serve the public.

Output

The product or service the system exports into its environment is output. Computers produce reams of printed paper output which provide answers to complex problems. Automobiles allow people to get from one geographic point to another. Police services help reduce crime rates. Manufacturing plants produce clothing, appliances, furniture, and other basic human needs. Labor unions produce increased salaries and fringe benefits for workers. Universities provide educated students, practical research findings, and personnel willing to serve the public. Whatever the primary reason for the organization's existence, it will be reflected in its environmental outputs.

Unless the balance can be shifted, all of us may have to walk to and from our work, our homes, and our schools. Organizations tend to collect more resources than they can use to ensure their survival. A university often requests more legislative funding than it actually needs, hoping that after cuts it will still have enough money to operate. A police department may be able to function with 300 officers but requests a budget from the city for 310. An automobile manufacturer may stockpile steel reserves in anticipation of an increase in the price of steel.

Interdependence

The nuts and bolts of systems theory is interdependence. As discussed earlier in this book, interdependence means the interlocking relationships between the parts of a system and the whole system. When one part of a system or subsystem is changed, the impact of the change is eventually felt throughout the organization, just as a stone thrown into a pond sends out a ripple. Since we have already amply discussed this concept, now consider examples of interdependent relationships in organizations.

A graduate teaching assistant at the University of New Mexico once read a poem containing profane language to his English class. Word of this act reached one member of the New Mexico legislature who loudly denounced this instructor, his deeds, and the entire university for apparently condoning this act. The legislator ultimately introduced a resolution into the legislature calling for reduction of the university's budget to *one dollar*. Although the motion failed, public attitude toward the university was negatively affected for several years. An attitude survey found that some people continued "to hold it against the university that swearing was allowed in class."

Another example followed from an actual legislative cut in operating funds at a university. It had the following results: certain academic programs had to be curtailed; several faculty positions were eliminated; and student enrollment in other programs increased. However, since there were fewer faculty to teach the increased numbers of students, enrollment limits were imposed on certain courses. The ultimate losers were the public whose children received a lower quality education than normally could be expected with a larger faculty.

In these illustrations, action at either end of the organization (the poem was at the bottom of the organization; the budget cuts were at the top of the organization) produced effects influencing the entire organization. Such is the nature of interdependence. Given this fact, it now appears naive, and even stupid, for a manager to say, "I don't care what's going on in other departments, I just want us to do a good job." The main lesson of the systems approach to organizations is that the manager's job and the organization's very existence may depend on those "other departments."

Organizational Goals and Measurement of Effectiveness

The degree to which an organization achieves its goals is the degree to which it is judged effective. Often, achieving the goal is not enough if the quality of the product or service reduces the value of the goal. Thus, the pants manufacturer's goal of 14 percent more pants during the first quarter may be achieved, but having to replace 50 percent of the zippers may reduce the overall effectiveness of the company. This is precisely why most organizations have the equivalent of a quality control unit which monitors such factors as work errors, accidents and safety records, number of complaints, and so forth.

Some of the measures of organizational effectiveness, depending upon the type of organization, are as follows:

1. Employee turnover (e.g., U.S. Army)
2. Absenteeism (e.g., the Finnish automobile industry)
3. Number of grievances (e.g., a school union)
4. Employee attitudes (e.g., a manufacturing company's morale)
5. Quality of work (e.g., the number of errors in checking-account balances in a bank)
6. Safety record (e.g., the number of accidents of a trucking company)
7. Productivity (e.g., the number of automobiles produced per unit of time)
8. Return on investment (e.g., the percentage of profit returned to a company for its investment in a new product)
9. Performance (e.g., employee appraisal ratings by superiors)
10. Employee commitment (e.g., the purchase of Employee Stock Option Plans within a large industry)
11. Community satisfaction with an organization (e.g., the complaints an airline receives)
12. Satisfaction of supplier with organization (e.g., the number of orders sold to a chemical company)
13. Consumer satisfaction (e.g., the number of complaints a department store receives)
14. Ability to identify problems or opportunities (e.g., the number of suggestions a manufacturing company gives rewards for)
15. Social responsibility (e.g., the amount of money a computer company donates to the community symphony)
16. Quality of life (e.g., the number of employees and families for whom a large industry provides graduate education)
17. Environmental impact (e.g., the amount of pollution a steel company produces)

Whatever measures are most appropriate for it and its goals, an organization must assess its effectiveness in order to cope with its environmental demands.

Communication Implications of Organizational Structure

Structure refers to the network of relationships and roles found throughout the organization. Structure enables the organization to meet its objectives effectively and in an orderly manner. Thus, structure provides the stability, predictability, and regularity necessary for an organization to function without anarchy. Structure also provides an interesting communication paradox: the extreme formality or cumbersome size or bewildering complexity of some structures can act as a communication block, filtering and distorting potentially useful information. McPhee (1985) emphasized that structure communicates constraints that organizational members face in the communication process. On the other hand, informal structures tend to allow more information to flow across their network paths than people can handle, which leads to overload. The major communication implication of structure, then, is that the structure most suitable for present organizational needs will allow important information to flow freely without overloading relevant decision makers.

In the 1950s, one of my client organizations was a relatively small midwestern university having a few thousand students and two hundred faculty. Following a merger with the state education system, the course offerings of the university changed, and so did the student clientele. The university began to attract several thousand additional students who were nontraditional undergraduates (older and employed), most of whom wanted to attend night sessions. The organizational structure—a relatively informal, highly centralized network centering around the offices of the president and academic vice president—was no longer suitable for the growth needs of the university. The president, used to the "good old days," still conducted much of his official business in the corridors, which he frequently roamed "to see who was around." His staff of one secretary and one administrative assistant were constantly harried by memos, letters, and phone calls, mostly from faculty and deans awaiting replies to earlier requests. To compound matters, the president spent 60 percent of his time lobbying for funds with the state legislature. *But* he retained final authority for most academic decisions. The academic vice president and his staff (one secretary and one assistant) were intimidated by the president and his style and, therefore, made no major decision without "checking with the boss." The council of deans met frequently, but usually only to debate inconsequential matters. In desperation, and out of frustration due to lack of attention, faculty and administrators constantly sent the president reprints, papers, and copies of extensive studies. When I arrived to interview the president I found him bent over, picking up a stack of papers from the floor where he had filed and tossed several dozen documents sent to his office. His opening remarks to me were, "Look at all this stuff! I can't understand why they keep sending it to me!"

Life in the 1950s must have been reasonably pleasant for this president. His environment was stable and the structure of his university was suitable for his needs. The peace so lulled him that he failed to notice the rapid changes in his environment. His organizational structure, once adequate, was no longer appropriate, and his failure to adapt led in time to the crisis I found. In short, the lack of formalized structures—namely, gatekeepers, decentralized decision makers, and additional staff—created an unbearable overload situation in which little progress toward achieving goals could be realized.

Sometimes managers may believe they are coping with shifting environmental influences by adapting their structure, only to find they have chosen the wrong adaptation. Such was the case of a large commercial bank. To compete more successfully with other banks (which offered checking accounts to take advantage of a change in local laws), the bank decided to involve its several thousand employees more fully in a campaign to attract customers. The bank chose to create a new structure—called, coincidentally, a "communication network"—in which relevant information from top management was to be filtered through "network persons" to employees. The bank, however, neglected to adequately prepare the "network personnel" for the large volume of additional information; the new tasks of reading, synthesizing, and translating; and the new behavior of meeting with employees in groups. The result was disaster. The network personnel typically received their packets of information and promptly filed them in a wastebasket. Morale problems mounted among employees who felt left out of the network, and the bank's share of the market declined even more.

Again, we find an organization reacting to sudden shifts in its environment rather than planning ahead for the possible. The explosion that occurred was predictable, because the bank hastily implemented a new structural artifact *after* its market status had been affected by new laws.

Another financial institution is in a relatively stable state, enjoys a large share of its market, but has an ineffective communication system. The top six executives who run the two-thousand-employee organization recently designed and implemented a corporate plan based on an outline of the financial and management goals for the coming five years. Amidst the plaudits for "finally telling us where we're going" were comments from subordinates: "Where do we fit into this plan?" "Why weren't we asked for our opinion on this matter?" These are the clues that reveal a limited upward-directed input system and indicate a top management group behaving in secrecy and not willing to listen. Adherence to a highly formal structure, a common practice in financial institutions, may work in times of low uncertainty, but watch out when the prime lending rate drops 1 percent!

A U.S. senator's office with only thirty employees had a surprisingly high degree of differentiation among its personnel and no significant integrating mechanisms. As a result, the press secretary rarely knew what constituent requests an aide was working on because the aide infrequently told him. On one occasion the press secretary learned from someone else about a difficult constituent request the aide had just completed. I asked the aide why she had not checked with the press secretary, and she replied, "He's too busy, and what I'm doing isn't that important." Such a situation could be explosive at election time!

Matrix Organizations

A matrix organization is one with a multiple chain of command. The distinguishing hallmark of a matrix is the two-boss manager. The matrix organization first evolved in the aerospace industry and is now in use wherever an organization must share resources, process large amounts of information, and focus on more than a single dimension of professional disciplines.

A matrix works particularly well in small organizations with a history of informality in their communication patterns. While the matrix is formal, it preserves many of the advantages of an informal organizational structure by encouraging cross-function communication and innovative thought and action. A concept basic to all discussions of matrix organizations is the distinction between divisions and resources. Broadly speaking, resources can be thought of as "inputs" to the matrix and divisions as the "outputs." Divisions are typically organized to combine all the business functions logically needed to serve the requirements of the respective customer groups while avoiding duplication of efforts through sharing resources. Resources are typically organized around the technical, professional, and function skills by means of which the divisions serve their customers. The divisions and the resources must work together to get the whole job done. Usually, the chief executive officer (CEO) or his or her designee has the responsibility of directing all the groups toward common objectives. However, powerful support for this also comes from within the matrix organization. Selected managers have responsibilities and reporting points in both divisions and resources. It is through these "two-boss managers" that significant integration of an organization is achieved.

One of the two hundred largest industrial corporations in the United States, with assets in excess of $2 billion and more than 30,000 employees in North America and Europe, recently adopted a matrix organizational structure. Since a matrix is a powerful way of organizing resources to focus on relatively short-term projects, and since this corporation is a

A matrix works particularly well in smaller organizations whose history consists of informality in their communication patterns.

large, diversified system confronting a rapidly changing market, the matrix is a good structure for their current needs. Notice in table 2.1, which illustrates their matrix, that members of the manufacturing department report both to the corporate manufacturing head and to the head of profit center 1. The matrix system is also a good warning mechanism of potential problems in authority, power, communication delegation, and control. Ambiguities in such areas typically cause conflicts which tax the interpersonal skills of most managers and require negotiation and confrontation instead of avoidance behavior.

A matrix is not a loose association of people. Every person has reporting points and is accountable for specific goals or tasks. In many instances, the matrix assigns more responsibility than authority to an individual. It is, therefore, an excellent environment in which to train general managers. Notice how in figure 2.6, the two-boss manager actually works.

A matrix permits flexibility and a degree of informality but also requires that attention be paid to the special requirements of direct flow of information and personal interaction at all levels. A price associated with this type of structure is that the "boss" (or bosses in a matrix) is not automatically informed if he or she is not required to be a part of the communication channel. However, the need to avoid surprises is not reduced. Employees have the responsibility for keeping supervisors informed when communicating directly across the organization. To do this well requires a clear understanding with each boss about what must be discussed before taking action, what should be discussed simply to keep informed, and what can be omitted from discussions when everyone is busy.

Table 2.1 Sample Matrix Organization

Corporate Unit/Resource	Profit Centers (PC)/Divisions				
	PC 1	PC 2	PC 3	PC 4	PC 5
Manufacturing					
Employee Relations					
Administration and Finance					
Technology (research and development)					
Marketing					

Figure 2.6 Two-boss manager in matrix organization.

Communication Implications of Organizational Restructure

Managers and organizations who desire to become more proactive in coping with potential shifts in organizational structure that may have an impact upon their communication systems should consider the following questions. Some were adapted from Farace and Danowski. Questions 1–5 apply at the *systems level:*

1. Does the current structure of the organization allow it to meet its objectives? Can alternative structures better facilitate communication flow and organizational effectiveness?
2. What are the major sources of information from the environment? Can organization-environment stresses be alleviated by reducing redundant organization-environment links? Can alternative mechanisms be created to improve communication flow between the organization and its environment?
3. Do the work, innovative, social, and grapevine networks of the organization differ? In what respects are such differences beneficial or harmful to organizational effectiveness?
4. What should be done when discrepancies between actual and expected networks occur? Form new groups? Change existing groups or eliminate their functions? Retain existing groups because they serve useful integrative functions?

5. Which groups are well connected? Which groups are not? Should groups be isolated? be integrated? Do groups isolated from the total organization experience information underload? Are certain groups too highly connected to other groups in the organization, perhaps causing information overload? Are there too many links through which information must pass to reach certain groups, increasing the likelihood of information distortion?

Questions 6–8 apply at the *group level:*

6. Are certain groups too large? too small? Are the internal communication patterns of groups too restricted for optimum task accomplishments or member morale? Are groups dominated too much by one or two individuals? Or is the internal communication pattern too loose and unrestricted to accomplish particular task objectives?
7. Is the group structure sufficiently controlled? Are the paths of communication between any two group members too long to be effective?
8. In groups dominated by a few individuals, do those persons have the necessary communication skills and training for the role?

Questions 9–11 apply at the *individual level:*

9. Who are the key communicators in the organization? Are their patterns of communication consistent with their prescribed job functions? If not, what are the reasons for the inconsistency? Should their functions be changed? Should their skills be changed? Is such change possible?
10. Who are the liaisons? Are the persons performing these roles the ones expected to do so because of their place in the organizational chart or because of their job descriptions? Do the liaisons serve an integrative or supervisory function? If the liaisons do not have the management role, should their functions be changed? Do the liaisons need more responsibility or clearer authority or additional skills to best carry out their roles? Are there a sufficient number of liaisons to provide effective coordination of work group activities?
11. Who are the isolates? How many individuals are isolated from communication flows? Do certain individuals fail to communicate about work-related matters? Are new channels of communication needed to integrate the isolates into the organization?

One of my clients, a large organization with a central headquarters and seven regional sales offices, discovered the unfortunate fact that their regional sales offices had few links with each other. We were asking question 5 above: which groups, if any, were well connected? which were not? which were isolated? which were integrated? The significance of discovering the low level of communication among this organization's branch offices was the consequent revelation that there is no system of peer support, little opportunity for people to share common problems with one another, and more importantly, possibly find solutions to some of the common problems confronting regional sales personnel. Figures 2.7 and 2.8 illustrate this problem of low integration. Note in figure 2.7 how the contacts initiated by the regional offices as they attempt to reach the Detroit office are not reciprocated. These incomplete communications are further illustrated in figure 2.8, which shows how futile the initiated communications of the Chicago office have been.

Figure 2.7   Detroit office/regional office paths.

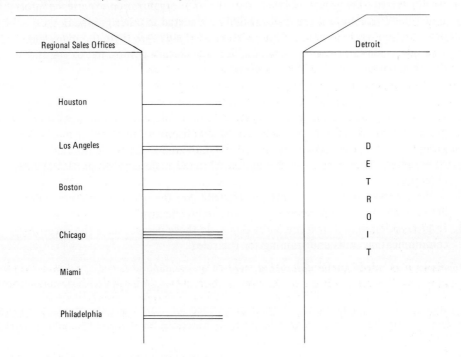

Figure 2.8   Chicago office/regional office paths.

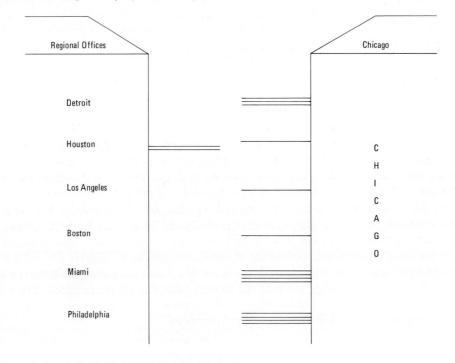

A further note about structure—up to this point we have talked about the communication implications of organizational structure. The organization that is truly coping ultimately lets the communication system dictate the structure of the organization. Just as a wise landscape architect often designs sidewalks for areas where grass has been trodden bare by footsteps, so does a proactive organization cope with the potential for future overload by designing structures to fit existing communication patterns.

Organization is not in itself an objective. An organizational form is selected to enhance the cooperation needed to achieve objectives through combined efforts. The role of management is the same regardless of organizational form: communicating objectives, establishing individual goals, and motivating for excellence in performance. In chapters 4 and 11 we examine closely network analysis—a system of gathering the information that can help organizations design their structures to best meet their current and projected needs.

SUMMARY

We are surrounded by manufacturing, service, governmental, social, and even criminal organizations. Understanding their components, structures, and relationships may improve the quality of our interaction with these organizations. An organization is defined as a network of interdependent relationships that can be viewed in accordance with the principles of three schools of thought: the classical school, the human relations school, and the social systems school.

The classical school focuses on the underlying structure and job functions of the people in the organization. Of prime interest to this school are the levels in the hierarchy, chain of command, job duty or role, division of labor, centralization, numbers of employees at each level of the hierarchy, line versus staff relations, and size and shape of the organization.

The human relations school of thought is concerned primarily with the people in the organization. Managers and scholars interested in this approach focus on such people-oriented variables as status, role, informal groups, social relations, morale, attitude, and personality.

The social systems school of thought concentrates on the relationship of the parts of the organization to the whole organization and the interlocking, interdependent nature of this relationship. The central theme of this school is that whatever affects one part of the system affects all parts. A model for viewing the organization as a system was presented and several key concepts to the theory were discussed: input, transformation, output, feedback, balance, and interdependence. The differences between open and closed systems were mentioned to show that an organization is an open social system by virtue of its interaction with its environment. Several communication implications for both structuring and restructuring an organization were mentioned.

EXERCISES

1. List three characteristics of each of the following groups which define them as organizations: (a) a social fraternity or sorority, (b) a basic chemistry class, (c) a drug store, (d) the Democratic or Republican Party.

2. Visit a local industrial or manufacturing plant. Ask the plant manager or the personnel manager for a copy of the organization chart. Discuss it with the manager. Try to meet as many of the people on the chart as you can. Ask them if they use or understand the organization chart.

3. While you are at this plant, meet with an hourly worker and his or her immediate supervisor. Ask them both if they can tell how many pieces of work are produced by that worker each day. Are there specific records and charts available? Are they posted so that others can see them? Is there a bonus system?

4. Visit with a police department or a military organization. How many of Fayol's principles of management do they follow? Talk with both management and employee representatives.

5. Design a formal organization chart for an organization to which you belong. Include both the chain of command and the job duties of the people in the organization. How many levels does the organization have? How many job functions? What is the average span of control for each manager?

6. Interview both an assistant to a manager and an assistant manager. Ask them what their specific duties are. What kinds of authority and responsibility does each have? What kinds of contacts and liaisons within the organization does each have? Who would you say is the more powerful individual?

7. Visit with either the personnel director or the training director of a local organization. What kinds of human relations training or practices does the organization use? Are there specific tests measuring managers' human relations skills and abilities? Ask this person what he or she thinks of *sensitivity training*. Report your findings to the rest of the class. Discuss the reactions you got to the phrase "sensitivity training."

8. Plant a message in an organization you belong to. Wait approximately one day and then interview six members of the organization. Ask each of them what portion of the message was heard and where, when, and through what medium it was heard. Using this information, chart both the formal and the informal organizational contacts for the six people.

9. Think of three organizations you have contact with. What is the primary function of each? What inputs help each to reach its objectives? Describe the transformation process each undergoes to reach its objective. List the concrete outputs each organization produces.

10. What are the major communication implications for organizations structured in a centralized versus decentralized manner? In a visit with a friend in an organization, discuss these implications. Does this person agree with you? Can he or she provide any examples?

11. What might be some of the costs and benefits to an organization which uses a matrix structure? What factors, internal to the organization, must be considered prior to the implementation of a matrix structure?

12. If you were trying to promote a matrix structure to an organization, how would you deal with the issue of people reporting to multiple bosses? For the organization you now belong to (or have in the past), would this dual authority reporting cause problems?

BIBLIOGRAPHY AND REFERENCES

Barnard, Chester. *The Functions of the Executive*. Cambridge, Mass.: Harvard University Press, 1938.
Bertalanffy, L., von. *Problems of Life*. London: Watts & Co., 1952.
———. "General Systems Theory." *General Systems* 1 (1956):1.
———. "General Systems Theory." *General Systems* 7 (1962):1–12.
Boulding, Kenneth. "General Systems Theory—The Skeleton of a Science." *Management Science* (April 1956): 202–5.
Boyer, Ernest. "The Bureaucracy Is the Message." *The New York Times*. November 11, 1979, 28 (Educ.).
Coch, L., and J. R. P. French. "Overcoming Resistance to Change." *Human Relations* 1 (1948):512–32.
Cooke, Morris. *Our Cities Awake*. New York: Doubleday, Doran & Co., 1918.
Dalton, Melville. "Conflicts Between Staff and Line Managerial Officers." *American Sociological Review* (June 1950):342–51.
Davis, Keith. *Human Behavior at Work*. New York: McGraw-Hill Book Co., 1972.
Deutsch, Karl. "On Communication Models in the Social Sciences." *Public Opinion Quarterly* 16 (1952):356–80.
Emerson, Harrington. *The Twelve Principles of Efficiency*. New York: Engineering Magazine Co., 1913.
Farace, R., and J. Danowski. "Analyzing Human Communication Networks in Organizations: Applications to Management Problems." Paper presented at a meeting of the International Communication Association, Montreal, 1973.
Fayol, Henri. *General and Industrial Management*. Translated by Constance Storrs. London: Pitman & Sons, 1949.
Fisher, B. Aubrey, and Leonard C. Hawes. "An Interaction System Model of Small Group Decision Making." Unpublished mimeographed manuscript, University of Minnesota, 1972.
Fleishman, E. A.; E. F. Harris; and R. D. Burtt. "Leadership and Supervision in Industry." *Ohio State Business Education Reserve Monograph* 33 (1955).
Gantt, H. L. *Work, Wages, and Profits*. New York Engineering Magazine Co., 1911.
Gilbreth, L. M. *The Psychology of Management*. New York: Sturgis & Walton Co., 1914.
Given, William B. *Bottom-Up Management*. New York: Harper & Bros., 1949.
Goldhaber, G.; M. Yates; D. Porter; and R. Lesniak. "Organizational Communication: State of the Art." *Human Communication Research* 5 (Fall 1978):76–96.
Graicunas, V. A. *Relationships in Organization*. Geneva: International Labor Office, 1933.
———. "Relationships in Organization." In *Papers on the Science of Administration,* eds. Luther Gulick and Lyndall Urwick. New York: Institute of Public Administration, 1937.
Gulick, Luther, and Lyndall Urwick, eds. *Papers on the Science of Administration*. New York: Institute of Public Administration, 1937.

Haire, Mason, ed. *Modern Organization Theory.* New York: John Wiley & Sons, 1959.

Healey, James H. *Executive Coordination and Control.* Columbus, Ohio: Bureau of Business Research, Ohio State University, 1956.

Herzberg, F. "One More Time: How Do You Motivate Employees?" *Harvard Business Review* 46 (January–February, 1968):53–62.

Huse, Edgar, and James Bowditch. *Behavior in Organizations.* Reading, Mass.: Addison-Wesley, 1973.

Ianni, Frances A. J. *A Family Business.* New York: Russell Sage Foundation, 1972.

Jablin, F. M. "Formal Organization Structure." In *Handbook of Organizational Communication: An Interdisciplinary Perspective,* eds. F. Jablin, L. Putnam, K. Roberts, & L. Porter, 389–419. Newbury Park, CA: Sage, 1987.

Katz, Daniel, and Robert Kahn. *The Social Psychology of Organizations.* New York: John Wiley & Sons, 1966.

Lawrence, P., and J. W. Lorsch. *Organization and Environment: Managing Differentiation and Integration.* Boston: Harvard University Graduate School of Business Administration, 1967.

Longenecker, Justin G. "Systems: Semantics and Significance." In *Contemporary Readings in Organizational Behavior,* edited by Fred Luthans. New York: McGraw-Hill Book Co., 1972.

March, J. G., and H. A. Simon. *Organizations.* New York: John Wiley & Sons, 1958.

McPhee, R. D. Formal structure and organizational communication. In *Organizational Communication: Traditional Themes and New Directions,* eds. R. D. McPhee and P. K. Tompkins, 149-178. Newbury Park, CA: Sage, 1985.

Mooney, James D., and Alan C. Reiley. *Onward Industry.* New York: Harper & Bros., 1931.

Parkinson, C. Northcote. *Parkinson's Law and Other Studies in Administration.* Boston: Houghton Mifflin Co., 1957.

Playboy Magazine, June 1970.

Roethlisberger, F., and W. Dickson. *Management and the Worker.* Cambridge, Mass.: Harvard University Press, 1939.

Rush, Harold M. F. "The World of Work and the Behavioral Sciences: A Perspective and an Overview." In *Contemporary Readings in Organizational Behavior,* ed. Fred Luthans. New York: McGraw-Hill Book Co., 1972.

Sayles, L., and M. Chandler. *Managing Large Systems—Organizations for the Future.* New York: Harper & Row, 1971.

Scott, William G. *Organization Theory.* Homewood, Ill.: Richard D. Irwin, 1967.

Sherman, Harvey. *It All Depends: A Pragmatic Approach to Organization.* Tuscaloosa: University of Alabama Press, 1966.

Taylor, F. *Principles of Scientific Management.* New York: Harper & Row, 1919.

Townsend, Robert. *Up the Organization.* Greenwich, Conn.: Fawcett Publications, 1970.

Weber, Max. *The Theory of Social and Economic Organizations.* Translated by A. M. Henderson and T. Parsons; edited by T. Parsons. New York: Oxford University Press, 1947.

Whyte, William F. *Human Relations in the Restaurant Industry.* New York: McGraw-Hill Book Co., 1948.

Wiener, Norbert. *The Human Use of Human Beings.* New York: Doubleday & Co., Anchor Books, 1950.

Wiio, Osmo. "Organizational Communication: Interfacing Systems." *Finnish Journal of Business Economics* 2 (1977): 259–85.

———. "Contingencies of Organizational Communication: Studies in Organization and Organizational Communication." Unpublished manuscript, University of Helsinki School of Economics, 1978.

3
ORGANIZATIONAL COMMUNICATION CLIMATE

In 1976 Steven Jobs and Stephen Wozniak, working in the former's garage in Los Altos, California, created the first Apple computer. Six years later, this company's almost 3,000 employees enjoyed sales approaching half a billion dollars. Under normal circumstances, we would expect such unusually fast growth in an organization to carry with it severe interpersonal constraints. However, at Apple these seem to have been minimized, primarily due to the efforts of a progressive management team headed by A. C. Markkula, president and CEO, whose "walk-around management" style enabled him to regularly mingle with his employees on the assembly line or in the cafeteria.

Although Markkula was replaced by John Sculley, formerly president of Pepsi-Cola, in an effort to allow Apple to keep up with the stiff competition from IBM, Markkula's and Apple's values, which all employees must adopt, still remain as descriptors of their corporate culture. These values, handed out to all Apple employees, include the following:

1. *Empathy for Customers/Users.* We offer superior products that fill real needs and provide lasting values. We are genuinely interested in solving customer problems and will not compromise our ethics or integrity in the name of profit.
2. *Achievement/Agressiveness.* We set aggressive goals and drive ourselves to achieve them . . . It's an adventure and we're in it together.
3. *Positive Social Contribution.* As a corporate citizen, we wish to be an economic, intellectual, and social asset in communities where we operate. But beyond that, we expect to make this world a better place to live.
4. *Individual Performance.* We expect individual commitment and performance above the standard for our industry. Only thus will we make the profits that permit us to seek our other corporate objectives.
5. *Team Spirit.* Teamwork is essential to Apple's success, for the job is too big to be done by any one person. Individuals are encouraged to interact with all levels of management, sharing ideas and suggestions to improve Apple's effectiveness and quality of life. It takes all of us to win. We support each other, and share the victories and rewards together.
6. *Quality/Excellence.* We care about what we do. We build into Apple products a level of quality, performance and value that will earn the respect and loyalty of our customers.

7. *Individual Reward.* We recognize each person's contribution that flows from high performance. We recognize also that rewards must be psychological as well as financial, and strive for an atmosphere where each individual can share the adventure and excitement of working at Apple.

8. *Good Management.* The attitudes of managers toward their people are of primary importance. Employees should be able to trust the motives and integrity of their supervisors. It is the responsibility of management to create a productive environment where Apple values flourish.

In 1984, Apple reported that John Sculley had become "Appleized," and Apple was listed as one of the 100 best companies to work for in America. (Levering, Moskowitz, Katz, 1984)

Sculley learned, and Markkula seemed to know intuitively what was emphasized in the paradigm of organizational communication presented in chapter 1—the importance of *people* and their attitudes, feelings, relationships, and skills. One of the seven key concepts in the definition of organizational communication in chapter 1 was *relationships.* Chapter 2 presented some of the key theories for the organization of people according to the roles and positions they occupy within an organization's formal and informal structures. Chapters 4 and 5 will focus on the communication behavior and skills of those people as they interact within the organization. This chapter is concerned primarily with the climate of the organization and how its environment influences the interaction of the members of the organization. We will study the people who belong to organizations, the relationships between their personal goals and those of the organization, and how these people can be better motivated to achieve both sets of goals.

The specific objectives are these:

1. To describe the concepts of organizational climate, communication climate, and organizational culture.
2. To describe the relationship between communication climate and overall job satisfaction.
3. To describe the relationship between "career pathing" and satisfaction with communication climate.
4. To present an overview of the human resources movement (which represents a philosophy for leadership and improvement of working relationships).
5. To describe, illustrate, and evaluate selected theories of leadership and human resources of the following researchers: Maslow, McGregor, Likert, Blake and Mouton, and Herzberg.
6. To list key propositions that evolved from the human resources movement.
7. To present and describe three new directions in human resources and motivation research.
8. To describe and evaluate Japanese models of human resources.
9. To present a specific case for analysis according to the key concepts discussed in this chapter.

Organizational Climate

Organizations that desire high productivity must depend upon their employees to achieve that outcome. As employees interact with their peers, subordinates, and supervisors, they gain insights and knowledge about the background, experiences, attitudes, and behavior of the other people. Based upon these inputs, relationships among the people in the organization become established. Such relationships may be friendly and affect the growth of the organization and its employees positively, or they may be hostile and affect both employees and organization negatively. On the other hand, relationships may have no effect upon the organization and its growth. Ideally, the climate and environment of the organization enhance relationships, to the mutual benefit of individuals and the organization.

What exactly does the term "organizational climate" mean? Most writers define climate in terms of the perceptions of an organization's members. For example, Tagiuri (1968) calls it ". . . a relatively enduring quality of the internal environment of an organization that (a) is experienced by its members, (b) influences their behavior, and (c) can be described in terms of the values of a particular set of characteristics (or attributes) of the organization." Litwin and Stringer (1968), after a series of studies, arrived at a set of dimensions of organizational climate:

1. *Responsibility.* Degree of delegation experienced by employees;
2. *Standards.* Expectations about the quality of one's work;
3. *Reward.* Recognition and reward for good work vs. disapproval for poor performance;
4. *Friendly, Team Spirit.* Good fellowship, trust.

In other words, organizational climate can be studied by observing the amount of individual autonomy and freedom experienced by individuals, the degree and clarity of structure imposed upon workers and positions, the organization's reward orientation, and the amount of consideration, warmth and support provided to workers (primarily from immediate superiors). Studies have tended to support the conclusion that the more positive the climate, the more productive the organization. (Campbell, *et al.,* 1970)

Research has shown that such relationships are not only desirable for organizational success, but are also extremely important to the very lives of human beings. In a nine-year study of 7,000 Californians, Lisa Berkman, an epidemiologist in the California Department of Health, found that people with few strong social relationships were two to four and one-half times more likely to die than were socially oriented people. Socially isolated men of all ages were more likely to die than were their gregarious counterparts. The risk for women between the ages of thirty and forty-nine years was about four and one-half times greater when strong social links were lacking. The study concluded that it makes little difference whether a social network consists mainly of a spouse, of friends, or of an *organization of some kind.* Do work organizations provide a climate for employees to build a social network? This outcome seems to depend upon the type of work.

A 1977 Opinion Research Corporation survey of 62,000 workers and 6,500 managers in 159 companies concluded that the answer is no. Thirty-eight percent of the hourly employees disliked their jobs, *but* 91 percent of the managers were satisfied with their work. Only 17 percent of the hourly employees and 45 percent of the managers felt that employees were dealt with fairly.

Organizational relationships may be friendly and affect the growth of the organization and its people positively.

Organizational relationships may be hostile and affect both the organization and its people negatively.

Unhappy American workers are a growing breed, according to an ongoing U.S. Department of Labor study. The study has been monitoring attitudes of 5,000 workers since 1966 and has found job satisfaction declining over the past several years. Workers who at one time reported that they were "highly satisfied" with their jobs are increasingly saying that they are only "somewhat satisfied" today. The study indicates that blacks tend to be less satisfied with work than other workers, and women seem to be more satisfied with their jobs than men. The study also says that higher-paid workers are generally happier employees.

Another statistic that indicates lack of job satisfaction is the national average of employee turnover—between 12 and 19 percent in most jobs. Particularly important to our study of relationships is the fact that the turnover rate is highest (19 percent) in smaller offices, where one would expect interpersonal relationships to be best, given the relative proximity of people.

Still more evidence of this growing trend comes from a 1984 study by Hay Management Consultants who interviewed 250,000 employees at 1,200 companies over an 8-year period. They found that employees at faster-growth companies with a more egalitarian attitude were more satisfied than their peers at slower growth companies whose organizational structures reinforced authority and control while inhibiting productivity and growth. They also found that work was a more satisfying experience for a manager than a non-manager, thus confirming the findings of both the Labor Department and Opinion Research Corporation. Hay reported that almost 80 percent of middle managers at slower-growth companies thought their company was a good place to work, while only 37 percent of non-management employees (professionals, clericals and hourly workers) agreed. One of Hay's most alarming statistics was that only about half of all non-management employees, in both fast and slow-growth companies, planned to remain with their company. As we will soon see, this contrasts very dramatically with the attitudes and loyalty found among Japanese workers.

Communication Climate

Research by Redding, Dennis, and others during the past fifteen years indicates that communication climate consists largely of the perceptions employees have of the quality of relationships and communication in the organization and of the degree of involvement and influence. Redding (1972) proposed that communication climate consists of five factors:

1. *Supportiveness.* Subordinates perceive that their communication relationship with their superior helps them build and maintain a sense of personal worth and importance.
2. *Participative decision making.* A generalized complex of attitudes that characterize a climate where employees are free to communicate upward with a true sense of influence.
3. *Trust, confidence, credibility.* The extent to which message sources and/or communication events are judged believable.

4. *Openness and candor.* Whatever the relationship (e.g., superior-subordinate, peer-peer, etc.), there is openness and candor in message "telling" and "listening."
5. *High performance goals.* Degree to which performance goals are clearly communicated to an organization's members.

Dennis (1975), building upon the work of Redding, defined communication climate as ". . . a subjectively experienced quality of the internal environment of an organization . . . which embraces members' perceptions of messages and message-related events occurring in the organization." Dennis tested for the existence of Redding's five communication climate factors in a study of 353 supervisory personnel from a large automobile manufacturing company and a major insurance company. He found support for only four of the five factors (supportiveness, participative decision making, openness and high performance goals). He did not find evidence that "trust" was a major factor in communication climate.

A basic tenet of communication climate is that an individual's cognitive and affective perceptions of an organization influence that individual's behavior in the organization. Major communication climate issues are concerned with the following:

1. Perceptions about communication sources and relationships in the organization:
   a. Are members satisfied with superiors, coworkers, and subordinates as sources of information?
   b. How important are these sources?
   c. Are the sources trusted?
   d. Are the sources open to communication?
2. Perceptions about information available to organization members:
   a. Is an adequate amount of information received from sources on important topics?
   b. Is the information useful?
   c. Is feedback on information sent to sources adequate?
3. Perceptions about the organization itself:
   a. How involved are members in decisions that affect them?
   b. Are goals and objectives understood?
4. Are people supported and rewarded for their efforts?
   a. Is the system open to input from its members?

Since much of the research on climate focuses on the boss-subordinate relationship, this subject is examined in detail in chapter 6, Dyadic Organizational Communication.

Communication Climate and Job Satisfaction

The importance of supportive climates in organizational communication is underscored by Redding, *"The 'climate' of the organization is more crucial than are communication skills or techniques (taken by themselves) in creating an effective organization,"* and by Schneider and Bartlett who list *managerial supportiveness* first on a list of factors influencing organizational climate. These findings appear to be consistent with the conclusion of Skinner that positive reinforcement helps develop desired responses, not merely reduce the chances of undesired responses. Nord claimed that positive reinforcement is likely to affect organizational relationships favorably rather than unfavorably.

Research conducted in the 1950s and 1960s offered moderate support for these views. For example, independently, Level, Sanborn, and Tompkins all described relationships between communication satisfaction and morale. In a major research program sponsored by the U.S. Navy, O'Reilly and Roberts discovered strong support for a relationship between both quantity and quality of communication and organizational performance. The data of Dennis, Richetto, and Wiemann also support a strong positive correlation between communication satisfaction and climate and perceived organizational effectiveness. DeWine and Barone (1984) found that as satisfaction with communication increased, positive perceptions of general organizational climate increased. They also found that as role conflict decreased, positive attitudes about climate increased. On the other hand, some researchers dispute these claims and criticize part of the research on both methodological and conceptual grounds.

Jablin, in a thorough review of the literature on communication climate, reported in 1980 that:

1. The study of communication climate has emphasized measurement of subjective (what does a person perceive to be happening?) rather than objective (what is actually happening?) phenomena.
2. Many measurements of the construct "climate" tend to overlap the construct "job satisfaction"; the former is more descriptive of the work environment, the latter of employees' reactions and feelings toward the environment.
3. Most climate studies have focused on the individual as the unit of analysis (perhaps due to the psychological heritage of much of the climate literature), while ignoring important communication-related activities at the work-group, organizational, and interorganizational levels.
4. Most climate research has proclaimed that organizations are dynamic, ongoing systems but has investigated communication behavior in organizations as a static entity.

In Europe, Osmo Wiio, chairman of the University of Helsinki's Department of Communication, heads an ongoing research effort that addresses these issues. Using a standard survey system called the OCD Communication Audit, Wiio has surveyed almost 10,000 members from all levels in thirty organizations. Wiio's approach to communication auditing is explained further in chapter 10. He argues that increases in message flow, or the openness of communication, may have a negative impact in some organizations due to overload or increased expectations. In one pre-post study, he found that dissatisfaction with the job and the organization actually increases as a function of a more open communication climate. He reasoned that the increase in communication raises employee expectations of participation in the decision-making process. When these expectations are not met, the result is greater dissatisfaction. Wiio concludes that the two factors may be related, but their relationship varies as a function of demographic and organizational contingencies.

The Work in America Institute of Scarsdale, New York has assembled 103 case studies that provide much documentation for these contingency views (Katzel, Bienstock, and Faerstein, 1977). For example, a large air freight company suffered from low morale, which was reflected in service, sales, and profits. In an effort to correct the problem, the company began a positive reinforcement program. Under the program, employee performance was audited and productive behavior was encouraged by praise and recognition from managers, who were provided with detailed instructions on various kinds of reinforcement.

The results: sales rose; savings over a three-year period amounted to $3 million; standards of customer service were met 90 to 95 percent of the time, as compared with 30 to 40 percent previously; container usage, which the company desired, rose from 45 to 95 percent.

At Bankers Trust Company, typists worked at the repetitive task of recording the transfer of stock ownership after sale or purchase, and monotony took its toll in errors and low levels of output. Realizing that the problem might be in the structure of the job rather than in the employees, the company began a job-enrichment program, which simply meant that the one-dimensional task was restructured to include related work and more responsibility.

The typists responded to the restructure, and after six months, production rates rose 92 percent in one section and more than 110 percent in two other sections. There was no increase in errors, even when some checkers' jobs were eliminated. The huge rise in productivity was not the only result. The reduction in the work force (fewer checkers) permitted the typists to assume the responsibility they apparently craved and also saved the company $300,000 per year.

One large chemical company changed its corporate management style to include the following eight responsibilities for its managers:[1]

1. All managers must set goals for their people.
2. All managers must train their people and help them become more effective in their job.
3. All managers must review their subordinates' progress in results and in goals and not appraise their activities or failures but actual achievement of their goals.
4. All managers must provide leadership. If they do not, groups will flounder, cooperative atmosphere will dwindle, and employees will work in their own direction.
5. All managers must constantly install new methods within their group and area of expertise to make their group continually more effective.
6. All managers must plan ahead. They must foresee opportunities and difficulties and develop action plans to resolve outstanding issues. Bosses are successful only when the people in their group are successful.
7. All managers must develop their people. Note that forced or artificial development is not implied, but rather opportunities and encouragement so that employees can improve as persons and as experts.
8. Finally, when appraising an employee's accomplishments, managers must use the financial and social standards they established for that employee.

Notice that all eight responsibilities contribute toward the building of a supportive communication climate.

---

1. Adapted and used with permission of the company.

Organizational Culture

Thus far, we have been talking about an organization's climate. Where climate is a measure of whether or not people's expectations of what it should be like to work in an organization are being met, organizational culture is concerned with the nature of those expectations. Culture is a pattern of beliefs and values shared by the members of an organization. Barnett (1988), in his review of the Organizational Culture literature, stated that "individuals are transformed into group members as a result of their interactions with other members of the group. It is through common social activities that the new members learn the meanings of the group's symbols and the generalized set of attitudes, values, and beliefs common to members of the organization." Typically, if employees' views are consistent with the organization's culture, then the climate will be positive. If there is a wide disparity between the culture and employees' values, the climate will be negative. Climate is often short term and may depend upon current management of an organization, but culture is usually long term, rooted in deeply held values and often very hard to change.

Kreps (1984) holds that culture is based upon an organization's development of "collectively held underlying logics and legends about organizational life and the organization's identity." He continues,

> These logics and legends are imbedded in and transmitted through formal and informal channels of organizational communication. Organizational culture is communicated to organization members and relevant others informally through interpersonal storytelling and gossiping using the organization's grapevine as a primary medium, and communicated formally through the use of advertising, slogans, organizational documents, group meetings, and public presentations. As an organization's identity emerges, organizational members interpret the organization's past, and present, making sense of the phenomena of organizational life and creating stories and legends about organizational activities. These stories and legends often provide a thematic base for the development of collective visions about the future development of the organization. Culturally derived explanations about what the organization is, what it does, how it goes about accomplishing its goals, where it has been, where it is going, and what role organization members play in these activities are essential elements in the development of an organizational identity.

Today, the study of corporate culture seems to be quite popular. Through the continued growth of organizational culture as a legitimate area of study, people such as management guru Peter Drucker have been proved wrong when they labeled many of these studies a "passing fad," which will last for only one year, while others have made a living advising companies on what type of culture will produce excellence. Rosabeth Moss Kanter (1983) has written about a "culture of pride" which, when coupled with a culture of success, would encourage firms to reach for new, innovative ways of operating. Perhaps the greatest voices preaching excellence to companies have been those of the former McKinsey & Co. consultants Thomas Peters and Robert Waterman whose book *In Search Of Excellence* has sold over 3 million copies in the U.S. They have identified forty-three American companies that, in their opinion, have become more successful than their counterparts, primarily due to the following eight attributes that define their cultures:

1. *Bias for Action.* A preference for doing something, anything, rather than losing good ideas through endless cycles of reports and committees.
2. *Staying Close to the Customer.* Learning what the customer wants and catering to him or her.

3. *Autonomy and Entrepreneurship.* Breaking the company into small companies and encouraging them to think independently and competitively.
4. *Productivity through People.* Creating in all employees the awareness that their best efforts are essential and that they will share in the rewards of the company's success.
5. *Hands-On, Value Driven.* Insisting that executives keep in touch with the company's essential business and promote a strong corporate culture.
6. *Stick to the Knitting.* Remaining with the businesses that the company knows best.
7. *Simple Form, Lean Staff.* Few administrative layers, few people at the upper levels.
8. *Simultaneous Loose-Tight Properties.* Fostering a climate where there is dedication to the central values of the company combined with tolerance for all employees who accept those values.

Since the book was published, however, many of these companies (e.g., Digital, Fluor, Hewlett-Packard, Levi Strauss, Revlon, Texas Instruments, Disney) have not exactly performed with excellence, prompting Peter Drucker to have dismissed *In Search of Excellence* as "a book for juveniles." Regardless of the long-term merits of Peters and Waterman's theories of what makes an excellent company, they certainly can't be faulted for studying the organizational cultures of the forty-three companies and attempting to identify the attributes that made them successful at the time.

George Barnett and I have developed an interview protocol we believe may be helpful to those who wish to study the culture of an organization. The questions include the following:

1. Tell me a little bit about your company. What kind of business are you in? With whom do you compete? What is your job here?
2. What is the mission of your company? What are you trying to accomplish? Are you accomplishing your mission? Why? Why not? What would you say are the goals and objectives of this company/department? Have you been achieving them? Why? Why not?
3. Are there any people in your company/division/department who are noted for their outstanding contributions? What have these "heroes" done? Are there any people here who are thought of as having had a negative influence on this company/division/department? What did these "villains" do?
4. When new people join this company/division/department, are there any words or phrases or specialized vocabulary with which they would need to become familiar?
5. (If they named a hero or villain) Earlier you mentioned _____ . Can you tell me a good or representative story or folktale about _____ that might help me better understand why he's described as a _____ ?
6. If you were to give a speech about this company/division/department to the Rotary Club (e.g.), what stories or folktales might you use to begin your speech?
7. Is there anything different or unique about the way things are done here, such as the way work is organized and accomplished? Is there anything different here at this company/division/department? Are the way decisions made unique? If I wanted to be successful here, what would I do? What would I not do?

8. Are there any rituals or ceremonies or special events that you see or participate in here? What about status symbols? Are there any? What do they mean? What impact do they have?

9. If the local newspaper were to run a story on this company, what kinds of things would they say? If you were to write the story, would you say anything differently?

10. If you were to hear good news about this company, how and from whom would you receive it? Now that you've heard it, to whom would you first tell it? How? What would be the good news? What about bad news? (Repeat)

The kind of data you would collect if you analyzed the culture of an organization would typically be qualitative by nature. You would then analyze your interview notes and draw interpretive conclusions.

Pacanowsky and O'Donnell-Trujillo (1982) describe the following set of indicators and displayers of organizational sense making that uncovers an organization's culture:

1. *Relevant constructs.* Each culture has its set of relevant constructs (objects, individuals, processes) used by organizational members. These constructs, such as "committee meeting," "seminar," and "Western Journal of Speech Communication," for a communication professor, identify the generic aspects of organizational understandings and serve as global indicators of how members structure their experiences.

2. *Facts.* Each organizational culture has its system of facts that members use to explain how and why the organization acts the way it does. These facts make up what might be viewed as the "social knowledge" of the organization.

3. *Practices.* Organizational members continually reveal the practices for accomplishing organizational activities, for "getting the job done." Practices known as "tasks" are often initially expressed formally by a supervisor, but come to be realized in the particular performances of organizational members as they become competent in the ways of their situated activities.

4. *Vocabulary.* Another distinguishing feature of any organizational culture is the particular vocabulary used by its members. This specialized vocabulary, sometimes called vernacular or argot, often provides clues as to what are the relevant constructs, facts, and practices of organizational life.

5. *Metaphors.* Useful displays of organizational culture related to vocabulary are the metaphors used by organizational members. As Lakoff and Johnson have argued, one's conception of reality is largely constituted in interlocking systems of metaphors. Organizational metaphors, when used by organizational members, may be helpful in understanding a sense of how members structure their experiences.

6. *Stories.* Each organizational culture also contains stories which members exchange on a regular basis. Stories about the personal successes or "screwups" of organizational members are not merely entertaining narratives but constitute organizational reality insofar as they signify possible future scenarios of organizational life. Other stories take on folkloric qualities which are used to substantiate organizational knowledge or pass on the unrecorded traditions or customs of organizational life.

7. *Rites and rituals.* Finally, each organizational culture develops various rites and rituals that orient members temporally and serve as occasions for sense making. Semiannual reviews, weekly staff meetings, and daily coffee breaks all constitute organizational rites and rituals that members regularly or occasionally participate in. Participation in such events provides access for members to a particular shared sense of reality. As members constitute their relevant constructs, practices, rituals, and so forth, they are also constituting parts of their organizational culture. These constructs, practices, and rituals are mini-accomplishments embedded in the larger ongoing accomplishment of organizational culture.

As an example of the way stories can become legends in an organization, the following story is often told at IBM about a security supervisor who dared to challenge Thomas Watson, Jr., the intimidating chairman of IBM's board. (Rodgers 1969)

> The supervisor was a twenty-two-year-old bride weighing ninety pounds whose husband had been sent overseas and who, in consequence, had been given a job until his return. . . . The young woman, Lucille Burger, was obliged to make certain that people entering security areas wore the correct clearance identification.
>
> Surrounded by his usual entourage of white-shirted men, Watson approached the doorway to an area where she was on guard, wearing an orange badge acceptable elsewhere in the plant, but not a green badge, which alone permitted entrance at her door.
>
> "I was trembling in my uniform, which was far too big," she recalled. "It hid my shakes but not my voice. 'I'm sorry,' I said to him. I knew who he was all right. 'You cannot enter. Your admittance is not recognized.' That's what we were supposed to say."
>
> The men accompanying Watson were stricken; the moment had unpredictable possibilities. "Don't you know who he is?" someone hissed. Watson raised his hand for silence, while one of the party strode off and returned with the appropriate badge.

While all stories may not be as revealing about a company's culture as the above, understanding as much about an organization's culture as possible will greatly help our understanding of how and why an organization communicates as it does.

Implications of Communication Climate for Career Pathing

The findings concerning communication and job satisfaction imply that employees must have the information necessary to do their jobs if they are to perform their roles adequately. To progress in an organization, however, they need to know more about the total system and how they fit into broader system objectives. If employees lack this information, they have no means of planning for advancement in the organization. They may see no clear "career ladder" and decide that their ability to progress in the organization is limited. Few employees are likely to stay satisfied with a job that offers limited opportunity for advancement.

The notion of "career pathing"—or identifying for the employee where the areas for advancement are and how to get there—is important in this regard. For career pathing to work, the supervisor or personnel counselor must be willing to share information with the employee about how the organization is run, what its objectives are, and how helping to meet those objectives is tied to advancement. The best career-path approaches offer alternative directions for advancement and allow the employee to choose among paths and goals. The findings on climate and job satisfaction indicate that one good way to identify employees who are ready for career pathing is to watch for those who express dissatisfaction and request information about the organization. They may be people ready to move up rather than troublemakers.

Another necessary condition for successful career pathing is that the organization *know* its objectives, its people, and the kinds of skills needed to meet the objectives. Information about the organization's technology, output, structure, and traditions can be combined with measures of performance and of past effectiveness to identify the present condition of the organization. Information about the education, experience, and aspirations of employees can identify the state of human resources. Examination of the economic, social, political, technological, and environmental conditions and trends confronting the organization can aid in determining the objectives that should be set to make the organization more effective as it confronts the environment. By putting this information together, the organization can determine where it is, who its people are, where it should go, and what it needs from its people to get there.

An example of a company with clearly identified and openly communicated objectives is Hewlett-Packard. Their objectives follow:

1. To achieve sufficient profit to finance company growth and provide the resources needed to achieve other corporate objectives.
2. To provide products and services of the greatest possible value to customers, thereby gaining and holding their respect and loyalty.
3. To enter new fields only when the ideas and technical, manufacturing, and marketing skills assure that a needed and profitable contribution to the field can be made.
4. To let growth be limited only by profits and ability to develop and produce technical products that satisfy real customer needs.
5. To help Hewlett-Packard people share in the company's success, which they make possible; to provide job security based on their performance; to recognize their individual achievements; and to ensure the personal satisfaction that comes from a sense of accomplishment in their work.
6. To foster initiative and creativity by allowing the individual great freedom of action in attaining well-defined objectives.
7. To honor obligations to society by being an economic, intellectual, and social asset to each nation and each community in which Hewlett-Packard operates.

A manpower analysis can help an organization specify the areas and levels of skills that will be needed to meet future objectives. The organization can determine those skills that must be brought in from outside the organization and those that can be developed in present employees. This information can then be communicated to employees so they know how to develop themselves and, therefore, how to advance in the organization.

Much of the foregoing discussion is summarized in the following steps:

1. The organization produces a long-range plan (usually three to five years) which outlines specific goals and objectives.

The organization determines its manpower needs from the projected goals and objectives.

2. The organization conducts a manpower analysis of current personnel to determine internal availability of human resources.
3. The organization computes the discrepancy between its available and its needed human resources for each major job category.
4. The organization determines its education (training and development) needs to advance internal personnel to fill needed job categories, *or* it begins external searches to fill needed jobs.
5. The organization communicates its manpower needs and educational requirements (courses, programs, qualifications, experience) to all internal personnel.
6. The organization receives applications and it interviews, screens, and prepares "ready-now" lists to help identify and plan career paths in accordance with both its own and its employees' advancement needs.

But career pathing will work only if employees perceive that their leaders' (supervisors') behavior leads to attainment of the employees' goals and clarifies the paths to these goals. House and Mitchell have developed a theory of leadership called "path-goal" theory, rooted in the assumptions of expectancy theory (Nebeker and Mitchell) that people are satisfied with a job if they think it leads to things that are highly valued, and they work hard if they believe that effort leads to things that are highly valued. The major propositions of path-goal theory follow:

1. A leader's behavior is acceptable and satisfying to subordinates if the subordinates believe the behavior is an immediate or future source of satisfaction to them.
2. The leader's behavior will motivate subordinates if satisfaction of subordinates' needs depends upon their effective performance *and* the leader's behavior creates an environment that supports, guides, coaches, and rewards subordinates for effective performance. House and Mitchell concluded that the "motivational functions of the leader consist of increasing the number of kinds of personal payoffs to subordinates for work-goal attainment and making paths to these payoffs easier to travel by clarifying the paths, reducing roadblocks and pitfalls, and increasing the opportunities for personal satisfaction en route."

The philosophy of establishing a climate where supportive relationships can thrive underlies the writings of many organizational behavioral scientists. Because these writers are concerned primarily with the control and motivation of human behavior in organizations, they are identified with the human resources movement. The remainder of this chapter is devoted to the central concepts and criticisms of this movement and to some new directions in human resources and motivation research.

Overview of Human Resources Approaches to Leadership and Management

The problem of managing employees in organizations is not new. What is new is the concern for the individual—his or her needs and personal psychology as they affect organizational needs of production and efficiency. Taylor and other scientific managers believed that the main obstacle to efficiency was the failure by management to adequately control employees' work output and sufficiently reward them for high production. Taylor devised certain methods to study jobs (time and motion studies, payment by results, production control systems) that he felt provided management with better ways of controlling employees' work output. He believed that the key to improving the organization's prosperity was to improve the prosperity of the worker. Therefore, it was easy for him to believe that workers saw themselves as "doers" and their managers as "organizers" if they were rewarded well enough. Although this approach to the management and motivation of employees seems naive to us now, many major industrial employers of the nineteenth and early twentieth century, including Henry Ford and John D. Rockefeller, accepted scientific management.

It remained for the universities to provide an alternative to "Taylorism" (as it was called). As mentioned in chapter 2, Elton Mayo, a professor of business at Harvard University, directed a series of experiments at the Hawthorne plant of the Western Electric Company near Chicago. Begun in 1927 and concluded in 1932, these experiments have had tremendous impact on the application of the behavioral sciences to management and industry. They were the first studies of the factors in the physical and social environments that affect the production and job morale of organizational employees. The experiments were at first concerned primarily with the effects of certain working conditions (job monotony, length of work day, length of rest periods, and amount of illumination) upon work output and employee efficiency. When the researchers interpreted their initial results and could find no relation between the variables, they attributed that fact to inadequate experimental design. Therefore, they formed a control group and a test group, and the next results revealed that both groups increased their output during the experiments. Even when the work day was lengthened, the number of rest pauses reduced, and the illumination reduced, output continued to increase. To quote Mayo, "The general upward trend, despite changes, was astonishing."

The researchers then decided to change their method. They believed that working conditions were not such a key factor as worker attitudes, social relations, and supervisory behavior. They recommended that attention be paid to the selection and training of supervisors and that a program of confidential interviews be instituted to give workers a chance to complain, suggest, or let off steam. In later experiments, the researchers investigated the process by which a *group* of employees controlled the pace of work to produce results satisfactory to the group, but not necessarily satisfactory to management. This was the first study of informal interaction, horizontal communication, and social organization of employees. The Hawthorne studies were criticized for being too clinical in interpretation of employee complaints and gripes (over 21,000 interviews were conducted). Many complaints seemed to be personal hang-ups rather than legitimate causes of unrest in the organization. Despite the criticism, the studies had an immeasurable effect upon future behavioral science research in organizations.

Throughout the 1940s and 1950s, emphasis on organizational research shifted from organizational to individual variables. The human relations school of thought, which emphasizes employee participation as a means to improve morale and thus production, devel-

Figure 3.1 Comparison of Miles's human resources model with the human relations model. (From R. Miles, "Keeping Informed—Human Relations or Human Resources?" *Harvard Business Review,* 1965. Reprinted with permission of the publisher.)

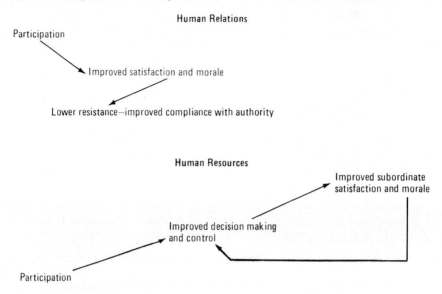

oped during this period. Some critics labeled such managers "the happiness boys," a natural reaction to this new philosophy of management. (This approach was explained in chapter 2, and we will not explore it further at this point.)

Despite the protests of advocates of human relations management that they were misunderstood, Raymond Miles, a researcher in the field, claimed that some of the criticism was justified because the researchers failed to emphasize certain concepts of their model. In a landmark article, Miles presented a new model which he called "human resources." Figure 3.1 presents both his model and the model of the human relations school.

The basic differences between human resources and human relations management are summarized in table 3.1.

Key Human Resources and Leadership Theories

The assumption from which Miles built his human resources model were derived from the work of Maslow, McGregor, and Likert. Let us look now at their theories of behavior, leadership, and management as well as those of other behavioral scientists.

Maslow

Underlying the model presented by Miles is a set of assumptions about basic human needs. One framework for studying human needs was developed by Abraham Maslow in 1954. Human resources writers are aware of its implications in organizations since fulfillment of basic needs is fundamental to the motivation of human beings.

Table 3.1 Two Models of Participative Leadership

Human Relations	Human Resources
Attitudes Toward People	
1. People in our culture share a set of needs—to belong, to be liked, to be respected.	1. In addition to sharing common needs for belonging and respect, most people in our culture desire to contribute to the accomplishment of worthwhile objectives.
2. They desire individual recognition, but even more, they want to feel a useful part of the company and their own work group or department.	2. Most members of our work force are capable of exercising far more initiative, responsibility, and creativity than their present jobs require or allow.
3. They tend to cooperate willingly and comply with organizational goals if these important needs are fulfilled.	3. These capabilities represent untapped resources which are presently being wasted.
Kind and Amount of Participation	
1. The manager's basic task is to make all workers believe that they are useful and important members of the department team.	1. The manager's basic task is to create an environment in which subordinates can contribute their full range of talents to the accomplishment of organizational goals. The manager must attempt to uncover and tap the creative resources of subordinates.
2. The manager should be willing to explain decisions and to discuss subordinates' objections to the plans. On routine matters, the manager should encourage subordinates to participate in planning and choosing among alternative solutions to problems.	2. The manager should allow and encourage subordinates to participate not only in routine decisions, but also in important matters. In fact, the more important a decision is to the manager's department, the greater should be the manager's effort to tap the department's resources.
3. Within narrow limits, the work group or individual subordinates should be allowed to exercise self-control and self-direction in carrying out plans.	3. The manager should attempt to continually expand the areas over which subordinates exercise self-direction and self-control as they develop and demonstrate greater insight and ability.
Expectations	
1. Sharing information with subordinates and involving them in departmental decision making will help satisfy their basic needs for belonging and for individual recognition.	1. The overall quality of decision making and performance will improve as the manager makes use of the full range of experience, insight, and creative ability in his or her department.
2. Satisfying these needs will improve subordinate morale and reduce resistance to formal authority.	2. Subordinates will exercise responsible self-direction and self-control in the accomplishment of worthwhile objectives that they understand and have helped establish.
3. High employee morale and reduced resistance to formal authority may lead to improved departmental performance. It should at least reduce intradepartment friction and thus make the manager's job easier.	3. Subordinate satisfaction will increase as a by-product of improved performance and the opportunity to contribute creatively to this improvement.

Source: Used by permission of the publisher. Adapted from R. Miles, "Keeping Informed—Human Relations or Human Resources?" *Harvard Business Review* 43 (July–August 1965):148–63.

Figure 3.2 Maslow's hierarchy of needs. (From P. Hersey and K. Blanchard, *Management of Organizational Behavior*, 1969, Prentice-Hall. Reprinted by permission of the publisher.)

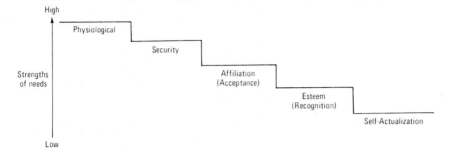

Maslow believes that basic human needs are arranged in a hierarchy according to their strength. Figure 3.2 illustrates this hierarchy of needs. The physiological needs are at the top of the hierarchy because they tend to have the highest strength until satisfied. These are the needs that must be met to sustain human life—for food and water, clothing, shelter— and in our society are most commonly satisfied by means of money. Thus, Taylor's theory is based almost entirely upon the physiological needs of man—reward employees sufficiently to satisfy their basic needs. He was right, of course, to the point at which the physiological needs are satisfied. When a person is no longer hungry, Taylor's theory runs into trouble.

As soon as the physiological needs are satisfied, which varies from person to person, the next level of needs—security—becomes predominant. This need represents man's desire to be free from danger in the present and in the future—the need for self-preservation. In the academic community, professors may satisfy their security needs when they receive tenure; students, when they graduate. A police chief involved in a student protest called in the National Guard, he said, "to protect the students involved"—interpret, "to provide the demonstrating students with security and freedom from danger."

As physiological and security needs become satisfied, affiliation (or acceptance) becomes the dominant need in the hierarchy. This need represents the need of human beings to belong, to be accepted, to be liked, to be respected by their friends. The Hawthorne studies revealed for the first time that in an organizational setting employees determine their own levels of efficiency satisfactory to the *group,* not to management. This is why when certain employees outproduced the group they were scorned by the group and labeled "rate busters," and those who underproduced and thus hurt the group's desired efficiency were labeled "chiselers." In both cases, the affiliation level of the group for deviants was very low.

Perhaps the next level of needs, esteem or recognition, explains why some Hawthorne employees became rate busters. It may be that after individuals achieve acceptance from their peers they feel the need to excel in the group to gain the esteem of their fellows. Professors who publish ten articles a year may do so to earn the recognition and esteem of their colleagues. However, other acts used to achieve esteem are not always positive. For example, union strikers who form picket lines may do so to satisfy this level of needs.

Self-actualization, the last need in Maslow's hierarchy, is the most difficult need to satisfy. Self-actualized persons have achieved their potential; that is, they have realized their full capability. Managers who enjoy managing satisfy this need by managing. Self-actualized terrorists satisfy the need by using destructive acts to defy authority. Soldiers may attain self-actualization by sacrificing their life for a buddy.

Many people questioned whether this hierarchy applied in all situations. Maslow believed that people do not all follow the prescribed order in the hierarchy. For example, some fulfill their affiliation needs before they satisfy their security needs.

What Maslow meant is that his hierarchy of needs is *typical* of the majority of people. Furthermore, acts that fulfill a need one week may not satisfy that need the following week. Terrorists who hijack a plane one week may want to blow it up the next week.

While Maslow's model appears to offer a rational framework within which to examine human behavior in organizations, there is little empirical evidence to support the theory and no research at all to test the model in its entirety. Maslow himself (1965) admitted the shakiness in applying his clinically developed theory to the organization:

> After all, if we take the whole thing from McGregor's point of view of a contrast between a Theory X view of human nature, a good deal of the evidence upon which he bases his conclusions comes from my researches and my papers on motivations, self-actualization, et cetera. But I of all people should know just how shaky this foundation is as a final foundation. My work on motivations came from the clinic, from a study of neurotic people. The carryover of this theory to the industrial situation has some support from industrial studies, but certainly I would like to see a lot more studies of this kind before feeling finally convinced that this carryover from the study of neurosis to the study of labor in factories is legitimate. The same thing is true of my studies of self-actualizing people—there is only this one study of mine available. There were many things wrong with the sampling, so many in fact that it must be considered to be, in the classical sense anyway, a bad or poor or inadequate experiment. I am quite willing to concede this—as a matter of fact, I am eager to concede it—because I'm a little worried about this stuff which I consider to be tentative being swallowed whole by all sorts of enthusiastic people, who really should be a little more tentative in the way that I am.

McGregor

The work of Taylor with its assumptions of scientific management, the Hawthorne studies and their emphasis upon the individual in the organization, and the framework for studying human needs proposed by Maslow all provided the foundation upon which Douglas McGregor developed his theory of human behavior in organizations. McGregor believed that traditional organizations—characterized by centralized decision making, hierarchical structure, and control of employee efficiency—assume certain facts about human behavior from which they derive organizational behavior. His conclusion was that if people desire external control, it is then only natural to provide such motivational control by dictating work loads and determining adequate salaries. McGregor (1960) extended this view of human behavior and its implications for managing employees to what he called Theory X. Its central principle is that an organization is controlled and directed through the exercise of authority.

In Theory X, which closely parallels the beliefs of Taylor, management concentrates its motivational efforts on satisfaction of physiological and security needs—the lower levels of needs. To close a school or keep it open during a snowstorm or during great student unrest is a decision made by a select body of people in order to control and direct the behavior of a much larger body of people and is an example of Theory X in operation.

Managers who adhere to the assumptions of Theory X will most likely employ the following communication behaviors in their organization:

1. Most messages flow in a downward direction from the top on through to the rest of the line organization.
2. Decision making is concentrated in the hands of a few people near the top of the organization.
3. Upward communication is limited to suggestion boxes, grapevines, and spy systems (employees who secretly report information about other employees to the manager).
4. What little interaction with employees takes place is with fear and distrust.
5. Downward communication is limited to informative messages and announcements of decisions, thus creating conditions for the grapevine to prosper as a means of supplementing the inadequate messages from above.
6. Since upward communication is almost nonexistent, decision making is usually based on partial, often inaccurate, information.

The net effect of these communication behaviors upon employees—which McGregor suspected would be the result—is to create an atmosphere of distrust, fear, and misunderstanding. Employees view with great suspicion communication to supplement the inadequate flow of information from the top. Eventually morale and production fall.

McGregor also began to doubt whether the higher levels of need can be ignored in any attempt to motivate satisfactory employee morale and high levels of production. He was greatly influenced by the findings of Elton Mayo and became convinced that individual behavior in the organization cannot be ignored. Thus, he hypothesized another set of assumptions about human behavior which, he believed, more accurately indicate how best to motivate people to work. He called these assumptions Theory Y and based them upon the concept of integration: ". . . the central principle which derives from Theory Y is that of integration: the creation of conditions such that the members of the organization can achieve their own goals best by directing their efforts toward the success of the enterprise."

Theory Y is based on Maslow's higher levels of needs: affiliation, esteem, and self-actualization. McGregor believed that there is more to job motivation than mere reward of salary and title. He also contended that workers prefer not to be directed and controlled externally but, rather, enjoy self-control and self-direction. Miles's approach to human resources derives essentially from McGregor's Theory Y. When managers allow employees in an automobile plant to determine the best schedule for producing cars—called flextime—they are operating on the assumption that the employees of the plant should decide personally the course of action that best suits their needs. This is essentially the assumption of Theory Y—integration of individual and organizational goals.

The manager who adopts Theory Y assumptions of human behavior will most likely be responsible for the following communication behavior:

1. Messages travel up, down, and across the organization.
2. Decision making is spread throughout the organization. Even important decisions involve input from members at *all* levels of the line organization.
3. Since feedback is encouraged in an upward direction—and management listens—no supplemental upward system is required.

Table 3.2   Assumptions of McGregor's Theory X and Theory Y

Theory X	Theory Y
1. The average person has an inherent dislike of work and will avoid it when possible.	1. The expenditure of physical and mental effort in work is as natural as play and rest.
2. Therefore, most people must be coerced, controlled, directed, and threatened with punishment if management is to get them to put forth adequate effort toward the achievement of organizational objectives.	2. External control and the threat of punishment are not the only means for bringing about effort toward organizational objectives. Employees will exercise self-direction and self-control in the service of objectives to which they are committed.
3. The average person prefers to be directed, wishes to avoid responsibility, has relatively little ambition, and wants security above all.	3. Commitment to objectives is a function of rewards associated with their achievement.
	4. The average person learns under proper conditions not only to accept but to seek responsibility.
	5. The capacity to exercise a relatively high degree of imagination, ingenuity, and creativity in the solution of organizational problems is widely, not narrowly, distributed in the population.
	6. Under the conditions of modern industrial life, the intellectual potentialities of the average person are only partially utilized.

Source: Douglas McGregor, *The Human Side of Enterprise* (New York: McGraw-Hill Book Co., 1967).

4. Frequent, honest interaction with employees takes place in an atmosphere of confidence and trust.
5. The flow of messages downward is usually sufficient to satisfy the needs of employees.
6. Decision making is based upon messages from all levels of the organization, and thus the accuracy and quality of the decisions are improved.

Because this communication system is open, an atmosphere of trust, reciprocity, intimacy, and growth precludes the need for such supplements as an informal grapevine. Employees recognize their input in the decision-making process and respond appropriately to management because they perceive their goals to be integrated with those of management. The assumptions of both Theory X and Theory Y are summarized in table 3.2.

Reaction to the publication of McGregor's theory was initially hostile. Critics accused McGregor of simplifying a complex situation by polarizing two theories of management and not admitting the possibility of linkages between the two theories. To answer some of his critics, McGregor (1967) stated:

Theory X and Theory Y are *not* managerial strategies: They are underlying beliefs about the nature of man that influence managers to adopt one strategy rather than another. In fact, depending upon other characteristics of the manager's view of reality and upon the particular situation in which he finds himself, a manager who holds the beliefs that I called Theory X could adopt a considerable array of strategies, some of which would typically be called "hard" and some would be called "soft."

McGregor tried to clarify that he was not creating a dichotomous either-or situation. He admitted the possibility that a manager might use parts of both Theory X and Theory Y, and further, that a manager might shift from one to the other, depending upon the situation and personnel involved.

Additional criticisms of McGregor's theory center around his basing the theory upon Maslow's hierarchy of needs—a point which Maslow himself made (as noted already). McGregor's basic principle is integration of individual and organizational goals. It assumes that most persons are motivated by the needs set out in Maslow's hierarchy. Eric Trist hypothesized that today's youth are motivated by different values and value systems from those that motivate their seniors in organizations:

> The industrial society emphasizes achievement, self-control, independence and endurance of distress. The postindustrial society will emphasize self-actualization, self-expression, interdependence, and the capacity for joy.

Tannenbaum and Davis agreed with Trist:

> It comes as a shock to discover that many of today's youth seriously doubt that something *should* be done just because it is technically possible to do it, that increased efficiency and output should be the major criteria of organizational and societal health, and that continuous and limitless acceleration is the hallmark of progress.

If Trist and Tannenbaum and Davis are correct, the possibility then looms that organizations may find it difficult if not impossible to integrate individual and organizational goals because of the different values of younger and older employees. McGregor's or any other theory based upon integration may, therefore, have difficulty withstanding the challenge of the postindustrial organization of the next decade.

Likert

Another approach to management within organizations was proposed by Rensis Likert and colleagues at the Institute for Social Research at the University of Michigan. Likert (1961, 1967) suggested that most management styles can be classified into one of four possible systems. System 1 and System 4 parallel McGregor's Theory X and Theory Y, respectively, and the other two systems fall somewhere between these two extremes of management theory.

System 1 is very similar to Theory X and scientific management theory. Management has no confidence or trust in employees, and subordinates respond accordingly by not discussing their jobs with their superiors. There exists an atmosphere of fear, threat, punishment, and occasional reward throughout the organization. Communication is mostly downward, subordinates distrust the messages, and any upward communication tends to be inaccurate. Most decisions are made at the top, and management attempts to control and direct subordinates. The result of this approach is development of an informal employee organization whose goals are generally different from those of management.

System 2 managers condescendingly place confidence and trust in their employees (similar to the relationship between master and slave). Most decisions are made primarily at the top of the organization, but there is room for some decision making and goal setting at certain lower levels. Most of the power and control remain concentrated at the top of the organization. Some interaction aimed at achieving organizational objectives takes place between employees and managers. Most of the information still flows downward within the organization, and most subordinates continue to view much of it with suspicion. Some upward communication exists but usually only what the boss wants or needs to hear. The rest is usually filtered and restricted. An informal organization usually develops, but its goals are not necessarily different from management's.

System 3 managers have substantial, but not complete, trust and confidence in their employees. Subordinates feel fairly free to discuss job matters with their superiors, and there is quite a bit of interaction between managers and employees. Communication flows both up and down within the system. Downward communication is often accepted by employees, but they may view it with some suspicion. Upward communication is generally accurate; the boss always hears what he wants to hear; and other information may be limited or cautiously given. Broad policies are decided at the top of the organization, but specific decisions are made at lower levels. An informal organization may develop, but its goals may be either congruent with or slightly resistant to those of management.

System 4 is analogous to Theory Y and the human resources approach of Miles. Management has complete trust and confidence in its employees. Decision making is widely spread throughout the organization. Information flows up, down, and across channels. Downward information is generally accepted; when it is not, open and candid questions are raised and discussed by employees and managers. Thus, much interaction takes place within the system. Upward communication is generally accurate, and management demonstrates that it is sincere in its efforts to monitor employee feedback. Motivation of employees is accomplished by heavy participation in decision making, goal setting, and appraisal. Generally, the informal and formal organizations are identical, and true integration of employee and manager objectives is accomplished.

In order to analyze an organization and make recommendations for change and renewal, Likert developed an instrument that enables managers to rate certain characteristics of their own systems as they currently operate.

Likert and associates tested this instrument in many different organizations. One of their findings is that System 4 organizations have the highest level of productivity of the four systems and System 1 organizations the lowest. Additionally, Likert reported that most of the managers he surveyed preferred to use System 4 but most of the companies they worked for used some other approach, usually System 1.

One of the key variables mentioned by Likert is the amount of participative decision making (PDM)—a term that refers to decisions made by the persons who must execute them. One criticism of Likert's theory was that he dealt with "allness" statements (e.g., "employees not at all involved in decisions related to their work"). These statements tend to disregard the contingencies of decision-making situations, which may vary from organization to organization. Also, some of Likert's language is called ambiguous (e.g., the term *participation* itself). However, in a survey of 318 managers, Greiner found "a surprising consensus . . . regarding the operational characteristics and effectiveness of participative leadership." Managers considered the following to be the ten most important characteristics:

1. Giving subordinates a share in decision making.
2. Keeping subordinates informed of true situations, good or bad and under all circumstances.

3. Remaining aware of the state of the morale of the organization and doing everything possible to keep it high.
4. Being easily approachable.
5. Counseling, training, and developing subordinates.
6. Communicating effectively with subordinates.
7. Showing thoughtfulness and consideration of others.
8. Being willing to make changes in the way things are done.
9. Being willing to support subordinates even when they make mistakes.
10. Expressing appreciation to subordinates when they do a good job.

Greiner's findings seem to indicate that even if PDM is a vague concept, many managers are still able to agree upon many of its characteristics.

Not only managers have an interest in PDM. When members of a famous symphony orchestra went on strike for several months, among the reasons given for the strike were these:

1. Musicians need to be consulted about their own management and development.
2. Management needs to gain competence and experience to make decisions about the repertoire musicians are allowed to develop for performance.
3. Long-range accord can be achieved only when the orchestra's executive structure periodically shares all vital financial information with the musicians.

Perhaps strikes such as these could be avoided if labor-management committees (LMCs) were more widespread. LMCs are panels established by mutual agreement in plants and offices to consider matters that affect both sides and lie outside the boundaries of their collective bargaining agreements. LMC agendas range from bus driver security, absenteeism, and energy conservation to cafeteria upgrading, workplace environment, plant layout, and housekeeping. Such meetings also furnish a forum for discussion of broader issues that may affect the entire industry and, therefore, are of mutual interest and concern to employer and union—matters like competition from foreign imports, new technologies, government regulations, and introduction of new product lines.

The LMC concept opens up channels of communication between employer and union that were not there before. The improved relationship that usually stems from such fresh communication frequently is reflected at the bargaining table when it is time to negotiate new labor contracts.

Other critics of Likert's theory accuse Likert and associates of studying only organizations with close links to the University of Michigan, thus limiting the general applicability of his findings. Finally, it is questionable whether PDM can be applied in organizations where economic incentives are not emphasized, such as government agencies.

Whether PDM can apply without economic incentives relates to the statements of Trist and Tannenbaum and Davis concerning changing value systems of present-day youth. The criticism of Likert's use of "allness" statements may have helped influence the management model developed by Blake and Mouton.

Blake and Mouton

Robert Blake and Jane Mouton of Scientific Methods, Inc. developed a two-dimensional grid analysis of leadership practices that managers can use. The theory for this model, generally called the managerial grid, is based on the research at Ohio State University, the University of Michigan, and the Group Dynamics Center.

In 1945, the Bureau of Business Research at Ohio State University developed a Leader Behavior Description Questionnaire that identified the dimensions of leadership in operation. Two dimensions of leadership emerged as predominant: initiating structure and consideration. *Initiating structure* refers to the leaders' behavior in delineating the relationship between themselves and members of the work group as they endeavored to establish well-defined patterns of organization, channels of communication, and methods of procedure. *Consideration* refers to behavior indicative of friendship, mutual trust, respect, and warmth in the relationship between leaders and their staff members. Initiating structure is task oriented and relates more to the needs of the organization (Theory X; System 1; scientific management). Consideration is people oriented and relates more to the needs of individuals within the organization (Hawthorne studies; human relations).

At about the same time the Ohio State team was studying leadership, the Michigan team concluded that two factors account for most of the variance when leadership is measured and identified: employee orientation and production orientation. Employee orientation is directly related to what the Ohio State studies called consideration, and production orientation is similar to initiating structure. A third group, under the direction of Dorwin Cartwright and Alvin Zander, concluded that all group objectives fall into one of two categories: achievement of a group goal and maintenance of the group. Achievement of a group goal coincides with the task-oriented concepts (production orientation; initiating structure), and maintenance of the group relates to people and their concerns (employee orientation; consideration).

Blake and Mouton based their grid theory on the approaches just discussed and generated five basic styles of leadership, or management, based on two factors: concern for production and concern for people. The five styles are presented in figure 3.3.

A 9/1 style of leadership (task) is typical of a manager with a very high concern for production (task) and a low concern for people. Efficiency is the prime concern, and human elements are subordinated to the needs of production. This is similar in theory to the System 1 manager, the Theory X supervisor, the philosophy of scientific management, and the leader who is high on initiating structure and concerned primarily with achievement of group goals and production orientation. The examples cited earlier and the communication behavior described for Theory X also apply to a 9/1 leader.

A 1/9 leadership style (country club) is typical of the manager who has a high concern for people but low concern for production. This manager is employee oriented, emphasizing consideration and maintenance of the group *but* at the expense of any organizational concerns for productivity and efficiency. Probably the critics who labeled such managers the happiness boys were thinking of the 1/9 manager. This manager abdicates decision making and smooths over conflict in an attempt to build a happy climate in which to motivate employees by flowery praise. A good example of the 1/9 style is the owner of a major league baseball team in the 1950s and 1960s who was concerned only with smoothing over conflict

Figure 3.3 The leadership grid.

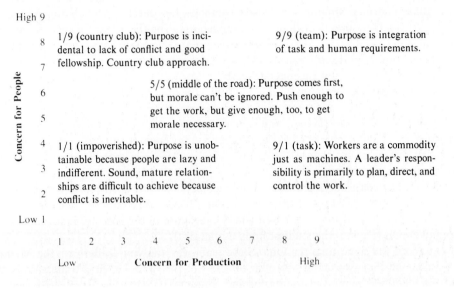

1/9 (country club): Purpose is incidental to lack of conflict and good fellowship. Country club approach.

9/9 (team): Purpose is integration of task and human requirements.

5/5 (middle of the road): Purpose comes first, but morale can't be ignored. Push enough to get the work, but give enough, too, to get morale necessary.

1/1 (impoverished): Purpose is unobtainable because people are lazy and indifferent. Sound, mature relationships are difficult to achieve because conflict is inevitable.

9/1 (task): Workers are a commodity just as machines. A leader's responsibility is primarily to plan, direct, and control the work.

and agitation in his team. Instead of resolving conflict among the players, he simply raised their salaries. Despite his generous treatment, the team seldom won a pennant. In fact, they finished in the second division during most of the two decades.

The 1/1 style of leadership (impoverished) is illustrated by managers who have low concern for both people and production. They avoid decisions, are neutral in conflict, maintain an atmosphere of apathy, and avoid feedback to employees. Their philosophy is to do the minimum amount of work needed to get the job done and keep employees satisfied: "People work best when you leave them alone!"

The 9/9 style (team) is characterized by managers with high concern for both people and production. They follow the axioms of Theory Y, System 4, and human resources and are high on both consideration and initiating structure. They are concerned with both employee and production orientations and strive to maintain the group while trying to achieve its primary task. These managers allow consensus in decision making, confront and resolve conflict, maintain an atmosphere of trust and acceptance, and encourage candid and spontaneous feedback from employees. They have truly mastered the concept of integration of individual and organizational goals.

The 5/5 style (middle of the road) is exemplified by managers who have a *moderate* concern for people and their production. They are on the way to acceptance of team management but, for whatever reason (personal, organizational, financial), stop short of complete integration. Their philosophy is be firm, but fair. They negotiate conflict by seeking compromise, and the result may be that employees think they are being manipulated rather than being trusted. Decision making is usually handled by majority rule unless the conflict is too great.

Managers with high concern for both people and product have a 9/9 style of leadership.

Herzberg

One of the most controversial theories in the human resources movement was that advocated by Frederick Herzberg of the University of Utah. Early motivation models were based on the assumption that individuals behave in ways that reduce the tension arising from unsatisfied internal needs. Consistent with these models is a definition of drive by Miller and Dollard as a strong stimulus that impels action. It is apparent that scientific management theorists apply this model when they advocate paying workers money for sufficient work output (adequate behavior). The money in turn enables workers to reduce the tension caused by such internal needs as hunger, sex, and shelter. This carrot-stick theory of motivation was questioned in the 1950s by some psychologists. One psychologist, White, developed the concept of "effectance motivation." According to Dalton, writing in 1959, such motivation "is innately satisfying and is not necessarily learned through association with some primary drive reduction." Later, Dalton (1971) added:

> . . . not only is there a tendency for individuals to act to control parts of their environment to fulfill their needs, but there is a tendency to explore, to find answers, to develop new skills, even when no other end is expected to be served (no incentive bonus, no promotion, no need satiation, unless we think of need for effectance). Working on a challenging task, an intriguing problem, or a new territory has value in and of itself, *if* the task is within that band of tasks or problems which lies just beyond the individual's present attained capacity.

Most of the writings of Herzberg support the analysis of Dalton. In an article critical of earlier models of motivation, Herzberg (1968) addressed the issue of positive KITA (Kick in the Ass):

> I have a year-old Schnauzer. When it was a small puppy and I wanted it to move, I kicked it in the rear and it moved. Now that I have finished its obedience training, I hold up a dog biscuit when I want the Schnauzer to move. In this instance, who is motivated—I or the dog? The dog wants the biscuit, but it is I who want it to move. Again, I am the one who is motivated, and the dog is the one who moves. In this instance all I did was apply KITA frontally; I exerted a pull instead of a push. When industry wishes to use such positive KITAs, it has available an incredible number and variety of dog biscuits (jelly beans for humans) to wave in front of the employee to get him to jump.

Herzberg spent several years developing and testing his theory of motivation, which is based on the writings of Harlow and White. Herzberg's methodology (the critical incident method) called for interviewing employees to gather data about times when they felt good or bad about their jobs. The interviewees were asked (Herzberg et al., 1959):

> Think of a time when you felt exceptionally good or exceptionally bad about your job, either your present job or any other job you have had. This can be either the "long-range" or the "short-range" kind of situation, as I have just described it. Tell me what happened.

Using Herzberg's technique, Myers reported getting both favorable and unfavorable responses to the question about job attitude. The following is a favorable answer given by an engineer:

> In 1959 I was working on a carefully outlined project. I was free to do as I saw fit. There was never a "No, you can't do this." I was doing a worthwhile job and was considered capable of handling the project. The task was almost impossible, but their attitude gave me confidence to tackle a difficult job. My accomplishments were recognized. It helped me gain confidence in how to approach a problem. It helped me to supervise a small number of people to accomplish a goal. I accomplished the project and gained something personally.

Here is an unfavorable response, given by an engineer:

> In December 1961 I was disappointed in my increase. I was extremely well satisfied with the interview and rating. I was dejected and disillusioned, and I still think about it. I stopped working so much at night as a result of this increase. My supervisor couldn't say much. He tried to get me more money but couldn't get it approved.

Based upon the data from his interviews, Herzberg identified two major factors that combine to motivate people to work. The first set of factors, having to do with motivational conditions intrinsic to work such as recognition and responsibility, he called "motivators." The second set of factors, having to do with the work environment, Herzberg called "hygiene." Influencing the development of hygiene are company policy and administration, supervision, relationship with supervisor, work conditions, salary, status, and security. Influencing the growth of motivators are achievement, recognition, work itself, responsibility, advancement, and growth. Herzberg contended that unsatisfied hygiene factors lead to dissatisfaction with a job. He did not claim, however, that workers will be motivated if all hygiene factors are satisfied. He concluded that motivated workers are those whose motivators are satisfied. Thus, the two kinds of factors, hygiene and motivators, can exist independently.

Table 3.3 Maslow's Need-Priority Model and Herzberg's Motivation-Hygiene Model Compared

Maslow		Herzberg	
Self-realization and fulfillment	*Motivation factors*	Work itself Achievement Possibility of growth Responsibility	
Esteem and status		Advancement Recognition	

Belonging and social activity		Status
		Interpersonal relations
		    Supervision
		    Peers
		    Subordinates
			Overlapping items

Safety and security	*Hygiene factors*	Supervision—technical Company policy and administration Job security	
Physiological needs		Working conditions Salary Personal life	

The similarities between Herzberg's model and Maslow's hierarchy of needs are shown in table 3.3.

Herzberg's two-factor theory of motivation has drawn much criticism in recent years. House and Wigdor summarized much of the research relating to Herzberg's model, including some of the major criticisms discussed in the literature. They identified three main weaknesses in Herzberg's theory: methodological bounds of the theory, faulty research foundation, and inconsistency with previous evidence. The first criticism centers on the use of the critical incident method to generate the raw data from interviewees. Vroom (1966) contended that people tend to take the credit when things go well and enhance their feelings of self-worth, but they protect their self-concept when things go poorly by blaming their failure on the environment. The second criticism deals with certain procedural problems: experimenter bias in the rating of the factors; lack of operational definitions for identifying satisfiers and dissatisfiers; and lack of reliability data. About the third criticism of the theory, its lack of data on the relationship between motivation and productivity, House and Wigdor concluded:

> At the present time, there seems to be general agreement among most researchers that the effect of satisfaction on worker motivation and productivity depends on situational variables yet to be explicated by future research.

House and Wigdor drew four conclusions concerning job satisfaction and dissatisfaction:

1. A given factor can cause job satisfaction for one person and job dissatisfaction for another person, and vice versa.
2. A given factor can cause job satisfaction and dissatisfaction in the same sample.

3. Intrinsic job factors are more important to both satisfying and dissatisfying job events than are extrinsic job events.
4. These conclusions lead to the conclusion that the two-factor theory is an oversimplification of the relationships between motivation and satisfaction and the sources of job satisfaction and dissatisfaction.

The work Wiio and I have done on communication satisfaction and distance from the source (mentioned in chapter 2) indicates a point similar to Herzberg's hygiene factor: that getting information from sources close by simply prevents dissatisfaction, it does not create long-term satisfaction. Information from distant sources (e.g., top management), which is similar to Herzberg's motivator factor, is necessary to create satisfaction. This will be further explained in chapter 4 in the discussion of amount and type of information most employees need to be satisfied and productive.

More evidence to support our "distance-direction" theory comes from a very recent study by Lesniak (1981), who found that subordinates with a close vertical communication relationship with their superiors can realize significant and tangible benefits. Such "inner-circle" members (called "cadre members" by Lesniak) were better informed, more involved with decisions dealing with policy and managerial problems, more satisfied with organizational outcomes, and enjoyed better relations with most organization members than did "outer-circle" members (called "hired hands" by Lesniak). The latter were less well informed, less involved, received information of lesser quality, complained more often, and asked for clarification of confusing work instructions more often than did the "cadre." In short, the communicative exchange process seems to build a feeling of employee commitment, which leads to higher motivation and performance.

Key Propositions Evolving from Human Resources Movement

By now you should be aware of the parallels among the models of effective management we have considered here. Recognizing that the research of Maslow, McGregor, Likert, Blake and Mouton, and Herzberg does indeed have parallels, Lee proposed the following label to synthesize their work: Modern Human Resource Management (MHRM), consisting of three main propositions. Redding summarized the propositions as follows:

1. Managers should trust their subordinates to perform jobs responsibly.
2. Managers should permit subordinates to participate in the making of their own jobs.
3. Managers should replace much of the mechanistic structure characteristic of most institutions with an organic approach to organization.

Redding himself proposed five components of what he called "the ideal managerial climate": (1) supportiveness; (2) participative decision making; (3) trust, confidence, and credibility; (4) openness and candor; and (5) emphasis upon high performance goals.

I suggest that two ingredients discussed in most of the previous human resources models, *trust* and *integration,* include all of the concepts mentioned by Redding and Lee. I suggest further that the two are interdependent. Integration of individual and organizational goals will probably fail without a certain amount of trust among all concerned parties. Figure 3.4 illustrates the relationship between trust and performance.

Figure 3.4 Relationship between trust and performance. (From W. Haney, *Communication and Organization Behavior: Text and Cases,* 3rd ed., 1973, Richard D. Irwin. Reprinted by permission of the publisher.)

Figure 3.5 How to break the destructive cycle. (From W. Haney, *Communication and Organization Behavior: Text and Cases,* 3rd ed., 1973, Richard D. Irwin. Reprinted by permission of the publisher.)

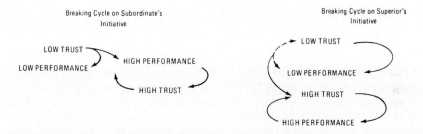

As figure 3.4 shows, the destructive cycle must be broken for the level of performance to be increased. Haney recommends two ways of breaking this cycle: at the initiative of the subordinate and at the initiative of the superior. Figure 3.5 illustrates this principle.

The first method for breaking the destructive cycle depends upon a subordinate's patience in tolerating a low-trusting manager by maintaining a high degree of performance, hoping that such action will convince the manager of the sincerity of the employee. The second way to break the cycle calls for a manager to respond to a low-producing employee by providing increased responsibility and trust. Both of these alternatives are difficult to initiate. Effective managers must decide what behavior is appropriate at a given time. As Haney points out, you don't throw an infant into the ocean and say, "Swim—I trust you!"

McGregor's answer to this dilemma is his concept of *integration*—which is the second concept referred to in most of the theories. If employees are allowed the freedom to satisfy their higher needs—esteem and self-actualization—and at the same time strive for organizational goals, a true integration of goals can be achieved. Figure 3.6 illustrates this concept and shows that when management and subordinates integrate their goals, the organization is the true winner. Hersey and Blanchard summarize integration as follows:

> . . . The individuals in the organization (both managers and workers) either perceive their goals as being the same as the goals of the organization, or . . . they see their own goals being satisfied as a direct result of working for the goals of the organization. Consequently, the closer we can get the individual's goals and objectives to the organization's goals, the greater will be the organizational performance . . .

Figure 3.6 Integration of the goals of management, subordinates, and organization-high organizational accomplishment. (From P. Hersey and K. Blanchard, *Management of Organizational Behavior,* 1969, Prentice-Hall. Reprinted by permission of the publisher.)

New Directions in Human Resources and Motivation Research

Three promising areas of research on the management of organizations in the coming decade are contingency leadership models, value differentiation management, and the charismatic (personality) factor in leadership. The chapter will then close with some comments on Japanese models, which are attracting much interest.

Contingency Leadership Models

The main proposition underlying contingency theories of leadership is that the appropriate type of leadership depends upon the circumstances. Perhaps the most widely known (and controversial) of the contingency models of leadership is that developed by Fiedler in the 1960s. Fiedler proposed that a leader's influence over a group was a function of the "favorableness" of the situation for the leader. The three factors that Fiedler believed contributed the most to an atmosphere of "favorableness" were position power (authority vested in the leader's position), task structure (degree to which the group's task can be specified in a step-by-step fashion), and the overall relationship between the leader and his or her group.

Some researchers have criticized Fiedler's model on both methodological and conceptual grounds (Graen et al.). Hill and Fiedler himself have suggested that other factors in determining leadership effectiveness are intellectual and technical abilities, motivation, and stress. Saha found considerable evidence to support that suggestion. Whether or not all of the contingencies that influence leadership effectiveness have been identified, few people have argued with Fiedler's basic premise. It has been supported by later work of Morse and Lorsch, who concluded that no one theory of management will suffice. Participative decision making may work in research and development organizations or with younger employees, and Theory X may be necessary when crises arise or during military maneuvers, for example. Morse and Lorsch concluded that the managerial style must be tailored to fit the task and the people. Redding supported this position, pointing out several factors that might influence the success or failure of a particular management style:

> It depends, that is, upon a wide variety of situational factors, ranging from the personalities and cultural backgrounds of organizational members to global variables like organizational technology and external forces in the total economy. . . . The task facing researchers is to discover *which* contingency factors exercise *what kinds* of effects upon what *people* and what kinds of *tasks,* with what kinds of effects upon overall organizational performance.

Luthans and Stewart introduced a general contingency theory of management in which literally hundreds of potential variables influencing organizational performance are presented.

Management consultant Warren Bennis has recently studied the behavior of ninety leaders of successful private and public-sector organizations. He has concluded that they all had four common themes associated with their behavior (1984).

1. *Management of Attention through Vision.*
   They were all clear about their vision, their dreams, to the point of being preoccupied with results. They saw the big picture.
2. *Management of Meaning through Communication.*
   They could all take their abstract visions and communicate them concretely so that others would understand and follow them.
3. *Management of Trust through Constancy.*
   They were all consistent in their behavior, even to the degree of being stubbornly persistent, thus enabling their followers to understand them and trust them.
4. *Management of Self.*
   Whatever style they had, they could deploy themselves to their organizations because they had a high self-regard. They knew their strengths and weaknesses and nurtured and developed their talents and skills so that they could determine the fit between what they were good at doing and what the organization needed.

Just as there is no one best way to manage, so is there no one best way to communicate. The communication process is influenced by many internal and external constraints from the organization and its subsystems. The constraints determine the status of the organization or its subsystems at any given time and are dependent upon the situation, that is, the state of the environmental suprasystem and the state of each subsystem. The communication process is thus contingent upon external and internal stimuli and upon the degree of freedom of states within the system allowed by the organizational constraints. Just as persons are different when they talk with a husband or wife compared to when they talk with a boss, so do organizations change when their communication contingencies change.

Table 3.4[2] identifies those internal and external contingencies that I believe most directly affect an organization's communication system. An organization that has maximized the effectiveness of its communication system will be in the best position to cope with a potentially unstable environment, internal or external to the organization.

Studies by Wiio in Finland and by me and my colleagues in the United States and Canada provide strong evidence in support of such a contingency view of organizational communication. From data obtained from more than thirty-five organizations (representing more than 40,000 workers), we have concluded that differences in communication effectiveness are a function both of type of organization and composition of work force (age, sex, edu-

---

2. Table 3.4 and the discussion of differences in communication effectiveness were adapted from Gerald Goldhaber et al., *Information Strategies: New Pathways to Management Productivity* (Norwood, N.J.: Ablex, 1984, Revised Edition).

Table 3.4   Communication Contingencies

Internal Contingencies	External Contingencies
1. Structural: degree of formality and type of structure chosen to organize the functions and relationships in the organization	1. Economic: amount of stability in current market competition and its impact upon capital resources available to organization
2. Output: amount of diversity and degree of quality in the products and services of the organization	2. Technological: degree of innovation in equipment and scientific research and development and their impact upon the organization
3. Demographic: degree of variation among the people working for the organization in such characteristics as age, sex, education, tenure, and supervisory status	3. Legal: degree of impact of local, state, and federal regulations, guidelines, and laws affecting organizational operations
4. Spatiotemporal: degree of variation in both spatial (design, amount, location, distance) and temporal (timing, timeliness) matters	4. Sociopoliticocultural: degree of impact of social, political, and cultural considerations upon the organization
5. Traditional: degree of conformity with organizational norms, history, and script	5. Environmental: degree of impact of climate, geography, population density, and availability of energy upon the organization

cation, tenure). Wiio stated, "In different organizational contingencies, different demographic variables showed significant relationships with communication variables." Among our findings were the following:

1. *Sex* does not seem to be a very strong demographic factor in organizational communication behavior. It seems to have some importance in improvement of upward communication, and it is important for banks and hospitals in furthering economic education.
2. *Age* seems to have more influence than sex: younger employees tend to receive less information and to want more than do older employees. Younger employees are more satisfied with their relationships but less satisfied with their jobs, in general.
3. *Job tenure* is also strongly related to communication behavior. Indications are that workers with the longest tenure need less and receive more information, and they also enjoy higher morale. (They may receive more useless information, which leads to overload.)
4. *Shift of work* is not strongly related to communication behavior. It is, rather, very selectively related to organizations, being particularly important in service organizations.
5. *Organizational level* seems to be generally important (more important in manufacturing industries than elsewhere). The higher the level, the more information people receive, particularly economic information.

6. *Level of education* is most important in public administration, the service branches, and manufacturing industries, and it influences employees' satisfaction with upward and downward communication and availability of economic information. As education increases, need to send information decreases, better relationships are enjoyed, and satisfaction with organizational outcomes increases. Employees with the least *and* those with the most education wanted and needed the most information.
7. *Union membership* is very selectively related to communication behavior. It seems to be most important in manufacturing industries and much less important in the service branches. In the printing industry, it is relevant in connection with organizationwide information; in banks and insurance companies, in connection with economic information.

Horan, in a study of 2,773 members of four U.S. organizations (two universities and two hospitals) and four Finnish organizations (two manufacturing and two service companies), has provided still more support for our contingency view of organizational communication. Horan found *no* general relationship between demographic and communication variables. No one demographic variable significantly correlated with any communication variable in all cases. He did find, however, some significant relationships in different contingencies and different organizations:

1. *Sex* was somewhat associated with communication variables. In the United States, women were more satisfied than men, but in Finland the reverse was true. Finnish women needed more information from more sources than did their male counterparts.
2. *Age* was the strongest and most general demographic factor related to communication variables. Generally the younger employees were the least satisfied and felt the greatest need for more information from more channels. The older the employee, the greater the satisfaction.
3. *Education* provided mixed findings, depending upon the country. In Finland those with the least amount of education were the least satisfied and most in need of information. In the United States, however, those with the least and those with the most education were *both* less satisfied than those with a medium amount of education. All of Horan's findings replicated the findings of Wiio and myself from other studies cited above.

Persons interested in organizational communication should, therefore, consider such questions as the following. *What are the contingencies under which organizations communicate best when confronting their environment?* Specifically, do different types of organizations have different communication needs? Do organizational internal contingencies (demographics such as age, sex, education, seniority, management level, and amount of communication training) affect communication needs? Are different demographics better predictors of communication need in types of organizations? Do different combinations of demographics and organization types produce different qualities of communication relationships and communication satisfaction?

Value Differentiation Management

Throughout this chapter we have pointed out that value differences between the youth of today and their elders can be detected everywhere. Managers may be wise to consider value differences among their employees before attempting to apply an MHRM (Modern Human Resource Management) theory which may assume a commonality of value orientation among employees.

A 1972 survey by Yankelovich (reported in the *Albuquerque Tribune*) of 1,244 college students interviewed on fifty campuses illustrates this point. According to the survey, 30 percent of all college students say they want to live outside the United States, primarily because of "an increasing belief among students that American society is a sick society." The report said, "Students have divorced their concerns about the state of the nation from their own personal fate. Withdrawing emotional involvement from social and political matters, they have channeled their feelings into their own personal lives, where they experience more control, less frustration, and greater contentment." This interpretation of the survey indicates that students are *avoiding* integration of their individual goals with those of the greater society as they perceive them. The survey stated:

> They do not believe that American democracy or justice functions even-handedly or as proposed in theory. They believe big business really runs the country, and such major institutions as political parties, the military, the penal system, and business need drastic reform.

Only one-third of the students retain moderate political values, condemn the use of violence, regard private property as inviolable, believe business should make a profit, and hold that social change should be achieved within the system. Of special interest to organizations is this finding in the survey:

> The greatest single erosion of relations to authority is the "boss" relationship. In 1968, 56 percent of the students did not mind the prospect of being bossed around on the job; in 1971 the figure was 36 percent.

More recent data from several sources show that our values have indeed changed over the years. The 1981 Harris Poll that measures confidence in our institutions found that major corporations achieved a 16 percent high confidence rating, only slightly better than the 12 percent rating for organized labor. In another 1981 poll done by the *Los Angeles Times,* 49 percent of the sample thought it was more important to do things that "give you personal satisfaction and pleasure" than to "work hard and do what is expected of you." A 1980 survey released by Connecticut Mutual Life Insurance Company reported that 63 percent of the national sample desired a "marriage of shared responsibility in which the husband and wife cooperate on work, homemaking and child raising" as opposed to a traditional marriage. These surveys seem to indicate that the values of present-day college students and others have changed drastically from those held by the majority of the organizational establishment. It is this change in values that may threaten both the functioning of some contemporary management theories as well as management of the United States itself.

An encouraging note for U.S. managers, however, is the research that indicates people acquire the values of the group they associate with. For example, Patty Hearst became a revolutionary when she associated exclusively with revolutionary types. In general, this means that the higher up persons are in the organization, the more they share its values. The problem, then, is with employees who are not "higher up in the organization"—the newer, younger employees and managers or hourly clerical workers without supervisory responsibilities. The difference in perceptions and values of younger supervisors (or hourly workers) compared to older managers can be illustrated by a classic study of adjustment to army life. In this study, officers tended to overestimate enlisted men's desire to be soldiers, their job satisfaction, and their pride in their outfit. Ninety-two percent of the officers said, "Most of the officers are the kind who are willing to go through anything they ask their men to go through." Only 37 percent of the men thought this statement to be true. The foremen in one company predicted that 30 percent of the workers would rank "not having to work too hard" important to their jobs. In fact, only 13 percent of the men gave this reply.

Attitudes toward work and personal value systems have changed radically in the past few years, but very few organizations seem to have altered their management and their reward systems. Younger workers and managers have less patience, greater expectations, increased interest in innovation and creativity, and desire for a voice in decisions. Younger employees today are the first workers who have been exposed to extensive career counseling. They expect clear and challenging career paths. To adapt to these changing values, organizations will have to come up with imaginative, innovative programs dealing with job hours, pay scales, job responsibilities, and work ethics. Harry Dennis and colleagues of The Executive Committee in Milwaukee developed a value analysis inventory for a hospital to compare values of its workers with those of its managers and values of its newer employees with those having longer job tenure. The information in this inventory will enable any organization to develop the innovative steps necessary to ensure its survival. The inventory is given in figure 3.7.

Lee Thayer wrote about what a leader is and what a leader actually does. "A leader is a person who enchants him or herself ("bewitches" himself or herself) with the story he or she tells. The story may be a theory, a painting, an idea, a political or social doctrine, a belief, an organizational "philosophy," or a creative description. In its telling, others may become enchanted with it. The more people who become enchanted with it, the more "truthful" or "right" it appears to be, both to the leader and to his or her "followers." It may then become institutionalized, and become a part of the way the world "is," the way the world is known, for future generations. We are first "led" by the ways the world might be, and then by the way the world "is." A leader revitalizes or changes our ways of "minding" the world. . . The leader is the meaning-giver, the myth-giver, and the compelling story-teller."

The Charisma Factor in Leadership

Charisma is perhaps one of the most misunderstood and abused concepts in modern parlance. Webster defines it as a "spiritual gift regarded as divinely granted to a person as a token of grace and favor" and as "a personal magic of leadership arousing popular loyalty or enthusiasm for a public figure." Charisma is leadership by virtue of personality. Max Weber was one of the first organizational scholars to discuss personality of leaders as influential in their appeal (he even called such people "charismatic" leaders). In 1500, Niccoli Machiavelli said in *The Prince* that "some persons always lack, despite their training, some personality traits needed to be a great leader." I agree with Saha, who, summarizing the work of Korman and Bass and Valenzi, said that "from our knowledge of personality-oriented theories, it appears inconceivable that personality is not important for determining behavior."

The problem with Webster's and other definitions of charisma is that they leave charisma up to the gods, the magicians, and heredity—which reinforces the notion that only heroic,

Figure 3.7 A value analysis inventory. (Adapted and used with permission of The Executive Committee. Milwaukee, Wisconsin.)

We all have values that influence the standards we set for ourselves and expect from others in our organizations. The values you communicate to your colleagues and subordinates are translated and incorporated into the organization in many different ways. Here is a method for identifying what a value is.

1. It is something you choose from among alternatives.
2. It is something you choose freely.
3. It is something you prize and are reluctant to give up.
4. It is something you tend to repeat.

Can you articulate your value position for each of the statements listed below?

1. How would you describe your value position toward the emphasis that should be given to a university hospital versus a community hospital?

( ) _____ ( ) _____ ( ) _____ ( ) _____ ( )
Low emphasis to a   High emphasis to a
university hospital   university hospital

( ) _____ ( ) _____ ( ) _____ ( ) _____ ( )
Low emphasis to a   High emphasis to a
community hospital   community hospital

2. How would you describe your value position with respect to your personal management style?

( ) _____ ( ) _____ ( ) _____ ( ) _____ ( )
Let the majority of input   Let the majority of decision
for decisions originate with me.   input originate with others.

3. How would you describe your value position toward the "sense of community" you want felt in the hospital?

( ) _____ ( ) _____ ( ) _____ ( ) _____ ( )
I prize individual initiative,   I prize group initiative and
achievement, commitment, and   collective achievement,
loyalty.   commitment, and loyalty.

4. How would you describe your value position toward organizational decision making?

( ) _____ ( ) _____ ( ) _____ ( ) _____ ( )
Decisions should be made by the   Decisions should be made by as
fewest number of people possible.   many people as possible.

5. How would you describe your value position toward spending versus austerity?

( ) _____ ( ) _____ ( ) _____ ( ) _____ ( )
A climate of austerity, thrift, and   A climate of free spending and
spending surveillance is most   minimum surveillance is most
desirable.   desirable.

6. How would you describe your value position toward recognition of status among people in the hospital?

( ) _____ ( ) _____ ( ) _____ ( ) _____ ( )
Status differences should be   Status differences should be
ignored as much as possible.   observed as much as possible.

Figure 3.7 *Continued*

7. What is your value position toward a philosophy of youthfulness versus maturity in the hospital?

( ) _____ ( ) _____ ( ) _____ ( ) _____ ( )

Experienced, seasoned, accomplished personnel are more likely to be hired.   Inexperienced, relatively unaccomplished personnel are more likely to be hired.

8. How would you describe your value position toward the profile you want your hospital to maintain with the public?

( ) _____ ( ) _____ ( ) _____ ( ) _____ ( )

A very low public profile   A very high public profile

9. How would you describe your value position toward the extent to which you want a paternalistic atmosphere in the hospital?

( ) _____ ( ) _____ ( ) _____ ( ) _____ ( )

Atmosphere strongly avoided   Atmosphere strongly encouraged

10. How would you describe your value position toward your desire and willingness to take risks?

( ) _____ ( ) _____ ( ) _____ ( ) _____ ( )

I have very little desire to take risks.   I have a very strong desire to take risks.

( ) _____ ( ) _____ ( ) _____ ( ) _____ ( )

I am very unwilling to take risks.   I am very willing to take risks.

John Wayne-types have charisma. If that were true, charismatic leaders would be people who had personal traits greater than the average person's but who were able at the same time to personify the public's desires. My research shows that the three personality types who display charisma are the hero, the anti-hero, and the mystic.

The **hero** is the type of person we wish we could be—the image idealized by the masses. He or she looks as we wish we could look and says things we wish we could say. The hero is bold and aggressive. We fantasize an ideal future and project our desires, goals, and wishes onto our heroes. For millions, poet and musician John Lennon, from his bold appearance, long hair, high-heeled boots, and experimentations with drugs, served as a hero.

The **anti-hero,** typified by Walter Cronkite, looks and sounds like us and does what we do. He is our uncle and our father. His attitudes and beliefs are ours.

The **mystic** is foreign to us. Henry Kissinger, with his Dr. Strangelove accent, is mystically charismatic. Many people cannot understand how an overweight, balding man can be attractive to many women. We are uncertain about his message. We cannot pin him down. He looks different from the rest of us, yet his foreignness has a strange appeal to us. Although we fear the unknown, we are curious enough to want to know more.

My research has identified five elements that I believe are the major factors underlying charisma.

Appearance. What does the person look like? How attractive is he or she to the masses? Does he or she look as most people wish they looked, as most people actually are, or is his or her appearance foreign and strange?

Steve Jobs, founder of Apple Computers and NeXt Computers, has created corporate myths and meanings for both companies, and thus enjoys a legion of loyal followers.

Sexuality.   What kind of sexual appeal does the person have? How sexually active is he or she perceived to be? Does he or she engage in bold sexual activities, normal activities (for married or single), or are we uncertain about his or her activity?

Message Similarity.   What are the person's goals, beliefs, and attitudes? What is he or she actually saying? Does the person say what we wish we could say, what we are now saying? Or are we unclear about the messages and uncertain about his or her stands?

Action.   How decisive is the leader? What kinds of leadership behaviors and activities does the person engage in? Are his or her acts bold and aggressive, what we'd expect, or are we surprised by his or her unusual, unexpected, or foreign mannerisms?

Imagery.   How effective does the person use the media to communicate style; to act; to role-play? Is the leader an aggressive speaker? Is his or her style plain? Or is it unusual? This may even be the most important element in charisma, especially given the importance of TV.

It is important to keep in mind that we are dealing with people's *perceptions* when we describe an individual's charisma. Further, it is important to realize that factors such as *time and place* can have a dramatic effect upon how we perceive an individual's charisma.

Table 3.5   The Charisma Theory of Leadership

Elements	Hero Type (Idealized)	Anti-Hero Type (Fits In)	Mystic Type (Foreign)
Appearance (looks and attraction)	Looks as people wished they looked	Looks like average person	Looks different from most people
Sexuality (perceived activity and appeal)	Bold activity	Average activity	Uncertain about activity
Message similarity (goals, beliefs, attitudes)	Aggressive message: says what masses wish they could say	Average message: says what most people have on their minds; wants what most people want	Uncertain about stands and what messages really are
Action (behavior, leadership, decisiveness)	Bold, aggressive acts	Expected, unsurprising acts	Uncertain and unexpected acts
Imagery (style—using media and nonverbal communication)	Bold and aggressive style; exciting speaker	Plain style; average speaker	Different style; unusual speaker

The theory, as summarized in table 3.5, has four propositions:

1. The amount and type of a leader's charisma is the result of the *perceptions* of the people who assess that charisma.
2. Perceptions of a leader's charisma will vary according to time, place, and other factors that affect that perception.
3. Leaders perceived to have the greatest amount of the right kind of charisma will be most effective.
4. Perceptions of charisma can be measured and enhanced, primarily through adept use of the media.

In order to determine the amount and type of charisma you may have as a leader or potential leader, my colleagues, Marshall McLuhan, Don Williams, and I have constructed a charisma test. The test, along with the key, should give you an idea of how your personality may affect your leadership style.

1. Do you look as most people wish they looked? Are you attractive to the masses?
2. Do you look as most people actually look? Do you tend to fit in with a crowd? Are you considered ordinary in appearance?
3. Do you look different from most people you know, but not conventionally beautiful or handsome? Is there some unusual feature about your appearance?
4. Do you have a large degree of sexual appeal to members of the same or opposite sex? Are you perceived as being sexually bold or aggressive?
5. Are you perceived as having the sex appeal of an average single or married person (depending upon which you are)? Are you perceived as engaging in sexual activities normal for a single or married person?
6. Are people uncertain about your sexual appeal and the amount and type of sexual activity you engage in? Are there questions or doubts among the voters about your sexuality, preferences, and activities?

7. Do your messages reflect what people wish they could say? Are you perceived as saying bold and aggressive things?
8. Do your messages reflect what people are actually saying? Are you perceived as saying what people expect you to say?
9. Are you perceived as being uncertain or unclear on your stands? Are people unable to identify your positions?
10. Are you perceived as a strong leader, a man or woman of action, a decisive person? Do you engage in bold or aggressive behavior?
11. Are you perceived as an average leader, a man or woman who does what is expected? Do you follow the crowd?
12. Are you perceived as an unusual leader, a man or woman who does the unexpected? Do you surprise people with your actions?
13. Are you perceived as a good actor or role player, one who effectively uses the media? Are you an exciting public speaker?
14. Are you perceived as an average public speaker? Is your speaking style plain and lacking distinction? Are you perceived as making only fair appearances on television?
15. Are you perceived as an unusual speaker who employs a strange style or unusual and different speaking techniques? Are you perceived as foreign when you appear on television?

If you answered "yes" to all or most of questions 1, 4, 7, 10, and 13, you are probably perceived as a hero. If you answered "yes" to all or most of questions 2, 5, 8, 11, and 14, you are probably perceived as an anti-hero. If you answered "yes" to all or most of questions 3, 6, 9, 13, and 15, you are probably perceived as a mystic.

Japanese Models of Human Resources

Much has been said and written about the success of Japanese business organizations compared to their counterparts in the United States. Before all U.S. companies switch from coffee and doughnuts to tea and rice cakes, a careful study of both the strengths and weaknesses in the Japanese system may be in order. First of all, we should take note of several distinguishing characteristics of the Japanese economy and culture that have influenced their management systems.

1. *Narrow industrial base.* Since World War II and its obvious devastation of the Japanese economy, Japan has chosen to concentrate its industrial efforts primarily in three areas: steel, automobiles, and consumer electronics (radio, TV, watches).
2. *Homogeneous population.* Japan is a very homogeneous country with regard to race, religion, language, and culture. In other words, workers and managers have few differences.
3. *Heavy reliance upon foreign raw materials.* Since Japan has to import most of its food and raw materials, it is particularly sensitive to foreign crises and international conflicts (e.g., oil embargoes).

4. *Respect for the individual.* The Japanese culture for centuries has imbued its people with dignity; its elderly population particularly have been accorded the utmost respect.

If we understand these economic and cultural realities in Japan, we can more easily understand some of their management "innovations." The United States has a broad industrial economy of industries and businesses which must compete at home and abroad; the narrow Japanese focus, on the other hand, allows for greater centralization of valuable resources, lower inventories, and higher profits. While the United States has a broad ethnic and cultural mix which does not lend itself easily to such "groupthink" ideas as worker-management councils and elimination of status differences between management and labor, the Japanese homogeneous culture promotes egalitarianism, harmony, and solidarity among all its people. The United States imports much less of its raw materials than does Japan (and almost none of its foodstuffs). An atmosphere of crisis management in Japan is a constant pressure on workers for high productivity and excellence in order to build a more independent Japan. Whereas the expansiveness of U.S. culture along with our management structure and labor union movement have encouraged tangible financial rewards as the main incentive to work, the much more crowded conditions of Japan have fostered respect for the individual and reverence for the elderly. This makes it easier for the Japanese to use compensation systems that rely more upon recognition than on cash.

Because of these economic and cultural factors, an atmosphere of mutual trust exists in most Japanese work organizations. Effective work teams are extensions of the intimacy necessary in Japanese life, and made possible by caring, support, and disciplined unselfishness. Some of the more publicized features of Japanese organizations include:

1. *Lifetime employment.* Most workers are guaranteed job security in return for reciprocal commitments to their employers.
2. *Seniority-based compensation.* While many U.S. companies believe that this system is counterproductive as motivation for younger employees, the Japanese believe it is indispensable in promoting good working relations between older and younger workers. Since older employees are no longer worried about their promotion and salary increases, or about being replaced by younger workers, they willingly share their knowledge and skills with the younger workers and cooperate in building cohesive work teams. Younger employees look forward to their delayed rewards.
3. *Participative decision making.* All those who will be affected by a decision are involved in making it. Even if sixty to seventy people are involved, they must reach a consensus in which all parties understand each other's point of view. They all may not prefer the final decision, but will agree to support it because they have had a chance to explain their viewpoints and listen to others. While a decision reached through consensus takes longer, it is usually faster to implement with fewer problems because of the commitment of all involved. This "ringi process" in which collective decisions pass from manager to manager, typically bottom-up, for their approval promotes joint responsibility for all decisions. No one can claim individual responsibility, and private "turfs" are thus minimized.

4. *Collective values*. Perhaps the greatest difference between U.S. and Japanese management systems relates to this striking difference between the individual freedoms desired by U.S. workers and the somewhat paternalistic reliance in Japan upon group values and teamwork. Where U.S. workers are usually rewarded financially for their productivity and input (piece-rate systems, suggestion boxes, etc.), the Japanese are more often rewarded with recognition and public gratitude.

The implications of the above organizational features for communication in Japanese companies have been studied by several researchers. Howard and Teramoto (1981) found a greater volume of total communications within Japanese corporations than in American ones; they reported that this increased volume of communication helped the Japanese members know and trust each other when carrying out their jobs. Similarly, Pascale (1978) in a massive study of several Japanese companies, their American subsidiaries and similar American companies found that the Japanese companies had a significantly higher number of face-to-face contacts. Pascale attributes this finding to the difficulty of adapting word-processing equipment to the Japanese language, thus making it more efficient for Japanese managers to use face-to-face communication rather than cumbersome written memos and reports. Further, the Japanese work space in most companies is quite crowded, forcing close contact among many workers regardless of their hierarchical placement in the company's structure. Still another reason for the heavy reliance upon face-to-face communication by the Japanese may be attributed to the unique Japanese negotiating procedure "nemawashi". In this process, all parties make interim arguments and take interim positions to which none may be committed—stages that precede movement toward a mutually agreed-upon position. Since written communication may imply a degree of commitment that may not exist, face-to-face communication is preferred. The process of "nemawashi" is further explained by Nakanishi in his excellent summary of differences between American and Japanese companies' communication systems. (1984)

Pascale and Athos (1981) contend that the Japanese reliance upon face-to-face communication, openness, lateral communication across functional areas, bottom-up information flow and participative decision making is due to their focus on people rather than systems. Using the framework developed by McKinsey and Co. of the 7 basic "S's", the basic elements which underlie organization and management, they contend that the Japanese rely more on style, superordinate goals, staff and skills whereas the Americans focus more on strategy, structure and systems. Pascale and Athos call the former the "soft S's" and the latter the "hard S's".

Recognizing that both Japanese and American organizations had strengths and weaknesses, Professors William Ouchi and Alfred Jaeger (then at Stanford University) did field studies which led them to hypothesize a hybrid organization which would include parts of both traditional Japanese and traditional U.S. organizations. They called it type Z. Japanese strengths in human resources, social cohesion, job security, and holistic concern for employees would be merged with U.S. strengths in speedy decision making, management innovations, risk-taking skills, and individual freedom. Rehder has summarized the characteristics of traditional American companies, traditional Japanese companies, and this new mixed type, as shown in table 3.6.

Table 3.6 Traditional and Emerging American and Japanese Organizations and Management Systems

Organization and Management Characteristics	Traditional U.S. System	Mixed U.S./Japanese Systems	Traditional Japanese
Organization Structure	Hierarchical bureaucracy with specialized and highly structured functions and positions; duties and responsibilities clearly defined in writing for each individual. Organization built around individual.	Hierarchical organization with moderate job specialization and increasing decentralization through the development of many organizational innovations, such as matrix and project teams, task forces, quality circles, job enlargement, ombudsmen, and facilitators.	Hierarchical organizations with loose, broad, general functions and informal job descriptions with strong reliance on internalized work group norms of cooperation, consensus seeking, and high group achievement standards. Organization built around groups.
Management Systems Centering management philosophy and expectations	Maximized return on investment through technological and individual efficiency. Employees dislike work but may be motivated by money if tasks are closely supervised. Organization goals therefore believed to be incongruent with employee goals.	High levels of performance and increased productivity can be achieved through the harmonization of employee and organization goals. Organization and employee goals are increasingly seen as congruent.	People seen as most valuable asset in order to achieve company goals of increasing their share of international markets. Organization and employee group goals are therefore seen as congruent to group goals.
Decision-making system	Decision-making system is highly centralized, top down, written, with extensive post-decision verbal communication to seek compliance.	Decision-making system is becoming less centralized and more informal consensus seeking. Written communications and individual responsibility continuing to predominate.	Decision-making system is highly decentralized, bottom up, informal, with verbal communications used to seek consensus and written system (Ringi) used as post-confirmation.
Management-employee relationship and control system	Management-employee relationship centered on formal work relationship. Employment commitment dependent on economic conditions and performance. Employee oriented to occupation or profession rather than organization. Individual, formal performance	Increased awareness and concern for employee as person and his or her welfare. Employee increasingly oriented to both occupation or profession and organization. Combining of informal individual and group goals decision making and controls with	Paternalistic relationship with employees and their families. Lifetime employment with reciprocal employee-company dependency and loyalty. Reliance on high group motivation and standards with social work controls. Joint management/employee

Source: R. Rehder, "What American and Japanese Managers Are Learning From Each Other," *Business Horizons,* April 1981:63–70.

Table 3.6 *Continued*

Organization and Management Characteristics	Traditional U.S. System	Mixed U.S./Japanese Systems	Traditional Japanese
	standards and controls. Advisory management/employee relationship predominates.	formal individual and group standards and controls. Greater congruence of organization and employee goals without extreme dependency of paternalistic organization. Less advisory (win-lose) relationships and more joint problem-solving (win-win) relationships between and within levels of organization.	problem solving used as way of reinforcing common goals.
Selection, compensation, and promotion	Employees selected primarily on basis of job-related formal education and/or practical experience and skills for specialized specific job with little or no employment security. Promotion and rewards primarily based on productivity as determined by management.	Employees selected both directly from schools and at various ages from other organizations with longer term employment expectation and commitment to development of employee. More promotion from within with broader and more jointly shared performance criteria.	Employees selected for lifetime directly from school, based on academic achievement, corporate examinations, and extensive screening program, including familial relationships and school ties. Promotion and compensation function of education, tenure, sex, and family responsibility until age 55. Broad group evaluation criteria.
Human resources training development	Human resources potential seldom fully recognized. Human resources training and development not carefully planned but intermittent with high levels of functional and technological orientation to improve individual performance. High career/job specialization.	Human resources potential increasingly recognized with commensurate in-house and outside training and development program growth. Greater emphasis on job enlargement and career planning as well as organization socialization. Technical training, research, and development also increasing.	Human resources seen as invaluable lifetime investment. Continuous in-house training and development key to both organization loyalty and technical development. Less job and career specialization with broader skills and management development as team member. Technical adaptation and development traditionally very well developed.

Ouchi identified thirteen steps necessary to convert an organization to Type Z:

1. Initiate the development of trust by encouraging candid discussion of Theory Z among managers and by personally displaying openness and integrity.
2. Work with managers to "audit" company objectives and strategies and identify inconsistencies in the theory and the practice of management philosophy.
3. Openly support the desired management philosophy indicated by the audit.
4. Create work structures (often in matrix form) that promote cooperation.
5. Develop interpersonal skills by recognizing and improving patterns of group interaction and group leadership.
6. Monitor progress toward change by formally testing for changed behavior in individuals and by obtaining observations from outsiders.
7. Involve the union in change of plans and processes.
8. Stabilize employment by distributing the burden of bad times among shareholders, managers, and employees.
9. Emphasize the importance of long-run performance by slowing monetary promotions and increasing nonmonetary evaluations.
10. Broaden career paths; promote understanding by de-emphasizing specialization.
11. Involve employees in the process of change *only after* visible results have been achieved from the above steps at the management level.
12. Solicit and implement suggestions from workers as a group.
13. Maintain open communication to promote continued growth of holistic attitudes.

Ouchi's step 12, to get group suggestions, has stimulated much interest in the United States in a Japanese technique called *quality control circles*—subsequently shortened to *quality circles* in the United States (probably to avoid any suggestion that they are a management tool for "control"). The technique was actually taught to the Japanese by an American quality control expert, W. Edward Deming. The quality circles are groups of six to eight (or more) employees who meet regularly: to solve problems related to the quality of goods/services; to improve methods of production; to improve worker morale and motivation; to stimulate teamwork; and to develop production skills among its members. Quality circles are currently the rage of U.S. industry, quite possibly due to their potential for saving companies millions of dollars. Toyota and Nissan reported that in 1980 they each saved millions of dollars from the fifteen to twenty suggestions per employee submitted via quality control circles, of which 85–90 percent were adopted. Comparison with General Motors, for instance, is startling: it typically receives less than one suggestion per employee per year and adopts less that 23 percent of them. What is even more dramatic about the Japanese success with this technique is that, unlike U.S. companies, which reward accepted suggestions with large cash stipends (even as high as $25,000), the Japanese rarely give any cash, choosing instead to give recognition and publicity to the contributors of ideas. (We will discuss QCs more fully in chapter 7, Small-Group Organizational Communication.)

It is important to remember that quality circles seem to work well in Japan probably because several cultural and economic differences discussed above have helped create a business climate appropriate for such techniques. If an organization simply imported this (or any Japanese) technique without the necessary understanding of the underlying values concerning human potential and long-term development of human resources, there would be little chance for lasting success.

Perhaps noted management consultant Edgar Schein (1981) said it best when he critiqued both Ouchi and Pascale and Athos' books, "We cannot produce cultural change simply by pointing to another culture and saying that some of the things they do would be neat here."

Unfortunately, many American companies have blamed their employees when productivity and/or quality declines. Martin Douglas, a GM auto worker for 16 years until he was laid off in the 1980 recession, has told us, in the *Los Angeles Times,* that this is not necessarily the fault of the workers.

> I am—or was—an American autoworker. I built General Motors cars for 16 years. Then, in March, I was laid off indefinitely. Although I don't think the major cause of the layoff was consumer's perception of my work ability, I believe that it was a factor.
>
> "When we lament the lack of quality in television programming, we don't fault the writers or cameramen; we blame the producers and network executives who put the shows on the air. By the same token, it is not the worker who determines the quality of a car but the executives in Detroit and the plant supervisors. . . .
>
> The worker who performs a certain task 320 times a day, 5 days a week knows more about the specifics of his particular job than anyone else. Yet, in 16 years, I have never been consulted or seen any other assembly line worker consulted on how to improve a job qualitatively or quantitatively. There are "suggestion programs," but their main concern is always how to save the company's money.
>
> I don't believe it is inherent in human nature to do a lousy job. Man innately wants to do good work, but he needs to be involved. He needs to know how his job relates to the work as a whole. Nothing is as frustrating as to not be able to do your job properly because a job earlier down the line was omitted. To instruct a worker in such a case to go ahead and do his job anyway is absurd. Yet, this happens, because the basic operating philosophy is to get the job done at any cost. . . .
>
> The autoworker can only build as good a car as he is instructed or permitted to build. Quality is not something to be concerned with only when there is a slack in production. We on the line take our cue from those in the head office. If they don't really care about quality, they can't expect us to either.

SUMMARY

In this chapter we discussed the climate, culture and environment of the organization and presented several viewpoints on how to enhance relationships which mutually benefit individuals and organizations. Relationship paradigms and propositions which emphasize supportive environments and climates for producing desired organizational relationships were introduced. Relationships between supportive climates and job satisfaction and career pathing were discussed. The human resources movement was discussed historically, and key figures and dates in the movement were identified. The theories and criticisms of Maslow, McGregor, Likert, Blake and Mouton, and Herzberg were discussed and illustrated, culminating in a list of the key propositions inherent in the human resources movement. Trust and integration were identified as fundamental to the success of most human resource theories. Three new directions in human resources and motivation research consider the contingencies of leadership and motivation, the value differences among employees, and charismatic influences on leadership. The Japanese approach to human resources was discussed.

A case for your analysis follows. The accompanying set of questions should help you analyze the case according to the key concepts presented in this chapter.

CASE STUDY[3]

Bill Brady is a vice president in a large financial institution and head of an eight-hundred-member department responsible for all administration (see fig. 3.8). There are three bureaus in the department, each headed by an assistant vice president: Jim Hammond, 57 years old, 32 years of service; Kevin McMahon, 46 years old, 28 years of service; and Mike O'Hara, 35 years old, 10 years of service. Bill, 60 years old, who has risen through the ranks during his 40 years of service, has been department head for the past 10 years.

A year ago the executive vice president of the area, Bill's boss, retired. His successor, Ben Sage, hired from outside, is both a financial and a computer expert. He is young, aggressive, creative and brought with him to the new responsibility a dynamic, loyal, bright personal staff from his former company. He supplemented this staff by selecting the best of the young turks from within his new division to form an efficiency review and operations planning group.

The environment within which the industry operates has undergone significant changes. A trend toward much larger accounts is evident; competition from banks for the smaller traditional accounts cuts into the market; and new business comes in much more slowly. It is a time of high inflation and high unemployment. Within the company itself the division is nearing the limit permitted by Securities and Exchange Commission regulations for administering accounts; employee turnover is low; and levels of staff are high (including many long-service employees). Administration costs are also rising and are among the highest in

Figure 3.8 An organization chart.

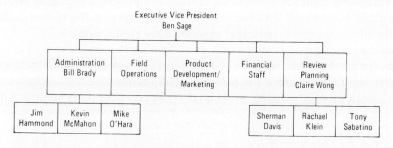

3. This case study was adapted from training materials used by a large financial institution.

the industry. The former executive vice president, Tom Wintersfield, was aware of these conditions and had discussed them often with Bill Brady. Bill had developed a plan to gradually reduce staff through attrition; to increase productivity through renegotiating performance standards, improving performance appraisals, and maintaining better contact with account representatives; and to improve service for customers by gradual computerization of many labor-intensive procedures. Tom, however, had felt that the plan was overly ambitious and too expensive and that it involved too much change too soon. Bill was optimistic when Tom retired and Ben Sage was appointed the new executive vice president. He became disillusioned and angry, however, when Ben brought new blood into the organization and set up a special group to effect change rather than consider the plan developed by Bill. He was especially annoyed when the efficiency review and operations planning group received credit and approval for recommending some of the very changes Bill had wished to incorporate in his own department, but for which he could not receive approval from Tom, the former executive.

Claire Wong is head of the review planning group, a vice president at the same level as Bill, and reports directly to Ben as a staff function. Bill also reports directly to Ben as a staff function. Bill also reports directly to Ben as head of one of five departments, administration; the other four are planning, field operations, product development/marketing, and financial staff. Claire's unit consists of three divisions, each headed by an assistant vice president: Sherman Davis, 31 years old, 5 years of service; Rachael Klein, 28 years old, 4 years of service; and Tony Sabatino, 43 years old, 20 years of service. The mission of Claire's staff is to study the operations of a work unit, determine which functions can be computerized, which jobs can be eliminated, and which functions can be combined to reduce the number of people needed to process forms; then to recommend immediate (not gradual) organizational changes that complement the long-range plan for the area.

Claire has budget to support the study and change recommendation phases for each of the five departments, but after the recommendations she submits to Ben receive his approval, the budgets of all department heads must support the implementation of change. Claire insists that all recommendations be reviewed with the department head—for example, with Bill—before they are submitted to her. She believes that the department head must be on board for any change to be effective. The review staff works directly with the bureau heads in Bill's department in studying the unit and in recommending changes. Jim, Kevin, and Mike, the bureau heads, were involved in developing Bill's original recommendation to Tom Wintersfield and still feel that its approach of gradual reduction represents the fairest and most reasonable approach in reducing costs and improving competitive position. They have known and worked well with the long-service employees in the bureaus and are conscious of the effect that quick, radical change will have on these people.

When the review group studies a unit, they often study it on site as well as use reports prepared by the bureau heads. When on site, they frequently perform some department functions to determine problem areas; the person normally responsible is given busywork meanwhile. The bureau heads do not always explain the presence of the study group and its mission to employees.

CASE QUESTIONS

1. What is taking place in the case? What is the current situation? What events led to this situation?
2. What could have been done to prevent some of the communication problems or at least diminish their consequences?
3. What can be done now?
4. What procedures, techniques, and measures would you suggest to prevent a recurrence of problems such as these?

BIBLIOGRAPHY AND REFERENCES

Albuquerque Tribune. (April 12, 1972): A-6.

Barnett, George, and Gerald Goldhaber. "Strategies to Improve the Organizational Culture of a Large Company." Private Report, SUNY-Buffalo, July, 1984.

Barnett, G. A. (1988). Communication and Organizational Culture. In G. Goldhaber and G. Barnett (Eds.) Handbook of Organizational Communication (pp. 101–130). Norwood, NJ: Ablex Publishing Corp.

Bass B., and E. Valenzi. "Contingent Aspects of Effective Management Styles." In *Contingency Approaches to Leadership,* edited by J. G. Hunt and L. S. Larson. Carbondale, Ill.: Southern Illinois University Press, 1974.

Beer, M. *Leadership, Employee Needs, and Motivation.* Columbus, Ohio: Bureau of Business Research, Ohio State University, 1966.

Benis, W. "Leadership Styles of Great Leaders." Speech Delivered at the International Communication Association Meeting, San Francisco, 1984.

Bennis, W. *Organization Development.* Rev. ed. Reading, Mass.: Addison-Wesley Co., 1969.

Bennis, W.; E. Schein; F. Steele; and D. Berlew. *Interpersonal Dynamics.* Homewood, Ill.: Dorsey Press, 1968.

Berkman, Lisa. "Social Relationships and Longevity." *Buffalo Evening News* 23 December 1977, p. 8.

Blake, R., and J. Mouton. *The Managerial Grid.* Houston: Gulf Publishing Co., 1964.

Butler, R. A., and H. F. Harlow. "Discrimination Learning and Learning Sets to Visual Exploration Incentives." *Journal of General Psychology* 40 (1957):257–64.

Campbell, J.; M. Dunnette; E. Lawler; and K. Weick. *Managerial Behavior, Performance and Effectiveness.* New York: McGraw-Hill, 1970.

Cartwright, D., and A. Zander, eds. *Group Dynamics: Research and Theory.* 2d ed. Evanston, Ill.: Row, Peterson, 1960.

Clark, J. V. "Motivation in Work Groups: A Tentative View." *Human Organization* 19 (1960):199–208.

Dalton, G. W. "Motivation and Control in Organizations." In *Motivation and Control in Organizations,* edited by G. W. Dalton and P. R. Lawrence, Homewood, Ill.: Richard D. Irwin, 1971.

Davis, K. *Human Relations at Work.* New York: McGraw-Hill Book Co., 1967.

Dember, W. N., and R. W. Earl. "Analysis of Exploratory, Manipulatory, and Curiosity Behaviors." *Psychological Review* 64 (1957):91–96.

Dennis, H. "The Construction of a Managerial Communication Climate Inventory for Use in Complex Organizations." Paper presented at a meeting of the International Communication Association, Chicago, 1975.

Dennis, H. S., III; G. M. Richetto; and J. M. Wiemann. "Articulating the Need for an Effective Internal Communication System: New Empirical Evidence for the Communication Specialist." Paper presented at the annual meeting of the International Communication Association, New Orleans, Louisiana, 1974.

DeWine, Sue, and Frank Barone. "Employee Communication and Role Stress: Enhancement or Sabotage of the Organizational Climate?" Paper presented at the meeting of the International Communication Association, May, 1984.

Douglas, Martin. "Auto Workers Can Only Do as Well as Head Office Permits." *Los Angeles Times,* July 24, 1980.

Dunnette, M.; J. Campbell; and K. Jaastad. "Factors Contributing to Job Satisfaction and Job Dissatisfaction in Six Occupational Groups." *Organizational Behavior and Human Performance* 2 (1967):143–74.

Fiedler, F. "Engineer the Job to Fit the Manager." *Harvard Business Review* 43 (September–October 1965):115–22.

———. *A Theory of Leadership Effectiveness.* New York: McGraw-Hill Book Co., 1967.

Fossum, D. "A Detailed Chronology of the Events Which Transpired on the Campus of the University of New Mexico from May 4, 1970, through May 13, 1970." Mimeographed handout, May, 1970.

Galbraith, J., and L. L. Cummings. "An Empirical Investigation of the Motivational Determinants of Task Performance: Interactive Effects Between Instrumentality-Valence and Motivation-Ability." *Organizational Behavior and Human Performance* 2 (1967):237–57.

Gantt, H. L. *Work, Wages, and Profits.* New York: Engineering Magazine Co., 1911.

Gibb, J. "Defensive Communication." *Journal of Communication* 11(1961):141–48.

Gilbreth, L. M. *The Psychology of Management.* New York: Sturgis & Walton Co., 1914.

Goldhaber, Gerald. "Network Newsmen: Who's Got the Most Charisma." *TV Guide* 29 (1981):4–10.

———. "The Charisma Factor: Using It to Win Elections." *Campaigns & Elections Journal* 2 (1981):4–17.

Goldhaber, G.; D. Porter; and M. Yates. "The ICA Communication Audit Survey Instrument: 1977 Organizational Norms." Paper presented at a meeting of the International Communication Association, Berlin, Germany, 1977.

Goldhaber, G.; H. Dennis; G. Richetto; and O. Wiio. *Information Strategies: New Pathways to Management Productivity.* Norwood, N.J.: Ablex, 1984, Revised Edition.

Goldhaber, G.; M. Yates; D. Porter; and R. Lesniak. "Organizational Communication: State of the Art." *Human Communication Research* 5 (Fall 1978):76–96.

Graen, G., et al. "The Contingency Model of Leadership Effectiveness: Antecedent and Evidential Results." *Psychological Bulletin* 74 (1970):285–95.

Graen, G.; J. Orris; and K. Alvares. "The Contingency Model of Leadership Effectiveness: Some Experimental Results." *Journal of Applied Psychology* 55 (1971):196–201.

Greiner, L. "What Managers Think of Participative Leadership." *Harvard Business Review* 51 (1973):111–17.

Halpin, A. *The Leadership Behavior of School Superintendents*. Chicago: Midwest Administration Center, University of Chicago, 1959.

Haney, W. *Communication and Organizational Behavior: Text and Cases*. 3d ed. Homewood, Ill.: Richard D. Irwin, 1973.

Harlow, H. F.; M. K. Harlow; and D. R. Meyer. "Learning Motivated by a Manipulation Drive." *Journal of Experimental Psychology* 40 (1950):228–34.

Harris, L. "Americans Losing Confidence." *Buffalo Evening News,* November 14, 1981, A-4.

Hersey, P., and K. Blanchard. *Management of Organizational Behavior*. Englewood Cliffs, N.J.: Prentice-Hall, 1969.

Herzberg, F. *Work and the Nature of Man*. Cleveland: World Publishing Co., 1966.

———. "One More Time: How Do You Motivate Employees?" *Harvard Business Review* 46 (January–February 1968):53–62.

Herzberg, F.; B. Mausner; and B. Snyderman. *The Motivation to Work*. New York: John Wiley & Sons, 1959.

Hill, W. "A Situational Approach to Leadership Effectiveness." *Journal of Applied Psychology* 53 (1969):513–17.

Hinrichs, J. R., and L. A. Mischkind. "Empirical and Theoretical Limitations of the Two-Factor Hypothesis of Job Satisfaction." *Journal of Applied Psychology* 51 (1967):191–200.

Horan, H. "Contingencies of Perceived Organizational Communication Effectiveness: A Comparison of American and European Organizations." Ph.D. dissertation, State University of New York-Buffalo, 1981.

House, R. J. "A Path-Goal Theory of Leader Behavior." *Administrative Science Quarterly* 16 (1971): 19–30.

House, R. J., and T. Mitchell. "Path-Goal Theory of Leadership." *Journal of Contemporary Business,* Autumn 1974: 81–97.

House, R. J., and L. A. Wigdor. "Herzberg's Dual-Factor Theory of Job Satisfaction and Motivation: A Review of the Evidence and a Criticism." *Personnel Psychology* 20 (1967):369–89.

Howard, N., and Y. Teramoto. "The Really Important Difference Between Japanese and Western Management." *Management International Review* 3 (1981):19–30.

Hulin, C. L., and P. A. Smith. "An Empirical Investigation of Two Implications of the Two-Factor Theory of Job Satisfaction." *Journal of Applied Psychology* 51 (1967):396–402.

Hunt, J. G., and J. W. Hill. "The New Look in Motivational Theory for Organizational Research." *Human Organization* 28 (1969):100–109.

Jablin, F. "Organizational Communication Theory and Research: An Overview of Communication Climate and Network Research." In *Communication Yearbook* 4 edited by Dan Nimmo, pp. 327–47. New Brunswick, N.J.: Transaction-International Communication Association, 1980.

Johnson, D. W. *Reaching Out*. Englewood Cliffs, N.J.: Prentice-Hall, 1972.

Kanter, Rosabeth Moss. *The Change Masters*. New York: Simon and Schuster, 1983.

Katz, D.; N. Maccoby; and N. Morse. *Productivity, Supervision and Morale in an Office Situation*. Ann Arbor, Mich.: Institute for Social Research, 1950.

Katzell, R.; P. Bienstock; and P. Faerstein. *A Guide to Worker Productivity Experiments in the United States 1971–1975*. Scarsdale, N.Y.: Work in America Institute, 1977.

Korman, A. "On the Development of Contingency Theories of Leadership: Some Methodological Considerations and a Possible Alternative." *Journal of Applied Psychology* 58 (1973):384–87.

Kreps, Gary. "Organizational Culture and Organizational Development: Promoting Flexibility in an Urban Hospital." Paper delivered at the meeting of the International Communication Association, San Francisco, 1984.

Lawler, E. E., and L. W. Porter. "Antecedent Attitudes of Effective Managerial Performance." *Organizational Behavior and Human Performance* 2 (1967):122–42.

Lawler, E. E., et al. "Managers' Attitudes Toward Interaction Episodes." *Journal of Applied Psychology* 52 (1968):432–39.

Lee, J. A. "Keeping Informed: Behavioral Theory vs. Reality." *Harvard Business Review* 49 (March–April 1971):20–28, 157–59.

Lesniak, R. "The Role of Vertical Communication Relationships in Traditionally Structured, Complex Organizations." Ph.D. dissertation, State University of New York-Buffalo, 1981.

Level, D. A. "A Case Study of Human Communication in an Urban Bank," Ph.D. dissertation, Purdue University, 1959.

Levering, Robert; Milton Moskowitz; and Michael Katz. *The 100 Best Companies to Work for in America.* Reading, Mass.: Addison-Wesley Publishing Co., 1984.

Likert, R. *New Patterns of Management.* New York: McGraw-Hill Book Co., 1961.

———. *The Human Organization.* New York: McGraw-Hill Book Co., 1967.

Lindsay, C. A., et al. "The Herzberg Theory: A Critique and Reformulation." *Journal of Applied Psychology* 51 (1967):330–39.

Litwin, G., and P. Stringer. "Climate and Motivation: An Experimental Study." In R. Tagiuri and G. Litwin (eds.) *Organizational Climate: Exploration of a Concept.* Boston: Harvard University Press, 1968.

Luthans, F., and T. Stewart. "A General Contingency Theory of Management." *Academy of Management Review* 2 (1977):181–95.

McGregor, Douglas. *Human Side of Enterprise.* New York: McGraw-Hill Book Co., 1960.

———. *Professional Manager.* New York: McGraw-Hill Book Co., 1967.

Machiavelli, Niccolo. *The Prince.* New York: The New American Library, 1952.

Maslow, A. H. *Motivation and Personality.* New York: Harper & Row, 1954.

———. *Eupsychian Management.* Homewood, Ill.: Richard D. Irwin, 1965.

Miles, R. "Keeping Informed—Human Relations or Human Resources?" *Harvard Business Review* 43 (July–August 1965):148–63.

Miller, N. E., and J. Dollard. *Social Learning and Imitation.* New Haven, Conn.: Yale University Press, 1941.

Morse, J. J., and J. W. Lorsch. "Beyond Theory Y." *Harvard Business Review* 48 (May–June 1970):146–55.

Myers, M. S. "Who Are Your Motivated Workers?" *Harvard Business Review* 42 (January–February 1964):73–88.

Nakanishi, Masayuki. "The Nature of the Japanese Productivity System: Its Implications to Organizational Communication." Paper delivered at the meeting of the International Communication Association, San Francisco, 1984.

Nebeker, D., and T. Mitchell. "Leader Behavior: An Expectancy Theory Approach." *Organizational Behavior and Human Performance* 11 (1974):355–67.

Nishiyama, K. "Japanese Quality Control Circles." Unpublished paper presented to the International Communication Association, Minneapolis, May 21, 1981.

Nord, W. R. "Beyond the Teaching Machine: The Neglected Area of Operant Conditioning in the Theory and Practice of Management." *Organizational Behavior and Human Performance* 4 (1969); reprinted in *Motivation and Control in Organizations,* edited by G. W. Dalton and P. R. Lawrence. Homewood, Ill.: Richard D. Irwin, 1971.

O'Reilly, C., and K. Roberts. "Interpersonnel Communication and Objective and Perceptual Assessments of Performance in Organizations." Mimeographed handout, University of California at Berkeley, 1976.

Ouchi, W. *Theory Z: How American Business Can Meet the Japanese Challenge.* Reading, Mass.: Addison-Wesley, 1981.

————. "Going From A to Z: Thirteen Steps to a Theory Z Organization." *Management Review* 70 (1981):8–16.

Pacanowsky, M. E., and O'Donnell-Trujillo, N. (1982). Communication and Organizational Cultures. Western Journal of Speech & Communication, 46, 115–130.

Pace, R. W., and R. Boren. *The Human Transaction.* Glenview, Ill.: Scott, Foresman, 1973.

Pace, R. W.; R. Boren; and B. Peterson. *A Scientific Introduction to Speech Communication.* Belmont, Calif.: Wadsworth Publishing Co., 1974.

Pascale, R. "Communication and Decision Making Across Cultures: Japanese and American Comparisons." *Administrative Science Quarterly* 23 (1978):91–109.

Pascale, Richard, and Anthony Athos. *The Art of Japanese Management: Applications for American Management.* New York: Simon & Schuster, 1981.

Peters, Thomas, and Robert Waterman. *In Search of Excellence.* New York: Harper and Row, 1982.

Porter, L. W. *Organizational Patterns of Managerial Job Attitudes.* New York: American Foundation for Management Research, 1964.

Public Opinion 4 (1981):21–31.

Redding, W. C. *Communication Within the Organization.* New York: Industrial Communication Council; Lafayette, Ind.: Purdue Research Foundation, 1973.

Rehder, R. "What American and Japanese Managers Are Learning from Each Other." *Business Horizons,* April 1981: 63–70.

Rodgers, W. *Think: A Biography of the Watsons and IBM.* New York: Stern & Day, 1969.

Roethlisberger, F., and W. Dickson. *Management and the Worker.* Cambridge, Mass.: Harvard University Press, 1939.

Rogers, C. R. *On Becoming a Person.* Boston: Houghton Mifflin, 1961.

Saha, S. "Contingency Theories of Leadership: A Study." *Human Relations* 32 (1979): 313–22.

Sanborn, G. A. "An Analytical Study of Oral Communication Practices in a National Retail Sales Organization." Ph.D. dissertation, Purdue University, 1961.

Schein, Edgar. "Does Japanese Management Style Have a Message for American Managers?" *Sloan Management Review* 22 (Fall, 1981):55–68.

Schmidt, W. H., ed. *Organizational Frontiers and Human Values.* Belmont, Calif.: Wadsworth Publishing Co., 1970.

Schneider, B., and C. J. Bartlett. "Individual Differences and Organizational Climate." *Personnel Psychology* 21 (1968):323–33.

Skinner, B. F. *Walden Two.* New York: Macmillan, 1948.

———. *Science and Human Behavior.* New York: Macmillan, 1953.

———. "The Science of Learning and the Art of Teaching." *Harvard Educational Review* 24 (1954):86–97.

Smith, P. B.; D. Moscow; M. Berger; and C. Cooper. "Relationships Between Managers and Their Work Associates." *Administrative Science Quarterly* 14 (1969):338–45.

Tagiuri, Renato. "The Concept of Organizational Climate." In R. Tagiuri and G. Litwin (eds.) *Organizational Climate: Exploration of a Concept.* Boston: Harvard University Press, 1968: 11–32.

Tannenbaum, R., and S. A. Davis. "Values, Man and Organizations." In *Organizational Frontiers and Human Values,* edited by Warren Schmidt. Belmont, Calif.: Wadsworth Publishing Co., 1970.

Taylor, F. *Principles of Scientific Management.* New York: Harper & Row, 1919.

Thayer, L. (1988). Leadership/Communication: A Critical Review and a Modest Proposal. In G. Goldhaber and G. Barnett (Eds.) Handbook of Organizational Communication (pp. 231–263). Norwood, NJ: Amblex Publishing Corp.

Tompkins, P. H. "An Analysis of Communication between Headquarters and Selected Units of a National Labor Union." Ph.D. dissertation, Purdue University, 1962.

Trist, E. "Urban North America: The Challenge of the Next Thirty Years." In *Organizational Frontiers and Human Values,* edited by Warren Schmidt. Belmont, Calif.: Wadsworth Publishing Co., 1970.

Vroom, V. *Work and Motivation.* New York: John Wiley & Sons, 1964.

———. "Organizational Choice: A Study of Pre- and Postdecision Processes." *Organizational Behavior and Human Performance* 1 (1966):212–25.

Weber, Max. *The Theory of Social and Economic Organizations.* Translated by A. M. Henderson and T. Parsons; edited by T. Parsons. New York: Oxford University Press, 1947.

White, R. W. "Motivation Reconsidered." *Psychological Review* 66 (1959):329.

Wiio, O. "Organizational Communication: Interfacing Systems." *Finnish Journal of Business Economics* (special edition) 2 (1977):259–85.

Wiio, Osmo; Gerald Goldhaber; and Michael Yates. "Organizational Communication Research: Time for Reflection?" In *Communication Yearbook* 4, edited by Dan Nimmo, 83–97. New Brunswick, N.J.: Transaction-International Communication Association, 1980.

PART TWO
THE PROCESS OF COMMUNICATION

Chapter 4   describes the transactional, personal, and serial nature of communication and discusses the primary methods, purposes, and networks used to create and exchange verbal messages within organizations.

Chapter 5   defines and describes the creation and exchange of nonverbal messages in organizations related to the physical behavior and appearance of the body, the human voice, and the environment.

4
CREATING AND EXCHANGING VERBAL MESSAGES

The following sentences were taken from letters written by wives, husbands, mothers, and fathers on file at the San Antonio Veterans Administration:

"Both sides of my parents are poor and I can't expect nothing from them, as my mother has been in bed for one year with the same doctor, and won't change."

"Please send me a letter and tell me if my husband has made application for a wife and baby."

"I can't get any pay, I has six children, can you tell me why this is?"

"I am forwarding you my marriage certificate and my two children, one is a mistake as you can plainly see."

"I am annoyed to find out that you branded my child as illiterate, it is a dirty lie as I married his father a week before he was born."

"You changed my little boy to a girl, does this make a difference?"

"In accordance with your instructions, I have given birth to twins in the enclosed envelope."

"My husband had his project cut off two weeks ago and I haven't had any relief since."

How often after assigning a meaning to a message do we assume that everyone else gets the same meaning simply because we know what we mean? In a popularly used teaching film on communication, a manager is upset with an employee for not following *explicit* instructions to do a "model job." When the worker joyfully displays his electrical-mechanical simulation "model," the boss angrily shouts, "I didn't ask you for this!" The employee proclaims, "But boss, you asked me to produce a model job, and that's what I did!" The now almost violent boss screams, "But I didn't mean that you should build a model. I meant that you should do a model job, a good job, an excellent job!" The employee interrupts, "But boss, that's not what you said!" In a final shout of despair, the boss yells, *"Don't listen to what I say, listen to what I mean!"*

Unfortunately, most of us are unable to read the minds of others, and our understanding of what people are trying to say is limited primarily to their words. Therein may lie part of the problem, for English words can have as many as *twenty-eight different meanings!*

Sometimes the results of misunderstanding the exact meaning of a word or phrase can be tragic, as in 1977 in the Canary Islands when two jumbo jet airplanes still on the runway were involved in a crash in which 567 lives were lost.

Sometimes misunderstanding exactly what a word or phrase means in the context in which it is used can have a tragic result, as in 1974 when a Boeing 727 crashed into a hilltop fifty miles north of Dulles Airport, killing all ninety-two persons on board. The investigation disclosed the cause of the crash to be the use by the air traffic controller of the expression "You are cleared for approach," which meant something different to the pilot.

On March 27, 1977, another plane crash occurred in which two jumbo jet airplanes still on the runway at the airport in the Canary Islands were involved. The consequences of still another communication failure in the airline industry were even more devastating—567 lives were lost. Transcripts of the conversation between the control tower and the pilots involved clearly indicate that imprecise use of language probably caused this tragedy. A KLM Royal Dutch Airlines 747 requested runway takeoff instructions from the control tower at about the same time a Pan Am 747 asked for similar instructions. The KLM pilot misinterpreted the tower's route instructions as clearance for takeoff. The tower, instead of reemphasizing that takeoff clearance had not been given or at least asking the pilot to repeat his last transmission, responded with, "O.K. Stand by for takeoff. I will call you." Stand by usually means "hold it" in airline language, but the KLM pilot may have interpreted the tower's use of O.K. as permission to take off. Judge for yourself whether the language was precise enough to prevent the crash.

In chapter 1, communication was defined as the creation and exchange of messages. A message was described as a series of symbols to which a receiver attaches meaning. In other words, messages deal with meaningful symbols about people, objects, and events generated during human interaction. Verbal messages were differentiated from nonverbal ones. In this chapter, verbal messages are discussed. Nonverbal messages are examined in chapter 5. This book is concerned primarily with messages within an organization. Chapter 8, however, considers communication external to the organization.

The specific objectives of this chapter are the following:

1. To present a message classification system for organizational communication
2. To define and describe the following concepts:
   a. the process of communication
   b. the transactional nature of communication
   c. the nature of communication rules
   d. the personal nature of communication
   e. the serial nature of communication
3. To describe and illustrate these concepts:
   a. new communication technologies and their effects
   b. various oral software methods for exchange of communication within an organization
   c. purposes for creation and exchange of messages within an organization
4. To describe various communication networks and relate them to concepts of organization theory
5. To define, describe, and illustrate the following two types of message networks within an organization:
   a. the formal network
   b. the informal network
6. To provide a set of guidelines for effective communication

Message Classification System

Several taxonomies are available for the study of message behavior. The method used in this book is presented in table 4.1. Much of my thinking in developing this classification system was influenced by Howard Greenbaum.

Since we will deal primarily with oral (software) methods of message exchange (as opposed to written messages or messages exchanged by such means as telephone, television, and telex), the message paradigm presented in table 4.2 encompasses only the first five variables listed in table 4.1.

Study of the paradigm will show that ninety-six different kinds of oral messages are possible. When one considers that a word can have twenty-eight different meanings and that interpretation of each message depends upon the individual situation and the viewpoint of the communicators, the complexity of the communication process becomes evident. As this process is described, you may come to wonder that human beings are ever able to communicate what they mean.

Table 4.1   Message Classification System

Variable	Classification
Message relationship	Dyad Small group Public
Message network	Formal (upward, downward, horizontal) Informal
Message purpose	Task Maintenance Human Innovative
Message receivers	Internal External
Message language mode	Verbal Nonverbal
Message diffusion method	Software (oral, written) Hardware

Table 4.2   Oral Software Message Paradigm

	Formal Network Internal and External	Informal Network Internal and External
Dyad		
Task	M	
Verbal and nonverbal		
Maintenance		
Verbal and nonverbal	E	
Human		
Verbal and nonverbal		
Innovative		
Verbal and nonverbal	S	
Small Group		
Task		
Verbal and nonverbal	S	
Maintenance		
Verbal and nonverbal		
Human		
Verbal and nonverbal	A	
Innovative		
Verbal and nonverbal		G
Public		
Task		
Verbal and nonverbal		E
Maintenance		
Verbal and nonverbal		
Human		
Verbal and nonverbal		S
Innovative		
Verbal and nonverbal		

The Process of Communication

A friend was once seated in an airplane next to an elderly man. Shortly after takeoff, the man asked my friend what he did for a living. "I teach communication at the university," answered my friend. The other passenger asked, "Are you in radio and television?" "No," replied my friend. "Do you help children with speech problems?" "No, I'm teaching students how to be better communicators when they meet people," my friend answered. The elderly passenger was silent for the rest of the trip. Just before the plane landed, the passenger said to my friend, "Hmmm, I'd better watch what I say." This conversation may help illustrate the difficulty of defining exactly what is meant by communication.

Definitions and models by the dozens exist; so even experts in communication cannot agree about the nature and limits of the discipline. In order to limit the uncertainty and ambiguity of the abstraction *communication,* we will adopt a broad definition: *the creation and exchange of messages.* Rather than debate the scope of communication, we will simply limit our discussion to the use of messages by human beings. We will consider communication to take place when one human being attaches meaning to a symbol(s) regardless of whether that human being originated the symbol(s). We will consider the notion of intentionality moot and presume that all messages, intentionally or unintentionally communicated by human beings, represent communication. The only other limit we place on the process is the locus— within a complex organization. In this book, we are dealing with human communication processes (message behavior) within complex organizations. Messages similar to those within an organization may well be communicated outside an organization, but our focus is on what happens to those messages within and because of an organization.

Rather than consider alternative definitions and models of communication currently in vogue, let us discuss some of the main traits of the communication process: the transactional, rule-based personal, and serial characteristics of communication.

Communication Is Transactional

In 1960, David Berlo signaled for many the beginning of a new era in communication by his book, *The Process of Communication.* It introduced the notion that communication is a dynamic, interactive process. Prior to that book communication was thought to be essentially a linear act in which information was transmitted from one person to another in a sequence of steps. Berlo refuted this static viewpoint as follows:

> If we accept the concept of process, we view events and relationships as dynamic, ongoing, ever-changing, continuous. When we label something as a process, we also mean that it does not have *a* beginning, *an* end, a fixed sequence of events. It is not static, at rest. It is moving. The ingredients within a process interact; each affects all of the others. . . .
>
> Communication theory reflects a process point of view. A communication theorist . . . argues that you cannot talk about *the* beginning or *the* end of communication or say that a particular idea came from one specific source, that communication occurs in only one way. . . .

Despite the popularity of Berlo's theory and later supportive research evidence for it, several writers still clung to a linear perspective of communication. One speech textbook paid lip

No two communication events are identical.

service to Berlo's concept of "interactive process" by adding a feedback loop to its model of communication. What had once been labeled a one-way, static model was now supposed to represent a process—by the addition of feedback. This relatively naïve viewpoint still maintained, however, that communication occurs in a *sequence of events*. In his best-selling management text Davis (1972) summarized his approach to communication as follows:

> Two-way communication has a back-and-forth pattern similar to the exchange of play between tennis players. The speaker sends a message, and the receiver's responses come back to the speaker.

Further into the book, the author defines communication as "the passing of information and understanding from one person to another."

Current thinking of communication researchers and theorists reemphasizes what Berlo labeled "a dynamic process" and defines communication as a *transactional* process. As used here, the prefix *trans-* denotes "mutual" and "reciprocal." *Trans-* is used rather than *inter-,* which means "between," to emphasize that communication is a reciprocal process in which both parties, sender and receiver mutually affect each other as they send and receive messages. Wilmot and Wenberg stated this idea simply when they said about the transactional process:

> All persons are engaged in sending (encoding) and receiving (decoding) messages *simultaneously*. Each person is constantly *sharing* in the encoding and decoding processes, and each person is *affecting* the other.

Inherent in this perception of communication are the beliefs that no two communication events are identical, that no communication event may be relived, that no communication event is isolated from its environment, and that no communication event is static or sequential. To further illustrate the simultaneous reciprocal influence of both parties on the communication situation, here is a section from the classic article on the transactional nature of communication by Barnlund. The scene is the waiting room of a doctor's office. Mr. A is awaiting the arrival of Dr. B.

As Mr. A glances about the office he may be aware of the arrangement of furniture, a worn carpet, a framed reproduction of a Miro painting, a slightly antiseptic odor, an end table covered with magazines. To any one of them he may attach significance, altering his attitude toward his doctor or himself. . . . All these cues are available potentially to anyone who enters the reception room. The perception of any specific cue, or the meaning assigned to it, however, will be similar for various people only to the extent that they possess the same sensory acuity, overlapping fields of perception, parallel background experiences, and similar needs or purposes.

A second set of cues consists of those elements or events that are essentially private in nature, that come from sources not automatically available to any other person who enters a communicative field. . . . In the case of Mr. A, the private cues might include the words and pictures he finds as he riffles through a magazine, the potpourri of objects he finds in his pocket, or a sudden twitch of pain he notices in his chest. . . .

Although no one else has yet entered the communicative field, Mr. A has to contend with one additional set of cues. . . . They consist of the observations he asks of himself as he turns the pages of his magazine, sees himself reflected in the mirror, or changes positions in his chair. . . . These cues are identified . . . as behavioral, nonverbal cues. . . . They comprise the deliberate acts of Mr. A in straightening his tie or picking up a magazine as well as his unconscious mannerisms in holding a cigarette or slouching in his chair. . . .

The communication process is complicated still further . . . by the appearance of a second person . . . , let us say Dr. B, who enters the reception room to look for his next patient. The perceptual field of Dr. B, as that of Mr. A, will include the public cues supplied by the environment. . . . These cues, however, will not be identical for both persons . . . because of differences in their backgrounds and immediate purposes. Dr. B may notice the time on the wall clock or the absence of other patients, and he may assign different valences to the disarray of magazines on the table or to the Miro print. In addition, Dr. B will be interpreting private cues . . . that belong exclusively to his own phenomenological field, such as his own fatigue at the moment, and these may alter the interpretations he attaches to Mr. A's conduct. Finally, there are the behavioral cues . . . that accompany his own movements to which he must be tuned in order to act with reasonable efficiency.

Even before any verbal exchange takes place, however, there will be a shift in communicative orientation of both individuals. As Mr. A and Dr. B become aware of the presence of the other (sometimes before), each will become more self-conscious, more acutely aware of his own acts, and more alert to the nonverbal cues of the other as an aid to defining their relationship. . . . The doctor, as he enters, may assume a professional air as a means of keeping the patient at the proper psychological distance; the patient, upon hearing the door open, may hastily straighten his tie to make a good impression. . . .

Dr. B, crossing the room, may initiate the conversations. Extending his hand, he says, "Mr. A! So glad to see you. How are you?". . . In a nonclinical environment where the public cues would be different, perhaps on a street corner . . . Mr. A would regard this message . . . as no more than a social gesture, and he would respond in kind. This, on the other hand, is a clinic. . . . Is this remark, therefore, to be given the usual interpretation? Even here, the nonverbal cues . . . of Dr. B, the friendly facial expression and extended hand, may reinforce its usual meaning in spite of the special setting. On the other hand, these words . . . may be interpreted only as showing the sympathetic interest of Dr. B in Mr. A. In this case, the message requires no answer at all but is a signal for Mr. A to come into the office. . . .

Communication is Rule-Based

People interact by exchanging messages, by meaningful symbolic transactions that use verbal or nonverbal cues. The more repetitious our communicative behavior, that is, the more often we assign similar meanings to symbols and agree with others about those meanings, the more patterned our behavior that reflects these meanings becomes. These patterns of behavior, then, reflect and reinforce our values, beliefs, and attitudes. To the extent that regular, habitual patterns of behavior are noted in our communication activities, we say that certain "rules" (norms, expectations, expressions of proper behavior) are in effect. (Farace, Monge, Russell, 1977) If these rules are followed extensively throughout an organization, we state that "communication policies" are in effect, especially if they are put in writing.

Cushman, King, and Smith (1988) explicated two propositions: (1) the interchange of information involves a transaction among symbol-using participants with the understanding with results being guided and governed by communication rules; and (2) communication rules form general and specific patterns that provide the basis for a scientific explanation and prediction of communication behavior.

Schall (1983) has defined communication rules as "tacit understandings (generally unwritten and unspoken) about appropriate ways to interact (communicate) with others in given roles and situations; they are choices, not laws (though they constrain choice through normative, practical, or logical force), and they allow interactors to interpret behavior in similar ways (to share meanings)."

According to Shimanoff (1980), communication rules are multifunctional: they function to coordinate, evaluate, interpret, justify, and predict interactive behavior. They identify what we "should" or "should not" do in an organization, in accordance with experience ("Lunch breaks will last one hour because we've always done it this way"), achieving objectives ("If you work on weekends, the boss will notice and give you a raise"), or ethics ("We should tell the people about the chemical dump, because it's morally correct to do so").

Cushman and Whiting (1972) have identified two classes of rules: content and procedural. Content rules are concerned with what words and symbols mean in a particular context to both parties in the interaction. Procedural rules relate to the protocols and means of communication (e.g., how long, who goes first, where do we talk, what medium or channel do we use, etc.). In order for co-orientation to occur in an interaction, both parties must agree on rules governing content and procedure of the interaction. For example, IBM has had a well-established dress code for years that requires males to wear suits and ties to work. By contrast, Apple Computer, with its relatively informal atmosphere has ignored such rules. If a former Apple executive were to join IBM as a new manager, he might be quite surprised when he attended his first business meeting wearing jeans. When people define a situation differently, that is, apply different rules, they will probably not co-orient to the event, and conflict may occur. In an organizational setting, rules can be stated generally and imply broad themes (e.g., "At Apple, we expect excellence from everyone") or stated more specifically so that they communicate the tactics of interaction (e.g., "Our work group will focus on developing a high quality new computer called Macintosh").

Shimanoff (1980) has further characterized communication rules as followable, prescriptive, and contextual.

1. *Followable.* People are physically capable of following rules, thus rule-generated behavior is controllable.
2. *Prescriptive.* Communication rules indicate what should or should not occur, thus opening up rule-generated behavior to evaluation and sanctions.
3. *Contextual.* Communication rules apply in all similar situations, thus, rule-generated behavior is contextual.

Thus far, we have been talking about rules that govern communication behavior in organizational settings. We have been discussing the ways and types of rules that determine the kinds of interactions that might take place in an organization. It is also possible to produce rules *by* communication. Tompkins (1984) has designated four kinds of rules that he contends have developed by the nature of the communication that takes place in the organization.

1. *Hierarchical Rules.* This includes high-level policies that are translated into increasingly concrete rules down through an organization's levels. These rules are generated by superiors-in-interaction and are regenerated by the process of interpretation and transformation at each stage of the scalar chain.
2. *Task Rules.* These guides for performing tasks are generated by industrial engineers and other experts and are taught to workers in training sessions and on-the-job (enabling workers to learn their jobs).
3. *Work-Group Rules.* Workers will interact with each other to define and enforce the limits of their obedience to the hierarchy of the organization, in order to achieve solidarity and cohesion.
4. *Individual Rules.* Typically, these rules are learned outside the organization by employees who make an implicit or explicit contract with the organization about what they will do for remuneration. (Organizations will try to screen out any workers whose individual rules are not friendly to the organization.)

It is very important for employees to have a clear understanding of what the explicit/formal as well as implicit/informal rules of an organization are if he or she is to avoid unwanted conflicts. Since communication is such a personal process, this may be quite challenging.

Communication Is Personal

No two people are alike. We are all products of different families and cultures. We all have different nervous systems. Because of such environmental and physiological differences, our perceptions are also different. Perception is the process by which we receive and organize sensory data from the environments. When we see an automobile hit a pedestrian or hear a telephone ringing or touch a baby's smooth skin or smell a cake baking in the oven or boldly taste a small sample as it cools, we are receiving information from the environment and determining how to classify and respond to it. Depending upon our individual needs, values, feelings, physical makeup, and past experience, we either respond to or ignore any one piece of information. For example, if our eyesight is slightly impaired, we may not see the speeding

HI THERE SWEETLIPS!

HOW 'BOUT A LITTLE KISS?

HISS

JUST MY LUCK. SHE HAS A HEARING IMPEDIMENT.

Our perception is influenced by our past experience and our physiology. (By permission of Johnny Hart and Field Enterprises, Inc.)

automobile. If we are waiting for an important phone call, we may race to the telephone before the first ring has ended. If we have never touched a baby, we may not notice the texture of its skin. If our nose is stuffed, we may not smell a cake. If we were punished as a child for sneaking a cookie from the cookie jar, as an adult we may be reluctant to sample a freshly baked cake. In all of these cases, our perception is influenced by *our past experience and our physiology*. Because of these differences in individual perception, we conclude that our communication behavior will be different as we are confronted with stimuli from the environment. Thus, since perception and behavior vary among people, communication is a highly personal process governed by unique interpretations of human messages.

When we realize how personal communication is, it becomes relatively simple to admit the highly *approximate* nature of communication. The best we may be able to hope for is to *approach* a common understanding.

Words and Meanings

Too often in an organization it is assumed that the only requirement for better communication is to make sure that all messages are expressed in clear, simple language. This naïve view of communication assumes that words in themselves have meaning. They do not. Thus far we have emphasized that people determine the measure of words by the way they use them. Therefore, since word meaning depends for the most part on context, people find it handy to allot whatever meaning they wish to words and messages. In fact, a study of the 500 most commonly used words found that a current dictionary identified 14,070 meanings for those words—about 28 meanings per word.

Despite the fact that meaning is not inherent in words, some bureaucrats behave as if it were. Laurence Peter defined "officialese" as a form of bureaucratic writing in which the words can be understood but not the sentences. He claimed there are two kinds of officialese: hard-to-understand officialese and easy-to-misunderstand officialese. To illustrate university officialese, he cited the answer of a university official to a question on a government application:

Question: What method is employed in selection of fellowship students?
Answer: A nonjudgmental ongoing reassessment of ego differentiation facilitates role adjustment to the interrelation of consensus work and social integration combining self-determination with an authoritative structured environment.

CREATING AND EXCHANGING VERBAL MESSAGES   131

I once saw an advertisement placed by a large university which specified that applicants for a teaching position should be able "to combine synchronic and diachronic analysis of events in a transcultural and holistic mode." Any gym teachers out there? At an academic conference, I heard a colleague describe himself as a "quantitative agnostic." When I asked him what that meant, he answered calmly, "I'm a mathematical primitive." But can he balance a checkbook?

Anyone who has dealt with government agencies knows that universities are not alone in the use of officialese. All accomplished government bureaucrats know that when they are confronted with a proposal to be rejected, they should say:

> While the initial study committee has made a skillful and in-depth analysis of the alternative resource mixes as they relate to the proposal in question, the optimal functions as reflected by the committee's thematic projections would suggest a nonaffirmative response if the executive office were forced to make an immediate decision. In view of the paramount importance of the multivious aspects of the proposal, it is my recommendation that a special task force be created with the assigned responsibility of appropriately developing sound administrative options to the proposed implementation decision. Reliable and tested administrative procedures would enhance the practicality of the proposal and add to it the incremental viability factors essential for the type of creative innovation that functions within established guidelines.

James Boren, who provided this example, has other guidelines for bureaucrats in his book, *When in Doubt, Mumble.*

Congressman Jack Kemp once asked former Budget Director Bert Lance whether the Carter administration had the right to terminate a missile project before receiving permission from Congress. Lance's officialese answer was this:

> As you know, the Impoundment Control Act of 1976 does not contain any provision governing the obligation or deobligation of funds proposed for recision during the forty-five-day period. A recision message is awaiting congressional action. There is no prohibition on terminating existing contracts, thereby deobligating funds, during this period.

> In the absence of express requirements with respect to obligation or deobligation of funds and in view of the recognition by Congress that funds could be withheld, there is no legal basis for precluding the Department of Defense from either refraining from obligating additional funds or terminating existing contracts during the forty-five-day period the related recision message is pending in the Congress.

How about "yes!"

The National Council of Teachers of English has established a Committee on Public Doublespeak to "honor" those bureaucrats who excel in their use of officialese. The Department of Defense once won for calling the neutron bomb, which kills every living creature within its reach but leaves physical structures unharmed, "a radiation enhancement weapon." Runners-up have included the Central Intelligence Agency for conducting experiments in brainwashing and behavior control under cover of an organization called the Society for Investigation of Human Ecology; and Health, Education, and Welfare secretary Joseph Califano, who advertised for "an extremely confidential personnel assistant . . . responsible for managing, performing, and supervising work related to the operation of the secretary's kitchen and eating area." He was looking for a chef!

Table 4.3 Gobbledygook Exercise

Webster's dictionary defines *gobbledygook* as "wordy and generally unintelligible jargon." Others have described it as a conglomeration of flossy, pompous, abstract, complex, jargonistic words we too frequently try to pass off as communications. Gobbledygook is almost always loaded with jargon of the writer's own professional interest—words seldom used by persons outside the writer's little word-world. It seems to stem from an ingrown (perhaps subconscious) professional desire to impress rather than to communicate, to be "proper" rather than personal and direct.

To show how easy it is to get balled up in the jargon of our own trade or profession, let's look at a little game we recently heard about. You play it with three groups of buzz words numbered from zero to nine:

Group 1	Group 2	Group 3
0. evaluate	0. educational	0. competencies
1. coordinate	1. diffusion	1. research
2. upgrade	2. program	2. implications
3. formalize	3. professional	3. planning
4. total	4. leadership	4. subject matter
5. balanced	5. clientele	5. role
6. finalize	6. differential	6. image
7. systematized	7. decision making	7. focal point
8. ongoing	8. innovative	8. flexibility
9. responsive	9. policy	9. programming

Now think of any three-digit number, and then from each of the above groups select the numbered word corresponding to each digit in the number picked. For example, take the number 220, and you get "upgrade program competencies." If you use 359, your phrase turns out to be "formalize clientele programming." Your phrases may lack real meaning, but most of them will have a ring of familiarity.

According to former U.S. Senator S. I. Hayakawa, earlier a student of Korzybski and the general semantics movement, no matter how good are the intentions of Congress about a law, by the time the legislation is proposed and the experts get through writing it in legal language, it becomes incomprehensible. Then, the regulatory agencies work on the law, and the language becomes even more complicated. Help may be on the way. New York State has passed legislation requiring plain language in all consumer agreements.

By now you must realize that officialese is the domain of gobbledygook. The exercise in table 4.3 is provided to help you become an instant expert in the use of gobbledygook.

Perceptual Differences

Many times the communication problem in an organization is not due to lack of clarity or not using the correct word but to differences in perception of those who are communicating. These differences can, and many times do, lead to severe conflict within the organization. For example, if a student believes that it is his duty to call the police when he observes a crime, but a policeman believes that the student will *not* call the police, we have the ingredients for a communication breakdown between that student and the policeman. This may be a critical breakdown because it may later influence that policeman's behavior when he deals with college students in both law enforcement and non-law enforcement situations.

I reported a research study which documents perceptual differences between police and college students in New Mexico (Goldhaber, 1972). For example, 75 percent of college students surveyed felt that long hair on students would affect how a policeman would treat them, but 81 percent of the police denied that long hair would have any effect upon their treatment of college youth. In another question, 95 percent of the students said they would call the police if they saw someone commit a murder, while almost 50 percent of the police estimated that less than 75 percent of the students would call the police. It was apparent from these answers, and others on the questionnaire of thirty-two items, that there was a large discrepancy between perceptions of attitudes and the attitudes themselves. I reached these conclusions:

> Perceptions of another person's attitudes toward you may dictate your actions toward that person; if the perception of the attitude is radically different from the actual attitude, then the actions taken by either party toward the other may be not only inappropriate, but also highly offensive.

Many studies have reported major perceptual differences between bosses and their subordinates—for example, the following findings in a study by Likert (as summarized by Huse and Bowditch):

> Although 85 percent of the supervisors believe their subordinates feel free to talk about the job with the boss, only half of the subordinates share this belief. More than 90 percent of the foremen and 100 percent of the top management feel that they always or nearly always tell subordinates about changes affecting them or their work. Only about half of the subordinates feel the same way.

Several studies I have directed report similar findings. For example, all of the top management in a police organization perceived that they could always freely and openly communicate with their employees (patrolmen), but only one-third of the patrolmen shared this belief. In another organization, all of the vice presidents and the president said they had an open-door policy which they felt was an effective communication channel between them and their subordinates, but only 20 percent of the subordinates shared this perception; and data on the frequency of interactions via this channel supported the subordinates' perceptions. One employee reported, "They don't have an open-door, they have a cracked-door policy!" In a third organization there was much conflict due to perceptual differences about the goals and objectives of the system. Top management assumed that middle management supported their desires for implementation of a new product line. When asked for their opinion, almost 90 percent of the middle managers believed that the new product was of questionable value and that top management was manipulating them into supporting their "preconceived objectives."

The basic conclusion of most of these studies is that people respond in different ways to messages because of differences in perception. Assumptions that do not take into account perceptual differences may lead to supposition of attitudinal structure and behavioral response that do not exist. Such assumptions may directly cause conflict and unwarranted hostility. If we remember that communication is a personal process, that no two people are alike, we may reduce the possibility for such confrontation.

Communication Is Serial

As little children, we may have played a game where one child whispers a story in the ear of another. Then the child who received the story whispers what she thought she heard into the next child's ear. This procedure continues until all children playing the game have heard and repeated a version of the story. The last child in the chain then loudly proclaims his

How Purchasing Ordered It
(Purchasing Department)

How Sales Representative Sold It
(The Order Desk)

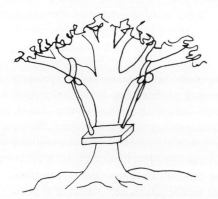

How Construction Installed It
(Engine Shop)

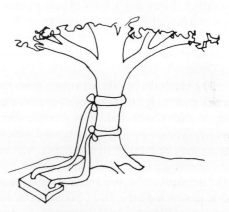

How Engineering Designed It
(The Factory)

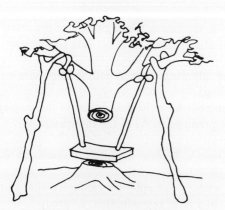

How Service Department Made It Work
(Airframe Shop)

What the Customer Wanted
(Whoopee)

"Messages in serial reproduction, like water in a great river, change through losses, gains, absorptions, and combinations along the route from the headwaters to their final destination." (Quotation and drawing from Pace and Boren, *The Human Transaction,* Scott, Foresman, 1973.)

CREATING AND EXCHANGING VERBAL MESSAGES   135

understanding of the story to everyone, usually accompanied by much giggling and joking about "how funny the story sounds now" or "how different from the original it now is."

This children's game, sometimes called telephone, illustrates much about the process of person-person-person communication. We call this process serial communication because it involves a step-by-step sequence in the replication of a message. As we view human communication, it is easy to see that almost all communicative behavior flows in this manner.

There is little difference between the telephone game and gossip about a neighborhood scandal, or the spread of rumors about a new company policy, or the boss sending an order down the organization through several channels, or even a manager who remembers a message from a spouse two weeks earlier. All these examples involve the process of one or more people sending messages to and receiving messages from one or more people that are reproduced through one or more channels until they reach their final destination.

Even the president of the United States is not immune to the distorting of serial communication. Every day a staff of seven people go through piles of newspapers, monitor the wire services and television networks, and assemble a news summary for the president to read. We will soon see what the potential for error is in the serial process. Then we may well speculate about the potential for information inaccuracies in the flow to and through the Oval Office.

The chain that exists between a manufacturer and his consumers also represents serial communication. A large corporation manufactures a product and distributes it to a warehouse or jobber, who sells it to a wholesaler, who sells it to a retailer, who sells it to the consumer. These four links may expand somewhat depending upon the product. For example, a carpet may be retailed to a designer, who sells it to a nightclub, whose patrons walk on it. When a message is sent along the product manufacturing/distribution chain, it is subject to all the weaknesses of the serial communication process. Pace and Boren described these weaknesses metaphorically: "Messages in serial reproduction, like water in a great river, change through losses, gains, absorptions, and combinations along the route from the headwaters to their final destination." The findings of other researchers support the river metaphor and Pace and Boren's conclusions:

1. Details become omitted, declining sharply in number at the beginning of the series and continuing throughout thereafter—but at a somewhat slower rate (sometimes called leveling).
2. Details, when retained, become highlighted, allowing them to gain in importance and meaningfulness (sometimes called sharpening).
3. Details become added for the purpose of embellishing the description of the message.
4. Details become modified to conform to the predispositions of the interpreter (sometimes called assimilation).
5. Statements that were previously qualified tend to become definite statements in later reproduction.
6. Details tend to be combined into a single, unitary concept—for example, what starts out as three different individuals becomes, in a later reproduction, a "group" (sometimes called condensation).
7. Details of events or happenings are described in the order in which one would *expect* them to occur rather than as they actually *did* occur.
8. Details are adapted so as to make the entire message or event seem plausible.

9. Certain phrases are adjusted to reflect the accepted style of expression used by the social level and stratum of the individuals collectively involved in the serial reproduction of the message.

When we discuss formal and informal organizational communication networks, several obstacles created by the serial process become more apparent. A few examples now, however, may help clarify some of these concepts. One example of details becoming lost or filtered out concerns three messages which were traced downward from their origin (top management) through seven management levels in a utility company whose organization I studied. Recall tests of most employees at the lowest level of management indicated that either they didn't know or had never received the messages. Follow-up interviews and some data from first-hand observation indicated the latter was true. In another organization, a men's residence hall at a large university, the hall manager instructed the supervisor of maids that the maids were "to knock on the doors of the men before entering, in order to guarantee their privacy." When the supervisor addressed her fourteen maids, she stated, "Now the little darlings don't want to be seen in their underwear, so be sure and knock before you go into their rooms. They probably will need the time to hide their booze and dope, anyway!" This is an example of both assimilating (changing the intent of the original message) and adding information in order to embellish the message. I once directed a study of communication in a bank. A message related to my study illustrates the phenomenon of assimilation. My instructions to the organization's liaison person working with me were to have the president send a letter of explanation to the bank officers immediately prior to sending them survey instruments. This procedure would allow me to use the authority channels of the bank both to explain the study and to help increase my return rate. The liaison prepared the surveys, placed them in envelopes, addressed them, and asked her assistant to take all 300 to the mail room for the envelopes to be sealed and to await further mailing instructions. The assistant gave the questionnaires to the clerk in charge of the mail room, who promptly sealed and mailed the surveys to the bank officers—before the president's letter had even been written! One hundred ninety-three officers called the president the next day to ask what was going on!

We know that because of the transactional and personal nature of communication, message reproduction is fraught with misperception and misunderstanding. The number of times a message is reproduced compounds the probability of distortion. The following discussions of message diffusion, purpose of message, and message networks should make it evident that the very dynamism of the communication process limits its effectiveness.

Diffusion Methods and the New Technologies

In chapter 1, method of diffusion was defined as the particular activity used to send a message. Usually diffusion is concerned only with two methods. Hardware methods make use of such devices as television, telephone, telex, walkie-talkie, radio, and computer. Software methods produce written and oral messages. Hardware methods depend upon electrical or mechanical power to function. Software methods rely on the ability of people to speak, listen, and write. Since this is a book on speech communication, we are primarily concerned with

There can be little doubt that the new communication technologies will allow more information to be processed, stored, retrieved, and transferred faster and cheaper.

oral software methods of diffusing messages. Written methods (e.g., letters, memos, bulletins, reports, newsletters, newspapers, proposals, minutes, announcements, manuals, policies) are discussed in other books. However, since tremendous advances in communication technology have been noted in the past five years, and since many of these new technologies are of particular concern to any large organization, we will briefly examine them and their effect upon efficiency and effectiveness.

The New Technologies

In the parts warehouse of Ford Motor Company in Petersboro, New Jersey, an employee picks up a package at the loading dock, reads the destination into a microphone, and puts the package on a conveyor belt, which then carries it to the correct storage shelf. Meat inspectors at six Wilson Foods Corporation packing plants weigh and grade hog carcasses as soon as the animals are slaughtered, and they dictate the information into a computer terminal that can receive oral information. The computer prints out a record of each farmer's hogs and later writes a check to the farmer. The process eliminates blood-stained paperwork and the inaccuracies of typing into a terminal.

The office of the future, available today in many organizations, is a highly automated environment where most clerical chores are performed electronically, with dramatic improvement in the productivity of managerial and professional personnel. Voice and video teleconferencing services via telephone lines and communication satellite links will increasingly replace person-to-person meetings and interstate travel. Memos and letters typed on paper will give way to computer-controlled electronic mail displayed on video screens, and clumsy, bulky hard-copy filing and photocopying systems will be supplanted by sophisticated electronic and microform systems for information storage and retrieval. Office workers will have easy-to-use computer terminals that will perform localized data-and word-processing functions. Almost all of these new services will be integrated into compact, uncomplicated executive workstations that look much like today's more specialized video terminals.

In an experiment that may delight all workaholics in the United States, Control Data Corporation has about 100 employees working at home or at satellite offices in an energy-saving, production-raising effort at "telecommuting," the electronic connection between home and office. Initial results showed that each participant reduced monthly auto driving by 500 miles for a $90 savings, and productivity increased up to 300 percent.

In another experiment with telecommuting, the state of California currently has 200 of its 145,500 employees working at home connected to their offices through computer terminals. The state is trying to get answers to the following questions:

1. Will the benefits of telecommuting (e.g., smaller offices, energy conservation, etc.) outweigh its costs?
2. How will isolation affect employees?
3. Will telecommuting also work well in "work centers" (leased office space near employees' homes)?
4. Who should own the terminals or personal computers?
5. How will the unions or other workers' organizations react?

This experiment and others like it may be quite important to our understanding of the effects of telecommuting. It may not always be positive. While working at home may sound ideal—no commuting, flexible hours, no dress codes, more time with the family, higher productivity, cheaper and better lunches, etc.—there may be some high costs. Some workers that I have interviewed have complained of isolation, increased stress due to fear of being isolated from the social and political network of the organization, weight gain due to proximity of the refrigerator, family problems due to increased number of hours "on the job." Until the research findings are in, and modifications are made, the 100,000 telecommuters from 450 companies in the United States may be accepting some unnecessary risks.

Most of the products and services that the new communication technologies make available for the automated office of the future fall into three categories: information processing, information retrieval, and information transfer.

Information Processing. Combined data-and word-processing functions via a terminal on the manager's desk is the way most organizations will be moving. The result will be not only efficient production of information, but visual display of that information with graphs and charts. The manager's personal computer, near his or her workstation, will be easy to use and designed for the manager's special needs. Letters and reports composed on the manager's word processor can be transmitted to another processor for printing. Information processing also includes dictating equipment, photocopiers, and printing devices. Some dictation equipment now includes keyboards, video screens, and telephone couplers to allow remote dictation and transcribing from anywhere in the world. Office copiers can be directly connected to computers and word processors to receiver output, choose the printed format and type styles, and then print material at high speed on paper or microform media. In their study on the implementation of word processing and action bias effects, Browning and Johnson

(1988) used word processing to examine how technological advancement affects the structure of an organization's culture. Their results stated that word processing can increase action bias in cultures.

Information Retrieval. Information retrieval products generally address the need to cut through the glut of paperwork that harasses almost every white-collar worker. They are designed to make paper-based memos, letters, reports, and filing systems obsolete. Surveys indicate that American businesses now deal with an estimated 325 billion documents, and the figure is growing at an estimated 72 billion pieces per year. The office of the future should greatly minimize the paralysis due to paper overload. Electronic filing systems are now being marketed that store information on computer tapes, microform products, videodiscs, and even in on-line computer memories. Computer-output microform allows computers to record output directly on microfiche, and computer-indexing allows easy retrieval. Laser-optical videodiscs have a highly advanced indexing system. Each of the 100,000 frames on a disc can be used to store information, and each frame can be individually read by the low-grade laser beam and displayed on a video monitor.

Information Transfer. Unlike the old methods of information transfer—travel, mail, and telephone—the office of the future will use electronic mail, facsimile devices, and teleconferencing to dramatically increase the organization's options. With electronic mail, workers can avoid typing memos and letters that must then be dispatched via messenger or post office. Instead, they can communicate with each other through video terminals by simply punching in a memo or message and directing it to a colleague's "electronic in-basket." The recipient could call up the message on the screen, answer the message via video, and/or forward his or her own memos to other parties as well. Electronic mail memos can be stored indefinitely, routed to multiple video terminals simultaneously, or printed on paper if needed. In addition, highly automated facsimile devices, able to transmit hundreds of pages per minute, can send letters and text material to dozens of locations simultaneously and can even be connected to electronic filing systems for instantaneous transformation into microform or videodisc. Travel costs of sending employees to meetings can be reduced by teleconferences via satellite links, which can be arranged for much less money. Executives assemble in an AT&T-operated teleconference room in a participating city. The rooms are equipped with soft chairs, soft lighting, screens, facsimile machines for transferring documents, voice-activated cameras, and even electronic blackboards that allow images in one city to be reproduced in others.

After its first three years, AT&T's new videoconference technology does not appear to be a big success, mostly due to the high costs ($1,200/hour and up for satellite transmission and $125,000 to $1 million to build private conference rooms) and poor marketing by AT&T (they initially tried to sell the technique as similar to face-to-face communication and people were disappointed after experiencing it). My own research has shown that people miss the nonverbal cues emitted in typical small-group meetings not detected by cameras used in the teleconference set-up.

Effects of the New Technologies. There can be little doubt that the new communication technologies will allow more information to be processed, stored, retrieved, and transferred faster and cheaper. There will undoubtedly be savings in time and money and increased overall efficiency in the management of information and the decision-making process. Re-

In the teleconference set-up, many nonverbal cues are missed by the camera, thereby inhibiting communication and robbing the participants of a sense of personal intimacy.

search on the effects of the office of the future done by Don Tapscott at Bell Northern Research in Toronto has shown exactly that. In an effort to measure workers' attitudes, time use, and communication patterns as a result of exposure to an integrated office system that provided electronic mail, information retrieval, word processing, administrative support, and data processing, he compared an experimental and a control group on relevant measures. The new technologies seemed to improve the users' communication flow, time use, access to information, attitudes toward office system technology, and quality of working life. However, much more research needs to be done before we can conclude that the new technologies are as effective as they are efficient. We need to ask the following questions:

1. Will the new technologies
    a. overload us with information?
    b. hamper our senses? (e.g., fatigue our eyes?)
    c. create new networks? destroy old networks?
    d. improve or harm worker morale?
    e. increase productivity?
    f. violate our privacy?
    g. create new status symbols and power bases?
2. Will the new technologies fail because of
    a. unfamiliarity with the products and techniques?
    b. low status associated with "keyboarding"?
    c. threats to secretarial personnel?
    d. diminished informal communication?
    e. people's overall need for "flesh" contacts?

In her study on organizational communication and technological innovation, Sandra E. O'Connell (1988) concluded with the following six hypotheses that deal with the role of technology and its influence on communication in the organization:

1. Opportunities for face-to-face contact will be diminished, and information from nonverbal cues will be reduced. Consequently, opportunities for random, spontaneous information sharing will be reduced. Managers will need to structure work and relationships to provide more opportunities for face-to-face contact to occur. Meaning will be derived from text and symbols.

2. More informal messages and "short-circuiting" of the hierarchy will occur as new formats are accepted due to the remote nature of an electronic network. Organization structure and formal information flow will be redefined.

3. Channel effects will mean that messages of affect and values will decrease. Digitized data, with less context and interpretation, will be the norm. Consequently, decision making may be impaired rather than enhanced. Ambiguity in interpreting information will increase, and the quality of decisions could decrease with the lack of organizational values and context. Organizations will need to work harder at communicating their values and corporate history. Managers will have to seek new ways of communicating the affective component of messages. New and improved decision-making skills will be needed.

4. Trust will play a changed role in communication. Trust develops with shared experience, values, give and take, and the result of human communication. Satellites, electronic mail, and networks could reduce the dimensions of trust to which we are accustomed. New communication networks may spring up in their place.

5. The computer imposes a discipline of linear thinking. Data is processed at speeds that increase with each new version of the chip. Consequently, people may develop less patience and tolerance for individual styles of communicating. Organizations may find themselves less tolerant of people who do not think or perceive in a strict linear mode. They will need to find ways to encourage and protect nonlinear thinking and communicating.

6. Expectations of work performance may be machine driven. As we become accustomed to the speed and accuracy of the computer, we may expect employees to have the same qualities and produce in a similar manner. Employees in some organizations will perceive this as dehumanizing and coercive. Unions will take up the human environment as an issue. New ways of defining and using performance standards will be needed.

We seem to be approaching a time when Marshall McLuhan's notion of the electronic global village is a reality with regard to organizational communication.

But to what effect? Preliminary research conducted in Canada and England shows that a teleconference, for example, may not be as effective as a "live" group meeting because of the absence of necessary nonverbal facial cues, which limited camera facilities make almost impossible to monitor. A major conclusion of a three-year, sixteen-organization study I directed in the United States and Canada is that *most employees want and need more inter-*

personal face-to-face contact, particularly with senior management, the very ones most likely to use the new technologies. Edward R. Murrow, long before communication satellites were a reality, put it this way:

> Communication systems are neutral. They have neither conscience nor morality . . . . They will broadcast truth or falsehood and . . . quality or junk with equal facility. Man communicating with man presents not the problem of how to say it, but, more fundamentally, what he is to say.

Perhaps one of the first signs that the information explosion may be producing a counter-revolutionary effect has come from a theatre in Rochester, New York. The GeVa Theatre has banned electronic watches that beep or chime from the theatre during performances. Management already had requested that doctors leave their beepers at the ticket booth. We will now see exactly how face-to-face diffusion methods help an organization exchange messages among its members.

Oral Software: Face-to-Face Diffusion Systems

Once an organization has specified its overall goals and objectives, along with its communication objectives, it may generate formal communication policies to help implement them. For example, an organization may identify one overall goal to be reduction of the level of decision making on several key issues. This goal leads to a specific communication objective of informing and seeking input and decision making from certain employees on select decisions. The communication objective may be translated into a specific formal policy such as, "All employees will be informed about what decisions their input and vote are sought"; or, more specifically, "The production department will meet monthly to make decisions relevant to their operation and future." Many organizations do not formalize their communication objectives; often the objectives are implied from observation of behavior within the organization. For example, in one business firm the engineering department met frequently with the manufacturing department to discuss issues of concern to both units. The frequency of these meetings *implied* an unwritten company policy: "Departments with mutual concerns should meet regularly to discuss these concerns."

Once the organization determines its policies (explicitly or implicitly), a particular communication activity implements that policy. Therefore, when we discuss diffusion methods, we are actually concerned with *specific organizational communication behavior.* In the example just given, the behavior was the monthly meeting of the two departments. Analysis of a behavior can be made at several levels. We can ask questions about the *activity itself:* Who is involved in the activity? How often does it occur? Under what conditions does the activity occur? Who initiates the activity? What is the content of each activity? We can also ask questions about the people involved in the activity. Such questions analyze each *individual's communication behavior:* What words did the participants use (sentences, phrases)? Who spoke the most? Did the participants ask questions? Did they make statements? What type of nonverbal communication was used (e.g., eye contact, facial expression, tone of voice, gesture, touch, dress, seating arrangement)? We can even analyze an organization's *total system of activities* by asking such questions as the following: Which activity is used the most? What activities are used for each purpose? How often do participants engage in each activity? Who is involved in each activity?

Thus, messages are diffused by communication activities that can be analyzed by examining the activity itself, the behavior of the individuals participating in the activity, and the total system of activities. Methods of analyzing behaviors are outlined in chapter 10, "Implementing Organizational Communication Diagnosis." Whatever method of analysis is used to examine message diffusion, the more commonly used criteria for such analysis are as follows:

1. Content of the messages transmitted in the activity
2. Timing (how often; time of month, week, or day)
3. Interaction conditions (room or spatial arrangement, location, noise conditions)
4. Participation (members involved, frequency of participation)
5. Initiation (who starts the activity?)
6. Preparation (amount of advance work)
7. Feedback (amount and frequency)
8. Direction of the activity (up, down, across, diagonal)
9. Purpose of the activity (decision making, information giving or receiving, informal)

Table 4.4 lists some common oral software communication activities. As can be seen, most oral software activities consist of meetings, interviews, and casual conversation in a variety of settings. Many organizations develop their own unique activity behavior, as indicated in table 4.5, which presents the communication activities of several organizations I have studied. The table uses the activity designations of the organizations studied. Table 4.5 shows that organizations vary considerably in the type of communication activity they use to diffuse messages. Several factors can influence their choice: cost, overall goals, specific needs, size of organization, time available, personnel available, and needs and feelings of employees.

Purposes of Messages

Message purpose has to do with the reasons (*why*) for sending and receiving messages within an organization and with the specific function (*what*) of each message. As just pointed out, messages are created and exchanged in response to an organization's goals, policies, and specific objectives. Several authors have identified their perception of the primary functions of messages in organizations. Katz and Kahn specified four communication functions: production, maintenance, adaptation, and management. Redding suggested three general reasons for message flow: task, maintenance, and human. Thayer presented four specific functions of message flow within organizations: to inform, to persuade, to command and instruct, and to integrate. Berlo identified three functions: production (getting a job done), innovation (exploring new behavioral alternatives), and maintenance (keeping the system and its components operating). Greenbaum discussed four key message functions: regulative, innovative, integrative, and informative-instructive.

I will discuss four types of messages: task, maintenance, human, and innovative.

Task messages are concerned with the products, services, and activities of specific interest to the organization, for example, messages about improving sales, markets, quality of service, and quality of products. Task messages include those that give employees all the

Table 4.4   Oral Software Communication Activities

Dyad

Informal conversation (casual, lunch, coffee break, water break)
Hiring interview and orientation interview
Goal-setting interview
Appraisal interview
Exit interview
Superior-subordinate discussion (problems, policies, solutions, etc.)
Informal meeting

Small Group

Brainstorming sessions
Decision-making meetings
Orientation and training groups
Regular department meetings
Directors or executives meetings
Special purpose meetings (crisis, budget, etc.)
Interdepartmental meetings
Problem-solving meetings
Informal meetings (luncheon, coffee break, retreats, rap sessions, etc.)
Quality circles

Public (internal)

Regular meetings of all department heads
Suggestion systems
Organization meetings
Staff meetings
Union meetings
Grapevine
Social functions (picnics, holiday parties, bowling teams, etc.)
President's meeting with all employees

---

information necessary to handle their jobs efficiently. Such activities as training, orientation, and goal setting are also considered task messages. In sum, task messages relate to the desired outputs of the system. For example, a job description communicated to a new employee in an orientation session constitutes a task message.

Maintenance messages pertain to policy and regulation of the organization. They help the organization to survive and self-perpetuate. Maintenance messages include commands, dictates, procedures, orders, and controls necessary to facilitate the organization's movement toward its system outputs. Whereas task messages relate to the *content* of the system output, maintenance messages relate to the *achievement* of the output. At its annual planning session, one company established a system goal of greater participation by employees in the generation of team-developed research proposals. In order to achieve this desired output, a set of committees was created, each with its own agenda and schedule. Messages governing the operation and regulation of these committees were maintenance messages. A specific example of this kind of message is this: "Committee X will meet weekly for a minimum of two hours."

Table 4.5 Sample Communication Activities (Oral Software)

Organization A

Orientation sessions
Job instruction
Order giving
Daily informal contacts
Training groups
Plant-wide meetings ("boss talks")
Grapevine
Round-table discussions
Face-to-face formal contacts
Department meetings

Organization B

Suggestion systems
Informal contacts
Commanders' call (monthly organization wide meeting)
Council meetings (gripe sessions)
Personal contacts (via open door)
Training sessions
Grapevine
Guard mount (information sessions on daily job duties)

Organization C

Biweekly rap session (president and any organization member)
Interviews (hiring and appraisal)
Advisory council (input prior to decision)
Face-to-face (via open-door policy)
Weekly meetings between president and organization's leaders
Monthly board of directors meeting
Weekly and biweekly committee meetings
Retreats and informal conferences (mountain resorts, motels, etc.)
Grapevine
Counseling sessions
Informal activities (lunches, dinners, social, athletic, lounges)

Organization D

Executive meetings
Hiring and firing interviews
Appraisal interviews
Grapevine
Information exchange meetings (department heads)
Daily face-to-face contacts

Human messages are directed at people within the organization and take into account their attitudes, satisfaction, and fulfillment. Human messages are concerned with feelings, interpersonal relationships, self-concept, and morale. Human messages include praise for superior achievement, appraisal interviews, conflict-solving sessions, grapevine activity, informal activities (rap sessions, luncheons, social-athletic activities), and counseling sessions. Organizations can generate a multitude of effective task and maintenance messages, but if the human category is neglected, severe morale problems that prove dysfunctional to the system's goals may ensue. A company hired a new manager with an impressive record for generating peak employee efficiency while also maintaining the system adequately. Shortly after his arrival, however, several employees became noticeably unhappy with his lack of sensitivity to their feelings. When the manager asked individual employees for specific examples of this behavior, they could not comply, but continued to assert that their feelings were being ignored and as a consequence they were no longer happy. Production continued to decrease as more and more employees complained via the grapevine to each other. Finally, the employees initiated a conflict-solving session with the manager to discuss their feelings. The outcome of the session was positive in that it gave the employees an opportunity to formally express their feelings of discontent to the manager, who promised to process the information and consider new behaviors for increasing his sensitivity to their feelings. The message behavior generated at this meeting was of the human type because it was specifically directed at improving interpersonal relationships.

Innovative messages enable an organization to adapt to its changing environment. New plans, activities, programs, directions, projects, and product suggestions generated during problem solving, planning, and brainstorming sessions are typical innovative messages. For example, one organization held an annual planning conference to set goals and objectives for the coming year. This conference, its agenda, and its message behavior constitute use of innovative messages.

A study by Schuler and Blank supports a positive relationship between adequate communication of task, human, and innovative messages and job satisfaction and worker performance. These researchers also found preliminary evidence of a negative relationship between overcommunication of regulative messages and job satisfaction. Their findings also indicate that employees at higher levels within an organization need more task and human messages because of the greater complexity of their tasks. Their results suggest, however, that human messages are more satisfying and conducive to overall performance than are the other three types of messages. This research is important, not only because the researchers show that different kinds of messages can be identified, measured, and related to satisfaction and performance, but also because of the implications for contingency theory. Each message type seems to interact with specific organizational levels to differentially affect employee satisfaction and performance. Organizations would be wise, therefore, to become sensitive to message differences in their employee motivation programs.

Message Networks[1]

Organizations are composed of numbers of people who occupy specific positions or roles. The exchange of messages between and among these people takes place over pathways called communication *networks* (or *nets*). A communication network may consist of only two people or an entire organization.

The *role* that individuals play in a communication system is determined by their structural relationship vis-à-vis other individuals in the system. This relationship is defined by the pattern of interaction connecting the individual to the flow of information in the network.

---

1. Parts of the discussion on message networks are adapted from Gerald Goldhaber et al., (1978).

Individuals who are relatively unconnected to the organization are called isolates.

In current network terminology, three or more individuals whose majority of interactions are with each other are termed a *group*. Group members whose interactions are with members of other groups are termed *bridges*. Individuals whose interactions are mainly with members of two or more groups but who are not members of any one group are termed *liaisons*. Individuals who are relatively unconnected to the organization are termed *isolates*.

In his exhaustive review of communication network analysis, Rolf T. Wigand (1988) concludes that the network approach has gained particular attention in recent years and is an organizational tool that is helpful in analyzing communication and behavior patterns within an organization.

Early field work in rumor transmission identified the existence of cohesive groups in which individuals having information relevant to the group communicated it rapidly to other group members but withheld the information from nonmembers. Davis (1953) found that some individuals are consistently excluded from the flow of rumors and seldom cited as sources. This indicates that there are different information roles within an organization: information sharing within a group, information transmission between groups, and relative isolation from information. Later rumor studies suggest that rumor transmitters (liaisons) are oriented more toward interaction while persons who receive rumors but do not transmit them are more task oriented. Persons who do not receive or transmit rumors (isolates) are more self-oriented.

Schwartz conducted a study of the characteristics of liaisons in a network of formal information flow. The results indicate that liaisons hold higher status positions than do nonliaisons and are more strongly represented in the management structure. Liaisons engage in more committee activity than their counterparts and belong to coordinating groups at higher levels in the organization. Liaisons are perceived by other employees to have a greater number and diversity of contacts in the system, and interaction with liaisons is perceived to have more influence in the power structure of the organization. These findings indicate that communication role as identified by sociometric choice has real consequences for an individual's degree of power and influence in an organization and that these consequences are readily apparent to others.

MacDonald investigated self-perception of liaisons and their perception of the communication system in the organization. His findings indicate that liaisons perceive themselves as having more contacts and more influence in the system than do nonliaisons. Liaisons and their contacts perceive that they possess more control over message flow, yet liaisons do not perceive that they possess more information, whereas their contacts perceive that they do. Liaisons perceive the communication system to be open and express greater satisfaction with the system than do nonliaisons.

At least with respect to liaisons, it appears that the relative function and position of individuals in the communication system constitute a socially identifiable role with specific attributed and enacted characteristics. Liaisons are perceived to exert greater influence, to control the flow of information, and to act as important integrators of groups and individuals. Further, liaisons recognize their role and its implications for themselves and the organization. They are oriented toward fulfilling their interactive role, perceive the system to be open to them, and are satisfied with the functioning of the communication system.

In contrast, Roberts and O'Reilly compared isolates and participants across three network types (authority, expertise, and social) and hypothesized consistent differences between liaisons and participants in conditions they termed antecedent to communication roles (status, tenure, personality, need for achievement and power) and conditions termed consequents of those roles (satisfaction, performance, commitment, perception of communication). In general, they found that participants have greater experience with the organization, while isolates are less mature and decisive and have a weaker concept of self and a higher need for security. Isolates tend to withhold information and are less satisfied with communication than are participants. They receive less redundant information and are less likely to summarize information and facilitate flow. Finally, isolates depend upon telephone and written channels more than do participants.

These findings portray isolates as less experienced, more insecure, and less motivated toward achievement in comparison with participants. They are less satisfied with communication and less likely to give active support to the transmission of information. Such a description stands in sharp contrast to that of liaisons, who appear to be at the opposite end of a continuum of willingness and ability to communicate.

Richards reported a comparative investigation of the distribution of network roles across eight networks in four organizations. The results are summarized in figure 4.1.

Richards's sample of organizations was heavily weighted by having a high percentage of nonparticipants or relative isolates. Thus, the average values are quite close to the upper ranges in this category. More instructive than the averages are the wide ranges in the distribution of roles across networks. The percentage of nonparticipants ranged from 27 to 50 percent. The percentage of liaisons ranged from 4 to 16 percent, and the number of group members ranged from 44 to 77 percent.

Greater variability in the distribution of roles was found in a large network study I conducted at a large Midwestern university (Goldhaber, 1977). Two networks (work-related information exchanged over formal and informal channels) were studied, and more than 75

Figure 4.1 Distribution of network roles across eight networks in four organizations. (From Richards, 1976.)

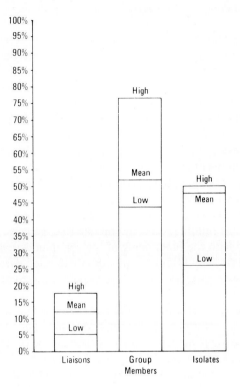

percent of a population of nearly 1,500 administrative, faculty, and staff personnel completed the survey documents. The results of the study are summarized in figure 4.2.

In this study as many as 93 percent of a network was made up of participants as compared with the average of 50 percent across the networks examined by Richards. In addition, the formal and informal networks in my sample were more integrated. Many more group members reported bridge links and links with liaisons than did group members in the majority of the networks in Richards's sample.

Understanding of the specific attributes of network roles is much greater than understanding of the comparative distribution of those roles. Major findings are the following:

1. Liaisons are more gregarious, influential, and satisfied members of communication networks than are isolates.
2. Liaisons hold higher official positions in the organization, and their integration with diverse groups and coordinating bodies further enhances their power.
3. Liaisons have been with the organization longer, know the system better, and perceive it to be more open to them than do isolates.
4. The role of liaison has social reality both to those who hold it and to others in the system. Liaisons and their contacts perceive the centrality, importance, and influence of this integrative role.

Figure 4.2 Comparative distribution of network roles across formal and informal information networks in a large university. (From Goldhaber, 1977.)

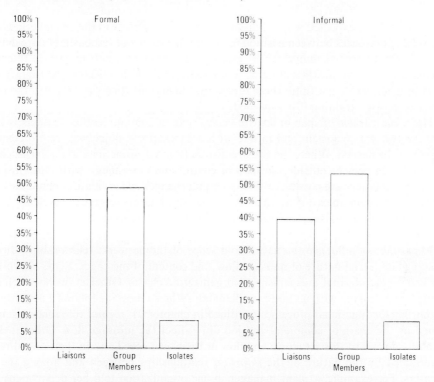

5. Isolates, on the other hand, are less secure in self-concept, less motivated by achievement, and less willing to interact than are network participants.
6. Isolates are likely to be younger and less experienced with the system and are not usually in a position of power in the organization.
7. Isolates tend to withhold information rather than to facilitate its flow.
8. Isolates perceive the communication system to be closed to them and are relatively dissatisfied with the system.
9. Less is known of group members as distinct from other participants. They tend to keep information relevant to the group within their own membership, although they pass information among themselves quite rapidly.
10. Group members are more homogeneous in attitudes and perceptions. As the integration of the group increases, the similarity of the members' need for involvement and information increases, as does the degree of shared belief about the group itself.
11. Much less is known about the distribution of these roles in a social system and how this distribution is affected by the type of network, the size of the system, and the nature of the organization. There is great variability in role distribution across these factors, probably due to wide differences in the methods of collecting network data.

Examination of network roles can aid in identifying the key communicators in an organization and can determine whether persons responsible for coordination of various functions are doing so effectively. Liaisons can be studied to determine whether the people in these roles would be expected to be a liaison because of their place in the official organization chart. When differences between position in the organization and responsibility are detected, more authority or responsibility can be given to those persons with important integrative functions in the communication system. When individuals with official responsibility for liaison-type functions do not fulfill these functions, the organization can establish the needed channels or provide training if it is needed.

Here, comparison of span of control versus span of communication contacts is useful. Where the two are congruent and in line with organizational objectives, reinforcement of linkages may be needed. Where the two are disparate and dysfunctional (i.e., too much communication with persons outside the span of control and not enough with those inside the span), several solutions are possible: establish certain channels, consolidate or eliminate others, establish direct communication mechanisms, or establish filters to reduce overload. The implications of network analysis for organizational restructuring were discussed in some detail in chapter 2.

Many factors influence the nature and scope of the network: relationships, direction of message flow, serial nature of message flow, and content of messages. Some networks are prescribed by such formal mechanisms as organization charts. Other networks, such as the grapevine, may emerge without notice or planning. When a message follows a net prescribed by scalar and/or functional processes (outlined in chapter 2), *formal* role relationships determined by the chain of command and job duty affect the message flow. Other messages may totally disregard this structure and flow at their own speed and in their own direction, as determined by the nature of the *informal* relationships between and among the communicators. For example, a plant manager in one organization told her department heads at their monthly meeting that the plant planned to produce a new product within a year. All department heads were to orally inform their foremen, who would, in turn, tell employees. The entire process of message diffusion was to take one week. Within twenty-four hours, more than 85 percent of the entire plant (350 employees) had heard the news. One department head called his wife during lunch to tell her the news. She immediately called four of her closest friends, who called other friends. Before the day was over, most of the wives had been informed of the news.

Had the message followed the prescribed channels over established nets, it would have been *formal* communication. Instead, it flowed via the grapevine and can therefore be considered *informal* communication. Let us now discuss these two network relationships—formal and informal—and the implications of each in an organization (a procedure for analyzing communication networks is given in chapter 10).

Formal Network Relationships

When messages follow official paths dictated by the organizational hierarchy or by job function, they flow in accordance with *formal network relationships*. These messages usually flow *up* or *down* the organization if the *scalar* principle of authority and hierarchy is employed and *across* the organization if the *functional* principle of job classification is adhered to. *Thus, the direction of the message is an indicator of the network relationship.*

Downward Communication

Downward communication refers to messages that flow from superiors to subordinates. Smith and others (1972) have this to say about downward communication:

> [It is] the most frequently studied dimension of formal channels. Authority, tradition, and prestige are implemented through downward communication. Those at the top of the organization are naturally concerned with the communication effectiveness of their downward-directed messages to employees. Downward-directed communication studies answer the question: To what extent do messages directed downward in the organizational structure obtain the kinds of responses desired by the managerial message sender? Downward communication sets the tone and establishes the atmosphere for effective upward communication.

In most downward communication, task and maintenance messages related to directions, goals, discipline, orders, questions, and policies, are used. Katz and Kahn identified five types of downward communication:

1. *Job Instructions.* Directives on how to do a specific task. For example, "Before you begin to jack the car up, loosen the lug nuts on the wheel; this will avoid the possibility of the car slipping off the jack."
2. *Job Rationale.* Messages about how a task relates to other organizational tasks. For example, "It is important that we all do a good job building the wings so that our plant in Boston will be able to attach them to the body of the planes."
3. *Procedures and Practices.* Messages pertaining to organization policies, rules, regulations, and benefits. For example, "After you have worked six months with us, you qualify for a one-week vacation with pay."
4. *Feedback.* Messages appraising how well individuals do their job. For example, "Mary, top management was really pleased about your beating the quota last week!"
5. *Indoctrination of Goals.* Messages designed to motivate employees by impressing upon them the overall mission of the organization and how they relate to these system goals. For example, "Congratulations, you now own a 'piece of the rock'!"

The following problems affect messages as they flow downward in an organization.

Reliance upon Written and Hard Diffusion Methods.　Despite research findings to the contrary, many organizations rely too heavily upon written and mechanical (hardware) methods for diffusing downward-directed messages. Expensive manuals, films, newsletters, public address systems, and booklets are used instead of personal contact and face-to-face communication.

Message Overload.　Related to the previous problem is the concept of overload. In some organizations (thanks to the ditto, mimeo, and copy machines) employees are overburdened with bulletins, memos, letters, announcements, magazines, and policy statements. Davis (1972) refers to this phenomenon as "overpublication," because employees tend to react by not reading or listening to the messages. Many employees may institute a highly selective screening process, which can cause important messages to be filed in the "circular" file. In one organization familiar to me most of the employees, after eight months of receiving countless messages every day, began to throw every message into the wastebasket *before* reading it. The wise manager should very carefully send only those messages that directly affect the employees involved. Of course, undercommunication should be avoided, because it also negatively affects morale.

O'Reilly has provided some interesting evidence that information underload is associated with lower satisfaction but higher performance. He also found that individuals who are overloaded with information express greater satisfaction with both their job and communications in general, but they are rated by their superiors as performing less well than those who receive less information.

Organizations seem to be taking steps to cope with information overload. Just as the President of the United States receives news syntheses, so do managers at Abbott Laboratories receive a monthly business information index that briefly summarizes more than 1,000 recently published books and articles. Managers then can request the complete works from Abbott's library. Abbott's top twenty-five or thirty executives also receive a monthly "clip" service that includes portions of as many as 100 articles relating to the company or to the health-care industry. General Motors is even more painstaking in disseminating news to its executives. A one-page "daily news line" is a kind of headline service that informs managers of breaking news. Another daily summary provides a cross section of what is being said about GM, the competition, or the industry. It usually runs to about six pages and is sent to 100 key executives.

Timing. Managers should consider the timing of messages and the potential impact of an improperly timed message upon employee behavior. Messages should be sent downward only at times mutually advantageous to both management and employees. The disastrous effect of a poorly timed message is illustrated by the action of a manager who announced the department salary schedule (with severe cuts for several employees) two hours before the department's annual spring picnic.

Filtering. Earlier, we talked about the serial nature of communication and the tendency of messages to be changed, shortened, and lengthened as they are relayed throughout a network. This effect can be seen plainly in messages that travel down an organization. The conclusion of various studies on this problem is that filtering can be due to various factors: number of links in a network, perceptual differences among employees, and lack of trust in a supervisor. Mellinger reported that employees who don't trust a supervisor may block the relay (or understanding) of supervisor messages. Pearce, who spent several years in research on interpersonal trust, defines trust of behavior operationally as follows:

> . . . deliberately constructing situations in which the other must choose between behavior which confers satisfactory outcomes on both or which confers extremely positive outcomes on himself but negative outcomes on the trusting person. This type of situation . . . occurs in social interactions such as those in which each person must choose whether and what to disclose about themselves. If one person tells the other significant things about himself, the other may use this as an opportunity to exploit him (by blackmail, ridicule or persuasive manipulations) or he may reciprocate the disclosure, making possible the development of a caring and helping relationship. If the other person refuses to exploit the one performing the trusting behavior, he has demonstrated his trustworthiness.

Tompkins summarized much of the literature on downward communication when he stated: "Widespread ineffectiveness is the rule, probably because of a variety of causes."

Based on my study of sixteen organizations, my conclusions concerning downward communication are these:

1. Most employees do not receive a great amount of information in their organization.
2. The primary information needs of employees include, first, more information about personal job-related matters and, second, information about organizational decision making. My finding is somewhat related to the "two-factor theory of motivation" of Herzberg (1966). I have called this finding my "two-factor theory of information." Information about personal job-related matters (e.g., how to do my job, my pay and benefits, etc.) is needed to *prevent dissatisfaction,* but it will NOT create satisfaction. Information about organization wide concerns (policies, plans, decision making, failures, etc.) is needed to *create satisfaction.*
3. The best sources of information are persons closest to employees and the worst are persons farthest from them. The greatest needs appear to be more job-related information from immediate supervisors and more organization-related information from top management. (See discussion of distance theory in chapters 2 and 3.)
4. Information from top management is of lower quality than that from other key sources. Although low-quality information is primarily a problem of top management, untimely messages reduce the quality of information from all key sources.

One of the most important implications of these findings for organizations is that a number of the job-related topics studied here involve areas of disclosure either mandated by law (e.g., pay and benefits) or required by many union contracts (e.g., job progress). Measurement of the perceived adequacy of information received on these topics can provide important indicators of compliance with these requirements. Where information on the topics related to the total organization is perceived to be inadequate (e.g., how decisions are made, mistakes and failures), management may consider implementing a formal policy on disclosure dealing with these issues.

In formulating a policy on disclosure, it is important to consider the risks and benefits of communicating sensitive information on how the organization is run (Steele, 1975). Disclosing information on organizational plans, decision-making processes, financial goals, innovations, or mistakes involves a number of direct and hidden risks. The presentation of this information requires that it be gathered, synthesized, and put into a comprehensive format, which involves management time and effort. The information may be misused for personal gain or leaked to competitors. Since some information may be negative, some employees may not react intelligently and may lose confidence in management. Formally disclosing future plans limits management's flexibility in changing or abandoning goals and objectives. Publicly owned corporations are under legal constraints concerning information released internally but withheld publicly.

The benefits of disclosure are improved understanding, more involvement with organizational goals, and greater efficiency. Properly handled disclosure can prepare employees for problem situations and make them more aware of the difficulties faced by management. Employees who are better informed about the way the organization operates are more confident in their ability to contribute to operations and are better contributors. When employees are kept informed of upcoming changes or innovations, they are more likely to offer their support.

After considering the risks and benefits of disclosure, management can arrive at a decision on the topics to be communicated and the means of communication. It is important that the decision reached is one that all parties involved find acceptable.

A communication system must be developed that guarantees the uniform and timely dissemination of accurate information. Meeting schedules can be coordinated across the hierarchy to guarantee that information from higher levels is passed to subordinates in all units in a similar manner. At each level, a uniform decision on how to communicate this information should be made so that no undue lag time or distortion of the information is involved. Check-back systems can facilitate transmission of accurate information and minimize confusion and rumor transmission.

The networks of interaction in the organization can be examined to identify key communicators, who can be contacted by their supervisors to aid in effective dissemination of information. This personal contact system may be used to augment more formal systems of communication. Where great distances or large numbers of people are involved, new technologies that can aid in rapid, uniform dissemination of information may be considered. Thus, management should consider the structural, personal, and technological forces that can be mobilized to implement a policy of disclosure.

I once studied the office of a U.S. senator whose downward communication was typical of the low-quality, top-management information just cited. He once requested an energy report from his senior aide, saying that he considered the report to have "top priority." The aide and his staff spent the entire night at the Library of Congress researching and preparing the necessary document. The secretarial staff came to work at five o'clock the next morning to type, copy, and collate the report before the senator arrived for his eight o'clock staff meeting. When the aide, exhausted but proud, handed him the report, the senator said, "What's this for? I won't need this report for another month, if ever." He then literally tossed the report to the side of his desk among a pile of papers. This behavior demoralized the staff for a week.

Upward Communication

Upward communication refers to messages that flow from subordinates to superiors. It is usually for the purpose of asking questions, providing feedback, and making suggestions. Upward communication has the effect of improving morale and employee attitude. Therefore, upward-directed messages are usually integrative or innovative. Smith and colleagues describe the function of upward communication as follows:

> [It] serves as feedback for management, giving clues regarding the relative success of a given message. In addition . . . upward communication can stimulate employees to participate in formulating operating policies for their department or organization.

Four reasons why management should value upward communication were pointed out by Planty and Machaver:

1. It indicates the receptivity of the environment for downward communication.
2. It facilitates acceptance of decisions by encouraging subordinate participation in the decision-making process.
3. It provides feedback on subordinate understanding of downward communication.
4. It encourages submission of valuable ideas.

The most effective method of encouraging upward communication is sympathetic listening during the many day-to-day informal contacts within the department and outside of the workplace.

Scholz (1959) considers upward communication indispensable for effective planning and motivation and as a source of decision-making information. Haire described upward communication as a method of allowing superiors to know subordinates; permitting diagnosis of misinterpretations; providing first symptoms of tension and difficulties; and permitting visibility of subordinates' views of superiors. Planty and Machaver also feel that upward communication is valuable to the employee, since it satisfies basic human needs, releases emotional tension and pressures, and is fundamental to democracy. This reasoning is but a short step from McGregor's concept of integration, which, he said, requires active and responsible participation of individuals in decisions affecting their career.

Planty and Machaver recommended that upward communication include messages relating to the following:

1. *What Subordinates Are Doing.* "We're working on the Smith account this week."
2. *Unsolved Work Problems.* "We still haven't been able to figure out why the engine won't work."
3. *Suggestions for Improvements.* "I think we should eliminate the fourth step in the process; we can save five minutes that way."
4. *How Subordinates Think and Feel about Jobs, Associates, and Company.* "I feel very upset every time Joe watches how I'm doing; he's always so critical."

Popular communication activities used to implement upward communication include counseling, grievance system, rap sessions, open-door policies, suggestion systems, opinion surveys, employee letters, social gatherings, and meetings.

When an organization installs a suggestion system, the following guidelines are helpful:

1. File the suggestions along with the documents used to evaluate the suggestions and include the date of the evaluation.
2. Include all rules that set limits for use, the evaluative criteria used in judging a suggestion, and a place for the employee's signature on the suggestion form.
3. Give each employee honest feedback on why his or her suggestion was or was not used.
4. Avoid a hasty request for suggestions to solve a particular problem; the request may be misinterpreted as extra work.

If these guidelines sound unduly cautious, consider the case of two employees who won more than $350,000 from their employer in court on their claim that the company had used their suggestion without giving them proper credit.

An example of the use of employee letters occurred when Admiral Zumwalt assumed command of the U.S. Navy. He began the practice of answering letters from enlisted men and officers by scheduling a regular column in the Navy newspaper in which the most pertinent questions were reproduced along with Zumwalt's answers. In another case, the president of a university had biweekly rap sessions with students. He merely sat in a lounge area of the student union building and informally spoke with any students who cared to chat with him about any topic of concern. Initial response to these sessions was encouraging. Thirty to forty students regularly showed up to meet the president. The governor of a state has bimonthly meetings with randomly selected faculty members of a major university—another example of upward communication. The meetings are informally structured and enable the faculty to provide the governor with *first-hand* information about the university.

It is vital that the information be first-hand because the same filtering process that affects downward communication also contributes to the distortion of upward-directed messages. Several researchers have reported on the problems inherent in upward communication. Two major problems deal with filtering and status. Employees tend to send upward those messages that enhance their credibility and status while they block or filter out those messages that may make them look bad. Furthermore, Read concluded that the more upward-mobility aspirations an employee has the less he or she tells the boss. Besides the tendency to filter bad news as it travels upward, the problem of status also inhibits many upward-directed messages. When administrators proclaim proudly, "My door is always open, but employees just don't seem to want to come in," they may forget that to hourly workers the open door of the vice president is just as intimidating as the closed door. Davis (1972) attributed these problems to the "scalar curtain":

> A manager often does not realize how great the upward communication barriers can be, especially for blue-collar workers. His status and prestige at the plant are different from the workers'. He probably talks differently and dresses differently. He can freely call a worker to his desk or walk to his workstation, but the worker is not equally free to call in his manager. The worker usually lacks ability to express himself as clearly as the manager, who is better trained and has more practice in communication skills. . . . The worker is further impeded because he is talking to a man with whose work and responsibilities he is not familiar. The result is that very little upward communication occurs unless management positively encourages it.

Figure 4.3 Classic communication pathway in a complex organization having pyramidal structure. Arrows indicate the communication steps when H talks to I.

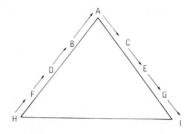

My own research on upward communication provides the following conclusions:

1. Employees do not have the opportunity to send a great amount of information in their organization.
2. Their primary needs include a greater opportunity to voice complaints and evaluate superiors.
3. Most employees want to receive more information rather than send information.
4. The farther up the organizational hierarchy employees are, the less follow-up they receive, particularly on information sent to top management.

According to Davis, the most effective method for encouraging upward communication is *sympathetic listening during the many day-to-day informal contacts within the department and outside the workplace.*

In one of the most extensive industrial programs of upward communication by a corporate leader, Hyatt Hotel president Patrick Foley regularly meets with employees from each hotel to discuss their "complaints." Foley always begins by explaining to the employees that "this isn't a witch hunt. I'm not here to cause any problems." He promises to look into every complaint and write a letter to each person afterward, explaining his position. The sessions usually last about three hours and involve small groups of employees, thirteen to sixteen in each group.

Horizontal Communication

Horizontal communication is the lateral exchange of messages among people on the same organizational level of authority. Messages flowing in accordance with the *functional* principle (see chapter 2) are horizontally directed. Such messages usually relate to task or human purposes: coordination, problem solving, conflict resolution, and information sharing. We know little about horizontal communication because of the absence of research in the area. Yet, few deny its importance in the operation of the entire communication system of an organization. As early as 1916, Fayol proposed his classic "bridge" of horizontal communication. Assume that figure 4.3 represents a typical complex organization and its pyramidal structure. If H wants to talk with I, she has to send the message to her supervisor, who in turn relays it to his supervisor, and so on. After the message goes all the way up and down the organization, it finally reaches I. This particular message flow takes *eight* different relays. Fayol recognized the waste of time and resources in this message network and therefore proposed a bridge between H and I. Figure 4.4 presents Fayol's bridge.

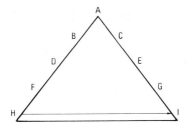

Now the message travels via only *one* relay, increasing both its accuracy and its speed. You may wonder why Fayol's bridge is not applied unilaterally throughout every organization. There are two answers: authority and overload. If all people were able to talk to all other people whenever they wanted to, the authority structure would be abolished. In many organizations (e.g., military organizations, hospitals, police) some authority is critical to the effective accomplishment of the system's goals. In one organization where employees could freely cross whatever organizational boundaries they desired, severe conflict and misunderstanding arose. The production manager frequently issued orders and directives to the engineering department. This caused the members of engineering to question whose authority governed them and what priority they should give the production manager's orders. Another problem associated with the expansion of Fayol's bridge to all possible participants is message overload—too many messages flowing in all directions without being screened or filtered. As a result, the system slows down and might even cease to function because of the burden of too many messages. Thus, Fayol offered a compromise between the rigidity of zero horizontal communication and the anarchy of total horizontal message flow.

Research by many persons since 1954 has identified the following purposes for horizontal communication within an organization.

Task Coordination.   Department heads may meet monthly to discuss how each department contributes to the system's goals. Team teaching and team writing in university communities are examples of task coordination.

Problem Solving.   The members of a department may assemble to discuss how to handle a threatened budget cut and may employ brainstorming techniques.

Information Sharing.   The members of one department may meet with members of another department to give them new data. One department at a university recently rewrote its entire curriculum. In order to inform other departments about these major revisions (which affected most segments of the university), the faculty held several meetings with representatives of the other departments to explain the new curriculum.

Conflict Resolution.   Members of one department may meet to discuss a conflict with the department or between departments. Resolution of such conflicts is especially important to the social and emotional growth of the members of the department. At a recent meeting of a department in a large organization, one member stated, "We need to give each other psychological support for our contributions to the overall department."

Despite the apparent importance of horizontal communication, several factors tend to limit its frequency: rivalry, group specialization, and lack of motivation.

Rivalry. In today's competitive organizations, data are not always shared because possessors do not want to lose their chance for advancement. Sometimes employees may fear that admissions of ignorance about an issue may cause them to lose face with co-workers. Rapidly changing organizations do not allow time for members to develop the mutual trust that might reduce rivalry and jealousy.

Specialization. Many organizations today seem to stress specialization and thus create a competitive atmosphere. When this occurs, managers are encouraged to further their own goals rather than to communicate with other managers on the same level in order to advance company goals. Although it does not specifically bar horizontal communication, a formal organizational structure favors vertical communication.

An example is an automobile parts manufacturing company in which the computer services unit had a very difficult time satisfying the exact needs of user departments, such as accounting and records. Whenever a user department requested a computer service, the computer personnel had to make several attempts before they achieved success. The problem was the initial contact. Personnel in computer services conveyed an attitude of condescension and apparent familiarity with the users' problems. The users were intimidated by this attitude and by their reluctance to appear ignorant when translating their needs into computer language. The problem was solved by hiring a liaison person whose total function was to bridge the horizontal communication gap caused by overspecialization.

Lack of Motivation. Management has not encouraged frequent horizontal communication, nor have they rewarded those who engage in such practices. As long as management perceives that its goals are being met, they may see little need for altering the communication system. Smith and colleagues (1972) supported this finding when they said: "Organizational payoff may result from sensitivity to superiors and subordinates rather than to peers."

Thus far, we have talked about the exchange of messages along *formally* prescribed pathways and directions. When messages deviate from such traditional networks, they are called informal messages.

Informal Network Relationships

The chairman of an academic department was visiting the retirement director of the university when the latter asked, "Have you heard about Professor Jones's decision to retire this year?" "No, I hadn't," replied the surprised chairman. "Well, it's true; he came in yesterday to fill out the required forms." The chairman left the next day for a conference in Montreal, where he saw Professor Smith from his department back home. "Professor Smith, I was just informed yesterday by the retirement director that Jones was retiring this year." Smith, equally dumbfounded by the news, asked, "Can we fill the slot this year?" The chairman replied, "I'll have to check with the dean on the phone tomorrow. If he says, O.K., then we can announce the job opening while we're here." That night at a party Smith met some friends from schools in New York, Boston, and San Francisco. After a couple of drinks, he told his friends about Jones's decision to retire, and that he *hoped* his dean would let them fill the job. After a lengthy conversation about budget cuts, deans, and the job market, Smith retired for the evening. At 6:45 A.M., Smith was awakened from a deep sleep by the ringing of the telephone. The person at the other end of the phone inquired about the *"opening* created at the department because of Jones's *resignation."* Smith angrily shouted into the phone, "There is no opening!" and hung up. A half-hour later the phone rang again and a different voice asked the same question. Before the morning was over, an exhausted Smith had received *thirteen* phone calls. One caller stated that he was awfully sorry to hear that *"Smith was leaving the department"* and that he hoped Smith *"wasn't fired."*

This pattern of communication illustrates the informal network that frequently operates within every complex organization. Messages which do *not* follow scalar or functional lines are classified as informal. Tompkins concluded that informal messages "are not rationally specified. They develop through accidents of spatial arrangements, personalities, and abilities of the persons. . . ." Many writers use the word *grapevine* as a synonym for this type of message behavior. Davis (1972) stated, "The term grapevine applies to all informal communication." Here is Davis's explanation of the term:

> The term "grapevine" arose during Civil War days. Intelligence telegraph lines were strung loosely from tree to tree in the manner of a grapevine, and the message thereon was often garbled; hence any rumor was said to be from the grapevine.

Research on the grapevine has produced the following findings.

The grapevine is fast. In the example just given, a message was generated in one country on Monday afternoon and spread to over twenty people (from several cities) who were attending a meeting in another country (2,500 miles away)—all within thirty-six hours. Since the grapevine does not follow formal channels and is usually more personal in transmission, the messages are free to travel as fast as the senders and receivers desire. Davis reported that in one organization 46 percent of the management group knew about one manager's newborn child within thirteen hours after the event. Walton (1961) also reported the grapevine to be the speediest channel for spreading messages among employees.

The grapevine is accurate. By counting the details of messages and determining which were true and false, Davis (1972) was able to report accuracy ranging from 80 to 90 percent for noncontroversial company information. Marting found that grapevine communication is at least 80 percent accurate. In his study at the U.S. Naval Ordinance Test Station, Walton found that about 78 percent of the employees tested thought that the information on the grapevine was correct at least half the time. Rudolph reported 80 percent accuracy for informal communication at a major public utility company. Despite the impressive research documenting the accuracy of grapevine-transmitted messages, many managers still believe that the grapevine is highly inaccurate.

My own research with the grapevine shows that of the employees surveyed in sixteen organizations, most tend to get more information than they want from the grapevine. They perceive the grapevine to be a fast, frequently used, but *not* accurate source of information that perhaps provides lower quality information than high-quality information from other sources. Davis believes that this is so because grapevine errors are usually dramatic and consequently are impressed more firmly on memory than day-by-day routine truths. Moreover, the inaccurate parts are often more important.

Consequently, Professor Smith may be ready to damn the grapevine for waking him at 6:45 A.M. with a "totally false story," but as it turned out, most of the phone callers had all the facts correct except for the question of whether the dean would allow the job to be filled. In times of tight job markets, it may be easy to see why unemployed students may slightly alter an original message. Situations fraught with anxiety or excitement may affect the accuracy of the grapevine, but its overall track record is impressive.

The grapevine carries much information. Whether management likes the grapevine or not, it is a fact of life in all organizations. Therefore, the wise manager should admit its permanence, gain from its advantages, and recognize its limitations. The grapevine offers a network for diffusing some messages that cannot normally be sent over formal nets.

For example, a lobbyist in Washington once explained the importance of partying with the powerful as a traditional way to get ahead: "If you sit next to a congressman for an hour during a dinner, it's like gold. You talk to him while he's relaxed, not about a bill but about something that interests him. By the end of the talk, he's kind of a friend. When you call him next, you can get an appointment." In fact, the importance of these informal contacts may be why many in Washington criticized the Carter administration for its reluctance to become part of the informal Washington network.

Another advantage of the grapevine is that it provides management with feedback about employee sentiment. The grapevine provides an outlet for the expression of emotionally charged messages that could foster hostility and anger among employees if they were suppressed. The grapevine also may help translate some of management's directives into language easily understood by employees. How often have you asked a fellow student or colleague, "What does this mean for us?"

The most negative attribute of the grapevine is that it also serves as the network over which *rumors* travel. Davis defined rumor as "grapevine information which is communicated without secure standards of evidence being present." Allport and Postman (1947) stated in their "basic law of rumor" that rumors spread as a function of both the *importance* and the *ambiguity* of the information pertaining to the topic at issue. A subject of high interest of which little information is known is susceptible to the spread of rumor. In one organization, employee salary raises were given without an explanation of how they were determined. Since salaries are of vital concern to most employees, the grapevine carried many stories about "favoritism," "lack of standards," and "randomness."

Once rumor begins, the best advice is to provide the facts to those most affected by its spread. This removes the ambiguity, provided that the facts are transmitted via a credible organizational source. Many organizations use telephone rumor-control systems to combat the spread of rumor. When an employee first hears a rumor, it can be anonymously reported to a central office via the telephone. If the facts are known, the employee is immediately informed of them. If they are not known, the employee can call back later. Meanwhile, it is the responsibility of the rumor office to trace the rumor. As calls come in, they can be logged as to when, where, and from whom the rumor was first heard. Similar rumor control systems worked effectively during times of civil unrest and disorder in such cities as Detroit, Albuquerque, and Boston.

Figure 4.5   The grapevine cluster.

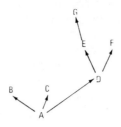

Some of the more interesting rumors related to large corporations that have recently spread around the United States are the following. McDonald's Corp. was said to be adding red worms to its hamburgers as a way of increasing protein content (the rumor actually lowered McDonald's sales in the Southeast). A woman trying on a Taiwanese-made coat in a K-mart store was supposed to have had her arm amputated after a snake (hiding in the coat) had bit her. It was rumored that Proctor & Gamble's corporate symbol, which contains a picture of a moon, indicates that P&G had been acquired by the Reverend Sun Myung Moon's Unification Church.

The grapevine travels by cluster. Another misconception about the grapevine is that its messages travel in a chainlike sequence from A to B to C to D, and so forth. Davis (1953) explained the grapevine flow in this way:

> A tells three or four others. . . . Only one or two of these receivers will then pass on the information, and they will usually tell more than one person. Then, as the information becomes older and the proportion of those knowing it gets larger, it gradually dies out because those who receive it do not repeat it. This network is a "cluster chain" because each link in the chain tends to inform a cluster of other people instead of only one person.

Figure 4.5 illustrates this pattern of communication.

As we have discussed earlier, those people who actively contribute to the life of the grapevine by passing messages are liaisons, and those people who receive and transmit messages poorly or not at all are called isolates. Walton called those people "centrals" and "peripherals," based upon their location in the communication network.

Much of what we have said in this chapter can be summarized by asking several of the following questions, many of which come from advice given in the classic work by Berlo. If you use these questions as guidelines in seeking information about your own interactions, you will be a more informed and probably a more effective communicator.

1. *Source of Message.* What communication skills does the source possess? What are the communicator's attitudes? What is the communicator's knowledge level? Does the communicator know too much or too little? What expectations does the communicator bring to the situation? What cultural background does the communicator come from? Is the source credible/believable for the situation and message? Is there more than one source for the message?

2. *Message.* What are the facts contained in the message? Are there too many or too few facts in the message? Does the message contribute to information overload or underload? Is the message clearly structured and presented so it minimizes receiver uncertainty? (Remember that the 500 most common words in the dictionary have 14,070 meanings—about 28 per word.) Is the message appropriate for the receiver and his or her skills, attitudes, knowledge level, and sociocultural background? What code is used to communicate the message—verbal, nonverbal, or both?

3. *Channel.* What is the best channel for the message, source, and receiver in the present situation? What channels are actually available for use? What channels are cost-effective? What channels do the sources and receivers prefer? What channel is likely to have greatest impact and accomplish the source's purpose? What channel is most appropriate for the message? Should the message be diffused orally, in writing, or both? Should the message be diffused nonverbally, physically, or via mass media?

4. *Receiver.* What communication skills does the receiver possess? Can the receiver read, listen, think, write? What is the likelihood that a typical receiver can understand the message and its implications? What are the receiver's attitudes toward her- or himself, the source, the message, the situation? What is the knowledge level of the receiver? Does the receiver understand the code in such a way as to minimize misperception, incorrect inference, and distortion? What expectations does the receiver bring to the communicative situation? What sociocultural background does the receiver come from? (The receiver is the most important link in the communication process. If the source doesn't reach the receiver with his or her message, then he or she might as well have been talking to no one.)

5. *Feedback.* Did the receiver actually receive the message? Did the receiver read or hear the message? Did the receiver understand the message? Did the receiver believe the message? Did the receiver act upon the message? How do you know that the receiver received, read, understood, believed, and acted upon the message?

6. *Noise.* Where did the process of communication break down? Was there noise or interference with the source, the message, at the channel, or with the receiver? Did the source send the message he or she wanted to and perceived he or she was sending? Did the receiver receive the message he or she desired and thought he or she was receiving? Was the message distorted because of a large number of links between sender and receiver? Were details from the message omitted, highlighted, added, or modified as the message traveled from source to receiver?

SUMMARY

Communication is the creation and exchange of messages. A message consists of symbols to which a receiver attaches meaning. Messages can be classified according to relationship (dyadic, small group, or public) network (formal or informal), purpose (task, maintenance, human, innovative), receiver (internal or external), language mode (verbal or nonverbal), and diffusion method (hardware or software).

We view communication as a dynamic process which is transactional, rules-based, personal, and serial. As a *transactional* process, communication involves the simultaneous and mutual sending and receiving of messages. This perspective carries the belief that no communication event is identical, relived, isolated from its environment, or static. As a *rules-based process,* communication patterns emerge that, if agreed-upon by all parties, produce co-orientation and limited conflict. As a *personal* process, communication admits to the uniqueness of people. Because of different nervous systems and environments, our perceptions are different. With differing perceptions, our behavior and interpretation of messages also differ. Thus, at best, communication is an approximate process by which the communicators attempt to approach a common understanding. As a *serial* process, communication involves a step-by-step sequence in which messages are replicated. One or more people send messages to and receive messages from one or more people. The messages are reproduced through one or more channels until they reach their final destination. Because of its serial nature, communication carries with it the possibility of message distortion and change.

In complex organizations, messages are exchanged via hard (mechanical and electrically powered) or soft (oral and written) methods. The new technologies, while certainly more efficient in their ability to transmit more information faster and more cheaply, raise many questions about their effectiveness. We emphasized oral software methods, such as meetings, conversations, interviews, grapevine, and social functions. These communicative activities or behaviors can be analyzed according to such criteria as message content, timing, interaction conditions, initiation, participation, and feedback. Most messages in organizations can be classified according to four purposes: task (related to products, services, outputs); maintenance (related to policies and regulations); human (related to attitudes, morale, and fulfillment); and innovative (related to new plans and ideas).

When messages follow official paths dictated by the organizational hierarchy or by job function, they flow in accordance with *formal* network relationships. People who exchange these messages are either participants (group members, liaisons, bridges) or nonparticipants (isolates) who differ in many attitudes and behaviors. Messages flow up, down, and across the organization. Downward communication refers to messages (usually task or maintenance) that flow from superiors to subordinates. Upward communication refers to messages that flow from subordinates to superiors, usually for the purpose of asking questions, providing feedback, and making suggestions. Horizontal communication is the lateral exchange of messages among people on the same organizational level of authority. Such messages usually relate to coordination, problem solving, conflict resolution, and information sharing.

When messages deviate from such traditional networks, they are called *informal* messages. A synonym for informal message behavior is *grapevine.* Research findings indicate that the grapevine is fast and accurate, carries much information, and travels by cluster. Besides providing a channel for emotional and non-job-related messages, the grapevine can provide management with important feedback about employee attitudes and morale. Unfortunately, the grapevine also carries rumor, which can be highly destructive to an organization. When faced with rumor spread, the best approach is to provide a clear, fast explanation of the facts.

EXERCISES

1. Use the word *fast* in at least ten different contexts. Compare your ten sentences with those of your classmates. How many different meanings of *fast* did your class identify? Discuss the implications of your findings.

2. Visit an organization with which you are familiar. Speak with the personnel manager or the public relations manager. Ask him or her for examples of dyadic, small group, and public communication activities (oral software activities) used in the organization.

3. Identify those personnel in your organization whose function is to coordinate all inter-unit activities (liaisons). List the activities associated with this role in terms of information processing, information retrieval, and information transfer.

4. Assume that you are the department head of an eleven-member department in a manufacturing organization that has seven departments and a total of 250 members. You are about to orient a new member of your department (who has just been hired today). Devise one example each of task, maintenance, human, and innovative messages you might use in the interview.

5. Talk with a close friend about any topic of your choice. Plan to have this conversation in a location where you will have some privacy for at least one-half hour. After your conversation, each of you should make a list of *all* stimuli that affected your conversation (e.g., time of day, location, outside noise, words used by you and your friend, culture, etc.). Each of you should compare lists and discuss the implications of having different lists or similar lists.

6. Go with a friend or two to a museum where you can look at paintings, particularly modern paintings. Describe what each sees in the paintings. Do you see different things? Why? Why not?

7. Repeat exercise 7 in chapter 1. What are the implications for serial communication?

8. How does your organization attempt to cope with information overload? Do you feel they are effective? List ways in which they can improve the handling of overload.

9. Speak with a member of top management (president, vice president, plant manager) at an organization of your choice. Ask this person to send a policy or job-related message downward throughout the organization, using normal channels. A week later, after the message should have reached its intended audience, interview five people at the lowest possible organizational level. Ask the following questions: Did you get the message? When? From whom? How? (What was the method of diffusion?) Tell the manager with whom you originally spoke the results of your survey.

10. Speak with someone you know at the bottom of the hierarchy in an organization (line worker, machinist, student). Repeat exercise 9 using a message appropriate for upward communication. After you speak with members of the top of the organization, let those members at the bottom know the results of your survey. Were there differences between exercise 9 and this exercise?

11. Based upon discussion in the text, do you think the benefits of corporate disclosure outweigh the costs? Think of an organization to which you belong. What types of information were not or are not disclosed that you believe should be?

12. Start a *harmless* rumor in an organization of your choice. Wait approximately one week and speak with five to ten members of the organization. Ask the following questions: Did you hear the rumor? What facts did you hear? When did you first hear the rumor? From whom did you hear it? Describe the circumstances. After you get your data, can you draw any conclusions about the spread of this rumor? How far did it spread, how fast, via what network, and via what diffusion method(s)?
13. Make a list of five explicit and five implicit communication rules that are followed in an organization with which you are familiar.

BIBLIOGRAPHY AND REFERENCES

Albaum, Gerald. "Horizontal Information Flow: An Exploratory Study." *Academy of Management Journal* 7 (1964):21–33.

Albuquerque Journal, 8 June 1973, p. 1.

Allport, Gordon, and Leo Postman. *The Psychology of Rumor.* New York: Henry Holt & Co., 1947.

Anderson, J. A. "Single Channel and Multi-Channel Messages: A Comparison of Connotative Meaning." *Audio Visual Communication Review* 17 (1969):434.

Anzieu, D. "Les Communications Intra-Groupe." In *Communication Process.* New York: Macmillan, 1965.

Barnlund, Dean C. "A Transactional Model of Communication." In *Speech Communication Behavior,* edited by L. Barker and R. Kibler. Englewood Cliffs, N.J.: Prentice-Hall, 1971.

Bartlett, F. C. "Experiments on Remembering: The Method of Serial Reproduction." In *Remembering.* London: Cambridge University Press, 1932.

Berlo, David K. *The Process of Communication.* New York: Holt, Rinehart & Winston, 1960.

Boren, James. *When in Doubt, Mumble.* New York: Van Nostrand, 1972.

Browning, L.D., and B. McD. Johnson, "Technology and Culture: Action Bias Effects in the Implementation of Word Processing." In *Handbook of Organizational Communication,* edited by G. Goldhaber and G. Barnett, 453-72. Norwood, NJ: Ablex Publishing Corp., 1988.

Burns, Tom. "The Directions of Activity and Communication in a Departmental Executive Group." *Human Relations* 7 (1954):73–97.

Cushman, D., and G. Whiting. "An Approach to Communication Theory: Toward Consensus on Rules." *Journal of Communication* 22 (1972): 217–38.

Cushman, D. P., King, S. S., Smith III, T. (1988). "The Rules Perspective on Organizational Communication Research." In G. B Goldhaber & G. Barnett (Eds.), Handbook of Organizational Communication (pp. 55-94). Norwood, NJ: Ablex Publishing Corp.

Davis, Keith. "A Method of Studying Communication Patterns in Organizations." *Personnel Psychology* 6 (1953a):301–12.

———. "Management Communication and the Grapevine." *Harvard Business Review* 31 (September/October 1953):43–49.

———. "Communication within Management." *Personnel* 31 (1954):212–17.

———. *Human Behavior at Work.* New York: McGraw-Hill Book Co., 1972.

Dewey, John, and Arthur Bentley. *Knowing and the Known.* Boston: Beacon Press, 1949.

DeWhirst, H. D. "Influence of Perceived Information-Sharing Norms on Communication Channel Utilization." *Academy of Management Journal* 14(1971):305–15.

Dwyer, F. M. "Adapting Visual Illustrations for Effective Learning." *Harvard Education Review* 37(1967):250–63.

————. "The Relative Effectiveness of Varied Visual Illustrations in Complementing Programmed Instruction." *Journal of Experimental Education* 36(1967):34–42.

Farace, Richard, and Donald MacDonald. "New Directions in the Study of Organizational Communication." Mimeographed handout, 1971.

Farace, Richard, Peter Monge, and Hamish Russell. *Communicating and Organizing*. Reading, Mass.: Addison-Wesley Publishing Co., 1977.

Goldhaber, Gerald, Donna Fossum, and Sally Black. "Police-Student Attitudes and Attitude Perceptions of Each Other." *Law and Order* 20 (April 1972):101–6.

Goldhaber, G., D. Porter, and M. Yates. "The ICA Communication Audit Survey Instrument: 1977 Organizational Norms." Paper presented at a meeting of the International Communication Association, Berlin, Germany, 1977.

Goldhaber, G., and G. Richetto. "A Communication Audit of a Midwestern University." Report to the president of the university, 1977.

Goldhaber, G., M. Yates, D. Porter, and R. Lesniak. "Organizational Communication: State of the Art." *Human Communication Research* 5 (Fall 1978):76–96.

Greenbaum, Howard. "The Appraisal and Management of Organizational Communication." Paper presented at a meeting of the Eastern Region of the American Business Communication Association, New York, May 1973.

Haire, Mason. *Psychology in Management*. New York: McGraw-Hill Book Co., 1964.

Haney, William. "Serial Communication of Information in Organizations." In *Concepts and Issues in Administrative Behavior,* edited by Sidney Mailick and Edward H. Van Ness. Englewood Cliffs, N.J.: Prentice-Hall, 1962.

Herzberg, F. *Work and the Nature of Man*. Cleveland: World Publishing Co., 1966.

Herzberg, F., F. Mausner, and B. Snyderman. *The Motivation to Work*. New York: John Wiley & Sons, 1959.

Higham, T. M. "The Experimental Study of the Transmission of Rumour." *British Journal of Psychology* (1951):42–55.

Horan, Hilary H. "A Communication Systems Analysis of KOB-TV." Paper presented at a meeting of the International Communication Association, Atlanta, April 1972.

Hunsicker, F. R. "How to Approach Communication Difficulties." *Personnel Journal* 51 (1972): 680–83.

Huse, Edgar, and James Bowditch. *Behavior in Organizations*. Reading, Mass.: Addison-Wesley, 1973.

Jackson, Jay. "Analysis of Interpersonal Relations in a Formal Organization." Ph.D. dissertation, University of Michigan, 1953.

————. "The Organization and Its Communication Problem." *Advanced Management* 24 (1959): 17–20.

Jacobsen, Eugene, and Stanley Seashore. "Communication Practices in Complex Organizations." *Journal of Social Issues* 7 (1951):28–40.

Katz, Daniel, and Robert Kahn. *The Social Psychology of Organization*. New York: John Wiley & Sons, 1966.

Lesikar, Raymond. *Business Communication*. Homewood, Ill.: Richard D. Irwin, 1972.

Likert, R. *New Patterns of Management*. New York: McGraw-Hill Book Co., 1961.

MacDonald, D. "Communication Roles and Communication Content in a Bureaucratic Setting." Paper presented at a meeting of the International Communication Association, Phoenix, 1971.

McGregor, Douglas. *The Human Side of Enterprise.* New York: McGraw-Hill Book Co., 1960.

Maier, N. R. F., W. H. Read, and J. Hooven. "Breakdown in Boss-Subordinate Communication." In *Communication in Organizations: Some New Research Findings.* Ann Arbor: Foundation for Research on Human Behavior, 1959.

Maier, N. R. F., L. R. Hoffman, and W. H. Read. "Superior-Subordinate Communication: The Relative Effectiveness of Managers Who Held Their Subordinates' Position." *Personnel Psychology* 26 (1963):1–11.

Marting, Barbara. "A Study of Grapevine Communication Patterns in a Manufacturing Organization." Ph.D. dissertation, Arizona State University, 1969.

Massie, J. L. "Automatic Horizontal Communication in Management." *Academy of Management Journal* 3 (1960):87–91.

Mellinger, G. D. "Interpersonal Trust as a Factor in Communication," *Journal of Abnormal and Social Psychology* 52 (1956):304–9.

Menning, J. H., and C. W. Wilkinson. *Communicating Through Letters and Reports.* Homewood, Ill.: Richard D. Irwin, 1972.

Minter, R. L. "A Denotative and Connotative Study in Communication." *Journal of Communication,* 18 (1968): 26–36.

Mortensen, C. David. *Communication: The Study of Human Interaction.* New York: McGraw-Hill Book Co., 1972.

O'Connell, S. E. "Human Communication in the High Tech Office." In *Handbook of Organizational Communication,* edited by G. Goldhaber and G. Barnett, 473-82. Norwood, NJ: Ablex Publishing Corp., 1988.

Odiorne, George S. "An Application of the Communication Audit." *Personnel Psychology* 7 (1954): 235–43.

Opinion Research Corporation. "Avoiding Failures in Management Communication." Research report of *The Public Opinion Index for Industry* (January 1963).

O'Reilly, C. "Individuals and Information Overload in Organizations: Is More Necessarily Better?" *Academy of Management Journal* 23 (1980):684–96.

Otto, M. C. "Testimony and Human Nature." *Journal of American Institute of Criminal Law and Criminology* 9 (1918–1919):98–105.

Pace, R. Wayne, and Robert Boren. *The Human Transaction.* Glenview, Ill.: Scott, Foresman, 1973.

Pearce, W. Barnett. "Trust in Interpersonal Communication." Paper presented at a meeting of the International Communication Association, Montreal, April 1973.

Peter, Laurence. *The Peter Prescription.* New York: Morrow, 1972.

Planty, Earl, and William Machaver. "Upward Communications: A Project in Executive Development." *Personnel* 28 (1952):304–18.

Read, William H. "Upward Communication in Industrial Hierarchies." *Human Relations* 15 (1962): 3–15.

Redding, W. C. "Position Paper: A Response to Discussions at the Ad Hoc Conference on Organizational Communication." Paper presented to the Ad Hoc Conference on Organizational Communication, University of Missouri at Kansas City, February 1967.

Richards, W. "Using G-Network Analysis in Research." Paper presented at a meeting of the International Communication Association, Portland, Oregon, 1976.

Roberts, K., and C. O'Reilly. *Communication Roles in Organizations: Some Potential Antecedents and Consequences.* Technical Report No. 11, Contract No. N000314–69–a–1054. Washington, D.C.: Office of Naval Research, July 1975.

Rudolph, Evan. "A Study of Informal Communication Patterns Within A Multi-Shift Public Utility Organizational Unit." Ph.D. dissertation, University of Denver, 1971.

Schall, Maryann. "A Communication-Rules Approach to Organizational Culture." *Administrative Science Quarterly* 28 (1983):557–81.

Scholz, William. "Communication for Control." *Advanced Management* 24 (1959):13–15.

———. *Communication in the Business Organization.* Englewood Cliffs, N.J.: Prentice-Hall, 1962.

Schuler, R., and L. Blank. "Relationships among Types of Communication, Organizational Level, and Employee Satisfaction and Performance." *IEEE Transaction on Engineering Management* 23 (1976):124–29.

Schwartz, D. "Liaison Roles in Communication Structure of a Formal Organization: A Pilot Study." Paper presented at a meeting of the National Society for the Study of Communication, Cleveland, 1969.

Schwitter, J. P. "Computer Work Groups: Problems." *Advanced Management Journal* 30 (1965): 30–35.

Scott, William G. *Organization Theory.* Homewood, Ill.: Richard D. Irwin, 1967.

Shimanoff, Susan. *Communication Rules: Theory and Research.* Beverly Hills, CA.: Sage, 1980.

Simpson, R. L. "Vertical and Horizontal Communication in Formal Organizations." *Administrative Science Quarterly* 4 (1959):188–96.

Smith, Arthur L. *Transracial Communication.* Englewood Cliffs, N.J.: Prentice-Hall, 1973.

Smith, Ronald L., Gary M. Richetto, and Joseph P. Zima. "Organizational Behavior: An Approach to Human Communication." In *Approaches to Human Communication,* edited by Richard Budd and Brent Ruben. Rochelle Park, N.J.: Hayden Book Co., Spartan Books, 1972.

Steele, F. *The Open Organization.* Reading, Mass.: Addison-Wesley, 1975.

Sutton, H., and L. Porter. "A Study of the Grapevine in a Governmental Organization." *Personnel Psychology* 21 (1968):223–30.

Swift, Pamela. "Keeping Up With Youth—New Expressions." *Parade Magazine,* 17 June 1973, p. 2.

Tapscott, D. "Investigating the Office of the Future." *Telesis* 1(1981):1–6.

Thayer, Lee. *Communication and Communication Systems.* Homewood, Ill.: Richard D. Irwin, 1968.

Tompkins, P. K. "Organizational Communication: A State of the Art Review." In *Conference on Organizational Communication,* edited by G. Richetto. Huntsville, Ala.: NASA, George C. Marshall Space Flight Center, 1967.

———. "The Functions of Human Communication in Organization." In the *Handbook of Rhetorical and Communication Theory,* edited by Carroll Arnold and John Bowers, 659–719. Boston: Allyn & Bacon, 1984.

Vardaman, G., and P. Vardaman. *Communication in Modern Organizations.* New York: John Wiley & Sons, 1973.

Walton, Eugene. "Communicating Down the Line: How They Really Get the Word." *Personnel* 36 (1959):78–82.

———. "How Efficient Is the Grapevine?" *Personnel* 28 (1961):45–49.

———. "Project Office Communications." *Administrative Management* 23 (1962):22–24.

Wenburg, John, and William Wilmot. *The Personal Communication Process.* New York: John Wiley & Sons, 1973.

Whipple, Guy Montrose. "The Observer as Reporter: A Survey of 'Psychology of Testimony.'" *Psychological Bulletin* (May 15, 1909):153–70.

Wigand, R. T. "Communication Network Analysis: History and Overview." In *Handbook of Organizational Communication,* edited by G. Goldhaber and G. Barnett, 319-59. Norwood, NJ: Ablex Publishing Corp., 1988.

Wilcox, Roger. *Oral Reporting in Business and Industry.* Englewood Cliffs, N.J.: Prentice-Hall, 1967.

Wilmott, William, and John Wenburg. "Communication as Transaction." Paper presented at a meeting of the International Communication Association, Montreal, April 1973.

5
CREATING AND EXCHANGING NONVERBAL MESSAGES

He winketh with his eyes, he speaketh with his feet, he teacheth with his fingers. (Proverbs) 6:13

Once I scheduled an appointment at 2:00 P.M. with an attorney to discuss a civil case. At 2:10 P.M., when he hadn't arrived, I asked his secretary if he was out to lunch. She smiled cunningly and said, "He'll probably be a *few* minutes late, as usual." I immediately became resentful and was convinced that he was having a few drinks while I was kept waiting. Finally, at 2:25 P.M. he entered the office, walked over to me, and introduced himself. Just as I expected to be taken into his office, he promptly excused himself to visit "briefly" with one of his partners. I remained standing, even though I felt rather awkward. After five more minutes, he returned and led me into his office. As I sat down, I noticed that he left the door open. I began to discuss the details of the case, during which time he both listened to me *and* signed about eight to ten papers on his desk. About ten minutes later the phone rang; he answered and said, "I'm sorry, I can't talk to you now; I'm with a client." No sooner had he hung up the phone than it rang again. This time he turned his swivel chair around so that his back was facing me. He spoke with his caller, a female friend, for about ten more minutes. When he resumed eye contact with me, I gave him a dirty look! He promptly buzzed his secretary and asked her to "hold all calls." He then got up and shut the door. Just as I thought he was settling down to finally give me the attention I was paying for (at $40 per hour), he placed both feet upon his desk, removed a brush from his desk drawer, and began to shine his shoes!

In this episode, much more was communicated than the words used as we discussed the case. In fact, the legal advice the attorney gave me was quite sound. Yet I left his office ready to file a complaint with the bar association. My feelings about this experience can be attributed to such nonverbal cues as the use of time (scheduling and ignoring an appointment); space (distance between my seat and his—behind a desk); facial expressions (lack of eye contact, dirty looks); objects (office furniture, clothing, hair length); tone of voice, gesture, and physical action (leaving the door open, answering and talking into the phone, turning his chair around, signing papers, and shining his shoes). Several other nonverbal cues were probably present, but beyond my level of awareness or recall.

The importance of nonverbal messages is underscored by Birdwhistell, who estimated that a computer could handle up to 10,000 bits of information when analyzing the signals emitted by two human beings. He predicted that the face alone is capable of producing some 250,000 different expressions. Harrison (1970) estimated that 65 percent of the social meaning in face-to-face communication is carried by nonverbal messages.

It is apparent that by its sheer quantity, nonverbal behavior is vital to the process of communication. In this chapter, as we study these nonverbal messages, our specific objectives are the following:

1. To define nonverbal messages
2. To describe the key functions of nonverbal messages
3. To present the system used in this book for analyzing nonverbal behavior
4. To define, describe, and illustrate the following kinds of nonverbal messages:
   a. messages elicited from physical behavior and appearance of the human body
   b. messages elicited from the human voice
   c. messages elicited from the environment

Definition and Function of Nonverbal Messages

Several authors have published definitions of nonverbal messages or communication. Eisenberg and Smith discuss messages without words. Mehrabian (1971) refers to silent messages. Wenburg and Wilmot talk of "all the cues that are not words." Applbaum and colleagues conclude that "talking without words . . . behavioral cues that are *not* part of our language code, but are transmitted by persons and the environment in communication situations . . ." are nonverbal communication.

In a review of the literature on nonverbal communication, Harrison (1972) asserts that definitions range in scope from the very broad in which nonverbal communication is applied to almost any stimulus that impinges on people to the very narrow in which nonverbal communication is restricted to only those behaviors that carry the *intent* to communicate. Harrison suggested, "The simplest solution is to define verbal communication as anything that uses written or spoken words, with nonverbal picking up any other kind of symbol." Knapp agrees, stating that nonverbal communication encompasses "those events in which words are not spoken or written."

In this book, we have defined communication as the creation and exchange of messages. We stated earlier that the emphasis is not on written messages. Therefore, as used here, the term *nonverbal message* applies primarily to those messages that are not spoken. Naturally, the study of vocal cues requires a spoken message, but our concern is with such cues as pitch, tone, and rate, rather than with a specific word or its meaning. In chapter 1, we presented our paradigm for organizational communication, showing that organizational communication involves the interaction of people and messages within a selected environment. Within this paradigm, each of the three key components—people, message, and environment—generates its own unspoken messages. People can communicate with their body and physical behavior. Manipulation of vocal tone, pitch, rate, and volume is a form of communication. Time, space, architecture, and artifacts are environmental means of communication. Table 5.1 presents the dimensions of nonverbal behavior with which we are concerned in this chapter.

In his text on small group communication Rosenfeld stated:

> Research in the area of nonverbal communication rarely focuses on the impact of nonverbal communication on small group interaction. Yet, the implications of research findings are relevant to the small group setting. . .

Table 5.1 Dimensions of Nonverbal Behavior

The Body and Its Behavior and Appearance	The Voice	The Environment
Face (mouth and eyes)	Volume	Space and territory
Gesture	Tone	Time
Touch	Rate	Architecture (building and room design, seating arrangement)
Posture	Pauses	
Shape	Nonfluencies	Objects (clothing, art, sculpture, artifacts)

If we substitute the term *organizational* in the two places where Rosenfeld says "small group," the statement becomes equally valid for the subject of this textbook. Despite the emphasis on anecdotal inference and the lack of "hard" research data for nonverbal communication in the organizational setting, we feel justified in discussing it because of the important functions it serves in the total communication process.

Functions of Nonverbal Messages

Most writers agree that nonverbal behavior serves many important functions in the total communication system. Harrison (1972) believes that nonverbal behavior defines and regulates the communication system, as well as communicates specific content. In other words, through nonverbal messages people discover such things as whether they are to communicate or not, what is appropriate to say, who speaks first, and what they are trying to say. Ekman (1965) has stated that nonverbal behaviors can repeat, contradict, substitute, complement, accent, and regulate verbal signals. Professors may show slides during a lecture that repeat, complement, or accent a point made verbally during the lecture. A warm hand placed on the shoulder of an anxious employee may substitute for the words, "That's O.K. I'm still on your side." Students who nod their heads in apparent agreement with a professor may encourage the professor to assume that they understand the lecture, and this behavior may regulate the length of the lecture. In many cases, a nonverbal message may contradict a verbal message. A professor may state verbally, "Be sure and ask me any questions about things you don't understand." Then during the course of the semester, he constantly lectures beyond the time allotted for class and interrupts questions by saying, while looking at his watch, "Sorry, time's up." Mehrabian (1971) stated that when this happens, it will probably be the nonverbal behavior that is believed:

> When any nonverbal behavior contradicts speech, it is more likely to determine the total impact of the message. In other words, touching, positions (distance, forward lean, or eye contact), postures, gestures, as well as facial and vocal expressions, can all outweigh words and determine the feelings conveyed by a message.

Keltner agrees with that statement:

> When information communicated through nonverbal channels contradicts information communicated through the verbal channels, the nonverbally communicated information seems to predominate in the interpretation of the person receiving the two sets of information.

As Keltner implies, "Actions speak louder than words."

Applbaum and colleagues differentiated verbal and nonverbal communication this way:

> Generally, verbal communication transmits basic content in communication situations, while nonverbal communication transmits feelings, emotions, likings, personal meaning, and preferences.

Stewart thinks the primary function of nonverbal communication is to provide relationship cues. He believes nonverbal behavior defines the persons communicating and the relationship between them.

It appears, therefore, that nonverbal communication is responsible for communication of feelings and attitudes, the substance of most interpersonal relationships. Here is an illustration of the feeling-oriented nature of nonverbal behavior. One manager, when confronted with negative feedback from all his employees about his management style, constantly demanded specific verbal examples illustrating his bad management. After several hours of presenting examples and having the manager refute each one logically, one employee shouted, "Damn it! We could go on here all night giving you examples. It's very hard to verbalize what's bothering us. It all relates to our personal feelings and the way you appear to relate to us. It's hard to talk about our feelings, but believe me, they are very real!"

One final note before we examine the three dimensions of nonverbal behavior in an organization. As McCroskey and colleagues have warned, "It is difficult to study nonverbal communication in isolation because of its close interrelationship with verbal signals." We must consider the context within which a nonverbal cue is generated *before* attributing meaning to it. Just as it is simple for two communicators to bypass each other's meaning because of the multiple interpretations possible for a particular word, so is it possible (if not easier) for a nonverbal cue to be mistakenly interpreted. Knapp (1978) summarized this position: "Nonverbal communication is so inextricably bound up with verbal aspects of the communication process that we can only separate them artificially. In actual practice this separation does not occur." Without this perspective, we may find ourselves in the position of two psychiatrists who confronted each other one morning in an elevator. "Good morning," the first psychiatrist said to the second. Looking perplexed, the second psychiatrist thought, "I wonder what he meant by that?"

The Body, Its Behavior, and Its Appearance

How many times have you used such expressions as "poker-faced," "looks can kill," "piercing look," "red-faced," "loudmouth," "nervous smile," "dancing eyes"? The "body talks" claims a best-selling book and a popular game. We use the language of our body (facial expression, gestures, posture, touching, body shape) to communicate our feelings and attitudes. Employees and managers skilled in reading body cues may gain new insights about each other.

Research indicates that body movement is a major predictor of interpersonal liking. Mehrabian (1971) stated:

> Greater liking is conveyed by standing close instead of far, leaning forward instead of back while seated, facing directly instead of turning to one side, touching, having mutual gaze or eye contact, extending bodily contact as during a handshake, prolonging goodbyes, or using gestures during a greeting which imply a reaching out toward the other person who is at a distance.

Beier and Sternberg analyzed the body language of fifty-one Salt Lake City couples married from three to six months, with these conclusions:

> . . . subtle cues in the interaction of newlyweds are measurable and can identify stress. Touch, eye contact, open and closed sitting positions, initiative in conversing . . . are prognostic and might help us make a reasonable prediction as to which of the marriages are likely to fail.

Research I conducted indicates that certain movements of the body aid male homosexuals in their attempts to meet other homosexual males. One thousand homosexuals in ten U.S. cities were interviewed and three key body cues were identified as "most helpful": gazing at length (greater than three to four seconds) into another male's eyes, extended mutual touching of the knee area, and tapping of toes (especially during men's room encounters).

Researchers have catalogued the nonverbal behavior of the body. Ekman and Friesen identified five types of body expressions: emblems, illustrators, regulators, affect displays, and adaptors. *Emblems* are common gestures used to substitute for words. For example, a policeman may raise his right hand with the palm extended outward as he stops a lane of traffic, or a catcher shows one finger pointed downward between his legs to signal his pitcher to throw a fastball. *Illustrators* accompany and complement spoken language. A fireman may point to a victim in a burning building as he says, "There he is!" A professor may hold up a book to her class as she says, "Here's your assignment." A parking lot attendant may point to a specific space as he tells the driver, "Park here." *Regulators* control oral interaction. Nodding heads may tell a professor to continue speaking; or eliminating eye contact may signal a speaker that the listener has lost interest in the topic. *Affect displays* are body cues that indicate the emotional state of the interactants. A little boy may stick his tongue out at his mother to show extreme displeasure with her. A foreman may wrinkle his brow, close his eyes partially, and become red-faced as he demonstrates anger at a piece of work done by a new employee. *Adaptors* are body movements learned in early childhood that have a specific purpose, but that a speaker may not notice. Scratching one's nose, wiping the sweat off the forehead, and chain-smoking are examples of adaptors.

Perhaps the best known classification of the movements of the body is that of Ray Birdwhistell, which he called *kinesics*. Birdwhistell developed and tested an observation system which enables one to observe and record the movements of the body from moment to moment. McCroskey and colleagues summarized his theory as follows:

> His research is based on the theory that kinesics constitutes a language much like one that is written or spoken. A gesture can be performed in sequence to provide the equivalent of a sentence or paragraph. . . . Birdwhistell's work seems to support three important conclusions: (1) Body movement can be observed and recorded—even on what appears to be a microscopic level; (2) the compilation of a list of gestures and their meanings is useless without reference to specific contexts; and (3) movements in the area of the eye combined with hand motions are the prime situation definers for our culture.

Emblems are common gestures used to substitute for words.

Illustrators accompany and complement spoken language.

Much of the research done on the physical behavior of the body can be conveniently grouped under four headings: face, posture and gesture, touching, and general shape of the body.

The Face

The face is probably the most visible indicator of emotions and feelings, yet one of the hardest to measure. We are aware of and can control many of our facial expressions, and yet we often unintentionally display a particular face. Compounding the measurement problem is the finding that the face is capable of conveying several emotions simultaneously, rather than just a single emotion.

The development of Ekman's Facial Affect Scoring Technique (FAST) enables researchers to identify six emotions (happiness, anger, surprise, sadness, disgust, and fear) by observing three areas of the face: the brows-forehead area; the eyes-lids-bridge of the nose area; and the lower face or cheek-nose-mouth-chin-jaw area. With a minimum of training (six hours), coders can become proficient in using the FAST technique. Knapp (1978) summarized some of the evidence generated by the use of FAST:

> (1) The best predictors for "happiness" are the lower face and the eye area; (2) the eyes are most revealing for "sadness"; (3) the eye area and the lower face tell us most about "surprise"; (4) "anger" is best identified by the lower face and the brows-forehead; (5) the lower face is the best predictor for "disgust"; and (6) "fear" identifications seem most heavily weighted in the eye area.

Perhaps the one area of the face which provides the most information is the eyes. Findings by numerous researchers reveal certain consistent factors, which McCroskey and colleagues summarized as follows:

1. Eye contact seems to occur under the following conditions:
   a. when people seek feedback concerning the reaction of other people
   b. when an individual wants to signal that the communication channel is open
   c. when an individual wants to signal need for affiliation, involvement, or inclusion.
2. Women seem to engage in more eye contact in a variety of situations than do men.
3. Eye contact seems to increase as the communicating pair increases the distance between themselves.
4. Eye contact is used to produce anxiety in others.
5. Eye contact is absent under the following conditions:
   a. when people want to hide their inner feelings
   b. when two parties are physically close to each other
   c. in competitive situations where there is dislike or tension or after recent deception
   d. when a speaker begins a long utterance or when listeners anticipate a long, boring utterance
   e. when an individual wishes to disavow maintenance of all social contact

Of particular interest to the study of organizational hierarchies and the status relationship are the findings of Hearn, which indicate that people of high status command much greater eye contact than do people of low status. Managers who do not receive much eye contact from their employees may not be perceived by the employees as high-status individuals.

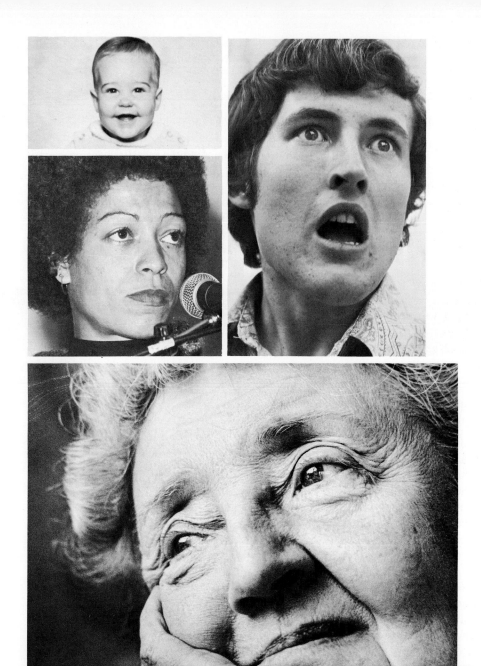

The face is probably the most visible indicator of emotions and feelings.

Gestures and Posture

As children in school, many of us were told by our teachers to sit up straight! We may even have been punished for exhibiting "bad posture." When one considers the work of Hewes, who identified over one thousand different postures, the question of "bad" versus "good" posture becomes somewhat silly. Efron has also reminded us of the complexity of observing posture by pointing out the severe cultural differences in body language. Harrison (1972), indicating the kinds of problems that can be encountered when we ignore the cross-cultural differences in the meaning of gestures, wrote:

> An American might make an "A-OK" sign with his hand in polite European company. In many cultures, that same sign is an obscene gesture representing the female genitalia. To a young woman, it is in effect a proposition; to a man, it is an accusation of homosexuality. Needless to say, the consequences of such a gesture were frequently far from "A-OK." In another instance, an American might offer food with his left hand. This is considered a grievous insult in certain parts of the world where the left hand is reserved for cleansing the body.

Knapp (1978) has pointed out that posture may provide information about such things as attitude, status, emotion, courtship, and warmth. Once again, the findings on status are of special interest in our study of organizations. Mehrabian (1968) concluded, "People relax most with a low-status addressee, second-most with a peer, and least with someone of higher status than their own." Mehrabian also found that men remain more tense when confronting a disliked man than a disliked woman. Perhaps this is evidence of male-perceived superiority of status over females.

Remland (1981) has reported that when superiors and subordinates communicate face-to-face, the unequal nature of the relationship (i.e., the higher status of the superior) is signaled nonverbally by the way the two parties use their bodies. Higher status personnel tend to behave in a more relaxed and inattentive manner than lower status employees. The former may "lean back in their chairs and look around the room while they appear to be listening." They tend to be more "easy going." They usually signal inattention by "not facing or looking at the subordinate, particularly when the latter is talking. Unresponsive head and facial displays (e.g., not smiling at a joke or not nodding in agreement) also reflect a subtle lack of involvement. The implicit message which is communicated nonverbally is: 'My body is more important than yours.' "

Touching

From infancy onward we all need to touch and to be touched. Spitz showed that infants do not grow normally unless they are touched by others. Parents touch their babies when they diaper, feed, burp, powder, and fondle them. Children are hugged by parents and close friends. Adolescents touch when they make love. Adults touch when they shake hands. The film *Second Chance* demonstrates the need for touch. In the film, a twenty-two-month-old baby girl whose parents have abandoned her is turned in to the hospital weighing only fifteen pounds and only twenty-eight inches tall. She demonstrated extreme retardation in motor ability and communicative behavior and is diagnosed as suffering from "maternal deprivation syndrome" attributed to lack of touching by her parents. After a volunteer substitute mother provides constant love, especially in the form of physical touching, for a few months, the baby shows marked improvement in height, weight, and motor ability.

As we grow older, physical touching is replaced by verbal and other nonverbal symbols (smiling, nodding heads, winking, gesturing). Parents admonish their children against touching with such familiar phrases as "Don't touch that!" "Don't play with yourself!" "Don't touch the TV, the vase, the cake, yourself." Especially frowned upon is the mutual touching of two males. Perhaps the success of the many T-groups and encounter groups, which stress bodily awareness and touching, can be attributed to the constant need for touching.

In one of the few studies done on touching, Jourard found that females touch and are touched more than are males. Friends of the opposite sex and mothers do most of the touching, while fathers limit most of their touch to the hands of others. In a church sermon Young proclaimed:

> Every human being needs to touch and be touched. Each of us has thoughts and feelings so deep and personal that words will simply not bear their weight. And yet, we long to communicate them, to share them with another. Our most intense joy is amplified and given permanence by being shared. Our deepest fears and anxieties are made endurable and manageable by being shared. But they can only be truly shared in their full depth and significance when they are shared in the totality of who we are. They cry out for touch.

> When your child comes to you, frightened and hurt, *tell* him you care, *tell* him you love him, *tell* him you are sorry. Then *touch* him. Take him in your arms and cuddle him. Then he will believe you. Then he will know you care.

Body Shape and Appearance

Tens of millions of dollars are spent annually by Americans on such personal care products as deodorant, mouthwash, soap, and perfume to combat such fatal illnesses as bad breath and body odor. Additional millions are spent on hair sprays, shampoos, and rinses designed to make our hair "sweet smelling, manageable, and dandruff-free." When we consider the purchase of lipstick, mascara, false eyelashes, toupees, undergarments, and false teeth, it becomes obvious that Americans are concerned about the shape and appearance of their bodies. Spoofing our concern for our bodies, Knapp (1978) painted the following picture:

> Mr. and Mrs. American awake and prepare to start the day. Mrs. American takes off her "night-time" bra and replaces it with a "slightly-padded-uplift" bra. After removing her chin strap, she further pulls herself together with her girdle. Then she begins to "put on her face." This involves an eyebrow pencil, mascara, lipstick, rouge, eye liner, and false eyelashes. Then she removes the hair under her arms and on her legs and places a hairpiece on her head. False fingernails, nail polish, and tinted contact lenses precede the deodorant, perfume, and endless decisions concerning clothes. Mr. American shaves the hair on his face, puts a toupee on his head and carefully attaches his newly purchased sideburns. He removes his false teeth from a solution used to whiten them, gargles with a breath sweetener, selects his after-shave lotion, puts on his elevator shoes, and begins making his clothing decision.

Some research justifies much of the behavior just described. Physical attractiveness appears to enhance one's initial credibility. Singer showed that some females use their physical attractiveness as a means of manipulating male instructors into giving them higher grades. He reported that attractive girls would sit in the front of the classroom, come up to the teacher after class, and make an appointment to see him during his office hours. Research showing similar behavior of male students with female instructors remains to be designed.

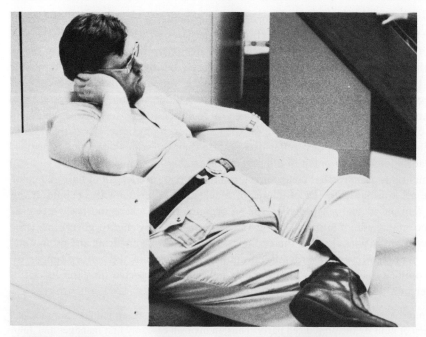

A system for classifying bodies according to their overall shape suggests three body types: the flabby endomorph, the frail ectomorph, and the muscular mesomorph.

Sheldon (1940) developed a system for classifying bodies according to their overall shape into three types of physique: ectomorph (frail, thin, tall), endomorph (fat, flabby, round), and mesomorph (muscular, athletic). Wells and Siegel demonstrated a belief among many people that "different temperaments go with different body builds." Looking at pictures of the three body types, subjects rated ectomorphs as thinner, younger, taller, more tense and nervous, and less masculine. Endomorphs were rated fatter, older, shorter, less good looking, and more talkative. Mesomorphs were rated stronger, more masculine, better looking, younger, and taller. It is obvious that Americans strive for the mesomorph physique. Books on dieting, for example, remain at the top of best-seller lists despite their questionable value or medical desirability. Leading men and women in movies are invariably mesomorphs.

Other dimensions of nonverbal behavior related to the body are length of hair and color of skin. We are all familiar with the problems of blacks and other nonwhite people in the United States. This used to be especially true in organizations, where mostly white employees achieved management status. During the 1970s, primarily due to government intervention, many organizations changed their policies and behavior about hiring and promoting nonwhite employees. However, interracial communication problems did not disappear by simply putting minority personnel in "white men's jobs." Jones reported his experiences as a black manager in a predominantly white corporation in this way:

> While prejudice exists in business, the United States norm against being prejudiced precludes an admission of guilt by the prejudiced party. Thus, in my own case, my first manager and John were more guilty of naivete than bigotry—they could not recognize prejudice, since it would be a blow to their self-images. And this condition is prevalent in United States industry.
>
> My experience points out that a moral commitment to equal opportunity is not enough. If a company fails to recognize that fantastic filters operate between the entry level and top management, this commitment is useless.

Length of hair was similarly prejudicial to young men seeking jobs in the late 1960s and early 1970s. Especially if they had hair below the ears or shoulders, they faced almost certain discrimination in many jobs. Some companies outlined appearance codes specifically addressed to hair length, beards, and sideburns.

The Human Voice

In chapter 4, we described a scene from a film in which a manager exclaimed to his employee, "Listen to what I mean, not what I say!" Listening to "what he means" can be accomplished by concentrating on the boss's voice and not on specific word choice. Such variables as tone, volume, breathiness, and pitch of the voice provide much information about a speaker regarding attitude, status, and feelings. Several researchers refer to the study of the human voice as *paralinguistics,* which they divide into segments (relating to vocal descriptors) and vocalizations. Segments are such qualities of the voice as pitch, volume, resonance, rate, and rhythm. Vocalizations are nonfluencies, unfilled pauses, and vocal characteristics such as laughing, yawning, and crying.

Much of the research on the human voice reveals a consistency among listeners in ability to predict certain characteristics about speakers. Kramer, for example, concluded that with information from the voice it is possible to predict physical characteristics (age, height, weight, body type), aptitudes and interests (values, vocation), personality traits (introverted, extroverted), overall personality (neurotics, normals), and adjustment and psychopathology. Nerbonne demonstrated that listeners can correctly identify a speaker's ethnic group (black versus white), education (high school versus college), and dialect region (Eastern, Southern, or general American). Addington found that the voice confirms many stereotype differences between men and women: "Male personality was perceived in terms of physical and emotional power, whereas female personality was apparently perceived in terms of social faculties."

Other researchers show that listeners can accurately identify certain emotions from vocal cues. The rate at which speech disturbances occur ("ah," sentence correction, sentence incompletion, repetition, stutter, intrusion of incoherent sound, tongue slip, and omission) relates to anxiety. My own research (1970) indicates that subjects in a state of anxiety exhibited more "non-ah" nonfluencies than did a control group. I found that such speech disturbances as "ah," "eh," "uhm," "uh," and the like have little relation to anxiety. In other research, my colleagues and I studied the nonfluencies of former President Carter during his presidential campaign debates against Ford in 1976 and Reagan in 1980. In most of the debates, Carter was more fluent than his opponents, indicating probably a lower level of anxiety and tension.

A vocal measure that does relate to anxiety is the pause. Goldman-Eisler (1955) suggests that utterances with few syllables per breath and much hesitation may indicate anxiety and tension. Mahl (1963) said that speech silence is an expressive attribute which is useful as an anxiety index. Geer found that people who experience anxiety in speaking have longer and more frequent periods of silence than do people not in an anxious state. Mahl (1964) concluded that intense anxiety is reflected in hesitant speech. Manther concluded that the number of pauses is influenced by the anxiety level of the speaker. Highly anxious speakers have more pauses. My own research (1970) shows that the average length of the pause for anxious speakers is greater than for nonanxious speakers.

Once again, it has been shown that status can be predicted from nonverbal behavior. Harms showed that adults listening to a forty-to-sixty-second speech sample can identify a speaker's status and credibility. Many listeners stated that they could do so after only ten to fifteen seconds of listening. Mehrabian (1968) has also provided some evidence relating to vocal cues and status:

> Utterance duration, for example, is a very stable quality in a person's speech; about 30 seconds long on the average. But when someone talks to a partner whose status is higher than his own, the more the high-status person nods his head the longer the speaker's utterances become. If the high-status person changes his own customary speech pattern toward longer or shorter utterances, the lower-status person will change his own speech in the same direction. If the high-status person often interrupts the speaker, or creates long silences, the speaker is likely to become quite uncomfortable. . . . If you have an employee who makes you uneasy and seems not to respect you, watch him the next time you talk to him—perhaps he is failing to follow the customary low-status pattern.

One final note about vocal cues. The findings in much research show that listeners' comprehension of a message is *not* significantly affected by extreme variation in volume, rate, and pitch, contrary to the belief of many teachers of public speaking. My own research on compressed speech (speeded speech) demonstrates that listeners can comprehend taped messages compressed to rates up to 350 words per minute. Other researchers have found high comprehension at even faster rates, with a moderate amount of listener training. My research on the 1976 Ford-Carter debates showed that Carter spoke about twice as fast as Ford, and was judged more effective overall by almost one hundred listeners.

Environment

Thus far, our investigation of nonverbal behavior in the organization has been limited to discussion of cues from either people's bodily behavior or their voices as they transmit messages. The third element in our paradigm of organizational communication is the environment. Here is where we find many nonverbal behaviors unique to the organizational setting. We shall consider such environmental influences as territory and space; time, building, room, and seating design; and artifacts and objects.

Territory and Space

A favorite children's fairy tale includes the following dialogue:

> They looked at the three chairs. "Somebody has been sitting in my chair!" cried Papa Bear in a huffy big voice.
>
> "Somebody has been sitting in my chair!" cried Mamma Bear in a middling-sized voice.
>
> "Somebody has been sitting in my chair and has broken the bottom out!" cried Baby Bear in a wee baby voice.
>
> The three bears looked in the room where the three beds were. "Somebody has been lying in my bed!" cried Papa Bear in a huffy big voice.
>
> "Somebody has been lying in my bed!" cried Mama Bear in a middling-sized voice.
>
> "Somebody has been lying in my bed, and *there she is!*" cried Baby Bear in a wee baby voice of astonishment.

There is very little difference between the reaction of Papa Bear and his family to Goldilocks's invasion of their home and the persons in the following situations. A middle-aged woman in New Mexico shot and killed a drunk man who was attempting to break into her house. In 1966, George Mahoney challenged Spiro Agnew for the governorship of Maryland with the slogan "Your home is your castle. Protect it!" Mahoney lost. In 1973, a colleague and I received a memo from the higher administration telling us to prepare to move from our offices to a different building. My colleague's response was, "I'll cling to my couch and force them to remove me bodily!"

In all of these examples, people (and bears) were claiming and defending a particular territory. Hall (1959) called this territoriality and predicted that animals and human beings will go to extremes to protect their territory. Rosenfeld (1973) characterized territoriality as assuming proprietary rights to a geographical area with no legal basis. Hall (1966) defined territory as "fixed-feature space because it is organized by unmoving boundaries, either visible or invisible."

High-status personnel usually (1) have greater territory, (2) protect their territory better, and (3) invade the territory of lower-status personnel.

According to McCroskey and colleagues, the concept of territoriality was of primary importance during the discussion on the size and shape of the negotiation table at the Paris peace talks in 1968:

> The United States (US) and South Viet Nam (SVN) wanted a seating arrangement in which only two sides were identified. They did not want to recognize the National Liberation Front (NLF) as an "equal" party in the negotiations. North Viet Nam (NVN) and the NLF wanted "equal" status given to all parties—represented by a four-sided table. The final arrangement was such that both parties could claim victory. The round table minus the dividing lines allowed North Viet Nam and the NLF to claim all four delegations were equal. The existence of the two secretarial tables (interpreted as dividers), the lack of identifying symbols on the table, and an AA, BB speaking rotation permitted the United States and South Viet Nam to claim victory for the two-sided approach. Considering the lives lost during the eight months needed to arrive at the seating arrangement, we can certainly conclude that territorial space has extremely high priority in some interpersonal settings.

Later in this chapter, we will examine seating arrangements in detail.

Mehrabian (1971) shows that there is a psychological advantage to being in one's own territory. We are all familiar with the home-team advantage in athletic contests. In one organization where conflict arose over the leadership of a particular manager, a meeting was scheduled to discuss the issues. The day before the meeting was to take place—in the manager's office—the employees requested a change in location. A new office was selected—that of a manager from a different department—even though the new location was not capable of seating all of the interactants. Thus, people may go to great extremes to protect or eliminate the home-territory advantage.

There appear to be three principles relating to territory and status in an organization. High-status personnel usually (1) have greater territory, (2) protect their territory better, and (3) invade the territory of lower-status personnel (Remland, 1981).

In many animal species, the dominant animal has a territory which is larger and more desirable than that of other species members. This principle holds for human beings as they interact within a complex organization where, according to Knapp (1978), those with higher status have more and better space and greater freedom to move about. Eisenberg and Smith concluded that the greater an individual's prestige, the larger the territory the individual will control. The pecking order at a university is a convenient illustration of this principle. Four or five graduate students can manage in the same size office allotted two faculty members or one department chairman. Deans have larger offices, and vice presidents even larger ones. In his classic study of a restaurant, Whyte also demonstrated a direct relationship between status and territory. Sommer predicted that in most organizations office size is determined by rank. Mehrabian (1971) links the amount of territory to both status and power in the organization, as follows:

> Higher-status persons of a social group have access to more locations and have more power to increase or restrict immediacy vis-à-vis others than the lower-status members . . . among persons of different status within the same institution, such as a school, a business, or a hospital, higher-status individuals are assigned larger and more private quarters.

The first principle relating territory to organizational status appears to be quite sound: *The higher up you are in the organization, the more and better space you have.*

The second principle states that individuals with higher status are better able to protect their territory than are those with lower status. You need only try to call the governor of your state on the telephone to illustrate this principle. You will probably first reach a switchboard operator, who connects you with the governor's office, where a secretary answers. The secretary then connects you with the governor's appointments secretary, who transfers your call to the governor's administrative assistant. Finally, after *four* transfers, you are connected with the governor—unless, of course, you've hung up or been told to "please call back." Attempts to reach any chief executive (president of a corporation, chief of police, U.S. senator, president of a university) will probably have similar results. As Mehrabian (1971) stated, "Persons of higher status determine the degree of immediacy permitted in their interactions with others. A person of lower status has less right to increase his immediacy with someone of higher status . . ." Mehrabian continued:

> The clue to status differences is the degree of hesitation and discomfort shown by the visitor at each stage as he is about to increase his immediacy to the person he visits. If the status differential is significant, he must wait for permission before he makes any major move in coming closer, or risk offending the higher-status other. He will be hesitant to presume familiarity by casually dropping into a seat as this implies relaxation and intention to stay on. Indeed, even when invited to sit, the visitor will still behave in a way that is consistent with his status in the situation as he sees it. If there is more than one visitor's chair, he will tend to sit at a distance from his host. . .

Eisenberg and Smith agree with Mehrabian: "The most important executive will control the area which is least accessible, sealed away from intruders by several doors and a handful of

The higher up you are in the organization, the more and better space you have.

minions." Fabun also emphasized the importance of location as a means of protecting one's territory:

> . . . the vertical distance between ground level and a person's office may act as an indication of his importance. Usually executive offices are located at or near the top of the building they occupy. Occupying a large room at the top of the building not only "says" a great deal about the person occupying it, but in part determines the kind of communication that can be carried on with him.

Research I conducted adds further support to the protection principle. I found that secretaries of several university administrators acted as communication barriers between their bosses and student visitors—*on direct orders from their bosses.* Thus, the second status-territory principle is established: *The higher up you are in the organization, the better protected your territory is.*

The reverse seems to be true for persons with lower status in the organization. The third principle allows for higher-status personnel to be able to freely invade the territory of those with lower status. When professors are forced to limit enrollments in their classes, the usual victims are the freshmen and sophomores. In several cases familiar to me, even when an underclassman was duly registered for the class, the upperclassmen exercised their territorial imperative and asked the professor for admission to the class. Eisenberg and Smith pointed out that etiquette is breached when subordinates enter the offices of superiors, "*but it is expected that the boss will saunter into the realm of any subordinates without there being the slightest complaint.*" The president of a university announced an open-door policy to encourage students to visit freely with him. After several weeks of almost no student visitors (except student government officials), the president decided to move the location of the rap sessions to the lobby of the student union. He was promptly surrounded by interested parties. Here, we see the third principle of territory and status in operation: *The higher up you are in the organization, the easier it is to invade the territory of lower-status personnel.*

Even though it may be unobtrusive, the overall effect of these three territorial principles is for superiors sending a message to subordinates, "My space is more important than yours." (Remland, 1981)

Whereas territory represents fixed-feature space, movable space, called "informal space" by Hall (1959), travels with us. Little called this our "personal distance," and Sommer named it "personal space." Rosenfeld (1973) defined personal space as "the space that you place between yourself and others." Hall (1969) labeled the study of personal space and distance *proxemics* and developed a model representing the four distances used by most Americans in their social and business transactions. Hall emphasized that these distances are culture bound; that within the American culture they are a function of the attitudes, feelings, and relationship of the interactants as well as of the context within which they communicate. The four distances are these: intimate, personal, social, and public.

Intimate distance (from touching to about eighteen inches) is the distance of love making and wrestling, comforting, and protecting and involves most of the sensory inputs, especially smelling and touching. Sometimes when we are in crowded elevators or subway trains we are unavoidably forced to interact with strangers at intimate distance. When this happens, our bodies seem to react almost automatically with such behaviors as tightening of muscles, pulling our hands rigidly to our sides, looking either up or down. One of our students rode the same elevator for one hundred trips and noted that most people looked either at the elevator floor or at the flashing numbers indicating approaching floors.

Personal distance (from eighteen inches to four feet) at the inner limits is reserved for close friends and intimates and at the outer limits for most interpersonal conversation. The relationship of the interactants, their feelings toward one another, dictates the distance between them. As Mehrabian (1968) points out, the more people like each other, the closer they sit or stand. With personal distance, touch is quite possible and feedback from visual interaction is available. The amount of space tolerated for conversation also varies from culture to culture. Hall (1959) concluded that Arabs require much less personal distance for conversation than do Americans, a factor that can cause a problem as the Arab moves ever closer to the American who keeps backing away. Each party may react negatively toward the behavior of the other without understanding his cultural-spatial needs. Hall (1959) stated:

> The intermediaries who arrange an Arab marriage usually take great precautions to insure a good match. They may even on occasion ask to smell the girl and will reject her if she "does not smell nice." . . . Bathing the other person in one's breath is a common practice in Arab countries. The American is taught not to breathe on people.

In another study related to social distance, Williams found that during conversation introverts keep people at a greater distance than do extroverts.

Social distance (from four to twelve feet) is the distance of most business interactions, both informal and formal. Closer distances are reserved for informal interaction, and Hall adds, "People who work together tend to use close social distance." It is also the distance used by people attending an informal social function. Farther distances are typical of more formal business and social encounters. Some large offices allow enough room for chairs to separate the interactants by as much as eight or nine feet.

Public distance (from twelve to fifteen feet or more) is well outside the circle of involvement. Vocal cues are more important when eye contact diminishes. Teachers use this distance in many lecture halls. Speakers use this distance in public appearances. Important speakers, such as the president of the United States, use the outer limits of public distance.

Space and Costs of Communication

Space has been linked to communication costs: office relocation outside a major metropolitan area (to save money in rent and salaries) may increase communication costs sufficiently to offset other savings. Several studies conducted in Europe during the last ten years confirm this point. Thorngren showed in Sweden and Goddard in England that after relocation most workers retain 30 percent of their former communication contacts. The Communication Studies Group in London estimated that after relocation, a civil servant's telephone costs increase by about 50 pounds per year. Pye developed a model for computing the approximate extra travel costs involved when relocated employees travel back to their former city for business meetings. Pye concluded that *the increased economic benefits, which in general are possible when a long distance move is made, do not offset the greater costs of communication.* Naturally, communication costs can be reduced if the need for the old contacts is diminished by regional decentralization of decision making, such as was done by the Prudential Insurance Company in the United States. Another alternative currently being experimented with in both England and Canada is to substitute telecommunication alternatives for travel. Preliminary findings indicate that about one-third of existing meetings consist of activities whose outcome is not significantly affected when the meeting is conducted via audioteleconference devices and that an additional 10 percent of existing meetings consist only of tasks whose outcome would not be affected by television-type visual teleconference devices. The effects of new spatial arrangement on communication costs of the majority of meetings still need to be accounted for. However, affected managers can probably figure out their organization's needs and balance these needs against potential costs.

Role Distance and Communication

My studies of U.S. and Canadian organizations have confirmed that role distance has a significant impact on organizational communication behavior. Both dissatisfaction with organizational communication and need for communication improvement increase with organizational distance. Some of my specific conclusions (derived from studies of sixteen organizations in the United States and Canada with samples of almost 4,000 employees) related to distance are as follows:

1. The farther up the organizational hierarchy an employee is, the less the follow-up regarding information sent to top management and also in response to requests.
2. The best sources of information are persons closest to employees (co-workers, immediate supervisors); the worst sources are persons farthest away (top management, boss's boss, formal management presentation).
3. Information from top management is of lower quality than that from other key sources.
4. The immediate communication climate is excellent and healthier than that of the organization at large (which limits openness, lacks sufficient incentives and rewards, and minimizes input, influence and advancement opportunities).

In sum, *dissatisfaction* with organizational communication seems to increase as organizational distance between communication sources and receivers increases.

Time

A second major environmental variable is the dimension of time. We are constantly reminded of its importance by such everyday sayings as "Time flies," "Time is money," "Don't waste time," "Take your time," "It's about time," "Time's up," and "Time out (in)." Our vocabulary is filled with words that refer to time: *soon, later, then, sometime, yesterday, today, tomorrow, now, immediately, early, late, last (week, month, year, season), next, behind, ahead.* We eat according to time (three meals a day at specific time intervals). We work and go to school on a time schedule (8:30–5:30 each day). We sleep according to time (seven to nine hours per night). We structure daily events, meetings, and reports and even get paid in accordance with time. Major events in our lives are structured by time—birth, christening, marriage, retirement, and even sometimes death.

Americans treat time with great respect, especially in organizations. Tardiness in school, for meetings, or with reports may be interpreted as an insult and be accompanied by negative consequences. Promptness is respected and usually rewarded. Professors often say, "If you hand your papers in on time, or earlier, I'll have a chance to read them all very thoroughly." As further evidence of the respect with which we treat time, simply remember how you felt the last time your phone rang at *3:00* A.M.

Halpin indicated some organizational interpretations of time as follows:

> Most organizations or cultures develop informal tolerance ranges for lateness; to keep a person waiting beyond the tolerance limit is a subtle way of insulting him. However, the handling of promptness and lateness can vary with the subculture and with the functions of the meeting.

Thus military officers are likely to arrive a few minutes ahead of the appointed time, whereas professors usually arrive from five to ten minutes after the set time. In the social sphere, only a yokel will arrive at a cocktail party at the stipulated time; whereas good manners require a guest to arrive at a dinner party not more than ten minutes late.

The treatment of time is also a function of status. Greater status may allow personnel to abuse the time of others while expecting rigid adherence to their own schedules. Thus, the head of one department in an organization was constantly late for meetings which he initiated, but on one occasion when his secretary arrived ten minutes later than he did, he promptly gave her a dirty look. Hall (1959) concluded that Americans of equal status usually allow five minutes before they expect an apology for tardiness.

Remland (1981) has found that higher status persons act in ways that control the time of others. The frequency of communication is often determined by superiors, superiors typically set the agenda for meetings, and the amount of time spent in a communication is more often determined by those of higher status. Remland concludes by saying that superiors are sending a very clear message to their subordinates, "My time is more valuable than yours."

Several American organizations are now experimenting with flextime, a system that increases employee flexibility in choosing their working hours. At Hewlett-Packard, for example, there are no time cards and no clocks to punch. Workers can begin work at any time between 6:30 and 8:30 A.M. Results are extremely encouraging:

1. Most workers fall into the habit of coming to work at one particular time every day.
2. Most workers arrive as early as possible—close to 6:30 A.M.
3. Most workers respect the honor system of no time cards and put in a full day's work.

Severe intercultural problems can arise in an organization due to different perceptions about time. In some cultures arriving on time is as insulting as being late is to most Americans. Latin Americans usually tolerate as much as a 45-minute wait before beginning a business meeting. Smith warns of possible misunderstanding between whites (who possess a "commercial" concept of time) and blacks (who possess a "hang-loose" concept). Smith warns that whites may view blacks as "irresponsible" because of this perceptual difference. Hall and Hall (1975) illustrated this very problem with the following story:

> The black is told to appear for a job interview at a certain time. He arrives late. The white interviewer concludes from his tardy arrival that the black is irresponsible and not really interested in the job. What the interviewer doesn't know is that the black time system isn't the same as that of whites. In the words of a black student who had been told to make an appointment to see his professor: "Man, you *must* be putting me on. I never had an appointment in my life."

A story was once told to my Finnish colleague, Osmo Wiio, about an American businessman who had made an offer to a Japanese company about a very large business deal. The business was so important that he decided to go to Tokyo to negotiate, and he was prepared to stay there several weeks if necessary. For a Westerner, the Japanese decision-making process is both incomprehensible and frustrating—and, above all, very slow. The man went around to see different people in endless negotiations. When he tried to push for a decision, he was met with a polite and evasive answer, "Soon." After hearing this answer *for six months,* he gave up and left almost in tears for losing perhaps the best deal in his life. After he left, the Japanese commented on his departure by wondering about his "strange hurry." In three more weeks, he would have had his deal.

Recognizing how important are the differences that can exist from one culture to another, Stull and Baird (1981) have introduced the following cultural awareness skills to make us more empathic and effective communicators when we confront intercultural situations.

1. *Showing Personal Respect.* The ability to demonstrate unconditional positive respect for others without acting ethnocentric or superior.
2. *Being Nonjudgmental.* The ability to see things as they "are" rather than as they "should be."
3. *Being Flexible.* The ability to tolerate ambiguity and to deal with the unexpected in a culturally appropriate/sensitive manner.
4. *Being Spontaneous.* The ability to drop expectations and to deal with individual situations perceptively on a "here and now" basis.
5. *Using Problem-Orientation.* The ability to encourage and obtain the input and participation of others to approach and solve problems in a culturally appropriate manner.
6. *Being Empathic.* The ability to "try" to see the world through the eyes of others, realizing that one's own view is personal; the ability to employ cultural relativism.

In June and January, Japanese businesses typically declare bonuses and thus provide a tremendous economic boost to the Japanese economy. Throughout the country workers rush to the closest department store to spend their bonuses on gifts for business and social contacts. It seems that the entire country moves into high gear as part of this elaborate plan to infuse new revenues into the hands of workers—all on a precise schedule. The Japanese appear to manage their time rather than being managed by it—a lesson U.S. businesspeople would best heed.

My studies have shown that the quality of information from most major sources in organizations is reduced because of poor timing. Messages typically arrive too early or too late to be of use to employees. Although distant sources (top management) are most guilty of this fault, few escape the behavior or its consequences. It seems that "slow news travels down and fast news travels up the organization." In one organization, for example, a middle manager summed up the feelings of most of his colleagues, "It seems that whatever reports or memos I send upstairs just seem to float around and disappear."

Just as *timeliness* has implications for communication, so does the *amount of time* spent in various activities. Symptomatic of information overload is the accompanying waste of time necessary to sift through irrelevant information to find the essential elements. This is the case concerning meetings. No meeting should last more than ninety minutes. After this length of time, fatigue and inattention reduce the quality of decision making. To fully understand the implications of this statement, assume that a meeting lasts three hours instead of ninety minutes. Attending this meeting are ten managers whose average salary is $50 per hour (including benefits). Does the extra ninety minutes produce at least $750 worth of decisions or solved problems? And that's just to break even! You can compute the cost of your hours and minutes from data in table 5.2. These figures represent just the cost. Most companies expect employees to produce at a rate of two to three times their cost. One simple way to increase productivity per unit of time is to follow the principles of time management.

Table 5.2 Employee Cost by Hours and Minutes

Yearly Salary	Cost per Hour[a]	Cost per Minute[a]
$10,000	$12.36	$0.21
20,000	24.73	0.41
30,000	37.10	0.62
40,000	49.47	0.82
50,000	61.84	1.03

[a] Including cost of benefits, cost of lost productiveness, and salary.

To get a rough estimate of the return on time invested for a number of tasks that confront you, follow these procedures:

1. List all the tasks by the day or week, whichever fits your personal and business requirements.
2. Estimate the relative value of each task on a scale of 1 to 10, with 1 being low task value.
3. Estimate the time available for each task.
4. Divide the task value by the time available for each task. This figure provides your return on investment values. The higher the number, the higher is the rate of return.
5. Using these returns on investment values, assign a priority order to your tasks. Group those tasks that can be done more efficiently when done in sequence.

Other techniques that can help you manage your time better are to use a pocket and desk calendar that lists important calls, meetings, appointments, and tasks in priority order; to use an alarm watch to signal the end of a meeting; to ask a secretary or friend to interrupt you after the meeting exceeds a preassigned time limit. As Hall (1959) has said, "Time talks," and what it has to say is of vital concern to all of us.

Building, Room, and Seating Design

Some buildings and rooms seem to encourage human interaction. They appear to have invisible signs posted that say, "Come in," "Hello," "Come closer," or "Welcome." Still others seem to communicate coldness and be saying, "No visitors," "Stay away," or "Keep out." I remember the living room of my youth, and its always new looking, always clean furniture, rugs, and fireplace. Few people ever sat on the chairs, and in fourteen years the fireplace was never once lit. Mehrabian (1971) reminds us of countless living rooms—"as beautifully furnished as a showroom but left just as unoccupied while the guests cluster happily in the kitchen and enjoy themselves there."

The design of buildings, rooms, and tables can do much to enhance or inhibit communication. Johnson (1987) emphasized the importance of the physical environments in organizations and that it has many potential impacts on organizational communication because it forms the context within which this communication occurs. A friend designed the Law School at the University of New Mexico to enhance interpersonal encounters. As you enter the building, you come into the middle of a circular foyer of approximately thirty feet in diameter. It is furnished with large, comfortable black leather chairs arranged in groups of three or four around coffee tables. Faculty, students, and administrators must all pass through the foyer to get anywhere in the building. Thus, the design of the building greatly facilitates human interaction.

Look at your classroom. Does it enhance human interaction? Chances are, the seats are lined up in rows and nailed to the floor. What kind of interaction does this arrangement encourage? Maslow and Mintz provided evidence linking the esthetic conditions of a room with certain human reactions. Subjects in a beautiful room tended to rate pictures of faces higher than subjects placed in an ugly room. Subjects in the ugly room finished the task sooner and had responses of monotony, fatigue, sleep, headache, discontent, irritability, and hostility. Subjects in the beautiful room had responses of comfort, pleasure, enjoyment, importance, energy, and a desire to continue the activity. It is apparent, therefore, that the esthetics of the room influenced the communication behavior of the interactants.

Many banks and large offices have partitions to separate customers from officers and employees. Additionally, they may have a regimented arrangement of furniture (side-by-side seating along a wall, or rows of desks arranged so each employee faces another's back). Some research has shown that workers in an open environment (without inside walls) tend to work at higher levels of productivity than workers in a closed environment. On the other hand, Eric Sundstrom and colleagues at the University of Tennessee at Knoxville recently reported that workers were happier and more productive when their office space was "more private than open"—perhaps because privacy enhances an employee's status and sense of identity, reduces distractions, and allows people to pay less attention to maintaining appearances and more to getting the job done. Osmond (1957, 1959) called areas that separate people "sociofugal" and areas that bring people close together "sociopetal." Mehrabian (1971) suggested designing sociopetal seating areas as follows:

> Maximum number of pairs of seats should be placed at intermediate levels of immediacy (that is, about four feet apart and oriented from face-to-face position to 90-degree angle).

Sommer called the concern for seating patterns and other spatial behavior "small group ecology." Much of the research in this area concludes that our seating behavior is quite logical, whether it is intentional or not. Sommer concluded that seating arrangements in small groups are primarily a function of the task, the relationship of the interactants, and the environment (amount of space). Strodtbeck and Hook reported that persons sitting at the head of a table are perceived more often as leaders of groups. Sommer showed that leaders selected the head of the table and other participants arranged themselves so they could see the leader. It is more important, according to Sommer, to be able to *see* leaders than to *interact* with them. Sommer reported that students in a seminar room are most silent when they occupy the chairs to the immediate left or right of the instructor. If you sit to the immediate left or right of a hostile person at a meeting, you are more likely to control that person's influence. Knapp (1978) summarized one of Sommer's findings:

> In typical straight row classroom settings, it seemed students sitting within eye contact range of the instructor participated more; students sitting in the center sections of each row participated more; participation tended to decrease from front to back; and participation decreased as class size increased.

It is apparent that the architecture of buildings, the design and arrangement of rooms, and the seating plans around tables contribute greatly to the environment of nonverbal behavior.

Furthermore, Davis (1984) emphasized that physical location can influence the information that one is privy to and the involvement of individuals in organizational events.

In 1974, the Volvo assembly plant in Kalmar, on the east coast of Sweden, began a revolutionary set of work experiments that focused on both enriching the workers' jobs and improving the quality of their working environment. The new plant was designed to meet the physical requirements of a more humanized work process. Instead of being in a large industrial plant, the teams work in small "workshops" where they see only their immediate team area. Each team has its own entrance and its own facilities: shower room, sauna, lockers, and coffee room. The noise level is cut so much that a private discussion can be held quite easily right in the work area. All heavy work is done with power tools, usually designed for the purpose. For general relaxation, the plant has table tennis, libraries, and even swimming pools. Live shrubs and coordinated colors decorate the work locations. Pehr G. Gyllenhammer, general manager of Volvo, Sweden, said, "It must be possible to create an environment which better meets the need of the modern man for meaning and satisfaction in the daily life. This goal must be reached without impairing efficiency."

Do the Volvo experiments work? Preliminary findings are encouraging. Absenteeism and turnover decreased. Job satisfaction and working skills increased. Fewer work errors were recorded, and Volvo maintains that its flexibility in production of automobiles is greater than before. Perhaps what occurred was a Hawthorne effect—any kind of attention given workers would reduce absenteeism and turnover. Nevertheless, Volvo showed increased production quality—fewer faults during production and fewer cars returned for repairs during the guarantee period.

Artifacts and Objects

When Ruesch and Kees developed their nonverbal classification scheme, they identified three types of language: sign, action, and object language. In one way or another, we have already considered the first two types. Object language pertains to the display of material things—clothing, artwork, room furnishings, and color—and such status symbols as reserved parking spaces, keys to the executive washroom, two secretaries, and so forth. Discussing status symbols in organizations, Porter stated:

> One of the most status conscious groups is the military. Here we find that the cut and makeup of their uniforms, the service stripes they wear, the medals displayed across their chests, the braid on their caps and their sleeves all have the same story to tell—what their experience has been and what their place is in the organization.

> To a great extent businesses have followed the lead of the military by the appointment of offices and the giving of service pins. The type of desk, the rug on the floor, the drapes on the windows, the water jug, the number of stars on the pin all tell the same story as the military symbols.

Sometimes the color of a room may affect the type of interaction that takes place there. Warm colors (yellow, orange, red) apparently stimulate creativity and make people feel more outgoing. Cool colors (blue, green, gray) encourage deep thought processes and may inhibit both the frequency and quality of communication.

We mentioned above the arrangement of furniture within an office and its effects upon interaction. The actual *presence* of certain furnishings may either promote or dampen communication. Many executives are refurnishing their offices today and adding such home furnishings as coffee tables, easy chairs, sofas, and artwork. Fast (1928) distinguished the formality of Johnny Carson, who uses a desk to separate himself from his guest, and the informality of David Frost, who abandons a desk and sometimes chairs. Executives today who are the most powerful have offices that show few if any signs that any work is performed there. They prefer a relaxed, living-room-library feeling that encourages a perception of their accessibility. One artifact that seems to communicate this desired perception is the fireplace. Sanford Weill, the chairman of Shearson/American Express, Inc., had a fireplace installed in his office in Manhattan's World Trade Center. Since his office is on the 106th floor of a 110-story building, it was necessary to channel a chimney through four floors to reach the roof. Other symbols of power in the executive suites are private bathrooms, complete with marble trimmings, and private dining rooms, complete with fine china and silver.

Some executives use objects to limit interaction. They create barriers with furniture or use plants, files, and clocks to protect them from possible intrusion. Some even position chairs, tables, typewriter stands, etc. in the way to create a circuitous route into their office—all intended to say to outsiders, "Bug off!"

Clothing also provides cues that influence interaction. Hoult has shown that one's clothing influences strangers more than it does people who know one well. Knapp (1978) agreed and suggested, "It is reasonable to assume that, in most instances, our perceptions of others are influenced partly by clothes and partly by other factors." Compton demonstrated a relationship between selection of clothing and status. People of higher status select their clothing more carefully. Many organizations are well aware of the impact of clothing upon their publics. The campus police at one university recently donned blazers instead of standard police uniforms. Several schools (high schools and colleges alike) have adopted formal dress codes. One high school specifically prohibits the wearing of such clothing as miniskirts, slacks, shorts, and blue jeans. One college dormitory in the Midwest prohibits male residents from entering the dining area unless they are wearing long pants, a shirt, shoes, and socks. The same university prohibits students from attending student union dances without socks. One pants manufacturer prohibits the wearing of the very blue jeans they manufacture.

John Molloy collected information about 15,000 executives and professional men, and his conclusions overwhelmingly indicate that the clothing you wear directly affects the credibility you have with various audiences. Molloy found that men are most likely to be *liked* when they wear suits of solid light gray or blue. He also found that solid dark blue suits give men the highest *credibility* with the largest range of audiences. In general, the darker the suit, the more authority it communicates. In an updated version of his research, Molloy suggested that women who intend to dress for success should, in general, avoid high fashion, dress conservatively, and, as he advised men, dress appropriately for the audience with whom they are interacting.

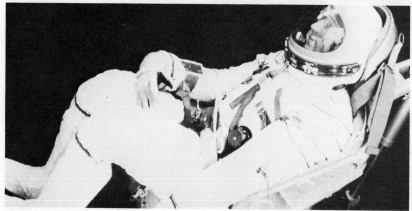

Clothing also provides cues that influence interaction.

SUMMARY

The quantity of nonverbal stimuli signals how important it is to the total process of communication. Nonverbal messages are outside spoken and written languages. Each of the three components in the organizational communication paradigm—people, message, and environment—can generate its own nonverbal behavior. People communicate with their bodies, vocal characteristics are the means by which messages communicate; and space, time, design, and artifacts are the communicators for the environment. Nonverbal communication is the communication of feelings and attitudes and should be interpreted only in the context of the total communication situation.

The study of the body and its behavior and appearance was pioneered by Birdwhistell, who called his science kinesics. Much of the research done on the physical behavior of the body can be conveniently grouped under four headings: face, posture and gesture, touching, and general shape of the body. The mouth and eyes provide much of the information about facial expression. Gestures and posture can be related to organizational status. Despite our hunger and need for touching, most of us do not employ this form of nonverbal behavior. The body can be described according to three shapes: ectomorph, endomorph, and mesomorph.

The human voice can be studied by examining such descriptors as pitch, tone, volume, rate, resonance, and rhythm and by studying such vocalizations as pause, nonfluencies, laughing, crying, and yawning. Examination of the voice is called paralinguistics and shows that listeners are able to predict certain characteristics about speakers, such as physical characteristics, aptitudes, personality traits, and psychopathology.

The third dimension of nonverbal behavior—the environment—is concerned with territory and space, time, design of buildings and rooms, and artifacts. Territoriality involves laying claim to and defending a certain area. Three organizational principles of territory and status were identified: personnel with high organizational status usually (1) have greater territory, (2) protect their territory better, and (3) invade the territory of lower-status personnel more easily. Personal space is the space you place between yourself and others. It is highly flexible and travels with individuals as a function of their culture, environment, relationship, and personality. Hall labeled the study of space and territory proxemics and identified four distances in which interaction takes place. Intimate distance (from touching to eighteen inches) is the distance of lovemaking, wrestling, comforting, and protecting. Personal distance (from eighteen inches to four feet) is reserved for close friends and most interpersonal conversation. Social distance (from four to twelve feet) is the distance of most business interaction, both informal and formal. Public distance (from twelve to twenty-five feet or more) is used for public speaking, teaching, and impersonal interaction.

Dissatisfaction with organizational communication increases as distance between communicators increases. Time is important to communication and is treated with great respect by Americans, who are usually punctual and insulted by tardiness. Time management can improve the returns on your time investments. Intercultural communication problems can arise when we deal with people from cultures who treat time differently.

The design of buildings, rooms, and conference tables can either enhance or dampen interaction. The Swedish experiments at the Volvo factory have shown that changes in working environment can increase job satisfaction and quality of production.

Artifacts and objects can communicate warmth, coldness, or status. Our clothing may affect how we are perceived and received.

EXERCISES

1. Visit an organization of your choice. Spend approximately *three* hours touring the facility. Keep a record of *all* the nonverbal behavior you observe. Follow the system established in table 5.1.
2. Watch at least two of your favorite television shows *without* sound. Can you tell what the people are saying? What they are doing? Keep a record of their behavior and compare it with that of a friend who watched the same two shows *with* sound. If you have access to a videotape recorder, record the shows and compare your original notes with the sound replay. This exercise can also be done with films.
3. Go to the airport and watch the flight personnel as they handle the traffic and assist the planes on their way to the terminal building. What kinds of nonverbal behavior do you observe? Repeat this exercise by watching a policeman as he directs traffic or a baseball coach as he signals his team.
4. Have a conversation with a friend about any topic of your choice. Neither one of you may say any words other than the nonsense phrase, "Garlic salt tastes good for breakfast." Were you able to communicate? What did you notice about each other's tone of voice?
5. Call the governor of your state (U.S. or state representative, U.S. or state senator) on the telephone. How many secretaries, aides, or assistants did you speak to? What did they say? How did they treat you? Did you get through? Now repeat this exercise by calling the president of your university, college, or organization where you are unknown. Discuss the results of your call this time. Finally, call the head of one department (personnel, engineering, or manufacturing) in a small organization with under fifty personnel. What were the results this time of your call? Did the status of each person you called influence the result of the call? Discuss the differences in the results of your calls.
6. Ride an elevator (in several buildings) when you can be certain it will be crowded. Accidentally touch someone. Do you notice any reaction? What do most people look at when riding on the elevator? What happens if you turn around and face all the people? How do they react to you now? Did anyone speak to you?
7. Examine three rooms (classroom and waiting rooms at an airport, hospital, or business firm). What do you notice about the furniture? About the arrangement of the chairs, if any? About the material the furniture is made of? What can you say about the general design of each room? Are there objects in the room? What purpose do they serve?
8. Visit an office of your choice. Examine the furniture and its arrangement. Is there a relationship between the furniture and the occupant of the office?
9. When you are visiting a close friend, sit in his or her favorite chair. Remain there and watch and then describe your friend's reactions.

10. Call a *very close* friend on the telephone at 3:00 A.M. What is his or her reaction to your call?
11. Watch the television newscasters on two or three stations. Do they dress differently? What impression does each communicate? Look at pictures of high government and corporate officials. What kinds of clothing do they wear? What impression does each communicate?
12. Read the *Wall Street Journal,* the *New York Times* business section, *Fortune, Forbes,* or *Business Week* for one or two weeks. Identify one company that is moving or planning a move (either an expansion of present facilities or a move to another location or country). Based upon the information available to you (if possible, call someone in that organization or visit someone there), what will the major communication costs be after the move has taken place?
13. You have just been promoted to assistant vice president of your organization. Your promotion has placed you *two* hierarchical levels over several of your friends (some of whom are one level below you as managers and some of whom are two levels below you as assistant managers). What new communication techniques or channels will you use to communicate with your friends? What will they do differently to communicate with you?

BIBLIOGRAPHY AND REFERENCES

Addington, David. "The Relationship of Selected Vocal Characteristics to Personality Perception." *Speech Monographs* 35 (1968):492–503.

Applbaum, Ronald L., K. Anatol, E. Hays, O. Jenson, R. Porter, and J. Mandel. *Fundamental Concepts in Human Communication.* San Francisco: Canfield Press, 1973.

Argyle, M., and J. Dean. "Eye Contact, Distance and Affiliation." *Sociometry* 28 (1965):289–304.

Argyle, M., M. Lalljee, and M. Cook. "The Effects of Visibility on Interaction in a Dyad." *Human Relations* 21 (1968):3–17.

Beier, Ernst, and Daniel Sternberg. "Body Language." *Parade Magazine,* 8 April 1973, pp. 5–6.

Birdwhistell, Ray. *Kinesics and Context.* Philadelphia: University of Pennsylvania Press, 1970.

Brooks, W. *Speech Communication.* Dubuque, Iowa: Wm. C. Brown Co. Publishers, 1971.

Compton, N. "Personal Attributes of Color and Design Preferences in Clothing Fabrics." *Journal of Psychology* 54 (1962):191–95.

Davis, T. R. "The Influence of the Physical Environment in Offices."*Academy of Management Review,* 9 (1984):271–83.

Davitz, J. R. *The Communication of Emotional Meaning.* New York: McGraw-Hill Book Co., 1964.

Davitz, J. R., and L. Davitz. "Correlates of Accuracy in the Communication of Feelings." *Journal of Communication* 9 (1959):110–17.

Diehl, C. F., and E. R. McDonald. "Effect of Voice Quality on Communication." *Journal of Speech and Hearing Disorders* 21 (1956):233–37.

Diehl, C. F., R. White, and P. Satz. "Pitch Change and Comprehension." *Speech Monographs* 28 (1961):65–68.

Duncan, Starkey. "Nonverbal Communication." *Psychological Bulletin* 72 (1969):118–37.

Efron, D. *Gesture and Environment*. New York: King's Crown Press, 1941.

Eisenberg, Abne, and Ralph Smith. *Nonverbal Communication*. Indianapolis, Ind.: Bobbs-Merrill Co., 1971.

Ekman, P. "Constants Across Cultures in the Face and Emotion." *Journal of Personality and Social Psychology* 17 (1971):124–29.

———. "Communication Through Nonverbal Behavior: A Source of Information About an Interpersonal Relationship." In *Affect, Cognition and Personality,* edited by S. S. Tomkins and C. E. Izard. New York: Springer Publishing Co., 1965.

Ekman, P., and W. Friesen. "The Repertoire of Nonverbal Behavior: Categories, Origins, Usage, and Coding." *Semiotica* 1 (1969):49–98.

Ekman, P., E. Sorenson, and W. Friesen. "Pan-Cultural Elements in Facial Displays of Emotion." *Science* 164 (1969):86–88.

———. "Facial Affect Scoring Technique: A First Validity Study." *Semiotica* 13 (1971):37–58.

Elton, M., et al. "An Approach to the Location of Government." Paper presented at a meeting of the Institute of Management Science, London, 1970.

Exline, R. V. "Explorations in the Process of Person Perception: Visual Interaction in Relation to Competition, Sex, and Need for Affiliation." *Journal of Personality* 31 (1963):1–20.

Exline, R. V., D. Gray, and D. Schuette. "Visual Behavior in a Dyad as Affected by Interview Content and Sex of Respondent." *Journal of Personality and Social Psychology* 1 (1965):201–9.

Fabun, Don. "The Silent Languages." In *Communications: The Transfer of Meaning,* edited by D. Fabun. New York: Macmillan, 1968.

Fast, Julius. "Can You Influence People through 'Body Language'?" *Family Circle,* November 1970. Reprinted in *Communicating Interpersonally,* edited by R. Wayne Pace et al. Columbus, Ohio: Charles E. Merrill, 1973.

———. *Body Language*. New York: Pocket Books, 1970.

Frye, Jerry, Gerald Goldhaber, and Bruce Bryski. "A Communication Analysis of Selected Nonverbal Dimensions of the 1980 Carter/Reagan Presidential Debate." Presented to the ICA Convention, Minneapolis, 1981.

Geer, J. H. "Effect of Fear Arousal upon Task Performance and Verbal Behavior." *Journal of Abnormal and Social Psychology* 71 (1966):119–23.

Goddard, J. "Organizational Information Flows and the Urban System." *Economic Appliquée* (1975):125–64.

Goldhaber, G. "The Effect of 'Ego-Involvement' on Selected Dimensions of Speech Production." Ph.D. dissertation, Purdue University, 1970.

———. "Listener Comprehension of Compressed Speech as a Function of the Academic Grade Level of the Subjects." *Journal of Communication* 20 (1970):167–73.

———. "Effects of Speech Compression Training on Listener Comprehension of Native Speakers of English, Spanish and Navajo." In *Time Compressed Speech: An Anthology and Bibliography,* edited by Sam Duker. Metuchen, N.J.: Scarecrow Press, 1973.

———. "Gay Talk: Communication Behavior of Male Homosexuals." In *Urban Communication,* edited by W. Arnold and J. Buley. Cambridge, Mass.: Winthrop Publishers, 1977.

Goldhaber, G., H. Dennis, G. Richetto, and O. Wiio. *Information Strategies: New Pathways to Management Productivity*. Norwood, N.J.: ABLEX, 1984, Revised Edition.

Goldhaber, G., J. Frye, T. Porter, and M. Yates. "The Image of the Candidates: A Communication Analysis of the 1976 Ford-Carter Debates." *Washington Post,* 14 November 1976, p. C-2.

Goldhaber, G., and C. H. Weaver. "Listener Comprehension of Compressed Speech When the Difficulty Rate of Presentation and Sex of the Listener Are Varied." *Speech Monographs* 35 (1968):20–25.

Goldman-Eisler, Frieda. "Speech Breathing Activity: A Measure of Tension and Affect during Interview." *British Journal of Psychology* 46 (1955):53–63.

————. "Speech Breathing Activity and Content in Psychiatric Interview." *British Journal of Medical Psychology* 24 (1956):35–48.

————. "Speech Analysis and Mental Processes." *Language and Speech* 1 (1958):59–75.

Haggard, E. A., and K. S. Isaacs. "Micromomentary Facial Expressions as Indicators of Ego Mechanisms in Psychotherapy." In *Methods of Research in Psychotherapy,* edited by L. Gottschalk and A. Auerbach. New York: Appleton-Century-Crofts, 1966.

Haiman, F. S. "An Experimental Study of the Effects of Ethos in Public Speaking." *Speech Monographs* 19 (1949):190–202.

Hall, E. T. *The Silent Language.* New York: Fawcett Publications, 1959.

————. *The Hidden Dimension.* New York: Doubleday & Co., 1966.

Hall, E. T., and M. Hall. "The Sounds of Silence." *Playboy Magazine,* June 1971. Reprinted in *Communicating Interpersonally,* edited by R. Wayne Pace et al. Columbus, Ohio: Charles E. Merrill, 1973.

Halpin, Andrew. *Theory and Research in Administration.* New York: Macmillan, 1966.

Harms, L. S. "Listener Judgments of Status Cues in Speech." *Quarterly Journal of Speech* 47 (1961):164–68.

Harrison, Randall. "Nonverbal Communication: Explorations into Time, Space, Action, and Object." In *Dimensions in Communication,* edited by J. Campbell and H. Helper. Belmont, Calif.: Wadsworth Co., 1970.

————. "Nonverbal Behavior: An Approach to Human Communication." In *Approaches to Human Communication,* edited by R. Budd and B. Ruben. New York: Spartan Books, 1972.

Hearn, G. "Leadership and the Spatial Factor in Small Groups." *Journal of Abnormal and Social Psychology* 54 (1957):269–72.

Hess, E. H. "Attitudes and Pupil Size." *Scientific American* 211 (1965):46–54.

————. "Pupillometric Assessment." In *Research in Psychotherapy,* edited by J. M. Shlien. Washington, D.C.: American Psychological Association, 1968.

Hess, E. H., and J. M. Polt. "Changes in Pupil Size as a Measure of Taste Difference." *Perceptual and Motor Skills* 23 (1966):451–55.

Hess, E. H., A. Seltzes, and J. Schlien. "Pupil Response of Hetero- and Homosexual Males to Pictures of Men and Women: A Pilot Study." *Journal of Abnormal Psychology* 70 (1965):165–68.

Hewes, G. W. "The Anthropology of Posture." *Scientific American* 196 (1957):123–32.

Hoult, R. "Experimental Measurement of Clothing as a Factor in Some Social Ratings of Selected American Men." *American Sociological Review* 19 (1954):324–28.

Johnson, J. D. "Effects of Spatial Elements of Physical Structure on Organizational Communication." Paper presented to the Organizational Communication Division of the Speech Communication Association, Boston, November, 1987.

Jones, Edward. "What It's Like to be a Black Manager." *Harvard Business Review* 51 (July–August 1973):108–16.

Jourard, S. M. "An Exploratory Study of Body-Accessibility." *British Journal of Social and Clinical Psychology* 5 (1966):221–31.

Kasl, S. V., and G. F. Mahl. "The Relationship of Disturbances and Hesitations in Spontaneous Speech to Anxiety." *Journal of Personality and Social Psychology* 1 (1965):425–33.

Keltner, John. *Interpersonal Speech-Communication.* Belmont, Calif.: Wadsworth Co., 1970.

Klinger, H. N. "The Effects of Stuttering on Audience Listening Comprehension." Ph.D. dissertation, New York University, 1959.

Knapp, Mark. "The Role of Nonverbal Communication in the Classroom." *Theory into Practice* 10 (1971):243–49.

———. *Nonverbal Communication in Human Interaction.* 2d ed. New York: Holt, Rinehart, & Winston, 1978.

Kramer, E. "Judgment of Personal Characteristics and Emotions from Nonverbal Properties." *Psychology Bulletin* 60 (1963):408–20.

Little, K. B. "Personal Space." *Journal of Experimental and Social Psychology* 1 (1965):237–47.

Longfellow, L. A. "Body Talk: The Game of Feeling and Expression." *Psychology Today* 4 (1970): 45–54.

McCroskey, James, C. Larson, and M. Knapp. *An Introduction to Interpersonal Communication.* Englewood Cliffs, N.J.: Prentice-Hall, 1971.

Mahl, G. F. "Disturbances and Silences in the Patient's Speech in Psychotherapy." *Journal of Abnormal and Social Psychology* 53 (1956):1–15.

———. "Exploring Emotional States by Content Analysis." In *Trends in Content Analysis,* edited by I. Pool. Urbana: University of Illinois Press, 1959.

———. "Measures of Two Expressive Aspects of a Patient's Speech in Two Psychotherapeutic Interviews." In *Comparative Psycholinguistic Analysis of Two Psychotherapeutic Interviews,* edited by L. A. Gottschalk. New York: International Universities Press, 1961.

———. "The Expression of Emotions on the Lexical and Linguistic Levels." In *Expressions of the Emotions in Man,* edited by P. Knapp. New York: International Universities Press, 1963.

———. "Some Observations About Research on Vocal Behavior." *Disorders of Communication* 42 (1964):466–83.

Manthei, Joan. "Correlation of Manifest Anxiety and Pausing Behavior." Mimeographed handout, Purdue University, 1970.

Maslow, A., and N. Mintz. "Effects of Esthetic Surroundings." *Journal of Psychology* 41 (1956): 247–54.

Mehrabian, A. "Communication Without Words." *Psychology Today* 2 (1968):52–55.

———. *Silent Messages.* Belmont, Calif.: Wadsworth Co., 1971.

Mills, J., and E. Aronson. "Opinion Change as a Function of the Communicator's Attractiveness and Desire to Influence." *Journal of Personality and Social Psychology* 1 (1965):73–77.

Molloy, John T. *Dress for Success.* New York: Warner Books, 1976.

———. *The Woman's Dress for Success Book.* Chicago: Follett Publishing Company, 1977.

Nerbonne, G. P. "The Identification of Speaker Characteristics on the Basis of Aural Cues." Ph.D. dissertation, Michigan State University, 1967.

Orr, David et al. "Trainability of Listening Comprehension of Speeded Discourse." *Journal of Educational Psychology* 56 (1965):148–56.

———. "The Effect of Listening Aids on the Comprehension of Time-Compressed Speech." *Journal of Communication* 17 (1967):223–27.

Osmond, H. "Function as the Basis of Psychiatric Ward Design." *Mental Hospitals* 8 (1957):23–32.

———. "The Relationship between Architect and Psychiatrist." In *Psychiatric Architecture,* edited by C. Goshen. Washington, D.C.: American Psychiatric Association, 1959.

Porter, George W. "Nonverbal Communications." *Training and Development Journal,* June 1969: 3–8. Reprinted in *Contemporary Readings in Organizational Behavior,* edited by F. Luthans. New York: McGraw-Hill Book Co., 1972.

Pye, R. "Effect of Telecommunications on the Location of Office Employment." *OMEGA* (1976): 289–300.

———. "Office Location and the Cost of Maintaining Contact." *Environment and Planning* 9 (1977): 149–68.

Reece, M., and R. Whitman. "Expressive Movements, Warmth, and Verbal Reinforcement." *Journal of Abnormal and Social Psychology* 64 (1962):234–36.

Remland, Martin. "Developing Leadership Skills in Nonverbal Communication: A Situational Perspective." *Journal of Business Communication* 3 (1981):17–29.

Rosenfeld, H. "Instrumental Affiliative Functions of Facial and Gestural Expressions." *Journal of Personality and Social Psychology* 4 (1966):65–72.

Rosenfeld, L. *Human Interaction in the Small Group Setting.* Columbus, Ohio: Charles E. Merrill, 1973.

Ruesch, J., and W. Kees. *Nonverbal Communication.* Berkeley: University of California Press, 1956.

Russell, S. P. *The Three Bears.* Racine, Wis.: Western Publishing Co., 1968.

Sheldon, W. H. *The Varieties of Human Physique.* New York: Harper & Row, 1940.

———. *The Varieties of Temperament.* New York: Harper & Row, 1942.

———. *Atlas of Man: A Guide for Somatyping the Adult Male at All Ages.* New York: Harper & Row, 1954.

Singer, J. E. "The Use of Manipulative Strategies, Machiavellianism, and Attractiveness." *Sociometry* 27 (1964):128–51.

Smith, Arthur. *Transracial Communication.* Englewood Cliffs, N.J.: Prentice-Hall, 1973.

Sommer, R. *Personal Space.* Englewood Cliffs, N.J.: Prentice-Hall, 1969.

Spitz, R. "Hospitalism: Genesis of Psychiatric Conditions in Early Childhood." *Psychoanalytic Study of the Child* 1 (1945):53–74.

Starkweather, J. A. "The Communication Value of Content-Free Speech." *American Journal of Psychology* 69 (1956):121–23.

Stewart, John, ed. *Bridges Not Walls.* Reading, Mass.: Addison-Wesley, 1973.

Strodtbeck, F., and L. Hook. "The Social Dimensions of a Twelve-Man Jury Table." *Sociometry* 24 (1961):397–415.

Stull, James, and John Baird. "Developing Cultural Awareness." A training program developed for Hewlett-Packard, 1981.

Sundstrom, Eric, R. Burt, and D. Kamp. "Privacy at Work: Architectural Correlates of Job Satisfaction and Job Performance." *Academy of Management Journal* 23 (1980):101–17.

Thorngren, B. "How Do Contact Systems Affect Regional Involvement?" *Environment and Planning* 2 (1970):409–27.

Trager, G. L. "Paralanguage: A First Approximation." *Studies in Linguistics* 13 (1958):1–12.

Utzinger, V. A. "An Experimental Study of the Effects of Verbal Fluency Upon the Listener." Ph.D. dissertation, University of Southern California, 1952.

Wells, W., and B. Siegel. "Stereotyped Somatypes." *Psychological Reports* 8 (1961):77–78.

Wenburg, John, and William Wilmot. *The Personal Communication Process.* New York: John Wiley & Sons, 1973.

Whyte, W. F. "The Social Structure of the Restaurant." *American Journal of Sociology* 54 (1949): 302–8.

Widgery, R. N., and B. Webster. "The Effects of Physical Attractiveness Upon Perceived Initial Credibility." *Michigan Speech Association Journal* 4 (1969).

Wiio, Osmo. "Time and Information—Intercultural Aspects of Human Communication." Paper presented to the World Communication Conference, Ohio University, 1979.

Williams, J. L. "Personal Space and Its Relation to Extroversion-Introversion." M. A. thesis, University of Alberta, 1963.

Wynne-Edwards, V. C. *Animal Dispersion in Relation to Social Behavior.* Edinburgh: Oliver & Boyd, 1962.

Young, Michael G. "The Human Touch: Who Needs It?" In *Bridges Not Walls,* edited by John Steward. Reading, Mass.: Addison-Wesley Co., 1973.

Zimbardo, P. G., G. Mahl, and J. Barnard. "The Measurement of Speech Disturbance in Anxious Children." *Journal of Speech and Hearing Disorders* 28 (1963):362–70.

PART THREE
INTERACTION FORMATS OF ORGANIZATIONAL COMMUNICATION

Chapter 6   identifies and describes the major types and purposes of dyadic organizational communication.

Chapter 7   identifies and describes key variables affecting small-group organizational communication and its effectiveness.

Chapter 8   describes and illustrates the major types and purposes of both public organizational communication activities and training.

6

DYADIC ORGANIZATIONAL COMMUNICATION

The telephone rang. It was the boss, "Frank, I want to see you in my office at 2:00 P.M. today!" As Frank hung up the phone, his hands began to tremble. "What did I do now? Where did I go wrong? How can I get out of this?" His stomach churned, his heart began to beat faster, and he started to sweat under his arms. For the next few hours, he could do no work, could eat no lunch, and could only feel helpless. "What could he possibly want from me? Where did I go wrong?" His thoughts drifted. Finally, at five minutes before two, he left for the boss's office. As he entered the large room, walked over to the boss, and extended his hand, the boss turned to him, smiled, slapped his back, and said, "Congratulations, Frank, that report you wrote last week was right on the money! We got the contract, and you're getting a fat raise. Nice job!" Frank fainted.

The boss-subordinate transaction is probably the most common communicative situation within a work organization. Research shows that the quantity and quality of such communication plays a most significant role in employee satisfaction. Could the transaction just described have been improved? Could the boss have given Frank more information on the phone to allay his fears? If we asked the boss for his evaluation of the situation, he would probably say, "I did a good job of communication. After all, I gave Frank a stroke. I recognized his good work." And if we asked Frank, he would tell us, "The boss likes to scare us. He likes to catch us off guard." If we asked Frank's secretary, she might say, "Frank is afraid of most people, especially of his boss, who likes to play games with his employees." As we will see, a number of variables affect such transactions, including the perception each communicator has of the other, their past experiences both with each other and in other situations, the nature of their relationship, the similarity of their backgrounds, the amount of trust each has in the other, the skills each employs in creating and exchanging messages, and even the total personality of each.

Thus far in the book, we have examined the organization and the process of creating and exchanging verbal and nonverbal messages within an organization. In the next three chapters we will study the major organizational relationships which promote the creation and exchange of these messages. In chapter 6, we focus on the two-party relationship—the dyad. In chapters 7 and 8, we look at small-group and public organizational communication. The specific objectives in this chapter are the following:

1. To describe the ingredients in successful dyadic relationships
2. To describe and summarize significant research on dyadic organizational communication, particularly as related to the boss-subordinate relationship
3. To describe ways of handling interpersonal conflict in organizations
4. To list and describe several techniques that may improve listening abilities of bosses and subordinates
5. To list and describe the steps necessary for implementing the following organizational techniques:
   a. job expectation technique (JET)
   b. management by objectives (MBO)
   c. managing up
   d. performance appraisal
6. To describe and illustrate the following organizational transactions:
   a. games commonly played in an organization, specifying the transactions, roles, and payoffs involved
   b. methods to stop game playing and improve interpersonal relationships
7. To describe and illustrate techniques for managing stress in organizational relations

Successful Dyadic Relationships

McCroskey once described organizational communication as "hot talk in cool buildings." In a speech some have described as "revolutionary for a corporate leader," Roger D'Aprix told an audience of corporate communicators that we must be honest, trusting, and loving in our organizational relationships. By "love" D'Aprix meant showing employees and co-workers that they have value and dignity and that you care for them: "You don't have to like them, but you do have to show them you care for them." How paradoxical it is that most of us would rather choke than share such love in an organization even though every one of us personally needs and responds to love.

Carl Rogers said that effective interpersonal relationships occur when both parties fulfill the following conditions:

1. Encounter each other personally, meeting on a person-to-person basis.
2. Empathize accurately with each other's private world and communicate that understanding significantly to each other.
3. Regard each other warmly and positively despite the particular behavior of either party at a given moment.
4. Regard each other positively and unconditionally, without evaluation or reservation.
5. Perceive the mutually experienced genuineness, acceptance, and empathy of each for the other.
6. Perceive that a mutually maintained open and supportive climate reduces the tendency to distort meaning.
7. Exhibit trustful behavior while at the same time reinforce feelings of security about each other.

Pace and colleagues (1974) developed a set of predictive propositions about interpersonal relationships based upon Rogers's work and added the following two conditions:

1. Accept responsibility for misunderstandings and seek actively to create overlapping meanings and perceptions.
2. Seek to accomplish the goals of interpersonal interaction (mutual satisfaction, self-confirmation, confirmation of the physical environment, desired change, and productivity).

Pace and Boren (1973) proposed the following ways to improve interpersonal relationships. They stated that interpersonal relationships tend to improve when both parties observe these standards:

1. Develop a direct personal encounter with each other by communicating feelings directly.
2. Communicate an accurate empathic understanding of each other's private world through self-disclosure.
3. Communicate a warm, positive understanding of each other through helpful styles of listening and responding.
4. Communicate genuineness toward and acceptance of each other by expressing acceptance verbally and nonverbally.
5. Communicate an outgoing, unconditional, positive regard for each other through nonevaluative responses.
6. Communicate an open and supportive climate through constructive confrontation.
7. Communicate to create overlapping meaning by negotiating for meaning and giving relevant responses.

In the foregoing statements and propositions of Rogers and Pace, one common element seems to be that a *supportive* climate must exist in order for effective interpersonal relationships to be maintained and improved. What is a supportive climate? Likert (1961) concluded that successful superiors are those who are perceived by their subordinates as follows:

> . . . supportive, friendly, and helpful rather than hostile. He is kind but firm, never threatening, genuinely interested in the well-being of subordinates and endeavors to treat people in a sensitive, considerate way. He is just, if not generous. He endeavors to serve the best interests of his employees as well as of the company.

> . . . He shows confidence in the integrity, ability, and motivations of subordinates rather than suspicion and distrust.

> . . . His confidence in subordinates leads him to have high expectations as to their level of performance. With confidence that he will not be disappointed, he expects much, not little.

At about the same time that Likert defined supportive climates, Jack Gibb was concluding eight years of research in interpersonal relationships in small group discussion. Gibb proposed two communication climates—defensive and supportive—and suggested that each can be identified by certain behaviors. According to Gibb, a *defensive climate* has the following characteristics:

1. *Evaluation* Passing judgment; blaming; praising; questioning standards, values, and motives.

2. *Control* Trying to do something to another; attempting to change an attitude or a behavior of another.
3. *Strategy* Manipulating and tricking others.
4. *Neutrality* Expressing lack of concern for another's welfare.
5. *Superiority* Communicating an attitude of superiority in position, wealth, intellectual ability, and physical characteristics; arousing feelings of inadequacy in others.
6. *Certainty* Being dogmatic; needing to be right; wanting to win.

A *supportive climate* has these characteristics:

1. *Description* Being nonjudgmental; asking questions for information; presenting feelings, events, perceptions, or processes without calling for or implying change for the receiver.
2. *Problem Orientation* Defining mutual problems and seeking solutions without inhibiting the receiver's goals, decisions, and progress.
3. *Spontaneity* Being free of deception; having no hidden motives; being honest and straightforward.
4. *Equality* Having mutual trust and respect; engaging in participative planning without influence of power, status, or appearance.
5. *Empathy* Respecting the worth of the listener; identifying, sharing, and accepting his or her problems, feelings, and values.
6. *Provisionalism* Being willing to experiment with one's own behavior, attitudes, and ideas.

The importance of a supportive climate in organizational communication is underscored by Redding: *"The 'climate' of the organization is more crucial than are communication skills or techniques (taken by themselves) in creating an effective organization."* Schneider and Bartlett also put *managerial supportiveness* first in a list of factors influencing organizational climate. These findings appear to be consistent with Skinner's conclusion that positive reinforcement helps develop desired responses; it does not merely reduce the chances of an undesired response. Supporting Skinner's position, Nord claims that positive reinforcement "is apt to produce favorable rather than unfavorable 'side effects' on organizational relationships."

The philosophy of establishing a climate where supportive dyadic relationships can thrive underlies much of the writing of many current organizational behavioral scientists, as the discussion that follows will show.

Dyadic Organizational Research

Research in dyadic organizational communication stems from the human relations, group dynamics, and motivational schools of industrial psychology and administrative science. The basic tenet is that an individual's cognitive and affective perceptions of an organization influence that person's behavior in the organization. Basic issues involve perceptions of organizational communication sources: Are people satisfied with superiors, co-workers, and subordinates as information sources? Are these sources trusted? Are they open? Are they credible? Other issues involve perceptions of information available to different organizational members: Is the important information received from different sources adequate? Is

The boss-subordinate transaction is probably the most common communicative situation within a work organization.

the information useful? Is it timely? Is there sufficient feedback on information sent to various sources? With respect to the issue of recognition and caring: How much input into their boss's decisions do members have? Are members supported and rewarded for their efforts? Are members listened to with empathy?

Research on relationships has focused on the perceived characteristics of the partners in a relationship. The perceptions of openness, honesty, trustworthiness, influence, understanding, and competence were among the variables studied. Much of the research concentrated on the superior-subordinate relationship, while some attention was given to peer relationships and relationships in general.

One tradition of relationships research involves the study of the degree of understanding superiors and subordinates have of the responsibilities, requirements, and problems inherent in each other's job. Browne and Nietzel investigated the ratings of organization members of the amount of responsibility, authority, and delegation at their own level and at the level of their immediate superiors and subordinates. Discrepancies between the estimates of superiors and subordinates of each others' jobs were used to infer the degree of ineffective communication. The results indicate that agreement between levels about responsibility, authority, and delegation is positively related to morale: superiors and subordinates whose perceptions of each others' jobs are in agreement evidence higher morale than do those whose perceptions are different.

Read studied the degree of understanding superiors have of the job-related problems faced by their subordinates as a measure of upward communication. This understanding was measured in relation to the perceived trustworthiness and influence of the superior from the subordinate's perspective and the subordinate's mobility aspiration. Read found that the accuracy of upward communication is greatest under conditions of high trust, but that high subordinate mobility aspiration and high perceived superior influence negatively affect trust and communication. This indicates that ambitious employees are likely to withhold information about job problems from their superiors, particularly when the superiors' motives and intentions are suspect and their perceived ability to influence an employee's advancement is great.

In a related study, Maier, Hoffman, and Read investigated agreement about job problems, trust of superior, and subordinate mobility aspiration among superiors who had previously held a subordinate's job and those who had not. Although one might expect a superior having prior experience with a subordinate's job would be more familiar with the job problems, the results replicate findings of Read's study. While trust is positively related to accuracy, mobility aspirations are negatively related, even among superiors and subordinates with similar job experiences.

Athnassiades (1973) found that the degree of distortion in upward flowing messages depends on subordinates' feelings of insecurity and their desire for promotion. A subordinate is likely to distort information when he or she has a high need to achieve; subordinates are less likely to distort when they have high job security.

These findings appear to mean that superiors fail to understand the problems faced at lower levels because employees are ambitious, suspicious, and tend to cover up these problems. Krivonos summarized the findings of the upward communication literature as follows:

1. Subordinates tend to distort information upward in a manner that pleases their superiors.
2. Subordinates tend to tell their superiors what they want them to know.
3. Subordinates tend to tell their superiors what they think they want to hear.
4. Subordinates tend to tell their superiors information that reflects favorably on themselves and/or does not reflect negatively on themselves.

One explanation for these findings, known as the "Pelz effect," is that a superior's influence over subordinates is related to the degree to which subordinates perceive that their boss has influence with his or her superior. (Pelz, 1952)

Another explanation for these findings is that superiors are not perceived as being receptive to this information, and the lack of openness results in low trust and poor communication. This relationship becomes even stronger for ambitious employees who are dependent on a superior for advancement. Roberts and O'Reilly (1974) found that *trust* in one's superior is the most important facilitator of open, upward-directed communication. Influence of the superior and mobility aspiration of the subordinate are not as strongly related to upward communication behavior as is trust.

Research on the degree of perceived openness of relationships with superiors constitutes another strong tradition in this area. Heron was among the first to stress the need for upward initiation of messages in an organization and to advise management that communication is a joint process.

Coch and French conducted a landmark field experiment on the effect of participation and group processes. They established conditions under which employees had varying levels of prior involvement in the process of changing to a new method of production. Conditions of involvement varied: from work group participation in planning and approval of change, to work group approval of preplanned change, to the announcement of change with no work group approval. The results dramatically demonstrated that learning and production rates for a new process are highest under conditions of participation and approval.

A coherent program of research on the relationships between communication and supervision was conducted at Purdue University under the direction of W. Charles Redding. Much of this research has direct implication for the issue of openness in an organization, as the following general findings indicate:

1. A positive attitude toward communication and skill as a communicator are positively related to the quality of supervision.
2. Willingness to receive communication, ability to listen, and responsiveness to input are positively related to the quality of supervision.
3. Better supervisors tend to be solicitous rather than authoritative in their communication.
4. Sensitivity to employee feelings and needs is positively related to the quality of supervision.
5. Willingness to share information, to give advance notice of changes, and to explain the reasons for policy are positively related to the quality of supervision.

The issues of trust, understanding, openness, and responsiveness in organizational relationships were treated as a unified concept of communication climate in recent research as discussed in chapter 3.

Dennis developed an item pool representing five components of communication climate: (1) supportiveness of superior-subordinate relationships, (2) quality of downward communication, (3) openness of superior-subordinate relationships, (4) quality and influence of upward communication, and (5) reliability of information from subordinates and peers.

The items relating to the quality of boss-subordinate relationships in Dennis's inventory follow:

1. Your superior makes you feel free to talk with him or her.
2. Your superior really understands your job problems.
3. Your superior encourages you to let him or her know when things are going wrong on the job.
4. Your superior makes it easy for you to do your best work.
5. Your superior expresses his or her confidence in your ability to perform the job.
6. Your superior encourages you to bring new information to his or her attention, even when the new information may be bad news.
7. Your superior makes you feel that things you tell him or her are really important.
8. Your superior is willing to tolerate arguments and to give a fair hearing to all points of view.
9. Your superior has your best interests in mind when talking to his or her bosses.
10. Your superior is a really competent, expert manager.

11. Your superior listens to you when you tell him or her about things that bother you.
12. It is safe to say what you are really thinking to your superior.
13. Your superior is frank and candid with you.
14. You can sound off about job frustration to your superior.
15. You can tell your superior about the way you feel he or she manages your work group.
16. You are free to tell your superior that you disagree with him or her.

Roberts and O'Reilly (1974) constructed a climate-type instrument based on the concepts advanced by Read. The measure contained factors relating to trust, influence, mobility, desire for interaction, directionality of contact, and the accuracy, summarization, amount, and overload of information. They correlated responses to these factors with organizational variables, such as job satisfaction, leadership consideration, organizational competence, and commitment. Correlation of overall job satisfaction was significantly positive with all of the communication items except for those dealing with the amount of upward communication and overload, where correlation was negative. In leadership style, positive correlation of the consideration dimension with trust, influence, mobility, desire for interaction, and amount of information received was significant. Perceived organizational competence correlated significantly and positively with trust, influence, mobility, desire for interaction, and accuracy of information received, and correlation of organizational commitment with these variables and amount of downward communication was also positive.

Thus, it is evident that perceptions of the quality of relationships and communication are highly related to factors central to organizational life. Climate measures of trust, supportiveness, openness, and influence have been shown to be correlated with perceptions of leadership, decision making, and organization as a whole.

Recent research on relationships has been concerned with the specific perceptions subordinates have of their superiors, with a great deal of attention being paid to the notion of credibility of supervisors. Richetto found that perceived credibility (expertness, trustworthiness, intent, and sociability) is the distinguishing characteristic of those sources most often turned to for task, political, and social information. Credibility is a more important factor than organizational status for Richetto's respondents, even for job-related topics.

Falcione (1974) conducted a factor analytical study of semantic differential items relating to supervisory credibility. Four factors accounted for 55 percent of the total variance and consisted of safety (honest, just, ethical, fair); competence (experienced, informed); extroversion (aggressive, active); and stability (calm, poised). In a later study, Falcione (1975) found that the safety factor is the most reliable of the four factors for predicting satisfaction with supervision.

In another investigation of specific perceptions of supervisors, Daly, McCroskey, and Falcione studied the construct of homophily, or perceived similarity. This is a multidimensional construct made up of perceived similarity in attitude, background, appearance, and values. In this study, the additional dimensions of perceived similarity of job type and personality were included with measures of satisfaction with supervision. This study indicated that attitude and value homophily are the most reliable predictors of satisfaction with supervision.

In a 1984 study, Tamayo and Lustig tried to identify the types of messages used by supervisors that lead to subordinates' satisfaction with both their supervisors and their jobs.

Although they only found limited support linking supervisory message behavior to job satisfaction, they found considerable support showing a relationship between the type of messages used by supervisors and subordinate satisfaction with the supervisor. Using Huseman, et al's message classification system (1978), they found that *rationales* (i.e., justifications or reasons for work or ideas) and *positive expressions* (i.e., casual, non-work related "small talk") had a major impact on satisfaction with the supervisor. According to the researchers, "the supervisor who had the ability to provide work-related justifications and nonwork-related nurturance was the person who provided the greatest degree of satisfaction to the supervisees."

In sum, perceptions of the relationships and the attributes of the members constituting the relationships are potent factors in an individual's evaluation of the job and the organization. These perceptions involve the degree of trust, openness, and influence in the relationship, as well as the credibility and similarity of the other member of the relationship. Related to these perceptions are evaluation of the quality of communication and perception of the organization as a whole. Perceptions of communication, particularly of specific topics of information in the organization, are important to an individual's feeling of involvement and commitment to an organization.

My own research shows that *the most important contributor to job satisfaction is the quality of the relationship employees have with their supervisors.* Most central to the establishment of high-quality boss-subordinate interpersonal relationships are the following:

1. A boss who praises subordinates
2. A boss who understands a subordinate's job
3. A boss who can be trusted
4. A boss who is warm and friendly
5. A boss who is honest
6. A boss with whom subordinates are free to disagree

As you review these items, you may find the basis for what Roger D'Aprix earlier called organizational love—behaviors demonstrating that people care for each other.

Kelly, in an extensive review of the literature on superior-subordinate communicative relationships, has developed five propositions about the nature of these relationships.

1. The type of messages that characterize the communication between a superior and a subordinate will influence their satisfaction with that relationship. As Jablin has found out, subordinates prefer messages that confirm, disagree with, or accede to their own positions rather than those that repudiate and disconfirm.
2. The satisfaction of subordinate and superior with their relationship will be affected by one another's communication style. Subordinates are more satisfied when their supervisors are friendly and attentive rather than dominating.
3. Subordinates differentiate managerial styles by the communicative behavior of superiors. Subordinates are particularly able to differentiate democratic, laissez-faire, and autocratic supervisors by their specific communicative behaviors.
4. The quality of communication between superiors and subordinates is more important than the quantity of messages exchanged in determining the degree of satisfaction with the relationship. The type of message and the role of the other person with whom you communicate, both as measures of quality, are more important than the number of messages exchanged.

The most important contributor to job satisfaction is the quality of the relationship employees have with their supervisors.

5. Feelings of trust or distrust have a significant impact on the nature of the superior-subordinate communicative relationship. As we have stated before, subordinates are more satisfied with supervisors whom they trust.

Jablin has found that certain structural variables may also affect the nature of the superior-subordinate relationship. He concluded that subordinates in the lowest levels of their organizational hierarchies perceive significantly less openness in superior-subordinate communication than do subordinates at the highest levels of their hierarchies. He also found a trend toward greater perceived openness in smaller organizations, perhaps due to the greater opportunities for interaction.

Organizational Implications for Dyadic Research

The previously mentioned findings and my own cited earlier raise some important issues for organizations. We already know that information from distant sources is perceived as less timely than information received from the grapevine in most organizations, and the transmission of information from top management often lags behind the transmission of rumors. To overcome this problem, sources and channels must be selected that can either transmit information faster than rumors or provide believable information to counter rumors.

Greater use of supervisors and co-workers as sources of information and influence may be a partial solution. These sources have the greatest ability to influence employees through group pressure, and the supervisor is in the best position to mobilize this pressure. Supervisors may not be taking full advantage of their relationship, perhaps because of a lack of awareness or skills. Though supervisors are trusted, they are not perceived as being open to disagreement or bad news, or willing to recognize the achievements of their subordinates. There is a necessary foundation of trust, but it is not being used to strengthen the relationship. If supervisors are made aware of the possibilities of their relationships and trained to make the most of these possibilities, they may be able to exert greater direct influence and to mobilize peer influence.

A common response to conflict in the work group is to bring in a higher authority to settle the dispute. While this may save wear and tear on immediate relationships, it can also lead to dissatisfaction. The higher authority may not have the influence of a strong relationship and may fall back on the use of formal rules and the power to sanction behavior. This may solve the immediate problem, but it can also irritate employees and reinforce a view of management as "heavy-handed." A supervisor who is skilled in handling conflict on a personal basis may avoid these negative outcomes without damaging the superior-subordinate relationship.

Before a supervisor can resolve conflict, however, he or she must understand exactly what the conflict is, along with its causes and context. Filley (1975), drawing upon the work of Pondy (1967, 1969), has suggested that conflict is a process involving two or more parties that follows a six-step process:

1. *Antecedent Conditions* are the characteristics of a situation that generally lead to conflict, although they may be present in the absence of conflict as well.
2. *Perceived Conflict* is a logically and impersonally recognized set of conditions that are conflictive to the parties.
3. *Felt Conflict* is a personalized conflict relationship, expressed in feelings of threat, hostility, fear, or mistrust.
4. *Manifest Behavior* is the resulting action—aggression, competition, debate, or problem solving.
5. *Conflict Resolution* or suppression seeks to bring the conflict to an end either through agreement among all parties or the defeat of one.
6. *Resolution Aftermath* comprises the consequences of the conflict.

Filley has shown that conflict is more likely to occur when the following occur: ambiguous jurisdictions (i.e., unclear role definitions); conflict of interest (i.e., one party wins when the other loses); communication barriers (especially those of time and space); dependence of one party (i.e., one party depends on another for resources or task performance, etc.); differentiation in organization (i.e., scalar, functional, or labor divisions); association of the parties (i.e., prior informal and formal relations); need for consensus (i.e., all parties must agree on a decision); behavior regulations (i.e., rules, policies, standardized procedures); and unresolved prior conflict.

Bechard (1967) has suggested a "confrontation meeting" as a means of possibly resolving conflict among individuals and groups or between groups. The steps follow:

1. *Climate Setting.* The first step involves setting the ground rules that will be used in the confrontation meeting. The manager shares with the participants the need for open discussion of issues and problems and outlines the broad goals he or she has for the meeting.

2. *Information Collecting.* Small groups are formed from people in different functional areas and managerial levels. It is stipulated that bosses and subordinates not be in the same work group. Top management generally meets as a separate group. Usually it is preferable to use a diagonal slice from the organization, that is, individuals representing different functional areas and different levels of the organization. The groups work for about an hour on the task of identifying problems, and a recorder lists the results of the discussion.

3. *Information Sharing.* Reporters from each small group place that group's findings on pieces of newsprint that are taped to the wall. The total list of items is categorized and reported to the entire group. At this point, the numerous problems that have been identified are categorized into basic problem areas so that they can be worked upon and problem solutions developed.

4. *Priority Setting and Action Planning.* In a brief general session, the meeting leader goes through the list of items, and the participants then form functional work teams reflecting the organization's structure. Each group is headed by the top manager in the group, and members are charged with these tasks: (1) to identify the problems related to their area and develop a list of priorities for these problems, (2) to identify problems and priority issues for top management, and (3) to determine action plans for solving these problems, giving first consideration to highest-priority items.

5. *Follow-up by Top Team.* The top management team meets after the groups have completed step 4 to review the first action steps and evolve a set of follow-up action plans, which are then communicated to the rest of the group within the next few days.

6. *Progress Review.* Follow-up meetings with the total management group are held periodically, generally beginning four to six weeks after the initial meeting to review the outcome of action plans resulting from the confrontation meeting. Top management plays an important part here by showing that it is committed to following up on problems that are identified in the confrontation meeting.

We will discuss the nature and resolution of conflict in more detail in chapter 7 when we focus on small-group communication patterns.

Another issue involves follow-up, or the responsiveness of individuals to information sent to them. Perceived lack of follow-up can lead to a lack of initiative on the part of employees and a management that is relatively uninformed about conditions at lower levels. There may be many reasons for a lack of follow-up, each with different implications for improvement.

A lack of follow-up may be unintentional, due to a lack of awareness, overload, excessive filtering at intermediate levels, or a lack of effective mechanisms to provide direct response. Where poor follow-up is unintentional, a number of improvements in the communication system can be made that guarantee messages sent to higher levels receive direct consideration and response. Speak-up programs, suggestion systems, prior input into meeting agenda and direct memo policies can be combined with formal, mandated response systems that show employees their problems and suggestions are being considered.

Where poor follow-up is intentional, the most sophisticated and efficient communication systems conceivable will not be effective. If management really does not want to receive or respond to input, no formal system can improve the situation. I once had a consulting relationship with such an organization. Mechanism after mechanism had been introduced to improve follow-up, yet all had fallen into disuse. Management was not willing to respond, and the employees knew it. Only after a commitment to a policy of feedback and disclosure had been gained from management, did any follow-up system show improvement.

Is it necessary for top management to gain the trust and support of employees? Why not just use the influence of the supervisor to keep employees informed and cooperative and leave top management free to set long-range goals and coordinate the whole organization? Increasing the visibility of top management is a time-consuming process and one that may have only limited results. For most normal operational purposes, a highly trusted top management may not be considered necessary.

The problem with employee trust and support is that it doesn't appear to be necessary until it is needed. Top management is often perceived as being responsible for the overall performance of the system. Where factors threaten that overall performance and require a coordinated or extraordinary effort on the part of all employees, there is a limit to the ability of individual supervisors to generate this effort. Where top management is perceived as untrustworthy or distant, their ability to gain the cooperation of employees will be impaired. The need for employee cooperation may come at a time of crisis for the organization, when there is no time to spend building trust. Thus, the question is not whether employee support is worth the effort, it is whether top management feels that their organization is so secure that they can afford to do without trust.

We will next examine specific techniques of listening that can, if mastered, lead to a climate of improved trust.

Listening Techniques to Improve Superior-Subordinate Relations

As we have pointed out before, managers who are perceived by their subordinates as "good listeners" tend to have better relationships and are trusted more by their subordinates. Sperry Corporation, a true believer in the importance of listening, has conducted a multimillion-dollar campaign telling consumers and their customers that they "understand how important it is to listen." One of their more popular ads states:

> Good listeners think more broadly—because they hear and understand more facts and points of view. They make better innovators. Because listeners look at problems with fresh eyes, combine what they learn in more unlikely ways, they're more apt to hit upon truly startling ideas. Ultimately, good listeners attune themselves more closely to where the world is going—and the products, talents and techniques it needs to get there. That's the selfish reason Sperry's committed to listening. To lead, you need a lucid vision of the future.

According to Lyman Steil, Sperry's communication consultant, we spend 80 percent of our waking time communicating, and listening accounts for about half of this time. Steil also contends that our listening efficiency, as measured by the amount of material understood and remembered by subjects forty-eight hours after listening to a ten-minute message, is no better than 25 percent on the average. Sperry apparently has accepted Steil's conclusions and has trained almost half of its U.S. employees in listening techniques since 1979. Whether

Table 6.1 Lyman Steil's Ten Keys to Effective Listening (From Sperry Corporation Listening Program materials by Dr. Lyman K. Steil, Department of Rhetoric, University of Minnesota and Communication Development, Inc. for Sperry Corporation, copyright 1979. Reprinted by permission of Dr. Steil and Sperry Corporation.)

The Ten Keys	The Bad Listener	The Good Listener
1. Find areas of interest	Tunes out dry subjects	Seizes opportunities; asks "What's in it for me?"
2. Judge content, not delivery	Tunes out if delivery is poor	Judges content; skips over delivery errors
3. Hold your fire	Tends to enter into argument	Doesn't judge until comprehension is complete
4. Listen for ideas	Listens for facts	Listens for central themes
5. Be flexible	Takes intensive notes using only one system	Takes fewer notes; uses four or five different systems, depending on speaker
6. Work at listening	Shows no energy output; attention is faked	Works hard, exhibits active body state
7. Resist distractions	Distracted easily	Fights or avoids distractions; tolerates bad habits; knows how to concentrate
8. Exercise your mind	Resists difficult material; seeks light, recreational material	Uses heavier material as exercise for the mind
9. Keep your mind open	Reacts to emotional words	Interprets color words; does not get hung up on them
10. Capitalize on the fact that thought is faster than speech	Tends to daydream with slow speakers	Challenges, anticipates, mentally summarizes; weighs the evidence; listens between the lines to tone of voice

or not exposure to a short course in listening has improved Sperry's overall productivity remains to be seen, but over 300 corporations have now called upon Steil to help them work on listening problems they have.

Although the approach of Steil and others to listening seems to have gained popular acceptance in many large corporations, it is important to note that the research on listening is quite sparse and somewhat inconclusive on basic issues, such as What is listening? What are the behaviors of good versus bad listeners? What are the effects and/or correlates of good versus bad listening? Steil's summary of "keys" to good listening is presented in table 6.1, along with descriptions of good and bad listeners. We caution you, however—much more research is needed in the entire area before any firm conclusions about listening can be made. Are you listening?

The remainder of this chapter deals with how organizations can establish effective dyadic relations by clarifying employee roles, establishing measurable objectives, and "managing up." Unfortunately, many members of organizations remain dishonest in their dyadic relationships. Therefore, we will examine a taxonomy that helps identify certain patterns of organizational dishonesty and game playing. Finally, the chapter concludes with specifics about ways to reduce game playing and enhance interpersonal relationships.

Job Expectation Technique (JET)

Much stress and conflict can and often does occur between bosses and subordinates due to misunderstanding about what an employee's job is or should be. My own research shows that role ambiguity is a leading cause of employee dissatisfaction. The job expectation technique (JET) was developed to help reduce such role ambiguity; it can also be quite helpful when a new team is formed or when a new member joins a group.

According to Huse, the following steps are involved:

1. *Determination that such a process is feasible.* After a study to reveal role conflicts or role ambiguities has been made, all group members must agree to employ JET or the technique will be ineffective.
2. *Establishment of goals and purposes.* Since about three hours are needed to adequately define the job of just one employee, management must commit several days to define both the prescribed and discretionary roles for each member of the work group, including the top manager.
3. *Selection of a meeting place.* An off-site location is necessary to avoid interruptions.
4. *Definition of the perceived job expectations.* The person whose job is to be discussed first lists on a flip chart the duties and responsibilities of the job as he or she perceives them. All other members can add their input and perceptions to the list. An outside consultant facilitates the process.
5. *Completion of the job expectation analysis.* When consensus has been reached on the job role, the employee then writes a description of the job activities and distributes it to all other members in order to maximize understanding and agreement.
6. *Completion of the job expectation analysis for each job.* The five steps just described are followed for each member of the group. Usually the easiest job is analyzed first and the job of the top manager last.
7. *Periodic review and analysis.* Annual review of all jobs should be scheduled and conducted, particularly to orient new group members.

Although limited research on the effects of JET has been conducted, the technique tends to reduce role ambiguity and conflict. One important use of JET is in establishing goals in a management by objectives program.

Management by Objectives (MBO)

Management by objectives (MBO) is a system for clearly establishing worker goals and reviewing performance as it contributes to the overall effectiveness of the organization and the desired career path of workers. MBO enables workers to know what is expected of them, to know how well they have done in meeting their goals, and to receive proper coaching and counseling that relates their performance to appropriate career paths. Although some authorities criticize the system for stressing measurement, not allowing sufficient time for meeting goals, using a reward-punishment psychology, and emphasizing red tape and paperwork, others have shown that it can work quite well, especially when the technique is customized for an organization. Usually, competitiveness is minimized, training is emphasized, and the entire organization benefits from the process.

According to Huse, the steps involved in implementing MBO are these:

1. *Work group involvement.* Members of the work group jointly define both group and individual goals and tasks and establish action plans for meeting these goals. JET can be a useful technique in this step. Without such work group commitment at the beginning, MBO will likely fail when dyadic interactions between subordinates and superiors occur later.

2. *Joint manager-subordinate goal setting.* After the goals of the work group have been outlined, the duties and responsibilities of individual employees are examined with their supervisor. It is here that both parties need to be careful that the goals are clear, realistic, and consistent with the organization's ethics, morals, and directions. Because subordinates and supervisors have different roles in the organization, it is likely that they will, and probably should, perceive events and tasks in a different manner. Sussman believes this may be healthy for the organization, since it allows a variety of viewpoints to be presented. While I agree with Sussman's conclusion, I believe the organization's overall effectiveness will be impeded unless the worker and supervisor can *agree* on what the employee's desired job role *should* be.

3. *Establishment of action plans for goals.* The action plan should be a specific statement created jointly by the supervisor and subordinate of how the goals are to be implemented. Minimally, an action plan should state the following:
   a. objective(s)—a clear, concise statement of the gains for the individual, group, and organization financially or otherwise
   b. background—the factors leading to establishment of the action plan (marketing information, competitive situation, economic outlook, risks involved, assumptions made)
   c. strategy—specific procedures for accomplishing the objective(s)
   d. resources—staff, equipment, buildings, software, new systems, time, and money needed to accomplish the action plan
   e. checkpoints—key decision and review dates listed in chronological order
   f. financial analysis—both short-term and long-term indications of income, expenses, and net income due to the plan

4. *Establishment of criteria, or yardsticks, for success.* The subordinate and superior must agree on the criteria in order to determine whether the action plan is completed successfully. These criteria can be both qualitative and quantitative and are necessary to ensure that both parties have the same understanding of what is expected. *This is the most important step in the entire MBO process.*

5. *Review and recycle.* Periodic review between the manager and the subordinate should take place. Subordinates should review their progress and discuss achievements and obstacles. Managers should discuss work plans and objectives for the future. There should also be additional general discussion about future career goals, hopes and ambitions, and fears and concerns of the subordinate. Typical questions *employees* ask during a career discussion follow:
   a. How am I doing on this job?
   b. What should I be doing to improve my performance?
   c. Am I becoming obsolete in my functional area?
   d. Is another work style likely to be more effective?

e. What can I do off the job to increase my potential? What courses can I take? What reading can I do?

f. Is my area of interest what the company needs now? In the future? When? How long?

g. Is my career goal realistic? What is the most likely timing of position changes?

Typical questions managers ask during a counseling session follow:

h. What type of work interests you?

i. Do you have strong preferences for manager versus individual contributor work?

j. What do you view as your strengths in this work? (If reply is inconsistent with the demonstrated performance, try to reconcile.)

k. What additional work experience do you feel you need?

l. What type of assignment do you visualize next? How soon?

m. Whom do you view as your strongest competitor for the next position? How do you think you compare with him or her?

n. What do you consider the most likely selection criteria for this next position?

o. What do you propose to do to better yourself for this next position?

Individuals who choose career goals beyond their current level of expertise and experience require additional development by participation in either external or internal programs, courses, and workshops.

6. *Maintenance of records.* Some people believe that the preparation and passing on to third parties of documents specifying goals, criteria, priorities, and due dates limit honest communication between managers and employees. Nevertheless, many organizations do use the procedure. Regardless of who sees the documents, they usually contain the following information:

a. statement of work and educational background

b. significant accomplishments and personal contributions

c. career and development plans

d. assessment of performance of present position

e. statement about potential long-range and short-range growth capabilities

f. development plans for an individual's training, transfer, and education

g. recommendations

Although much of the evaluation research on MBO programs has been positive, it is still too early to draw firm conclusions about the long-term effectiveness of MBO. Extensive longitudinal studies need to be initiated before such judgment will be possible.

However, Stewart and Cash (1978) have provided us with a summary of what we do know about performance appraisal interviews.

1. Sometimes it is not so much what is said in an appraisal interview as how the interview is handled by the interviewer.

2. What an interviewer thinks about the interviewee, and vice versa, influences the climate of the interview.

3. The more an interviewer points out areas of needed improvement to an employee, the more threatened and therefore the more defensive the employee becomes.

4. The greater the threat the more negative is interviewee attitude toward the appraisal process.

5. An annual performance appraisal has little value in terms of actually improving the interviewee's on-the-job performance; appraisals should occur at least semiannually.
6. Separating money from job improvement seems to have a positive effect on the employee.
7. Subordinates perform best when asked to set their own goals.
8. Increased participation in the appraisal process tends to improve the employee/boss relationship.
9. The greater the criticism, the greater the anxiety.
10. Praise can create anxiety and defensiveness.
11. Interviewees in general seem to have no specific interviewing style preference.
12. A problem-solving style of interviewing creates the least anxiety and defensiveness.
13. Regardless of the style employed by the interviewer, criticism appears to be the key factor in creating defensiveness.
14. Interviewees accept and desire discussion of performance weaknesses.
15. Women rate achievements of other women less favorably than similar ones achieved by men unless evidence of outside recognition is available.
16. Male administrators tend to discriminate against women in promotions, development, and supervision.
17. Administrators tend to find males more acceptable for management positions than equally qualified females.
18. When raters evaluate performances using objective criteria, they rate (a) high-performing blacks and whites equally, (b) low-performing males and females the same, (c) high-performing females significantly higher than high-performing males, and (d) low-performing blacks significantly higher than low-performing whites.

Managing Up

Gabarro and Kotter have developed a theory they call "managing up." It states that good relations with your boss involve mutual dependence and require managers to manage their bosses as well as their subordinates. Their research has shown that few managers take time to manage their bosses. Gabarro and Kotter recommend that the best way to manage your boss is to make sure you understand both your boss and his or her context and yourself and your needs. With regard to *your boss*, you should ask:

1. What are your boss's most important *organizational* goals and objectives?
2. What are your boss's *personal* goals and objectives?
3. What are your boss's strengths?
4. What are your boss's weaknesses?
5. What is your boss's preferred style of working? (Does your boss prefer memos? formal meetings? phone calls? etc.)
6. Does your boss thrive on conflict or try to minimize it?

You should also ask certain questions about *yourself:*

7. What do you need the most from work? What are your organizational and personal goals/objectives?
8. What are your strengths and weaknesses?
9. What style of work do you prefer?

Table 6.2   Managing the Relationship with Your Boss

Make sure you understand your boss and his or her context, including:

Your boss's goals and objectives

The pressures on your boss

Your boss's strengths, weaknesses, blind spots

Your boss's preferred work style

Assess yourself and your needs, including:

Your own strengths and weaknesses

Your personal style

Your predisposition toward dependence on authority figures

Develop and maintain a relationship that:

Fits both your needs and styles

Is characterized by mutual expectations

Keeps your boss informed

Is based on dependability and honesty

Selectively uses your boss's time and resources

---

10. Do you enjoy conflict or try to minimize it?
11. What is your predisposition toward dependence on authority figures?

Once you have objectively analyzed yourself and your boss, you are ready to develop and maintain a relationship that fits your needs and style, is characterized by mutual expectations, keeps your boss informed, is based on dependability and honesty, and selectively uses your boss's time and resources.

Table 6.2 summarizes Gabarro and Kotter's theory of managing up. Although quite time consuming, this behavior is very legitimate and may be the most crucial aspect of a manager's job.

Using data collected from 700 managers from private sector and government organizations over a seven-year period, Downs and Conrad (1982) identified eleven specific communication behaviors that they believe define "being an effective subordinate." They are the following:

1. *Encode clear messages.* Write and speak clearly.
2. *Provide feedback.* Confirm understanding, respond freely.
3. *Communicate in a timely manner.* On-time, prompt, current.
4. *Be brief and concise.* Get to the point, don't waste time.
5. *Listen.* Pay attention, listen carefully.
6. *Be factual and thorough.* Research topic, avoid inference, use adequate detail, don't filter bad news.
7. *Ask questions.* Seek details and clarification.
8. *Check perceptions.* Paraphrase, repeat, restate.

9. *Anticipate superior's needs.* Avoid surprises and trivia while informing to prevent problems.
10. *Volunteer input.* Provide new ideas, recommendations, act as sounding board.
11. *Follow instructions.* Take guidance and direction, carry out orders, follow through.

If a subordinate uses as many of these communication behaviors as possible when dealing with superiors, the chances are high that accurate communication will follow and conflicts will be minimized or prevented.

Managing Stress

The phone rings. The boss is on the other end yelling at you, "Jones, get up to my office now, and I mean now!" Or, you've just returned from your vacation and you enter your office to find 43 phone calls to return, 31 letters to answer and 11 reports to complete—all within the next 48 hours. Your throat and mouth start to dry out, the sweat begins to pour down your face, your heart begins to beat faster, your mind draws to a blank. You are experiencing *stress.*

According to most psychologists, the stress response is a nonspecific physiological and psychological chain of events triggered by any disruption to one's equilibrium or homeostasis. Typically, to restore balance due to stress, the body's autonomic nervous system and endocrine system combine to speed up cardiovascular functions and slow down gastrointestinal functions, resulting in a "fight or flight" response. Over long periods of time, this response can wear a person down and increase the likelihood of illness, disease, and emotional distress. How much distress and which illness will vary from person to person depending upon personalities, habits, backgrounds, family history, etc. We all need some stress to work at maximal levels, but at some point, and it varies across individuals, the amount of stress becomes both physically and psychologically destructive.

The sources of stress are varied and can occur both on the job and away from work. (Adams, 1980) The former can include such major, sudden events as major changes in policies or procedures, increases in the amount and pace of work, major reorganizations, *or* the more insidious sources which derive from daily pressures that build up, such as too much work and too little time, feedback only in response to bad work, unresolved conflicts, unclear role descriptions, and as I mentioned in chapter 4, information overload. This last continuing source of stress, information overload, may even be enhanced by the new communication technologies, which, ironically, were developed to decrease our workloads. As discussed in chapter 4, these new technologies may indeed, primarily due to their efficiencies in diffusing information, be a major cause of workers receiving too much information from too many sources. Perhaps our information society is nurturing a new disease called "infornoma." Just as we can get asbestosis from inhaling asbestos, so can we get "infornoma" from inhaling information. (My good friend, Frank Dance of the University of Denver, has suggested that perhaps the cure for "infornoma" may be an "infornectomy"—blinders or earplugs will also do the trick.)

Gherman (1981) cites that there are at least four general categories that come under major organizational stressors. They are (1) role-making dysfunction and conflict, (2) job factors, (3) physical working conditions, and (4) interpersonal relations. Gherman emphasized that living habits and attitudes can help you identify where your particular stress problem

If we structure our time to include activities such as establishing intimate relationships, having fun, and spending time alone, we can diminish the time available for game playing.

lies. There is a sharp difference in attitude and behavior between people who suffer from constant stress and those who don't. Executives who are under stress report such habits as taking tranquilizers, having two or more cocktails at lunch, using sleeping pills, rarely having weekends for family and self, hurried breakfasts, and heavy cigarette smoking. Stressed executives also report similar attitude characteristics: more fear of self-expression, more boredom, more suspicion that they are not receiving their due for efforts, more job security, more dissatisfaction with job progress, more dislike for colleagues, and a greater desire to retire by age fifty-five.

Stress can also be induced by sources away from the work organization. Such major events or changes as a serious illness, the death of a close friend or family member, even a marriage can produce the stress response, *or* again, it might be from the daily buildup due to general anxiety over children's behavior or concern over finances.

Whatever the sources or causes of stress, it is vitally important to each of us to recognize its presence and symptoms and be able to manage our stress before it leads to unwanted consequences. Most experts in stress recommend a combination of efforts or techniques to manage stress, usually involving diet, exercise, awareness, planning, and relaxation.

1. *Diet.* Eat a balanced diet with ample vitamins, minerals, etc. and a minimal amount of salt, sugar, saturated fat, refined white flour, and chemical additives; eat regular meals, don't smoke, and restrict caffeine and alcohol intake to moderate amounts.

2. *Exercise.* Do regular aerobic exercise to improve the cardiovascular system and regular recreational exercise to reduce tension.
3. *Awareness.* Understand your personal needs and desires.
4. *Planning.* Use effective time management techniques and have a good, long-term plan for career and life.
5. *Relaxation.* Use meditation, prayer, etc. to genuinely relax.

Berger (1986) suggests that regular exercise, in the form of jogging and swimming, are important stress-reduction techniques. In particular, people who swim report less tension, anxiety, depression, anger, and confusion, and more vigor, after swimming than before.

The above techniques will not necessarily produce immediate change in your condition or personality. However, by following these guidelines you may gradually change your life-style and, consequently, decrease the amount of stress.

In order to help you assess the degree to which you may be prone to or experience stress, I have devised the following set of questions (modeled after Adams, 1980). If you answer "yes" to most or all of these questions, you probably are either not being exposed to large amounts of harmful stress or you are able to cope well with the stress you now receive. If you answer "no" to most or all of these questions, you may profit from some of the techniques previously described to help you manage your stress.

Questions to Help Assess Your Level of Stress

1. Do you breathe easily and sufficiently?
2. Are you aware of your optimal stress level?
3. Do you love yourself and feel good about yourself?
4. Do you have enough supportive relationships?
5. Are you generally optimistic?
6. Do you generally take things (or make changes) one step at a time?
7. Do you avoid using the word "can't" improperly?
8. Do you avoid worrying about irrelevant matters or unchangeable circumstances?
9. Do you have a perspective that "it's *all* small stuff?"
10. Do you maintain a vigorous regular exercise program?
11. Is your diet balanced and nutritional?
12. Do you engage in some form of regular contemplation, such as meditation or prayer?
13. Do you have effective interpersonal skills?

SUMMARY

Successful dyadic encounters in an organization occur when both parties show mutual honesty, trust, and love. By remaining open and permissive with one another, each allows the other to grow and develop for the mutual benefit of the individuals and the organization. Ingredients necessary for successful dyadic organizational relationships were described and illustrated. Behaviors typical of both defensive and supportive climates were listed, with emphasis on supportive climates as they contribute to effective relationships. Major variables affecting dyadic encounters were discussed, with particular reference to homophily, feedback, trust, openness, accuracy, supportiveness, and credibility. Research strongly indicates that perceptions of relationships and attributes of the members of these relationships are potent factors in an individual's evaluation of the job and the organization. The most important contributor to job satisfaction was shown to be the quality of the relationship employees have with their supervisor. Central to an effective relationship with one's boss is the degree to which the boss gives praise; understands workers' jobs; is trusted; is warm, friendly, and honest; and allows disagreement. Supervisors who use positive expressions and provide ample justifications are particularly effective with their subordinates. Conflict was discussed along with the steps involved in reducing it.

Sperry Company's listening program, developed by Lyman Steil, was presented along with several techniques that Steil and the company contend will improve listening abilities. Job expectation technique (JET) as a means of reducing role conflict and ambiguity among employees was presented in detail. Application of JET to management by objectives (MBO) was presented and described, and the six steps necessary for a successful MBO program were identified. Additionally, the research on performance appraisal interviews was summarized.

Managing up is a technique by which you can reduce uncertainty between you and your manager, to make you both more effective. It involves gathering data about your manager's and your own needs, goals, strengths, weaknesses, and styles. Finally, the stress response was described along with several methods for managing unwanted organizational stress.

EXERCISES

1. Observe a class taught by a stranger, preferably in an academic discipline new to you. Was the atmosphere defensive or supportive? List specific behaviors exhibited by the instructor and/or the students that led to your conclusion.
2. Interview an employee of the university (a secretary, grounds keeper, physical plant worker, administrator), and ask this person to describe his or her specific job duties. Next, interview the immediate supervisor to find out his or her understanding of the employee's job duties. Compare the two interviews and discuss their discrepancies.
3. Ask the employee you interviewed for exercise 2 to mark Dennis's sixteen-item checklist measuring the quality of supervisor-subordinate relationship. Note the specific items and the total number of items checked. Then, have the employee's boss mark the same inventory in the way he thinks the employee would. List and discuss the discrepancies.
4. Think about a situation in which you are experiencing conflict. What are the causes/sources of the conflict? How can it be resolved?
5. List strategies for improving communication from "distant" organization sources. Are there different strategies for different sources? Why?
6. Simulate a work organization in the class and complete the JET for all persons included in the simulation.
7. Think about a former or current supervisor. Outline a strategy for "managing up" in this dyadic relationship.

8. Complete an action plan for either a part-time job or a simulated job (preferably a job you plan to have after graduation).

9. Divide the class into dyads. Conduct career discussion interviews in which one member of each dyad plays the role of the manager and the other member plays the employee. Use the questions under step 5 (review and recycle) in the discussion of MBO as the basis for the interview.

10. Describe the kinds of strokes you give and receive at work or in school. Discuss the kinds of strokes others give. Are you satisfied with the kinds and amount of strokes you give and receive? Relate the kinds of strokes you give and receive to Herzberg's two-factor theory of motivation discussed in chapter 3.

11. You have performed a needs analysis for an organizational division and have identified listening as the problem specific to this unit. Design a listening workshop listing the skills you believe should be taught and improved.

12. Think about the stress you are experiencing. Perhaps by completing the stress questionnaire in this chapter you can assess your level of stress. How can you reduce it?

BIBLIOGRAPHY AND REFERENCES

Adams, John. "Improving Stress Management." *Social Change* 8 (1980).

———. "Groundrules for Survival: or How to Stop Being a Victim." *OD Practitioner* 12 (1980).

Albuquerque Journal, 4 April 1972, p. C-1.

Athnassiades, J. "The Distortion of Upward Communication in Hierarchical Organizations." *Academy of Management Journal* 16 (1973):207–26.

Beckhard, Richard. "The Confrontation Meeting." *Harvard Business Review* 45 (1967):149–55.

Berger, B. G. "Use of Jogging and Swimming as Stress-Reduction Techniques." In *Human Stress,* edited by J. Humphrey. Vol. 1, New York: AMS Press Inc., 1986.

Browne, C., and B. Nietzel. "Communication, Supervision and Morale." *Journal of Applied Psychology* 36 (1952):86–91.

Coch, L., and J. French. "Overcoming Resistance to Change." *Human Relations* 1 (1948):512–32.

Daly, J., J. McCroskey, and R. Falcione. "Homophily-Heterophily and the Prediction of Supervisor Satisfaction." Paper presented at a meeting of the International Communication Association, Portland, Oregon, 1976.

D'Aprix, R. "Business and Society: Friends or Foes?" Paper read at a meeting of the Industrial Communication Council, Washington, D.C., October 1976.

Dennis, H. "The Construction of a Managerial 'Communication Climate' Inventory for Use in Complex Organizations." Paper presented at a meeting of the International Communication Association, Chicago, 1975.

Downs, Cal, and Charles Conrad. "Effective Subordinacy." *Journal of Business Communication* 19 (1982):27–37.

Falcione, R. "The Factor Structure of Source Credibility Scales for Immediate Superiors in the Organizational Context." *Central States Speech Journal* 25 (1974):63–66.

———. "Subordinate Satisfaction as a Function of Perceived Supervisor Credibility." Paper presented at a meeting of the International Communication Association. Chicago, 1975.

Filley, Allan. *Interpersonal Conflict Resolution.* Glenview, Illinois: Scott, Foresman and Company, 1975.

Gabarro, John, and John Kotter. "Managing Your Boss." *Harvard Business Review* 58 (1980):92–100.

Gherman, E. M. *Stress and the Bottom Line* NY: AMACOM Publishers, 1981.

Gibb, J. "Defensive Communication." *Journal of Communication* 11 (1961):141–48.

Goldhaber, G., and M. Goldhaber. *Transactional Analysis.* Boston: Allyn & Bacon, 1976.

Goldhaber, G., D. Porter, and M. Yates. "The ICA Communication Audit Survey Instrument: 1977 Organizational Norms." Paper presented at a meeting of the International Communication Association, Berlin, Germany, 1977.

Heron, A. *Sharing Information with Employees.* Palo Alto: Stanford University Press, 1942.

Huse, E. *Organization Development and Change.* St. Paul, Minn.: West Publishing Co., 1975.

Huseman, R., J. Hatfield, and R. Gatewood. "A Conceptual Framework for Analyzing the Communication-Productivity Relationship." Paper presented at the Academy of Management meeting, San Francisco, 1978.

Jablin, Fred. "Message-Response and 'Openness' in Superior-Subordinate Communication." In *Communication Yearbook II,* edited by Ruben. New Brunswick, N. J.: Transaction-International Communication Association, 1978, 293–309.

———. "Formal Structural Characteristics of Organizations and Superior-Subordinate Communication: An Exploratory Study." Paper presented to the International Communication Association, Minneapolis, 1981.

Kelly, Lynne. "A Critical Review of the Literature on Superior-Subordinate Communicative Relationships." Paper presented to the International Communication Association, Boston, 1982.

Krivonos, P. "Distortion of Subordinate to Superior Communication." Paper presented at a meeting of the International Communication Association, Portland, Oregon, 1976.

Likert, R. *New Patterns of Management.* New York: McGraw-Hill Book Co., 1961.

———. *The Human Organization.* New York: McGraw-Hill Book Co., 1967.

Maier, N., L. Hoffman, and W. Read. "Superior-Subordinate Communication: The Relative Effectiveness of Managers Who Held Their Subordinates' Positions." *Personnel Psychology* 26 (1963): 1–11.

Nord, W. R. "Beyond the Teaching Machine: The Neglected Area of Operant Conditioning in the Theory and Practice of Management." *Organizational Behavior and Human Performance* 4 (1969). Reprinted in *Motivation and Control in Organizations,* edited by G. W. Dalton and P. R. Lawrence. Homewood, Ill.: Irwin-Dorsey, 1971, 352–77.

Pace, R. W., and R. Boren. *The Human Transaction.* Glenview, Ill.: Scott, Foresman, 1973.

Pace, R. W., R. Boren, and B. Peterson. *A Scientific Introduction to Speech Communication.* Belmont, Calif.: Wadsworth Publishing Co., 1974.

Pelz, Donald. "Influence: A Key to Effective Leadership in the First Line Supervisor." *Personnel* 29 (1952):209–17.

Peter, L., and Raymond Hull. *The Peter Principle.* New York: Morrow, 1969.

Pondy, L. "Organizational Conflict: Concepts and Models." *Administrative Science Quarterly* 12 (1967):296–320.

———. "Varieties of Organizational Conflict." *Administrative Science Quarterly* 14 (1969):499–506.

Read, W. "Upward Communication in Industrial Hierarchies." *Human Relations* 15 (1962):3–15.

Redding, W. C. *Communication within the Organization.* New York: Industrial Communication Council; and Lafayette, Ind.: Purdue Research Foundation, 1972.

Richetto, G. "Source Credibility and Personal Influence in Three Contexts: A Study of Dyadic Communication in a Complex Aerospace Organization." Ph.D. dissertation, Purdue University, 1969.

Roberts, K., and C. O'Reilly. "Failures in Upward Communication." Manuscript, University of California, Berkeley, 1973.

Roberts, K., and C. O'Reilly. "Measuring Organizational Communication." *Journal of Applied Psychology* 59 (1974):321–26.

Rogers, C. R. *On Becoming a Person.* Boston: Houghton Mifflin, 1961.

Schneider, B., and C. J. Bartlett. "Individual Differences and Organizational Climate." *Personnel Psychology* 21 (1968):323–33.

Skinner, B. F. *Science and Human Behavior.* New York: Macmillan, 1953.

Stewart, Charles and William Cash. *Interviewing: Principles and Practices.* 2d ed. Dubuque, Iowa: Wm. C. Brown, 1978.

Sussman, L. "The Relationship between Message Distortion and Job Satisfaction." *The Journal of Business Communication* 12: (Summer 1974):25–29.

Tamayo, Michele, and Myron Lustig. "The Relationship of Employee Job Satisfaction to Supervisor Message Type." Paper presented at the meeting of the International Communication Association, San Francisco, 1984.

Trenk, Barbara. "Listen Up." *US Air Magazine,* (September 1981):20–26.

7

SMALL-GROUP ORGANIZATIONAL COMMUNICATION

Consider the following event as it was described in the *Albuquerque Journal.*

> New Yorkers, who in recent years have been categorized collectively for their reluctance to "get involved," apparently have had a change of heart.
>
> The generalized smear on New Yorkers' consciences resulted from the refusal, several years ago, of neighbors to respond to the screams of Miss Kitty Genovese for help moments before she was stabbed to death on a street in Queens Borough.
>
> Thursday night three men grabbed a purse from a 19-year-old girl while she was talking with a friend at a street corner, and one of the trio knocked her to the ground when she started screaming.
>
> "We don't want a Kitty Genovese in this neighborhood," shouted a passerby. In moments a hundred New Yorkers, more or less, were pursuing the three offenders. One of the pursuers was swinging a tire iron at the fugitives.
>
> The purse snatchers boarded a taxicab, but the pursuers surrounded the cab and refused to let it take off until police arrived. The three suspects were arrested and charged promptly with assault and robbery. Perhaps the days of law and order—and citizen involvement—are on their way back.

This collection of brave New Yorkers constituted a *group.* Had the "hundred" strangers continued on their way, despite the girl's call for help, their encounter would have been no more intimate than that of a large crowd of people standing in line at a theater, watching a football game, walking to work, or shopping in a large department store. We would have called them an aggregate, a collection of individuals with nothing in common.

However, these hundred people were different. They had a common purpose. Each passerby recognized the existence of and necessity for all the others. Perhaps, alone, none would have helped the girl, but together the one hundred seemed to communicate a common purpose. As Lewin said, "Each member recognizes the existence of every other member as an essential part of the total group, and his behavior reflects their expectations." Homans defined a group as "a number of persons who communicate with one another often over a span of time, and who are few enough so that each person is able to communicate with all the others, not at secondhand, through other people, but face-to-face . . ." Cartwright and

Zander called a group "a collection of individuals who have relations to one another that make them interdependent to some significant degree. . . ." Applbaum and colleagues have pointed to five characteristics of groups in general: interaction of communication, common goals or purposes, set of norms, set of roles, and interdependency.

We can see that, according to Applbaum and associates, the hundred New Yorkers constituted a group. They certainly interacted primarily via nonverbal cues (facial expressions, shouts, touch), and they all attempted to rescue the nineteen-year-old girl—their common purpose. They unofficially established their group norm by following the command of one passerby, "We don't want a Kitty Genovese in this neighborhood." One of the people adopted the role of persecutor ("swinging a tire iron"); others assumed the role of capturers ("surrounded the car"), while all assumed the role of "involved citizens." The actions of all probably affected the actions of each, and vice versa. The courage each displayed perhaps came from the collective bravery of the group.

In this chapter, we are concerned with *small groups*. Scott defined the small group as "a restricted number of people, usually fewer than seven, who enjoy personal interaction over a fairly long span of time" and who have "a . . . degree of commonality of interest often expressed as a goal upon which there is mutual agreement." Olmstead suggested twenty as the upper limit of a small group. Bales (1950) said that a small group exists, not according to any specific numbers, but when the members establish a psychological relationship with each other. Hare agreed that numbers alone do not create a small group; he insisted that face-to-face interaction is the primary defining characteristic.

We define a small group as Applbaum and associates did: "two or more people communicating face-to-face, with each member aware of the presence of each other member within the group." Our specific objectives in this chapter follow:

1. To define *group* and *small group* in terms of social systems
2. To identify and describe the types of small groups within organizations
3. To describe and illustrate quality circles
4. To describe and exemplify the following group variables:
   a. functional roles
   b. leadership
   c. networks and group ecology
   d. problem-solving and decision-making skills
   e. conformity and cohesion
   f. conflict
5. To describe and illustrate the assessment of group effectiveness

The Small Group as a Subsystem

Just as in chapter 2 an organization was defined as a social system, so can a group be defined in the same way. Both organizations and groups are composed of interdependent and interrelated subsystems. Both are open and dynamic, having inputs, outputs, operations, feedback, and boundaries. Both maintain balance through feedback, and both have a multiplicity of purposes, functions, and objectives, some of which are in conflict. In this book, we view

Figure 7.1 The group as a subsystem.

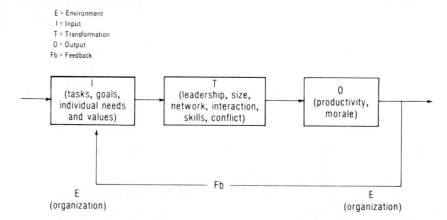

E = Environment
I = Input
T = Transformation
O = Output
Fb = Feedback

the organization as the larger system and a group as an interdependent *subsystem*. Thus, the organization as a whole becomes the environment for the group as a subsystem. Figure 7.1 presents a diagram of the group as a subsystem.

Huse and Bowditch also defined a group as a subsystem within an organization. They identified four characteristics of a group within this framework: common purpose, interaction, awareness of one another, and self-perception as a member of the group. They believe that groups form in organizations to help achieve organizational goals, to expedite the flow of information, and to serve certain personal needs. Following Maslow's hierarchy of needs (see chapter 3), they listed four specific individual needs that groups satisfy:

1. *Security needs.* The power and security within the group provides protection.
2. *Social needs.* The sense of belonging generated by a group provides affiliation.
3. *Ego needs.* A sense of accomplishment, recognition, and competency results from the problem-solving and decision-making opportunities within a group.
4. *Self-actualizing needs.* Feedback from group members provides insight into one's behavior.

Huse and Bowditch concluded:

. . . man's social and ego needs are both satisfied and reinforced by his participation in groups. Certain needs can be satisfied only by the group; therefore, man turns to the group in order to satisfy his needs. Furthermore, by providing feedback, the group can help the individual meet his highest self-actualizing needs.

Rosenfeld summarized Schutz's theory of fundamental interpersonal relations orientation (FIRO) as a possible rationale for joining groups. Schutz identified three interpersonal needs that must be satisfied through interpersonal relationships in order to avoid insanity: (1) *inclusion,* our need to belong, to establish and maintain effective interpersonal relations; (2) our need for power, called *control;* and (3) our need for love, *affection.* Schutz claimed that each of these three needs is expressed as well as wanted. Individuals need to include, control, and love as well as be included, controlled, and loved. Through meaningful interaction, commitment, loyalty, problem solving, decision making, and constant feedback, a group provides individuals with ample opportunity to satisfy all three needs.

Figure 7.2 The FIRO theory.

	I Inclusion	C Control	A Affection
Expressed e (toward others)	I join other people, and I include others.	I take charge; I influence others.	I get close to people.
Wanted w (from others)	I want people to include me.	I want people to lead me.	I want people to get close and personal with me.

Sample FIRO Statements

	I Inclusion	C Control	A Affection
Expressed e (toward others)	I try to be with people. (Usually, often, or sometimes.)	I try to take charge of things with people. (Most people, many people, or some people.)	I try to have close relationships with people. (Usually or often.)
Wanted w (from others)	I like people to invite me to things. (Most people or many people.)	I let other people decide what to do. (Usually, often, sometimes, or occasionally.)	I like people to act close and personal with me. (Most people or many people.)

Figure 7.2 summarizes the FIRO theory and presents sample statements that subjects would agree with in order to be placed in a particular category.

The following story illustrates how the needs for inclusion, control, and affection can be fulfilled. Twelve neighbors lived on the same street for several years, during which time their mutual transactions were restricted to "Hello," "How are you today?" or "Nice weather, today, isn't it?" One day a new neighbor moved onto the street, and within a month the children of the new neighbor were involved in several criminal actions affecting the old neighbors. Houses were broken into, property was stolen and/or vandalized, children were verbally and physically abused, and drugs were openly solicited. Finally, the original twelve neighbors held a meeting to discuss what course of action to take. During the first hour of the meeting, which was held at the home of one of the neighbors, most of the people screamed about how "unsafe the neighborhood is" or how "we never had any trouble before *they* moved in" or how "frightened the children now are." During the next two hours, one of the neighbors volunteered to list all the actions that could be attributed to the behavior of the new neighbors. After the list was generated, the group agreed that something had to be done "before things get out of hand." The neighbors agreed to meet again the following week to continue their discussion about this matter.

The meeting provided the opportunity for all three of Schutz's needs to be satisfied. The *inclusion* need was met since all attended the meeting. Several of the neighbors wanted to "take the law into their own hands"; one even suggested "going over to them with a baseball bat or a gun." All of the neighbors wanted to do something. Whatever the level of action, it was apparent that all desired to express some *control*. The group expressed *affection* toward one another by actively listening to all members talk about the problem, by respecting each person's feelings about the condition of the neighborhood, and by agreeing to continue meeting. One neighbor stated, "It's too bad we had to meet one another under these circumstances."

Types of Groups in Organizations

"It seems that I spend most of my time in committee meetings." "I never have any time for anything—but committee meetings." "If the boss calls one more meeting, I'll hit the roof!" "I stopped going to meetings—they're a waste of time!" These statements are representative of surveys I conducted at twenty-five organizations to assess reactions of employees and managers toward meetings. The overall response seemed to be negative. Most managers felt that meetings took too long and accomplished too little. (Statistics verify at least that meetings take too long.)

Tillman found that 94 percent of organizations with more than 10,000 employees have formal committees. Kriesberg reported that executives typically spend an average of ten hours per week in formal committee meetings. My own research at a large university shows that the average tenured faculty member served on one college committee, two to three departmental committees, one university standing committee, and two to three subcommittees *simultaneously* (and also attended departmental, college, and university faculty meetings). The number of hours per week they spent in committee and other regularly scheduled meetings was eleven. When nonscheduled and informal meetings are included, it is easy to understand why faculty members reported that they were "tired of all the committee assignments." One faculty member said that he barely had time left to prepare for his classes. It is apparent that meetings account for much of the time expended in organizations.

The time given to other small-group activities must also be accounted for. Brooks identified five types of groups which can exist in an organization: primary groups, casual groups, educational groups, therapeutic groups, and problem-solving groups.

A *primary group* is usually an individual's family and closest friends. It is through primary groups that individuals achieve intimacy and deep social encounters. It is possible, although infrequent, for primary groups to exist within work organizations. Close friendships may develop among a small group of colleagues who choose to spend much of their nonworking time in each other's company.

A *casual group* forms for mutual exchange of ideas and social conversation. Its purpose is to establish informal friendly relations rather than to accomplish a particular task. Typical organizational casual groups are those formed during coffee and lunch breaks. Additional casual groups might grow from informal rap sessions, retreats, bowling and golf teams, company picnics, and spread of rumors via the grapevine.

An *educational group* provides opportunity for instruction and study. If you are in a class now, your class is probably an educational group. Weekly book clubs were founded so that members can read and react to new publications. Orientation and training sessions in many businesses are considered educational groups.

A *therapeutic group* is a means used by social workers, psychologists, psychiatrists, and counselors to facilitate behavior change among their clients. The group serves as a supportive environment where individuals have the option of gaining new self-awareness. Group members provide feedback which is used as a gauge to recognize and measure change. The closest analogue to this type of group in an organization is sensitivity training and transactional analysis, whose objectives (according to Huse and Bowditch) are the following:

1. To increase individuals' interpersonal competence by helping them become more aware of their own feelings and emotions and those of others
2. To give individuals a greater awareness of their own and others' role within the organization, to increase their willingness to deal with and achieve collaborative relationships with others, and to help them increase their organizational interpersonal competence
3. To assist the organization in doing a better job of diagnosing, defining, and working on organizational problems and to help the organization improve through the process of working on the training of *groups rather than of individuals*

A *problem-solving group* is assigned specific tasks. Such groups usually have a structured agenda that reflects the nature of the group's goals and an unstructured, hidden agenda that reflects the personal needs of the members of the group. Within an organization, groups such as committee meetings, staff meetings, decision-making meetings, information-sharing meetings, brainstorming sessions, conferences, executive meetings, and budget meetings are problem-solving groups. Since the problem-solving group is probably the most common group in the work organization, it is used as the frame of reference for the discussion of key group variables later in this chapter.

Another way of viewing small group activities within an organization is according to the particular network over which messages travel. In chapter 4, we distinguished between the formal network, in which messages follow official paths dictated by the organizational hierarchy or by job function, and the informal network, in which such scalar and functional lines are ignored. Most primary and casual groups can be classified as informal small groups. Educational, therapeutic, and problem-solving groups can be considered formal groups. Many small group communication activities found in complex organizations reflect the group typologies previously discussed. Formal small group activities in organizations include quality circles, brainstorming sessions, as well as training programs and decision-making meetings. Examples of informal small-group activities would include informal meetings, rap sessions, luncheons, and social events like annual company picnics.

Key Group Variables

Several factors influence the outcome of small-group activity. Among them are variables relating to both group input and group transformation. We will now examine each of these variables plus some of the methods of evaluating group effectiveness.

Functional Roles

Researchers in group dynamics have generally identified two primary roles assumed by certain members of a group: the task role and the maintenance role. Task roles relate to completion of the group's immediate goals, such as making a decision, solving a problem, or completing a project. We know from the work of Schutz and others that members join groups to fulfill other needs too. The socioemotional needs of certain members of the group are satisfied by the maintenance role they assume. The maintenance relates to the feelings of the group members rather than the successful accomplishment of the group's objectives. Groups which fail to take into account the socioemotional needs of the members often find that these needs subtly complicate task interactions. When this happens, we say that the group's hidden agenda influences its behavior. Hidden agendas are the private emotions and motives of the group members. One group structured an agenda to solve a particular problem. After an hour of discussion, one member called for a vote. A quick vote was taken and the meeting was adjourned—in time for this member to make his golf date.

Bales (1954) recognized these two functional roles, which Kelly summarized as follows:

> Groups work through three phases: clarification ("What is it?"), evaluation ("How do we feel about it?"), and decision ("What are we going to do about it?"). Second, to work through this process, the group selects two people to fill two roles—the task specialist who talks in terms of "Let's zero in on the problem," and the human relations specialist who is usually warm and receptive, and acts as a "first-aid" man to help alleviate group tension without diverting it too much from its primary task.

Benne and Sheats detailed specific behaviors that task-oriented and maintenance-oriented group members follow. They identified a third role, self-serving behavior, which is actually dysfunctional for the effectiveness of the group.

Task behaviors include such activities as the following:

1. Initiating (defines the problem, sets the rules, contributes ideas), for example, "I think the problem is that the foreman's temper is too short."
2. Information giving and seeking (asks for or offers opinions and beliefs about their own or the group's attitude toward a suggestion), for example, "I think we had a situation like this last year."
3. Opinion giving and seeking (asks for or offers opinions and beliefs about their own or the group's attitude toward a suggestion), for example, "I think that your example needs more facts."
4. Elaborating and clarifying (provides additional information about a particular suggestion or idea), for example, "I think Dick is trying to say that the facts are kind of obscure right now."
5. Orienting and summarizing (reviews the significant points covered in an attempt to guide the direction of the discussion), for example, "Since it's so late now, hadn't we better move on to the second point?"
6. Consensus testing (checks to see if the group is ready to make a decision), for example, "I think I hear the group favoring the first point. Is this so?"

Maintenance behaviors include the following:

1. Harmonizing (resolves differences and reduces tension, sometimes with the use of humor), for example, "Hey, you guys, if I wanted to hear an argument, I would have invited my wife to the meeting."
2. Compromising (offers a compromise on an issue or change in position), for example, "Isn't there a position we can all live with?"

3. Supporting and encouraging (praises, agrees with, and accepts the contributions of others), for example, "I really like your idea, Sally."
4. Gatekeeping (facilitates interaction from all members), for example, "John, what do you think about Sally's idea?"
5. Standard setting and testing (checks out the group process, people's feelings, group norms, and the like, to evaluate the operation of the group), for example, "I feel that there's a lot of hostility in this room. Do others share my perception?"

In addition to group task and group process, members may assume a self-centered role which facilitates solving individual problems. These self-serving behaviors include the following:

1. Blocking (refuses to cooperate by rejecting all ideas), for example, "I don't like John's idea any more than I liked Sally's."
2. Withdrawing (remains indifferent, daydreams, avoids the topic), for example, "Why don't we work on this problem ourselves?"
3. Dominating (interrupts, monopolizes conversation, is authoritative), for example, "Now just a minute, Tom, I think we should do it my way!"
4. Being aggressive (boasts, criticizes, fights), for example, "I'm not interested in your opinion! You've been wrong ever since we started!"

Leadership

Closely related to functional roles in a group is the concept of leadership. We used to believe that good leaders exhibit certain traits, such as responsibility, status, capacity, honesty, and self-confidence. However, current research findings indicate that leadership is more a function of the relationship among members of the group. Pace and Boren defined leadership as doing those things that facilitate group interaction and that move the group toward completion of the task. Effective leadership necessitates accomplishing both objectives. As we have just seen, objectives can be functionally assumed by any group member; therefore, it is theoretically possible for *any member to assume a leadership role at any time*. In keeping with the two primary group roles—task and maintenance—we usually define the two group leaders as the "task" leader and the "socioemotional" leader.

As Bales (1954) has pointed out, it is quite difficult for one person to assume both roles:

> At the end of the group's first meeting, there is one chance in two that the task leader will be the most liked. At the end of the second meeting the chances are reduced to one in four. At the end of the third they are one in six, and at the end of the fourth they are only one in seven.

Davis has reminded us, however, that in organizations the central locus of power is usually the boss or manager—the person with the highest status. In fact, in many organizations "leaderless" groups may be dysfunctional in the accomplishment of a group task. In organizational environments when leadership of the group is in doubt, the group becomes preoccupied with the leadership problem and makes negligible progress toward its goal until that problem is solved.

"Leaderless" groups may be dysfunctional in the accomplishment of a group task.

Various organizational leadership and managerial styles were discussed in chapter 3. Therefore, here we will add only Tannenbaum's leadership continuum. Tannenbaum (1958) identified seven possible leadership behaviors, ranging from the total authoritarian to the extreme democratic for managers:

1. To make a decision and announce it
2. To sell their decision
3. To present their ideas and invite questions
4. To present a tentative decision, subject to change
5. To present a problem, get suggestions, and make a decision
6. To define limits and ask the group to make the decision
7. To permit subordinates to function within the limits defined by superiors

We have viewed leadership as a function that can be assumed by several group members throughout the life of the group, by whoever facilitates either accomplishment of the group's objectives or resolution of its feelings.

Networks and Group Ecology

In this section, we are concerned with the effects of patterns of both message flow and physical distance on group productivity. Message flow refers to group networks, and physical distance refers to spatial arrangements. We will see that both influence the functioning of a group.

Group networks determine the paths that are open for the flow of messages. The first studies of group networks were done by Bavelas and Leavitt. Bavelas varied the pattern of communication and tested a circle, a line, a star, and a Y configuration by measuring the

Figure 7.3 The communication networks used by Leavitt.

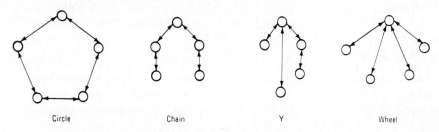

Circle   Chain   Y   Wheel

speed and accuracy of solving a particular problem and the satisfaction of group members with the solution. He found that the Y pattern has fewest errors and solves the problem fastest. The circle has the highest morale and the Y pattern the lowest. Bavelas also found that persons in central positions report the highest morale, while morale of persons in the peripheral positions is lowest. Leavitt separated five subjects by carefully placing vertical partitions around a table. Subjects could pass only written notes to one another in accordance with one of the following four patterns of communication: circle, chain, Y, and wheel, as shown in figure 7.3.

Each group of five subjects was given a card containing five different symbols out of a set of six. The problem called for discovering which symbol was held in common by all members. After each subject indicated awareness of the common symbol, the experimental trial was ended. Subjects then filled out a short questionnaire. Dependent variables measured included number of errors, number of messages, speed, and morale. Results indicate that the wheel network is fastest and most accurate; the circle is slowest, uses more messages, and has the lowest accuracy. However, the circle does have the highest group satisfaction.

We generally refer to the wheel, the chain, and the Y networks as highly centralized because one person is central to all the messages, wherever they flow. The circle is considered a decentralized network because no one person is central to the message flow. Later research supported the speed of the centralized networks over the decentralized networks. However, other researchers reported that decentralized networks are faster when the problem is more complex. Shaw's summary of eighteen studies leaves little doubt that the complexity of the task is a critical factor in determining the relative effectiveness of different communication networks. The decentralized network was found to solve complex problems not only faster, but with fewer errors than do other networks.

In a synthesis of the literature on communication networks, Smith generated the following propositions:

1. Initially, highly centralized networks tend to commit the fewest errors.
2. The number of errors committed in a network decreases as a function of familiarity, systematic distribution of information, and authoritarian leadership.
3. The number of messages sent decreases as a function of high centrality.
4. Group morale increases as a function of low centrality and nonauthoritarian leadership.
5. Propensity for leadership is a function of high centrality.

6. Highly centralized networks make fewer answer changes than low centrality networks.
7. A low centrality communication network is most efficient when complex problems must be solved, whereas a centralized network is most efficient when simple problems are to be solved.

Based upon Smith's propositions, it would seem that an organization should use a *centralized network* when the problem is simple, it wants minimum messages and errors, and is looking for a leader. When the problem is complex, an organization should use a *decentralized network,* if high morale and flexibility are desired.

Although most of the research just discussed was conducted in laboratory settings, it has many implications for organizations regarding the adequacy of present network structures.

Network analysis can aid in determining whether current organizational structure allows for effective information flow and coordination of interdependent units. The external links of an organization can be examined to determine whether important sources of information are monitored effectively, whether redundant or unimportant sources overload the system, and whether present mechanisms for dealing with external contacts can handle these exchanges effectively. Comparison of formal and informal networks can indicate areas where rumors are abundant and necessary work-related information is scarce; thus, the best path for communicative efforts to alleviate such conditions can be determined. Change in the communication system can, where necessary, establish links or consolidate redundant or weak contacts.

Network analysis can show whether work groups are too large or too poorly integrated to operate effectively. Groups that are isolated from the system and groups that are connected to the system only through a series of indirect links can be identified and greater communication resources can be focused in these areas.

When Scharpf's idea of networking on the basis of task interdependency is used, groups that work together can be consolidated or connected formally to facilitate interaction and to streamline the official structure. When graphics programs developed by Lesniak and colleagues are used, the interactive structure can be visually represented within the official organizational chart. Direct comparison between these structures show where intraunit and interunit coordination may be poor due to formation of rival groups or lack of interunit contact. Moreover, the connections between management and other organizational levels can be examined for the entire organization and also for specific groups in order to determine whether the official span of control is similar to the span of communication contacts.

Groups are also influenced by the spatial arrangements and physical distances when members are seated near one another. This study, called *group ecology,* was discussed in some detail in chapter 5. Steinzor was one of the first to study the effect of spatial arrangement upon group interaction. He found that members speak more to people seated directly opposite them than to those occupying adjacent seats. However, when a strong leader was present, Steinzor found the reverse to be true. In a later study, Sommer (1959) found that leaders in small discussion groups gravitated to the head position at rectangular tables. Strodtbeck and Hook reported that members of a jury who sat at the head of the table were rated as having greater influence on the decision process than people at the sides. Hare and Bales concluded that subjects who rate high on dominance tend to sit in more central seats and do most of the talking. Sommer (1967) stated: "High-status, dominant individuals in American culture gravitate to the head position, and people who occupy the head position participate more than people at the side positions."

Problem Solving and Decision Making

Should problems be solved and decisions be made by individuals or by groups? Which method is more effective? The answer to these questions is vital to the operation of an organization because of the net costs involved, such as time, money, and morale. An executive earning $40,000 a year costs an organization approximately $50 per hour (including benefits and a productivity factor of two-to-three times salary). If five such executives are tied up in a problem-solving meeting for three hours, the cost to the organization is $750. When only one executive is involved in making the decision, the cost is only $150. Simple arithmetic tells us that the group costs $600 more than does an individual. Is the cost worth it? Will the group produce a decision that will justify the additional cost?

Several researchers have attempted to answer such questions. Davis believes that an average group does produce more ideas and better-quality ideas than an average individual working alone. However, as Bouchard and Hare have pointed out, "When group output is compared with output of the *same number of persons* working individually, individual output (adding each person's *different* ideas only) is higher than the group output . . . ." Bunker and Dalton concluded that it depends upon the situation—that certain kinds of groups can be more effective than individuals in solving certain kinds of problems. They believe that the *nature of the task* is the key factor. Groups typically do better than individuals with tasks that require pooling of data, but individuals do better with tasks that divide labor and bring the results together. Barnlund compared groups with individuals on certain problem-solving tasks and reached these conclusions:

1. Majority decisions, when deadlocks are evenly divided between right and wrong answers, are not significantly different from those made by the average individual and are inferior to those of the best member of the group working alone.
2. Group decisions, reached through cooperative deliberation, are significantly superior to decisions made by individual members working alone and to majority rule.

In a recent summary of the research on strengths and weaknesses of groups, Maier identified the following group assets:

1. *Greater pool of knowledge and information.* Groups know more than individuals.
2. *Greater number of approaches to a problem.* Individuals get into ruts in their thinking, but group members can avoid this by multiple inputs.
3. *Participation in problem solving increases acceptance of the solution.* Members who participate in decisions tend to support them.
4. *Better comprehension of the decision.* Groups making decisions need no relay and translator since they made the decision.

He also identified several group liabilities:

1. *Social pressure.* Members try to be accepted by other members of the group.
2. *Valence of solutions.* Both critical and supportive comments.
3. *Individual domination.* One or two members may talk more than their share.

4. *Conflicting secondary goal: winning the argument.* Winning becomes more important than finding the best solution.

He listed the following factors as possibly being either assets or liabilities, depending upon the skill of the discussion leader:

1. *Disagreement.* Hard feelings or conflict resolution may result.
2. *Conflicting interests versus mutual interests.* Disagreements may arise regarding solutions for different problems.
3. *Risk taking.* Groups are more willing to assume risks than individuals, called the "risky shift phenomenon".
4. *Changing position.* If persons with constructive solutions change, the decision may suffer more than when those with less constructive solutions change.

If an organization decides to call upon the resources of a small group to solve a problem or make a decision, certain techniques can enhance the quality of the decision or the solution. Brooks, Schein, Pace and Boren, and others have published models for group problem solving, most of which follow the original model developed by Richard Wallen. In sequence, the usual steps to follow are these.

Identify and Analyze the Problem.   Reduce the problem to terms and examples recognizable to most of the group members. You might find that there is a problem, confusion over the nature of the problem, or disagreement over the importance of the problem. It is best to agree on such matters before more time is spent looking for solutions. Too often, a group may confuse the symptoms of the problem with the problem itself. One university department received notice that many of its major students were changing to other programs. Analysis of the problem revealed that the drop in that department's enrollment wasn't the *real* trouble, but the curriculum the faculty offered. Rather than waste time lamenting over lost students, the faculty tackled the more severe problem of reconsidering its curriculum.

Generate Possible Solutions.   Once the problem is identified and understood, the group may begin the task of solving it. Sometimes groups generate specific criteria or standards for an acceptable solution before they generate solutions. This may limit the thinking of the group because they suggest only solutions that meet their criteria. Of course, some groups may be able to work within some very carefully defined limits. If this is the case, then all members should have a clear understanding of the criteria. In other situations, the group should be turned loose to generate as many solutions as possible within the time available.

One technique of generating a quantity of alternative ideas is brainstorming. The following are rules to follow in brainstorming sessions:

1. *Set a time limit.* Usually ten minutes to one hour.
2. *Designate one person as group recorder.* Or use a tape recorder.
3. *Generate as many ideas as possible within the time limit.* Quantity is desired—even wild ideas may trigger more practical ones.
4. *Avoid evaluation, criticism, and all forms of judgment (good or bad) until the session is over.*

Earlier in this chapter, we discussed a group of neighbors who met to discuss the criminal behavior of the children of a new neighbor. During one meeting the following suggestions were made for resolving the problem: burn their house down; go to their house and reason with them; go to their house with a baseball bat and gun; seek legal counsel; get a court injunction banning their children from all further unlawful activities; buy their house and force them to leave.

Evaluate Solutions.   After the list of possible solutions has been generated, it is time to review the merits and feasibility of each suggestion. At this point, criteria can be developed according to the group's needs (unless standards have already been developed). Each potential solution should be tested, using personal experience, expert opinion, current surveys of existing data, and planned scientific research. (In the example, the neighbors quickly discarded several of the suggestions, because one criterion they had established was to remain within the law.) After all possible solutions have been reviewed and evaluated, the group is ready to make a decision, selecting the idea which will provide maximum benefit and minimum detriment.

Cost-Benefit Analysis.   Sometimes evaluation can be made easier by using a systematic approach, such as a cost-benefit analysis. The following steps are useful in doing this analysis:

1. Identify all relevant criteria affecting the decision (e.g., money, time, people, energy, climate, laws, and geography).
2. Define each criterion in the specific context of the decision (e.g., "For the purposes of this discussion, geography will denote the northeastern United States").
3. Weight each criterion on a 1-to-5 scale, 1 being minimum importance and 5 being maximum importance.
4. For each potential solution, indicate whether the application of each criterion is advantageous (a benefit) or disadvantageous (a cost). *It may be both.*
5. For each potential solution, weight all criteria on a value scale of -100 to $+100$ as follows:
   -100 = maximum disadvantage (greatest cost)
   $+100$ = maximum advantage (greatest benefit)
   0 = neutral (no benefit; no cost)
6. For each potential solution, multiply the importance weight (1 to 5) times the value weight (-100 to $+100$) for each criterion.
7. Sum the total scores for each solution.
8. Rank order the solutions, the highest scores getting first rank, and so forth. You now have a list of solutions ranked in order of their potential benefits to you in accordance with your own predetermined criteria. You are ready to make a decision.

Table 7.1 provides a form for simplifying a cost-benefit analysis and a sample analysis. Choice A in the table has more total points than choice B. Therefore, choice A will probably be more beneficial.

Table 7.1 Cost-Benefit Analysis

Potential Solutions

| Criteria | Impor-tance Weight | Choice A Value | | | Choice B Value | | |
| | | Benefit | Cost | Weight | Benefit | Cost | Weight |
	Low 1 2 3 4 5 High	Low High 0—+100	Low High 0——100	× Value	Low High 0—+100	Low High 0——100	× Value
1. Energy	5	60	0	+300	40	0	+200
2. Money	3	40	−100	+120 −300	0	−80	−240
3. Time	4	0	−100	−400	0	−10	−40
4. People	2	100	0	+200	10	0	+20
5. Space	1	0	0	0	0	0	0
6. Law	4	0	0	0	0	0	0
7. Technology	4	30	−10	+120 −40	30	−10	+120 −40
8. Culture	3	0	0	0	0	0	0
9. Politics	2	0	0	0	0	0	0
10. Ethics	5	100	0	+500	50	0	+250
11. Climate	3	20	−5	+60 −15	30	−5	+90 −15
12. Traditions	4	50	0	+200	10	0	+40
13. Other (e.g., *family*)	5	80	−10	+400 −50	20	−20	+100 −100
14. Other _____							
15. Other _____							
16. Other _____							
				+1900 −805			+820 −435
TOTALS				+1095			+385

In both choices, some of the criteria are of little consequence (space, law, culture, and politics). For one criterion, technology, choice A and choice B have about equal impact. Although choice B is less disadvantageous for time, choice A is far more beneficial for family, traditions, ethics, and people. In short, although choice B has half the disadvantages of choice A, it also has half the advantages. Therefore, choice A is overall about twice as beneficial as choice B.

Make a Decision. The method by which a group arrives at its final decision is a function of the amount of time available, the past history of the group, the kind of task being worked on, and the kind of climate the group wants to establish. Pace and Boren outlined seven commonly used decision-making strategies, all of which are some form of authority, voting, or consensus:

1. *Decision through bypass.* An idea is suggested but not discussed or voted upon. This process continues until the group decides to adopt one idea.
2. *Decision through power.* The person with the most power in the group either decides alone or endorses someone else's suggestion. (The President of the United States generally operates in this manner.)
3. *Decision through vocal coalition.* Railroading, which is a decision by a loud minority, illustrates this behavior. A boss may propose an idea, turn to the top two assistants for support, and then look to the group for endorsement. By this time members of the group may feel too threatened to volunteer a different opinion.
4. *Decision through majority vote.* Often the simplest way to arrive at a decision is to take a vote or to poll all the members. The idea receiving more than half of the votes (through secret ballot, voice vote, or show of hands) wins. This form of decision making, while highly democratic, may prematurely cut off discussion or set up an unwarranted win-lose coalition, the effect of which may be felt long after the vote.
5. *Decision through plurality.* Sometimes a majority is impossible, and rather than spend additional time, a group may decide to accept the idea supported by the greatest number of its members.
6. *Decision through consensus.* Seeking consensus is usually the most effective form of decision making, but it usually takes the most amount of time. Schein has defined consensus as follows: "If there is a clear alternative which most members subscribe to, and if those who oppose it feel they have had their chance to influence, then a consensus exists." Note that Schein does not define consensus as a unanimously agreed-upon solution. Ideally, in consensus Schein believes that group members may behave in the following manner: "I understand what most of you would like to do. I personally would not do that, but I feel that you understand what my alternative would be. I have had sufficient opportunity to sway you to my point of view but clearly have not been able to do so. Therefore, I will gladly go along with what most of you wish to do."
7. *Decision by unanimity.* While it is infrequently employed, this form of decision making represents complete agreement by all members on whatever solution is produced.

Since 1971, Graphic Controls Corporation, a Buffalo-based manufacturer of recording charts and other products used with electronic equipment for the visual presentation of data, has practiced decision making through consensus in the top two levels of management. Indications are that it uses this technique to a greater extent than do most U.S. organizations. William Dowling has described Graphic Controls' application of consensus management:

> Moreover, Graphic Controls realizes that for such an agreement to be sincere and "to take"— not to be something to which everyone pays lip service while some simultaneously make mental reservations to subvert it subsequently—it must be preceded by a process that takes all members' needs into consideration, hears dissenters out at length, strives for solutions that reconcile opposing views, and attempts to secure the commitment of any members who are still dissatisfied. Only after this process is completed do you have the commitment to act.

Does it work? After consensus was implemented, Graphic Controls' sales doubled and profits increased by eight times the 1971 level. However, a cause-effect relationship is almost impossible to demonstrate since there was no controlled research design. Graphic Controls recently allowed the measurements of its program to be made public. Table 7.2 presents a summary of some of those measurements, which indicate significant improvements in both worker attitudes and organizational effectiveness.

Conformity

Group pressure, or conformity to the established norms of a group, is apparently strong enough to lead people to condone or even perform criminal acts. In his classical experiments, Asch demonstrated the profound effect group pressure has on individual judgment. A group of stooges were instructed to proclaim publicly that the length of one line was equal to another line even though the two lines were not equal. Experimental subjects were unaware of the involvement of the stooges, and one-third of the subjects conformed to the group estimate, *even though they knew it was wrong.* Asch concluded that groups can influence individuals to conform to established norms. This conclusion becomes more dramatic when one realizes that Asch used noncohesive groups.

Schein defined a norm as a set of assumptions or expectations held by the members of a group or organization concerning what kind of behavior is right or wrong, good or bad, appropriate or inappropriate, allowed or not allowed. Rosenfeld defined conformity as the degree to which an individual's behavior corresponds to group norms. Groups can establish *explicit* (formal, usually verbalized) norms, such as IBM's dress code prohibiting the wearing of colored shirts, or *implicit* (unspoken but understood and accepted) norms, such as a civic club's norm that a tie and jacket be worn at its weekly meetings. Work groups may have established norms governing appearance, length of meetings, topics to discuss, degree of formality at meetings, type of decision-making strategy, and even propriety of the language used at meetings.

Individuals usually conform to the norms of the group having the greatest impact upon them at a given time. For example, my research on homosexual behavior in ten U.S. cities demonstrates that many homosexuals assume the behavior of their intimates only when in the direct company of these intimates. When interacting with members of the general community, particularly at work, homosexuals behave conventionally.

Rosenfeld summarized some of the key variables affecting the amount of conformity in groups:

1. Personality characteristics which may predispose group members to conform:
    a. degree of submissiveness (submissive people conform more)
    b. level of self-confidence (high degree of self-confidence equals low degree of conformity)
    c. authoritarianism (closed-minded people conform more readily to higher authority than open-minded individuals)
    d. intelligence (greater intelligence results in lower conformity)
    e. originality (greater originality equals lower conformity)
    f. need for achievement (lower need for achievement results in high conformity)
    g. need for social approval (higher need for approval results in greater conformity)

The basic elements of a good quality of work life are a safe work environment, equitable wages, equal employment opportunities, and opportunities for advancement.

Highlights

	1975	1976	1977
OSHA accidents	2.5%	2.0%	1.7%

A smaller percentage of the work force suffered serious injuries on the job in 1976 and 1977. The great majority of employees also said they were safe from physical danger at work. Some 8% reported that dangerous or unhealthy conditions were a problem for them.

	1975	1976	1977
Wages		*	*

*(increased beyond inflation rate)

Wages per hour increased the past two years. Overall, 62% of the work force felt that their wages were fair in comparison to those paid by other organizations in the area. 72% said their wages were sufficient to meet monthly expenses.

	1975	1976	1977
Female employment	30.5%	32.0%	34.3%
Minority employment	7.5%	8.7%	8.6%

Female employment increased the past two years. Overall, 72% of the female employees reported they were treated fairly on the job. The percentage of minority employees increased in 1976 but not in 1977. Overall, 84% of the minority employees said they were treated fairly on the job.

	1975	1976	1977
Promotions	7.0%	11.1%	10.9%

The percentage of employees promoted increased in 1976 but not in 1977. 61% of the employees said they were satisfied with their chances for advancement.

The relationship between a corporation and its people can also be measured in the way working life is satisfying to employees and contributes to their well-being on—and off—the job.

Satisfaction	% Satisfied		
	1975	1976–77	difference
Pay	69.9%	71.0%	1.1%
Fringe benefits	69.0	89.5	20.5
Job security	76.8	76.1	−0.7
Working conditions	71.2	77.2	6.0
Co-worker relations	88.2	89.1	0.9
Accomplishments	80.5	77.7	−2.8
Chances to develop skills	72.4	74.6	2.2
Overall job satisfaction	93.7	90.2	−3.5

Most employees were satisfied with their working lives in both 1975 and 1976–77. During this time, there was a significant increase in satisfaction with fringe benefits and a small increase in satisfaction with working conditions. Other changes were insignificant. Overall job satisfaction is higher than that recorded in Gallup polls and the Institute's own survey of the national work force.

Absenteeism and Turnover

Absenteeism went from 3.7% to 2.8% of the scheduled work hours during the three-year period. Turnover was reduced from 12.7% to 9.3% of the work force from 1975 to 1976. In 1977, it increased to 12.9%. Counting the loss of Business Forms Division employees, 33.3% of the work force left in 1977.

Work and the Quality of Life

Working life contributes, in some measure, to the quality of life. Overall, 95% of the employees expressed satisfaction with their lives. 57% of the work force were members of community, church, or social organizations, and the vast majority reported voting in local and national elections. 70% of the employees said their jobs today were preparing them with the training and experience they need for their jobs in the future. Nationally, fewer workers feel as optimistic about their employment future.

2. Intragroup variables which seem to affect conformity:
   a. cohesion (greater cohesion equals higher conformity)
   b. attractiveness of the group (the more attractive a group is to members, the greater will be their conformity)
   c. importance of the group (more importance equals higher conformity)
   d. amount of interaction (greater interaction produces higher conformity)
3. External pressures which seem to affect conformity:
   a. group size (conformity increases as size increases to four or five members and decreases when the number of members exceeds five)
   b. group structure (decentralized networks which allow greater group interaction produce higher conformity)
   c. difficulty of the problem or task confronting the group (more difficult tasks produce higher conformity)
   d. newness of situation (newer situations produce greater conformity if they resemble previously successful situations)
   e. pressure for consensus (greater pressure produces greater conformity)
   f. degree of crisis or emergency (crises produce high conformity)
   g. degree of situational ambiguity (more ambiguous situations result in higher conformity)

Hollander found that a leader could deviate from a group's norms as a function of how well he had contributed to the group's goals in the past. Calling his theory "idiosyncracy credit theory," Hollander stated that if a leader has conformed in the past, he has earned credits (similar to bank credits). As credits build up, the leader can deviate from the group without fear of reprisal.

Deviance from the norms of a group, however, usually results in ultimate ejection of the deviant member from the group.

Wenburg and Wilmot identified five sequential steps taken by most groups as they handle deviants (nonconformists):

1. Delay action (do nothing and hope that such members will automatically "get back in line").
2. Talk among themselves and use light humor with deviants.
3. Ridicule deviants (recognizing their behavior as different and shameful).
4. Apply "serious" persuasion (severe criticism or even threat).
5. Ignore, isolate, and finally reject deviants.

The following incident in the 1960s illustrates the five steps in action. A young member (named Joe) of a local civic organization decided to let his hair grow longer (below the ears). After the members had ignored Joe for four weeks, one of the officers placed a pair of scissors under Joe's lunch plate. Several other group members joined the festivities and everyone seemed to have a good time joking about haircuts, barbers—and hippies. Two more weeks passed and Joe still wore long hair. Some of the members of the club then openly ridiculed his appearance; one member even called Joe's wife and complained, "Joe is disgracing the reputation of the club." At the next meeting, the treasurer of the club approached Joe and warned him that if he didn't get a haircut by the next meeting, the membership was going to consider raising his dues. Joe quit the club that week.

Concerning haircuts, all of the members of that civic club had a common norm—except Joe. We might say that the group was a highly cohesive unit. The more closely a group conforms to its norms, attitudes, and values, the more *cohesive* it is. Shepherd defined cohesion as "the quality of a group which includes individual pride, commitment, meaning, as well as the group's stick-togetherness, ability to weather crises, and ability to maintain itself over time." As evidence of the importance of group cohesion to organizations, Schachter and associates found that cohesion is directly related to group productivity. High-cohesion groups are better able to determine the level of group production than are low-cohesion groups. According to Schachter, a high-cohesion group can have low production.

To determine whether a group you belong to is highly cohesive, Wenburg and Wilmot have suggested asking yourself such questions as the following: How many good friends do I have who are members of this group? If I had to choose between this group and another specific group to which I belong, which would I choose? Do I really feel that I belong to this group? The answers to these questions will give you much information about the group's cohesion. If the answers you and other members give are mixed, the inconsistencies probably indicate potential conflict. As we will see, internal conflict and competition can decrease the amount of cohesion in a group.

Conflict

One undesirable side effect of the famous Hawthorne studies (see chapter 3) was that conflict within organizations was perceived as bad. Frequently called the "happiness boys" because of their adherence to this principle, human relations managers of the 1940s and 1950s soon learned the naïveté of this philosophy. They soon realized that not only is conflict inevitable in an organization, but a minimal amount of conflict is desirable. Kelly reflected on this point of view:

> The human relations school fails . . . to recognize the importance of conflict as a creative force in society . . . the idea that conflict is always bad warrants closer examination. Perfect organizational health is not freedom from conflict. On the contrary, if properly handled, conflict can lead to more effective and appropriate adjustments.

Lorenz argued that controlled aggression may be necessary for human survival. Bach and Wyden identified three advantages of constructive aggression in marriage dyads: (1) partners can know where they stand; (2) they can recognize current conflict and learn to resolve it; and (3) each partner can be reminded of existing tolerance limits on all dimensions of the intimate system. Kelly has recommended that executives admit their aggression and anxiety and then begin to *manage* group conflict rather than suppress, ignore, or avoid it. Huse and Bowditch agreed with Kelly and said that "productive conflict" occurs when the following conditions are met:

> . . . there is open discussion and confrontation concerning ideas about tasks and projects. In this case conflict is regarded as a problem to be worked through using problem-solving methods. Here, a win-lose situation is avoided, and ideas are freely discussed and pooled in order to come up with a better solution than could be arrived at by a single group.

Taken together, all of these writers agreed that some conflict is beneficial to the health of a group or an organization. The following example supports such a conclusion. An academic department recently rewrote its entire curriculum. During the process of generating

Some conflict is beneficial to the health of a group or an organization.

ideas for new courses, two radically different philosophies emerged. Heated discussion often prevented rational decision making. Finally, it was agreed that one member from each group would meet to seek compromise and generate the best possible document for the entire department. The result (after an all-night meeting) was a curriculum both sides felt was superior to all previous suggestions.

Sources of conflict exist throughout an organization. Applbaum and co-workers suggested four causes:

1. Group members work closely and are interdependent.
2. Group members differ greatly in creativity.
3. Group members have different values and needs.
4. Groups face decisions central to their continuity.

Haiman suggested that groups may develop two kinds of conflict: *intrinsic* (conflicts over meanings, evidence, reasoning, and values) and *extrinsic* (conflicts over personal needs, defensiveness, feelings, and intentions).

Thus far, we have been talking about conflict *within* a group. In an organization, groups come into contact and interact with other groups in a number of ways: weekly meetings that bring department heads together; informal gatherings (picnics, socials, athletic events, coffee breaks) that bring members of different departments together; sales meetings that are attended by members of several organizational subsystems; conferences that are attended by all members of various groups. When these groups interact, formally or informally, conflict may be inevitable. As Neilsen has indicated, intergroup conflict may occur because of different personal characteristics, different interpretations of the amount of reward or status to be distributed throughout the organization, different perceptions and experiences, and competition for scarce organizational resources.

A desirable side effect of *intergroup* conflict is the effect it usually has on *intragroup* cohesion. Rosenfeld has explained this effect as follows:

> Intergroup conflict, unlike intragroup conflict, is often beneficial to the groups involved. While intragroup conflict usually tears a group apart, decreases its task activity, and produces a negative attitude toward the group's product, intergroup conflict brings group members together, increases the group's task activity, and causes members to positively evaluate their product.

Putnam and Poole (1988) state that the context in which the groups exist and the relationships that link the groups together are the dominant components of intergroup conflict. Some of the strategies employed in intergroup conflict management include structural interventions and process interventions. Structural interventions typically involve a change in the organizational structure and reallocating resources to the groups. This may be accomplished through the development of formal rules for behavior and by placing constraints on communication networks. However, the increase in formality of the group process among the groups involved in conflict often results in structural changes that may produce conflict as well. Process interventions used in intergroup conflict management involves the elimination of group boundaries and using superordinate goals to unify the groups. However, using this strategy to redirect the conflict and to create stronger relationships between the groups may not eliminate the underlying conflict between the groups.

If we have to live with either intergroup or intragroup conflict, what is the best way to manage or resolve such conflict? Pace and Boren suggest ways of handling intragroup intrinsic and extrinsic conflict. Differences in intrinsic conflict can be resolved by the use of clarification and verification (reality testing) and by broadening one's value system. Differences in extrinsic conflict can be resolved "through the establishment of mutual respect, openness, trust and trust worthiness, supportive intentions and behaviors, and a willingness to take risks attendant upon the revelation of self-knowledge to others." Schein described a conflict-reducing technique developed by Robert Blake:

1. Each group separately describes its own image of itself and its image of the other group.
2. Through representatives these images are then reported by each group to the other. Both groups now have new data about how each perceives the other.
3. The next state is not to react, but to meet separately to consider what kind of behavior on the part of each group may have led to the image the other group holds.
4. These behavioral hypotheses are then shared and discussed openly by both groups.
5. In the final stage the groups work together toward reducing the discrepancy between self-image and the image held by the other groups by planning how to relate differently toward each other in the future.

Neilsen listed seven strategies for reducing intergroup conflict, ranging from physical separation to intense interaction:

1. *Physical separation.* Reducing the opportunity for interaction.
2. *Limited interaction.* On selected issues with superordinate goals and decision-making rules previously established.
3. *Use of integrators.* Individuals seen by both groups as high-status people.
4. *Third-party consultants.* Neutral high-status parties who mediate direct negotiations between representatives of both groups.

5. *Negotiation without consultants.* Direct negotiation without third parties.
6. *Exchange of members.* Clarification of issues and familiarity of each group is gained, thus reducing perceptual differences.
7. *Multilevel interaction.* Intense interaction between both groups.

Huse and Bowditch reported an approach that reduced manufacturing costs in one plant. For one afternoon, the plant was shut down and *all* employees were assigned to problem-identification groups and encouraged to generate a list of key problems facing the organization. At the end of the afternoon, each group reported its findings to all other groups. Two weeks later, the plant shut down again, and a specific set of problems identified from the earlier meeting was assigned for solution. For the next two months, the plant shut down every Friday afternoon so the groups could "work on their list of problems." Through this team effort, morale and productivity rose, while costs and absenteeism dropped.

Cushman & King (1985) have identified the rule-governed myths, rituals, and social dramas that may be employed to resolve conflict (from a rule-based cultural perspective) in organizations within the United States, Japan, and Yugoslavia. In Japan: myth=nemawashi; rituals=one-on-one consultation, ringi and go-betweens; social drama=cultural isolation. In United States: myth=rugged individualism; rituals=conciliation, mediation, fact-finding, arbitration; social drama=appeal. In Yugoslavia: myth=self management; rituals=rituals of the socio-political community, the worker's council and the joint committee; social drama=social drama of the socio-political community.

In sum, conflict exists within groups, between groups, and within the organization as a whole. Successful groups and organizations learn how to manage conflict through open confrontation and effective interaction.

Effectiveness of Small Groups in Organizations

Leaving the discussion of some important factors that influence the operation and output of small groups in organizations, we will now consider briefly how to assess group effectiveness.

Schein has listed six criteria for determining whether a group developed maturely and functions smoothly. He believed that the following criteria allow a group to monitor its progress and identify its main weaknesses:

1. Does the group have the capacity to deal realistically with its environment and is it independent of its environment to an optimal degree?
2. Is there a basic agreement within the group about ultimate goals and values?
3. Is there in the group a capacity for self-knowledge? Does the group understand why it does what it does?
4. Is there an optimum use of the resources available within the group?
5. Does the group have the capacity to learn from its experience? Can it assimilate new information and respond flexibly to it?
6. Are the group's internal processes integrated—communication, decision making, distribution of authority and influence, and norms?

Table 7.3   Bales's Group Interaction Analysis

Maintenance Behaviors	Task Behaviors	Self-Serving Behaviors

1. Positive reactions
  a. Shows solidarity
  b. Shows tension release
  c. Shows agreement
	2. Answers
	  a. Gives suggestions
	  b. Gives opinions
	  c. Gives information
	
	3. Questions
	  a. Asks for information
	  b. Asks for opinions
	  c. Asks for suggestions
		4. Negative reactions
		  a. Shows disagreement
		  b. Shows tension
		  c. Shows antagonism

Bales (1954) developed a system for assessing group interaction that has been widely used. Based on the theory that all human interaction in the small-group setting can be viewed as a sequence of questions, answers, and positive and negative reactions to the questions and answers, Bales generated an instrument that enables observers to assess group process. As can be seen in table 7.3, Bales's approach closely parallels the three functional roles assumed by group members discussed previously: task behaviors, maintenance behaviors, and self-serving behaviors. Negative reactions exemplify self-serving behaviors; positive reactions exemplify maintenance or group-building behaviors; and asking questions or giving answers exemplifies the task role of members.

Using a specific form and scoring procedure, an observer is able to analyze the interaction patterns of a small group. Bales suggested rough guidelines to use when determining whether a particular group has done well:

1. About 50 percent of all remarks made in meetings are answers, while the remaining 50 percent consist of questions and reactions. (Such a balance may indicate successful communication.)
2. There are about twice as many positive reactions in most meetings as there are negative reactions, yet a balance between positive and negative reactions may be more desirable.
3. Rates of disagreement and antagonism that are too high are sure indicators of trouble.
4. Too much agreement (and not enough disagreement) may be an indication of either a lack of involvement or a threatening, inhibiting atmosphere.
5. Groups in a smoothly operating condition tend to show relatively high rates of suggestion. (The rate of negative reaction usually increases along with the rate of suggestions given.)

For a small group wanting a complete computer analysis of its interaction patterns, Lashbrook and Bodaken developed a program called *process analysis* for *five*-person groups (PROANA 5). It includes variables of member participation, network usage, clique formation, detrimental cliques, communication propensity, leadership, member isolation, and member dominance.

Participative Decision-Making Groups

In recent years, much attention has been focused on worker participation in organizational decision making. Over the past decade, many forms of participation have emerged around the world. Monge and Miller (1988) have created a typology of the four major programs used to increase the amount of worker input into organizational matters. The first type is referred to as European industrial democracy, which allows workers to elect representatives who participate on committees at various levels throughout the organization. This type of program is typically found in West Germany and socialist countries, such as Yugoslavia. The second type, frequently found in the United States, is the Scanlon System. Scanlon Systems typically involve the use of employee committees, or work groups, to include workers in everyday decisions regarding innovations within the workplace. The third type is the Chinese Down-the-Line program, which was initiated during the cultural revolution in China and was designed to decrease the role of the state in the industrial system and increase worker participation and organizational independence. This form of participation is different to most because the main emphasis is getting higher level employees involved in the work of their subordinates. Workers elect congresses, which represent all demographic types in the work force. These congresses deal with a wide range of organizational issues, such as the election of managers, performance appraisals, and acceptance of management proposals. The last form of participation, quality circles, was originally used in Japan and has caught on strongly in the United States.

Motorola Corporation has frequently run the following ad in the *Wall Street Journal:*

Many factors contribute to productivity: producible designs, superior tools, clever processes, minimal regulations. But, heading the list is people. Most of us are aware of the impressive productivity improvements Japanese companies have realized with their people by using teams of cooperating workers called Quality Circles. Wisely, hundreds of American companies now are duplicating these efforts in their factories. At Motorola, over a decade ago, we initiated a plan of our own. Today we call it the Participative Management Program (PMP), and it reaches beyond the factory floor. We believe it has helped us achieve the same, and often better, quality and productivity results for which Japanese companies get credit.

PMP is an effective way to get the individual worker more involved, responsible, informed, and therefore, more productive. Any individual worker can suggest things about any job he or she does that a supervisor may not know as well. As management listens and acts, quality and output rise. In PMP, teams of employees meet frequently, sometimes daily, among themselves and with support groups to tackle the basics. Everyone is encouraged to define problems and suggest solutions. The management listens, contributes, acts. Each team operates to high, published standards which it participates in setting. The teams measure their improving performance to these standards daily, weekly, monthly. And everyone benefits. Employees who want to can communicate additionally by submitting written recommendations. These are posted on prominent bulletin boards and must be answered in 72 hours. Not just with words, but with changes in tools, procedures or policies when humanly possible.

The results have been dramatic. Quality, output, and customer service are way up. Costs are down. Our jobs are more satisfying.

Another organization, RCA, has used quality circles to increase productivity and help people with extremely boring jobs gain more interest in their daily routine. Groups of six to eight people were assembled in different locations around the United States. Each group met on company time in a company location and, with assistance from the personnel department, picked its own facilitator and met either weekly or biweekly to look at their work activity and identify ways of improving productivity. All ideas were written, and several were implemented. RCA has raised some questions, however, about its own use of quality circles (QC):

1. Do QC groups need their supervisors?
2. Do QC groups still need their union?
3. Is RCA ready to implement the ideas generated from the QC groups?
4. Does RCA give QC groups the information they need to evaluate their own ideas?
5. Do the QC groups, particularly the leaders, have the necessary skills in problem solving, brainstorming, and group dynamics, in general, to facilitate effective meetings?

What are quality circles? The description here will expand somewhat on that in chapter 3. The quality circles used in Japan and elsewhere are small groups of employees, usually six to eight, who voluntarily meet to solve problems relating to the quality of goods and services produced by a company. Usually the employees are from the same organizational work unit, and the problems they discuss relate generally to a product or service as well as to the specific responsibilities that unit has for the product or service. The idea originated with an American, William Deming, who was instrumental in helping the Japanese economy recover after World War II. In 1982, there were over 100,000 registered QCs in Japan compared with about 1,500 in the United States. Lawler and Mohrman have estimated that in 1985 over 90 percent of the *Fortune* "500" companies had quality control programs in their structures. Although the reaction of American business leaders to these groups has been almost uniformly positive (e.g., AT&T, Xerox, Ford Motor Co., Honeywell, General Motors), acceptance is not universal, particularly among labor unions. In Britain, for example, Ford's attempt to introduce QCs was rejected by the unions because Ford bypassed them in the process of design and implementation of the QCs. The unions suspected that Ford was trying to increase *productivity* (which they viewed as a change in working conditions) instead of just *quality*. One auto union leader in Buffalo, Thomas Fricano, has commented on QCs: "We keep our guard up to make sure this is not utilized to take away any contractual provisions. The concept works and it works very well as long as both sides exhibit integrity. If management tries to use it to bust the union, we'd move to quickly do away with it. On the other side, if labor uses it to try to extort demands from the company, they'd do away with it. But, you've got to be on your guard."

Other questions arise, particularly in times of economic distress. Can collaborative approaches survive if workers perceive that their cooperation in cutting costs and improving quality and output does not result in greater job security? In early 1982, the United Automobile Workers union (UAW) entered into an historic agreement with the Ford Motor Company in which the union, for the first time in history, traded real benefits and salary increases for job security. If this pact is the forerunner of others in the automobile and other industries (particularly those faced with extreme foreign competition), it represents a dramatic shift in labor-management relations in the United States.

If QCs are to work well in an organization, the following steps should be taken:

1. *Management must be committed to QCs.*
2. *QCs must be part of a long-term strategic plan for growth and development in an organization.*
3. *Participants in QCs must be trained adequately in participative problem-solving, group dynamics, and communication techniques for small groups.*
4. *QCs should start with a few work units and, as effectiveness increases, they should spread throughout the company.*

However, Lawler and Mohrman reported in a 1985 study that most of the companies they observed had ineffective quality control programs, programs which because of several design factors, were destined to self-destruct. They believe that some of the problems that most often lead to destruction of a Quality Circle program include:

1. Middle managers often resist or reject the new ideas generated by quality circles. This results in the QC participants becoming discouraged with the entire program.
2. Managers who accepted the ideas generated by the quality circles did not necessarily implement those ideas. This resulted in a serious loss of credibility of both the program and management.
3. Groups run out of problems to address, particularly after management has resisted or accepted without implementing most of their new ideas.
4. Groups whose ideas are actually implemented are disappointed when they receive no financial rewards for contributing to the organization's savings produced by their QC ideas.

Lawler and Mohrman conclude that "circles encounter many threats to their continued existence. Because of these threats, it is not likely that managers will institutionalize and sustain programs over a long time."

Despite Lawler and Mohrman's very real concerns with quality circles, there are many groups in existence that are successful and do take into account many of the points raised. One such QC program is that developed by Niagara Frontier Services, Inc., a major supermarket chain from the Northeast. A summary of this program is presented at the end of this chapter.

Effective Small-Group Organizational Communication Programs

In order to see how small group communication is used in different organizations, we will look at four companies with successful programs.

Pitney Bowes Corporation, an international manufacturer of mailing and other office equipment headquartered in Stamford, Connecticut, established a massive employee communication program designed to maximize the opportunity for employee input. For about one hour each month, all 18,000 employees stop work and meet in groups of about a dozen with their section supervisor. Since Pitney Bowes has no labor unions, the meetings are not labor-type meetings. Wages are not on the agenda. The supervisor may discuss a problem, or an employee may bring one up. New policies, new programs, and suggestions are frequently talked over. The following week each department head meets with the section supervisor and elected employee representatives (one per section) to discuss unsettled problems. The next week the department heads, along with an elected employee representative, meet with division heads about problems that are still unresolved. A week later the group vice presidents meet with the division heads and an equal number of employee representatives. Minutes of all meetings are printed and posted on bulletin boards. Fred Allen, chairman of the board of Pitney Bowes, commented, "We think our kind of participation means more than the European kind, where employees may have two or three members of the board on their side, but the employee representatives can be outvoted at any time."

Xerox Corporation, an international manufacturer of copiers and other office equipment, also headquartered in Stamford, Connecticut, developed one of the most extensive and successful total communication programs among U.S. corporations. A major element in the Xerox program are the employee communication meetings. There are three types of meetings, each with its own purpose:

1. *Information only meeting.* Information is disseminated downward and no dialogue is expected. No restriction other than space is placed on the number of people who can attend the meeting.
2. *Workshop meeting.* These are work sessions in which problems are discussed and solutions proposed. Usually no more than fifteen people are present at such meetings.
3. *Participative or dialogue meeting.* The major focus is the sharing of ideas, information, and opinions. Management provides information, answers questions, and listens to the views of participants. The primary idea is to promote understanding between managers and employees about work goals, priorities, and procedures. Usually thirty-five to fifty people attend such meetings.

Xerox provides its managers with a handbook to prepare them for conducting these meetings. Included in the handbook are the following instructions:

1. Always be candid: Answer questions and comments truthfully; if you can't answer because information is confidential or proprietary, say so; if you don't know the answer, say that, too. It is helpful, however, if you can make a commitment to obtain an answer. You're not expected to have all the answers; often, in fact, your subordinates can provide the details and the answer.

2. Be well prepared: One of the best ways to prepare yourself is to invite the participants to submit questions several weeks before the meeting. There are two advantages. First, you know what's of interest to the participants, and, second, some attendees find it difficult to stand up and ask a question spontaneously at a meeting. The presubmitted questions permit people to prepare their questions with care and gives you an equal opportunity to develop a careful answer.

3. Encourage participation: As the meeting leader, you set the tone: so it's up to you to put the audience at ease and to encourage their frank participation. One way to do that is to be open and informal in your answers. You can help break the ice by tackling a difficult question early in the meeting—perhaps using a presubmitted question. The audience will get the message that you *are* willing to discuss troublesome matters candidly.

It can also be helpful to ask the audience to challenge your answers—to seek clarification— or follow up when they don't feel you've fully answered the question.

4. Treat participants as mature, responsible people: Don't talk down. Questions or comments may seem irrelevant to you, but they are important to the person making them.

One final word. You may have to modify somewhat the previous suggestions in order to meet your special needs or style. By all means do so, keeping in mind that the basic purpose of the meeting is an exchange of ideas, information, and opinions.

Xerox also provides a checklist for managers to use sequentially, beginning a month before a meeting. This checklist may be helpful to any organization undertaking such a program of meetings:

Three to four weeks before the meeting:

- Set date and time.
- Reserve location for meeting.
- Prepare list of attendees; mail invitations and forms for presubmitted questions.
- Order refreshments.
- Arrange for audiovisual material and/or signs, if required.

Two weeks before meeting:

- Collect presubmitted questions and route for answering.

One week before meeting:

- Prepare copies of presubmitted questions to distribute at meeting.
- Place agenda, any prepared remarks, and questions and answers in a three-ring binder and give to the speaker three days before the meeting.
- Confirm arrangements for meeting room and refreshments.

Day before the meeting:

- Get supplies ready: meeting questions, critiques, sharpened pencils, pads, ashtrays, and so forth.

Day of the meeting:

- Take supplies to the meeting at least one hour before it begins.
- Check that refreshments are ready.
- Distribute presubmitted questions before meeting; mail critiques to attendees immediately after meeting.

Within two weeks after the meeting:

- Tabulate and analyze critiques.

A program called the "Number 1 Team" program was introduced at one of General Motors' plants in 1966. The original objective was to establish goals for each department in conjunction with the hourly-rated employees and to solicit their efforts to achieve those goals through small-group meetings. The supervisor attended the original meetings with his or her department when the goal was introduced. After that, meetings were conducted by an employee acting as a conference leader. This system lasted about one year, until all departments had achieved their goals (they received a free luncheon in recognition). The concept of regular meetings was then expanded throughout the plant. The main purpose of the expanded meetings was to establish better rapport between supervisors and employees and to improve the overall esprit de corps in the plant.

Meetings were held in small groups of five to seven in a relaxed atmosphere to discuss subjects of the group's choosing (e.g., current events, sports, problems at the plant, status of their work unit). The only formality observed was the time and place of the meeting. Discussions lasted about one hour, were scheduled by the supervisor, and included coffee and careful minutes for soliciting feedback and answers to questions. Although problems of the

Figure 7.4 Team meeting evaluation form.

Moderator _____   Team _____

Meeting Location _____   Date _____

Meeting Length _____   Topic _____

Environmental Factors   *Comments*

1. Room comfortable?   _____

2. Able to hear?   _____

3. Effective use of visual aids?   _____

4. Refreshments served?   _____

Meeting Dynamics

1. Moderator adequately prepared?   _____

2. Extent of team participation?   _____

3. Purpose of meeting explained?   _____

4. Feedback encouraged?   _____

5. Adequate notes taken?   _____

6. Discussion kept on the topic at hand?   _____

7. Team apprised of performance?   _____

8. Problem priorities established?   _____

9. Items requiring follow-up?   _____

10. Adequate summarization?   _____

11. Other?   _____

Evaluated by: _____

plant were discussed, the initial focus of the meetings was more informal, in order to lay the groundwork for future discussions of a more substantive nature. The do's and don'ts established for these meetings follows. The evaluation form used is shown in figure 7.4.

Do:

1. Encourage free discussion on the general subject of our industry and what we can do individually and collectively to improve our position.

2. Maintain just enough control of sessions so that each person has an opportunity to express his or her views if they choose.

3. Let the conferees know that these meetings are for the purpose of establishing better communications and understanding among the members of the department, supervision and service personnel.

4. Approach the sessions with the idea that nothing concrete in the way of specific job improvements is expected or required to result from the employees' comments. Primarily interested in feedback to plan future programs based on employee needs and desires.

5. Limit the size to a comfortable number—5 to 7, more if you can handle them.

6. Select groups of employees in your department that work together as units. Analyze your group rather than scheduling by convenience.

7. Be firm, but not overbearing if company policy is called into question.

8. Follow up on any specific requests for information made by an individual—seek help from No. 1 Team Coordinator when you cannot accomplish on your own.

9. After several sessions, try to analyze discussions for common interests—any desire on part of employees to correct or change a condition that exists.

Don'ts:

1. Don't try to hold a controlled formal meeting with opening speech or lecture, but be prepared to start the discussion by requesting employees' ideas on how we can plan future programs that will be mutually beneficial.

2. Don't argue or take sides during a discussion on controversial issues—don't ridicule others' opinions.

3. Don't assume a superior or condescending attitude toward the group—you are part of it.

4. Don't make general policy statements if you are not positive that you are correct.

5. Don't allow any one member to monopolize the discussion—including yourself.

6. Don't assign values to the meetings either positive or negative—"These meetings will solve our problems" or "I don't know why we're here—let's have coffee and get back to work." Until some discernible pattern evolves, treat initial meetings as rap sessions.

7. Don't take a "stab" at answers to questions that may come up—write them down and get the correct answers later.

8. Don't have such loose control that the meeting resembles a small mob.

Niagara Frontier Services, Inc. is primarily a food services company and parent company to Tops Friendly Markets, one of the largest supermarket chains in Western New York. The following Quality Circle program was developed by Jack Mitchell, a member of the Human Resources and Organizational Development Department of NFS. Information about NFS' program, its structure and answers to key questions about the program are presented in their entirety as an example of an effective QC program.

Keys to the NFS Quality Circle Program

In the development of our Quality Circle program, we feel there are some essential points which you, the future participant, must be aware. The most important point to remember is that this requires effort from everyone, both management and worker alike. Through everyone's cooperation we feel the program can be quite successful. Some of the major areas essential to the program are:

1. *A People Building Philosophy.* There should be a desire by all employees to help one another develop and grow. This is a team effort and requires the effort of many separate talents. Use this circle as a means of developing both yourself and those around you.
2. *It Is Voluntary.* The Q.C.'s are designed for the company's as well as your benefit. The benefit to the company is a reduction in cost and better quality output. The benefit to you is an increased say in the decisions affecting your job.

   As such, you have complete freedom to take advantage of it, if you want to. Feel free to join, drop out or just make suggestions to a Quality Circle.

   We'd like you to volunteer because we feel you can contribute to our success.
3. *Projects Are Circle Efforts—Not Individual.* A Quality Circle is a team effort and projects which are chosen should be of interest and value to all members. Don't use the circle as an opportunity to "air your own problems." The focus should be on those problems affecting the entire group.
4. *Your Creativity Is Encouraged.* All ideas are welcome in a circle. No idea is considered too "crazy" to be ignored. Remember, even from the wildest ideas come practical solutions.
5. *Projects Are Related to Your Own Work Area.* We recognize that you are the expert at what you do. No one is in a better position to know the problems that need to be corrected. Quality Circles will not have you getting involved in areas of little importance to you. Look around and identify some potential problems that you can offer to the circle group. Some of your co-workers (and circle group members) may see the same "problems" and the circle offers you an opportunity to correct them.

Program Structure

For our program to be successful, it is important that it be well structured. As Quality Circles begin to be implemented at NFS, you'll notice that some individuals will be performing certain distinct roles in the process. The roles being performed in the Q.C. program include:

1. The Steering Committee
2. The Facilitator
3. Circle Leader
4. Circle Group Members

1. *Steering Committee.* The committee is a group of people at the management level who represent various divisions in the overall operation. Their function is to set the rules and regulations for circle teams. The committee will help determine where the program will begin and identifies areas that circle groups will initially be involved in. They typically meet on a monthly basis to keep an update on circle activities and solve any problems that members may have.

2. *Facilitator.* The role of the facilitator is to coordinate all circle activities. He is not a member of any particular quality circle. The facilitator is responsible for working closely with circle leaders and helping them in any way possible. He will train circle leaders, help solve group problems, and serve as a link between top management and the circle.

3. *Circle Leader.* The circle leader is responsible for the operation and performance of the Quality Circle. The main job is to conduct meetings and assure that they run smoothly. In running the meeting, the leader: sets an agenda; makes sure everyone participates; keeps minutes; assigns tasks; and keeps an update of what all group members are doing.

   The individuals selected as leaders must be willing to serve in this role. The circle leader can change at any time and if you have a desire to lead, you should notify the facilitator immediately.

4. *Circle Group Members.* This will be your role as you initially participate in the Quality Circle program. You will be in a circle with some or all of your co-workers on the job. As a member of a circle team your responsibilities include: participating at meetings; collecting data; analyzing data; developing and implementing problems, solutions, and developing management presentations.

It is important to remember that the circle is a joint effort. You are not doing anything alone. There will be others who will be relying on your commitment and involvement. Abide by the circle codes of conduct: Be on time, listen to other's ideas, don't monopolize group conversation, and if you have to criticize, criticize ideas and not people. The end result will be a smoothly running team and a better problem-solving effort.

Quality Circle Questions and Answers

The following are some answers to frequently asked questions regarding quality circles.

What Is It?

A group of people who voluntarily meet together on a regular basis to identify, analyze, and solve quality and other problems in their own work areas.

Where Do Members Come From?

Ideally, members of a particular team should be from the same work area, or who do similar work, so that the problems they select will be familiar to all of them.

How Many Members Are In a Team?

An ideal size is seven or eight members. The size can vary from as few as three members to as many as about fifteen members. The size will never be so great that each member cannot have sufficient time to participate and contribute at each meeting.

Figure 7.5 The problem-solving process.

| Problem Identification | → | Problem Selection | → | Problem Analysis | → | Recommendation to Management |

What Are the Objectives?

- Reduce errors and enhance quality
- Inspire more effective teamwork
- Promote job involvement
- Create a problem-solving capability
- Build an attitude of "problem prevention"
- Improve communication
- Develop harmonious manager/worker relationships
- Develop a greater safety awareness
- Promote cost reduction

How Is the Program Organized?

The program is an integrated system made up of several parts:

- The members themselves
- The circle leaders
- The facilitator (program coordinator)
- Steering committee

How Long Do Meetings Normally Last and How Often Are They Held?

As a rule of thumb, meetings occur once a week and each meeting lasts for approximately one hour. However, some organizations have introduced variations. An example is a half-hour meeting once a week. Another variation is to hold a one or two hour meeting every two weeks.

How Does the Process Work?

Figure 7.5 graphically depicts the steps involved:
  Problem identification can result from any of the following:

- The members
- Management
- Staff or technical experts

Typically, several problems are identified. The problem selected is determined by circle members. Analysis is performed by the members, with assistance, if needed, by the appropriate technical experts.

  The members make their recommendation directly to the manager using a technique described as "The Management Presentation." This technique is described in greater detail in a later section of this book.

What Takes Place During a Meeting?

Any of several activities may occur during a meeting such as the following:

- Identifying a theme or problem to work on
- Analyzing a problem
- Preparing recommendations for implementing a solution
- Participating in a presentation to management

How Should Members Approach Problems?

Members should approach problems with a positive attitude—one that says, "We can do it!". There is a tendency to shrug off problems with, "Why bother, management will not listen anyway." The fact is that many recommendations are approved by management. Open discussion and brainstorming, with everyone participating in a positive and cooperative manner, will shed new light on any problem.

What Is a Steering Committee?

The steering committee sets goals and objectives for the team activities. It establishes operational guidelines and controls the rate of expansion.

Who Should be On the Steering Committee?

Representatives from major departments within the company should be members of the steering committee. The facilitator will also be a member.

What Is a Facilitator?

The facilitator is the individual responsible for coordinating and directing team activities.

What Are General Problem Areas Selected by Members?

Virtually anything which affects the quality of your work is a candidate for problem analysis.

What Is the Management Presentation?

A management presentation is where the members describe to their manager what project they have been working on and what recommendations they wish to make concerning it. Participants use charts that they have prepared. This event represents a most exciting form of participation, communication, and recognition to all.

When Is a Management Presentation Made?

A presentation should be made to:

- Show completed projects
- Make recommendations
- Provide status on long-term projects

SUMMARY

Groups were defined as collections of individuals whose relationships with one another make them interdependent to some degree. A *small group* consists of two or more people communicating face-to-face, each member aware of the presence of all other members within the group. A group can also be defined as a subsystem within an organizational system, with input (goals and people's values and needs), transformation (leadership, size, network, interaction), output (productivity and morale), and feedback.

People join groups to satisfy certain personal needs (security, social, ego, self-actualizing). Groups exist for primary, casual, educational, therapeutic, and problem-solving reasons. Organizational group activities follow either a formal network (problem solving, decision making, meetings, quality centers, councils, conferences, training sessions) or an informal network (rap sessions, social events, grapevine, retreats).

Several factors influence the outcome of a small-group activity. Among them are variables relating to both group input and group transformation. Group members assume three *functional roles*: task, maintenance, and self-serving. Most groups have at least two *leaders,* one fulfilling the task functions and the other meeting the socioemotional needs of the group. Thus, it is theoretically possible for any member to assume the role of group leader at any time. Group *network* also influences group output. Highly centralized networks (wheel, chain, Y) tend to make the fewest errors, send the fewest messages, take the least time, and have the poorest morale. Decentralized networks (circle) produce higher morale, more messages and errors, take longer, and generally work better for complex tasks. Seating arrangements were also shown to be an indicator of status and leadership in the group.

Depending upon the nature of the task, most groups are more productive than individuals. A group *problem-solving* model was described based on four steps: identifying and analyzing the problem, generating several possible solutions, evaluating the solutions, and making a decision. Several alternatives for arriving at a decision ranging from withdrawal to unanimity were presented. Group pressure, or *conformity,* was shown to be an important factor in the functioning of the small group. Several personal, intragroup, and external variables were identified as influencing and being influenced by conformity. *Conflict* was proposed as an inevitable outcome of intragroup and intergroup interaction; in fact, some conflict may be desirable for the health of a group or an organization. The successful executive learns how to manage conflict rather than ignoring or avoiding it. Intergroup conflict was shown to have desirable outcomes on intragroup cohesion. Techniques ranging from complete isolation to intense interaction were suggested for resolving conflict.

The assessment of group effectiveness was briefly discussed, and a description of Bales's process interaction method was given. According to Bales, most groups interact by asking questions, giving answers, and reacting to these questions and answers positively or negatively. Paralleling the three functional roles—maintenance, task, and self-serving—Bales developed an instrument and suggested criteria for group process measurement. Actual small group organizational communication programs were described.

EXERCISES

1. List the number of groups to which you belong. Think of the most effective group. Why do you think it is so effective? What specific factors influence your choice?
2. Look at your list for exercise 1. Which groups would you say are small? Give reasons for your answer. What is needed to turn any of these groups into an aggregate? How many aggregates do you participate in each day?
3. Which of your needs are satisfied by the group you think is most effective?
4. Visit an organization of your choice. Spend at least one entire day observing the whole organization. How many group activities did you observe? Did they have a specific name or purpose? Were they formal or informal? If you can, observe one group for at least thirty minutes to an hour. How large was it? How often did each member participate? Did one member dominate discussion? Did all members have a chance to speak? Did the members appear to be happy with the group? Try to interview one or two of the group's members after you leave the group. What were their reactions to the group? to you?
5. Observe another group for at least one hour. This can be a campus group or a government agency meeting or a business staff meeting. Were all three functional roles assumed? Did one person act as leader? How did you know? Which functional role(s) did this person assume? Did the seating arrangement have anything to do with the selection of the group's leader(s)?
6. Think of the last group meeting you were a member of. List all rules (do's and don'ts) for an effective small-group meeting that were violated.
7. Set up three or four small groups (three to five members). Replicate Leavitt's experiment as described in this chapter. Were your results the same as Leavitt's? Which network was most productive? Which took the most time? Which made the fewest errors? Which resulted in the most satisfied members?
8. Arrange a brainstorming session for four to six people. Ask for suggestions on how to solve one of the following problems: air pollution in Los Angeles, atmospheric atomic bomb testing by France, the growing shortage of gasoline, or the high cost of college tuition. Be sure that no idea is evaluated. Set a time limit (ten minutes to one hour) and use one member as the recorder (or use a tape recorder). How many ideas did your group generate? How did the members feel about this activity? Repeat this exercise for a group of four to six individuals. Ask each one *alone* to generate his or her solutions. Add the total of all the individuals. Which generated more solutions? the group? the individuals (taken together)?
9. Observe one of the following meetings: a faculty meeting, a student senate or faculty senate meeting, a staff meeting, a department meeting, or a committee meeting. How were most decisions made? Were the members satisfied with the format? What other norms were you able to identify? Did most members observe them? How did the group handle deviates? How was conflict resolved? What did the leader(s) do about conflict?
10. Identify a decision you are about to make that has at least two alternate solutions. Compute the cost-benefit analysis for each alternative to determine the most beneficial solution.

11. Adapt Bales's process analysis format to observe and analyze one of the groups you investigated previously. Compare the group's interaction with the criteria established by Bales. Do you consider it an effective group?

BIBLIOGRAPHY AND REFERENCES

Albuquerque Journal, 17 June 1973, p. 20.

Allen, F. "Winning and Holding Employee Loyalty." *Nation's Business,* April 1977, pp. 40–44.

Asch, S. E. *Social Psychology.* Englewood Cliffs, N. J.: Prentice-Hall, 1952.

Bach, G., and P. Wyden. *The Intimate Enemy.* New York: Morrow, 1968.

Bales, R. F. *Interaction Process Analysis: A Method for the Study of Small Groups.* Cambridge, Mass.: Addison-Wesley, 1950.

Barnlund, Dean C. "A Comparative Study of Individual, Majority, and Group Judgment." *Journal of Abnormal and Social Psychology* 58 (1959):55–60.

Bavelas, A. "Communication Patterns in Task-Oriented Groups." *Journal of Acoustical Society of America* 22 (1950):725–30.

Benne, K. D., and P. Sheats. "Functional Roles of Group Members." *Journal of Social Issues* 4 (1948):41–49.

Bouchard, T. J., Jr., and J. Hare. "Size, Performance, and Potential in Brainstorming Groups." *Journal of Applied Psychology* 54 (1970):51–55.

Brooks, W. *Speech Communication.* 4th ed. Dubuque, Iowa: Wm. C. Brown Publishers, 1981.

Bunker, D., and G. Dalton. "The Comparative Effectiveness of Groups and Individuals in Solving Problems." In *Managing Group and Intergroup Relations,* edited by J. Lorsch and P. Lawrence. Homewood, Ill.: Richard D. Irwin, 1972.

Cartwright, D., and A. Zander, eds. *Group Dynamics: Research and Theory.* New York: Harper & Row, 1968.

Cushman, D.P., and S. S. King. "National and Organizational Cultures in Conflict Resolution: Japan, The United States, and Yugoslavia." In Communication, Culture, and Organizational Processes, International and Intercultural Handbook 9 (1985), edited by W. Gudykunst, L. Stewart, and S. Ting-Toomey. Beverly Hills, CA: Sage.

D'Aprix, Roger. *Employee Communication Meetings—A Handbook.* Stamford, Conn.: Xerox Corporation, 1970.

Davis, K. *Human Behavior at Work.* New York: McGraw-Hill Book Co., 1972.

Dowling, William F. "Consensus Management and Graphic Controls." *Organizational Dynamics* 5 (Winter 1977):23–47.

Goldhaber, G. "Communication and Student Unrest." Report to the President of University of New Mexico, 1971. Typewritten.

Guetzkow, H., and H. Simon. "The Impact of Certain Communication Nets upon Organization and Performance in Task-Oriented Groups." *Management Science* 1 (1955):233–50.

Haiman, F. *Group Leadership and Democratic Action.* Boston: Houghton Mifflin Co., 1951.

Hare, A. P. *Small Group Research.* New York: The Free Press, 1962.

Hare, A. P., and R. F. Bales. "Seating Position and Small Group Interaction." *Sociometry* 26 (1963):480–86.

Hirota, K. "Group Problem Solving and Communication." *Japanese Journal of Psychology* 24 (1953):176–77.

Hollander, E. "Conformity, Status and Idiosyncracy Credit." *Psychological Review* 65 (1958):117–27.

Homans, G. *The Human Group.* New York: Harcourt, Brace & World, 1950.

Huse, E., and J. Bowditch. *Behavior in Organizations.* Reading, Mass.: Addison-Wesley, 1973.

Kelly, J. "Make Conflict Work for You." *Harvard Business Review* 48 (July–August 1970):103–13.

Kriesberg, M. "Executives Evaluate Administrative Conferences." *Advanced Management* 15 (1950):15–17.

Lashbrook, W., and E. Bodaken. "PROANA 5: A Venture in Computer Assisted Instruction in Small Group Communication." *Computer Studies in the Humanities and Verbal Behavior* 2 (1969):98–101.

Lawler, E., P. Mirvis, W. Clarkson, and L. Randall. "How Graphic Controls Assesses the Human Side of the Corporation." *Management Review,* October 1981, pp. 54–63.

Lawler, E., and S. Mohrman. "Quality Circles after the Fad." *Harvard Business Review* (January–February, 1985):65–71.

Lawson, E. D. "Reinforced and Non-Reinforced Four-Man Communication Nets." *Psychological Reports* 14 (1964):287–96.

———. "Reinforcement in Group Problem Solving with Arithmetic Problems." *Psychological Reports* (1964):703–10.

Leavitt, H. J. "Some Effects of Certain Communication Patterns on Group Performance." *Journal of Abnormal and Social Psychology* 46 (1951):38–50.

Lesniak, R., M. Yates, G. Goldhaber, and W. Richards. "NETPLOT: An Original Computer Program for Interpreting NEGOPY." Paper presented at a meeting of the International Communication Association, Berlin, Germany, 1977.

Lewin, K. "Field Theory and Experiment in Social Psychology: Concepts and Methods." *American Journal of Sociology* 46 (1939):868–96.

Lorenz, K. *On Aggression.* New York: Harcourt, Brace & World, 1966.

Madron, T. *Small Group Methods and the Study of Politics.* Evanston, Ill.: Northwestern University Press, 1969.

Maier, N. R. F. "Assets and Liabilities in Group Problem Solving: The Need for an Integrative Function." *Psychological Review* 74 (1967):239–49.

Maslow, A. *Motivation and Personality.* New York: Harper & Row, 1954.

Monge, Peter, R., and Katherine I. Miller. "Participative Processes in Organizations." In Handbook of Organizational Communication, edited by Gerald Goldhaber and George Barnett. Norwood, NJ: Ablex, 1988.

Mulder, M. "Communication Structure, Decision Structure, and Group Performance." *Sociometry* 23 (1960):1–14.

Neilsen, E. "Understanding and Managing Intergroup Conflict." In *Managing Group and Intergroup Relations,* edited by J. Lorsch and P. Lawrence. Homewood, Ill.: Richard D. Irwin, 1972.

Olmstead, M. "Orientation and Role in the Small Group." *American Sociological Review* 19 (1959):741–51.

Osborn, Alex. *Applied Imagination.* New York: Charles Scribner's Sons, 1953.

Pace, R. W., and R. Boren. *The Human Transaction*. Glenview, Ill.: Scott, Foresman, 1973.

Putnam, L., and M. S. Poole. "Conflict and Negotiation." In *Handbook of Organizational Communication: An Interdisciplinary Perspective,* edited by F. Jablin, L. Putnam, K. Roberts, and L. Porter. Newbury Park, CA: Sage, 1988.

Roethlisberger, F., and W. Dickson. *Management and the Worker*. Cambridge, Mass.: Harvard University Press, 1939.

Rosenfeld, L. B. *Human Interaction in the Small Group Setting*. Columbus, Ohio: Charles Merrill, 1973.

Schachter, S. "Deviation, Rejection, and Communication." *Journal of Abnormal and Social Psychology* 46 (1951):190–207.

Schachter, S., N. Ellertson, D. McBride, and D. Gregory. "An Experimental Study of Cohesiveness and Productivity." *Human Relations* 4 (1951): 229–38.

Scharpf, F. "Does Organization Matter? Task Structure and Interaction in the Ministerial Bureaucracy." Paper presented at a meeting of the ECPR Conference, Louvain, Belgium, 1976.

Schein, E. *Process Consultation*. Reading, Mass: Addison-Wesley, 1969.

Schutz, W. *FIRO: A Three-Dimensional Theory of Interpersonal Behavior*. New York: Holt, Rinehart & Winston, 1958.

Shaw, M. "Communication Networks." In *Advances in Experimental Social Psychology*. Vol. 1. Edited by L. Berkowitz. New York: Academic Press, 1964.

———. *Group Dynamics*. New York: McGraw-Hill Book Co., 1971.

Shepherd, C. *Small Groups*. Scranton, Pa.: Chandler Publishing Co., 1964.

Smith, Val. "Communication Networks." Mimeographed handout. University of New Mexico, 1973.

Sommer, R. "Studies in Personal Space." *Sociometry* 22 (1959):247–60.

———. "Small Group Ecology." *Psychological Bulletin* 67 (1967):145–52.

Steinzor, B. "The Spatial Factor in Face-to-Face Discussion Groups." *Journal of Abnormal and Social Psychology* 45 (1950):552–55.

Strodtbeck, F., and L. Hook. "The Social Dimensions of a Twelve-Man Jury Table." *Sociometry* 24 (1961):297–415.

Tannenbaum, R., and W. Schmidt. "How to Choose a Leadership Pattern." *Harvard Business Review* 36 (1958):95–101.

Tillman, R., Jr. "Problems in Review: Committees on Trial." *Harvard Business Review* 47 (May–June 1960):162–72.

Wenburg, J., and W. Wilmot. *The Personal Communication Process*. New York: John Wiley & Sons, 1973.

8

PUBLIC ORGANIZATIONAL COMMUNICATION

The chairman of the board of a large commercial bank calmly faced his audience—one thousand stockholders assembled at corporate headquarters for the annual stockholders' meeting. After a stale joke or two, he got to the essence of the meeting and reported to the restless audience, "Due to a continued pattern of poor returns on several real estate investments, we are unable to announce a dividend at this time." As he finished saying that for the seventh consecutive quarter there would be no dividend, the stockholders erupted with loud, angry shouting, which culminated in a resolution to withhold executive management's salary raises for the year. Although the resolution failed, the chairman lost more than his pride at that meeting. The next day the price of the bank's stock fell three points, causing unrest among several hundred bank officers who were heavily invested because of the bank's stock option plan. Coverage by the local news media of the stockholders' meeting was extensive and negatively skewed. The bank's public relations director logged almost one thousand calls within a week from anxious customers questioning the bank's very solvency.

Contrast the foregoing scene with activities of Citibank, a multibillion-dollar bank headquartered in New York City. That bank replaced its long-form consumer loan contract, written in the finest of officialese, with a simple one-page form written in conversational English and also in Spanish for Spanish-speaking customers. Citibank also sent out cards to its delinquent loan customers asking whether they preferred a court trial to the opportunity of giving their side of the story without going to court. Citibank has also begun inviting consumer advocates to its planning meetings to discuss ways of handling such issues as computerized electronic banking.

BankAmerica, in what is one of the nation's most far-reaching programs in corporate disclosure, has published its disclosure code. One of its objectives is to give the public ready access to information the corporation currently provides in its routine reporting to regulatory agencies. It has also published the following basic principles under which its disclosure decisions are made (BankAmerica, 1976):

1. Customers for deposit services of BankAmerica are entitled to the information necessary to understand and evaluate the terms, conditions, availability and safety of these services.

2. Borrowers are entitled to know the standards for credit eligibility and all information necessary to evaluate the credit extended, including all charges, the methods by which they are calculated and the conditions and obligations involved.

3. Investors in the securities of BankAmerica Corporation and its subsidiaries are entitled to the information necessary to judge the quality of their investments, the adequacy of management and the value of their holdings.

4. Those whose funds BankAmerica manages in a fiduciary or agency capacity are entitled to the information necessary to judge the quality, costs and results of the services it renders.

5. Customers for the specialized financial services provided by BankAmerica are entitled to the information needed to evaluate the terms and conditions and the quality of the services offered.

6. Employees of all BankAmerica companies are entitled to the information necessary to make informed decisions about their pursuit of personal objectives within the organization.

7. The vendors, suppliers and other businesses with which BankAmerica deals are entitled to information necessary to make sound business contracts with the corporation. This includes information about policies on agreements and transactions, competitive practices, nondiscrimination practices and standards of fairness.

8. The public is entitled to the information necessary to judge the value and adequacy of BankAmerica's contributions to economic and social well-being and its adherence to legal and ethical standards.

Montgomery Ward has been working actively with consumer representatives to help pass legislation aimed at correcting unfair billing procedures. J. C. Penney Co. regularly holds consumer education seminars. Avon Corporation publishes a booklet in plain English and in Spanish explaining the rights of people sued for nonpayment of debts. Unfortunately, this kind of corporate behavior is representative of only a minority of business organizations and the way they communicate with their publics. A Harris Poll concluded that 44 percent of Americans believe that business leaders are not responsive to failure of products to fulfill consumer expectations. That same poll showed that almost half the country believes the White House, the military leaders, the Supreme Court, and the state government leaders are out of touch with the nation and its people. Congress fared worst. Fifty-eight percent of the respondents believed that the Congress is not in tune with the country.

A poll conducted for the American Management Association and published in the *Wall Street Journal* (1981) found that 36 percent of the business journalists in the United States think executives "often lie" to reporters while only 7 percent of the public relations directors in the United States think so. Similarly, 71 percent of the executives polled considered themselves "usually accessible" to the media, but only 27 percent of the reporters thought executives were easy to reach. These data indicate that an environment of suspicion exists between corporations and members of the press who must report what corporations have to say to the public.

Who constitutes the "public?" With whom must an organization—any organization—communicate in order to be in touch? Who are the public, and what do they want? Who in an organization must do the communicating? How must they communicate? How often? With what media? At what expense? To what end? These are just some of the questions addressed in this chapter on public organizational communication.

It is apparent that organizations have several publics to whom they are now accountable. No longer can an organization limit its communication efforts to employee memoranda, customer advertising campaigns, and consumer public relations programs. The proactive organization of the 1990s will regularly confront and be confronted by government publics

The proactive organization of the 1990's will regularly confront and be confronted by a variety of publics; much of the communication will take place via the electronic media.

(regulatory agencies, legislatures, common councils); financial publics (analysts, fund managers, individual investors, bankers); stockholder publics (employees, institutions, general public); customer publics (consumers, suppliers); employee publics (unions and trade associations, nonunion employees, managers); special interest publics (lobbyists, consumer-advocacy groups, environmental protection groups); and even the general public (neighbors, television and radio stations).

Robinson defined *public* as any group of people who have a common interest. Borden and associates refer to public messages as those intended to reach many people or that have the potential of reaching many people:

> Generally a public message concerns matters that have relevance to a group or groups of people; it contains meaning that is in the public domain.

Thus far in this book, we have been studying the creation and exchange of dyadic and small-group messages. The third relationship identified as important to organizational communication involves the public flow of messages—either within the organization or between the organization and its environment. The specific objectives in this chapter are the following:

1. To define and describe the nature of public organizational communication.
2. To relate the study of public organizational communication to the social systems paradigm presented in this book.
3. To define, describe, and illustrate the purposes, value, and frequency of public organizational communication.

4. To present, describe, and illustrate the major types of public organizational communication activities within an organization.
5. To describe the techniques used to measure the effectiveness of public organizational communication.

What Is Public Organizational Communication?

Public organizational communication involves the exchange of messages with large groups of people using face-to-face or mediated channels. In chapter 4, our model of organizational communication was limited to software methods of message diffusion. In this chapter, the concern is not with such technological, media-oriented public organizational communication activities as television, radio, film, telephone, videocassette, and microfilm. Since most organizational advertising uses some form of mediated message, it too is primarily outside the focus of this book.

What remains is primarily the face-to-face contact between the organization and its external environment and between one member of the organization and a large group of personnel from the same organization. Both utilize *public speaking* as the major tool for accomplishing their objectives. Dance and Larson refer to this type of communicative activity as "person-to-persons speech communication" because one person engages in speech communication with a group of other people:

> When one individual speaks to others, concentrating more on what they have in common rather than on what differentiates one from another, he is involved in person-to-persons speech communication.

Brooks described this type of behavior as "monological" because one person is usually involved in sending a message to a public.

The qualities that differentiate public organizational communication from dyadic and small-group communication are the following:

1. *Communication is source (speaker) oriented.* Whereas in dyadic and small-group organizational communication a reciprocal relation between communication source and receiver is involved, in public organizational communication the importance of the speaker is emphasized; that is, the speaker dominates the relationship.
2. *Large groups of receivers are involved.* A dyad is two people, and a small group, for most purposes, often has no more than five to seven members. Public messages are intended to interest many people, from two hundred or so to several million. No arbitrary limit can be set for the size of a public group. In the change from small group to group to large group to public group, when face-to-face communication with all group members becomes difficult or impossible, the group is considered to be public. Speakers adjust their communication behavior to accommodate such groups.
3. *There is less interaction between speaker and listeners.* It should be noted that the decrease in interaction is a direct function of the speaker-oriented nature and increased number of participants in public organizational communication. As Brooks said, "It is not possible to know each person specially as an individual person as it is in the case of the small group and dyadic situations."

4. *Language is more general.* In public organizational communication, speakers must use language with general appeal because of the large size of the audience. Usually, a speaker researches the character of an audience and then speaks in the generalities that appeal to those particular listeners as a group and does not try to appeal to each listener. Dance and Larson summarized these differences:

> Person-to-persons speech communication differs from other levels of speech communication in that it is characterized by greater specificity of intent on the part of the source, more centralized control of the communication process, and more well-defined expectations on the part of the receivers.

Public Organizational Communication within the Social Systems Model

Earlier in this book, the organization was described as an open system that inputs energy, converts it to output, and transmits it back to the environment. The open system model demands interaction between the organization and its environment. Organizations receive inputs from their environment (workers, raw materials, information) and send outputs into their environment (products, services, pollution). Few organizations can survive without being cognizant of their potential markets, suppliers, users, publics, and government regulations. We began this chapter with a description of the problems encountered by a banking institution that ignored the feelings and attitudes of a significant part of its environment—its stockholders. The impact of this behavior on the public was soon felt throughout the bank.

In order to describe the system of interest, it is necessary to specify the boundary of the system. The boundary gives the system a spatio-temporal reference by separating the components of the system from its environment. From a communication perspective, the boundary is often defined as a break in the degree of access to shared information. Usually, the boundary is determined by a discrete difference between what is going on within its limits and what is occurring in the environment.

Tushman and Scanlan have called those people who bring information into an organization and diffuse it throughout "boundary spanning individuals." They state that "boundary spanning occurs in a two-step process by individuals who are able to gather information from external areas and disseminate that information to their colleagues. These key individuals are seen as among the most competent individuals in their unit, and they have specialized characteristics to facilitate communication with distinct external areas." Figure 8.1 illustrates their model of boundary spanning.

In order to help businesses identify and bring relevant information into their organizations, several enterprising individuals have become "information brokers" who thrive by helping firms get the facts they need. In the past ten years, over 300 information retailers have sprung up, most notably in Washington, D.C. to help businesses find their way through the federal bureaucracy. Over 20,000 persons, at a cost of more than $9 billion, routinely gather information for the federal government. Americans easily get angry at federal spending, regulation, and government bureaucracy in general. Yet they fail to take advantage of the government as a resource for information on practically everything, most of it available free or at little cost.

Figure 8.1   Schematic of informational boundary-spanning model.

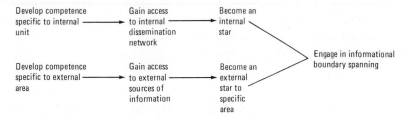

Contingencies that Affect Communication[1]

Contingencies that affect all organizations were listed in chapter 3. Table 8.1 shows the relationship between the external contingencies and various publics an organization must confront because of a contingency. As a shift in any of the external contingencies occurs, new informational demands are placed upon an organization. Organizations must be able to sense a change in their environment and to meet the change—create and exchange messages internally among relevant departments and units and externally to important publics—or they will not survive.

Let us examine each contingency to see its effect on public organizational communication.

Economic Factors.   Many managers view the economy as the most critical contingency affecting their organization. Rates of inflation and unemployment affect the size and shape of their labor force, the availability and cost of capital needed for growth and expansion, and their ability to market their stocks and bonds to the investing public. Knowledge of its various financial publics—stockholders, suppliers, customers, financial exchanges, brokerage houses, security analysts, banks, insurance companies, financial publications—can help an organization cope with traditional economic cycles.

Witness the crisis state of many American universities as they faced the recessions of 1974–1975 and the early 1980s. As never before in their history, they were forced to consider wholesale retrenchment, firing of tenured faculty, and phasing out of entire academic programs. When the bottom fell out of New York State's borrowing market, sending its credit and bond interest rates skyrocketing, the legislature was forced to cut back the budget of the State University of New York by several million dollars and virtually close down construction on one of its newer campuses. The university made plans to eliminate programs, faculty, and staff. Thus, economic conditions affected goals, outputs, demographics, and even structure and amount of space of the university. The impact on communication was that already overloaded faculty and administrators were forced to become involved in dozens of new meetings ("What criteria should be used to retrench departments?"); new memoranda ("Here are the reasons why we should survive"); and new lawsuits ("You can't break my contract").

---

1. Parts of the discussion in this section were adapted from Goldhaber et al., *Information Strategies: New Pathways to Management Productivity* (Norwood, N.J.: ABLEX, 1984, Revised Edition)

Table 8.1 External Organizational Communication Contingencies and Publics

External Contingencies	External Publics
Economic: amount of stability in current market competition and its impact upon capital resources available to organization	Customers Analysts Fund managers, individual investors, bankers, stockholders
Technological: degree of innovation in equipment and scientific research and development and the impact upon the organization	Trade associations Competitors Suppliers Research and development associations
Legal: degree of impact of local, state, and federal regulations, guidelines, and laws affecting organizational operations	Regulatory agencies Legislatures City councils, congress
Sociopoliticocultural: degree of impact of social, political, and cultural considerations upon the organization	Politicians Minority and special interest groups Consumer advocacy groups Unions, media
Environmental: degree of impact of climate, geography, population, density, and availability of energy upon the organization	Environmental protection groups Neighboring citizens groups Lobbyists

Source: Gerald Goldhaber et al., *Information Strategies: New Pathways to Management Productivity* (Norwood, N.J.: ABLEX, 1984, Revised Edition).

Although the university could have done little to prevent the economic conditions causing the problems, it was guilty of ignoring the crisis until its only option was stress. Contingency plans should have been drawn up in advance of the recession. Intelligence should have been gathered and people's reactions determined. Most universities are now more aware of the limited amount of money "in the pot" and have lobbying efforts underway to persuade legislators and other donors to give them their "rightful" share.

Private sector profit-making organizations have always viewed the economy with respect, probably because of its direct link to their survival, whereas universities and hospitals, for example, have typically gone through intermediary parties for major funding. As costs increase dramatically, hospitals must now become more aware of their potential clients—the public—and their competition—other hospitals. They must, as one farsighted hospital in northern Wisconsin has been doing for three years, regularly survey the public to identify its needs, its preferred services, and its concern for costs versus patient care. Even banks, typically secure in shifting economic conditions, are now engaging in extensive media campaigns to attract new customers and provide new services (supermarket banking, electronic banking).

A large commercial bank once hired me to conduct a market study to identify the major reasons customers select a bank for a loan. They were also interested in the major demographic and psychographic characteristics associated with their own (and their competitors') current and projected loan customers. This kind of planning is highly commendable in an organization. It is proactive, not reactive, management. Another bank, unfortunately,

Even banks can make poor decisions without market data. (By Toles for the Buffalo Courier-Express © 1981. Reprinted by permission.)

did not collect sufficient market data before it made a major decision to recall hundreds of mortgages in order to cope better with the losses it was realizing from paying out higher interest rates to investors than it was collecting from borrowers (mortgages, etc.). The public outcry was immense, ranging from angry protests to demonstrations to boycotts of the bank by other customers. After an agonizing week of negative reaction to their decision, the bank reversed itself and announced it would not recall the mortgages after all. Perhaps, with adequate measures of the public's pulse on this issue, the bank could have either avoided the decision or planned better for the public's reaction.

Recently, Al Reis and Jack Trout (1986) wrote about the economic factors involved in the marketing of an organization. They emphasized that for an organization to be successful today, it must become competitor-oriented. It must look for weak points in the positions of its competitors and then launch marketing attacks against those weak points. Many recent marketing success stories illustrate this.

For example, while others were losing millions in the computer business, Digital Equipment Corporation was making millions by exploiting IBM's weakness in small computers. Pepsi took advantage of its sweeter taste to challenge Coke in the hotly contested cola market. At the same time, Burger King was making progress against McDonald's with its "broiling, not frying" attack.

Reis and Trout went on to state:

> The true nature of marketing today involves the conflict between corporations, not the satisfying of human needs and wants. If human needs and wants get satisfied in the process of business competition, then it is in the public interest to let the competition continue.

Another factor in building a successful marketing strategy is an organization's internal communication system. Internal communications should not merely be used as a strategy for cultivating relationships among personnel, but also as a means by which personnel may build, maintain, and convey the firm's reputation in the marketplace. In an article published in *The National Law Journal,* it is stated that a good proportion of the marketing problems law firms face are the result of poor internal communication. In an environment such as this, personnel must keep abreast of the ongoing activities of other personnel in order to know what services may be provided by the firm. Internal communication programs, such as firm meetings, departmental presentations, video conferencing, firm retreats, and house organs should be utilized to orientate personnel to effective marketing of their own organization.

Technological Factors.   Organizations in England and Canada use new telecommunications technologies to reduce travel costs due to relocation away from a metropolitan area. Technology influences our behavior by creating uncertainty in our organizational lives. Research and development departments to monitor technology and develop response mechanisms to process the impact of technological changes are established. However, even with sophisticated research and development units, overload soon occurs, because the pace of technological innovation is now on a scale of ten to one, according to some estimates. This means that technological changes that at one time would have taken ten years are now developed within a year.

Present-day managers must be statisticians, accountants, operations researchers, cost-benefit analysts, financial planners, computer programmers, and systems thinkers in order to cope with the high uncertainty in their technological environment. Not only are computer technologies changing, but communications and even filing systems are also finding new methods of operation. Microfilm now allows an organization to save almost four times its present filing space and eight times the retrieval time, while practically eliminating lost document problems. Telex transmission allows a manager to send business correspondence by telephone, which means that a small long-distance phone charge is exchanged for the higher cost of sending a letter. Word-processing systems, conference calls, videocartridge memos, and recorded telephone messages all contribute to a new communication environment.

Another technology that has become a part of this new communication environment is the facsimile machine. The recent infiltration of "fax" machines into the business world and their relative low cost has made these machines more available and therefore a more viable means of communication. The rapid transmission speed of these machines, and their affordability for many small businesses and homes, is changing the way people conduct business in America. Many firms use facsimile as a supplement to the telephone, where detailed information, and graphic images, can be exchanged rapidly, via a process that allows individuals to communicate without high phone bills. The facsimile is the start of a new revolutionary form of "image communications" that allows organizations to strengthen their communication systems and become more competitive.

How effective are these new developments? We do not know because they are too new and the research is not yet complete. However, we do know that successful organizations keep informed about new technologies: what their competitors use; what will improve their services to customers and suppliers; and what leading universities and private research and development organizations are developing.

Legal Factors.   Hundreds of organizations are confronted with local, state, and federal laws and regulations, many of which have direct implications for their very survival. Ten years ago, the Occupational Safety and Health Administration (OSHA), the Employee Retirement Income Security Act (ERISA), the Employee Stock Ownership Plan (ESOP), and the Equal Employment Opportunity Commission (EEOC) were unknown, but today they affect millions of people and account for billions of company dollars spent to comply with their regulations.

No organization seems able to escape the "long arm of the law." Pharmaceutical companies must clear all potential carcinogens with the Food and Drug Administration; utility companies must seek approval for rate increases from their public service commission; automobile manufacturers must conform to specifications for emission standards while attempting to meet other guidelines governing fuel economy; and school systems must conform to guidelines for desegregation. In Albuquerque, building heights are regulated by the city council (to protect the view of the mountains); in Virginia, tobacco companies are forced to print health warnings on all cigarette packages.

Recently, safety warnings on products have become a concern for many organizations. Product warning messages, or safety communications, are another form of communication. In keeping with our definition of organizational communication offered in chapter 1, we may now define safety communication as the creation and exchange of messages that allow individuals to cope with environmental uncertainty in their relationship with the product at hand. Effective warnings are defined as messages that communicate to consumers that there is some danger associated with their use of a product. The near epidemic rates of product liability lawsuits suggest that many product warnings may not adequately inform consumers of the risks involved in using a given product. However, an effective warning, and therefore a manufacturer's liability, rests on the ability of the warning message to be understood by the product user not on whether they complied with the message.

Recent theoretical developments in understanding the effects of product warnings have focused on humans as information-processing systems (Lehto & Miller, 1986). A key element of our definition of safety communication is uncertainty. As defined in chapter 1, uncertainty refers to the difference between information available about the safe use of a product and the information an individual needs to use a product safely. Before consumers use a product that poses a health risk, they need information related to the nature of the risk, and how they should use the product to avoid the risk. If the consumer does not have the needed safety information, it may be the duty of the manufacturer to provide it. Although manufacturers, retailers, and consumers agree that consumers need to be warned about health risks associated with a product, there is substantial disagreement over the most effective method for transmitting safety information to reduce consumers' uncertainty about how to use a product safely.

The most critical facet of consumer information processing is the product users' uncertainty about the product. An individual's uncertainty about the product determines whether the consumer will purposely seek information about the products' safe use as well as the objective or purpose for processing product safety information. Whether an individual actively seeks product safety information is a function of his or her familiarity with the product, provided they have not been injured themselves or seen anyone injured while using the product (Goldhaber & deTurck, 1988). The more familiar the individual is with the product, the less likely they will perceive the product as hazardous and, therefore, be less likely to notice or read a product warning message. In addition, product familiarity may also create a boomerang effect, such that products with warning messages indicating a high degree of risk may indicate less perceived risk to a familiar user. Uncertainty also influences the objective by which an individual processes a warning message. An individual with a high degree of uncertainty about a product may be more likely to process safety information with the objective of how to use the product safely. Hence, the individual will take more time reading the warning message as well as have better recall of the contents contained in the warning message.

Sociopoliticocultural Factors. The laws to which most organizations conform were brought about by social, cultural, and political pressures. For example, the Equal Employment Opportunity Commission evolved after turbulent years of protest of inequalities. Lobbying and protest efforts of many environmental groups preceded the restrictions and pollution controls issued by the Environmental Protection Administration. An organization must be aware of these influences and their specific impact upon daily jobs. Monitoring of such influences is particularly important for large multinational corporations, which operate in many countries.

Although we have probably been shocked by such bribery scandals as that involving Lockheed Aircraft and the Japanese government, students of Japanese politics and culture are probably far less surprised. Influence peddling in Japan has been part of the accepted norm of doing business for years. Japanese workers qualify for a better job according to how much high-quality education they have and "who they know." Friends are always rewarded during the gift-giving season immediately after the bonuses are given.

Another difference between Japanese and U.S. organizations, pointed out in chapter 3, is the preoccupation of Japanese business with group involvement and consensus-seeking behavior in its decision-making process. Japanese businessmen emphasize analysis of problems, whereas Americans emphasize solution. Because of the frequent opportunities for input and because of the attempts to provide Japanese workers with almost lifetime security with a company, many Japanese workers answer proudly, "I'm a _____ man!" when asked where they work.

Not only must organizations with their networks of people adapt to foreign cultures and political systems, they must also deal with their own organization as a separate sub-culture with norms, values, and attitudes of its own. This is especially acute for large organizations, such as American Telephone & Telegraph, which has more than a million employees.

Several organizations today recognize their social responsibility toward the community within which they interact. For example, IBM for years has supported two small schools in North Carolina and Texas.

Mobil Oil Corporation has published many advocacy advertisements that discuss political issues, and Equitable Assurance Society has done likewise. In addition to the public relations benefits, these measures offer such organizations an opportunity to get a closer reading on the pulse of their communities—information they can readily use in predicting environmental trends.

Taiani—in one of the first major studies of how corporations identify their expected social behavior, the factors that influence their social behavior, and the role of communication in this process—found strong support for the role of a boundary spanning agent previously identified by Tushman and Scanlan. Among Taiani's conclusions were the following:

1. Organizations identify the social or role behavior expected of them from their internal and external environments—their publics.
2. Organizations are more likely to contribute to publics seeking their support if there is a great degree of perceived overlap or interface between the goals and objectives of the organization and those of the public group seeking its support.
3. Organizations perceived the role of communication in this process to be: to establish a system or network of interpersonal relationships; to identify, shape, and monitor attitudes, perceptions, demands, and expectations; and to disseminate relevant and timely information within the organization.

Environmental Factors.   Organizations today must attend to the overall quality of life of their employees and their families and of the community. More and more attention is being given to problems of pollution of air and water and impact on the land as results of an organization's activities.

Another environmental concern, one of the most important, is the amount and type of energy available to fuel the machinery and heat the buildings that organizations use.

Another environmental element to be carefully considered is the weather. In the severe winter of 1977, a major blizzard required alterations in numerous organizational communication systems. When the weather forced schools and hospitals to close, parents and children and families of patients had to be informed. Buffalo, New York, worst affected city in the United States, was immobilized. Snowmobiles were the primary means of transportation, and organizations with employees stranded at work had to find and borrow, rent, or buy such equipment. Informal communication networks (social as well as rumor) were rapidly established to handle the overload due to the sudden unstable weather conditions.

Perhaps the most important environmental concern today is the amount of energy available to fuel the machinery and heat the buildings that organizations use.

Internal Activities

General Electric Company regularly schedules an activity called Boss Talk, where the plant manager interacts with all employees for a general briefing and question-answer session. The organization as a whole (all the employees) can be seen as the environment within which the boss interacts (as a system). Thus, Boss Talk becomes the mechanism the manager uses to maintain a balance between system inputs (ideas and suggestions from employees) and system outputs (decisions, problem solving, promotions, and product lines determined by the boss).

Many companies here followed Pitney Bowes's example of establishing jobholder meetings, held about the same time of the year as stockholder meetings, to allow employees to ask questions of company officers. Usually a panel of top executives answer questions either submitted in writing in advance or asked from the floor at the meeting. Sometimes unsigned questions written on cards are collected at the meeting, and the most frequently asked questions are submitted to the panel for answers. With very large corporations, executives use television to address simultaneously several hundred thousand employees in different locations. When an executive cannot answer a question, a written answer is typically provided as soon as the information is available. A division of Carborundum Company regularly uses such meetings to make top management visible to employees. To date, union efforts within this division have not been successful.

Robinson distinguished between the internal and external publics of an organization:

> Some publics, such as employees, are part of an organization and are called *internal* publics. In contrast, customers are an example of an *external* public—as suppliers, retail dealers, and the community. Internal and external publics will differ from one organization to another.

As Zelko and Dance pointed out, external communication (message behavior dealing with external publics) has traditionally been the concern of the company's public relations department and perhaps the advertising and sales departments. As we have seen, this traditional view has changed dramatically in recent years.

Importance and Frequency of Public Communication in Organizations

Good public relations has become extremely important to most businesses and industries today, since never before has big business been held in such low esteem. In a recent poll, Americans ranked big business sixteenth in terms of honesty, dependability, and integrity— just above politicians, labor leaders, advertising agencies, and bureaucrats. The strong antibusiness attitude today was summed up by Robert Kirby:

> This hostility is real. College professors don't love us. The news media don't trust us. The government doesn't help us. Some special-interest groups wish we weren't even around.

> And each one of these creates an ever-expanding ripple of hostility—professors to their students, citizens' groups to the government, government to the news media, and media to the general public. Suddenly we look around and wonder why it is so lonesome out here in businessland.

> Unfortunately, this kind of hostility is encountered by all companies, including those that are regarded as model corporate citizens. In other words, it's a pervasive phenomenon, this antibusiness feeling.

William Ylvisaker advocated a strong speak-out approach for big business to counteract this negative attitude:

> If business doesn't speak out to present its ideas and viewpoints, who will? The answer is "no one." Business cannot afford to sit on its collective hands and say, "Let someone else do it," or "It's too difficult a job for us," or "We don't want our views known." Every voice heard is a step toward more respect for the business world.

Zelko and Dance cited as the advantages of public organizational communication: internally, "efficiency of operations"; externally, "a better public image." Most big businesses and industries have a public relations or public information office to handle advertising, press releases, special events, tours, and showings. The growth and development of hundreds of industrial speakers' bureaus throughout the United States is also evidence of the importance of goodwill to industry.

The available figures on the frequency of public communication activity by U.S. businessmen and professionals are an indicator of the value many organizations place on this form of human interaction. Zelko and Dance reported that in 1964, in the Bell System program alone, "more than 5,000 speakers spoke to audiences totaling over 12,000,000 all over the United States. . . . Smith, Kline and French Laboratories has 500 people in their speakers' bureau who have talked to over 7,000 organizations." They travel around the United States without extra compensation to spread goodwill and give facts about the drug industry. Since its bureau was begun in 1959, employees have given more than twenty thousand talks to a total audience of more than a million people—at a cost of about three dollars for each talk.

Hundreds of organizations maintain speakers' bureaus. I contacted several and was informed by all that their speakers were more active than ever. The figures we will later examine on organizational speech training programs further reinforce the importance that organizations place on public communication. Westinghouse Electric Corporation uses a group of articulate nuclear engineers to carry the facts about nuclear power to civic groups, talk shows, newspapers, and college campuses in states where the matter is an issue. In 1976, their public campaign offset the efforts of opposition groups in all seven states in which the issue was debated.

Grala recommended that a company interested in starting a speakers bureau consider the following five important factors: training, promotion, press relations, follow-up, and management support. For a successful operation all five are necessary.

Now that the Employee Retirement Income Security Act (ERISA) is law and organizations must communicate clear and complete information about pension and benefits programs to all employees, many companies have suddenly accepted the importance of public organizational communication. Since fringe benefits now exceed one-third of an organization's payroll, translating to about $4,000 per employee per year in the United States, most organizations have much to gain from accurately communicating this information to employees. Huseman and co-workers believe that most benefits communication programs try to accomplish one or more of the following objectives:

1. Make employees aware of the benefits program.
2. Make employees understand the benefits program.
3. Make employees aware of the cost of the benefits program to the employer.
4. Make employees aware that the benefits plan is competitive with the plans of other companies.
5. Make sure that the benefits program creates goodwill among employees.

Their survey of communication programs about benefits revealed that many organizations have used the following media:

Regular employee meetings	Pay envelope inserts
Intermittent employee meetings	Check stubs
Personal counseling services	Letters to employees' homes
Word of mouth	Posters
Booklets and brochures	Notices on bulletin boards
Benefit manuals	Slide presentations
Employee publications	Motion pictures
Computerized statements	Filmstrips
Annual reports	Closed circuit television
Reports (other than annual)	Commercial television and radio

Whichever media were used, it is clear that passage of the Employee Retirement Income Security Act (ERISA) has caused a major shift toward more organizational communication.

Image Making and Industrial Positioning

In the late 1950s and early 1960s, bumper stickers asked: "Would you buy a used car from Nixon?"—"Tricky Dick"—"How's tricks, Dick?" In the late 1960s and early 1970s, the bumper stickers proclaimed: "Nixon's the one"—"Protect law and order with Nixon."—"Four more years." In the aftermath of Watergate, bumpers displayed such signs as: "Four more years—with two off for good behavior," "Protect law and order—impeach the President," and "Don't blame me, I'm from Massachusetts." Within ten years of Nixon's resignation, he was active once again in foreign affairs, writing a new book, taking trips (authorized and unauthorized) to visit heads of state, and offering "free" advice to the president on how to deal with other nations. Over a period of twenty years Richard Nixon's image has been defined, redefined, and redefined again.

Just as politicians must rely upon public communication to create, reinforce, and redefine their personal images, so must organizations use public communication to create or redefine images about their services and products. General Motors, which spent millions in 1977 on a national campaign stressing its good service and calling its repairmen "Mr. Goodwrench," was forced to reconstruct its image when one customer had his Oldsmobile serviced and discovered it had a Chevrolet engine!

Throughout history companies have been more concerned about their stock shares and profit margins than about their identities. Now few would deny the importance of public organizational communication in image building and other areas. As Holm stated:

> Its people must be in touch with agents, suppliers, purchasers, stockholders, government agencies, donors, counterparts in other organizations, and a very important public of some sort. Professional and vocational affiliations must be maintained, an understanding public must be cultivated, business contacts must be kept fresh, and customers or patrons must be sought and satisfied. External communication becomes the vital counterpart of internal communication.

Especially since about 1970 and the greater emphasis on social responsibility, corporations have been taking positions to be visible and reflect their personalities to society. Another cause has been overcommunication. The more than 300,000 brand names in circulation and the welter of logos create such visual pollution that it is ever more difficult for a company to stand out. Given the primacy of the visual medium—television—companies, corporations, and products all need identities of their own.

There are over 10,000 individual products or brands on display in an average United States supermarket. Already in Europe they are building super supermarkets (called hypermarkets) with room for displaying 30,000 to 50,000 products.

Because of the heated competition of manufacturers for the public's attention, they spend millions of dollars each year on advertising looking for positions, or holes in the marketplace.

Al Reis and Jack Trout coined the term "positioning" and have defined it as, "how you position the product in the mind of the prospect." They feel that because the public is continually bombarded with conflicting messages from advertisers and because so little of the message is going to get through to the prospect anyway, an advertiser must ignore the sending side and concentrate on the perceptions of the prospect, not the reality of the product. Reis

During the past twenty years, Richard Nixon's image has been defined, redefined, and redefined again.

and Trout continue, "The basic approach to positioning is not to create something new and different, but to manipulate what's already in the prospect's mind. To retie the connection that already exists."

Oldsmobile campaigned to redefine its image from a luxury car designed for the older, more established car buyer to the new and exciting "Youngmobile" for the sports-minded youth of today. To capitalize on the youth movement of the 1960s and 1970s, Pepsi Cola created the "Pepsi generation." The oil industry tried to redefine its image in the 1970s from mass polluter to concerned environmentalist. Ford Motor Company responded to the Nader-influenced consumer complaints about automobiles by a campaign to redefine its image as an organization that "listens." Even social movements try to redefine their images. Gay Liberation has sought to alter the popular image of a limp-wristed, timid, secretive homosexual to an open, militant activist. My own research revealed a militant group of male homosexuals in the San Francisco area whose function was to patrol the streets in the gay districts of the city looking for persecutors of homosexuals. Their primary weapons in this campaign were the club and chain.

Allegheny Airlines had grown to become the sixth largest U.S. carrier in terms of passengers served. Yet the company suffered from a "rinky-dink" image. Research had shown that when it comes to airlines, consumers feel that "big is better." So Allegheny became a "big" carrier—U.S. Air—with its jets and ground vehicles repainted in bright modern colors, terminals refurbished, employee uniforms redesigned, and a new slogan, "It takes a *big* airline to fly more flights than TWA." As a result of the new image, U.S. Air's passenger traffic increased sharply along with its employees' morale.

Occasionally, a state attempts to improve its image as New York did recently with its "I love New York" campaign, a series of televised commercials highlighting the vacation spots of the state. Or a city tries to improve its image, as Buffalo did with its campaign "We're talking proud." Buffalo's Chamber of Commerce conducted a survey and found that

Occasionally a city tries to improve its image, as Buffalo, New York, did with its compaign, "We're Talking Proud."

the people of Buffalo had a generally favorable attitude toward the city and were somewhat angry about what they considered unwarranted attacks on its image (particularly in jokes by Johnny Carson). To defuse the myths and rumors with facts, the chamber ran a series of TV, radio, and newspaper ads (a few on network TV when the Buffalo Bills football team was playing on ABC-TV's "Monday Night Football"). The ads gave many reasons why "we should all be proud of living in Buffalo." The campaign seemed to be effective and was expanded to coincide with the massive urban revitalization program underway in the city.

Positioning products and organizations may be the most important element in successful marketing today. The ultimate goal of positioning is to create an image that will place the organization at its proper position within the market it serves. To do it successfully, an organization must build a reputation of responsibility, not adopt a manipulative public relations program. It must take into account its positive aspects and unique characteristics and stress them. The general question organizations should ask when considering positioning themselves is: *What is it about ourselves or our products/services that we want people to perceive?* The questions that logically follow are:

1. What position, if any, do we already own in the market's mind?
2. What position do we want to own?
3. What organizations must we beat to establish that position?
4. Do we have the resources to gain and hold that position?

Positioning, then, is the identity an organization wants perceived by its relevant publics, typically customers.

Organizations should probably avoid attempting to occupy positions held by strong competitors. Just as smart hockey players often concede Wayne Gretzky his two to three goals or assists every game, and basketball players give Dr. J his routine fifty points, so should companies like RCA and GE tread very cautiously before tackling IBM in the computer industry (as they attempted to do—very unsuccessfully).

A large broadcasting chain hired me to identify the perceived image of one of its leading news anchorpersons and compare it to his competitor's image. We found that our client's anchor was perceived as honest and credible, but not liked for it; his opponent was perceived as friendly and nice. Since the competition was already perceived with the important attribute "friendliness," we recommended that our client avoid trying to capture this attribute from the competition and instead concentrate on developing strategies that would endear its anchorperson to his audience for important traits he was already perceived as having—honesty and credibility.

Rein (1972) warned, "An axiom of redefinition strategy is that *behavior* change must accompany the verbal assertion of an image change." If the computer-buying public tests the new image of "Sperry Listens" and discovers that the behavior of executives doesn't conform to the promises of public relations personnel, Sperry may be faced with a loss in credibility (and a drop in sales). Of course, they may then redefine their image once again.

During the past twenty years, Richard Nixon's image has been defined, redefined, and redefined again.

Types of Public Organizational Communication Activities

We know that public communication is a valued and frequently used activity by many organizations. Table 8.2 lists several popular public organizational communication activities that many organizations use. In all of these activities, a speaker assumes primary responsibility for encoding and delivering a message to a large group of people. We will now see how labor unions, universities, and businesses and industries use public organizational communication.

How Labor Unions Use Public Communication

Labor unions have a national membership of more than twenty million people and yet are probably the organization least studied by communication experts. The influence of public communication upon the growth of the labor movement needs little elaboration. Just mentioning such names as John L. Lewis, Walter Reuther, James Hoffa, and George Meany is enough to demonstrate how effectively public speaking has served the labor movement. Zelko and Dance commented:

> Through the years of their development and increasing influence, unions have pridefully been able to point to their leaders as capable speakers who could well represent them to the public and to management. Much evidence exists to show that union leaders have risen to places of

Table 8.2   Common Public Organizational Communication Activities

Internal Activities	External Activities
Supervisory or department head meetings	Goodwill speeches
Suggestion systems	Commercial speeches and advertising
Organizationwide meetings (boss talks, jobholders' meetings)	Political speeches
	Lobbying
Union meetings	Civic and social club presentations
Grapevine	Convention and conference presentations
Social functions (picnics, holiday parties, awards banquets, etc.)	Formal public speech (special occasion)
	Television and radio interviews
Oral technical reports and presentations	Testimony before legislative bodies
Training programs	Addresses to stockholders
Orientation sessions	
Briefing and information sessions	

influence in their unions because of their ability as speakers. They were strongly motivated to speak out in their own meetings and to become noticed by others, and in general it can be said that they have worked harder than many members of management to improve their speaking ability.

Dee analyzed the five major activities in which the active union member is most frequently involved: organizing, bargaining, administering and policing agreements, participating in union meetings, and representing the union to other groups. Examination of each activity shows that there is heavy reliance upon public communication to meet the objectives.

Organizing includes those activities in which the labor activist attempts to build the membership of the union. While most of the communicative interaction is of the interpersonal variety, organizers often deliver speeches to nonunion members assembled for meetings of one form or another. The labor organizer uses persuasive arguments, specifically those stressing the economic advantages of union membership.

Bargaining is also primarily an interpersonal task that involves meetings, informal conversations, and planned persuasive encounters. However, when a union makes its formal presentation to management, it relies upon public organizational communication (sender-oriented format). Furthermore, the final agreement must then be presented to the union membership for their approval, a task which may involve public speaking of the persuasive type.

Administering and policing the agreement involves the actual operation of the agreement under working conditions. Union members must know and understand the terms of the agreement, which means that union leaders rely upon speeches to inform. In arbitration, if it occurs, formal presentation of arguments, facts, and opinions, another public communication activity, is used.

Participating in union meetings includes presenting reports, answering questions, and listening to an occasional speech. Parliamentary procedure is usually enforced, and attendance at such meetings is quite low.

Representing the union before other groups probably calls for the greatest use of public communication skill and ability. Here the union member must face a variety of audiences for a variety of purposes. Frequently, the union representative encounters an audience with

When a union makes its formal presentation to management, it relies upon public organizational communication.

values quite divergent from those of the working man and woman. The union representative must be able to deal face to face with such friends *and* foes as politicians, civic leaders, and other union members.

Based upon his analysis of labor union public communication behavior, Dee recommended that "training should stress such skills as organization of ideas, conversation, sensitivity, and adaptation of the needs and wants of listeners, semantics, and listening." The results of a survey conducted by Knapp and McCroskey seem to support Dee's recommendations. They sent questionnaires to a sample of university administrators (administering labor education programs), to all fifty AFL-CIO State Central Body presidents, and to 140 research and/or education directors of the unions themselves. According to Knapp and McCroskey, "The three groups sampled . . . were unanimous in rating the importance of oral communication abilities as 'vital' or 'quite important' for union officers and shop stewards." There was much agreement that union stewards had the greatest need for such training; strong support for public speaking, discussion leadership, and participation; little support for interviewing. *Public speaking was ranked as the area in which training was most needed.*

Not all researchers, however, support this finding. Koehler and Marsh examined many of the curricular offerings in labor education institutes. They did not believe the courses in these institutes (primarily in public speaking, parliamentary procedure, and discussion) reflected the true needs of labor in the area of communication. They questioned the ability of labor personnel (whose survey data provided the input from which the curriculum was derived) to understand "the communication needs of labor":

> First, the assumption that labor members know what they need with regard to communication is not valid. To most of them, communication is synonymous with public speaking. They find it next to impossible to conceptualize the total communication process of their organization. What is most disturbing is that after they have had the opportunity of being a participant in our present curriculum they still have a similar perception of communication as they had prior to the program.

How Universities Use Public Communication

During most of the academic year 1971–1972, the nation's campuses were quiet. Many spokesmen for higher education claimed that campus unrest was a thing of the past. Indeed, with the advent of the eighteen-year-old vote, which gave 25 million youths "political power," and with the winding down of the Vietnam War (a key issue in previous riots), much of the impetus for campus unrest was reduced. The educator-prophets who had predicted doom for the university were apparently wrong.

Then in April 1972, the Vietnam War escalated and so did campus disturbances. The *Chronicle of Higher Education* reported that "students on eighty campuses boycotted classes during a one-day national student strike April 21. On at least ninety other campuses there were war protests . . . which called for the strike." Closely associated with the escalation in campus unrest was a growing negative attitude of the public toward the nation's colleges and universities. Linowitz pointed out the relation between unrest on campuses and public condemnation of universities:

> Widespread disruption on the nation's campuses had angered the American public. As dissatisfaction grew, so did the specter of punitive measures: reduced financial support, restrictive legislation and harsh laws for handling even peaceful demonstrators, and political intervention in the affairs of educational institutions.

It is easy to see how important public attitude is to the future of American universities. It is also easy to see how, with massive press and television coverage, a person's attitude can be formed after watching five minutes of a demonstration—without ever leaving the living room. Bittner and associates reported:

> American colleges and universities have received considerable exposure in the mass media during the past few years. Much of this exposure has been limited to broadcast and newspaper coverage of student demonstrations and campus unrest—coverage which a few angry administrators have labeled distorted, biased, and nonrepresentative.

They reported how one college president expressed his feelings of dissatisfaction with the manner in which the press arbitrarily report sensational news stories about riots but delete stories about positive university accomplishments:

> It is understandable that the press feels compelled to cover controversial stories on the campus, many of them involving burning issues of the day in our society. However, it is difficult to understand and abide the press's refusal to give adequate and constructive coverage of the positive achievements of higher educational programs of teaching, research, and public service.

The Scranton Report warned that if the schism between students and the community is not mended, the survival of the nation will be threatened.

We know from attitude research that once an attitude is formed and reinforced, it can be quite difficult to alter it. To illustrate this point, in a survey I directed, one New Mexico citizen proclaimed that he would never send his children to the university because of "all the dirt and filth taught by the professors!" He referred to a minor episode that had occurred on the campus *four years* before the survey! Data from the survey indicated that many citizens shared this man's view. The public's attitude toward a university, no matter how flimsy the evidence to support it, has grave implications for the university's budget, especially if the school receives funds from the state legislature.

There is little difference between the plight of the university as it confronts its public and other organizations as they interact with the same public. Universities affected by negative attitudes resulting from campus unrest are similar to oil companies facing attack from angry environmentalists, to automobile manufacturers being chastised by misled consumers, and to the federal government suffering from post-Watergate lack of credibility. In all of these cases, the organizations are forced to interact with large groups of people to whom they are accountable.

When we use the social systems model, we can see that it is important for a university, as a system in need of balance, to maintain close contact with its public—that is, the environment in which it exists. Dedmon agreed with this position and chastised universities for ignoring their public relations homework:

> Most universities have been slow in developing the public relations operations required to help develop and communicate an identity of the institution to a relevant public. To the contrary, public relations work is generally viewed by the academician and a large segment of the administration as both degrading and inappropriate in an academic institution. Vice presidents charged with public relations generally, and development specifically, are according to some studies the least satisfied of all university administrators. Obtaining funds and communicating with the public is, in short, a kind of necessary evil.

Dedmon's observation was written before much of the campus unrest of the 1970s. Recognizing the damage to their image because of the riots, many universities subsequently made remarkable progress. Kansas State University developed a program of parents' seminars, held in six Kansas cities, to bring parents and university administrators, students, and faculty together to discuss issues pertinent to university life and education. The chancellor of the university traveled approximately 5,000 miles throughout Kansas in 1970, giving talks to alumni, parents, and prospective students. The University of Arkansas instituted a policy of holding briefing meetings throughout the state to inform voters and others about the university. The University of South Carolina set up a group called University Associates to meet periodically with the university administration. Composed primarily of alumni and non-alumni supporters of the university, the group functioned chiefly to squelch rumors. The University of New Mexico established a series of annual conference-retreats at a university-owned mountain resort. State legislators, alumni, faculty, students, administrators, and influential citizens from New Mexico attend the conferences. The weekend meetings include informal rap sessions, cookouts, formal gatherings, and small-group discussions on topics of concern to each group.

One form of internal public communication used at the university is that old "jug and mug" teaching device—the classroom lecture. Despite its known ineffectiveness as a teaching technique and as a linear communication activity, universities still use the lecture as the primary means of educating students. With the increasing emphasis on higher enrollments, budget cuts, and loss of faculty positions, the lecture is attaining new prominence as the most economical way to teach large numbers of students.

When students are unhappy with a lecturer, they may resort to heckling in order to fluster and anger the professor. Rein described this student tactic:

> The student who decides to "get" the professor waits for an opportune time in the lecture, and then attacks. He may, for instance, yell "Bullshit" at a particular opinionated point. Or

he may counter the professor's argument with a stream of references: "That's not what Bronkowski says," or "Have you read 'Howl'?" A variation is to use the obscure reference: "Did you read _____?" The question is asked in a mocking manner with a cute, upturned inflection at the end.

Rein provided as an example an actual dialogue between a professor and student in a communication theory class:

Professor: Let me place this communication model on the blackboard. (He proceeds to draw the model.)

Student: What's it good for?

Professor: Well . . .

Student: Bullshit. (nervous laughter from class)

Professor: I think eventually we will be able to predict certain kinds of strategies before they occur.

Student (shouting): So you can control our behavior and our lives?

Professor: If you'll allow me to finish, I'll be glad to answer . . .

Another student: You are finished.

Other class members (after sparse laughter): Give him a chance. Come on. (etc.)

Professor: I wasn't serious about the model (put-on). It's not my model (cop-out).

To combat the inaction of several universities about setting up effective public relations programs and to help universities with existing programs, I made the following recommendations after a one-year study of the communication channels between university and public. These recommendations are intended to supplement such mechanical communication activities as news and sports releases, publications, and bulletins. Some of them may be more relevant for publicly supported institutions.

1. The university should schedule an annual (or biannual) retreat at a location other than the campus (mountain or seashore resort, hotel, motel, ranch). The retreat should include members of the university faculty and administration, students, and community leaders from around the state (legislators, businessmen, and opinion leaders and spouses). Agenda for the retreats should be informal and should include small-group discussions as well as large gatherings.
2. The university should establish a university speakers' bureau to provide university staff, student, and faculty speakers for any service, civic, or educational group in the state—at no cost (other than transportation) to the requesting group.
3. Key student, faculty, and administration leaders should form a "university amigos" team to conduct handshake tours around the state. A similar concept can be developed by the alumni association and include "friends of the university."
4. Faculty-student teams should visit high schools for the double purpose of recruiting future students and informing the high schools about current academic developments (in each university department).

5. The university should establish a parents' committee (possibly through the student affairs office or the orientation office) for the purpose of improving communication between the university and the parents of the student body. A newsletter for parents should also be considered.

6. The governor of the state should meet informally (and off the record) with members of the university faculty, student body, and administration. The meetings can be held alternately at the governor's office and the university, should have no structured agenda, and should involve different university personnel each time. The plan developed at the University of New Mexico has proved quite successful and can serve as a model for such meetings.

7. The state legislature should establish a legislature-university communication committee whose *sole* purpose would be to conduct information exchange sessions with campus representatives (both on and off campus). The committee should function much like the governor's group described in item six.

8. The university should establish a legislators' day on campus, inviting legislators to be the guests of the university. Functions can include campus tours, orientation lectures, athletic events, social events, and attendance at classes.

9. Members of the university community should establish an active lobby to promote the best interests of the university during any hearings concerning legislation (especially financial) affecting the university.

10. The university placement office should attempt to improve relations between employers within the state and university graduates. A first step to reduce the possible exodus of university graduates from the state may be to schedule a job conference for such employers and university graduates, at which employers and students discuss job needs, employers recruit students, and students explain why they may want to leave the state.

11. The university should establish a research and development center to make certain services available to the public, such as data banks and translation of complex research findings, and to provide certain research services, in such areas as environment, leisure, government, business, and criminal justice. The overall purpose of the center would be to make the university more relevant to the needs of the public.

12. The university should establish a method of surveying or polling the general community (or voting public) annually. Such a poll can be handled by survey researchers on campus and should monitor feedback, measure attitudes, and compile comparative data to assess the impact of long-term changes at the university. Information so generated will assist the university in planning public relations efforts and in identifying geographic pockets of negative public attitude as well as possible causal factors. Figure 8.2 is a survey instrument that I have used successfully at two universities.

In the final analysis, no matter how sophisticated a communication campaign the university develops, it should recognize that every student, faculty member, administrator, janitor, secretary, and staff member connected with the university is actually a separate channel of communication. If universities learn to use their own human resources to improve their external image, they will have little need to do more to accomplish their purpose.

Figure 8.2 Survey questionnaire for university feedback.

1. When were you last on campus?
    - ☐ within past month   ☐ within past six months
    - ☐ within past year   ☐ within past five years
    - ☐ more than five years ago   ☐ have never been on campus

2. Which of the following services or events of the university have you used or attended during the past year?
    - ☐ cultural events (concerts, exhibits, speakers)
    - ☐ clinics (dental, psychological, speech, etc.)
    - ☐ athletic events or facilities
    - ☐ libraries
    - ☐ workshops, seminars, symposia
    - ☐ evening courses
    - ☐ campus radio station
    - ☐ none
    - ☐ other (specify)_____

3. What is the number of students enrolled at the university?
    - ☐ less than 10,000   ☐ 10,000–15,000   ☐ 15,000–20,000
    - ☐ 20,000–25,000   ☐ more than 25,000 ☐ don't know

4. From which source(s) do you get most of your information about the university?
    - ☐ students
    - ☐ friends
    - ☐ newspapers
    - ☐ radio
    - ☐ television
    - ☐ alumni publications
    - ☐ official university catalogs
    - ☐ student newspapers
    - ☐ other (specify)_____

5. To be admitted to the university's freshman class, a high school senior must have
    - ☐ an excellent high school record   ☐ a good high school record   ☐ a below-average high school record
    - ☐ a very good high school record   ☐ an average high school record   ☐ a poor high school record

6. How is construction on the campus financed? (Please check one.)
    - ☐ bonds paid back by student tuition and fees   ☐ gifts to the university by individuals and business
    - ☐ tax dollars provided to the university   ☐ don't know

7. Where does the university rank as an employer in its part of the state?
    - ☐ one of top three employers   ☐ one of top ten employers   ☐ don't know
    - ☐ one of top five employers   ☐ one of top twenty-five employers

8. From which area does the university draw most of its students? (Check one.)
    - ☐ western New York   ☐ metropolitan New York City area   ☐ don't know
    - ☐ upstate New York   ☐ outside New York State

9. What are the areas in which you would like more information about the university?
    - ☐ academic programs
    - ☐ community services and programs
    - ☐ cultural events
    - ☐ athletics
    - ☐ evening courses
    - ☐ other (specify)_____

Figure 8.2 *Continued*

10. In your opinion, how important are the following functions of the university?

    Instruction: unimportant ☐ ☐ ☐ ☐ ☐ very important
                                   1 2 3 4 5

    Research: unimportant ☐ ☐ ☐ ☐ ☐ very important
                                   1 2 3 4 5

    Public service: unimportant ☐ ☐ ☐ ☐ ☐ very important
                                   1 2 3 4 5

11. How would you describe the university?
    ☐ conservative   ☐ moderate   ☐ liberal   ☐ radical

12. Do you think the university is important to the region's economy?
    ☐ yes   ☐ no   ☐ don't know

13. If you have had the opportunity to evaluate the work of the university's graduates, how would you rate their capability on this scale? (If you have had no contact with its graduates, leave blank.)
    very low ☐ ☐ ☐ ☐ ☐ very high
              1 2 3 4 5

14. How important do you consider athletic teams such as basketball and hockey at the university?
    ☐ very important   ☐ important   ☐ not important   ☐ no opinion

15. Are you in favor of construction of the new university campus?
    ☐ yes   ☐ no   ☐ no opinion

16. Do you feel that the university faculty makes worthwhile contributions to this community?
    ☐ yes   ☐ no   ☐ no opinion

17. Do you think the university provides a quality education for its students?
    ☐ yes   ☐ no   ☐ no opinion

18. How would you rate the university as an academic institution?
    ☐ outstanding   ☐ above average   ☐ average   ☐ below average   ☐ poor

19. Which of the following best describes your feelings about the university?
    ☐ like it very much   ☐ like it   ☐ dislike it   ☐ dislike it strongly   ☐ no opinion

20. Do you think the university should accept more students from this area?
    ☐ yes   ☐ no   ☐ don't know

21. Would you send your son or daughter to the university?
    ☐ yes   ☐ no

22. Do you think the university is serving the needs of the people of this area?
    ☐ yes   ☐ no

23. Are you a graduate of the university?
    ☐ yes   ☐ no

24. Have you ever attended the university?
    ☐ yes   ☐ no

25. Your age:
    ☐ below 21 years   ☐ 21-25 years   ☐ 26-35 years   ☐ 36-45 years   ☐ 46-59 years
    ☐ 60 or over

26. Your sex:
    ☐ male   ☐ female

27. Your race or ethnic group:
    ☐ white   ☐ black or Negro   ☐ native American or Indian   ☐ Spanish-speaking
    ☐ Oriental   ☐ other_____

Figure 8.2 *Continued*

28. Your marital status:
    ☐ single   ☐ married   ☐ widow or widower   ☐ separated   ☐ divorced

29. The approximate income of the head of your household:
    ☐ under $10,000   ☐ $10,000–$14,999   ☐ $15,000–$19,999
    ☐ $20,000–$24,999   ☐ $25,000–$34,999   ☐ Over $35,000

30. How much education have you completed?
    ☐ eighth grade   ☐ two-year college or business, technical, or vocational school
    ☐ high school   ☐ bachelor's degree program in college
    ☐ some college   ☐ graduate or professional school

31. How long have you lived in this area? _____ years

32. What is your occupation? Please be specific (for example, high school teacher, auto mechanic, pharmacist) _____

33. If you could change one thing about the university, what would it be? _____

How Businesses and Industries Use Public Communication

Probably no kind of organization uses public communication more than business and industry. Besides the hundreds of millions of dollars spent annually for advertising and promotion of products, industry spends a great deal to create a favorable climate for the marketing of its products. Dedmon, who was critical of university negligence of public communication, has no such feelings about business and industry.

> Industry knows it must communicate with the general public in order to . . . market its products. It knows that it must guard against restrictive legislation. Most large industries are so concerned about their public image that they maintain expensive public relations departments employing some of the nation's foremost communication experts.

Holm reported several problems about which business and professional people have expressed concern:

1. How can we get the customers of our bank to feel the genuineness of our interest in them?
2. How can we get citizens of the town to take pride in the new plant we have located here?
3. How can we overcome the feeling of some of the public that our rates are too high?
4. What should we tell our employees about the coming changes in our operation?
5. How can we get our clients to see the virtues of the policy we propose in contrast to their own ideas?
6. How can we get better cooperation in keeping people from leaving cars on the main streets in a blizzard?

The solution to each of these concerns involves the use of some form of public organizational communication, primarily externally directed. Here is how some organizations solved similar problems.

Television stations are required by Federal Communications Commission (FCC) regulations to ascertain regularly whether they are meeting the needs of the community. Stations must go to the community at large and to community leaders to gather the information, usually for them to develop a plan for service over the next three years. Ideally, this forces broadcasters to interact with their public—typically through interviews, surveys, market analyses, fan mail, and informal contacts. Unfortunately, the FCC leaves selection of the methodology to the discretion of the licensee, and some stations use very slipshod data-gathering efforts.

Since the Occupational Safety and Health Act was passed in 1970, many companies, particularly those that manufacture potentially dangerous substances, have a medical staff, both to help maintain employee safety *and* to communicate better with the federal government. For example, a large chemical company established these goals for its corporate health program:

> Avoid unnecessary loss of profit due to regulatory actions against specific products; ensure that employees and persons living or working in proximity to production facilities are not exposed to hazardous levels of physical, chemical, or biologic agents handled or made in the facility or in the effluents from these facilities; we should ensure that the users of our products are aware of, and that they are adequately protected from, the effects of exposure to our products in use and disposal and have the expertise, responsible attitude, and capabilities to promptly handle and utilize toxic substances. We should be able to reduce occupational and nonoccupational insurance costs by improved preventive health care in a manner designed to prevent occupational and nonoccupational illnesses.

In order to meet these goals, the chemical company must communicate regularly with both federal and state government offices, including the Environmental Protection Agency; the Occupational Safety and Health Administration; the National Institutes for Health; the Department of Health and Human Services; and the several state agencies and legislatures in every state in which they operate or do business. The company also maintains regular communication with trade associations, professional societies, news media, academic communities, and consultants. This becomes a massive job and takes great skill, time, and effort.

Another audience of vital importance to all publicly held businesses and industries is the financial community, particularly security analysts who recommend stock purchases to potential investors, usually large institutions. This audience is important, because if a stock is underpriced (selling at a low price-earnings ratio) a company would be at a disadvantage in acquiring another company; or an employee profit-sharing plan invested in the company's stock could suffer (as happened in the bank example given at the beginning of this chapter); or the company could itself become a bargain acquisition for another company. In 1971, a manufacturer of batteries and other industrial products conducted an image study among security analysts, and the findings were very disappointing. Most analysts were unfamiliar with the company, did not know what it manufactured, did not think it was innovative, and did not recommend its stock to investors. The company began a major external public organizational communication program designed to reach financial analysts that included advertising in *Fortune, Business Week, Forbes, Wall Street Journal, Barron's, Scientific American, Time,* and *U.S. News and World Report.* The results were excellent. Within five years the price-earnings ratio of the stock increased from six to ten, an indication of renewed interest in the stock.

The increasing importance of interaction between organizations and government is underscored by a story from Niagara Falls. Several companies in the city, led by the president of a large manufacturing company, formed the City Management Advisory Board (CMAB) to provide free consulting advice on management techniques to their economically belabored community. A group of nineteen high-level executives met at least a half-day each week with city government officials to solve problems in the areas of finance, cost control, procurement, data processing, energy conservation, public protection, garbage disposal, community renewal, personnel, cash forecasting, and public works and utilities. The results of this highly innovative public organizational communication program were astounding! In 1975, before CMAB was formed, Niagara Falls ran a budget deficit of $1.5 million, and the city was paying 9.3 percent interest on its notes. In 1976, after CMAB had been in operation for only seven months, the city had a *surplus* of $748,000, and the interest rate on its notes was 4.88 percent.

In addition to maintaining their public relations efforts designed to promote good will and a favorable image for themselves, many organizations today are recognizing and utilizing their right to "free speech" as described in a landmark case tried in 1978 before the U.S. Supreme Court—*First National Bank of Boston vs. Bellotti*. In this case the court said that the First Amendment applies to corporations as well as to individuals. Corporations have the right, according to this verdict, to make their voices heard on issues, regardless of whether the issues are germane to their business interests. Many companies, led by Mobil Oil and its aggressive vice president for public affairs, Herbert Schmertz, are now attempting to apply the court's interpretation to the use of the mass media, primarily television, as a channel for diffusing their messages related to issues and their advocacy positions on those issues.

However, many companies still rely on oral face-to-face communication to convey their messages. Holm believes that "public speaking is a common and widespread necessity in business, professional, and industrial spheres, and that almost anyone may be called on, sometimes with very little advance notice, to make a speech." Holm cited the following advantages of public speaking in organizations:

> The person who has something to say and can say it well often finds that he has enhanced his reputation and his career. He has shown a willingness to meet responsibility which may lead to greater and more challenging responsibilities. He becomes more valuable to his employer, he aids associates and customers, he promotes good will for his business or profession, and he makes a positive contribution to his community.

Zelko and Dance identified several types of oral communication with the public, such as speeches to groups, sales interviews and presentations, informal contacts, professional contacts, and participation in civic or social organizations. There are five major public speaking situations in which business and industrial personnel most frequently interact: (1) informal meetings, (2) semiformal meetings, (3) formal meetings, (4) conventions, and (5) goodwill or public relations activities.

Informal meetings are casually held, rarely scheduled, but highly important to both management and employees. A manager may choose to discuss safety or sales with employees, or a salesman may wish to address a group of purchasing agents. In a friendly, informal atmosphere workers can become acquainted with one another.

Semiformal meetings require more planning, and usually speakers are introduced at such meetings. Holm included such activities here as "tell" or "sell" meetings, symposia, panels, training sessions, short courses, and briefing sessions. Several speakers may appear at a semiformal meeting, and many make a presentation instead of a formal speech. Howell and Bormann differentiated a presentation from a public speech on the basis of purpose of the presentation:

> . . . to secure a favorable response from those who have the decision-making power to accept or reject the proposal being presented. The proposal may offer an innovation, it may present a revised budget, the speaker may be "selling himself." . . . the communicator has a vital stake in the outcome. He knows he must make and defend his proposal in the give and take of a decision-making conference; that his success or failure depends on his ability to effectively inform and convince his peers or superiors and win them over to his point of view.

Another form of presentation common at a semiformal meeting is the oral technical report. Wilcox described the oral technical report as directed toward a special audience, having limited scope as well as presentation time, and delivered extemporaneously with personal and clear language for instant understanding. The main purpose of the oral technical report is to inform by means of exposition with data and other facts. Wilcox said that a well-organized report that uses appropriate visual aids will accomplish its purpose.

My graduate seminar in organizational communication consultation meets every semester with different organizations in their corporate headquarters. Our presentation usually consists of case studies of communication problems currently experienced by the company—Celanese Corporation; Union Carbide Corporation; Equitable Assurance Society; Arthur D. Little; Graphics Control; Xerox Corporation; Hooker Chemical Company; Towers, Perrin, Forster and Crosby; and others. Our oral technical reports provide an opportunity for these organizations to engage in public organizational communication with the academic community, an audience many companies are now trying to engage in dialogue. These conversations are also an opportunity to bring the university more in touch with what is happening inside organizational boundaries.

A formal meeting is usually the highly structured speaking engagement typical of dinners, banquets, and other ceremonies, such as, Holm has suggested, plant anniversary parties, ribbon-cutting ceremonies, acceptance or retirement dinners or meetings, and local and regional business meetings. Civic organizations hold weekly formal meetings, often with a scheduled speaker after lunch or breakfast.

An example of a formal meeting is the annual managers' day meeting held by a large manufacturer, during which its several hundred managers assemble to hear company financial and project status reports and future plans and an outside speaker. The later informal dialogue in workshop sessions is designed to break down formal barriers.

Another formal meeting, mentioned earlier, is the stockholders' meeting. Wise executives today are prepared in advance to handle the usual stockholder questions. Government regulations, energy shortage, business ethics, and dividend questions are the most likely candidates today. Haskins and Sells, a certified public accounting firm, contends that executives should be ready to answer the following stockholder questions:

1. How much does the company spend each year to comply with the regulations of government agencies?

2. What are the potential effects on the company of increased regulation in such areas as environmental standards, energy policies, and the extension of antitrust laws?
3. How adversely will production or sales be affected by energy shortages?
4. Can the company use alternative sources of energy?
5. What impact will deregulation of natural gas and other fuels have on the company?
6. Has the company developed a code of conduct for its personnel that bars illegal gifts at home and abroad?
7. Are the company's internal controls adequate to prevent or detect illegal or questionable payments, fraud, inventory shortages, or accounting errors?

Conventions are held in the United States by the thousands each year and are attended by millions. Professional societies, academic associations, technical meetings, and trade shows account for most. Naturally there is ample opportunity for numerous public speeches during the several days most conventions last. Unfortunately, many convention speakers look better than they sound. In a convention paper, Spielvogel poked fun at convention speakers:

> Convention speaking is a "big" business. Figures obtained from the New York Convention and Visitors Bureau reveal that in 1970 in New York City alone there were 815 conventions, accommodating 2,705,000 listeners . . . there are as many as 10,000 business meetings, conventions, corporate meetings a year. That's a lot of speech making.

> Recent observations have led me to conclude that hotels servicing luncheons and dinners to convention audiences have done more with infraray heating units to improve the food than have "warmed over" speakers, who should know better, have done about their talks.

Spielvogel recommended that conventions would be improved if the speakers were screened as carefully as the subject matter they speak about.

Military organizations (especially the U.S. Army and Navy) maintain active speech bureaus. Even hospital personnel are beginning to reach out to the public as they become more aware of the personal needs of their patients. However, all of this activity will be to little avail if the speakers are incompetent or ill prepared.

Measuring the Effectiveness of Public Organizational Communication

I once asked the training directors of three major airlines engaged in an expensive training program, "How do you know you're getting your money's worth? How do you know the training will do what it's supposed to do?" None of the three was able to provide an answer. All three admitted that they would have no data to support whether the training programs altered the behavior of the airlines' personnel.

Unfortunately, this is the case for much public communication training. The literature is sparse on measurement of effectiveness. Two studies reported in the mid-1960s provide some data. Irwin and Brockhaus tested the effectiveness of two public relations speeches about Bell Telephone Company. They assessed the impact of the speeches on five hundred adult women, measuring interest patterns, attitude changes, and information gains. Of primary importance was their finding that for both speeches the posttest attitude toward the telephone company was significantly more positive than the pretest attitude.

In a related study, Williams and Sundene also attempted to measure the effectiveness of a public relations speech about Bell Telephone Company. Approximately three hundred listeners were tested for attitude change before and after the speech. Results indicated that the speech was effective in improving attitudes toward the company and also attitudes toward the speech and speaker. While the two sets of results correlated significantly, no causal relation was demonstrated.

Robinson believes that survey research is an excellent means by which a public relations practitioner obtains feedback in order to function more efficiently in solving public relations problems. Public opinion polls I directed for the University of New Mexico and State University of New York/Buffalo were just such surveys. The primary objectives were the following:

1. To increase the public's interest and support of the university through the participative process.
2. To discover areas in which each university was deficient in projecting a favorable image to the voting public.
3. To accurately measure the voting public's opinion of the universities.
4. To help justify the fiscal existence of the universities to the legislature as publicly supported institutions of higher education.

Studies like these are necessary if an organization is to have any certainty about the effectiveness of its public communication program.

A colleague and I designed a measurement program for a professional basketball team interested in both designing and evaluating a public organizational communication program. The survey focused on specific reasons why people buy tickets and attend entertainment events. Preliminary study indicated two distinct populations of potential buyers: businessmen buying for their corporations, and the general public buying for their own use. Because promotional efforts can vary according to the target population, the businessmen and the general public were to be sampled separately. Table 8.3 outlines the procedures and objectives of this measurement program.

Table 8.3   Procedures and Objectives of a Professional Basketball Team Measurement Program

Procedures	Objectives
Program to assess the following factors:	
1. Knowledge levels of various season ticket plans and prices	1. To make concrete recommendations for content of the messages used to persuade people to buy tickets
2. Acceptable ranges for ticket prices	2. To provide summaries of the responses of the businessmen and general population sampled
3. Attitude toward basketball, team (players and management), auditorium, and entertainment in general	
4. Factors that influence patterns	
5. Kinds of incentives that will stimulate ticket purchase	
6. Preference for media and television channel for sports information	

I have conducted several dozen market studies for clients whose main needs were to identify *who* their market was demographically (age, sex, income, etc.) and psychographically (social, economic, and psychological values and indicators) and to discover *what* traits, attributes, or characteristics the market desired in the product or service.

SUMMARY

Public organizational communication involves the transmitting of messages to groups of people using face-to-face or mediated channels. In this book, we are primarily concerned with two kinds of message flow: between one member of an organization and a large group of people from the same organization and between the organization itself and its external environment. Both kinds use public speaking as a major tool in accomplishing their objectives.

At least four characteristics distinguish public organizational communication from dyadic and small-group communication: (1) it is source oriented; (2) large groups of receivers are involved; (3) interaction between communicator and receivers is less; and (4) language is more general. Public organizational communication can also be viewed as part of the social systems model in which interaction between an organization and its public is necessary to maintain systems balance.

Organizations use public organizational communication to create, reinforce, and redefine their image when necessary. Activities used in public organizational communication can be classified as internal (suggestion systems, union meetings, social functions) or external (goodwill speech, advertising, lobbying). Organizations such as labor unions, universities, businesses, and industries all use public organizational communication in their daily interaction. Of particular importance to business and industry are such activities as informal meetings, semiformal meetings, formal meetings, conventions, and public relations activities.

EXERCISES

1. If you are at a university or college, has it experienced significant pressures or changes in the past five years? If so, discuss these changes and awareness of them on the part of students and the public.

2. Think of two organizations. What publics are they responsible to? In what ways do they interact with their publics?

3. Visit an organization of your choice. Talk with the public relations director and ask the same questions given in exercise 2. If the organization is one you used for exercise 2, compare your answers with those of the public relations director. If possible, ask the public relations director to take you along during his or her next public appearance. Describe the audience, the speech, and the speaker. Do you think the speech was effective?

4. Attend a public speech. Compare this communicative situation with a small-group or dyadic experience you have recently had. Describe how the situations were different. In what ways were they similar?

5. Think of a product, service, social movement, or politician that recently redefined an image. Describe the old image. Describe the new image, identifying the specific changes in the redefinition. Was the purpose of the redefinition to appeal to a new audience?
6. What are the major goals of "positioning" an organization?
7. Contact the marketing director of a local organization. Find out how that company obtains information on its market position and how they use this information.
8. Visit with an organization which maintains an active speakers' bureau and talk with the director. How many speeches were given last year? How many speakers were used? How many organizations are reached each year? Does the director think the number will increase next year? Give reasons for the success or lack of success of the speakers' bureau.
9. Think of another organization. List as many public organizational communication activities as you can, both external and internal, for the organization. Use oral software techniques only. After you've composed your list, call or visit with the communication director, personnel director, or public relations director of the organization. Ask this person to prepare a similar list. Compare your list, the director's list, and the lists of class members.
10. Think of your group of peers. Identify which individuals in this group you would consider "boundary spanners." Why did you choose these individuals?
11. You are president of the Jones Chemical Company. Your company has just discovered that an old chemical dump in which you dumped toxic chemicals twenty-five years ago has suddenly become a problem to residents of the community whose homes have been built over the old dump. Chemicals are seeping into their basements. Who will your company communicate with as it confronts this crisis? What techniques of communication will your company use? What are the pros and cons of these techniques?
12. Contact the personnel director of a local organization. Find out the amount of money that organization spends yearly on paperwork done to comply with federal, state, and local government regulations.

BIBLIOGRAPHY AND REFERENCES

BankAmerica Corporation Voluntary Disclosure Code, 1976.

Bittner, John, et al. "College Administrators Reactions to News Coverage of Campus Unrest." Paper presented at the International Communication Association Convention, Phoenix, Arizona, April 1971.

Borden, George, R. Gregg, and T. Groce. *Speech Behavior and Human Interaction.* Englewood Cliffs, N.J.: Prentice-Hall, 1969.

Brooks, William. *Speech Communication.* 4th ed. Dubuque, Iowa: Wm. C. Brown Publishers, 1981.

Chronicle of Higher Education, May 1, 1972, p. 1.

Dance, Frank, and Carl Larson. *Speech Communication: Concepts and Behavior.* New York: Holt, Rinehart & Winston, 1972.

Dedmon, Donald. "A Comparison of University and Business Communication Practices." *Journal of Communication* 20(1970):315–22.

Dee, James P. "Communication Needs of the Active Union Member." *Journal of Communication* 18(1969):65–72.

Goldhaber, Gerald. "Communication and Student Unrest." Part 2. Report to the President of University of New Mexico, 1972. Typewritten.

Goldhaber, G. M., and M. A. deTurck. "Effects of Consumers' Familiarity with a Product on Attention to and Compliance with Warnings." *Journal of Products Liability* 2, (1988):29–37.

Goldhaber, Gerald, H. Dennis, G. Richetto, and O. Wiio. *Information Strategies: New Pathways to Management Productivity.* Rev. Ed. Norwood, N.J.: ABLEX, 1984.

Grala, William. "Industry's Best Defense: the Speakers Bureau." *Public Relations Journal* 20(1964): 12–13.

Haskins and Sells. "What Stockholders May Ask at Your Annual Meeting." *Nation's Business,* April 1977, pp. 4–6.

Holm, James. *Productive Speaking for Business and the Professions.* Boston: Allyn & Bacon, 1967.

Horan, Hilary. *"A Statewide Survey of Public Opinion toward the University of New Mexico."* Master's thesis, University of New Mexico, 1972.

Howell, William, and Ernest Bormann. *Presentational Speaking for Business and the Professions.* New York: Harper & Row, 1971.

Huseman, R., et al. "Communicating Employee Benefits: Directions for Future Research." Paper presented at a meeting of the International Communication Association, Chicago, 1978.

Irwin, John, and Herman Brockhaus. "The 'Teletalk Project': A Study of the Effectiveness of Two Public Relations Speeches." *Speech Monographs* 30 (1963):359–68.

Kirby, Robert. "Adversity, Hostility and Corporate Communication." In *Cross Currents in Corporate Communications.* No. 6. New York: Time-Life Books, 1977.

Knapp, Mark, and J. McCroskey. "Communication Research and the American Labor Union." *Journal of Communication* 18 (1968):160–72.

Koehler, J. W., and Fred Marsh. "Organized Labor: An Analysis of Communication Needs." Paper presented at the International Communication Association, Phoenix, Arizona, April 1971.

Lehto, M.R., and J. M. Miller. Warnings. Fundamentals, Design, and Evaluation Methodologies. Vol. 1. Ann Arbor, MI: Fuller Technical Publications, 1986.

Linowitz, Sol. *Campus Tensions: Analysis and Recommendations.* Washington, D.C.: American Council of Education, 1970.

National Journal of Law, May 23, 1988, p.39.

New York Times, April 27, 1988, p.1.

Redding, W. C. "The Empirical Study of Human Communication in Business and Industry." In *The Frontiers of Speech-Communication Research.* Edited by Paul Ried. Syracuse, N.Y.: Syracuse University Press, 1965.

Rein, Irving. *Rudy's Red Wagon.* Glenview, Ill.: Scott, Foresman, 1972.

Reis, A. and J. Trout. *Positioning: The Battle for Your Mind.* New York: McGraw-Hill, 1981.

Robinson, Edward. *Public Relations and Survey Research.* New York: Appleton-Century-Crofts, 1969.

Scranton, William. "Text of the Findings of the President's Commission on Campus Unrest." *Chronicle of Higher Education,* October 5, 1970.

Spielvogel, R. "Convention Speakers Should Sound as Good as They Look." Paper presented at the International Communication Association Convention, Phoenix, Arizona, April 1971.

Taiani, V. *The Role/Functions of Organizational Communication in the Area of Corporate Social Behavior.* Unpublished doctoral dissertation, Buffalo, N.Y., State University of New York-Buffalo, 1981.

Trout, J., and A. Reis. *Marketing Warefare.* New York: McGraw-Hill, 1986.

Tushman, M., and T. Scanlan. "Boundary Spanning Individuals: Their Role in Information Transfer and Their Antecedents," *Academy of Management Journal* 24 (1981):289–305.

Wall Street Journal, 6 July 1981, p. 15.

Wendel, W. "Private and Public Partnership: The Desperate Case of Niagara Falls." *Harvard Business Review* 55 (November–December 1977):6–8.

Wilcox, Roger. "Characteristics and Organization of the Oral Technical Report." *General Motors Engineering Journal* 6 (1959):1–12.

Wilkenfeld, J. "Hooker Chemical Plastics Corporation's Corporate Health Plan." Mimeographed. Niagra Falls, N.Y.: Hooker Corporation, 1977.

Williams, F., and B. Sundene. "A Field Study in Effects of a Public Relations Speech." *Journal of Communication* 15 (1965):161–70.

Ylvisaker, W. "Expanded Horizons for Corporate Communications." In *Cross Currents in Corporate Communication.* No. 6. New York: Time-Life Books. 1977.

Zelko, Harold, and Frank Dance. *Business and Professional Speech Communication.* New York: Holt, Rinehart & Winston, 1965.

PART FOUR
ORGANIZATIONAL COMMUNICATION DIAGNOSIS AND CHANGE

Chapter 9 describes and illustrates the planning of organizational communication diagnosis, dealing especially with the consultant's role.

Chapter 10 describes and illustrates the procedures and techniques for implementing organizational communication diagnosis, especially as related to communication auditing.

Chapter 11 describes and illustrates the procedures for implementing organizational communication changes, especially training techniques and evaluation.

Chapter 12 describes and illustrates various organizational communication career paths and the necessary preparation for their achievement.

9

PLANNING ORGANIZATIONAL COMMUNICATION DIAGNOSIS AND CHANGE

Imagine the following dialogue between a professor and a class of graduate students:

Professor Jones: On the twenty-third of this month there will be no class.

Student A: Why?

Professor Jones: I will be away from campus on a consulting trip.

Student B: Which company will you be working for?

Professor Jones: A large corporation in the East.

Student C: What will you be doing there?

Professor Jones: Helping them with their communication problems.

Student D: Can you give us any more information about this?

Professor Jones: I'm afraid not. I don't want to violate the confidence of the company. After you graduate and begin to do some consulting, you'll see what I mean.

It is highly likely that dialogue like this has echoed through many U.S. universities and has contributed to the many myths surrounding the art of consulting. In chapter 4, we discussed the grapevine and suggested that one reason for its existence is the lack of substantive information from management sources. One might speculate similarly about the national grapevine concerning communication consulting. The absence of textbooks, journal articles, convention papers, and university-level courses on communication consulting helps to promote rumors and myths. Because of this void in the literature, many students must do what Professor Jones said: set forth *almost totally unprepared* if they want to start a consulting firm or supplement a teaching income by serving as "an expert consultant." No wonder Argyris (1970) said the following about consultants and consulting firms:

> The consulting organizations can point with pride to the fact that they have earned millions of dollars without introducing new ideas about organizations, management, or change. Moreover, most hold the same change strategies as their clients and breed the same forces of organizational dry rot in their own systems.

The study of consulting is important because most organizations rely upon either an internal or external consultant to help plan organizational communication diagnosis and change. This chapter will answer specific questions and present certain facts about the art of consulting. In chapter 10, specific techniques for both internal and external consultants to use when actually conducting a diagnosis are described. Chapter 11 explains how consultants and organizations actually go about implementing the changes recommended in the diagnosis. Chapter 12, the last chapter in the book, presents specific career paths and discusses both internal and external consulting careers in organizational communication.

Most of the data in this chapter were derived from a handful of books and articles (primarily in fields other than communication), from my personal experience, and from experiences of colleagues. The specific objectives of the chapter are as follows:

1. To describe organization development (OD) as a framework within which consulting may occur.
2. To define, diagram, and exemplify three models of communication consulting: purchase, doctor-patient, and process.
3. To describe and illustrate the factors affecting the establishment of the consultant-client relationship (e.g., making contact, designing contracts and setting fees, initial meetings, etc.).
4. To define and illustrate the diagnostic and prescriptive functions of communication consulting.
5. To list, describe, define, and illustrate the types of communication consulting intervention activities.
6. To list and exemplify problems encountered by the communication consultant during intervention activities.
7. To list and illustrate ethical considerations of communication consultants during intervention activities.
8. To describe and illustrate the factors affecting the termination of the consultant-client relationship.

Organizational Development (OD)

Organizational development (OD) is a method of changing an organization and its beliefs, values, attitudes, and structure so that it can better adapt to the changing and turbulent environment of coming decades. You may find it helpful to know that management of change in an organization as a technique began only in the late 1960s. As evidence of the fast growth of this discipline, the publishing company, Addison-Wesley first released in 1969 only six volumes in its now classic OD series. Today there are a total of sixteen volumes in this series, including such topics as alternative work schedules, career dynamics, and multi-national issues. Burke and Schmidt defined OD as a

> *process* which attempts to increase organizational effectiveness by integrating individual desires for growth and development with organizational goals. Typically, this process is a planned change effort which involves a total system over a period of time, and these change efforts are related to the organization's mission. Key terms in this rather broad definition are: *process, planned change, total system,* and *organizational mission.*

Process indicates the dynamic nature of organizational change. *Planned change* indicates that various kinds of planning, implementing, and evaluating similar to that used in introducing a technical change are involved. *Total system* indicates that the entire organization and all its interdependent parts will be affected by the change (as discussed in chapter 3, change within a subpart, no matter how small, affects all other parts of a system). *Organizational mission* means that the change must take into account both the major goals of the organization and individual employee goals and integrate the two so that maximum use of human resources results.

French and Bell (1978) have defined OD as

> . . . a long range effort to improve an organization's problem solving and renewal processes, particularly through a more effective and collaborative management of the organization culture with special emphasis on the culture of formal work teams—with the assistance of a change agent and the use of the theory and technology of applied behavioral science, including action research.

Gordon Lippitt, who has been quite active as an OD consultant, has offered his definition (1982):

> Using knowledge and techniques from the behavioral sciences, organization development attempts to integrate individual needs for growth and development with organizational goals and objectives in order to make a more effective organization.

After reviewing the above definitions of OD, you might ask what is it that OD professionals actually do? Exactly where in the organization are they located? What are their titles? McDermott (1984) surveyed 1,000 OD professionals and found the following organizational titles to describe them:

—Vice President, Human Resources
—Director, Administrator or Manager of Training and Development
—Management Consultant
—Training Coordinator/Specialist
—Employer Relations and Organization Development Manager/Specialist
—Organization Development or Organization Effectiveness Consultant (Associate)
—Human Resource or Organization Planning Manager
—Industrial Psychologist
—Staff Development Consultant
—Professor of Management/Organizational Behavior
—Director of Education
—Personnel Programs Manager
—Director of Creative Worklife Center
—Director of Management Development
—Director of Corporate Services

Bennis (1969) has claimed that one reason why present-day (and future) organizations need OD is to handle major changes in managerial behavior effectively. According to Bennis, these changes are:

1. A new concept of the human being based on increased knowledge of complex and shifting needs, which replaces an oversimplified, innocent, pushbutton idea of the human being.

2. A new concept of *power* based on collaboration and reason, which replaces a model of power based on coercion and threat.
3. A new concept of *organizational values* based on humanistic-democratic ideals, which replaces the depersonalized, mechanistic value system of bureaucracy.

The foregoing list makes it apparent that OD *must* take into account incorporation of new values into an organizational system—for example, the values of younger employees, as mentioned in chapter 3. In fact, when asked about the possible reaction of students to OD, Bennis stated:

> We've heard a lot in recent years about students—particularly the brighter ones—turning their backs on business as a career. I think it's clear that the younger generation is not attracted to conformity, it's not attracted to interests narrowly defined around profit concerns or to being enmeshed in a hierarchical system with limited responsibility. As a matter of fact, if there's one distinguishing characteristic of the student activists as well as many other young professionals, it is their *anti-hierarchical* values.

> In contrast, organization development concepts encourage people to develop their potentialities within the organizational framework and emphasize individual responsibility and problem-solving. These are all much more congruent with the younger generation's and problem-solving. These are all much more congruent with the younger generation's needs and goals. I think any company with a strong organization development program is missing the boat in its recruiting effort if it fails to publicize its organization development approach to managing. This would be a real plus to young people in making a decision about a job.

What Bennis said is not significantly different from the results of the Yankelovich survey on student values mentioned in chapter 3. He advocates OD as a method for organizations to use in setting up change that will be sensitive to the values of the youth of today. I agree with Bennis, both because OD takes account of *value differences* and because it utilizes the *systems approach*. Figure 9.1 illustrates the systems approach.

In figure 9.1, the change agent, in a collaborative relationship with the human resources of the system, applies valid knowledge and introduces programs for change, which should improve the systems' outputs.

An organization has the choice of hiring an outside consultant or of using its own internal resources. Sometimes one choice is advantageous, sometimes the other. An *outside* consultant should be hired when the following circumstances pertain:

1. The organization needs objective data in a specialized area from a credible expert.
2. Because of excessive office, fringe benefit, overhead, and other costs the organization cannot afford to hire a full-time staff member with the knowledge needed to accomplish the change.
3. The organization is unwilling to make a career path commitment for a full-time staff member.
4. The organization is unwilling or unable to give a full-time staffer the necessary *power* to conduct the necessary consultation.
5. The job must be done quickly—for example, the company is fighting for survival or is on the verge of a major expansion—and an outsider can save critical time.

Figure 9.1 Organizational development (OD) as a systems approach. (Source: Warren Bennis, *Organization Development,* © 1969, Addison-Wesley, Reading, Massachusetts.)

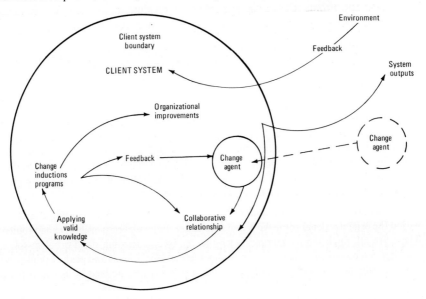

Dover has cautioned about some potential problems when an organization hires an outside consultant, particularly for studies in which data are gathered and fed back to the client. Among them are the following:

1. The consultant may be naïve or ignorant of the nature of the organization being studied (e.g., its union-management relations, its personnel practices, etc.).
2. The consultant may not understand differences that may exist between units of the organization.
3. The consultant may not have a good liaison with an internal resource, such as a behaviorally trained manager, who can help formulate appropriate solutions to problems diagnosed by the consultant.
4. The consultant may report the data to the "wrong" audience (e.g., staff personnel may not use the information as effectively as line officers—CEO, etc.).

Organizations may choose to look to internal resources in order to avoid such problems. *Internal* resources should be used when these circumstances pertain:

1. The organization is involved in introducing new technology. Since an outsider would have to be trained at the organization's expense, it is more cost-effective to invest organizational money in its own technical staff, especially when the technology will have long-range impact.
2. People with expert knowledge, credibility, objectivity, and power within the organization (whose jobs can be covered by other employees without too much disruption during the consulting operation) can solve the problem.

3. The problem doesn't require an independent viewpoint or comparison with the diagnoses and solutions of other organizations.
4. The organization finds it financially cheaper in the long run to use internal resources.

No consultant should be used when the circumstances are these:

1. The consultant is intended to serve as a scapegoat for an unpopular or unfruitful decision.
2. The management of the organization wants to "shake things up."
3. The management of the organization is basically inept.
4. The management has already made a decision and is looking for outside support.
5. The organization simply wants to enhance its image by hiring an outside expert.

Many companies maintain their own consulting staffs, who work either alone or with outside consultants.

Regardless of whether an organization uses an internal or external consultant, it should ask itself several questions *before* it begins any program of organizational change:

1. How does the organization manage change now?
2. What are some of the major internal or external changes the organization must deal with now and in the future?
3. Who are the change leaders, officially and unofficially, in the organization? What are their social, demographic, and psychographic characteristics, past and present?
4. How do successful leaders operate in the organization? What methods, skills, and tools do they use?
5. What specific strategies, techniques, tools have been effective in managing or communicating about change in the organization?
6. What are some options for effective interventions in the future?

Since OD usually relies so heavily upon the consultant, this chapter uses OD as the conceptual framework for describing the activity of the communication consultant. First, let us examine three models of communication consulting.

Communication Consulting Models

A survey of the literature on organizational consulting reveals three general behavioral models for consultants: purchase, doctor-patient, and process. In the pages that follow, each of the models is defined, diagrammed, and illustrated in terms of the communication consultant.

Purchase Model

In the purchase model, the client (the manager, the organization, the department) defines a need within the system based upon a diagnosis conducted within the system and by the system. Then the client approaches the consultant to purchase the service or information to meet the organization's needs. After the consultant provides the service or the information, the client usually terminates the relationship. Figure 9.2 illustrates the purchase model.

Figure 9.2 Purchase model of consulting.

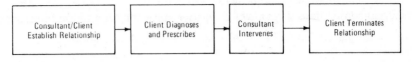

Figure 9.3 Doctor-patient model of consulting.

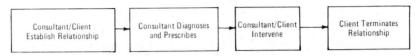

In this model the roles of both consultant and client are well defined and develop in a linear sequence. Illustrations of this model include the following: (1) Client purchases a communication training program from the consultant (to meet the training needs already diagnosed by the client). (2) Client purchases a survey of communication attitudes among employees. (3) Client purchases a set of recommendations on how to improve upward communication in the system. (4) Client purchases the consultant's recommendations on how to improve meetings.

According to Schein, the success of this model depends upon how accurately clients have diagnosed their own needs, communicated them to the consultant, assessed the consultant's capability of meeting these needs, and thought through the consequences of the consultant's intervention and recommendations.

Doctor-Patient Model

In the doctor-patient model, the client complains of an "illness" and describes symptoms without really knowing what is wrong, much as when someone consults a medical doctor. The role of the consultant is primarily to diagnose and prescribe (and occasionally help implement). The consultant is usually hired to "look over the organization," tell what is wrong, and suggest a remedy. The client then usually terminates the relationship. Figure 9.3 illustrates the doctor-patient model.

The main difference between the purchase model and the doctor-patient model is that in the former, diagnosis is done by the client, in the latter, it is done by the consultant. Caplan has discussed mental health consultation models (from which the doctor-patient model was derived) in this way:

> Since the primary goal is to improve the client, the consultant's fundamental responsibility is to make a specialized assessment of the client's condition and to recommend an effective disposition or method of treatment to be undertaken by the consultee. The consultant's attention is centered on the client, whom he will probably examine with whatever methods of investigation his specialized judgment indicates are necessary in order to arrive at an adequate appraisal of his difficulty.

In the most common example of the doctor-patient model, the communication consultant administers a departmentwide or organizationwide communication audit and produces a report telling the organization "what is wrong" and "what to do about it." This model

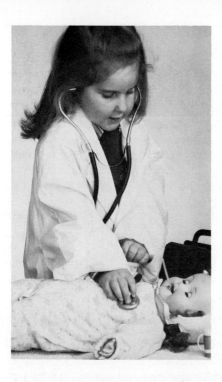

In the doctor-patient model, the client complains of an "illness" and describes symptoms without really knowing what is wrong, much like consulting a medical doctor.

may fail miserably if the consultant gets inaccurate information or if the client refuses to accept the diagnosis or prescription—which may occur in defensive organizations where employees are reluctant to talk with consultants or tell them the truth, or if defensive managers do not heed the consultant.

Process Model

In the process model, the consultant and the client are jointly involved in all steps of the interaction. Both consultant and client establish relationships, diagnose and prescribe, intervene, and terminate relationships. As figure 9.4 shows, the process model does not follow a linear sequence; any step may lead to the next step or to any other step in the process. All steps are interdependent. For example, immediately after establishing a relationship, both parties may agree to terminate the relationship (a form of intervention). Schein defined process consultation (PC) as follows:

> A set of activities on the part of the consultant which help the client to perceive, understand, and act upon process events which occur in the client's environment.

Inherent in this model are the assumptions that managers do not know what is wrong, do not know what kinds of help are available, are sincere in their desires for improvement, and will be more effective if they learn to diagnose their own problems. Also inherent in this model are the assumptions that consultants work jointly with members of the organization, provide alternatives for the client to consider, and are expert in diagnosis and in establishing a helping relationship with clients.

Figure 9.4 Process model of consulting.

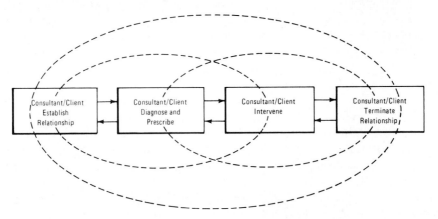

Argyris (1961) saw the chief responsibility of the process consultant as follows:

> . . . as helping an organization solve its problems in such a way that it becomes more competent in solving the same or a similar class of problems without the continued help of the consultants.

Once outside consultants are hired, management tends to think of them as internal staff. They are expected not only to provide new ideas, but also to *implement* those ideas. That is a mistake! Consultants *should* play the devil's advocate and raise questions that insiders are afraid to raise or cannot raise because they lack the knowledge. They should also provide guidance in finding answers. However, putting the ideas into motion is *management's job*.

No matter how well outsiders study a company, they cannot know it as well as management itself does. Consultants have little chance of getting a program to work, since they lack the necessary leverage that insiders have. Even solutions packaged by the best consultants must be modified to fit each company's unique situation.

Recognizing that many people have interpreted the consultant's role as that of a "change agent" (as described in many OD models), Argyris (1970) later stated:

> Change is *not* a primary task of the interventionist. To repeat, the interventionist's primary tasks are to generate valid information, to help the client system make informed and responsible choices, and to develop internal commitment to these choices. One choice that the clients may make is to change aspects of their system. If this choice is made responsibly, the interventionist may help the client to change. However, the point we are making is that change is not a priori considered good and no change considered bad.

In sum, in the standard models (purchase and doctor-patient), consultants are the ones who provide expert advice or services. It is they who are primarily responsible for solving the problems of the organization. In the process model, consultants help the organization to use its own resources to solve its own problems. Schein explained the difference in this way:

> The standard consultant is more concerned about passing on his knowledge, the process consultant is concerned about passing on his skills and values.

As an example of how the process model works, I will describe a study I did for a major newspaper. The client wanted me to conduct a network analysis of their organization. I taught two of their researcher/liaisons (in a three-day intensive period) the skills needed to conduct and interpret the study. We then jointly administered the study. I drafted a survey instrument with them. They mailed the survey forms to the participants, who completed them and sent them directly to me for computer analysis. My colleague, Richard Lesniak, and I mailed the computer output to them for their initial study. They phoned us with several questions over a two-week period, and Lesniak and I made a short trip to their headquarters. During this trip, we worked closely with the client to complete interpretation of the data. The client drafted the final report, sent it to us for feedback, and then completed it and distributed it to appropriate personnel. After distribution of the report, the client contacted Lesniak or me several times with additional questions and comments. Only once did the client attempt to deviate from our process model. They tried to get us to give them some specific recommendations about reorganization. However, we insisted that their knowledge was far superior to ours (as Dover has suggested). I believe that this client now has the skills and values to implement future studies of this type, and can also develop and implement recommendations from the present study.

The remainder of this chapter deals with the four components of the process model and provides detailed examples of how to use this model as a communication consultant.

Establishing Relationships

Establishing a relationship between the consultant and the client usually involves three steps: making contact, holding an initial meeting, and designing a contract.

In the doctor-patient model, the client complains of an "illness" and describes symptoms without really knowing what is wrong, much like consulting a medical doctor.

Making Contact

Most consultant-client contacts are made directly or indirectly or by referral. Some direct contacts are friends who ask the consultant to assist in their organization; potential clients who participate in training programs or workshops administered by the consultant; or people who hear a convention paper or other presentation by the consultant. For example, as a member of a speakers' bureau, I addressed a civic group on management communication problems. One of the members of the club approached me after the meeting and asked if I would call him at his office to discuss some of the problems of his organization. On another occasion, a potential client who heard me deliver a paper on compressed speech at a national convention asked me to design a training program for her organization. Also, a participant in a transactional analysis workshop that I conducted asked me to consider designing a workshop for his organization.

Other direct contacts are clients who read books, articles, or papers by consultants in which they find material related to their organization. For example, management at two university systems on the West Coast read my articles on university communication systems and asked me to help design their research programs. A group of researchers needing help on a grant project might read pertinent articles by a communication consultant and contact the consultant.

Referrals, the third general way for a consultant to be contacted by potential clients, are from other consultants (who may be unable or are too busy to aid the client); from other organizations (who have heard about or have worked with the consultant); from individuals within an organization (who are familiar with the consultant or his or her reputation); and from friends or colleagues of the consultant (who are aware of his or her capabilities). For example, a government agency asked me to design a set of workshops because a consultant friend was too busy to take on the responsibility. Again, a bank familiar with my work in another organization contacted me. Sometimes consultants are contacted by an organization simply because it has heard of the consultant. An organization is wise to avoid selecting a consultant strictly on the basis of recommendation by previous clients. An equally good source are professionals who have worked with the candidate.

It should be apparent by this time that contacts can come at any time from many sources, some when least expected. This should underscore a general maxim for consultants: You never know who is in the audience!

If you are interested in starting a career as a consultant, one way to get your name known is to join the local organizations that are relevant to your profession, such as the *local chapter* of the American Society of Training and Development, or the International Association of Business Communicators, or the Public Relations Society of America. Attending their meetings regularly and even volunteering to perform some services for them will make you known, at least informally, to many of their members (who may be potential clients). You could, after a short time, offer to be responsible for one of their programs. This would give you a chance to exhibit your professional capabilities to your colleagues and potential clients. You could also volunteer to give a speech to a nonprofit organization, again as a way to get your name known in your community.

The consulting business, either fortunately or unfortunately, depending upon your perspective, is one in which personal contact, word-of-mouth, references, and referrals are more likely to generate potential clients than are direct marketing strategies (e.g., advertising, direct mail, publicity, etc.). In fact, it has been my experience and observation that *the more direct effort the consultant engages in to generate business, the less business is likely to be generated.*

One of my favorite indirect methods of developing future business is to fly first class on airplanes. The type of person who flies first class is more likely to talk with you (perhaps due to the almost partylike atmosphere on many first-class flights, especially wide-body jets) and is also more likely to be a decision maker in business, industry, or the professions. In short, one can meet future clients on a first-class airplane trip.

Initial Meeting

Once contact has been established, I like to hold an initial meeting with the client system. At this meeting, I usually decide if I am indeed going to become the consultant. Therefore, it is somewhat important to establish in as much detail as possible the nature of the problem, the nature of the commitment to me, and the nature of my commitment to the organization. In order to accomplish these purposes, I insist that members of the organization who are at or close to the top of the power structure of the organization be present at this initial meeting,

STOCKWORTH
by Sterling and Selesnick

Panel 1: MY RESEARCH SHOWS THERE'S A HIDDEN HIERARCHY IN YOUR COMPANY.

Panel 2: AN INVISIBLE NETWORK OF SPIES, WHISPERERS, GOSSIPS AND STORYTELLERS.

Panel 3: IMPOSSIBLE.

Panel 4: YOU'RE OUR ONLY CONSULTANT.

STOCKWORTH reprinted by permission of Sterling and Selasnick, Inc.

If you are interested in starting a career as a consultant, one way to get your name known is to join the local organizations that are relevant to your profession.

plus the contact members and any other members of the organization who may help define the problem or will work with me later. Argyris (1970) supports this point of view:

> If the interventionist is to have the best possible opportunity to help the client system generate valid information, make free and informed choices, and develop internal commitment, he should strive to begin at the highest level in the organization necessary to accomplish these tasks. Given the proposition that pyramidal systems centralize information at the top, power and choice then tend to be at the top. If the system is not pyramidal in structure, the point of entry may be lower.

If the consultancy is to be successful, the involvement of top management is absolutely critical and essential.

One final note about the initial meeting relates to *where it should take place.* Although some consultants don't object to holding this first meeting on site at the client's office or in his organization, I prefer to hold this meeting in my office. Since I may know very little about my potential client (he or she may be using me for his or her own power needs, he or she may be a major part of the problem, etc.) at the time of this early contact, it is absolutely vital for me to maintain complete control of the situation. Using *my* home turf will give me a nonverbal spatial advantage that may come in handy, particularly if the person who contacted me is not being totally honest and forthcoming with me.

Designing a Contract

The details concerning the nature of mutual commitments and expectations are usually part of the contract between consultant and client. Such contracts also include reference to the details of the service to be provided, the number of days of involvement, and the fee. Weisbord (1973) has defined a contract as:

> . . . an explicit exchange of expectations, part dialogue, part written document, which clarifies for consultant and client three critical areas:
>
> 1. What each expects to get from the relationship
>
> 2. How much time each will invest, when, and at what cost
>
> 3. The ground rules under which the parties will operate

Both the client and the consultant should attempt to be as specific as possible concerning the nature of the service to be provided, clarifying all terms or concepts unknown to either party. For example, the consultant may desire to teach members of the training department how to conduct a communication audit throughout the organization. In order to do this effectively, the consultant needs to have time releases for employees being taught the procedures, access to records, freedom to call meetings and conduct interviews, adequate work space, secretarial assistance, and the like. All of the consultant's needs should be specified in the contract. On the other hand, the client may expect some "private" advice on how to communicate better with certain members of the organization or some support for a new communication training program. It is important to discuss all commitments and expectations *before* the consultancy begins, in order to minimize disappointment and avoid possible breach of contract or of ethics. If the consultant and client cannot agree on all relevant expectations, this may be cause for the relationship to be terminated at this point. Both parties should be ready to take this step if an unsatisfactory relationship appears imminent.

The details of the service to be provided influence the number of days needed, and consequently the nature and amount of the fee. For example, a request to teach organizational personnel how to audit their communication system (and supervise the audit) may require as many as sixty days. Sometimes, this can be spread over a long period of time—for example, two days a week for six months. At other times, depending upon availability of the consultant and immediate needs of the organization, the work can be done in sixty consecutive days (e.g., during a summer vacation). Of course, if the organization needs time when the consultant is unavailable, the consultant terminates the relationship after having made an appropriate referral. The consultancy may take as little time as one day: the relationship may be terminated early, the work may require a simple task such as observing one meeting, or a one-day workshop may be all that is needed.

The last element to be specified in a contract is the nature and amount of the fee. An average fee for expert consultants is $750–$1,500 per day (plus expenses), but this varies, depending upon the nature of the service, the time available, the financial capability of the organization, and the distance to be traveled. In some cases, consultants may charge by the hour (an average going rate today is approximately $100 to $200 per hour). In many cases, the consultant has no input in setting the fee because the organization has a standard rate which is nonnegotiable. For example, many federal government agencies and departments have uniform consultant rates ranging from $250 to $500 per day (plus expenses). As a general rule, consultants should set their fees in accordance with the amount of time available: the less time, the higher the rate. One final note on setting fees concerns the ethics of helping clients who cannot afford high rates. I consider a consultant to be a professional similar to a doctor, an attorney, or a psychologist. Depending upon the time the consultant has available, I believe consultants should *not* refuse clients simply because they cannot afford the fee. Possible alternatives to monetary repayment exist and should be explored by both client and consultant: student placement for internships, hiring of students, research outlets (for faculty and students). Of course, consultants whose time is extremely limited should make every effort to refer clients to other sources of assistance. If an organization has difficulty paying a fee, it may ask the consultant to help reduce *other* costs in the operation.

Overall, it is best *not* to use a consultant under the following circumstances:

1. The proposal is vague and omits specifics about objectives, steps in reaching the objectives, extent of the organization's involvement, specific role of the consultant, and fee.
2. The project is the first of its kind for the consultant.
3. There is conflict between the consultant and members of the organization's staff.

Sometimes the process of making contact and eventually ending up with a contract can take a long time. One client of mine, a large computer company, hired me to help them conduct a communication audit of their U.S. personnel. Several months went by between the first contact and the eventual contractual agreement, during which time the following events took place. The client telephoned to see if I was interested; asked me and others to submit brief resumes; asked a few of those who submitted resumes to submit outline proposals with a general estimate of the costs; asked those whose costs were judged to be reasonable to submit a more detailed proposal; asked the best proposal writers to be interviewed at their home-base locations; asked the best interviewees to come to the corporation's headquarters (at the consultant's expense) for a meeting with the communication audit committee; asked for a final bid from the "finalists"; and ultimately awarded me the contract. (After this long process I wasn't sure how "happy" I was to win the contract.)

As a check on whether the consultant has acted appropriately during the period of time when a relationship is being established, the following questions should be answered:

1. Did the consultant assess the client's needs adequately?
   a. Were appropriate initial contacts made with the client?
   b. Were the client's real concerns and desired results identified?
2. Was the project precisely defined?
   a. Was the size and scope of the project, along with the client's costs and benefits, correctly estimated?

3. Is the consultant providing the client with "real" assistance?
   a. Is the consultant familiar with his or her own strengths and deficiencies in assisting clients with similar projects?
   b. Is the consultant helping the client identify project objectives and measures of success?
4. Has the consultant obtained the actual support of the client?
   a. Does the client support the project's design?
   b. Does the client agree to the consultant's terms (costs, timetable, services), either orally or in writing?

Diagnosis and Prescription

In the diagnosis and prescription phase of the process model, the consultant joins with the client system (and their resources) to help the client system understand the nature of and possible solutions to the problem. In keeping with the process model, it should be remembered that this step occurs at all points in the model and can influence all other components in the model. For example, diagnosis begins during establishment of relationships between client and consultant and continues throughout until the relationship is terminated. Weisbord (1976) has proposed the following six categories for use in an organizational diagnosis. Each represents an area where the consultant will probably want diagnostic information from his or her client:

1. *Purposes*. What businesses are we in?
2. *Structure*. How do we divide up the work?
3. *Leadership*. Does someone keep the boxes in balance?
4. *Relationships*. How do we manage conflict among people? With technologies?
5. *Helpful Mechanisms*. Have we adequate coordinating technologies?
6. *Rewards*. Do all needed tasks have incentives?

One major tool open to the communication consultant for use during the diagnostic stages of the model is the communication audit referred to in chapter 10. Primary data-gathering methods and instruments used in this audit are observation (of meetings, work situations, and conferences); interviews (of employees and managers); and questionnaires (surveys, attitudinal measures, and knowledge tests). The general output of a communication audit is a report highlighting the strengths and weaknesses of the communication system, together with a set of recommendations prescribing new behaviors.

Unfortunately, many clients believe that the prime responsibility for conducting this audit belongs to the consultant ("who is getting paid to do this!"). This kind of thinking is consistent with the purchase and the doctor-patient models for consulting. Argyris (1970) commented on this approach:

> One of the most frequent manipulations attempted by clients is to demand that the interventionist shortcut the three primary tasks and get on with change. Industrial organizations seeking help to overcome a crisis see little need for careful diagnosis. Governmental representatives giving money to help correct inner-city problems focus on change, not on diagnosis.

Sometimes consultants may be intimidated by clients who demand results, and they may promise specific outcomes for their consultancy. Argyris (1961) stated:

> The interventionist can promise to do his best to develop a valid diagnosis of the organization. However, he cannot promise any solutions ahead of time. Most clients understand this position. Many clients will question the competence and ethical posture of a group that promises ahead of time its certain help in terms of recommendations for action and of possible benefits. Many administrators have been hurt by interventionists who have made promises they could not fulfill.

This problem can be avoided (or minimized) if careful statements of commitments and expectations are made during initial meetings between clients and consultants. Strict adherence to the process model, which calls for *joint* diagnosis and prescription, also avoids the problem.

Use of the process model during diagnosis and prescription is shown in table 9.1, which is a communication audit design provided by Organizational Associates, a consulting firm composed of communication experts from western United States. Note that this design calls for constant interaction between consultant and client, and notice the implications for voluntary behavior change by the client system.

The following questions may help the consultant determine the extent to which he or she has acted appropriately during the diagnostic phase of the process:

1. Has the consultant appraised the overall situation?
2. Has the consultant identified appropriate sources for data or information?
3. Has the consultant designed an appropriate method for data gathering?
4. Was the data collected and analyzed in accordance with accepted research standards?
5. Was the data fed back to the organization in a manner that they could use so they could "own" it?
6. Did the consultant protect all of his or her information sources?

Intervention Activities

In this discussion of the process model, we are concerned with the actual implementation of behavior change within an organization. We will identify, describe, and exemplify types of client-consultant intervention activities that lead to behavior change. In later sections of the chapter, both practical and ethical considerations during intervention are considered. Intervention is discussed in detail in chapter 11.

Turner (1982) has suggested a hierarchy of eight fundamental objectives for most consultancies:

1. Providing information to a client
2. Solving a client's problems
3. Making a diagnosis, which may necessitate redefinition of the problem
4. Making recommendations based on the diagnosis
5. Assisting with implementation of recommended solutions
6. Building a consensus and commitment around corrective action
7. Facilitating client learning, that is, teaching clients how to resolve similar problems in the future
8. Permanently improving organizational effectiveness

Table 9.1   Sample Design of Communication Audit Following Process Consulting Model

Item I. The Organization-Comunication Audit: A Point of View

Outside consultants who study management operations and communication practices in organizations usually obtain data, look for problems, suggest corrective procedures to top leaders, and leave. With reference to an organization-communication audit, Organizational Associates prefers to function differently.

In the first place, we make the assumption that outside consultants can never comprehend the "real" management operations and communication practices in an organization on a short-term, temporary basis. An alternative is to hire the outside consultant as a full-time employee within the organization for a minimum of one year; the consequence, of course, is that the consultant is no longer an "outsider." We assume that employees *know* the organization better than an outside consultant can in a month's or even three months' period of time. The major implication is that employees must be taught by the outside consultants to analyze their own problems.

In the second place, we make the assumption that no outside consultant can make an enduring change in the behavior of any individual in an organization. Behavior change in adults is a complex, slow process. Moreover, changes in behavior are a private, internal affair; that is, no one can force another person to change his behavior. Ultimately, the individual must persuade himself to change. Other people or things can be instrumental in the self-persuasion process. The major implication is that, should problems be detected by outside consultants, they cannot change the behavior of individuals in the organization. At best, outside consultants can *facilitate experiences* which allow individuals to change their own behavior.

The above implications provide a rationale for an organization-communication audit as outlined below.

Item II.   Projected Outcomes of the Organization-Communication Audit

In a healthy, productive organization, members and nonmembers should be able to influence the operation of the organization. Appropriate individuals should (1) know the organization's objectives, (2) have an opportunity to evaluate and change the organization's objectives, (3) understand what takes place in the organization, and (4) help analyze problems in the organization and participate in making decisions about corrective actions. In short, a healthy, productive organization is a place where meaningful work is accomplished when people in the organization fuse their personally meaningful objectives with the objectives of the organization. The above criteria for a healthy, productive organization are seldom met without effective management-employee and organization-client communication systems.

The proposed audit could identify major problems that hinder reaching the criteria essential for a healthy, productive organization. Consultants could facilitate systematically a process whereby members of the organization learn the full dimensions of identified problems and learn to correct these and future problems. During this process, the consultant would gradually exit from the organization. Thus, the goal of generating an on-going system whereby individuals in the organization eventually become their own organization-communication consultants would be attained.

Source: Organizational Associates, a communication consulting group. Used with permission of Organizational Associates.

According to Turner, the first few objectives are those that are most understood and requested by clients. Unfortunately, many consultants desire to achieve the higher objectives even though their consultancy may not lead to these achievements.

I agree with the overall philosophy of behavior change discussed in the sample audit design prepared by Organizational Associates (table 9.1). To repeat: because of the personal nature of behavior change, the primary role of the consultant should be to facilitate the individual's recognition of problems and to create an atmosphere in which behavior change can take place (if the individual desires). Argyris (1971) defined the intervention function of the consultant as entering "an ongoing system of relationship, to come between or among persons, groups, or objects for the purpose of helping them." According to Argyris, in order

Item III. Specific Procedures and Techniques to Be Used in Organization-Communication Audit

1. *Feasibility study:* On-site feasibility study by staff consultants.

2. *Introductory meeting:* Initial meeting with unit (all personnel) to preview philosophy, assumptions, expectations, and procedures associated with organization-communication audit project.

3. *Administer profile instruments:* Administer to all personnel R. Likert's *Organizational Profile,* semantic differential, and attitude scales, generating data on key organizational variables and communication systems.

4. *Follow-up of profile instruments:* In-depth, follow-up exploration of dimensions of profile within the organization, using structured and semistructured interviews, obtrusive and unobtrusive observations, communication logs, and checklists.

5. *Complementary units—data collection:* Secure data from complementary units, the public-community, and related groups concerning perceptions of the organizational effectiveness and communication practices of the organization being studied. This will be achieved through structured interviews, the semantic differential, and other measuring techniques. Random samples will be used where appropriate and possible.

6. *Analysis and meshing of data:* Determine how in-depth data (point 4) and complementary units (point 5) data compare with profile results (point 3).

7. *Data analysis meeting:* Meeting to share data with unit (all personnel) and invited guests; examine, delete, elaborate, and identify problem areas; item-by-item analysis of all data.

8. *Interim report:* Staff consultants complete interim project report and distribute to all unit personnel and selected individuals, *if desired.*

9. *Task groups formed:* Form task groups comprised of all unit personnel and invited participants, *if desired.*

10. *Task groups evaluate:* Task groups meet and review data in terms of personal meaning for them; enumerate problems and alternative means for corrective action. (Staff consultants available on site.) Task groups prepare reports.

11. *General meeting of task groups:* Meeting to share task group reports: elected personnel collate reports following oral summaries into single document.

12. *Final report:* Staff consultants prepare final report evaluating organization-communication audit and task group activities and supplying recommendations.

13. *Final report meeting:* Meeting of unit (all personnel) and invited guests where unit administrator responds to task groups' and consultants' reports and discusses the management of alternatives or recommendations.

14. *Turnover to organization:* Staff consultants meet with administrative staff to review procedures for members of the organization to assume full responsibility for continuing organization-communication audit and long-range basis.

for intervention activity to be successful, the consultant should possess the qualities of confidence, perception, understanding, sympathy, and acceptance; should trust his or her own experience; and should be able to grow. Specific behaviors necessary to achieve these qualities are owning up to, being open toward, and experimenting with ideas and feelings; helping others to own up to, be open, and experiment with ideas and feelings; contributing to the norms of individuality, concern, and trust; and communicating in observed, directly verifiable categories, with minimal attribution, evaluation, and internal contradiction.

The more common types of intervention activities used by communication consultants who follow the process model are procedural input, theoretical input, nondirective counseling, direct feedback, and process sessions.

Procedural Input

Procedural input comes closest to following the standard purchase and doctor-patient models, because it calls for direct information from the consultant. However, if the consultant avoids solving the organization's problems and limits intervention to *assisting* the organization in solving its own problems, the assumptions of the process model will not be violated. For example, if a client wants to learn how to design and administer a communication audit, it would be acceptable for the consultant to tell the client how to draw samples, design questionnaires and interview schedules, act as a process observer at meetings, analyze the content of written materials, and so forth. The consultant must, however, avoid actually performing these tasks for the client.

Theoretical Input

Clients may be in need of relevant information in order to solve their problems. In such cases, as an expert in the process of communication (more than clients), the consultant may provide this information. After the data have been disseminated, the client should react to and discuss the theoretical input and how it relates to his specific organization. The form of the theory input varies and can include brief lectures, brief oral comments by the consultant, written comments by the consultant, and reprints of articles or books. For example, an organization may identify a problem dealing with communication networks and direction of flow of communication (see chapter 4). However, the members of the client group may have difficulty conceptualizing network theory adequately to solve their problem. The consultant may provide the client group with literature on the subject that can expedite the helping process.

Nondirective Counseling

This activity may be appropriate to use with clients who have difficulty perceiving their actual communication behavior as others see it. Consultants must be careful to avoid directly telling clients their opinion of the clients' behavior. A better approach is to ask clients how they see themselves. Schein has suggested such questions as, "What does that comment mean to you in terms of how you see yourself?" "Can you think of anything you do which might give people that impression?" "What do you think the person who made the comment was trying to get across to you?" "What might you do differently to create a different reaction?" "Do you see anything in your own behavior which you could change?" "Do you really want to change your behavior?"

Direct Feedback

If a client group is sufficiently secure in its role and position, one intervention activity that can provide much pertinent information is a direct feedback session. In such a session, consultants summarize their perception of how individuals see the group (based on the consultants' own interviewing data). The group is then invited to react to the summary. By having a consultant act as an intermediary, a group can avoid situations that might directly threaten individuals and result in dishonest or minimal feedback. The feedback may be limited to individuals or include the group as a whole. It should be noted, however, that if a group is defensive and not ready to deal with feedback, even when processed by the consultant, the activity will prove fruitless. A group must be ready to examine the feedback, seek out possible behavioral indicators for the feedback, and make decisions about doing something about the feedback.

Process Sessions

As a group becomes more adept at solving its own communication problems, it may want to schedule regular sessions at the end of each meeting or conference to evaluate the communication process that just took place. A short period of time (fifteen to thirty minutes) after each meeting can be allotted for this purpose. Then, as the client representatives continue to grow in analytical ability, they may occasionally (one or two times a year) wish to devote entire sessions (half a day or a weekend) to analyzing the interpersonal communication behavior of the members of the group, relating it to the organizational setting. Such meetings should be scheduled away from the organization (at a motel, lodge, or retreat) in order to encourage informality. They can be a good opportunity for the consultant to review the group's progress in problem solving.

The following questions may help the consultant check his or her skills during the intervention activities used in the organization:

1. Were objectives established that were appropriate to the systems, resources, relationships, policies, etc. of the organization?
2. Were alternative methods and/or approaches to achieving the objectives identified, and was/were the most appropriate alternative(s) selected for the particular organization.
3. Were resources needed and available to the consultant, in order to accomplish the objectives for change, such that shortfalls could be avoided?
4. Did the consultant establish a timetable for change that showed the total time required and the priorities of various steps in the change process?
5. Has the consultant correctly identified both the finances needed and their source, along with the benefits to the client?
6. Has the consultant established techniques to measure the program's quality and timing?

Practical Problems of Intervention

In all of the foregoing intervention activities, individual and organizational factors may inhibit consultants in reaching the primary goal of helping an organization solve its communication problems. We will mention a few such factors and provide examples.

Management's Demand for Action

We mentioned previously the possibility of a client system wanting "immediate action" or "a solution to its problem" or "help pretty quick." In such cases, the consultant may feel intimidated and thus may succumb to management's values by providing direct input into the problem area. This is a violation of the process model and soon results in some members of the organization perceiving the consultant as "trying to play both ends against the middle."

Lack of Organizational Cooperation

Once consultants begin to work, they may find certain members of the organization unwilling to cooperate with them. For example, some employees may not answer questionnaires, may avoid interviews, may discredit a consultant to other members of the organization, or may not tell the truth when answering questions. If consultants are too overt in trying to win the trust of a certain subgroup, they may be perceived as a "friend of management" or "an ally of labor." They must be careful to straddle both camps in such a way that they alienate neither management nor labor.

Violation of Process Model by Consultant

There is always the danger that consultants (perceiving themselves as expert in communication) may become too directive in giving suggestions, advice, feedback, and information. They may forget that they are filtering all of their suggestions through their own frame of reference, which may limit their objectivity. Consultants may also find that some members of the organization either challenge or do not accept their advice, which puts them in the position of having to defend their input rather than facilitate the growth of the client.

Ethical Considerations of Consulting

Redding, in a semihumorous explanation of undesirable consultant behavior, identified three broad categories of incompetence: the "Bungler," who is honest but stupid; the "Quack," who is incompetent and careless; and the "Felon," who is highly expert in both incompetence and fraud. It would appear that the matter of ethics during communication consulting should be addressed. Unfortunately, some "experts" frequently dispense solutions despite their ignorance of the problems. At a recent meeting of a professional society, I heard a speaker endorse a particular communication tool as the best way to train managers in human relations. I asked him, "How do you know your approach is what your client needs?" He replied, "Because I'm the expert in the field." I pursued, "How do you know that it works?" He indignantly responded, "That's not my problem. I'm just the trainer!" At the same meeting, a woman introduced herself to me as a communication consultant. When I pressed her for her credentials, she finally admitted having a bachelor's degree in English literature and a master's degree in political science, but stated, "I read a lot to keep up with the field."

Argyris (1971) wrote of the ethical considerations that can impede a consultant's work with an organization:

> The more an interventionist realizes that he is violating his own ethics, the more he realizes that he is lowering his own standards, the more he senses that he is responding to the anxieties of the client rather than confronting him with these anxieties, the more he may feel conflicted. He may select to reduce the conflict by changing his objectives. He may now conceive of successful intervening as remaining within the existing values of the clients, as becoming the eyes and ears or right arm of management, as conceptualizing the problems in ways that satisfy those in the client system who pay for the services, and as minimally confronting the client with values and ideas which, although valid, may be upsetting. This is the stereotype that many behavioral scientists have of the role of the typical consultant. . . . Unfortunately, there is too much evidence which suggests that many consultants do conceive of consulting in this manner. As a managing partner of one of the largest consulting firms in the country told the writer, "That concept of consulting is the best formula for success."

What is ethics and what ethical considerations are important for the communication consultant? Ethics pertains to the "rightness" or "wrongness" of selected behavior according to certain standards of behavior. A consultant faced with the question Should I or shouldn't I. . . ? is probably confronting an ethical consideration. Here is how Hays defined ethics for the communication consultant:

> . . . those principles and standards which guide the choices of alternative behaviors in the conduct of consulting with clients regarding the process of communication in an organization. Ethics here deals with the conduct that is approved or disapproved. It covers the range of any behavior which can be judged worthy or unworthy. What in the long range is judged good for the client, good for the consultant, and good for the profession will be the criteria for the code of ethics developed by this assemblage.

Benne (1959) identified three ethical problems of consulting: problems arising within the consulting relationship; intrusion from other professional associations; and intrusion from civic and personal moralities of the consultant. For the communication consultant, these can translate into personal ethics, organizational ethics, and professional ethics.

Personal Ethics

Individual consultants may have a personal code of ethics governing how they behave within an organization. Both religious and civic convictions contribute to this behavior. For example, a consultant who identifies with a radical cause may find it difficult to consult adequately and efficiently with an organization actively involved in fighting that cause. This raises a major ethical question: Should consultants be permitted to determine which clients they accept and which they do not? Argyris (1970) commented on this issue:

> Medical doctors and lawyers discovered many years ago that one way to keep their respective professions alive and viable in a society was to offer their aid to anyone who needed it. To be sure, there are medical doctors and lawyers who refuse to take lower-class clients, but these refusals are subject to investigation by the local medical or legal professional societies. Such denial of help is not condoned by fellow professionals.

Schein took issue with Argyris, suggesting that the consultant decide for her- or himself whether to see all clients:

> Only if the consultant can personally accept the norms, goals, and criteria of the organization can he justify helping the organization to achieve them. If the consultant feels that the organization's goals are unethical, immoral, or personally unacceptable for some other reason, he can choose to attempt to change them or terminate the relationship, but this choice should be made.

I support Argyris on this issue and recommend that consultants, *since they are professionals,* not refuse assistance to any client for financial, political, or personal reasons. The only justification for refusing to help a client should be the consultant's lack of time—in which case a referral should be made. Of course, once a relationship has begun, if both parties do not conform to the behaviors stated during the contract, then either party should feel free to terminate the relationship.

Organizational Ethics

Here we refer to the standards of behavior to which the consultant should conform while engaged in intervention activity within an organization. Once their work is underway, consultants may decide that the purchase or doctor-patient model makes clients dependent upon them and, further, that this dependency is healthy because it increases both the time commitment and the fee. Consultants may reveal information obtained from employees to high-level management. While they may feel that management needs the information, the disclosure nevertheless violates the confidence of employees who are also part of the client system. Consultants may simply decide that their findings are publishable and therefore submit the data to a journal *prior to* securing permission from the client. All three types of consultant behavior during intervention raise ethical questions. While employed as a consultant for a large bank, I was confronted with an ethical dilemma of the second type described above. After months of data collection, I was confronted by the bank's CEO who posed the question, "What should I do? Should I fire Pete, based on the data he gave you?" Of course, if I were to reveal the information Pete gave me regarding his views of the organization it would be a violation of his confidence and a breach of organizational ethics. In situations like these, it is best to explain to your client the ethics that guide your intervention and inform your client that choices like that are up to him or her and should be based on the information the intervention reveals.

Professional Ethics

Here the behavior standards of the consultant are set forth by the professional association. As pointed out by Benne (1959), this is difficult to monitor, since communication consultant training overlaps several disciplines (psychology, sociology, anthropology, and business administration and management). The two major professional communication associations (International Communication Association (ICA) and the Speech Communication Association) do not (as of this writing) have a code of ethics governing communication consultants. Hays has recommended that such a code conform to the behavioral objectives approach discussed in chapter 11. Hays's classification system of ethical communication behavior, which can be used in drawing up a code of ethics, is given in table 9.2. Note the kinds of behaviors in which ethics is a consideration.

Until a code of ethics is prepared and arbitration powers are given to a major professional association, the behavior of communication consultants is governed only by the culture of the organization in which they work and their own personal ethical standards.

Recognizing the absence of a code of ethics in the field of communication, Redding (1984) has offered us five guidelines to which he believes all training should adhere:

1. *Respect for the integrity of the individual (trainee).* Trainees are treated with dignity (e.g., rote learning of tasks and prescriptive drills are de-emphasized in lieu of dialogue that stresses the contributions of the trainee.
2. *Providing opportunity for self-actualization.* Training activities help trainees reach their true potential.
3. *Encouraging the exercise of critical faculties.* Trainers encourage trainees to keep an open mind toward the organization's goals by allowing ample opportunity for dialogue and expression by trainees.

Table 9.2 **Hays's Suggested Ethical Classification System for Communication Consultants**

I. Classifications of Skills

A. The communication consultant must pass written examinations dealing with various facets of communication in the organizational setting developed by the professional organization.
B. The communication consultant must file a report with an ethical standards committee for each consultancy.
C. The communication consultant must make available to the client a feedback device whereby data about client reaction is reported to the professional organization.

II. Classification of Behaviors Related to Fees

A. Fees must be negotiated and decided upon in advance of the consultancy.
B. Communication consultants will not accept any fees for any referrals.
C. No fees will be accepted from suppliers.
D. Fees will not be tied to any cost reduction.

III. Classification of Information Collection

A. The consultant will be able to list the objectives that management has for employing a communication consultant.
B. The consultant will have measures of reliability and validity for all measurement instruments.
C. Communication consultants must attend one official training session every two years to update their knowledge of existing information and attitude measurement instrument.
D. No data will be published without the permission of the client.

IV. Classification of Analysis or Prediction

A. All predictive and analytic statements must be in writing, and a written justification must be given—except in those cases where the client expressly requests the consultant to give only oral reports.
B. Communication consultants must label all analytic or predictive statements as based on quantitative probability theory, expert consensus, or personal opinion.
C. Communication consultants must update predictive skills and knowledge of techniques by taking an official short course once every two years.

V. Classification of Training Activities

A. Training programs should be developed so that the objectives match the needs of the problem analysis results.
B. Training programs should utilize criterion-referenced behavioral objectives.

VI. Classification of Personal Behavior of Consultants

A. Consultants will not seek employment from a client.
B. Consultants will observe all local, state, and federal laws while in the process of consulting.
C. Consultants serving competing firms at the same time will do so only with the knowledge and consent of both.
D. Consultants will read widely in the field in order to pass a yearly refresher test.

Source: Adapted from Ellis Hays, "A Behavioral Objectives Approach to the Development of a Code of Ethics for Communication Consultants." Paper presented at a meeting of the International Communication Association, April 1972.

4. *Devoting explicit attention to ethical problems and issues.* Trainers include a discussion of ethics (applied to both the organization and the training experience) by de-emphasizing ends-over-means objectives.
5. *Concern for long-term development of trainees.* Trainers keep trainees' career paths and potential in sight by linking the training to their future career goals instead of just their immediate jobs.

Termination of Consultant-Client Relationship

Throughout this chapter, we have stressed that the main role of the communication consultant following the process model is to help develop diagnostic skills within the client system. Should the consultant (and the client) feel that these skills have been developed or improved sufficiently, this may be the opportune time to begin termination of the consultant-client relationship. In keeping with the process model, termination should be a joint decision made after careful deliberation by both parties. Furthermore, the decision to begin termination of the relationship does not necessarily mean that the consultant never returns to the organization. One useful method is to phase out the relationship over a period of time. For example, the consultant reduces involvement with the organization from two days a week to one or even a half-day a week for a month or so, and then to a half-day once a month, and so forth, until the relationship is finally terminated. In this manner, both the client and consultant can gauge whether the client system has the autonomy necessary to diagnose its own communication problems. After termination has begun, the consultant's time can be increased if necessary without beginning again the entire process of establishing the relationship. Once termination is completed, the consultant may desire periodically (twice a year) to contact the organization (without trying to *sell* his or her services) to check its progress.

You are reminded, of course, that both consultant and client should have the right to terminate a relationship at any time the conditions of the original contract are violated. If termination becomes necessary, the consultant should schedule a meeting with top management to discuss the reasons for termination. If management initiates the termination, it too should bring the reasons to the attention of the consultant. When either consultant or client consider termination to be premature, reasons for this judgment should be presented in an atmosphere of free discussion.

Consultants who are dependent upon a relationship for its monetary worth may find it difficult to objectively argue for continuation of a relationship clients desire to terminate. However, if a relationship is based upon mutual trust, then termination should not present many problems for either party.

SUMMARY

Organization development (OD) as a framework within which the communication consultant usually operates was discussed. Three models of communication consulting (purchase, doctor-patient, and process) were defined, exemplified, and diagrammed. Factors affecting the establishment of the consultant-client relationship were described: making contact; initial meetings; and designing a contract. Recommended fee schedules were presented, along with the recommendation that monetary considerations not limit the selection of a client system. Diagnostic and prescriptive consultant functions were defined and illustrated. A sample communication audit following the process model was presented. Common types of intervention activities used by the communication consultant (procedural input, theoretical input, nondirective counseling, direct feedback, and process sessions) were listed, described, and illustrated. Management's demand for action, the organization's lack of cooperation, and the consultant's violation of the process model were described as possible inhibitors of the consultant's primary task, which is to help the organization diagnose its own communication problems. Personal, organizational, and professional ethics considerations were listed and illustrated as they pertain to the communication consultant. A sample code of ethics relating to skills, fees, information collecting, analysis and predicting, training, and personal behavior was presented. Factors affecting termination of the consultant-client relationship were described, with emphasis on the mutual trust upon which the relationship should be built.

EXERCISES

1. Interview the following people in your community:
   a. a communication consultant who is also a university or college professor;
   b. a professional communication (or management) consultant not affiliated with a university or college;
   c. a manager of an organization who recently employed a communication (or management) consultant.
2. Ask them to describe their most recent consultant-client relationship. Ascertain which consultant model (purchase, doctor-patient, process) was followed in the relationship.
3. You have been hired by a local government agency (police, social services, educational), and your primary task is to institute a new communication training program. Outline a consulting plan that follows each of the three models (purchase, doctor-patient, process). Give the advantages and disadvantages of each model. How will you establish your relationship? Describe the contract you design. What fee will you charge?
4. Outline a diagnostic plan of action for the foregoing consulting job. Explain how you plan to involve the client in the plan. Will you produce a written report with recommendations?
5. You have been hired to evaluate the weekly staff meetings of a large corporation. After observing three months of meetings (twelve meetings), you are ready to begin intervention. Describe the types of activities you plan to follow. What will you do *first?*
6. On the job (exercise 4) you encounter a defensive client system whose members deny all of your observations. Furthermore, some of the members of management now question your presence and worth to the organization. What is the *first* thing you should do?
7. As an external consultant, what are some of the problems you might encounter in interpreting and feeding back data to your client?
8. From the consultant's point of view, what are some of the "dangers" associated with the process model of consultation?

9. Develop a code of ethics for communication consulting. Does it differ from the one presented in this chapter?
10. List the steps you should follow when you are ready to terminate your relationship with two organizations who hired you (see exercises 2 and 4).
11. You are going to embark upon a structured organizational development program within your organization. What are some of the questions and issues you might address by doing so?
12. So, you've quit your job, mortgaged the house, and sold the car in order to move to a new city to embark on a career as an organizational consultant. You have no clients and no contacts. How might you go about getting yourself known and establishing some business contacts?
13. When should a company hire or not hire a consultant? If a consultant is hired, when would it be best to hire an external consultant? When would it be best to use someone already in the organization?

BIBLIOGRAPHY AND REFERENCES

Argyris, Chris. "Explorations in Consulting-Client Relationships." *Human Organization* 20 (Fall 1961):121–33.
————. *Intervention Theory and Method: A Behavioral Science View.* Reading, Mass.: Addison-Wesley, 1970.
Benne, Kenneth. "Some Ethical Problems in Group and Organizational Consultation." *Journal of Social Issues* 25 (1959):60–67.
————. "Theory and Method in Applying Behavioral Science to Planned Organizational Change." *Journal of Applied Behavioral Science* 1 (1965):337–59.
————. "Changing Organizations." In *The Planning of Change.* 2d ed. Edited by Warren Bennis, Kenneth Benne, and Robert Chin. New York: Holt, Rinehart & Winston, 1969.
Bennis, Warren. *Organization Development: Its Nature, Origins, and Prospects.* Reading, Mass.: Addison-Wesley, 1969.
Bennis, Warren, Kenneth Benne, and Robert Chin, eds. *The Planning of Change.* 2d ed. New York: Holt, Rinehart & Winston, 1969.
Burke, W. Warner, and Warren H. Schmidt. "Primary Target for Change: The Manager or the Organization?" In *Organizational Frontiers and Human Values.* Edited by Warren Schmidt. Belmont, Calif.: Wadsworth Publishing Co., 1970.
Caplan, Gerlad. "Types of Mental Health Consultation." In *The Planning of Change,* 2d ed. Edited by Warren Bennis, Kenneth Benne, and Robert Chin. New York: Holt, Rinehart & Winston, 1969.
Dover, C. J. "Some Problems in Interpreting Data Collected by External Consultants/Researchers." Paper delivered to the International Communication Association convention, Minneapolis, May 1981.
Downs, C., and M. Larimer. "The Status of Organizational Communication in Speech Departments." Unpublished manuscript, 1973.

Ferguson, Charles. "Concerning the Nature of Human Systems and the Consultant's Role." In *The Planning of Change*. 2d ed. Edited by Warren Bennis, Kenneth Benne, and Robert Chin. New York: Holt, Rinehart & Winston, 1969.

French, W., and C. Bell. *"Organization Development: Behavioral Science Interventions for Organization Improvement*. 2d ed. Englewood Cliffs, N.J.: Prentice-Hall, 1978.

Hays, Ellis. "A Behavioral Objectives Approach to the Development of a Code of Ethics for Communication Consultants." Paper presented at a meeting of the International Communication Association, April 1972.

Lippitt, Gordon. *Organization Renewal: A Holistic Approach to Organization Development*. 2d ed. Englewood Cliffs, N.J.: Prentice-Hall, 1982.

McDermott, Lynda. "The Many Faces of the OD Professional." *Training and Development Journal* (February 1984):15–24.

Redding, W. Charles. "The Ethical Considerations of Consultants and Graduate Students in Organizational Research." Paper presented at a meeting of the International Communication Association, April 1972.

———. "Professionalism in Training—Guidelines for a Code of Ethics." Paper presented at the Speech Communication Association meeting, Chicago, 1984.

Schein, Edgar. *Process Consultation: Its Role in Organization Development*. Reading, Mass.: Addison-Wesley, 1969.

Tilles, S. "Understanding the Consultant's Role." *Harvard Business Review* 39 (1961):87–99.

Turner, Arthur. "Consulting is More Than Giving Advice." *Harvard Business Review* (September–October 1982):120–129.

Weisbord, Marvin. "The Organization Development Contract." *Organization Development Practitioner* 5 (1973):1–4.

———. "Organizational Diagnosis: Six Places to Look for Trouble with or without A Theory." *Group and Organization Studies* 1 (1976) 430–47.

Wright, David, and Suzanne Sherman. "A Survey of Organizational Communication at the Graduate Level in Speech Communication Programs: Initial Report." Unpublished report, 1970.

10
IMPLEMENTING ORGANIZATIONAL COMMUNICATION DIAGNOSIS: THE COMMUNICATION AUDIT

When an accountant audits the books of a large organization, he or she determines its financial health by computing the ratio of cash resources and reserves to cash flow. Generally, the higher this ratio, the greater are the chances for financial health of the organization. Such periodic audits help organizations select their investments, determine future markets for their goods or services, and plan their growth. In short, forecasts developed from these audits help organizations prevent crises, and thereby also ensure their survival.

When a doctor gives a patient a physical examination, the physician assesses the patient's health by comparing his or her vital signs with the norms for healthy people of the same age and sex. Repeating this examination regularly gives doctor and patient advance notice of developing ailments and may help forestall more serious conditions and lengthen the patient's life span.

Just as checkups by accountants and physicians provide clients with information necessary to maintain health, so too does a communication audit provide an organization with

Just as an accountant audits the books of a large organization to determine its financial health, so does a communication consultant audit an organization's communicative climate to assess its health.

advance information which may prevent a major breakdown. Few people would deny the importance of effective communication in maintaining a healthy organization, but until recently organizations have expended surprisingly little effort in the preventive maintenance that a regular communication audit would offer.

In this chapter, our objectives are the following:

1. To list the benefits for organizations and researchers of a communication audit.
2. To present alternative plans for conducting a communication audit.
3. To describe and illustrate the primary data-gathering and analysis tools used in a communication audit.
4. To list and illustrate practical problems associated with data gathering in a communication audit.
5. To describe and illustrate the seven steps involved in writing a communication audit report.

Benefits of a Communication Audit

Organizations that conduct a communication audit will derive valid information about their communication systems. With this information, they will become aware of current behaviors and practices and also the likelihood of future successes and failures. They can take the initiative in planning for their future rather than defensively react to communication crises. Valid information gives an organization the freedom to choose from alternatives which path it wants to follow as it grows and develops. By replacing guesswork with accurate data, an organization can recognize potential problems. Audit data can be used in the following ways:

1. To compare the premeasurement and postmeasurement status of their communication system and determine the impact of new communication programs.
2. To assess the impact of ongoing programs, such as those mandated in 1974 by the Employee Retirement Income Security Act (ERISA).
3. To compare presurvey and postsurvey data to determine the impact of organizational innovations (restructuring, addition of a computer, new organizational development programs).
4. To identify the current organizational structure as an aid to successful reorganization.
5. To identify key communication groupings prior to restructuring—especially important for large transnational corporations that make overseas assignments.
6. To identify major communication costs (telephone calls, meetings, postage, air travel) involved in expansion into other states or countries.
7. To develop new communication training programs geared to solve organizational problems identified by the audit.

Organizations with access to data from a communication audit will be able to answer many of the following questions:[1]

1. What environmental factors affect the organization's communication system?
2. What structural factors affect the organization's communication system?

---

1. Some of these questions were submitted by Don Faules, Evan Rudolph, Darrell Piersol, Wayne Pace, and Carl Larson during their participation in an International Communication Association Audit project (1972); others are from Thayer (1967) and Farace and MacDonald (1971); and some are mine.

3. What is the impact of stress and fear upon the effectiveness of communication activities in the organization?
4. What is the relationship between mechanization and communication activity?
5. How can computers be used better to simulate organizational communication problems and activities?
6. What nonverbal communication variables exist within the organization?
7. What is the effect of change on communicative interaction and behavior?
8. How can formal and informal communication patterns be identified and standardized?
9. What are the differences between intershift and intrashift communication patterns within the organization?
10. What is the effect of isolation on such variables as organizational interaction? morale? productivity?
11. What are the most effective communication media under specific conditions?
12. What are the communication preferences of individuals concerning superiors? subordinates? peers?
13. What is the relationship between the levels of the organization and the amount of information received at these levels?
14. What is the effect of timing (opportune; inopportune) of communication of important events on morale and productivity?
15. What is the effect of intergroup relationships on the decision-making process in the organization?
16. How much change in the organization is realistic? attainable? practical?
17. What is the effect of changing values and value systems upon the communication system of the organization?
18. What are the role and function of power groups in the organization?
19. What standards or norms should be developed to assess the effectiveness of the organizational communication system?
20. What is the cost (time; money) expended to process efficiency of information sources?

Students and researchers interested in the study of organizational communication should also be able to answer other questions with data from a communication audit such as the following. These questions are grouped according to the study area by which they are typically classified in the literature: homophily studies, apprehension studies, credibility studies, contingency theory studies, network studies, and communication and organizational effectiveness studies.

Homophily Studies. Can communication needs be predicted by homophily? Specifically, do employees who are more homophilous with their immediate supervisors have lower communication needs than those who are less homophilous with their immediate supervisors? Can communication frequency and strength of interaction be predicted by homophily? Specifically, do employees who are more homophilous with their immediate supervisors talk more or less often with those supervisors than do employees who are less homophilous with their supervisors? Do the former have stronger or weaker links and more or less cohesive work groups than the latter? Do workers have better communication relationships with those communication sources most homophilous with them?

Apprehension Studies. Is communication isolation a function of communication apprehension? Specifically, do isolates score higher on measures of apprehension than centrals? than liaisons? than group members? than bridges? Do measures of apprehension predict frequency of interaction? importance of interaction? What role does seniority on the job play in communication apprehension? Are employees with more seniority more or less apprehensive? Do other demographics influence apprehension (age, sex, supervisory status, education, communication training)?

Credibility Studies. Does credibility of source affect communication needs of receivers? Do sources with high credibility have employees with low communication needs? Is there a relationship between source credibility and homophily? Specifically, are more homophilous sources perceived as being more credible than less homophilous sources?

Contingency Theory Studies. Do different types of organizations have different communication needs? Do organizational internal contingencies (age, sex, education, seniority, management level, amount of communication training) affect communication needs? Are cultural differences (national, regional, racial, etc.) associated with differences in communication needs? Does managerial leadership style affect communication needs? network roles? If so, what are the internal and external contingencies?

Network Studies. Does network role influence or determine communication satisfaction? communication need? worker performance? Specifically, do isolates have greater communication needs than centrals? than liaisons? than group members? than bridges? Do isolates perform better than centrals? than liaisons? than group members? than bridges? Do they have better relationships? higher morale? greater job satisfaction? Are communication isolates also physical isolates? Specifically, are isolates physically closer to centrals, to work group members, to bridges, or to liaisons? Are homophilous groups physically closer than heterophilous groups?

Communication and Organizational Effectiveness Studies. Does communication effectiveness influence organizational effectiveness? Specifically, do employees, groups, and organizations with lower communication needs have lower absenteeism? lower turnover? higher supervisory and subordinate ratings? produce products and/or services with fewer errors? have fewer grievances and complaints? experience higher job satisfaction than those of higher communication needs?

In short, the conduct of a communication audit has several concrete benefits both for the organization which invests its financial and human resources and for the student or researcher or auditor who invests time in the collection and analysis of the audit data. The following are three plans for conducting a communication audit.

Greenbaum Conceptual Structure

Greenbaum has proposed an appraisal or auditing procedure which relates to both the overall communication system and to specific communication activities that constitute the parts of the system. Table 10.1 summarizes Greenbaum's conceptual structure.

Table 10.1   Greenbaum Conceptual Structure for the Appraisal of Organizational Communication Systems

Section A. Structure Relating to the Overall Communication System	Section B. Structure Relating to Specific Communication Activities
1. Objectives, plans, and policies	1. Nature and objectives
2. Implementation methods and responsibilities	2. Performance criteria and procedural instructions
3. Measurement methods	3. Standards of performance
4. Organizational situation factors	4. Measurement methods
5. Supportive communication programs	5. Activity situational factors
	6. Supportive communication programs

There is an advantage in considering the overall communication system first and studying specific communication activities later. Such an approach provides classified locations for workers who are interested in general communication and attitudinal temperatures of an organization and for those particularly interested in a special communication process within an organization. Further, the preliminary study of the surrounding organizational environment is a necessary prerequisite for a more complete understanding of specific communication activities. Also, such an approach permits questions from two different viewpoints: (1) How well is the entire communication system working? Does the communication system have the elements required to achieve objectives? (2) What are the efficiency and effectiveness of specific activities? Which activities require support? What is the nature of that requirement? We will discuss the macroapproach and microapproach and then present a work plan for implementing a communication audit.

Structure Relating to Overall Communication System

The macro aspect of communication system appraisals (see table 10.1, section A) requires that attention first be given to organizational objectives and plans in order to determine the explicit or implicit communication policies. Communication policies are important. They represent management guidelines for utilization of specific communication activities intended to move the organization toward its goals.

After objectives and communication policies have been determined, the problem is to determine whether the organization has provided the necessary implementing activities. This task can be approached by taking an inventory of communication activities and making the appropriate analysis. The analysis includes classification of such activities by levels (individual, small group, organizationwide) and by functions (informative, regulatory, persuasive, integrative). Chapters 1 and 4 give more information about both functions and levels of communication activities. The analysis of activities should continue with other tests to the point where a judgment is possible as to whether the communication activities within the organization are adequate, inadequate, or more than adequate to implement the communication policies. Such a judgment will not be necessary or even possible until the attitudes and feelings of the organization members are examined by means of surveys, statistical indicators, and regular operational feedback.

In the appraisal of the overall communication system, it is of great importance to examine the means for maintaining and developing the system. Does a specific person have centralized staff responsibility for the communication function and is there periodic accountability? Is the communication function treated in a formal manner by top management and does it have a place in the goals plan of the organization? If no formal controls are explicitly related to the communication function, how does the organization process problems relate to communication? What procedures are followed for the introduction of innovative communication methods? Where is the responsibility for the overall communication system?

These questions related to the responsibility for the overall communication system can be answered by an examination of the organization structure, background, and leadership. The data derived from this examination, together with general material on environmental influences related to leadership behavior, constitute a core of information that may be termed "organization situational factors." (Much of the information in chapter 3 on the human resources movement relates to an organization's situational factors.) These factors—together with the knowledge obtained as to plans, policies, implementation methods, responsibilities, and attitudes—provide the basis for consideration of change proposals and supportive communication programs for the overall communication system. Examples of such programs are presented in chapter 11 in the discussion of communication training programs.

Structure Relating to Specific Communication Activities

The micro aspect of communication system appraisals (see table 10.1, section B) concentrates on individual communication activities. After an explicit statement of the nature and objectives of the activity has been made, a particular communication activity should be analyzed as to pertinent performance criteria in order to develop practical procedural instructions for the conduct of that activity. The criteria to be considered include the elements of communication theory relating to content, media, channels, timing, interaction conditions, direction, participation, initiation, preparation, feedback, clarity, redundancy, and other subclassifications of communication behavior.

It is necessary to establish instructions for how to carry out an activity. It is also necessary to determine standards for satisfactory performance of the activity in order to later judge the quality of specific communication activity, both in its constituent parts and in its entirety. In some cases, performance standards may be explicit and mutually determined, as in the case of a formal work-planning program. In other cases, the standards may be mostly implicit.

The caliber of the *actual* performance of the communication activity is determined through one or more data-gathering techniques (questionnaire, interview, observation, etc.) discussed in the next section of this chapter.

When the data supplied through the measurement of actual performance are compared with established standards, it is possible to highlight specific deviations deserving further study. These exceptional items should be investigated in order to identify necessary changes in policies and/or activities, plus training and other supportive actions for the specific communication activity. Next, we consider the variables that are situational to individual activities: communication skills, perceptual and conceptual abilities, motivational influences, and formal structure and leadership policies within the organization.

Work Plan for a Communication Audit

Table 10.2 presents a generalized work plan for a communication audit. The work plan is an outgrowth of the previous discussion of both the macro and micro aspects of communication system appraisal. The audit work plan can be used throughout the entire organizational system or within a particular subsystem or unit. It is intended as a guide for the student, researcher, or communication manager in evaluating the communication system.

Table 10.2   Work Plan for a Communication System Appraisal

Section A. Overall Communication System
Stage I. Fact Finding

---

1. Determine organizational objectives, organizational policies, and communication policies.

2. Inventory the communication activities and classify in relation to specific communication policies.

3. Identify the nature of communication system controls and the organization function vested with communication as a key responsibility.

Stage II. Analysis

---

1. Study the communication activities in terms of levels, objectives, functions, channels, and other class types.

2. Utilize appropriate measurement techniques to judge the strengths and weaknesses of the overall communication system.

3. Note the strength and weaknesses of the overall system in relation to organization situational factors including structure, processes, and leadership.

Stage III. Evaluation

---

1. Summarize the data obtained and arrive at conclusions concerning the adequacy of existing activities to implement policies.

2. Recommend necessary changes and/or supportive communication programs and furnish details as to implementation.

Section B. Specific Communication Activities
Stage I. Fact Finding

---

1. Determine the nature and objectives of the activity.

2. Ascertain the procedural instructions for the activity with reference to applicable communication performance criteria.

3. Arrive at performance standards constituting satisfactory performance for each procedural instruction.

Stage II. Analysis

---

1. Employ appropriate measurement techniques to estimate actual performance and deviation from standards.

2. Study deviations representing important weaknesses in the communication activity and give attention to the activity situational factors influencing communication behavior.

Stage III. Evaluation

---

1. Summarize the data obtained and arrive at conclusions concerning the adequacy of the specific communication activity to meet the objectives set for that activity.

2. Recommend corrective measures furnishing details as to implementation and/or report on the presence of organization situational factors preventing accomplishment of objectives.

Work Plan for Appraisal of the Overall Communication System

Stage I of table 10.2, section A has the fact-finding purpose of determining organizational objectives, policies, and communication activities, as well as ascertaining the nature of communication system controls. An example of the linking of policies to activities is shown in table 10.3.

Experience indicates that it may be easier to inventory communication activities than to determine organizational objectives and policies, since the latter are frequently not explicitly recorded. Even where written organizational objectives and policies do exist, it is still necessary to test their validity by determining whether they represent the present attitudes of management.

Identification of communication system controls may result in a listing of responsibilities of operating line and staff members of the organizations. Where the communication function has been recognized, the staff responsibilities may be held by the personnel department or the public relations department. Where the communication function has not been recognized, the personnel area is the best place to start looking for managers with internal communication responsibilities. In all cases, it is important to carefully note the nature and extent of such responsibilities, as well as the specific goals and objectives of the managers holding communication responsibilities.

Stage II (analysis) of table 10.2 has the purpose of studying the inventoried communication activities in respect to functions served within the overall system and determining the strengths and weaknesses of the general system. An example of this classification appears in table 10.4.

Table 10.4 divides approximately thirty communication activities into twelve classifications formed by the matrix of four communication objectives and three levels of communication. This starts to give an understanding of the functions served by the existing methods of implementation utilized by an organization. For some organizations, there may be many blank spaces opposite the "informative" and "integrative" communication objectives. For organizations that employ communication activities in all categories, there may be a question of quality rather than variety. Obviously, other classifications and forms of communication activity analysis are possible and should be applied.

To judge the general effectiveness of the communication system, investigators usually have employed the questionnaire, the interview, observation, and other techniques directed to an overall consideration of the attitudes of employees toward communication practices and associated organizational variables. These and other techniques are discussed in the next section.

In all cases it is important to supplement the general organizational knowledge accumulated in the fact-finding phase by facts of organization history, structure, management processes, and leadership to gain the broadest understanding of what is called "organization situational factors." This is entirely consistent with the approach discussed by Likert (see chapter 3), which treats communication as an intervening variable caused by certain organizational factors and which influences still others.

Stage III (evaluation) of table 10.2 has the purpose of summarizing the findings and the analysis of the previous stages and coming to a conclusion about the adequacy of the existing activities in the implementation of policies. The findings may indicate a lack of

Table 10.3   Communication Activities Implementing Communication Policies

Company Policy	Activities
1. To provide effective internal communication channels, encouraging employees to express their views and recommendations (to encourage individual development and organizational growth and success).	Work group meetings Interdepartmental meetings Supervisor-subordinate scheduled meetings Exit interviews
2. To transmit to all employees present corporate policies, practices, and plans or any planned changes thereof, so there is every opportunity for employees to offer their suggestions and revise their practices to conform to such changes.	Companywide publications Bulletin boards Employee pamphlets Quarterly staff meetings Work group meetings
3. To discuss with each new employee, both prior to hiring and during the first three weeks of employment, the full range of employee policies and working conditions, so the new employee accepts the position with the full knowledge of company practices and reaches a productive level of performance in a minimum of time.	Hiring interview Company brochure Benefits brochure Orientation interview

Table 10.4   Classification of Communication Activities by Level and Objectives

Objectives	Level of Communication		
	Interpersonal	Small Group	Organization
To inform	Hiring interview Exit interview Orientation Oral and written reports	Work group meeting Executive meeting Supervisory training program	House publication Bulletin boards Employee pamphlets Grapevine
To regulate	Supervisor-subordinate scheduled meeting Annual review	Executive meeting Crisis meeting	Policy statements Company memos Union contract
To persuade	Problem solution Expression of viewpoint on policy	Work group meeting Executive committee	Employee pamphlets Supervisory staff meetings
To integrate	Annual review Informal lunch	Work group meetings Interdepartmental meetings Coffee break discussions Informal lunches	House publications Newsletter Social events Grapevine

Table 10.5 Performance Criteria, Procedural Instructions, and Performance Standards for the Internal Communication Activity of Employee Orientation

Area of Performance Criteria	Procedural Instruction	Performance Standard
Content Direction Timing	Provide for the general orientation of new employees—within the department and relative to the entire organization.	Within five working days of hiring
Feedback Content Timing	Encourage new employees to indicate problems promptly so difficulties may be overcome quickly.	Formal once-a-week brief interview for minimum of first three weeks
Initiation Content Controls Timing	Arrange for self or senior skilled personnel to train new employee in job details. Employ procedure chart as a guide and reference.	Orient in two weeks Train in sixty days
Initiation Participation Interaction conditions Timing	Introduce employee to individual members of group and do everything possible to ensure that new member is socially accepted by group. Utilize methods appropriate to position.	Immediately on date of start

certain activities appropriate to communication policies; or existing activities may not be sufficiently comprehensive; or certain desirable objectives may be overlooked and others overstressed; or the activities may be present but results are not being obtained.

Beyond the statement of findings, recommendations must be set forth. Such recommendations may be triggered by the discovery of certain weaknesses in the system, but they must be molded in light of organization objectives, policies, and situational factors.

Work Plan for Appraisal of a Specific Communication Activity

Stage I, section B of table 10.2 has the fact-finding purpose of determining the nature and objectives of the activity, relevant performance criteria, procedural instructions for the conduct of the activity, and performance standards. As stated in the discussion of conceptual structure, a particular activity should be analyzed in terms of the communication elements: content, media, timing, interaction conditions, direction, participation, initiation, preparation, feedback, redundancy, linking, and controls. Performance criteria will help determine procedural instructions, and performance standards applicable in the circumstances can be deduced. A limited example of this kind of factfinding for the internal communication activity of employee orientation is presented in table 10.5.

Note in table 10.5 that four procedural instructions were developed from a checklist of possible performance criteria (with the aid of an experienced member of the organization in this area of responsibility). Eight performance criteria were considered most important during the give-and-take consideration of the procedures presently employed by this organization. In this manner, it was possible to formulate a written procedure and performance standards for a communication activity that had been used previously without detailed instructions or standards. In some organizations with extensive systems support, facts concerning communication activities are more readily available. Explicit statements may be present in the procedure manual, but it is important to determine whether management's current thinking is still in accord with such statements; and it is essential to identify the performance standards relating to the communication activity.

Stage II (analysis) has the purpose of studying the particular communication activity in order to determine if performance is up to standard. This is done by means of appropriate data-gathering and data-analyzing techniques. Once there is an indication of current performance, the situations representing serious deviations from previously established standards need to be isolated and the situational factors that influence communication behavior in that particular activity need to be studied.

Stage III (evaluation) has the purpose of summarizing the findings and analysis relative to the specific communication activity and reaching a conclusion about the adequacy of the present performance to meet the objectives and the performance standards previously set for that activity. If the activity has a serious weakness and is to be retained, the evaluation might include a recommendation for supportive communication programs. However, all communication problems are not communication centered. The cause of the difficulty or weakness may arise from such factors as organizational policy, leadership, and structure. In such instances, the data collected in the appraisal of the overall communication system provides important information to apply in arriving at conclusions concerning a particular communication activity.

Measurement Tools Used in Communication Audits

In 1971 the International Communication Association (ICA), a nonprofit professional communication society, started its communication audit project in response to the lack of standardized procedures for assessing organizational communication systems.[2] The ICA audit developed a standardized system of five measurement instruments in order to establish a normed data bank to enable comparisons between communication systems of various organizations. It was hoped that through these comparative studies of different organization's communication systems an external validation of many organizational communication theories and propositions could be ascertained. In 1979, the ICA audit ceased to exist as an official ICA-sponsored activity and the five instruments and the procedures used in the audits became part of the public domain.

---

2. Information in this section is adapted from Goldhaber (1976; 1978); Goldhaber and Krivonos (1977); Goldhaber and Rogers (1979); and Goldhaber et al. (1984). In 1979 the ICA audit ceased to exist as an official ICA-sponsored activity. All instruments and procedures are in the public domain.

Table 10.6   Questionnaire Survey Topics

Topic	Number of Items
1. Amount of information received and needed from others on selected topics.	26
2. Amount of information sent and needed to be sent to others on selected topics.	14
3. Amount of follow-up or action taken and needed on information sent to others.	10
4. Amount of information received and needed from selected sources.	18
5. Timeliness of information received from key sources.	6
6. Amount of information received and needed from selected channels.	16
7. Quality of communication relationships.	19
8. Satisfaction with major organizational outcomes	13
9. Demographic information	12
Total	134

The five measurement tools from the ICA audit, which are commonly used today, can be used independently, or in any combination depending on the needs of the organization. These common tools for measuring an organization's communication system are a questionnaire survey, interviews, network analysis, communication experience analysis, and the communication diary.

Questionnaire Survey.   The survey consisted of 122 items, including 12 demographic questions plus up to 34 questions of any type determined by the organization. The reliability of the scales on the 134-item set range from a low of 0.73 to a high of 0.92. The validity of these scales was based upon their self-evident relationship to organizational communication, their ability to predict organizational outcomes, and their consistency with previously validated measures of organizational communication. Respondents could indicate their perception of the *current status* of their communication system as well as their needed or *ideal status*. This greatly helped the identification of communication uncertainty in the organization. Table 10.6 summarizes the topics and item distribution on the survey. Table 10.7 illustrates the survey format. Table 10.8 presents a sample from the computer output used to analyze the survey data.

Table 10.7 Sample Format of ICA Communication Audit Survey

Receiving Information from Others

Topic Area	This is the amount of information I receive now					This is the amount of information I need to receive				
	Very Little	Little	Some	Great	Very Great	Very Little	Little	Some	Great	Very Great
How well I am doing in my job	1. 1	2	3	4	5	2. 1	2	3	4	5
My job duties	3. 1	2	3	4	5	4. 1	2	3	4	5
Organizational policies	5. 1	2	3	4	5	6. 1	2	3	4	5
Pay and benefits	7. 1	2	3	4	5	8. 1	2	3	4	5
How technological changes affect my job	9. 1	2	3	4	5	10. 1	2	3	4	5
Mistakes and failures of my organization	11. 1	2	3	4	5	12. 1	2	3	4	5
How I am being judged	13. 1	2	3	4	5	14. 1	2	3	4	5
How my job-related problems are being handled	15. 1	2	3	4	5	16. 1	2	3	4	5
How organization decisions are made that affect my job	17. 1	2	3	4	5	18. 1	2	3	4	5
Promotion and advancement opportunities in my organization	19. 1	2	3	4	5	20. 1	2	3	4	5

Notice that 51 percent of the respondents perceived that they were getting a lot of information about their "job duties"; the mean score (on the five-point scale) was 3.37, as compared with the norm of 3.56. In contrast, 73 percent felt that they needed more information on their "job duties"; the mean score here was 3.94, close to the norm of 4.00. We would conclude, then, that the respondents are getting less information than they need on "job duties." The rest of the survey would be interpreted in this manner.

Interview. Randomly and/or purposively selected members of the organization were asked to participate in one-on-one interviews, the principal purpose of which was to corroborate and/or expand concerns reported in other audit tools. Two interview schedules were used: the first survey was structured to provide exploratory information using open-ended questions; a follow-up guide was specifically tailored to each organization to explain findings revealed through the use of other audit tools. Most interviews lasted one to one and one-half hours. All were conducted confidentially (sometimes tape recorders were used to facilitate data analysis). Table 10.9 presents the exploratory interview used in an audit.

Table 10.8   Sample Computer Output for Survey: Receiving Information from Others

Topics Rank-Ordered Positively with Respect to Current Quality

Rank	Percent	Sample Mean	Norm Mean	Persons	Question from ICA Communication Audit Survey
1	51.105	3.37	3.56	1,920	My job duties
2	49.133	3.30	3.55	1,814	Pay and benefits
3	44.669	3.23	3.50	1,655	How my job relates to the total operation of my organization
4	42.130	3.15	3.46	1,590	Progress in my work
5	39.207	3.05	3.35	1,464	Organizational policies
6	37.530	2.96	3.38	1,398	How I am being judged
7	32.335	2.84	3.20	1,199	How my job-related problems are being handled
8	31.943	2.88	3.23	1,179	Important new service or program developments in my organization
9	30.084	2.84	3.24	997	How technological changes affect my job
10	29.145	2.66	3.23	1,081	Promotion and advancement opportunities in my organization
11	25.000	2.54	3.10	927	How organization decisions are made that affect my job
12	24.686	2.65	3.10	905	Specific problems management faces in my organization
13	22.300	2.59	3.06	826	Mistakes and failures of my organization

Topics Rank-Ordered Positively with Respect to Needed Quality

Rank	Percent	Sample Mean	Norm Mean	Persons	Question from ICA Communication Audit Survey
1	77.717	4.08	4.13	2,846	Pay and benefits
2	75.838	4.06	4.11	2,806	How I am being judged
3	74.763	4.00	4.04	2,758	How my job-related problems are being handled
4	74.722	4.01	4.08	2,755	How organization decisions are made that affect my job
5	73.064	3.94	4.00	2,726	My job duties
6	72.903	3.99	4.06	2,685	Promotion and advancement opportunities in my organization
7	71.816	3.93	3.96	2,701	Progress in my work
8	70.538	3.91	3.95	2,624	Organizational policies
9	69.698	3.89	3.94	2,560	How my job relates to the total operation of my organization
10	62.660	3.76	3.82	2,294	Important new service or program developments in my organization
11	56.986	3.63	3.73	2,080	Specific problems management faces in my organization
12	53.965	3.54	3.70	1,783	How technological changes affect my job
13	53.932	3.56	3.68	1,982	Mistakes and failures of my organization

Table 10.9   ICA Communication Audit Exploratory Interview Guide

In the following questions, we are talking about communication. Although *communication* can have several different meanings, depending upon the context, we use the term quite broadly to include any message sent or received in your organization.

1. Describe your job (duties, function). What decisions do you usually make in your job? What information do you *need* to make those decisions and from where should you get it? What information do you *actually* get to make those decisions and from whom? Are there formal (written) or informal policies in your organization which determine how you get this information? Should any policies be added, changed, or abandoned?

2. What are the major communication *strengths* of this organization? Be specific.

3. What are the major communication *weaknesses* of this organization?

4. Describe the *formal* channels through which you typically receive information about this organization? What kinds of information do you tend to receive? How often?

5. Describe the *informal* channels through which you typically receive information about this organization. What kinds of information do you tend to receive? How often?

6. How often, if ever, do you receive information about this organization which is of low value or use to you? If and when you do, what kinds of information do you receive? Be specific. From whom do you receive this?

7. What would you like to see done to improve information flow in this organization? Why hasn't it been done yet?

8. Describe the way decisions are typically made in this organization.

9. When conflict occurs in this organization, what is its major cause? How is conflict typically resolved?

10. Describe the communication relationship you have with your immediate supervisor. Your co-workers. Middle management. Top management. Your subordinates (if appropriate).

11. How do you know when this organization has done a good or bad job toward accomplishing its goals? What measures of effectiveness are used in this organization?

   Data are qualitatively analyzed, with summaries of the responses grouped and specific conclusions drawn.

Network Analysis. Respondents indicated the extent to which they typically communicated with each individual in their unit or department (or with key individuals outside their unit). A computer examination of all communication links identified that operational communication network (for rumors, social, and job-related messages) and placed individuals in communication roles of isolate, liaison, or group member. The instrument was completed in a group session lasting about thirty minutes. Table 10.10 presents a sample network analysis form. Figures 10.1 and 10.2 illustrate the nature of the output from an audit network analysis.

Communication Experience. Respondents described critical communication episodes they felt were representative of typically successful or unsuccessful incidents. From these descriptions and the type of incidents they represented, a set of examples were developed to help illustrate *why* a given unit or department experienced good or bad communication. These qualitative data added much richness to, and provided for, information from other

Table 10.10 ICA Communication Audit Network Analysis Instrument

During a typical workday, I usually communicate about work-related matters with the following people through the following channels:

	Identi-fication	Formal Organizational Structure	Informal (Grapevine) Organizational Structure
Executive		*How important is the communication?*	
Stenographer-secretary	0001	___ A B C D E	___ A B C D E
Senior stenographer	0002	___ A B C D E	___ A B C D E
Executive secretary	0003	___ A B C D E	___ A B C D E
Assistant executive director	0004	___ A B C D E	___ A B C D E
Assistant manager	0005	___ A B C D E	___ A B C D E
Telephone operator	0006	___ A B C D E	___ A B C D E
Executive director	0007	___ A B C D E	___ A B C D E
Administration and Finance			
Assistant director for administration	0008	___ A B C D E	___ A B C D E
Typist	0009	___ A B C D E	___ A B C D E
Accounting clerk	0010	___ A B C D E	___ A B C D E
Accounting clerk-typist	0011	___ A B C D E	___ A B C D E
Assistant accountant	0012	___ A B C D E	___ A B C D E
Senior accountant	0013	___ A B C D E	___ A B C D E
Typist	0014	___ A B C D E	___ A B C D E
Stenographer	0015	___ A B C D E	___ A B C D E

Key: A = not at all important
      B = somewhat important
      C = fairly important
      D = very important
      E = extremely important

audit tools. Respondents completed this instrument in group or individual sessions lasting about one hour. All data were computer analyzed confidentially. Table 10.11 presents a sample of the computer analysis provided with these data; figure 10.3 presents the audit communication experience form.

Communication Diary. Each participant was asked to maintain a diary of specified communicative activities (conversations, phone calls, meetings, written materials received and sent, etc.) for a one-week period. Forms were provided to simplify the recording of these communication events. Cumulative time required per person for the entire week was ap-

Figure 10.1 Sample ICA network analysis output. (Based on work by Richard Lesniak and others, 1977.)

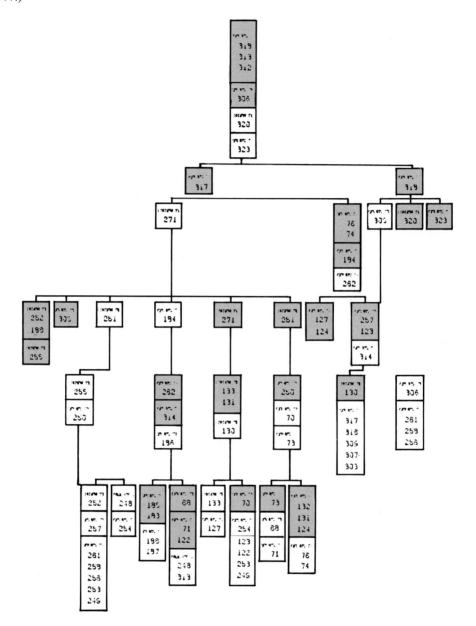

Figure 10.2 Sample netlink output: group, liaison, and special person links. (Based on work by Richard Lesniak and others, 1977.)

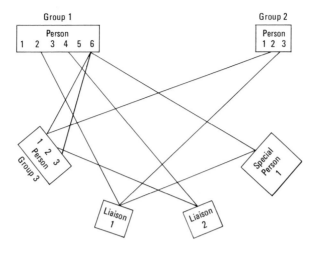

Table 10.11   Communication Experiences Analyses Frequency Breakdown by Category

Communication Experiences Regarding the Adequacy of Information

Sub-category	Frequency Negative		Frequency Positive		Immediate Supervisor		Subordinate		Co-Worker		Top Management	
2.1	9	75.0%	3	25.0%	1	8.3%	0	0.0%	5	41.7%	6	50.0%
2.2	2	100.0%	0	0.0%	1	50.0%	0	0.0%	0	0.0%	1	50.0%
2.3	3	75.0%	1	25.0%	2	50.0%	0	0.0%	1	25.0%	1	25.0%
2.4	2	40.0%	3	60.0%	2	40.0%	1	20.0%	1	20.0%	1	20.0%
2.5	0	0.0%	2	100.0%	1	50.0%	1	50.0%	0	0.0%	0	0.0%
2.6	3	100.0%	0	0.0%	1	33.3%	0	0.0%	0	0.0%	2	66.7%
Totals	19	67.9%	9	32.1%	8	28.6%	2	7.1%	7	25.0%	11	39.3%

Sample Incident
I lack information concerning departmental philosophy and goals because I am not included in monthly departmental meetings or other special meetings. Last month a meeting was held which I didn't know about. As a result, I didn't give my co-workers vital information they needed to do their jobs.

Figure 10.3   ICA communication audit communication experience form.

While you were filling out the previous section, the questions may have brought to mind a recent work-related experience of yours in which *communication* was particularly ineffective or effective. Please answer the questions below and give us a clearly printed summary of that experience.

A. To whom does this experience primarily relate? (Circle *one*.)
   1. subordinate   2. co-worker   3. immediate supervisor
      4. middle management   5. top management

B. Please rate the quality of communication described in the experience below (circle *one*):
   1. effective   2. ineffective

C. To what item in the previous section does this experience primarily relate?
   _____ (put in the item number)

Describe the communicative experience, the circumstances leading up to it, what the person did that made him or her an effective or ineffective communicator, and the results (outcome) of what the person did. PLEASE *PRINT*. THANK YOU.

_____

_____

_____

_____

_____

_____

_____

proximately one and one-half hours, including a short training period. These data were confidentially analyzed by computer. They provided indications of actual communication behavior among individuals, groups, and the entire organization. Figure 10.4 presents the audit diary form, and table 10.12 (p. 364) presents a sample computer printout summarizing one person's interactions for a week.

Figure 10.4 ICA communication audit communication diary form.

Your name _____ Date _____

Other party _____
_____
_____

	Communication							
	1	2	3	4	5	6	7	(etc.)
Initiator								
Self	—	—	—	—	—	—	—	
Other party	—	—	—	—	—	—	—	
Channel								
Face-to-face	—	—	—	—	—	—	—	
Telephone	—	—	—	—	—	—	—	
Written	—	—	—	—	—	—	—	
Kind								
Job-related	—	—	—	—	—	—	—	
Incidental	—	—	—	—	—	—	—	
Rumor	—	—	—	—	—	—	—	
Length								
Less than 3 minutes	—	—	—	—	—	—	—	
3 to 15 minutes	—	—	—	—	—	—	—	
15 minutes to 1 hour	—	—	—	—	—	—	—	
Over 1 hour	—	—	—	—	—	—	—	
Qualities								
Useful	—	—	—	—	—	—	—	
Important	—	—	—	—	—	—	—	
Satisfactory	—	—	—	—	—	—	—	
Timely	—	—	—	—	—	—	—	
Accurate	—	—	—	—	—	—	—	
Excessive	—	—	—	—	—	—	—	
Effective	—	—	—	—	—	—	—	

Key Audit Logistics and Timetable

In order to complete a communication audit within a reasonable time (usually about three months), the timetable shown in table 10.13 was suggested.

While the audit was being conducted, the ICA had recommended that the organization establish an audit liaison committee composed of a diagonal slant of seven to nine persons whose functions were the following:

1. To help implement audit logistics (set up interviews, etc.).
2. To receive interim audit reports.
3. To communicate preaudit, audit, and postaudit information to the organization (via newsletters, memos, meetings, etc.).
4. To receive final audit report.
5. To begin to assign priority to conclusions and recommendations.

Table 10.12   Sample ICA Diary Output

Personal Profile of Jane Smith		Confidential
Number of interactions during week	268	
Average interactions per day	67.00	
Share of interactions during week		6.63 percent
You initiated 49.63 precent of your interactions		
Number of face-to-face interactions	167	
Percent of face-to-face interactions		62.78
Number of telephone calls	62	
Percent of telephone calls		23.31
Number of written communications	21	
Percent of written communications		7.89
Number of intercom communications	15	
Percent of communications by intercom		5.64
Job-related interactions	187	69.26 percent
Innovative interactions	35	12.96 percent
Informal interactions	3	1.11 percent
Other kinds of interactions	45	16.67 percent
Less than 3-minute interactions	170	65.38 percent
3 to 15-minute interactions	69	26.54 percent
15 minute to 1-hour interactions	8	3.08 percent
Interactions over 1 hour	13	5.00 percent

63.06 percent of your interactions were useful
51.79 percent of your interactions were important
 8.58 percent of your interactions were private
 7.09 percent of your interactions were in conference

Table 10.13   ICA Communication Audit Timetable

Activity	Duration
Finalize contract; prepare tools	1 week
Conduct exploratory interviews	1 week
Transcribe interviews and prepare for analysis	1 week
Analyze exploratory interviews	1 week
Administer survey, communication experiences, and network anlaysis questionnaires	1 week
Analyze survey, communication experiences, and network analysis data	2 weeks
Preliminary interpretation of data; formulation of follow-up interview guide and communication diary log	1 week
Conduct follow-up interviews; administer communication diary	1 week
Transcribe interviews and prepare for analysis; prepare diary data	1 week
Analyze follow-up interviews and communication diary	1 week
Interpret data; draw conclusions; prepare recommendations; write final report	2 weeks
Present final report (orally and in writing); discuss future steps	2 days
Total Elapsed Time	**13.2 weeks**

Feedback of Results and Follow-up

The results of the audit were reported orally and in writing to appropriate personnel. A brief report containing conclusions and recommendations was prepared for general organizational dissemination. A detailed report written in accordance with customary conventions for the reporting of survey-participant data (i.e., percentages, tabular presentations, and content summaries) was also provided, primarily for the audit liaison committee and other appropriate personnel. Unless other information was specifically requested, descriptive statistics were the only calculations applied to the data.

After top management had reviewed the results, the data were commonly shared next with other subordinate supervisory personnel in the organization. Then, the findings of the audit (both favorable and unfavorable) were condensed and distributed, with recommendations, to all members of the organization. Next, a committee (usually the audit liaison committee) was typically formed to study the audit results and make recommendations to management. Finally, an action program to implement approved recommendations was undertaken.

The following recommendations have been implemented by some of the ICA clients:

1. Addition of new formal channels of communication (newsletters, videotape playback of key memoranda, new bulletin boards, new meeting structures, new telephone systems).
2. Development of communication goals, objectives, and policies and the disclosure of these to employees.
3. Open disclosure policies on certain topics of information.
4. Improvements in informal communication (luncheons with key executives, social events, rap sessions, open-door policies).
5. Hiring or shifting of personnel to improve the communication function in the company.
6. Addition of liaison personnel to facilitate horizontal communication between computer users and computer personnel.
7. Changes in the amount of information communicated about career paths and the personnel function (job postings, pay ranges for certain positions, training and development programs available for certain career paths).
8. Better upward input solicited by top management to improve the planning process, both short and long range; development of specific mechanisms to generate such input in a nonthreatening way.
9. Improvement in the quality of the quarterly officers' meetings; adding question-answer periods and open discussion.
10. Retraining of certain management personnel in communication skills (writing, listening, public speaking, interviewing, group discussion, problem solving, brainstorming).
11. Better and more periodic monitoring of the company's external image as perceived by significant publics (consumers, stockholders, politicians, community leaders).

Data-Gathering and Data-Analyzing Techniques Used in Communication Audits

Presentation in this section of the major techniques used in communication audits to gather and to analyze data will follow this pattern:

1. Definition of the technique.
2. Examples of its use.
3. Strengths and weaknesses of the technique.
4. Description of nature of data generated by the technique and list of appropriate analysis techniques.

Most of the commonly used data-gathering techniques in communication audits can be grouped into *three* broad categories: observation techniques, questionnaire-interview techniques, and content-analysis techniques.

Observation Techniques

Observation techniques involve perceiving and recording the behavior of either yourself or other people. When we observe and record our own behavior, we are involved in a duty study; when we observe the behavior of others, we are acting as a trained observer. Techniques and instruments in organizational communication have been developed for both approaches.

Duty Study. The duty study—also known as self-recording technique, communication log or communication flow sheet—provides respondents with a means of recording their own communication behavior, either continuously or periodically. Burns was one of the first to use this technique. He obtained information about communication activities of executives, who recorded it in the following categories: length of time an interaction lasted, persons involved in the discussion, subject of the discussion, and initiator of the encounter. Burns reported that he encountered few problems with the technique in gathering data on direction of communication and amount of time spent in various types of communication activities. The categories for observing communication behavior evolve out of discussion between the researcher(s) and the respondent(s). For example, in an audit of a college within the University of New Mexico, I asked an administrator to record his communication behavior for three weeks, using the same categories as in the Burns study. The record was to include also the media used in the interaction, where the interaction took place, and whether feedback was requested.

Gearing and Hughes have recommended the following rules for collecting observational data:

Rule 1. Record as much as you can about the entire situation, including the actors, their behaviors, the context, and the setting of those behaviors.

Rule 2. Record to the greatest extent possible your personal reflections on the event, including questions, comments, explanations, judgments, and conclusions.

Rule 3. Keep your factual descriptions separate from your personal reflections.

Rule 4. Immediately after you have finished observing, expand your record to include as much detail with as much clarity as possible.

Rule 5. Review your observational record within twenty-four hours of its recording to make final editing or factual changes before closing out that record.

The main advantages of the duty study are the following. It provides detailed information about the *amount* of communication, the *network* utilized, and the *direction* followed. It avoids observer bias. It avoids reliance upon memory. Its chief disadvantages appear to be the following. It takes a lot of time, and thus may be impractical. It generates a large amount of data, some of which may be unusable. It depends upon respondent trust and willingness to cooperate. It does not give information about message distortion, rate of message flow, and redundancy of the network.

Data generated by the duty study are primarily nominal (frequency), and thus their analysis is limited to descriptive and nonparametric statistics. For example, the *average* (mean) length of time involved in an activity, the *percentage* of time spent interacting with certain people, and *differences* in topics of discussion between various people can be computed in terms of their *significance*. Key statistics used in these analyses are *mean, median, mode, variance, standard deviation, shape of the curve of distribution* (kurtosis), *percentages,* and *chi-square* (used to compute significance of differences between frequencies). Most of these statistics can be computed simultaneously by a computer program called Statistical Package for the Social Sciences (SPSS) Codebook.

Trained Observer. Trained observers perceive and describe the behavior of people other than themselves. This technique is similar to the duty study, but respondents do not have to record their own communication behavior. Several researchers have used versions of the trained observer technique. Roethlisberger and Dickson in the famous Hawthorne studies (cited in chapter 3) used data collected in the Western Electric plan over several years duration and called their approach "living-in." Piersol introduced his version of this technique in a study of communication behavior of foremen in a large corporation and called his approach the "shadow technique." He recommended that only people who trusted the observer enough not to deviate from their normal behavior be shadowed. Sanborn used the shadow technique to follow executives of a large retail corporation for four hours each, recording all noticeable oral communication behavior. In the research at the University of New Mexico, in addition to having the administrators record their own communication behavior, I also recorded their behavior on several occasions and trained two secretaries to act as observers. This approach enabled us to get three perceptions of the same behavior for validation purposes.

The chief advantages of this technique are similar to the duty study: it provides a convenient method for describing the communication load of key personnel; it provides information about networks and directions; and it allows for no respondent contamination. Its main weaknesses are that it takes a lot of time; it requires training of observers; and it carries some risk of causing behavior to deviate from normal patterns.

The data and the data analysis are similar to those in the duty study.

Questionnaire-Interview Techniques

Questionnaire-interview techniques generally seek data about respondent's perceptions, attitudes, and knowledge about information within the organization. Many of the same principles apply to the construction of both interview schedules and questionnaires. First the information-seeking interview-questionnaire is considered, and construction techniques, common usage problems, and research studies that used these techniques are discussed. We will then refer briefly to several measuring instruments that use questionnaire-interview techniques.

A questionnaire is a *written* instrument that seeks information about a person's attitudes, knowledge, and perceptions. Various kinds of questions can be constructed for a questionnaire:

1. Example of an open-ended question:
   What is your opinion of the recent election?
2. Example of a closed question:
   Do you agree with the policies of the present administration?
3. Example of a forced-choice question:
   Would you rather vote for . . . or . . . ?
4. Example of a question using a Likert scale:
   What is your reaction to the present administration's foreign policy? Check one:
   __ strongly agree __ agree __ no opinion __ disagree
   __ strongly disagree
5. Example of a question using a semantic differential scale:
   For each of the following pairs of adjectives, please circle the number between them which comes closest to expressing your attitude toward the candidacy of Edward Kennedy:

cold	1	2	3	4	5	6	7	hot
fast	1	2	3	4	5	6	7	slow
active	1	2	3	4	5	6	7	passive

6. Example of a checklist:
   Please check each adjective in the following list which applies to your personality:
   __ warm __ cold __ pleasant __ unpleasant __ angry __ loving
7. Example of a multiple-choice item:
   When you get a letter, how soon do you answer it?
   __ immediately __ within one day __ within one week
   __ longer than one week __ never

Most of the same techniques can be used to construct an interview. The main difference is that an interview is a *live* exchange between a questioner and a respondent. Of course, some interviews are nothing more than an opportunity for the questioner (interviewer) to simply read questions from a schedule and record the answers of the respondent (interviewee). Other interviews allow for much interaction between the interviewer and the interviewee. The interview has the distinct advantage over the questionnaire of allowing interviewees to ask questions of interviewers when they do not understand a particular question.

Questionnaire-interview techniques generally seek data about the respondent's perceptions, attitudes, and knowledge about information within the organization.

Many problems of the questionnaire-interview can be avoided if auditors adhere to some of the following steps in designing and using these techniques. Anderson has recommended that researchers specify their research goals, draft and field-test a pilot instrument, and then revise it for final use. Parten has recommended using simple words and concise, unambiguous questions that lend themselves to tabulation and statistical treatment; avoiding questions which beg the answer; minimizing the amount of writing required of respondents; and making internal validity checks. If the population is too large for all of it to be included or *all* of the population may not be able to participate in a study, appropriate sampling procedures and guidelines should be used.

When used appropriately, questionnaires have the advantage of permitting collection of a lot of information in little time; interviews have the advantage of allowing interaction between auditors and their respondents.

Many auditors have problems with the questionnaire-interview techniques. The more common problems concern how to code open-ended questions into appropriate and quantifiable categories; how to get a return rate representative of the population; how to avoid biased responses due to question construction and/or interviewer techniques (leading questions or suggested answers); how to avoid interpretation difficulties (from overgeneralization of results, failure to cross-tabulate key variables); and how to avoid cross-cultural misunderstandings (especially due to language choice).

A related problem that researchers face is the reading difficulty involved in their questionnaire, or the readability of the questionnaire. The more difficult the questionnaire is to read the less likely your results will be accurate. One method for assessing the readability of questionnaire surveys is the Gunning Fog index. The fog index is the reading grade level that is necessary for the reader to be able to comprehend the content of the questionnaire survey. To calculate the fog index the designer must take a systematic sample of 100 words from the questionnaire survey. Then divide the number of words by the number of sentences to get the average sentence length. Then count the number of words containing three syllables or more to get the number of hard words. Add these two factors together and multiply by a constant of .4.

Fog Index = .4(% of three-syllable words and over + average sentence length).

Another common problem many auditors face involves qualitative analysis of non-quantifiable data. Too often researchers believe that if data cannot be quantified, it should be discarded.

Questionnaire-interview techniques have been used in a variety of studies in organizational communication. In a classic study of organizational structure, Jacobson and Seashore relied heavily upon the interview as a data-gathering technique. The Hawthorne studies researchers gathered their nonobservation data primarily via the interview. In a study I directed in New Mexico, Horan used a mail questionnaire to measure attitudes of voting citizens toward the university. To avoid a return below what was needed, an intentionally large sample (over 4,000) was selected in order to guarantee a return of the needed 384 (we received 388). Unfortunately, many researchers do not have the financial resources to generate samples of this size. Other researchers have used questionnaire-interview techniques. Lull and co-workers surveyed seventy top executives concerning their communication media preferences. Level used questionnaires and interviews to analyze the total communication activity of an urban bank. Zima used both techniques to compare and contrast the satisfaction with counseling communication of nonfactory and factory supervisors. Minter used interview techniques primarily to measure managers' attitudes toward communication and other variables.

Other research instruments have been developed that use some of the previously mentioned techniques. Two of the more commonly used instruments in communication audits are episodic communication channels in organization (ECCO) analysis and network analysis.

Episodic Communication Channels in Organization (ECCO) Analysis

ECCO analysis was developed by Keith Davis in 1952 as an instrument to analyze and map communication networks and measure rates of flow, distortion of messages, and redundancy. Figure 10.5 presents an example of an ECCO analysis instrument as used by Rudolph.

The administration of the instrument is relatively simple. Respondents are asked to fill in the ECCO form in the presence of the researcher. This generally takes three to four minutes and can be done at the place of work. When respondents have questions, they are free

Figure 10.5 Example of an ECCO analysis instrument.

Prior to receiving this questionnaire did you know the information in the box below *or any part of it?*

<u>(Message)</u>

Please *Check One:*

_____ Yes, I knew all of it.

_____ Yes, I knew part of it. If so please list the numbers of the parts you knew

___ ___ ___ ___ ___.

_____ No, I did not know any of it.

If your answer above was ''Yes, I knew all of it'' *or* ''Yes, I knew part of it,'' please complete the questionnaire by providing the information requested below.

If your answer above was ''No, I did not know any of it'' you have completed the questionnaire. Please return the questionnaire to me or drop it in the information box. Thank you very much for your cooperation.

If you had the information in the box, *but* the facts you heard were different, please write the facts you heard next to the associated number.

1. _____
2. _____
3. _____
4. _____
5. _____

Question 1

From whom did you *first* receive the information in the box? Please place the source's code number (from your code sheet) on this line _____. Remember that by using the code number *you never identify* the specific person who gave you the information, because *each* code number is assigned to *several* persons (in the operator group).

Question 2

Where were you when you first received the information in the box above? Please check one:

(11) _____ At my desk board or other location where I carry out my job duties
(12) _____ Elsewhere in the room where I work
(13) _____ Outside this room but still working
(14) _____ Away from my unit department but still working
(15) _____ Away from my unit department but not while working (coffee break, etc.)
(16) _____ Away from the building and while not working for this company

Question 3

How long ago did you first receive the information in the box? Please circle the approximate time:

Today	Yesterday	3 4 5 6 7	days ago
		2 3 4 5 6	weeks ago

Question 4

By what method did you first receive the information in the box above? Please *check only one* of the following methods:

Written or Visual Methods

Source: E. Rudolph, ''An Evaluation of ECCO Analysis as a Communication Audit Methodology'' (paper presented at a meeting of the International Communication Association, 1972). Used with permission of Evan Rudolph.

Figure 10.5 *Continued*

(20) _____ Personal letter from the company
(21) _____ Letter, memo, or service program
(22) _____ Annual Report
(23) _____ News I
(24) _____ Mountain Bell Magazine
(25) _____ Tempo-70
(26) _____ Company film
(27) _____ Public newspaper or magazine
(28) _____ Company records

Talking or Sound Methods

(29) _____ Talking with one other person in his presence
(30) _____ Talking over the telephone
(31) _____ Talking (and listening) in a small group of two or more
(32) _____ Attending an organized meeting or conference
(33) _____ Overhearing what someone else said
(34) _____ Radio or television

Miscellaneous

(35) _____ I did it or I originated the information or decision
(36) _____ Other, please explain

Thank you very much for your cooperation. Please return the questionnaire to me or drop it in the information box.

to converse with the researcher. Questionnaires are then coded, tabulated, and analyzed by means of appropriate statistical techniques.

ECCO analysis is a convenient, fast, reliable field instrument. It allows for respondent-researcher interaction when necessary or desired. It is relatively inexpensive, simple, and clear. It deals with concrete messages rather than with perceptions or attitudes. Its major disadvantage appears to be that it sometimes takes several weeks for a message to be totally diffused within an organization, which may affect respondent recall of the facts.

Network Analysis

Although the ICA audit used network analysis as one of its five measurement tools, the study of communication networks is neither unique to organizational communication research nor a recent development by communication scholars. Grounded in the laboratory studies of communication networks as conducted by sociologists and psychologists, network analysis is now possible in large, complex organizations because of advances in computer technology and the work of Richards and Lesniak et al.

The *goals* of network analysis are as follows:

1. To identify the particular pathway through which information flows in a particular organization.
2. To compare these operational pathways (communication networks) with planned or formal networks identified on organization charts or in job descriptions.

3. To determine potential bottlenecks and gatekeepers of information by comparing actual communication roles of key personnel (isolates, liaisons, group members) with expected roles provided by job descriptions or organization chart placement.
4. To use the foregoing information to help an organization operate more effectively as it attempts to meet its goals.

The major *products* of a computerized network analysis are these:

1. Computer-generated maps of all operational communication networks relevant to a particular audit.
2. Computer-generated comparison of actual with expected networks.
3. Computer identification of all organizational personnel as work-group members, liaisons between groups, or isolates within the organization.
4. Computer-generated comparisons of actual with expected communication network role.

As with the communication audit network analysis, data are collected when respondents, using a self-reporting form, indicate the extent to which they typically communicate with each individual in their unit or department (or with individuals outside their unit). They do so either by checking names on an alphabetical roster or, in larger organizations, by writing in the names of the persons with whom they frequently communicate. Additional data are often collected about the frequency, importance, and effectiveness of the interaction. The instrument is typically completed in group sessions lasting about thirty minutes, including instructions. Data are then keypunched and analyzed by computer.

When interpreting the data from a network analysis, you may combine these findings with those of a survey instrument to ask such questions as the following: Does network role influence or determine communication satisfaction? communication need? worker performance? Specifically, do isolates have greater communication needs than centrals? than liaisons? than group members? than bridges? Do they have better relationships, higher morale, and greater job satisfaction? In a broader sense, data from network analysis may be used to answer questions about the entire organization, about certain groups, and about specific individuals.

The use of network analysis as an audit technique has been criticized (see Bernard and Killworth [1977], for example). The major criticisms can be summarized as follows (Jablin, 1980).

1. The technique relies primarily upon subjective recall of subjects to identify sociometrically their main communication contacts. Basically, the critics contend that people do not know, with any degree of accuracy, those with whom they communicate, and, consequently, cannot validly complete the network analysis survey form. Objective measures (i.e., actual phone records, copies of memoranda, etc.) are, according to the critics, a more valid way of identifying networks.
2. Additional error in the measurement can be detected when people do not reciprocally indicate that they communicate with each other. Some people may forget all their contacts; others may under- or overstate their contacts; others may just make simple mistakes. Conservative network analysts typically would drop all unreciprocated links from their analyses; more liberal analysts would assume reciprocity and supply the missing half of the data.

3. Most network analysis methodologies require the use of census data rather than the usual random samples used in most surveys. The reasoning is that, with a census, you are less likely to have missing links and important gaps in the true structure of the organization. However, there is a pragmatic problem associated with getting data from almost all members of an organization.

Content Analysis Techniques

Content analysis techniques seek to analyze the content of messages. Budd, Thorp, and Donohew defined content analysis as "a systematic technique for analyzing message content and message handling." Essentially, the technique involves selecting the written communications you wish to study; either sampling or using the entire universe, developing categories for measurement; measuring the frequency of appearance of the category(ies) in accordance with appropriate coding rules; applying appropriate statistical tests to the data; and drawing final conclusions from the data.

Several examples of use of the techniques in organizational communication exist. Colby and Tiffin used content analysis techniques to assess the readability levels of various organizational documents. Dee analyzed common themes appearing in a union newspaper. Funk used content analysis in the attitude questionnaire data generated in his study of industrial foremen. Purdom did content analysis on messages sent through the formal channels of a health organization. I used content analysis in my study of the employment manuals of two companies. My categories consisted of two types of words—negative words (e.g., *cannot, never, no, don't,* etc.) and command words (e.g., *always, must, essential, required,* etc.), selected because of their apparent relation to McGregor's Theory X (see chapter 3). I programmed a computer to "count" these words in the text of the two manuals, to compute the differences between the two manuals, and to run the appropriate statistical test (chi-square) on the frequency data. In this case, the categories for analysis were selected in advance of the coding and counting portions of the study. In another study in which the entire communication system of a college at the University of New Mexico was audited, I used content analysis techniques to study the written memos of the organization. The category of analysis was commonly occurring themes within the memos. In this study, the specific themes evolved from the initial investigation of a sample of the memos.

This example of defining categories in a *post hoc* manner illustrates the use of qualitative analysis (mentioned above as something many auditors find to be a problem). Holsti has listed several possible uses of qualitative analysis for content analysis techniques:

> He may want to read over a sample of his data to get a "feel" for the types of relevant symbols or themes. Prior to coding, he may also read over the data to identify any idiosyncratic attributes which, if not taken into account, might adversely affect the results. After coding and data analysis have been completed, he may want to check the "face validity" of the quantitative results by rereading parts of all of his documents. . . . Thus the content analysis should use qualitative methods to supplement each other.

Timm and Barker recently surveyed communication researchers and auditors to determine the extent to which they use these and other data-gathering tools. Table 10.14, adapted from their paper, summarizes their findings. The remainder of this chapter is concerned with the problems associated with gathering data in a communication audit and the mechanics of writing the audit report.

Table 10.14 Comparison of Communication Auditing Techniques

Technique	Ease of Use			Quality of Data			Costs	
	To Design	To Administer	To Process Data	Quantification	Reliability Validity	Skills Required	Materials	Time
Questionnaire predesigned	N/A	easy	easy	good	varies with design	low	low to moderate	low
own design	fairly difficult	easy	easy	good	varies with design	moderate	low to moderate	low
Interview free response	easy	difficult	difficult	difficult	usually good	consider-able	low	high
structured	fairly difficult	easy	easy	good	varies with design	moderate	low to moderate	high
Observation	easy	moderate	difficult	difficult	unpre-dictable	high	low	high
Critical Incident	easy	difficult	difficult	difficult	unpre-dictable*	moderate	low	high
Content Analysis	difficult	difficult	difficult	good	good	high	quite high including computer	high
Network Analysis	easy	easy	easy if computer program used	good if computer program used	—	low to moderate	fairly high including computer time	low
Duty Study	easy	easy	consid-erable	adequate on most data		low	low	high
ECCO Analysis	easy	easy	fairly difficult	good	good	moderate	low	low

*Depends on respondent's training and motivation.
Source: P. Timm and R. Barker, "Communication Auditing in Organizations: Where Do We Stand?"
(Paper presented at a meeting of the International Communication Association, 1976.) Used with the permission of P. Timm and R. Barker.

Communication Gradients

Developing communication gradients is a new technique for examining communication structure within organizations developed by Johnson (1988). Communication gradients are a representation of communication intensity within the physical boundaries of an organization. Communication intensity measures, such as frequency of contact, average frequency of individual contacts, response satisfaction, and importance of communication, can be correlated to an individual's work station and rest stations to determine where and between whom communication is taking place within the organization. Illustrative data is used to generate sample gradient plots of the four communication intensity measures and the rich visual imagery produced is used to analyze the effects among the variables.

Practical Problems in Gathering Data

Kerlinger stated that the main weaknesses of field research are of a practical nature. Few researchers would deny that there are some practical concerns—gaining entry into an organization; maintaining rapport within the organization; designing the study to match the constraints of time, money, and available resources; designing a schedule of research activities that coordinates the available time of professor, graduate student, and sponsoring organization; deciding who will control all original raw data and eventual publication of the findings; and selecting research topics that integrate researcher and organization needs. The following case study illustrates some of these practical limitations.

To *gain entry,* I contacted an industrial organization in Albuquerque for the purpose of placing a team of five graduate students in the company to conduct a research project during the fall semester. I, rather than the graduate students, made the initial contact because I have found that an organization prefers to deal with a professor, at least initially, in order to be reassured that the project is sanctioned and will receive adequate expert direction. When I made the initial contact, I spoke on the telephone with the president of the company. I believe that dealing with "the man in charge"—president, general manager, plant manager, district manager—saves a lot of time in setting up a research project. Usually, this person refers me to a subordinate who will act as liaison between the organization and the research team. The fact that the referral is communicated downward with authority enhances our opportunity to conduct the research.

After the initial commitment from the organization, I scheduled a meeting of the research team, the organization's liaison (the president or his designated subordinate), and me, held at the organization. At this meeting, we discussed the *nature of the research project* and the specific needs of the research team. There was a lengthy discussion about the topic to be studied. The organization had a specific proposal it wanted to study (lateral breakdown of communication among five departments within the organization), and the research team had prepared a proposal of what they hoped to study (differences between actual employee attitudes and their supervisors' perceptions of those attitudes). Usually, we adhere to the desires of the organization because of our need to gain entry into a field organization. In several cases, however, I believed that the research topic proposed by the organization was too trivial to be studied by a team of graduate students, and therefore, a research topic beneficial to both researcher and organization had to be selected. In the case discussed here, we agreed to the organization's proposal with minor alterations.

Now that we had gained entry and selected a research topic, other practical matters had to be discussed. Of prime importance to this organization was our *guarantee that all results of the study would be kept confidential* within the organization and the research team. I usually try to convince an organization that if we publish data, their identity will be protected by appropriately disguising name, location, and product. In this case, however, the organization was insistent that the results remain unpublished. Another tack is to guarantee the organization the right to preview, edit, and even censor material before publication. With this company, we decided not to push for publication rights because we believed that they would deny us entry if we persisted. In such situations, a decision must then be made by the researchers: Is it more important to gain entry and a field opportunity for students, and so forth, than to guarantee publication of significant findings? Usually we opt for entry over publication.

Also discussed at this initial meeting was who would assume *costs* of the research. Normally, these are limited to duplication costs, transportation costs for the research teams, and space requirements at the organization (office, desks, typewriters). Since the organization is getting a free communication study, it normally agrees to assume these minor costs. In the example under discussion, this proved to be the case. Of more importance to this organization was the *time* factor. It wanted an estimate of the number of hours per week our research would take and the total amount of time their normal operation would be interrupted. We had to reassure them that interruption would be kept to an absolute minimum. Our time needs were important also, because we had to work within the confines of one semester.

Finally, an agreement was reached (and put into writing) between us and the organization. I had to promise to be available for all emergency considerations and consultations, primarily to assist in maintaining rapport between the organization and the students. The study was conducted within fifteen weeks, and the results were prepared in writing and distributed to the organization and the students (with *Confidential* written in bold type on the front cover).

In this case example, the practical problems of gaining entry, choosing a research topic, guaranteeing confidentiality of results, paying costs, assessing time, and maintaining rapport were involved. Other problems could just as easily have been encountered, and field researchers should be equipped to handle them or face the possibility of discontinuing their research.

Several of my students have encountered the following additional practical problems in relation to one study or another: poor interaction with the organization's gatekeeper (liaison); not all members in an organization being aware of the field study; time pressures; researchers' need for information about field study; and lack of group cooperation during the study. These problems are explained in detail in the discussion that follows.

Poor Interaction with the Organization's Gatekeeper.   Once a contact or liaison person has been established with the organization, it is incumbent upon both the researchers and the gatekeepers to maintain adequate communication throughout the study. Gatekeepers should be aware of their own and the researchers' responsibilities and role during the study. In this way, perhaps, some of the problems reported by one of my students could be avoided:

> Our biggest problem in the communication audit was with our gatekeeper. He was a political appointee who went to great lengths to vocalize about how he was going to assist our team in the successful completion of the audit. In the final analysis, however, he continually prevented us from successfully completing our tasks in the company. He said he would inform all the department managers of our purpose and assured us that they would give us complete cooperation in their different departments. It turned out that he did not even mention us to them, except in the company newspaper (which nobody seemed to read). He was supposed to contact those people whom we were scheduled to interview, but when he arrived at the assigned time for the interviews, not one of our scheduled people had been notified. He assured us that he would have our questionnaires printed and available in his office for us to distribute by 6 A.M. The questionnaires were printed, but he had changed the wording on several of our items and left the questionnaires in the print shop. We needed to get a security guard to open the door for us. All this time, employees were entering the plant for the morning shift, and the graveyard personnel were leaving the plant. We thus missed many of the people we wanted to measure. Finally, his crowning achievement was taking the questionnaires out of the deposit boxes and reading them at the same time that employees were putting them into the boxes (after we promised everyone confidentiality).

Not All Members in an Organization Being Aware of the Field Study.   Adequate effort should be taken to guarantee that *all* members of the organization are notified in advance of the purpose of the study, the names of the researchers, their length of stay, and any expected duties of organizational members during the study. In this way, you may be able to prevent situations similar to the following from happening:

> When I got to the plant for my first interview, it became apparent to me that the man I was supposed to talk with had no idea who I was or why I was there. This pattern continued as I began to interview more and more people. I found that I was spending most of my time explaining my identity and purpose. Needless to say, most of the people didn't trust me and checked me out with their boss.

Time Pressures.   One of the biggest problems cited by my students was the fact that they didn't have enough time to complete their audits. They attributed this to the lack of time-phase outline, the demands of a field study (travel, time at the organization), lack of cooperation within their group, and lack of knowledge about conducting a field study.

Researchers' Need for Information about Field Study.   Many students stated that they found it difficult to learn how to conduct a field study at the same time that they were conducting a study in an organization. To combat this problem, we have implemented a two-semester sequence in which the first course explains the methodology of a communication audit and the second provides the opportunity for actually conducting an audit in an organization.

Lack of Group Cooperation during the Study. Probably because of the pressures of time and lack of knowledge, several groups reported that they "had trouble getting along together" and that this inhibited their efficiency. One student reported it this way:

> We would start out and then we would lose a group member. As soon as we'd start, someone else would quit. In each case we had to go back and try to pick up the pieces and start again. The group became hostile and then apathetic toward themselves and the project. Meetings were missed, assignments weren't done, and people were always fighting with each other.

Sometimes, even the best preparation cannot prevent some problems. In one audit, we were delayed for more than a year because of a strike. In another, just as the contract was to be signed, the chief liaison in the organization was killed in a plane crash, and we had to start negotiations again. In one study, just as the interviews were scheduled to begin, several prospective interviewees refused to be interviewed because of fear of reprisal. Interviews were scheduled in a park at night in order to guarantee confidentiality. In another audit the union refused to allow its members to complete the survey for fear of breaches of confidentiality. To overcome this fear, a union representative was stationed at the location where the questionnaires were returned so that he could see us actually collect them and place them in a sealed carton and then move the carton into our car. In one organization, as we were about to begin the interviews, we were informed that the entire study would have to be conducted in both French and English to conform with the bilingual requirements of the government.

Writing the Audit Report

It is *not* the intent of this section to discuss the mechanics of writing research reports. Ample sources for this purpose are available, among which the following are especially recommended. Kerlinger (pp. 690–97); Lesikar (pp. 321–506); Menning and Wilkinson (pp. 487–658); Turabian; and Wilcox. The intent here is to present an approach for summarizing results of a communication audit within an organization.

Table 10.15 presents a sample table of contents for a report of a communication analysis. This example was adapted from one used quite successfully (according to student comments) at the University of Montana, Department of Speech Communication. It was devised by R. Wayne Pace when he was there.

Section I (field of study) puts the specific study into the content of the field of organizational communication. This section may provide for later linkage of the study with existing theory. Section II (organization studies) is mostly descriptive and sets the geographic context within which the study was conducted. Section III (methods, procedures, data-gathering techniques) provides auditors with an opportunity to explain exactly how they conducted the study. If this section is adequately and clearly explained, other auditors should be able to replicate the study. Section IV (analysis and findings) allows auditors to present and interpret their data, linking it to previously stated objectives, policies, and earlier research. Section V (summary, conclusions, and suggestions) provides the reader of the report

Table 10.15   Table of Contents for Report of Communication Analysis

I.   Field of Study
    A. Nature of formal organizations
    B. Definition of communication
    C. Nature of communication in organizations
    D. Summary
II. Organization Studies
    A. Description of production and marketing, including the kind of service, size, location, and environment of organization
    B. Description of structure, including an accurate organization chart of formal channels and staff positions
    C. Definition of special organization activities, including incentive systems, union relationships, and community programs
    D. Identification of communication objectives and standards
    E. Summary
III. Method, Procedure(s), and Data-Gathering Techniques
    A. General approach
    B. Subjects
    C. Research instruments and tools
    D. Specific procedures
IV. Analysis and Findings
    A. Nature of data and types of data-analysis techniques used
    B. Communication policies
    C. Communication attitudes
    D. Communication practices
    E. Effectiveness of communication program
V.   Summary, Conclusions, and Suggestions
    A. Summary of entire study
    B. Conclusions warranted by findings
    C. Suggestions for improving communication
VI. Bibliography
VII. Appendixes

with a synopsis of the entire study. Experience shows that this section may be the only one some organizations read. Therefore, the auditor should take particular pains to present the key conclusions and recommendations. Often this section appears *first* in the report. Section VI (bibliography) should contain all primary and key secondary sources of the auditor in the study. Section VII (appendixes) is a good place to present instruments used (in total), original data collected, and procedural papers (instruction sheets).

The auditor should spend considerable time writing so it is a clear report. Many hours spent in an audit may be wasted if the reader is unable to read the report of the findings or if key components of the audit are left out due to haste.

After the report is written, it must be presented to the organization. Consistent with the process consultation model discussed in chapter 9, table 10.16 outlines a feedback session format developed for the ICA communication audit. Notice that the organization receives the report *before* the feedback session takes place. Notice also that the responsibility for generating priorities and recommendations is upon the members of the organization, *not* upon the facilitators. Only when it assumes this responsibility will the organization be able to use the data from its communication audit to enhance its development and growth.

Table 10.16   Feedback Session Format for the ICA Communication Audit

I. Prior to Feedback Session

A. Prepare client audit committee.
1. Send client an agenda and explanation of tasks along with the final report (i.e., explain rating scale to be used in ranking recommendations).
2. Give client a coding sheet for ratings to facilitate summarizing its recommendations.
3. Have client read report and attach ratings in advance of session, according to criteria of money, time, people, urgency, and personal commitment.

B. Separate behavior of rating the "problems" from behavior of rating the "recommendations."
1. Give the client the conclusions about the separate problems (referenced according to appendices and tables) and then have it rate the problems.
2. Give the client the recommendations derived from the separate problems (referenced to each problem), and then have it rate the recommendations.

C. Have the client generate other recommendations (individually) in advance, linking them to specific problems, and attach a priority to them.

D. Have facilitator prepare in advance standard work sheets for calculating sums, means, ranks, and priorities, and prepare either overhead transparencies or flip-chart sheets with key words and column headings so all remaining to be done is to assign problems or recommendations and their priorities.

E. Have facilitator prepare in advance transparencies or flip charts on findings and recommendations (generated in final report).

II. During Feedback Session (in small groups, with minimum of two facilitators)

A. Summarize key conclusions and recommendations (facilitator does this in 15 minutes, using prepared flip charts or transparencies).

B. The client submits its ratings for both problems and recommendations to one facilitator (who compiles means, etc. on a flip chart) while another facilitator solicits and writes on flip chart new recommendations—takes about one-half hour.

C. Both facilitators lead discussion on reactions of client to problems and recommendation (to be summarized anonymously and later sent to top management) (about 15 minutes).

D. Both facilitators lead discussion on former recommendations and solicit ratings on new ones (15 minutes).

E. First faciliator collects from clients written statements specifying "implementation steps to be taken" for key recommendations; second facilitator prepares flip chart of priorities for new recommendations (15 minutes).

F. Both facilitators lead discussion on new recommendations, using flip charts, and collected "implementation steps," which are attached to summary recommendations of priorities (15 minutes).

G. Session concludes by summarizing the day, emphasizing the importance of follow-up, outlining next steps: for example, using the audit committee in follow-up, typing a summary of each part of the session and giving it to all participants and top management, meeting with top management, explaining the need for follow-up and action plans to help during follow-up, and the like.

SUMMARY

In this chapter, we presented the benefits for both organizations and researchers of a communication audit. Two plans were presented in detail, the Greenbaum conceptual structure, and the communication audit. The most commonly used techniques were classified into three broad categories—observation, questionnaire-interview, and content analysis, communication gradients were also discussed. Several data-gathering techniques were then described and exemplified. Key data-analysis techniques (and computer programs) were cited. Practical problems associated with data collection were described in detail. An outline for writing the report that presents the findings of the audit was presented.

EXERCISES

1. Select an organization with which you are familiar. Discuss the benefits of a communication audit for the organization.
2. What are some of the practical implications of the communication audit which have actually been implemented over the years?
3. Select *one* department within this organization. Does the department have explicitly or implicitly stated communication policies? If you do not know, ask one employee in the department (preferably someone you know). What key communication activities does the department use? Classify these activities according to level (interpersonal, small group, etc.) and function (informative, regulatory, etc.).
4. What data-gathering techniques would you use to measure the effectiveness of the just-named communication activities? Describe how you would implement your measurement process. List the specific instruments you would use. How long would it take you? What kind of data would you generate? How would you analyze the data? Are computer programs available to help your analysis?
5. Discuss the practical problems you could confront in collecting the data.
6. How would you present the findings of your brief audit to the managers of this department? What form would the report take? How inclusive would it be?
7. What are some of the criticisms which have been aimed at the communication audit over the years?
8. Now design an audit for an entire organization. Be sure you plan to use at least one data-gathering approach from each of the three broad categories mentioned: observation, questionnaire-interview, and content analysis. What period of time do you expect the audit to require? How many people are needed to help you? What organizational resources will you need?

BIBLIOGRAPHY AND REFERENCES

Anderson, Ken. "Questionnaire Construction." Paper presented at the Speech Communication Association, San Francisco, 1971.

Ayres, H. J. "A Review of Some Techniques Used to Study Communication Variables in Organizations." Paper presented at a meeting of the International Communication Association, Atlanta, 1972.

Bernard, H., and P. Killworth. "Informant Accuracy in Social Network Data II." *Human Communication Research* 4 (1977):3–18.

Budd, R. W., R. K. Thorp, and L. Donohew. *Content Analysis of Communications.* New York: Macmillan Co., 1967.

Burns, Tom. "The Directions of Activity and Communication in a Department Executive Group." *Human Relations* 7 (1954):73–97.

Colby, A. N., and J. Tiffin. "The Reading Ability of Industrial Supervisors." *Personnel* 27 (1950):156–59.

Davis, Keith. "A Method of Studying Communication Patterns in Organizations." *Personnel Psychology* 6 (1953):301–12.

Dee, J. "Oral Communication in the Trade Union Local." *Journal of Communication* 10 (1960):77–86.

Downs, Cal. "Research Methods in Organizational Communication: A Review and Proposals." Paper presented at a meeting of the Speech Association of America, New York, 1969.

Farace, Richard, and Donald MacDonald. "New Directions in the Study of Organizational Communication." Manuscript, 1971.

Funk, Frank. "Communication Attitudes of Industrial Foremen as Related to Their Rated Productivity." Ph.D. dissertation, Purdue University, 1956.

Gearing, F., and W. Hughes. *A Training Program in Improving Observational Skills.* Mimeographed report, State University of New York/Buffalo.

Goldhaber, G. "Communication and Student Unrest." Part 1. Report to the President of the University of New Mexico, 1970. Typewritten.

———. "Communication and Student Unrest." Part 2. Report to the President of the University of New Mexico, 1972.

———. *Improving Institutional Communication.* San Francisco: Jossey-Bass, 1978.

———. "The ICA Audit: Rationale and Development." Paper presented at a meeting of the Communication Association of the Pacific, Kobe, Japan, 1976.

Goldhaber, G., and D. Rogers. *Auditing Organizational Communication Systems: The ICA Communication Audit.* Dubuque, Iowa: Kendall/Hunt, 1979.

Goldhaber, G., and P. Krivonos. "The ICA Audit: Process, Status, and Critique." *Journal of Business Communication* 15 (Fall 1977):41–56.

Goldhaber, G., H. Dennis, G. Richetto, and O. Wiio. *Information Strategies: New Pathways to Management Productivity.* Norwood, N.J.: ABLEX, 1984. Rev. ed.

———. "A Content Analysis of Two Employment Manuals—With Implications for Theory X-Y Management Assumptions." *EPS* 11 (1971):1–8.

———. "A Communication Audit of the Albuquerque Police Department," Unpublished report, 1972.

Greenbaum, Howard. "Organizational Communication Systems: Identification and Appraisal." Paper presented at a meeting of the International Communication Association, Phoenix, 1971.

———. "The Appraisal of Organizational Communication Systems." Paper presented at a meeting of the International Communication Association, Atlanta, 1972.

Gunning, R. *The Technique of Clear Writing.* New York: McGraw-Hill, 1952.

Holsti, Ole. *Content Analysis for the Social Sciences and Humanities.* Reading, Mass.: Addison-Wesley Co., 1969.

Homans, H. G. *The Human Group.* New York: Harcourt, Brace & Co., 1950.

Horan, H. "A Public Attitude Survey toward The University of New Mexico." Master's thesis, University of New Mexico, 1972.

Jablin, Fred. "Organizational Communication Theory and Research: An Overview of Communication Climate and Network Research." In *Communication Yearbook* 4. Edited by D. Nimmo. New Brunswick, N.J.: Transaction-International Communication Association, 1980.

Jacobson, E., and S. Seashore. "Communication Practices in Complex Organizations." *Journal of Social Issues* 7 (1951):28–40.

Johnson, J.D. "On the Use of Communication Gradients." In *Handbook of Organizational Communication.* Edited by Gerald Goldhaber and George Barnett. Norwood, NJ: Ablex, 1988.

Kelly, Charles. "Actual Listening Behavior of Industrial Supervisors as Related to Listening Ability, General Mental Ability, Selected Personality Factors and Supervisory Effectiveness." Ph.D. dissertation, Purdue University, 1962.

Kerlinger, Fred. *Foundations of Behavioral Research.* New York: Holt, Rinehart & Winston, 1964.

Lesikar, Raymond. *Business Communication: Theory and Application.* Rev. ed. Homewood, Ill.: Richard D. Irwin, 1972.

Lesniak, R., M. Yates, G. Goldhaber, and W. Richards. *"NETPLOT:* An original computer program for interpreting NEGOPY." Presented to the International Communication Association, Berlin, Germany, 1977.

Level, Dale. "A Case Study of Internal and External Communications Practices in an Urban Bank." Ph.D. dissertation, Purdue University, 1959.

Lull, P. E., F. Funk, and D. Piersol. "Business and Industrial Communication from the Viewpoint of the Corporation President." Manuscript, Purdue University, 1954.

Menning, J. H., and C. W. Wilkinson. *Communicating through Letters and Reports.* Homewood, Ill.: Richard D. Irwin, 1972.

Minter, Robert. "A Comparative Analysis of Managerial Communication in Two Divisions of a Large Manufacturing Company." Ph.D. dissertation, Purdue University, 1969.

Moser, C. A. *Survey Methods in Social Investigation.* London: Heinemann Educational Books, Ltd., 1966.

Newcombe, Judson F. "Inherent Problems in Utilizing the Survey Method in Descriptive Research: Interpretation and Utilization of Results." Paper presented at a meeting of the Speech Communication Association, San Francisco, 1971.

Pace, Wayne R. "An Analysis of Selected Oral Communication Attributes of Direct-Selling Representatives as Related to Their Sales Effectiveness." Ph.D. dissertation, Purdue University, 1960.

Parten, Mildred B. *Surveys, Polls, Samples.* New York: Harper & Row, 1950.

Piersol, Darrell. "A Case Study of Oral Communication Practices in a Midwestern Corporation." Ph.D. dissertation, Purdue University, 1955.

Purdom, Paul. "Organization Decentralization in a Government Executive Agency as Measured by Communications: A Study of the Community Health Services of the Philadelphia Department of Public Health." Ph.D. dissertation, University of Pennsylvania, 1963.

Pyron, Charles. "The Construction and Validation of a Forced-Choice Scale of Measuring Oral Communication Attitudes of Industrial Foremen." Ph.D. dissertation, Purdue University, 1964.

Redding, Charles W. "Research Setting: Field Studies." In *Methods of Research in Communication,* edited by Phillip Emmert and William Brooks. New York: Houghton Mifflin Co., 1970.

Richards, William. *A Manual for Network Analysis: Using the NEGOPY Network Analysis Program.* Palo Alto, Calif.: Institute for Communication Research, Stanford University, 1975.

Rudolph, Evan. "An Evaluation of ECCO Analysis as a Communication Audit Methodology." Unpublished manuscript delivered at the International Communication Association Convention, Atlanta, April 1972.

Sanborn, George. "An Analytical Study of Oral Communication Practices in a Nationwide Retail Sales Organization." Ph.D. dissertation, Purdue University, 1961.

Thayer, Lee. "Communication and Organization Theory." In *Human Communication Theory.* Edited by F. Dance. New York: Holt, Rinehart and Winston, 1967, 70–115.

Timm, P., and R. Barker. "Communication Auditing in Organizations: Where Do We Stand?" Paper presented at ICA Convention, Portland, 1976.

Tompkins, Phillip. "An Analysis of Communication between Headquarters and Selected Units of a National Labor Union." Ph.D. dissertation, Purdue University, 1962.

Turabian, Kate. *A Manual for Writers of Term Papers, Theses, and Dissertations.* 4th ed. Chicago: University of Chicago Press, 1976.

Wilcox, Roger. "Characteristics and Organizations of the Oral Technical Report." *General Motors Engineering Journal* 6 (1959):8–12.

Zima, Joseph. "The Counseling-Communication of Supervisors in a Large Manufacturing Company." Ph.D. dissertation, Purdue University, 1968.

11

IMPLEMENTING ORGANIZATIONAL COMMUNICATION CHANGE

In chapters 9 and 10, we discussed planning and implementation of organizational communication diagnosis intended to give an organization valid information about the status of its communication system. At this point, it becomes the responsibility of the organization and its leaders to take steps to reinforce, strengthen, or change its communication system, consistent with the findings of the diagnosis. Consultants can advise. Advisers can raise questions. However, only the organization itself can take responsibility for its future.

One frequently made recommendation that evolves from communication diagnosis is that the organization provide training for certain individuals. The thinking goes like this. Communication is a human phenomenon, and if there are communication problems, they are people problems: people can be trained. I do not necessarily disagree with this thinking; I only caution that training is not the *only* answer. For example, if senior management does not wish to disclose certain facts about its operation, no amount of supervisor training is going to "open up the system." If the intercommunication system does not work, training middle-line managers will not solve the problem. If morale is low because of the low credibility of top management, personnel training will not create the needed trust. If the organization needs to be restructured because job duties overlap or some workers duplicate the work of others, training the personnel director will not be a sufficient solution.

Training is an appropriate solution when certain communicative skills need improvement, such as listening, providing feedback, organizing, making decisions, solving problems, brainstorming, and resolving conflicts. The behavior involved in making decisions, for example, can be identified, described, demonstrated, practiced, reinforced, observed, and evaluated. Since training can affect so many communicative behaviors, this chapter is devoted to clarifying the methods and techniques of successful communication training.

"We've got to save money—cut the training budget!" How often has the president of an organization uttered these words? It seems that whenever an organization suffers financially, training is among the first areas to be cut back. Given the orientation expressed in chapter 3 about the importance of the human resources within an organization, such logic seems to represent the false economy. Bass and Vaughan have supported this position:

> Training should be viewed as an investment in the company's most valuable resource—people. Yet, too often, the tendency has been to consider it an expense to avoid wherever possible. . . . Technical knowledge requires constant updating, and as new techniques appear, retraining becomes a vital necessity.

Sussman and his colleagues conducted a study of the nature and extent of communication training among members of Pittsburgh's chapter of the American Society of Training and Development (ASTD). Among his conclusions were the following:

1. Training personnel feel that communication training is *very* important, more so today than in the past.
2. Although training personnel feel that communication training is *very* important to an organization, an average of only 35 percent of the members of the organization receive such training.
3. Most people who receive communication training occupy line and staff positions.
4. Listening and writing are perceived as the most important communication skills.
5. The major goals of communication training are facilitation of the exchange of information and increased productivity. Facilitation of human relations and reduction of interpersonal and intergroup conflict are secondary goals.
6. Most respondents feel that the major barriers in implementing communication training programs are upper management's lack of recognition of communication problems or a lack of action directed toward such problems when they are recognized.
7. Almost all respondents (91 percent) feel that communication ability is a skill that can be learned. Only 4 percent feel that communication ability is best developed by years of experience on the job.

Too often, companies purchase training programs without regard for both current and future needs of the organization. As this happens, it is no wonder that an organization may view training as a low priority item. It is our position in this chapter that training, especially communication training, fulfills an important need within an organization and that the need can be assessed *prior* to development and/or purchase of a training program and the results can be evaluated *after* such a program is administered. Our specific objectives in this chapter follow:

1. To define training and relate its functions to various consulting models
2. To describe the following training factors:
   a. both a general training model (GTM) related to other instructional models and a communication training model (CTM)
   b. ways of assessing the behavioral capabilities of individuals as well as organizational training needs
   c. key communication training techniques, with examples and resources for each technique
   d. methods and principles of evaluating the success or failure of a communication training program and its impact upon all components of the CTM.
3. To define and state the criteria for writing behavioral objectives for a training program
4. To list examples of communication training informational objectives
5. To outline a plan for a communication training program in transactional analysis

Training can be defined as any job-related instructional program designed to improve knowledge, skills, and/or attitudes of organizational members. Naturally, communication training is limited to those instructional programs designed to improve a participant's communicative behavior, knowledge, and attitudes. Training by an outside consultant can be

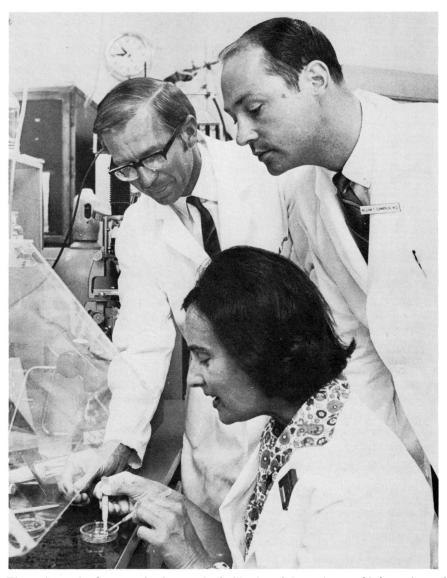

The major goals of communication are the facilitation of the exchange of information and increased productivity.

administered within the framework of any of the three popularly used consulting models, as discussed in chapter 9. They are the purchase model, in which an organization buys a particular training program from a consultant; the doctor-patient model, in which the consultant diagnoses the ailments of the organization, prescribes a particular training program, and administers it; and the process consultation model, in which the consultant and members of the organization together diagnose and remedy an organization's ills. Since training involves instructional methodologies quite similar to those used in other teaching settings (school,

Figure 11.1   The general training model (GTM).

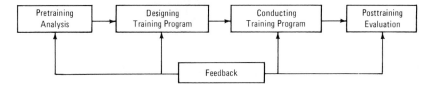

college, university), we will borrow heavily from previously developed theories of teaching behavior for the general training model (GTM) and the communication training model (CTM).

General Training Model (GTM)

One of the earliest general models of teaching behavior was developed by Glaser who listed four components: instructional objectives, entering behavior, instructional procedures, and performance assessment. A similar model was developed by DeCecco, who added a feedback loop to Glaser's basic model. Kibler, Barker, and Miles presented their general model of instruction (GMI), which also included four components (plus feedback): instructional objectives, preassessment, instructional procedures, and evaluation. In all of these models, instructional objectives (or some variant of this concept) were listed first, despite DeCecco's comment that "although the model gives priority to the selection of instructional objectives over the assessment of entering behavior, in practice these two components must interact." Brooks and Friedrich adapted most of these models to the teaching of speech communication and proposed a model that first lists *capabilities* (preassessment; entering behavior), followed by instructional *objectives,* instructional *strategies, evaluation,* and *feedback* (COSEF). It is the COSEF model that we use in our general training model (GTM). Figure 11.1 presents the GTM.

   Pretraining analysis refers to the assessment of an organization's current status and needs in relation to change and development. The scope of an assessment varies. It can include a total systems analysis, or such minor preassessment as examination of an organization's job descriptions (from which role behaviors are inferred). In a typical consulting-training situation in an organization, pretraining analysis normally precedes all other components in the GTM. The second component, designing a training program, incorporates the instructional objectives of the training program. Here is where we apply the results of organizational analysis in order to build improvement into the design. The third component, conducting a training program, refers to the actual administration of the program, including all instructional procedures and techniques. Post-training evaluation consists of both short-term and long-range assessment of the degree to which the training objectives were met. The last component, feedback, indicates how the evaluation data affect the other four components.

Figure 11.2 The communication training model (CTM).

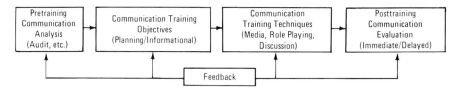

Communication Training Model (CTM)

We will not apply the GTM to communication training. Figure 11.2 presents the communication training model (CTM) to which we refer in the remainder of this chapter.

In the CTM, pretraining communication analysis can be a communication audit (described in detail in chapter 10) or any other subjective or objective measurement procedure. Obviously, the more valid and reliable the organization's communication system, the more accurately will the training program reflect current and future needs of the system. *We recommend that an organization conduct the most scrupulous assessment within its means in order to avoid wasting future resources on unneeded or unmet training needs.* The second component in the CTM, communication training objectives, refers to both the planning and informational objectives of the program. This component in the model dictates the techniques to be used in administering the program and also in measuring its effectiveness. Communication training techniques, the third component, include all instructional procedures (lecture, discussion, media, role playing) used to accomplish the objectives of the program. Posttraining communication evaluation (either immediate or delayed), the fourth component, utilizes attitude measuring instruments; teacher-made tests to measure cognitive achievement; observation systems employing peer, subordinate, and supervisory input; and so forth. Feedback, the fifth component, influences all four components in the CTM. According to Nadler (1986) it is necessary to have feedback after each step in a training model, such as the CTM, so that the designer may receive evaluation to do the following:

1. Determine if the design, up to this point, meets the needs and criteria established by earlier steps in the model.
2. Identify the individuals who should be involved in the process, and receive specific feedback from them.
3. Modify the design, if necessary, based on the feedback.
4. Obtain necessary approval from those concerned to proceed with the next event in the model.

The rest of this chapter deals with the components of the CTM, defining each one, providing examples in existing training programs, and listing appropriate resource information.

Pretraining Communication Analysis

Before members of an organization undergo training, it is essential that the following questions be answered: *Who* needs training? *What* kind of training do they need? Analysis of the current communication behavior, skills, and attitudes throughout the organization is one method of finding answers to these questions. In chapter 10, we proposed the communication audit as a procedure for accomplishing this. For example, in one organization where I conducted a communication audit, the results of the audit indicated that cultural variables were causing a major communication problem in middle management. The members in two departments consistently bypassed each other because the managers did not understand that cultural variables can influence the meaning of words. A member of one department attributed his negative feelings toward a member of the other department to the fact that the member continually pointed a sharp object at him. To him this was a threatening form of nonverbal behavior, and it inhibited effective verbal communication between the two. Based on the results of this audit, I devised a one-week session that emphasized intercultural communication variables.

Not all organizations have the resources to conduct a systemwide communication audit. Sometimes only one or two measurement techniques are employed prior to a training decision. I once conducted a training session for an organization after it had surveyed (via written questionnaire) its employees in three departments on their communication attitudes and feelings toward management. Results of the survey indicated that very few of the employees in the three departments believed that their bosses "really listened to us." Consequently, a training program was devised to emphasize the importance of and the skills required for effective listening on the job. In another organization, the manager who hired me had conducted preliminary interviews with her staff and decided to train several key employees in "communication." Since I needed more information about the specific needs of the organization, I randomly selected eight of the twenty-nine employees for in-depth interviews. Furthermore, I read their official job descriptions and spent fifteen hours observing them as they conducted their daily jobs. From this data I concluded that their specific needs centered around interviewing techniques, especially formation of questions. (They spent more than 80 percent of their working time conducting information-giving and information-getting interviews.)

Sometimes an organization, following the purchase model of consulting, believes that it has correctly diagnosed its need and simply wants a training program for a specialized area. If I believe I can help, based upon the information provided me, I agree to this arrangement. For example, a government agency hired me to conduct a one-day workshop on the fundamentals of transactional analysis (TA). The training director told me that the trainees simply "needed help in human relations and wanted to learn about transactional analysis." Since distance was a problem, I was unable to visit the organization before the workshop and had to rely primarily upon letters and the telephone. I requested information about whom I was to train (job descriptions, role relationships) and then applied many of the principles of transactional analysis to their particular organizational needs. In another organization where similar circumstances prevented me from first-hand observation or a more total organizational analysis, I relied upon written documents to help me prepare videotapes that presented case material related to the organization's particular needs. Although this procedure worked under those circumstances, it is not recommended as a matter of course.

The foregoing examples should illustrate that preassessment of an organization's communication training needs is not always a simple matter of conducting a study, examining the results, and designing a training program to cure the weaknesses. Usually, the trainer must rely upon whatever resources the organization has for the purpose of preassessment. Bass and Vaughan have suggested several sources of data to assist in assessment of training needs: observations, management requests, interviews, group conferences, comparative studies, questionnaire surveys, tests of job knowledge, supervisors' reports on performance, personnel records, business and production reports, review of literature concerning the job, and the evaluator actually performing the job.

Once a preassessment of communication training needs is made, the needs must be translated into specific instructional objectives.

Communication Training Objectives

Communication training objectives refer to the desired behavior of a trainee after undergoing training. Training objectives allow the trainer to predict exactly what the trainees will be able *to do* after participating in a training program. The focus of communication training objectives, like all behavioral objectives, is on the after-training behavior of the trainee. Objectives are important to the trainer, because they greatly facilitate the planning of instruction (selecting the best training technique), the designing of appropriate evaluation procedures, and the motivating and directing of trainees as they participate in the program.

Much empirical support exists for establishing behavioral objectives. In a classic study, Mager and McCann (1961) compared achievement and training time of three groups of students. One group selected and arranged its own course content; the second group used material selected and organized by the instructor; the third group was given a list of behavioral objectives, and members were allowed to instruct themselves, using any technique they chose. Training time for the third group was 65 percent less than for the other two groups, and there was no loss in achievement. Other researchers also support the use of behavioral objectives in instructional situations.

Criteria for Writing Communication Training Objectives

Many times, an organization requests a training program in order to fill a broad organizational goal, for example, to improve upward communication, to improve listening behavior of managers, to increase manager sensitivity, or to improve interpersonal relations between managers and their subordinates. It is apparent that these goals can be met in a number of different ways. The trainer who is sincerely interested in helping an organization reach its goals should translate broad general goals into specific instructional objectives. For example, if management states, "We need to improve our interpersonal communication," the trainer should ask such questions as, What behaviors would illustrate an improvement in "interpersonal communication"? What specifically will trainees be able to do after their interpersonal communication has been improved?

Mager (1962) identified three criteria necessary for specifying behavioral objectives: final observable behavior of the trainee, important conditions governing accomplishment, and standard of acceptable performance (success). Observable behavior refers to what the trainee will have to do to demonstrate accomplishment of the objective. Mager listed several objective verbs to use in constructing objectives: *write, recite, identify, differentiate, solve, construct, list, compare, contrast,* and *orally describe.* Trainees enrolled in a training program designed to improve interpersonal communication within their department can be asked to do the following. First, identify three instances where they perceived a breakdown in communication. Second, describe the three instances, listing the persons involved, when the instances occurred, where the instances occurred, and the task involved. Third, compare and contrast the three instances using the three principles; list causes of the breakdown; and suggest orally ways of solving the problems. The process may include role playing (acting out) the instances or preparing videotapes that illustrate the instances. Unfortunately, many organizations and trainers prefer to use more implicitly stated objectives, described by such subjective verbs as *know, understand, appreciate, enjoy, believe, like, have faith in,* and *really understand.* Such words present many problems in evaluation and design of training programs, because these words are open to different interpretations.

The second necessary behavioral objective criterion is to list the *important conditions* governing the objectives, for example, time limit, setting, logistics, and materials. Such conditions might be stated as follows: "Given a list of three situations, . . . "; "Using the videotape equipment in this room, . . . "; "Before the training audience, . . . "; "Given the following references, . . . "; "Given three hours, . . . " These are all conditions under which the trainee must demonstrate that the objective(s) have been achieved.

In addition to stating the desired end behavior and the conditions for producing it, a behavioral objective should contain some standard of acceptable performance. The trainee must know at what level the objective is or is not met. This is frequently stated in terms of time limits or percentages or frequencies of correct responses. For example, a trainee may be given thirty minutes to correctly identify the cause of a communication breakdown in a given situation; a test of understanding may specify 80 percent correct to pass; a manager may be given three days to orient employees to new policies. Without such explicit criteria of success, it is impossible to measure the extent to which the instructional objectives are achieved.

Training Objectives

Some writers claim that not all three of the aforementioned principles are necessary to write behavioral objectives. Kibler, Barker, and Miles have suggested that, for the purpose of communicating the instructional objectives to others (i.e., students, trainees, managers), it may not be necessary to specify the important conditions and the criteria of success. They call these objectives *informational objectives* and advise that they be constructed *after* the instructor has devised objectives in accordance with all three criteria (called *planning objectives*). Planning objectives serve the purposes just outlined for behavioral objectives (planning, evaluating, and motivating), while informational objectives are for the purpose of communicating. An example of a planning objective is this:

> Given three videotaped situations (derived from local department information), in 30 minutes the trainee will be able to identify three sources of communication breakdown, correctly describe the main cause(s) of the breakdown, and suggest ways to eliminate each breakdown.

In this example, the observable behavior is "to identify sources of communication breakdown," "describe the cause(s)," and "suggest ways to eliminate the breakdown." The conditions surrounding the accomplishment of the objectives are "given videotaped situations" and "derived from local department information." The criteria for success are "in 30 minutes," "three sources," "correctly," and "ways."

When these planning objectives are stated for informational purposes, the conditions and the criteria for success are left out:

> The trainee will be able to identify sources of communication breakdowns, describe the main cause(s) of the breakdowns, and suggest ways to eliminate the breakdowns.

Throughout this textbook, each chapter has begun with a statement of objectives. Since only observable behavior of readers is stated, the objectives are informational. This is the type of objective that most often appears in textbooks, syllabuses, and training outlines. Several examples of informational objectives which I have used in past training programs are as follows:

1. Define the goal of transactional analysis.
2. Define and recognize the three ego states.
3. Define and recognize the three types of transactions.
4. Identify the six ways people spend their time.
5. Identify and describe common games people play.
6. Recognize and describe ways to stop game playing.
7. Describe the relationship between perception and downward communication of information.
8. Identify ways to stop rumors.
9. Compare and contrast the classical model of organization with the general system model.
10. Compare and contrast the factors listed by Herzberg as hygienic with those listed as motivators.
11. Complete the transactional analysis test for recall and attain a score of 90 percent correct.
12. Identify and describe nonverbal indicators of status in an organization.
13. Compare and contrast the purposes and media of upward, downward, and horizontal communication in an organization.
14. List and describe the common media used in an organization for written communication.
15. Identify the components of an effective feedback system.
16. List the steps involved in designing a communication audit.
17. Complete the managerial grid test and locate your scores on a grid.
18. Compare and contrast individual decision making with group decision making.
19. Differentiate ways of expressing feelings verbally from expressing feelings nonverbally.
20. Describe ways of resolving interpersonal and group conflicts within an organization.
21. Describe the process of communication, listing key components and sources of overload.
22. List several common stereotypes that contribute to intercultural breakdowns in communication.
23. Identify different cultural nonverbal messages.

Now that instructional objectives for communication training programs have been discussed, let us list and describe key communication training techniques used to implement these objectives.

Communication Training Techniques

Communication training techniques are the instructional procedures or approaches the trainer uses to accomplish the behavioral objectives of a program. The key question asked by the trainer at this point in the CTM is, "*How* shall I administer a training program to meet the organization's needs?" Unfortunately, many trainers answer in the words of McLuhan, "The medium is the message," and concentrate on the technique as an end in itself. Bass and Vaughan (1966) commented on this approach to training:

> Commonly employed industrial-training techniques mix age-old practices with many twentieth-century innovations. Medieval-style lectures, after dominating three-quarters of a sales meeting, may be followed by a trio of sales trainees acting out roles in which two of them carry on negotiations with a customer while the third member watches. Unfortunately, much of the training in these programs is of a faddish nature; often they are much more concerned with training *methods* than with training *needs*. Fascination with a particular technique or the training staff's personal experiences and limitations may determine the nature of the program more often than a consideration of optimum learning circumstances.

They recommend that training techniques conform to the following criteria:

1. Provide for the learner's active participation.
2. Provide the trainee with knowledge of results about his or her attempts to improve.
3. Promote by means of good organization a meaningful integration of learning experiences that the trainee can transfer from training to the job.
4. Provide some means for the trainee to be reinforced for appropriate behavior.
5. Provide for practice and repetition when needed.
6. Motivate the trainee to improve his or her own performance.
7. Assist the trainee in his or her willingness to change.

What Bass and Vaughan have recommended can be summarized as follows: *Select instructional techniques that are appropriate in creating optimum learning conditions for meeting the objectives of the training program.* Several techniques used in communication training programs are discussed next, and examples and resources are listed for each technique.

Lecture

Probably no training technique is used and misused more than the lecture, a live oral presentation made with the intention to transmit information to trainees. Probably the reason it is used a great deal is that it is an economical means of communication. Large numbers of people can receive the same information at one time. However, as we learned in chapter 4, communication is a dynamic process involving the interaction of sender and receiver. The lecture is one-way communication (except during the question-answer period, if any) that in no way guarantees the successful reception and understanding of information. A training program centering around McGregor's Theory X-Theory Y model is an example of the lecture technique. The trainer begins the program with a one-hour lecture on the basic assumptions of McGregor's theory, pausing during the last fifteen minutes for questions from the audience (who have been busy during the lecture taking notes).

Bass and Vaughan have presented an excellent critique of the lecture:

> The lecture generally consists of a one-way communication: The instructor presents information to the group of passive listeners. Thus, little or no opportunity exists to clarify meanings, to check on whether trainees really understand the lecture material, or to handle the wide diversity of ability, attitude, and interest that may prevail among the trainees. Also, there is little or no opportunity for practice, reinforcement, knowledge of results, or overlearning.
>
> Ideally, the competent lecturer should make the material meaningful and intrinsically motivating to his listeners. However, whether most lecturers achieve this goal is a moot question.
>
> The above limitations, in turn, impose further limitations on the lecture's actual content. A skillful lecture may be fairly successful in transmitting conceptual knowledge to a group of trainees who are ready to receive it; however, all the evidence available indicates that the nature of the lecture situation makes it of minimal value in promoting attitudinal or behavioral change.

It would also appear that paperback books and copy machines are relatively inexpensive means of providing trainees with whatever information the lecturer would present live. Then, with the free time, the group can interact and discuss the readings. Another substitute for the live lecture is to use videocassette information recorded in advance, speeding up the rate of transmission by means of the compressed speech technique and, thus, taking less time than a live lecture. The compressed speech technique is discussed next.

Lecture Replacement and Review.   The compressed speech technique can be used as a substitute for a live lecture. Information put on cassettes and compressed can be played back by trainees at their convenience (even at home). If the training program includes lectures, the compressed tapes can serve as a quick review of the lectures, thus allowing trainees the opportunity to reexamine information they may have missed the first time around. Since compressed speech allows information to be presented in smaller units of time (up to 50 percent less time), the trainee is free for other study and review, and the instructor is free to incorporate discussion, demonstration, and other techniques which encourage trainee-instructor interaction.

Reading Improvement Programs.   Many industrial training programs are marketed to improve reading skills, rates, and comprehension. Research has already demonstrated that compressed speech can serve as a means of boosting the reading rate of slow readers. The trainee listens to the information over earphones while reading the same material; by gradually incrementing the aural presentation, the compressed speech serves as a pacer for increasing the reading rate. This same principle can be applied by using slides synchronized with the compressed tapes. This method is especially useful for blind trainees whose reading is limited to cumbersome braille (80 words per minute) and standard talking books (150 to 175 words per minute).

Listening Improvement Programs.   In chapter 6, the importance of listening in the communication process was considered. Nichols has stated that managers spend 40 percent of their time on the job listening at only 25 percent efficiency. Furthermore, good listening (as pointed out in chapter 6) is fundamental to the success of upwardly directed communication systems. It has been established that we think four times faster than we speak; this difference between thought speed and speaking speed creates what Fessenden labeled "spare time." Such spare time is the major cause of bad listening habits (the mind wanders when someone is talking) and why we can't pay attention to any one stimulus for a long period of time. If listeners were thoroughly trained and constantly exposed to compressed speech, the amount of spare time, and the accompanying probability of attention loss, would be reduced. Compressed speech training programs which enable marked improvement in overall listening ability have been devised.

Hardware Uses. Compressed speech is especially useful when different kinds of equipment—teaching machines, automated message systems, dictaphone machines, radio systems—are used in a training program. When a teaching machine is used in conjunction with programmed instruction, compressing the audiotapes will reduce both the cost and time of the program. Many large organizations have automatic message systems that are accessed by dial telephones. At any time of the day, an employee can dial a particular number and get the company "news" of the day. This type of system is a great asset in quieting the grapevine. Compressed speech is applicable here because it allows the company either to put more information on the system or to save time in the transmission of tapes. When a dictaphone belt is compressed, a secretary can receive more information from the boss within a given time. New methods of typing allow secretaries to greatly increase their typing speed. If a compressed speech device instead of an ordinary dictaphone record is used, secretaries can become even more efficient. Some organizations use radio or loudspeaker systems to transmit important announcements, speeches, and reports. This information can be edited and compressed for the employees with great savings of time. Satellite communication systems will make possible compression of telephone calls, thus allowing more calls to be transmitted. In the not too distant future, compressed videocassettes will be available for use in training programs. Actually, it is or will soon be possible to compress all electronically transmitted information. Perhaps the time saved by compressing information will give us more time to enjoy the aesthetic value of the information.

Media Techniques

Several other techniques in vogue today in training programs are film, videotape, audiotape, slides, telelecture, projectors, chalkboard and easel, and TelePrompTer.

Film. Sixteen-millimeter films have been used in training programs for several years. Films that relate directly to a concept covered in the program, that are preceded by a short discussion and followed by reactions, and that do not cover too much material are effective training aids. Many films are available free or for minimal rental charges from film centers around the country. Whenever possible, the instructor should preview the film before showing it.

Videotape. Videotape techniques are particularly useful in communication training workshops where attention is focused on individual improvement of communication skills. Decision-making situations can be videotaped and played back to allow individuals to "see themselves as others see them." Nonverbal behavior can be focused on if the volume is turned down during playback. Role-played scenes can be videotaped either live or in advance (with access to studio and actors) and are particularly useful for analyzing communication breakdown (as described earlier under behavioral objectives). Because relatively inexpensive systems are available, many organizations use a video system throughout the organization for sending memos and other messages. Videotape is particularly helpful in public-speaking training. Today, videodiscs are fast becoming as popular as videotape, primarily because more information can be stored on them.

Audiotape. Most of the uses of compressed speech just discussed relate to audiotape in training programs. In other uses of audiotape, prerecorded sounds can be replayed to illustrate perceptual differences among employees listening to sounds of the environment. Training exercises can be audiotaped and replayed by trainees at home. Speeches used in public-speaking training can be audiotaped and replayed for analysis and discussion. Inexpensive cassette tapes and very small tape recorders make this training aid very practical.

Slides. Used alone or with an audiotape accompaniment, 35mm slides are an asset in discussing nonverbal communication and other similar topics. When this technique is used, a photographer is needed, film and developing services must be purchased, a script for the slides must be developed, and much overall planning is needed. The end product, which might be a ten-minute presentation, may well be worth the time and money involved.

Telelecture. The telelecture is a conference-call system that allows a group of trainees to listen to one or more speakers from various places in the country. The guest speaker or resource person phones the training session at a prescribed time. The incoming call is amplified through a loudspeaker system to any number of listeners, who can respond individually and simultaneously via special microphones placed around the room. This technique is particularly inexpensive if the organization's telephone system has wide area telephone service (WATS line), which allows unlimited calls for a flat monthly rate. Today, with the marriage of telelecture and television, we now see much use of teleconference techniques, which, as stated in chapter 4, may not always be the best method to use for disseminating information.

Projectors. Included in this category are such familiar machines as the *overhead projector,* which projects special transparencies on a screen without requiring a darkened room (an asset in rooms without special curtains); the *opaque projector,* which projects pictures, books, charts, diagrams, and maps but needs a darkened room; the filmstrip projector, which shows a series of 35mm pictures; and the 8mm (or super 8mm) projector, which shows homemade movies that can be inexpensively tailor-made for training programs. Of course, all of these projectors must either be rented or purchased, and the user must know in advance how to operate the machine and have the presentation materials in appropriate form.

Chalkboard and Easel. There is hardly an instructor unfamiliar with the chalkboard, on which instructors using chalk can reproduce instantly any information they wish. It is especially useful during lectures and discussions to summarize comments, list ideas, and out-

Figure 11.3 A matrix from the classic game Prisoner's Dilemma. (Source: J. W. Pfeiffer and J. E. Jones, 1970. Used by permission of University Associates Press.)

Choice	Score
AC	Both win 3 points
CB	Person one wins 6 points Person two loses 6 points
DA	Person one loses 6 points Person two wins 6 points
DB	Both lose 3 points

Person One

	A	B
Person Two — C	+3 / +3	+6 / −6
Person Two — D	−6 / +6	−3 / −3

line results. Naturally, it is best when instructors write on the chalkboard without turning their backs and without squeaking the chalk. An easel is used in the same manner and for the same purpose, except that the writing is with wax pencil and pages must be flipped.

TelePrompTer. A TelePrompTer is a machine on which a speech typed in large type is placed on a movable disk and by means of mirrors is reflected on a one-way screen visible only to speakers as they face an audience. It is an excellent device for helping speakers learn the importance of maintaining eye contact with an audience. A speaker can also take the machine on speaking engagements to use in delivering a speech, since a manual control permits a speaker to regulate the rate of speaking. The TelePrompTer is best used in a formal situation with a large audience in which the speaker is separated by some distance from the audience. The device is used regularly in television. Its only major drawback is expense— well over $6,000. The special typewriter that produces the large type accounts for much of the cost.

Overall, it is to the advantage of the trainers to use whatever media techniques are available, *provided they support a training objective.* According to Felsenthal, the primary strengths of media techniques (especially films) are to stimulate discussion, clarify abstract concepts, and illustrate specific points. The chief disadvantages appear to be that availability is uncertain, cost is sometimes prohibitive, preparation is time-consuming, and misuse and overuse are widespread.

Games and Structured Experiences

A game is a competitive experience played by participants in an environment simulating that of the organization. Players sometimes, but not always, use computers. A classic game is Prisoner's Dilemma, the goals of which are to illustrate trust and the effects of betrayal of trust to contrast the effects of interpersonal competition and interpersonal collaboration. Teams of two people select one of two possible choices on a matrix (see figure 11.3), each member acting alone and not communicating with the other. After each member has made a selection, both members simultaneously pass their written choices over to the other person and then tally the score for the move. The score is determined by the two selections. The process is repeated for several moves, and then a brief period of oral face-to-face communication occurs, followed by additional moves. Final scores are tallied, and a winner is declared.

After playing the game, the groups are brought together for a discussion about the effects of high and low trust on interpersonal relations and on the merits of competition versus collaboration in organizational interactions. Players are encouraged to share their feelings and reactions about themselves and the other player, about each other's behavior during the game, and about whether trust was violated or built. Major conclusions resulting from this game are that trust is very often hard to build but very easy to destroy, and that inappropriate trust is just as dysfunctional as no trust at all.

Another example of a training game is the nonverbal communication game Body Talk (published by *Psychology Today*). It requires players to express their feelings nonverbally in accordance with whatever card they draw from a deck of cards marked with appropriate body parts and emotions. The object is to get rid of all your cards by correctly identifying the emotions acted out by other players and by accurately communicating your emotions to the other players. Common emotions depicted in this game are shyness, fear, frustration, anger, hope, joy, warmth, and love.

A *structured experience* is a collaborative experience-based learning situation in which learning goals are specified beforehand. Pfeiffer and Jones have discussed the structured experience:

> [It does not] imply that participants are being manipulated; it simply means that the intended learning is facilitated by a design . . . they are designed for the serious business of helping participants to learn about themselves, about how they relate to each other, about how groups operate, and about the human side of organization.

The most important aspect of the structured experience is the postexperience discussion and follow-up in which participants process what took place and relate it to their organizational experiences. This places a large responsibility on the trainer to be sure that all usable data generated from the experience gets processed by the group. Pfeiffer and Jones have suggested several ways of guiding this information-processing stage of the experience:

1. Have participants interview each other about what was learned.
2. Form subgroups (small reaction groups).
3. Have one group observe another group in a group-on-group design.
4. Use an empty-chair design to have people talk about what they learned.
5. Have reports from observers who used process observation sheets.
6. Establish panels (groups of observers) to interact after the structured experience in discussing their independent observations of the event.

A structured experience that relates to rumors (discussed in chapter 4) is the rumor clinic, which illustrates the distortions that occur as information is communicated from the original source through several individuals to a final destination. A message is read to the first of five or six individuals while the other participants remain out of hearing distance. That person repeats the message to another participant while the rest remain out of hearing distance—and so on, until each one has heard a message.

The audience hears everything and keeps notes on additions to, deletions from, and distortions in the original message. Figure 11.4 shows the type of tally sheet used by a group during this exercise. After the exercise is finished, the trainer leads a discussion on the applications and implications of the rumor clinic structured experience. This exercise can be audiotaped or videotaped to increase the accuracy of tracing the message through its many destinations. Besides discussing what happens to a rumor in the organization, the group can also discuss ways of stopping a rumor.

Figure 11.4 Observation form used in conducting a rumor clinic. (Source: J W. Pfeiffer and J. E. Jones, 1970. Reprinted by permission of University Associates Press.)

Rumor Clinic Observation Form

Sample Message:

"I cannot wait to report to the police what I saw in this accident. It is imperative that I get to the hospital as soon as possible."

"The semi truck, heading south, was turning right at the intersection when the sports car, heading north, attempted to turn left. When they saw that they were turning into the same lane, they both honked their horns but proceeded to turn without slowing down. In fact, the sports car seemed to be accelerating just before the crash."

Participant	*Additions*	*Deletions*	*Distortions*
1			
2			
3			
4			
5			
6			

Another kind of structured experience is based upon the classic work of Leavitt and Mueller on feedback. In this experience, one demonstrator tells a group of trainees how to draw a set of geometric figures. The group cannot ask questions of the demonstrator. Then, a second demonstrator performs a similar task with respect to different geometric figures, but this time the group can interrupt at any time and ask questions. Measures of time, accuracy, and predicted accuracy are taken on both experiences and compared afterward. Usually, this experience demonstrates that with feedback the project takes longer, but the increased actual and expected accuracy (morale) may offset the loss in time.

Case Study

In this technique of communication training, trainees are given a written document outlining specific organizational communication problems. Written cases can vary in length from one to fifty pages (or more), depending upon the complexity of the situation and the amount of resource materials provided for the case. Participants are usually given the case individually and allowed time to study and analyze it, to outline the key problems, and to suggest solutions. Then, the individuals are brought together to discuss their many solutions. Sometimes the best solution is based upon the input from one or two group members, not upon group consensus. In chapter 3, the following questions were suggested for the case study:

1. *What* is taking place in the case? What is the current situation?
2. What events led to this situation? What are the *underlying assumptions* of the communicators involved?
3. What *could have been done* to prevent some of the communication problems or at least diminish their consequences?
4. *What can be done now?*

Role Playing

In role playing, a *real* organizational experience or problem is selected, and the participants in the training program act out the various parts of the people involved in the situation. Only the situation is provided for the actors; therefore, dialogue is generated spontaneously during the experience. Persons can role-play themselves or anyone else they interact with during the course of the job. Thus, it is an excellent technique for gaining insight into one's own behavior and empathy with others in various organizational interpersonal encounters. The technique allows for participants to switch roles (role reversal)—especially useful in a conflict situation—to illustrate communication principles or to study real-life situations which evolve from a particular training group. Role playing can be combined with the case-study method by asking participants to act out persons involved in the case they are studying. The experience can be videotaped and played back for analysis, or role-playing situations can be videotaped in advance of the training session and analyzed later by the trainees. After the role playing is over, a certain amount of analysis usually follows, which can vary from almost no analysis to a complete, detailed description of all behaviors of all participants.

Some role-playing problems may arise because participants are afraid to act out a scene, think the activity is silly, overdramatize a scene and thus call attention to the method rather than to the purpose, or receive positive reinforcement for acting ability rather than for insightful analysis of the situation.

Most of these problems can be overcome by preparing tapes of situations in advance with trained role players as actors. I used this technique in preparing a set of videotapes for a training program on intercultural communication problems. In one tape the actors role-played a communication breakdown due to language problems. The showing of the tape was preceded by a discussion of the principles involved in the intercultural problem. I then asked the group to diagnose the taped situation and suggest causes of the problem and possible solutions. Next, we either live role-played the correct way of handling the communication interaction, or we played a videotape scene that suggested a solution to the problem. This technique limits the use of role playing to analysis of communication principles selected in advance of the training program. The trainer, of course, must be careful to select only those principles that relate directly to the objectives of the program.

I was once retained by a large chemical company to help improve the interpersonal skills of a key patent attorney in their organization. My training colleague, Paul Kowalewski, and I decided to rely primarily upon videotape and role playing as our major training interventions. We diagnosed that it would probably require considerable effort on the part of both the trainers and the trainee to confront behaviors that, while not necessarily effective for the trainee, had been practiced by him for over twenty years. Often, if a trainee can observe others and himself role-play situations, the trainee's recognition of behaviors that others perceive may be speeded up. Videotape helps provide accurate feedback, particularly to well-defended trainees who resist a trainer's personal comments. It is very important when using role playing and videotape that the trainer identify specific behaviors that the trainee can recognize and improve. Table 11.1 summarizes the specific nature of the feedback that we gave to our client in the previously mentioned case.

Any behavior can be modified if a person becomes aware of its existence. Use of videotape and practice with modeling of new behaviors will help in the training. Practice outside of training will help reinforce new behaviors.

Table 11.1   Sample Feedback after Role Playing

I. Poor Listening Behaviors
- A. Poor eye contact (avoids looking directly at other person's eyes).
- B. Interrupts other person, not allowing him or her to complete a sentence.
- C. Tends to smile or smirk when talking or listening rather than use neutral or supportive expression (effect may be condescension).
- D. Tends to talk too much in interview, not giving other person opportunity to talk.
- E. Tends to look at notes or documents, as though reading while other person is talking.
- F. Overall effect is to discount other person by not listening well.

II. Poor Questioning Behaviors
- A. Asks few questions; tends to lecture or dominate talk of interview.
- B. Tends to ask leading or loaded questions ("I don't think this makes a difference, does it?") rather than neutral questions ("Does this make a difference?").
- C. Avoids clarifying techniques; postpones clarifying either to show other person you understand OR to bring the interview to a close ("Let's think about this later" rather than, "What can we do now?").
- D. Tends to ask and answer his own questions rather than give other person opportunity to answer question ("Well, you seem to have found . . ." rather than "What did you find?" or "Did you find . . .?").
- E. Interview tends to ramble; needs to proceed in a well-organized manner; with an opening, transitions, summary, etc.
- F. Nonverbal behaviors tend to discount or be inconsistent with verbal behaviors when asking questions ("You said you had one other point" [with a smirk, which discounts other point to be made by other person]).

Programmed Instruction

Programmed instruction is self-instruction by trainees who work independently (sometimes in a small group). The information is presented in small units called frames, each frame requiring an immediate response and providing immediate feedback (answers). Frames are arranged in a sequence that will best meet the specific goals of the program and still allow trainees to work independently at their own pace. The following is a frame used in a transactional analysis program.

The Parent ego state is either critical or nurturing. The Child is fun loving or adapted. The Adult is like a computer and regulates the other two ego states. The three ego states are the ___ , _____ , and _____ .	Parent Adult Child

The answers shown on the right would remain hidden until after the trainee responds.

Bass and Vaughan summarized the advantages of programmed instruction as follows: speed of learning is increased; amount of information trainees retain is increased; control by management of the entire program is increased because it specifies the objectives of the program; cost estimates are more accurate; training is more consistent; and mass instruction calling for assembled groups of trainees is no longer necessary.

The main disadvantages appear to be these: much time and expense are needed to generate a program; information in most programs is limited to factual materials; and actual meaning can be obscured because of the fragmented presentation of information.

Discussion Techniques

Discussion techniques can be used in conjunction with all of the foregoing training techniques. Since a detailed presentation of the discussion technique is given in chapter 7, only some of its primary advantages in training are mentioned here. The major advantage the discussion has over the lecture is the opportunity for feedback and interaction among all trainees. If a group is too large, the trainer may then decide to divide it into smaller buzz groups whose purpose is to react to a structured experience, lecture, or film. Representatives from each buzz group report to the larger group. Leaders of discussion groups must be trained to facilitate interaction so no one member, including themselves, can lecture to or dominate the group.

Behavior Modeling Techniques

Behavior modeling is a training intervention that relies upon positive models of behavior being presented for coping with real, on-the-job applications. Byham and Robinson have identified several elements that describe most behavior modeling programs.

1. The subject matter is targeted to *real* needs of the group by identifying, before training, the difficult interactive situations faced by the trainees.
2. Small groups (usually six people) are trained at one time.
3. Only one difficult human interaction situation is learned at a time.
4. A step-by-step approach for handling each difficult interaction situation is provided.
5. A positive model using the step-by-step approach shows learners how each difficult situation can be handled.
6. Practice in handling the difficult situations is provided to the learner in the classroom.
7. Confidence is developed as trainees develop new skills they had not previously used in their difficult encounters.
8. A receptive and supportive on-the-job environment is built so that the trained person does, in fact, use the skills on the job.

Table 11.2 illustrates how Byham and Robinson have recommended using behavior modeling to improve work habits. Table 11.3 shows other situations which Byham and Robinson believe behavior modeling training techniques would be effective. Table 11.4 presents one of their typical training schedules. Table 11.5 shows a detailed module from a training program.

Table 11.2   Example of Interaction Modeling Critical Steps for Improving Work Habits

1. Describe in detail the poor work habit you have observed.

2. Indicate why it concerns you.

3. Ask for reasons and listen openly to the explanation.

4. Indicate that the situation must be changed and ask for ideas for solving the problem.

5. Discuss each idea and offer your help.

6. Agree on specific action to be taken and set a specific follow-up date.

Table 11.3   Commonly Used Interaction Modeling Modules

Orienting the new employee	Delegating responsibility
Improving employee performance	Setting performance goals
Improving work habits	Reviewing performance goals
Improving attendance	Motivating the average performer
Reducing tardiness	Teaching an employee a new job
Maintaining improved performance	Handling customer (client) complaints
Utilizing effective follow-up action	Handling emotional situations
Utilizing effective disciplinary action	Handling discrimination complaints
Handling employee complaints	Taking immediate corrective action
Overcoming resistance to change	Gaining acceptance as a new supervisor

Table 11.4   Typical Interaction Modeling Training Schedule

Performance Goals Program
(11 3-hour Sessions)

Day 1	Introductory module	45 min.
	Setting performance goals	1 hour 45 min.
	Setting performance goals/assignment	15 min.
	2 to 7 days intersession	
Day 2	Setting performance goals (continued)	1 hour 15 min.
	Reviewing performance goals	1 hour 35 min.
	Reviewing performance goals/assignment	10 min.
	2 to 7 days intersession	
Day 3	Reviewing performance goals (continued)	1 hour 15 min.
	Delegating responsibility	1 hour 35 min.
	Delegating responsibility/assignment	10 min.
	2 to 7 days intersession	
Day 4	Delegating responsibility (continued)	1 hour 15 min.
	Improving employee performance	1 hour 35 min.
	Review module/assignment	10 min.
	2 to 7 days intersession	
Day 5	Improving employee performance (continued)	1 hour 15 min.
	Review module	1 hour 45 min.
	2 to 7 days intersession	
Day 6	Review module (continued)	1 hour
	Utilizing effective follow-up action	1 hour 55 min.
	Utilizing effective follow-up action/assignment	05 min.
	2 to 7 days intersession	
Day 7	Utilizing effective follow-up action (continued)	1 hour 30 min.
	Maintaining improved performance	1 hour 25 min.
	Maintaining improved performance/assignment	05 min.
	2 to 7 days intersession	
Day 8	Maintaining improved performance (continued)	1 hour
	Motivating the average performer	1 hour 55 min.
	Review module/assignment	05 min.
	2 to 7 days intersession	
Day 9	Motivating the average performer (continued)	1 hour
	Review module	1 hour 50 min.
	Handling discrimination complaints/assignment	10 min.
	2 to 7 days intersession	
Day 10	Review module (continued)	40 min.
	Handling discrimination complaints	2 hour
	Diagnosis and application/assignment	05 min.
	2 to 7 days intersession	
Day 11	Handling discrimination complaints	45 min.
	Diagnosis and application	2 hours 15 min.

Table 11.5 A Typical Interaction Management Module: Allocation of Time

Administrator announces the interaction skill being considered, and the participants read an overview of the interaction skills .... 5 min.

Administrator describes critical steps in handling the interaction .... 7 min.

Administrator shows a motion-picture film or videotape of a supervisor effectively handling the interaction with an employee .... 8 min.

Administrator and participants discuss how the critical steps were handled in the film (or tape) and discuss on-the-job situations where similar situations occur and where the critical steps could be applied .... 5 min.

Three participants take turns in skill practice sessions by role-playing supervisors, with roles provided. Their behavior in handling interaction situations is observed by the other participants and the administrator using specially prepared observer guides. The use of positive reinforcement by the observers helps to build confidence and skill in the role-playing supervisors .... 50 min.

Participants write their own interaction situations based on job-related problems, using forms provided in the workbook .... 10 min.

Participants take turns in skill-practice session by role-playing the employee in the participant-written situations, while other participants role-play supervisors using the interaction skills. The skill practice sessions are observed and discussed .... 55 min.

Participants read a summary of the ideas covered. Using specially designed forms, they plan on-the-job applications of the interaction skills. The administrator hands out a "critical steps" card for participants to utilize on the job .... 10 min.

According to Robinson, the technique is one of the best-researched technologies in adult education (see Byham et al., Gaines and Salmon, and Kraut). It is a sound learning theory managers actually use on their jobs and organizations tend to keep on using after several years of experience. Its major drawback is cost: one instructor for a group of six people, and compared with other training interventions, the amount of classroom time is long (time is needed to identify, practice, and incorporate new behaviors). As with most training interventions, careful planning should precede implementation, and on-the-job reinforcement should follow training.

Communication Training Evaluation and Feedback

Evaluation should provide feedback about whether the training techniques were adequate, whether the objectives were met, and whether the trainer correctly diagnosed (via the communication audit, for example) the training needs of the organization. Unfortunately, few training programs incorporate evaluation systems that provide feedback at all of these levels. Most evaluation is limited to a brief attitude scale administered to trainees at the end of the program, which asks whether they felt the program was valuable, worthwhile, meaningful, and relevant. This philosophy seems quite inconsistent with an organization's willingness to expend great amounts of time and money on a training program to improve the behavior of individuals and the organization. It seems illogical not to be concerned with the measurement of the behavior to be modified and improved; yet many organizations today have this attitude.

Kelly and Baird (1984) have suggested four organizational "realities" that make it very difficult for trainers to evaluate their training.

1. Organizations may not want extensive quantitative or qualitative evaluation.
2. Extensive evaluational procedures cost organizations in terms of time and dollars.
3. Organizations often don't know what training is supposed to improve.
4. Extensive evaluation methods may be threatening to management.

After training is completed, the organization should be concerned with the following questions:

1. Were the trainees adequately prepared for the program? Were the training objectives compatible with organizational goals?
2. Were the trainees adequately motivated to learn the material in the program?
3. Were the training techniques valid and professionally administered?
4. Did the training techniques actually result in the objectives being met?
5. Were the trainees sufficiently trained so that their behavioral change will positively affect organizational goals?
6. Did the training results transfer to on-the-job activity?

Management should seek answers to all of these questions if it is to know whether its money and time might have been wasted. Odiorne has reported that most management training utilizes one of four measurement techniques to evaluate its training: (1) opinion survey, which economically and simply collects data on employee attitudes toward the organization, its members, and its goals; (2) objective measurement of performance, which measures productivity as a function of training; (3) staff evaluation, which appraises performance in job settings; and (4) overall appraisal of growth of all participants and their effect on the total organization. There are problems of validity and reliability in making such measurement. Kirkpatrick listed four evaluation steps which should be included in any evaluation system: reaction, learning, behavior, and results. I endorse Kirkpatrick's system as feasible for assessing the impact of communication training programs.

Reaction. Reaction indicates trainee attitude and feeling about the training program and its goals and procedures. Bass and Vaughan have suggested that reaction be assessed in accordance with the following: use a reaction form that assesses predetermined goals in an easily quantifiable manner; allow the trainees to remain anonymous, provide space for trainees to write in subjective comments not covered by rating scale items; and allow sufficient time for the trainees to complete the form. Figure 11.5 shows a reaction sheet I used in a transactional analysis workshop.

One of the major problems with reaction sheets as mechanisms for evaluation is that trainees may overestimate their knowledge, skills, or awareness when they complete a pretest instrument. Then, when they complete the posttest measure of training effectiveness, comparison of the pretest and posttest data may underestimate the effectiveness of the training program. This "response-shift bias" can be corrected by a new approach to self-report measurement called "pre-then-post testing." Basically, the trainee still completes the pre-test and posttest but, in addition, completes a "then" measure *after* training. The trainee is asked to reflect back to his or her level of performance or awareness prior to training and re-rate

---

Figure 11.5   A reaction instrument used in a transactional analysis workshop.

Please circle the number which corresponds to your feelings about this workshop on transactional analysis.

1. Was the information presented useful to you in your present job?

   Low   1   2   3   4   5   High

2. Did the course hold your interest?

   Low   1   2   3   4   5   High

3. Were the instructional techniques (films, discussions, exercises, etc.) adequate to meet the objectives of the program?

   Low   1   2   3   4   5   High

4. Was the instructor competent?

   Low   1   2   3   4   5   High

5. Did the workshop accomplish its objectives as stated by the instructor?

   Low   1   2   3   4   5   High

Figure 11.6   Instructions for administration of the "then" instrument.

This questionnaire gives you the chance to re-evaluate your skill level before the training began. Think back to the beginning of this program. Now that the training is over, how would you rate yourself as having been before?

You may *remember* how you rated yourself on these skills when you took the pre-test at the beginning. *Do not* simply tell us (from memory) how you *used* to see yourself. Rather, we want these ratings to be your current opinion of how you *should* have rated yourself (in light of your new understanding or awareness of yourself). There *may or may not* be any difference between your old pretest rating and this re-evaluated one. Don't worry about whether your re-evaluated ratings agree or disagree with your earlier ones.

Your results will not be seen by the ABC Corporation and your answers will be kept strictly confidential. So please answer as honestly as possible.

---

himself or herself. Mezoff has provided a typical set of instructions given to a trainee about to complete a "then" measure (see figure 11.6). Table 11.6 provides Mezoff's comparison of the standard pre-post training results with the proposed pre-then-post results. As the table shows, trainees tended to underestimate their learning experiences in the traditional pre-post method. Research by Howard and others has confirmed the superiority of this evaluation technique.

Learning.   Whether trainees comprehended the information presented in the training program can be assessed by objective tests that measure facts, principles, and concepts. In the transactional analysis workshop, I used a standardized multiple-choice test on the funda-

Table 11.6 Comparison of Pre-Post Results with Pre-Then-Post Results

Pre-Post Results (Scale from 0-to-10)

Item	Pretest	Posttest	Pre-Post % Increase
Listening skills	5.69	7.62	34.0*
Knowledge of self	7.00	7.84	12.0
Perceptiveness of others	6.31	7.31	16.0
Ability to interpret Nonverbal communication	5.92	7.15	21.0

Then-Post Results (Scale from 0-to-10)

Item	Pre	Then	Post	Then-Post % Increase
Listening skills	5.69	5.38	7.62	41.0*
Knowledge of self	7.00	5.62	7.84	40.0*
Perceptiveness of others	6.31	5.42	7.31	35.0*
Ability to interpret Nonverbal communication	5.92	4.69	7.15	52.0*

*Statistically significant at $p < .05$ level.

mental concepts of transactional analysis. Ideally, this test is administered both before and after training to allow examination of the difference in scores that could be attributed to training.

Behavior.   Actual changes in on-the-job behavior and transfer of learning from the training situation to the job setting can be measured by collecting performance appraisal data from peers, subordinates, superiors, and trainees themselves. Both immediate and long-range assessment of this variable are important. In one training situation, I interviewed several trainees and their peers, subordinates, and superiors both immediately (one week) after training and during three-, six-, and twelve-month periods following training.

Results.   Results are the organizational goals the training program was designed to improve or achieve. Measurements of production, turnover, absenteeism, grievances, and morale are usually collected for this variable. One extremely time-consuming and expensive way to measure results is to conduct a posttraining audit of the communication system. An overall estimate of results is whether the organization's communication policies are being implemented.

Whatever system of evaluation the communication trainer uses, we recommend that extensive evaluation be planned and carried out with the best available research designs. Otherwise, the organization may be signing a blank check for an untested improvement program.

Table 11.7 illustrates a comprehensive system I developed to evaluate the use of transactional analysis training by airlines. Notice how reaction, learning, behavior, and results are all assessed.

Table 11.7   A Plan for Evaluating a Training Program

I. Objectives

The goals of this project are to describe, analyze, and evolve a model of airline personnel and public communicative relationships and to assess the use of TA training as it facilitates effective and supportive interpersonal interaction during these relationships. Our overriding purpose is to answer the question: *Does TA training make a difference in the behavior of airline personnel?* Our specific objectives are to:

1. Develop an airlines personnel communicative needs profile (CNP) analyzing, describing, and evaluating communicative interaction between airlines personnel and select segments of the public. The primary output from the CNP will be a catalog of interaction situations and communicative behaviors engaged in by airlines personnel.
2. Analyze existing TA training programs and units to determine whether they are intended to change or modify the actual communicative behaviors identified in the CNP. The primary output from this objective will be an analysis of the extent to which TA training meets *actual* communication needs.
3. Determine the relationship between TA training and the following:
   a. changes in *information* about communicative behavior and their impact on human relationships
   b. changes in *behavior* of airline personnel when interacting with selected segments of the public
   c. changes in *sales,* for both initial and returning customers
   d. changes in *customer satisfaction and employee morale*

II. Method

The objectives of this project will be accomplished by airline personnel and communication and TA specialists in three phases: audit, analysis of existing training programs, and evaluation of impact of existing training programs.

A. Audit of Communicative Behavior

The first phase of the project will consist of assessing the communicative behavior occurring between airline personnel and the public in an effort to arrive at an airline personnel communication needs profile (CNP). The *first step* in the process of developing CNP will be to identify basic attitudinal sets that influence the communicative behavior of airline personnel. This will be done by administering selected attitudinal measures to a sample of the population. Semantic differential scales will be developed by the project staff, and published measures, relevant to the project goals, such as Haney's Uncritical Test or Coffman's Test, will be adopted and used.

The *second step* will be to inventory communication interaction situations and role relationships between airline personnel and members of the public. This inventory will serve as a checklist for later classification of specific communicative behaviors, and be accomplished by:

1. Interviewing a sample of airline personnel and the public
2. Observing airline personnel-public interactions
3. Securing self-reports recorded on tally sheets
4. Videotaping interaction situations

The *third step* will be to develop an analytical system for evaluating communicative interaction situations and role relations. Criteria and classification guidelines will be drawn from Berne's transactional analysis model.

The *fourth step* will be to identify dominant, highly significant airline personnel communicative behaviors reflected in the situations identified in the inventory developed in step two, above, by:

1. Interviews with a sample of airline personnel and the public
2. Field observations of airline personnel by trained process observers
3. Self-reports based on communicative behavior check sheets
4. Audio, video, and audiovideo recordings of airline personnel interaction with members of the public

Table 11.7   *Continued*

II. Method

The *fifth step* will be to analyze samples of specific communicative behavior using the criteria and analytical system developed during step three. The objective of the analysis will be to arrive at a catalog of communicative behaviors that facilitate and deter effective interpersonal interaction in airline personnel-public relationships. Comparisons, contrasts, relationships, and patterns within the recorded data will be identified. Senior members of the International Transactional Analysis Association will be used as third-part evaluators of recorded samples and process observer forms.

The *sixth step* will be to develop the communication needs profile (CNP) of airline personnel, based on the analysis of the interaction data. The CNP will result in a tabulation of verbal and nonverbal behaviors that relate to effective and ineffective communication in specific airline personnel-public interaction situations. The CNP will then be used to analyze and evaluate existing TA training programs used by the airline.

In addition to developing a CNP, the preceding set of procedures will also generate other useful materials, including:

1. Videotapes of field experiences to be used directly in training modules and from which simulated situations and role-played scenes can be developed.
2. Field-tested process observation instruments to be used in identifying communication behaviors of airline recruits and for evaluation during inservice progress reviews.
3. Pretraining and posttraining measurement tasks to be used in evaluating the training program. Before training, subjects can view samples of videotaped situations and be asked to identify observed communication behaviors in effective and ineffective interaction. After training, subjects can replicate the task on a different set of tapes to arrive at an improvement score (e.g., the number of correctly identified behaviors) which would indicate the degree to which an airline employee can describe, analyze, and evaluate desirable communicative behavior.

B. Analysis of Existing TA Training Programs

The second phase of the project will consist of analyzing the existing TA training programs and units to determine whether they meet the *actual* communication needs identified in the CNP. The four steps necessary to complete this phase are:

1. Examine outlines and written materials of existing TA training programs.
2. Participate in an existing TA training program(s).
3. Interview a sample of trainees.
4. Compare the behaviors *intended* for training with those identified in the CNP.

C. Evaluation of Impact of Existing Training Programs

The third phase of the project will consist of evaluating the TA training program by determining its relationship with actual behavior on the job as well as attitudinal, morale, and sales data from both the public and airline personnel.

To assess the *information gain* in communicative behavior, written examinations, recognition of concepts and behaviors in written and audiopictorial incidents, and analysis of simulated situations will be used. To assess the *behavior change* by airline personnel, observations of trainees exhibiting behaviors in simulated situations and in field situations and self-reports of trainees interacting on the job will be used. To assess changes in *sales,* pretraining and posttraining statistics on both total and repeat sales will be examined. To assess *customer satisfaction,* pretraining and posttraining statistics on letters and calls of complaint and commendations, as well as actual interview data, will be examined. Finally, to assess *employee morale* during and after training, appropriate attitude measures will be taken.

Outline for a Training Workshop

Table 11.8 presents an outline for a one-and-one-half-day transactional analysis (TA) workshop. Transactional analysis has been successfully used as a tool for teaching managers and other employees more effective ways of communicating both with other members of their organization and with the different publics with whom they interact (consumers, legislators, stockholders, suppliers). Many large companies have developed extensive TA training programs but, unfortunately, most programs in use have limited long-term application. Consequently, almost no research on evaluation of the long-term potential of TA as a management training tool has been conducted. The few reported studies are encouraging, however. Morse and Hall conducted an extensive TA evaluation while working for a large electronics company. The financial gains attributed to TA training were as follows:

1. $46,000 saved in reduced turnover costs
2. $20,000 increase in sales in a one-year period
3. $102,000 savings in increased productivity

Nykodym evaluated a transactional analysis training program administered to the systems data processing division of a large organization. In a tightly controlled experiment, he used the highly valid and reliable Survey of Organizations instrument in a pretraining and post-training design, with a control group to evaluate subordinate perception of TA-trained supervisors. Results support the effectiveness of the training. Despite some minor problems in matching demographics in his control group with demographics in the experimental groups, his design is encouraging for future evaluation of transactional analysis programs.

Some of the questions that need to be answered before transactional analysis can be acclaimed a truly effective long-term organizational communication training approach are as follows:

1. What are the differences in using transactional analysis therapeutically and nontherapeutically, especially in organizational development?
2. To what extent does the Parent-Adult-Child (PAC) model identify and differentiate organizational behaviors? Does any differentiation cluster according to type of organization, for example, volunteer service organization, political lobby group, labor union, federal regulating agency, public school, or other?
3. How does transactional analysis as an intervention tool compare with other tools, such as team building, job enrichment, survey feedback, diagnostic meetings, and so on?
4. Do managers whose styles differ structure their time differently? engage in different transactional emphases? stroke differently? play different games? have different scripts?
5. How specifically can transactional analysis be used to translate other organizational development theories, for example, Likert, Herzberg, Maslow, McGregor, Blake and Mouton, Lawrence, Lorsch, and others?
6. Do organizations who use transactional analysis differ on such system outputs as productivity, morale, absenteeism, and tardiness?

Table 11.8   Outline of Transactional Analysis Training Program

Pretraining Analysis

Interview five members of the group to be trained.
Examine job descriptions for all trainees.
Interview three management members of the organization (other than those to be trained).
Design training program objectives.

Training Objectives

By the end of this workshop the trainee should be able to:
1. Define the goal of transactional analysis.
2. Define and recognize the three ego states.
3. Define and recognize the three types of transactions.
4. List the six ways people spend their time.
5. Define and identify common games people play.
6. Recognize and practice ways to stop game playing.
7. Describe the basic concepts of life scripts and life positions.

Training Techniques

Objective 1: lecture—discussion—buzz group
Objective 2: lecture—discussion—structured experience film, slide—tape
Objective 3: lecture—discussion—structured experience
Objective 4: lecture—discussion—buzz group-structured experience—film
Objective 5: lecture—discussion—structured experience, role-playing film
Objective 6: role playing—discussion—videotape
Objective 7: lecture—discussion—film—videotape-structured experience

Training Administration

Group limited to 20 members. Workshop lasts 1 1/2 days. Training facility equipped with necessary media equipment, moveable chairs, dark curtains, etc. Program costs $250 per trainee.

Posttraining Evaluation

1. Reaction: administer reaction sheet immediately after training program.
2. Learning: administer standardized multiple-choice test immediately after training (and three months later).
3. Behavior: interview five trainees immediately after training, three months, and six months after training. Also interview trainees' peers, superiors, and subordinates (three and six months).
4. Results: Check on implementation of organization's communication policies directly related to training program.

7. Does the script of the founding father of the organization actually fit the script of the organization? Can the scripts of the organization's current leaders be compared directly with the script of the organization?
8. Is the public image of an organization actually enhanced when it uses transactional analysis concepts in the design of its advertisements?
9. Do such adult-programmed behaviors as consensus making, team building, and Theory Y actually offer more individual freedom and higher efficiency than rigid adherence to organizational hierarchies?

SUMMARY

Chapter 11 has defined training and related its functions to such consulting models as the purchase model, the doctor-patient model, and the process consultation model. A general training model (GTM) was presented and translated into a communication training model (CTM). Five components of the CTM (pretraining communication analysis, communication training objectives, communication training techniques, posttraining communication evaluation, and feedback) were discussed. Methods of assessing the behavioral capabilities of individuals as well as organizational training needs were related to designing training objectives. Criteria for writing behavioral objectives for training programs were defined and exemplified, differentiating planning from informational objectives. Several techniques commonly used in communication training programs were listed, along with application for each technique. Methods and principles for evaluating the success or failure of communication training programs and their impact upon all components of the CTM were considered. Table 11.8, in which a transactional analysis training program is outlined, is also a summary of the chapter.

EXERCISES

1. Interview the training director of a local organization. Ask what this person's definition of training is. Ask how this person assesses training needs in the organization, the techniques used in conducting a training program, and how the program is evaluated. Compare the answers with the information in the text.
2. Compare the CTM with other training models with which you are familiar.
3. Select a local organization with which you are familiar. Suggest three ways to make pretraining measurements of existing organizational behaviors.
4. Write five information objectives for a communication training program. Write planning objectives for each of these informational objectives.
5. Select three training techniques and briefly describe how to use each one in the planning objectives given in exercise 4.
6. Select two methods of evaluating the successes of a training program that implements your objectives and uses the foregoing techniques. Be sure to specify both immediate and delayed evaluation techniques. Briefly describe your evaluation system.
7. Obtain the design of a communication training program (from a training director, consultant, or textbook). Evaluate it in accordance with the criteria discussed in the text (see the components of the CTM). If you are unable to locate a communication training design, then use any training outline you can find and apply the components of the GTM in your evaluation of it.
8. What is behavior modeling? Give an example of how it can be used to successfully teach skills in an organizational setting.

9. You have done a needs analysis and documented that your organization is in need of formal communication training programs.
   a. List what you would include in these programs.
   b. Outline a strategy for selling a proposal for these training programs to top management.
10. You have just conducted a training seminar in your organization. You now want to get to the bottom line and find out if it made a difference. How might you go about assessing the effects of this training intervention?

BIBLIOGRAPHY AND REFERENCES

Amidon, Edmund, and Ned Flanders. *The Role of the Teacher in the Classroom: A Manual for Understanding and Improving Teachers' Classroom Behavior.* Minneapolis: Amidon, 1963.

Bass, Bernard, and James Vaughan. *Training in Industry: The Management of Learning.* Belmont, Calif.: Wadsworth Publishing Co., 1966.

Bormann, E., W. Howell, R. Nichols, and G. Shapiro. *Interpersonal Communication in the Modern Organization.* Englewood Cliffs, N.J.: Prentice-Hall, 1969.

Brooks, William, and Gustav Friedrich. *Teaching Speech Communication in the Secondary School.* Boston: Houghton Mifflin Co., 1973.

Byham, W., D. Adams, and A. Kiggins. "Transfer of Modeling Training to the Job." *Personnel Psychology* 29 (1976):345–49.

Byham, W., and J. Robinson. "Interaction Modeling: A New Concept in Supervisory Training." *Training and Development Journal,* (Feburary 1976):1–13.

Campbell, Donald, and Julian Stanley. *Experimental and Quasi-Experimental Designs for Research.* Chicago: Rand McNally, 1963.

Carroll, John. "A Model of School Learning." *Teachers College Research* 64 (1963):723–33.

———. "School Learning Over the Long Haul." In *Learning and the Educational Process.* Edited by J. D. Krumboltz. Chicago: Rand McNally, 1965.

DeCecco, John. *The Psychology of Learning and Instruction: Educational Psychology.* Englewood Cliffs, N.J.: Prentice-Hall, 1968.

Fairbanks, Grant, W. Everitt, and R. Jaeger. "Method for Time or Frequency Compression-Expansion of Speech." *Transactions of the Institute of Radio Engineers, Professional Group on Audio* AU-2 (1954):7–12.

Fairbanks, Grant, N. Guttman, and M. Miron. "Effects of Time Compression upon the Comprehension of Connected Speech." *Journal of Speech and Hearing Disorders* 22 (1957):10–19.

Felsenthal, Norman. "Media Resources for Human Relations Training." In *The 1972 Annual Handbook for Group Facilitators.* Edited by J. William Pfeiffer and John Jones. University Associates Press: Iowa City, 1972.

Fessenden, Seth. "Levels of Listening." *Education* 75 (1955):288–91.

Fletcher, H. *Speech and Hearing.* New York: Van Nostrand, 1929.

Foulke, E., C. Amster, C. Nolan, and R. Bixler. "The Comprehension of Rapid Speech by the Blind." *Exceptional Children* 29 (1962):134–41.

Gaines, D., and W. Salmon. "Does What You Do Make a Difference?" *Journal of Bank Training,* (Spring 1979):1.

Glaser, Robert. "Psychology and Instructional Technology." In *Training Research and Education.* Edited by R. Glaser. Pittsburgh: University of Pittsburgh Press, 1962.

Goldhaber, G. "Is Your Organization OK?" Paper presented at a meeting of the International Communication Association, Phoenix, Arizona, 1971.

Hanneman, Richard, and William Garvey. "A Technique for the Investigation of the Practical Limits of Speeded Speech." *American Psychologist* 4 (1949):304.

Harrison, G. V. *The Instructional Value of Presenting Explicit versus Vague Objectives.* Santa Barbara: California Educational Research Studies, University of California, 1967.

Howard, G. "Response-Shift Bias: A Problem in Evaluating Interventions With Pre-Post Self-Reports." *Evaluation Review* 1 (1980):93–106.

Howard, G., and P. Dailey. "Response-Shift Bias: A Source of Contamination of Self-Report Measures." *Journal of Applied Psychology* 64 (1979):144–50.

Kelly, Nan, and John W. Baird. "Evaluation of Training: The Ethics of Accountability." Paper presented at a meeting of the Speech Communication Association, Chicago, 1984.

Kibler, Robert, L. Barker, and D. Miles. *Behavioral Objectives and Instruction.* Boston: Allyn & Bacon, 1970.

Kirkpatrick, D. L. "Techniques for Evaluating Training Programs." *Journal of American Society of Training Directors* 13 (1959):3–9; 21–26.

Kraut, A. "Behavior Modeling Symposium: Developing Managerial Skills Via Modeling Techniques: Some Positive Research Findings—A Symposium." *Personnel Psychology* 29 (1976):325–28.

Leavitt, H. J., and R. Mueller. "Some Effects of Feedback on Communication." *Human Relations* 4 (1951):401–10.

Mager, Robert, and J. McCann. *Learner-Controlled Instruction.* Palo Alto, Calif.: Varian Associates, 1961.

———. *Preparing Objectives for Programmed Instruction.* Belmont, Calif.: Fearon Publishers, 1962.

Mezoff, B. "How to Get Accurate Self-Reports of Training Outcomes." *Training and Development Journal,* (September 1981):56–61.

Miles, D. T., R. Kibler, and L. Pettigrew. "The Effects of Study Questions on College Students' Test Performance." *Psychology in the Schools* 6 (1967):25–26.

Morse, John, and Robert Hall. "Organizational Development and Transactional Analysis: The GT&E Experience," In *Transactional Analysis.* Edited by G. Goldhaber and M. Goldhaber. Boston: Allyn & Bacon, 1976.

Nadler, L. *Designing Training Programs: The Critical Events Model.* Reading, Ma.: Addison-Wesley Publishing Co. 1986.

Nykodym, Nick. "Transactional Analysis: A Communication Strategy of Planned Organizational Change." Paper presented at a meeting of the International Communication Association, Chicago, 1978.

Odiorne, George. *How Managers Make Things Happen.* Englewood Cliffs, N.J.: Prentice-Hall, 1961.

Orr, David, and H. L. Friedman. *Research on Speeded Speech as an Educational Medium.* Progress Report Grant No. 7-48-7670-203. Washington, D.C.: U.S. Department of Health, Education, and Welfare, 1964.

Pfeiffer, J. W., and J. E. Jones. *A Handbook of Structured Experience for Human Relations Training.* Vol. 2. Iowa City: University Associates Press, 1970.

Robinson, J. "Will Behavior Modeling Survive the '80's?" *Training and Development Journal,* (January 1980):1–5.

Stolurow, Lawrence, and Daniel Davis. "Teaching Machines and Computer-Based Systems." In *Teaching Machines and Programmed Learning Part II: Data and Directions.* Edited by R. Glaser. Washington, D.C.: National Education Association, 1965.

Vaardaman, George T., C. Halterman, and P. Vaardaman. *Cutting Communication Costs and Increasing Impacts.* New York: John Wiley & Sons, 1970.

Wealbesser, Henry, and H. Carter. "Some Methodological Considerations of Curriculum Evaluation Research." *Educational Leadership Research Supplement* 26 (1968):53–64.

12
CAREER PATHS IN ORGANIZATIONAL COMMUNICATION

Roy Foltz, vice president of one of the largest communication consulting firms in America, once told an audience of industrial communicators the story of a communication executive who, during his *exit* interview, asked senior management for its perception of communicators in general. The management consensus:

> Communicators are not "business" people. They don't look at the bottom line. They're moralizers. They're more concerned with communications processes than with business itself. Their loyalty lies with their profession. They never keep within their budgets. They're always looking for more money. They cause more problems than they settle.

But who are these communicators? What positions in business, industry, government, and education do they hold? How do they get hired for these positions? What career paths do they follow? In their 1974 survey of organizational communication university programs, Downs and Larimer reported, "There is a trend for communication graduates to seek non-teaching jobs or consulting opportunities, and training in organizational communication prepares students for diverse job opportunities." The wide variety of jobs available to students with a background in organizational communication is illustrated by the following job titles that appear in advertisements in the *New York Times, The Wall Street Journal,* and *Chronicle of Higher Education:* personnel director, management trainee, recruiting officer, public relations director, community relations officer, training director, communication director, public information director, counselor, sales coordinator, instructional specialist, organizational development specialist, consultant, group process facilitator, human relations director, human resources director, employee relations director, employee development specialist, newsletter editor, survey specialist, student affairs director, assistant to . . . and internal communication director. These listings make it apparent that there *are* careers in sales, training, recruiting, management, and research, as well as in education, for people trained in organizational communication.

In this chapter the objectives are as follows:

1. To list and describe the jobs held and skills needed by organizational communication professionals
2. To describe and illustrate the training and educational preparation needed to qualify for these jobs

3. To specify and illustrate the steps necessary in applying for a job in organizational communication, including preparation of the cover letter and résumé and key questions to ask during the interview
4. To describe the steps in developing *your* career path in organizational communication
5. To reemphasize the underlying philosophy of this chapter as it is reflected in the thoughts of an expert corporate communications director who explains his concept of the future role of organizational communicators

Jobs

Consider the following scenario:

Student: I would like to major in organizational communication.

Professor-advisor: Fine. Here's a list of the courses you should take for your B.A. degree.

Student: Just one question. What will I be able to do when I graduate?

Professor-advisor: Go to graduate school.

Five years later this student, now in graduate school, again approaches his advisor.

Student: I have almost completed my graduate course work in organizational communication. What will I be able to do when I graduate with my M.A. degree?

Professor-advisor: Get a Ph.D.

Three years later the student, now completing his Ph.D. program, once again approaches his advisor.

Student: I will graduate this year. What will I be able to do when I receive my doctoral degree?

Professor-advisor: Teach organizational communication at some college or university. However, the job market doesn't look too promising this year.

Only a few years ago, this kind of exchange between students and advisors was only too frequent and, unfortunately, is still far too common in some disciplines. However, at this writing, the field of organizational communication is beginning to come into its own as a recognized discipline with a well-defined content oriented toward specific career paths, most of them noneducational.

Before discussing noneducational jobs, the responsibilities of a typical organizational communication teaching position are described:

1. To develop and teach courses in organizational communication.
2. To direct and conduct research studies in organizational communication.
3. To develop organizational contacts in the community for use in placement of student interns and research projects.
4. To evaluate the effectiveness of teaching, research, and intern programs.
5. To help students find suitable organizational communication employment.

While the academic requirements for a teaching position depend upon the specific program, a master's degree and probably a doctoral degree would be required. According to the Downs and Larimer survey, there are many opportunities in academic programs, but far more organizational communication jobs are available in nonacademic areas.

As evidence of the potential in private industry for communication positions, a 1975 Marshall Consultants' survey of Fortune 500 companies revealed that corporate communications budgets (excluding corporate and product advertising) were up in 51 percent of the cases, were the same in 16 percent, and decreased in the remainder. Half of the companies reporting an increase indicated growth above the (then) 10.6 percent inflation rate, with many approaching a 40 percent increase in their budget. Forty-one percent anticipated further increase, while only 8 percent anticipated a decrease.

As further evidence of the growth of the field of organizational communication, the International Association of Business Communicators (IABC) surveyed its members in 1987. Among its major findings were the following:

1. Communication salaries, budgets are up; employee motivation, economic factors dominate issues.
2. Male/female salary differences continue to decrease.
3. Communication budgets near $500,000; communicators optimistic about future.
4. Employment increasing in not-for-profit and healthcare sectors, down in corporations; more communicators are self-employed.
5. Many communicators fill newly created jobs.
6. Manager and director are most frequently cited title.

The data from the IABC and the Marshall surveys indicate ample opportunities awaiting both undergraduate and graduate students specializing in organizational communication. These job opportunities can be found in internal communication positions, external corporate communications, consulting, publishing, training, media, and research (Petrie et al, 1975). In the IABC survey of 1987, communicators from the United States and Canada, the United Kingdom, Hong Kong, and Australia were polled with regards to their job titles (see table 12.1). It was found that manager and director were the most frequently cited job titles for communicators in these geographic regions.

The job descriptions and titles, in the following ads, published in 1981,[1] provide a general overview of the range of professional jobs available in organizations. Notice that most of these jobs require extensive experience. A person entering the job market for the first time would probably work *for* someone holding a job similar to one of the following. These advertisements indicate both the available career paths and salary ranges in the profession.

FREELANCE WRITERS WANTED—To write multimedia training programs (audio, video, workbook exercises, facilitator-guided activities) in management and selling skills, for the organizational development market.

WRITER/CONSULTANTS—One of country's top consulting firms needs communication professionals. Primary focus on employee communications program in benefits and compensation. Firm serves over 60% of Fortune 500. Looking for people who can take legal-sounding information, make it understandable, attractive, concise. Want writers who empathize with audience. Ideal

---

1. These advertisements were taken from the Industrial Communication Council (ICC) Newsletter, December 1981.

Table 12.1 Communication Specialist Job Titles

	US/Canada	UK*	HK*	Australia*
Manager	19.7%	14.8%	22.7%	25.0%
Director	19.3%	25.9%	22.7%	8.3%
Editor	15.0%	11.1%	—	8.3%
Coordinator	9.3%	3.7%	—	4.2%
Consultant	7.5%	22.2%	9.1%	16.7%
Specialist	5.6%	3.7%	—	—
Vice President	3.3%	7.4%	4.5%	—
Supervisor	2.8%	—	—	—
Officer	2.1%	—	—	8.3%
President/Executive Director/CEO	1.8%	—	4.5%	4.2%
Editorial Assistant	1.5%	—	—	—
Freelancer	1.4%	—	—	—
Educator	1.1%	—	4.5%	—
General Manager	.6%	—	4.5%	—
Graphic Artist/Designer	.4%	—	—	—
Managing Director/Secretary	.1%	17.4%	9.1%	20.8%
Photographer	.1%	—	—	—
Other	8.2%	3.7%	18.2%	4.2%

*Denotes small sample size

candidate has 2–5 years communication experience; superior writing, interpersonal and analytical skills; strong creative abilities; and a natural motivation to excellence. Send resume and salary history in confidence.

SENIOR NEWS SPECIALIST—Fortune 500, high-technology corporation, located in Manhattan, is expanding its Media Relations department and is seeking a high-energy professional to join as Senior News Specialist. Knowledge and/or interest in the high-tech industries, strong writing skills, and ability to build lasting relationships with corporate and divisional executives are key elements of this position.

DIRECTOR, GROUP COMMUNICATIONS—Diversified, high-technology company based in New England offers an opportunity to build communications programs for major operating groups. Direct/liaison between corporate and divisions, manage programs, strategize with senior management. Future opportunity to head all communications. Salary: $100–125M compensation package.

GENERAL MANAGER-SOUTHEAST ASIA—Our client, a prestigious, international PR counseling firm, seeks energetic General Manager to head their Southeast Asian office. Individual should possess knowledge of SE Asia, ability to adapt to different cultures and workstyles, and PR agency background. Responsibilities will include supervising staff and developing new business opportunities. Interface with fellow Asian general managers in providing a regional PR service. Compensation package: $50M ($40–45M base).

COMMUNICATIONS CONSULTANT—International management consulting firm with Connecticut office seeks Communications Consultants with several years of solid writing and editing experience. Background in corporate publications, internal and external, important, as well as ability to deal effectively with clients. Salary: to $50M.

FINANCIAL PUBLIC RELATIONS—Two major New York City PR agencies are seeking experienced financial PR specialists to deal with the investment community (particularly analysts and registered representatives) plus the media. Programming, strategy development, and client liaison on a daily basis are among the responsibilities. One post, with a large agency, pays up to $42K. The other position, with a mid-size firm, pays up to $38K.

DEPUTY PR MANAGER—Large midtown corporation seeks a deputy manager to assist the DPR in administration, budgeting, and supervision of writers and media placement specialists. Five to seven years of managerial experience preferred. To $46K.

SENIOR SPEECH WRITER—Major NYC company needs a senior speech writer experienced in dealing with top management on a variety of business and social issues. Must be methodical, well organized, and with a flair for the spoken word. Conservative company with fine growth ahead. Excellent opportunity. To $40K.

SEVERAL PR OPPORTUNITIES—The following positions are only some of the opportunities for which we are actively seeking qualified professionals to fill. If any of these positions are of interest to you, or if you would like to be considered for other non-listed positions—send 4 resumes noting salary and geographic preferences. All correspondence is held in the strictest confidence. Positions are located in the NY metro area, unless noted otherwise.

STAFF VP, PR (Pa.)
(financial services) ....$65+M

TECHNICAL PUBLICATIONS EDITOR (Pa.)
(electric/engineering) $35–40M

COMMUNICATIONS CONSULTANT (Conn.)
(management consulting) $30–45M

ASSOCIATE EDITORIAL DIRECTOR (Mass.)
(previous experience needed) $45M

ACCOUNT GROUP SUPERVISOR (Mass.)
(industrial/automotive) $40M

PRODUCT PUBLICIST (Ohio)
(food/consumer goods) $25.5M

PUBLIC RELATIONS DIRECTOR
(high fashion) $25–35M

INTERNAL COMMUNICATIONS/CONSULTANT
(banking/financial services) $32–37M

ACCOUNT EXECUTIVES—VARIOUS
(financial/video/office equip/community relations/auto) $24–40M

COMMUNICATIONS CONSULTANT/WRITER
(insurance/management) $25–30M

MANAGER, PUBLIC AFFAIRS
(drug/health) $25–35M

SENIOR COMMUNICATIONS CONSULTANT
(previous experience needed) ....$50+M

MANAGER, INVESTOR RELATIONS
(different industries) $35–40M

ACCOUNT SUPERVISOR/CLIENT RELATIONS
Major public relations firm seeks experienced professional to service major brokerage account.
Must have financial experience with sound knowledge of Wall Street.

From these job titles and descriptions the following facts seem apparent:

1. Both theoretical understanding of communication and specific (technical)
   communication skills are necessary for success in nonacademic organizations.
2. Communication skills and knowledge are not enough. It is also necessary that the
   communication specialist be trained in the applied social sciences: economics, political
   science, management, and education.
3. Entry-level communication positions tend to require technical skills (writing, editing,
   photography), but advancement to an executive position appears to require both
   specialty training and a generalist outlook.

Figure 12.1 shows a recent advertisement for a director of Corporate Communications.
Note that in addition to the normal communication duties of writing, training, and development, the job also requires expertise in developing, administering, and interpreting surveys.

Some practitioners treat the field of organizational communication more generally,
preferring to speak of the holistic element of the communication function in most management positions. For example, O'Connell listed the following events as requiring effective internal communication: introducing a new product; moving an office to another city; merging
with another organization; changing managers; adopting a new pension plan; and defining
career alternatives. It is obvious that anyone in the organization may be involved in both the
planning and executing of the communication function for these events.

Another career possible for communication students is in the area of consulting. The
following enumeration illustrates the possibilities in and many ways of using communication
skills in this career:

1. Diagnose organizational communication systems, using survey, interviewing, or
   observational techniques. Identify strengths and weaknesses in communication
   systems and make specific recommendations for improvement.
2. Conduct survey-feedback sessions for small and large groups of managers and other
   employees.
3. Develop communication action plans identifying strategies and objectives, tactics and
   needed resources, and logistics and target dates.
4. Facilitate implementation of communication action plans for large and small
   organizations, including formal and informal channels.
5. Design, implement, and evaluate training programs for team building and conflict
   resolution; for conference, meeting, and leadership skills; for public speaking and
   business presentations; for interpersonal communication and transactional analysis;
   for interviewing techniques and appropriate dress for corporate situations.

Figure 12.1   Ad for Director of Corporate Communications.

Director
Corporate Communications

$54,000-$60,000 + Significant Benefits

The continuing success of our Long Island based Fortune 500 company has created a new position for a uniquely talented, thoroughly experienced professional to establish and manage a "STATE-OF-THE-ART" corporate communications system for 30+ locations throughout North America.

The role requires the:
- Development, application and interpretation of climate/attitude surveys
- Writing, production and editing of in-house video
- Editing of the corporate journal
- Coordinating and development of communication skills for top executives

We will consider ONLY those applicants who can substantially demonstrate the following:

☐ Degrees in communications related skills, e.g. M.A.—Speech Communication
☐ Technical experience of running a video studio
☐ Excellent spoken and written communication skills
☐ Editorship of in-house journal
☐ Considerable public relations campaign work, e.g. a political campaign
☐ Significant personal management skills
☐ Production and interpretation of multi-dimensional scaling for climate and attitude surveys (SPSS)

The compensation package is realistic. All replies will be held in strictest confidence. Only those resumes which include full details of the above credentials will be considered.

6. Conduct manpower analyses and determine appropriate manpower and career development programs to implement corporate goals and plans and facilitate the development and implementation of such programs.
7. Analyze communication patterns, information flow, and interpersonal transactions in present organizational structure for use in large system reorganization and/or measurement of impact of major innovations; assist in the reorganization of large organizations.
8. Design and implement measurement of customer service and satisfaction with products, using scientific survey and polling techniques.
9. Counsel corporate and political leaders on appropriate television, radio, and public speaking behavior.

According to a speech presented by Norm Leaper, President of the IABC, at the IABC Convention in 1987, organizational communication is used as a buzz word to describe all problem-solving functions in today's organization. The communication responsibilities of an organization are being taken on by entire departments created for that purpose. These departments usually exist under names, such as corporate relations, corporate communication, public affairs, or external affairs. Despite this new concern of the organization, which students of organizational communication are employed to satisfy, many IABC members have reported that they have left the corporate scene and become self-employed, often with their own consulting practice.

In 1986, the IABC interviewed more than a dozen top public relations professionals and communication leaders. The results, published in the IABC monthly magazine *Communication World,* concluded:

1. The field will continue to grow professional. Public relations people increasingly will shed their poor reputations and become management consultants.
2. Organizations will want their entry-level employees to know as much about finance and marketing as they do about media relations.
3. More and more communicators will be trying to get their messages to their target audiences by using the most effective medium available.
4. More communicators will specialize, becoming experts in finance, law, high technology, travel, or another area.
5. More women will enter the field.
6. More computers and word processors will be in use.

The field of organizational communication is also becoming brighter for women. While the number of women have increased in the field the top salaries are still drawn by the older men. According to *PR Reporter,* the median public relations salary in 1986 was $35,000, but women were still making $14,000 less than men. Some experts feel that as the industry grows the salary gap will close. However, to do this, women will have to become more aggressive in asking for the salaries they deserve, and instead of competing with each other, they must align themselves in professional networks (including affiliations with professional societies within their field) to work together to solve their problems.

However, the report published by the IABC in 1987 indicates that although the salary disparity still exists, women communicators received salary increases nearly twice as large as their male colleagues from 1985. Women's salaries increased by a 8.6 percent gain as opposed to a 4.7 percent gain in male salaries. According to the report "with all factors being equal, women now earn $5,500 less than men, which is a 16.4 percent decrease in the salary disparity since 1985."

For individuals seeking internal communication positions, an important indication of the commitment of a communication department to excellence in employee communication is the existence of a communication plan or statement of goals for the organization. The following goals,[2] which are the goals espoused by a large communications organization, illustrate this kind of commitment.

---

2. From the goals of the Xerox Corporation Information Systems Group (ISG) and its department, developed by Roger D'Aprix, department director, and used with permission of Roger D'Aprix.

Business Results, Strategy.   Communicate, within security limitations, the business results and business strategy of ISG. Pay particular attention to major new-product results and sales programs; publicize the performance of ISG individuals who attain notable results in any of our priority programs. Emphasize competitive pressures and our success in dealing with them.

Job Pressures.   Encourage ISG people to understand and adapt to increasing job pressures resulting from more effective competition and rising costs. Urge improved personal productivity, cost consciousness, and customer awareness.

Affirmative Action.   Portray affirmative action as a long-term Xerox business objective important to the success and integrity of our business.

Self-Development.   Urge ISG people to do a better job of self-development and to assume responsibility for their own careers. At the same time, communicate the fact that as the business matures, the growth rate will necessarily be slower, affecting career opportunity accordingly.

Two-Way Communication.   Encourage honest two-way communication and productive interpersonal relationships.

Security.   Help ISG people understand the need for observing strict security procedures for the protection of their own and the company's property and confidential information.

Social Action.   Encourage ISG people to participate in constructive social action.

In order to implement these goals, the corporation has developed an extensive communication program, which integrates written and face-to-face channels.

Educational Preparation

The previously listed job descriptions, titles, and advertisements indicate that an organizational communication curriculum should meet the following requirements:

1. Have a broad liberal arts or humanities base.
2. Stress the applied social-behavior sciences.
3. Incorporate both theory and practical courses.
4. Provide practical courses that develop specific skills in spoken, print, and telecommunication media.

Undergraduate courses should include the following:

1. Introduction to organizational communication: an overview of important theories and directions in the field.
2. Business and professional speaking: mechanics of oral communication skills necessary in organizational interactions.

3. Conference techniques and group discussions: skills needed to participate in and/or lead both small groups and large meetings and conferences (small-group skills are particularly important, given the Goldfine and O'Connell finding that most organizational communication departments do not exceed ten people).
4. Interviewing: theory and skills needed to understand, conduct, and evaluate various job-related interviews, such as hiring, appraisal, and exit.
5. Communication auditing: research skills needed to evaluate a communication program.
6. Mechanics of business writing: skills needed to produce successful memos, reports, proposals, and letters (taught preferably by a person with a background in journalism).
7. Introduction to public relations and advertising: the mechanics of a PR and advertising program (could consist of two courses).
8. Research methods and statistics.

Supporting courses in audiovisual aids; film, slide, and tape production; mass media; video instruction; organizational theory, behavior, and development; industrial sociology and industrial psychology; and accounting and economics should also be taken.

At the graduate level, if the master's is the final degree (as it probably should be for those not desiring an academic career), perhaps more theory could be stressed in such courses as the following: organizational communication theory, communication auditing and other research procedures, theories of diffusion, network analysis, institutional communication and public relations, and decision making.

Practical courses such as the following could be taken: communication training and consulting, applied communication, and internship in organizational communication.

Supporting courses for the master's degree include additional study of organizational behavior, theory, and development (usually taught in schools of business or management), survey research methods, marketing, public administration and public policy, and human resources planning.

Finally, at the doctoral level, where the career path is primarily educational or research oriented, individual instruction, independent study, internship, and small enrollment seminars focusing on specific issues in the literature should be taken. Such supporting course work as the following should also be taken: computer programming, analysis of organizations, organizational development, research methodologies, and advertising and public relations theory. Either through an internship or special seminars, it is also desirable for doctoral students to visit the headquarters of several organizations to see firsthand the nature of organizational communication jobs for which they are preparing.

Applying for a Job

Whether you elect to canvas several dozen organizations or to focus on a few carefully selected sites, you will need to prepare a cover letter and a résumé. Later, you will need to know key questions to ask when you are invited for an interview.

The Cover Letter[3]

The purpose of the cover letter is to arouse interest in reading your résumé. It is a personal introduction to the résumé (which is often very general and duplicated in quantity). There are three major considerations when writing cover letters.

1. A good cover letter is:
   a. *Brief.* Generally three-quarters page of typing should be the maximum length unless you have something special to say to the reader.
   b. *Enlightening.* Do not repeat the information that is in the résumé. Instead, use the cover letter to call attention to something especially relevant that appears on your résumé. Tell something that the reader would like to know before beginning to study your résumé.
   c. *To the point.* As with your résumé, do not waste words. Make each word count and come right to the point.
   d. *Personal.* The cover letter should not be mass produced. It should be individually typed and, wherever possible, addressed to a specific person in the organization. It should contain expressions that make the reader feel that you have a sincere desire to work in his or her organization.
2. The cover letter (and résumé) should project the following qualities about yourself:
   a. *Organized.* It should show that your thoughts are rational and well ordered.
   b. *Professional.* You should convey the image of professionalism by referring to your accomplishments, credentials, and career ambitions. Neatness counts. Typos and spelling errors are a reflection on your professionalism.
   c. *High self-concept.* If you don't feel good about yourself, the reader will not feel good about you. Your cover letter should make the reader feel that you like yourself (but do not overdo it).
   d. *Positive attitude.* You should try to convey a positive attitude about everything. People like other people who feel there is hope for the future. Do not dwell on unpleasant past experiences or jobs, the failing economy, or any other negative view of life. Whatever you want to talk about in your cover letter (or résumé), look on the bright side.
3. The cover letter should contain the following information (in addition to the items contained in Rogers's cover letter outline in figure 12.2 and sample cover letter in figure 12.3):
   a. *A personalized career objective.* Keep the company or organization that you are applying to in mind and consider placing this career objective in the cover letter instead of in the résumé.
   b. *Supplemental résumé information.* Refer to something relevant that appears in the résumé and expand on that information in order to make it appear especially significant to the reader. Do not repeat the résumé. The cover letter should contain specific information that does not belong in the résumé.
   c. *Specific notation indicating that response is awaited.* You should close your letter with a notation such as "I am looking forward to hearing from you in the near future" because it places the burden of response on the reader.

---

3. Material on the cover letter and the résumé was developed by Phil Samuels in 1982 and is used with his permission.

Figure 12.2 Outline for a cover letter. (Source: Don Rogers, Associate Professor, Department of Management, State University of New York at Geneseo, 1977. Used with permission.)

Heading	Address City, State, Zip Code Date

Name, Title
Department
Organization   **Inside Address**
Address
City, State, Zip Code
Dear (Mr., Ms., Mrs., Miss, Dr., etc.): **Salutation**
Paragraph I: **Arouse Interest; State Purpose**
Paragraph II: **Summarize Qualification; Describe Enclosure**
Paragraph III: **Suggest Action;**
Yours truly,   **Complimentary Close**
Name   **Signature**
Encl.   **Postscript**

Figure 12.3 Cover letter to accompany a résumé. (Source: Don Rogers, Associate Professor, Department of Management, State University of New York at Geneseo, 1977. Used with permission.)

222 Broadway Avenue
Los Angeles, California 22222
February 2, 1982

Dr. Donald P. Rogers
Vice President, Campaign Development
Communication Campaign Consulting Corporation
4226 Ridge Lea Road
Buffalo, New York 14226

Dear Dr. Rogers:

For your company to remain viable you need people who can communicate effectively, organize efficiently, and research diligently. I can do those things and I can do them for Communication Campaign Consulting Corporation as a campaign research and development manager.

Enclosed is a résumé which details my qualifications for a position as a research and development manager. Please note that both my education (B.S. expected from U.C.L.A. in management) and experience (work and school experience) have prepared me for a career in management. My abilities to lead, to organize, and to supervise others are evidenced by success in the jobs I have held and by positions of trust in the organizations I have joined.

I think that you will agree that I would be a good candidate for this position. I would like to talk personally with you about the job. To arrange an interview please call me at 222-222-2222. I am looking forward to hearing from you in the near future.

Awaiting your reply,

Johnson Edward Doe

Johnson Edward Doe

Encl.

CAREER PATHS IN ORGANIZATIONAL COMMUNICATION   429

The general format for a cover letter should be constructed in the following manner.

First Paragraph: State how you heard about the job (if applicable). After researching the company, talk about some of their positive points that have attracted you to their organization and how you can see yourself contributing to their organization.

Second Paragraph: Expand your skills, abilities, education beyond that mentioned in your résumé. Try to make specific to the organization that you are applying to.

Third Paragraph: Thank them and ask for an interview. Either wait for them to call, or tell them that you will be calling them. The latter option should be employed especially when you are out of town and will be visiting their area.

The Résumé

Your résumé should consist of a one or two-page summary of your career objectives, capabilities, and accomplishments. It should be action oriented and stress what you can do and have done.

There is not one best format for writing a résumé, but there are some specific considerations when designing the résumé that is right for you. Remember, the major purpose of a résumé is to make the reader curious enough about the writer to offer a job interview. (Most people do not get actual job offers from their résumés.) With that in mind, make your résumé specific enough to describe your skills and qualifications and intriguing enough to make the reader curious and interested.

1. Make sure *every* word, phrase, or blank space serves a purpose. It takes many drafts for a résumé to become perfect. For every word or phrase, ask yourself: "Why do I want them to know this information? Will this information make the reader want to meet me? Is there a more effective way to present this information?"
2. By using uppercase and bold letters in various places, you can control what stands out when the reader glances at your résumé. Before you put the dates of employment in your margins (as so many people incorrectly do), ask yourself whether that is the first thing you want the reader to notice.
3. Do not include a personal data section unless there is something special you want to highlight. How will your height, weight, or marital status get you an interview?
4. Before you put a career objective on your résumé, be sure you really want it there. When duplicating a résumé, a career objective will probably be too general to be effective. Save your career objective for your cover letter, where you can personalize it for each organization.
5. It is a good idea to have a skills section that lists some specific functions you can fulfill.
6. Have many people read and criticize each draft of your résumé. Get advice from people in the business world. You do not have to follow everyone's advice, but you should weigh all options.

Figure 12.4 consists of a format for a résumé and figure 12.5 gives a résumé using the format suggested in figure 12.4.

It goes without saying that *everything* on your résumé should be truthful. We have heard much about public personalities, even writers from the nation's top newspapers, forging their credentials, faking their résumés, and, in general, being dishonest about some part of

Figure 12.4 Format for a résumé. (Source: Don Rogers, Associate Professor, Department of Management. State University of New York at Geneseo, 1977. Phil Samuels, State University of New York—Buffalo, also contributed. Used with permission.)

[Name]

Home: Work:
  [Street]   [Department]
  [City]   [Organization]
  [Phone]   [Street]
                                            [City]
                                          [Phone]

Special Skills: Communication
Evidence of ability to listen, give speeches, conduct interviews, participate in conferences and discussions
Evidence of ability to use mass media techniques to produce print, radio, television, film, videotape, etc.

Leadership
Evidence of ability to motivate, supervise, and help people to achieve defined goals

Organizing
Evidence of ability to plan, conduct, and evaluate projects

Research
Evidence of ability to conduct, analyze, and interpret research projects

Mechanical
Evidence of ability to use mechanical devices and critical-analytical techniques

Education: [Degree]   [School]   [Date]
Major and minor studies:
Activities and honors:

Work and Related Experience: Title: Employer: Dates:
Duties and Responsibilities:

Affiliations and Activities: [High school interests, activities, hobbies]
[College interests, activities, hobbies]
[Current interests, activities, hobbies]
[Professional and other memberships]

References: On request [or from a collection source]

[DO NOT INCLUDE: Personal Data, physical handicaps, arrest record, salary requirements, preferred location, availability to travel, or the word *Résumé*]

Figure 12.5 Sample résumé.

HOWARD MARC GARTENBERG

Address: 100 Gefilte Rd.
Buffalo, New York 14214
(716)555–1234

Special
Skills:

1) The ability to design, conduct, and evaluate training programs or short courses in:
   a) Group Dynamics, Problem Solving and Decision Making
   b) Interpersonal Communication
   c) Principles and Methods of Interviewing
   d) Public Speaking
   e) Effective written and oral message strategies
   f) Critical Listening
   g) Persuasion
2) The ability to assess employee perceptions and attitudes through both survey directed feedback and group problem solving methods.
3) The ability to coordinate, develop, and write for various internal and external employee publications, and to assess their effectiveness.
4) The ability to conduct wage and benefit surveys and administer payroll.
5) The ability to interview and screen prospective employees.
6) The ability to conduct perceptual and attitudinal studies concerning an organization's image among the public sector.
7) The ability to develop and evaluate various marketing and advertising strategies, including segmentation and media mix.
8) The ability to develop and evaluate various public/community relations programs.

Education:

M.A. in Communication
Major Area of Emphasis: Mass Media Theory and Research
Minor Areas of Emphasis: Organizational Behavior, Marketing, Statistics
State University of New York at Buffalo

B.A. in Psychology and Communication (Graduated Cum Laude)
State University of New York at Buffalo

Work
Experience:

MANAGER, TRAINING AND DEVELOPMENT
Niagara Frontier Services, Buffalo, N.Y. (1981–Present)

DIRECTOR OF RESEARCH
Goldhaber Research Associates (1979–1981)
485 Fifth Avenue, Suite 1042, New York City, New York 10017
As director of research for this national public opinion and market research organization, I designed and conducted research projects. Duties included hiring, training, and supervising support staff and personnel, as well as instrument design and data analysis. Projects have included various market research studies and local and national political polls.

Figure 12.5 *Continued*

TEACHING ASSISTANT
State University of New York at Buffalo (9/77–6/79)
Duties included organization, preparation, and instruction of basic course in communication, as well as participation in ongoing research.

SURVEY RESEARCHER
State University of New York at Buffalo (9/76–6/77)
In this position I constructed, administered, and analyzed various media usage and impact surveys.

CORPORATE TAX AUDITOR
Programmed Tax Systems, Mineola, New York
(1/74–4/75)
Was promoted to this position after serving as assistant to quality control. Tasks included dealing with support staff, checking forms for proper itemization, and administering corrections where necessary.

Related Experience:
Assisted in the design and implementation of an industrial positioning and market segmentation study for a major national corporation.

Authored and delivered papers at several professional association conventions.

Participated in ongoing seminar devoted to the investigation and evaluation of various communication and organizational development programs. Seminar involved travel to and meetings with practitioners in several national and international corporations.

Served as vice-president of the Communication Graduate Student Association, and was elected to and served on a University-wide search committee to appoint a new departmental chairperson.

Wrote for campus newspaper *The Spectrum.*

Wrote for hometown newspaper *Bellmore Life.*

Founder and co-editor of home-based literary/news magazine *Matches & Trees.*

Disc jockey for campus radio station.

Organized news bureau and served as news director for that station.

Was promoted to and served as program director for that station.

Wrote, prepared, and delivered news broadcasts for college television station.

Professional Memberships:
International Communication Association
American Society for Training and Development
American Marketing Association

References:
Available upon request from:
University Placement and Career Guidance
State University of New York at Buffalo
Hayes Annex C
Buffalo, New York 14214

their careers. The risks are enormous, the penalties are severe, and a reputation for dishonesty could follow you for several years. Be absolutely certain that whatever you have stated about yourself on your résumé, in your cover letter, or during your job interviews is absolutely truthful and easily verifiable.

The Interview

When you are invited to a company (or to your university placement center) for an interview, you should prepare yourself for this critical event by researching the company and practicing key questions. Good sources for material about an organization are *Standard and Poor's Register of Corporations, Dun and Bradstreet's Book of Corporation Management, Fortune, Forbes, New York Times, Wall Street Journal, Business Week,* and local newspapers in the city where the organization is headquartered. You should also write to the company's corporate or public relations department for a copy of the most recent annual report, the current organizational chart, and a list of the major job positions and descriptions (probably available in the personnel department). If the company is a publicly traded organization, most stock brokerage firms would probably assist you in this research. You would be wise to check the company's earnings record and the recent performance of its stock, which are usually key indicators of the financial health of an organization.

Armed with this information, you are ready for the interview. Appropriate dress is important. Men should wear a suit, preferably a dark-colored (navy blue, dark gray, blue or gray pinstripe) three-piece suit, with a white or blue shirt and a solid or striped tie. Women should wear a conservative, dark-colored suit or dress and avoid tight-fitting clothing and pantsuits.

Downs and Tanner, in a study of decision making in the selection interview, have concluded that the interviewee should:

1. Be articulate, organized, and enthusiastic in answering questions.
2. Analyze strengths and weaknesses comfortably.
3. Sell yourself but avoid overkill.
4. Remember that everyone has had problems, so do not try to avoid all mention of them.
5. Be aware that your specific experiences do not determine your acceptance, but what those experiences tell about you as a person is extremely important.

I recommend that on a job interview you should be direct. Do not try to be what you are not. If you know the answers, give them. If you do not know the answers to some of the questions, be smart enough to say so. When you are invited to ask questions, you should seek facts, information about the organization's product line, where the organization stands in its field, what its growth potential is, etc.

The following probes and questions you could ask the interviewer will help to get the in-depth information you will need to make a decision. Do not be afraid to take the lead in this inquiry. Such questions will probably impress the interviewer with your thoroughness and interest.

1. Describe the company, its structure, services, products, and growth (profits, return to stockholders, earnings per share). Where within this structure is the communication function?

2. Describe the position for which I am applying. What are the duties and budgetary and decision-making constraints? What support staff will I have? Is there a written job description? May I see it? Why is there no written job description? Who makes the decision about my budget? What criteria are used in making this budget decision? What are the key "make-or-break" points in my job?
3. Describe your job. [Directed to interviewers only if they will work as a colleague or supervisor.] What are your duties? What are your decision-making and budgetary constraints? What is your relationship with the chief executive officer? What kind of support staff do you have?
4. Describe the major internal and external interfaces associated with my job. What are the potential sources of conflict? How is conflict resolved in the department? What are the ages and duties of other key personnel with whom I will interact?
5. What are the toughest problems I will face in my job during the first six months? What are the toughest problems you will face in the next six months? [Asked of interviewers only if they will be working with or supervising you.] What solutions have been attempted for these problems? Why haven't they worked?
6. What standards and measurements will be used to evaluate my performance in this job? How often will I be evaluated and by whom? When will my next salary increase be forthcoming? What is the expected career path for this position? What will my next position in this organization be?
7. In what manner will I be able to maintain my professional development? Will I be budgeted for travel to meetings of professional societies? Will I maintain relationships with universities? Will I be given time for personal development through courses and training programs?
8. How much travel is associated with this job? What budget exists for this travel? How large an entertainment budget will I have? What travel accommodations does this company expect me to maintain?
9. What will my salary be? What fringes and prerequisites will I receive in addition to my salary? Will I be reimbursed for moving expenses? Is there a dental, medical, retirement, disability, insurance, or stock option plan?
10. What assistance will you give me in relocating my family in this city? Will you assist me in selling my old house and purchasing my new one? Will you assist my spouse in visiting different neighborhoods and schools? Do you plan to have my family visit your company prior to my being hired?

Naturally some of these questions and/or probes may be more appropriate in applying for an advanced position in the organization, but most will provide ample information to help you make the right decision. Before you leave the interview, know what the next step will be. If you are not told, ask. Do not make the mistake of saying, "I just want a job. I'll do anything." Persons with that attitude are not good prospects because they haven't thought through what they want to do.

Perhaps the most difficult aspect of the job interview is knowing when it is over. When the personnel manager, for example, says: "Mr. Jones, thank you for coming in, you will be hearing from us," the interview is over. You may ask an additional question or two, but continuing to fire questions will probably eliminate you from further consideration. Virtually no one gets a job without an interview. Knowing how the interview game is played may not get you the job, but it will get you a lot closer than most of the competition.

Other Job Aids

Although it is usually more helpful in seeking second and third positions, the services of a search firm may be used. These firms typically charge their fees to the client organization. They collect a résumé and a statement of career goals, salary objectives, and geographical constraints from applicants and then match available candidates with existing jobs, arranging for interviews in the client organization only if they think a potential match between an applicant and an organization is possible. Usually, a search firm will interview you extensively to determine the kind of a person you are and how good the fit between you and an organization will be before referring you to a client organization. You should always check the reputation of the search firm with both the chamber of commerce and other people who have used the firm. Be wary of search firms who refuse to identify their client organization, or at least the type and size of the company, and firms that indicate they will have to "sell" you to the client. If the search firm lacks substantial information about the company, the position, and the internal environment, it would be best to avoid using that firm. If you are satisfied that the search firm is professional, it may be able to help you negotiate the best possible package for your career.

A final avenue of assistance in application for a job in organizational communication is to join some of the major professional communication societies, such as the following:

International Communication Association (Organizational Communication Division), PO Box 9589, Austin, Texas 78766

Industrial Communication Council, PO Box 3970, Grand Central Post Office, New York, New York 10017

Academy of Management (Organizational Communication Division), PO Box KZ, Mississippi State, Mississippi 39762

Speech Communication Association (Organizational Communication Division), 5105 Backlick Rd., Annandale, Virginia 22003

American Business Communication Association, 317-B David Kinley Hall, University of Illinois, Urbana, Illinois 61801

International Association of Business Communicators, 870 Market Street, Suite 928, San Francisco, California 94102

Public Relations Society of America, 845 Third Avenue, New York, New York 10022

OD Network, Block/Petrolla Associates, 1011 Park Avenue, Plainfield, New Jersey 07060.

In addition to helping you maintain professional and personal contacts, these associations for the most part maintain placement services which can identify where the jobs of most interest to you are.

Planning Your Career

After you have been hired in your first organizational communication position, you will begin to think about the eventual career path to follow. The steps involved in successful career planning usually consist of knowing yourself, knowing the choices available to you, and developing yourself for these jobs. Providing the choices available is usually the function of the personnel department, which should post job openings, maintain files of employees interested in transfer or advancement (sometimes called a "ready now" list), and actively communicate job openings to both employees and their immediate supervisor. In developing yourself, you should identify the training and education required to advance toward the career you desire. This means enrolling in training programs, taking college courses, joining community projects, accepting special assignments, and becoming a member of task forces. It may even mean going back to school full-time or part-time to get a degree. However, no amount of education or knowledge of available jobs and career paths will help you advance if you are not aware of your own desires, motivations, and potential. To help you gain such insight, here are a series of short exercises developed by Sandra O'Connell, noted career counselor in organizational communication. Once you feel you have sufficient insights about your own desires, you are ready to begin the search and advancement toward what promises to be a most rewarding career. Good luck!

Career Analysis[4]

Past accomplishments. Consider your school and work history up to now. Make a list of your peak accomplishments. A peak accomplishment is defined as something you did or played a major part in doing, that you especially enjoyed, and that means something to you. Choose accomplishments that gave you a sense of satisfaction. Include some from each period in your life: childhood, school, early work, and current position. Accomplishments may be in the area of school, hobbies, volunteer work, and regular or part-time jobs. A peak accomplishment is not the same as a peak experience. Sharing a sunset with a friend is a peak experience, but unless you played a major part in seeing this happen, it is not a peak accomplishment.

Review your list and select the three which are most meaningful to you in that they reflect the best of your skill and ability.

Write about each of the top three accomplishments in detail. Answer the question, What specifically makes this accomplishment important to me?

Factors of Strength and Interest. Examine the three top accomplishments and underline the words (especially verbs) that indicate what functions or actions you actually performed. List your major actions, that is, what you do that seems to lead to a peak accomplishment. Rank them in the order of how each contributes to your sense of accomplishment.

---

4. The career analysis information appearing on pages 437–38 is used with the permission of Sandra O'Connell, President, O'Connell Consulting (Arlington, Virginia).

One of the methods in career analysis is to choose your peak accomplishments, things you did or played a major part in, that you especially enjoyed, and that mean something to you.

Motivation.   The purpose of this section is to identify what seems to motivate you to reach your peak accomplishments. Note what was important to you about each: what was the payoff? personally? professionally? etc. Rank your motivating factors in terms of importance to you in the future.

Career Planning Inventory.   Fill out the following form:

	What I do well	What I dislike doing	What I do not do well	What I would like to learn	What I would like to stop doing
At work					
Outside work					

The one thing I want most to accomplish is:

The Future

I will close this chapter (and the book) with a speech by Roger D'Aprix[5] that summarizes much of the information in this chapter and provides a glimpse into the future for those of you desiring a career in organizational communication. What will the field offer? What should the role of the corporate communicator be? What values are important to this role? A meaningful and arousing set of answers is provided.

I approach this talk this morning with some concern. My reason for that concern is that this is basically a sequel to what I said last year at our annual meeting. And everyone knows that sequels often leave an audience wishing they had *not* asked for more.

In this case, however, I do feel a responsibility to elaborate on the point I was trying to make in Washington. If you were there, you might recall that I urged people in our business to be less concerned with print and more oriented to the task of human organization. At the end of that speech I uttered some nice words about the need for us to help management build better human relationships with the people they employ.

I confess to you that before I gave that talk I felt a bit uncomfortable about my message. I was worried that I might be seen as a little bit crazy in a profession that has traditionally prided itself mainly on its skills in writing, photography, and design. So I was pleased when a number of you were kind enough to comment favorably on what I had said. And even to see it as novel and original.

But I got my comeuppance at the cocktail party following that session when one member of the audience expressed his appreciation for the sentiments I had expressed and then said pointedly, "But what the hell did you mean?"

I'm grateful today to have the opportunity to try to tell him and you what I think I mean.

In the years ahead I see three separate, but closely related, needs for our profession to address. The first is becoming increasingly evident each year. It is the need for our huge institutional organizations to be more responsive to human values both inside and outside their corporate walls. The days when an organization could justify its existence and its behavior merely by pointing with pride to the bottom line are over. Like it or not, prepared for it or not, the successful executive must make his or her organization more fit for human habitation now and in the years ahead. That trend is underway, and it can only gain momentum as time goes on.

The second need for our profession to address is the issue of *who we are*. We must stop trying to be journalists, on the one hand, or house-organ soloists, on the other. Our profession is coming of age. And if we are to be ready—as Tevye says so beautifully in *Fiddler on the Roof*—we had better understand "who we are and what God expects of us."

The third need I believe we must address is a product of the other two. A corporate organization that is beginning to pay greater attention to human needs can be served best by a communicator who understands his or her responsibility to *make change comprehensible*. In my view that requires intensive and intelligent communication planning. Unfortunately, despite all of the words we have uttered in recent years about the need to plan our communication efforts, that remains the most poorly developed or understood skill in our business. I'll return to that point later on.

So there are the three needs I would cite for our profession in the years to come: the need for the organization to be driven by human as well as financial values, the need for us to comprehend our organizational role, and the need for us to become creative and imaginative communication planners. Let's look a little more deeply.

---

5. From Roger D'Aprix (1977). Used with the permission of Roger D'Aprix.

The trouble with organizational communication is its thin philosophical foundation. If the truth were known, I would bet that most people in the business world still believe that the main reason you communicate with people at work is to make them happy and productive. And it drives them crazy when people who are well-informed are not happier and more productive as a result.

The reason really is very simple. We have advocated respect for human values merely as a *means to use people* more effectively. Rarely do the motivation experts argue the intrinsic worth or the human dignity of people as the justification for respecting human values in our organizations. I suspect the reason is that they believe, rightly or wrongly, that such justification would be rejected by bottom line-oriented senior management.

Unhappily, there is a long-standing tradition in employee communication that this kind of verbal flimflam is the essence of our work. We should communicate with people so that they will not be distracted by misinformation and rumors. So that they will have "high morale" and be loyal to the organization. And so that they will be motivated to be more productive.

I think I know how we got to this juncture. Most senior executives, like the rest of us ordinary mortals, have a need to be liked and respected. They also have a desire to take as little flak as possible. As a profession struggling to win respectability within our various organizations, we fell into the old trap of promising them what they wanted. "Sure, we can take care of your recognition problems. Of course, we know how to make the work force more productive. Absenteeism? Don't give it a thought. We'll run a story on it. People think you're making too much money? We'll educate them to the facts of profit and overhead. Don't trouble yourself." And on and on with the promises we couldn't hope to keep.

And, of course, when the embarrassing questions come back about how we're doing, the response is easy. "Well, you know it really is impossible to *measure* communication and its effects on the work force. By the way, how do you like your latest message to employees that I wrote for your signature for this month's issue . . .?" And so it goes.

It's not really that we have more charlatans per square inch in this profession than in others. The fact of the matter is that we have some really talented people who are very effective communicators.

Where I believe we have gone astray is not bothering to understand or define our organization roles sufficiently. It has always intrigued me that in most of our professional meetings we spend our time talking about better and better technique with little regard for *why* we do what we do. And yet that's the really interesting question.

Too many of us don't know whether we are journalists . . . the voice of management . . . representatives of the employee public . . . or just hired guns. That confusion, unfortunately, often shows through in our work. And it certainly is evident at every gathering of communication professionals where we tend to ignore communication philosophy in favor of technical discussions about how we can produce better media.

Those of you who know me have heard me hold forth in the past about our responsibility to address the sense of alienation the contemporary worker often feels from his or her work. Or more accurately from his or her work organization.

The large, impersonal work organization will continue to be the fate of most workers in highly industrialized societies. Regardless of the profession or the work they choose, there is practically no way our children and our grandchildren can avoid working within large, often bureaucratic, organizations. In my view, the only thing that can make that kind of work experience bearable is a sense of the meaning of one's work and its significance to the whole.

I don't care how modest or large your contribution—to take satisfaction of any sort from it— you must understand its significance in terms that mean something to you. I acknowledge that the intensity of that need vary from person to person, but I still believe that the need is universal.

From that sense of meaning of work comes a sense of hope for the worker in his or her work life. And this, I believe, is where we come into the picture with our professional skills. By ourselves, we can do little to attack the larger problems I'm trying to define. The reason is that media can only serve as the backdrop for the worker's day-to-day experiences on the job and with the person who is managing him. We fool ourselves if we exaggerate our influence with our readers or listeners. At best, we reinforce their own daily experience on the job. At worst, we contradict it.

Where this all leads me is to the belief that we can function most effectively as communicators by counseling our own managements on the total process of communication. Together we must address human needs for information, for understanding, and ultimately for *hope*. That kind of communication, I believe, can only take place within a human relationship which we can reinforce with our various media.

That argues to me that we must address the heretofore unaddressed problem of interpersonal communication between a manager and the people he or she manages. And that's exactly the kind of communication most of us have steered clear of. Why we have done so is not hard to understand. It's too inaccessible. It's too hard to influence it in any way *we* can understand.

And yet it is the line manager who has the most influential communication role in any organization. That that fact has only been dimly understood by everyone concerned is only too evident.

The proposition that we should care about other people, be sensitive to their needs, and be concerned with how we communicate with them is not popular or well received in most organizations. The unspoken question is: Why? What will it do for *me?* What will it mean in accomplishing work goals? Aside from the need to cooperate with other people in doing the work, why should *I* worry about such matters?

There is, in fact, a feeling that concerns of this sort may get in the way of getting the job done. There is the unmistakable view in most institutional organizations that nice guys finish dead last. The way to success, says the organizational folklore, is to be combative and aggressive. And not to trust or care about others. Such attitudes normally lead to an environment that is hostile and even brutal. It is an environment that most of us, if we think about it, personally despise.

I have no glib answers for changing all of this. If there is an answer, it is to be found in our private views of human nature. But where I finally come out is the premise that even in our work organizations we must learn to act with concern and love for other people.

For the hardheaded business person who responds only to winning the game and to the fluctuations in the bottom line which tell him whether he is winning or losing, such behavior may be close to unthinkable. And yet, damn it, that's what all of us want for *ourselves.* We want to be valued, to be recognized, and to be treated fairly. And we want this simply because we believe we have it coming.

I said earlier that communication professionals are often confused about their roles and their responsibilities. Through the years I have thought long and hard on this subject. After lots of reflection I have concluded that the role that makes the most sense to me is to try to be an interpreter of change. I now reject the idea that we should try to be organizational journalists or mere purveyors of information. I once believed that role made sense, but I think people need more raw information. They need some sense of what the information really means in their lives.

Most organizations are uncomfortable with raw information or raw news. Management wants information to be complete—and to be massaged so that it answers more questions than it raises. I think that's a legitimate want, given the fact that information can disrupt as well as satisfy.

That may offend your journalist's heart, but I think the key to all of this is the difference between *reactive* and *proactive* communication. Most journalism, by definition, is reactive. It is merely reporting what has happened without much regard for what it means. It tends to thrive on the offbeat, the titillating, and the novel. At least, that's what it has tended to in most public journalism. Often it leaves the reader a sense of incompleteness, confusion, or even despair.

Proactive communication, on the other hand, tries to anticipate change and explain it as part of a rational process. It tends to anticipate problems and opportunities and to talk about them in terms that mean something to the audience. In short, it is geared to the issue of meaning and hope.

The proactive communicator must become a student of his or her organization. What does such a change mean in the marketplace? What does it mean in the larger society? What effect will it have on the structure and operation of the organization, not to mention its very mission? What will it do to the work force and to the organization's ability to provide jobs?

Several things are implicit in this kind of communication. One of the most important is a carefully developed communication plan which is married to the organization's long-range plans. That communication plan must reflect the organization's personality, its problems, and its priorities.

The number of people in our business who wing it day after day without any plan other than perhaps a story budget for their publication is incredible. If challenged on that score, many of them would sniff at the planning process and retort that they are journalists. Their job is to report the news in the organization.

In the first place, they're wrong about that, and in the second place, I suggest to you that this cavalier attitude toward planning has hurt us badly with our managements. How can they take us seriously when the extent of our plans for the future is what stories to run when? Or what new media or gimmicks we can propose for next year? I submit to you that no other area of an organization is allowed to function in this way. I believe we pay a price with the people who fund us and who decide our worth when we don't visibly marry our efforts to their problems and goals.

I also believe that we in employee communication are now in a position to occupy the communication spotlight. Our management needs us more than ever before. My fear is that as a profession we are not ready; that we are not up to the challenges. The mere fact that so many of our colleagues in this business simply don't know the first thing about communication planning . . . or that they continue to wallow in self-pity about their management's reluctance to turn them loose as organizational journalists . . . gives me pause. The fact that so much of our professional training in meetings and workshops focuses on technique reveals a very limited understanding of the possibilities of our business.

It is not going to be easy to persuade our own managements that this is what employee communication is really all about. They will naturally question what, if anything, we can do to pave the way for acceptance of change. They will undoubtedly continue to see us in the role of media experts to be called on only to focus our media on particular problems one at a time.

However, those of us who are able to understand and carry off the role of proactive communicator will, I think, be able to exploit the full potential of this profession to relate people's humanity and their work lives. In particular I think we have a golden opportunity in the whole area of interpersonal communication between line manager and the people he or she is managing. It's not too unusual in these times to find competent communication staffs, in our large companies particularly, producing slick management newsletters, artful television programs on videocassettes, elaborate telephone message systems, and a host of other programs in addition to the traditional newspaper or magazine.

The problem, however, is that you can't build employee relationships at the other end of a television monitor any better than you can at the other end of a newspaper. This is a human problem to be resolved by human beings face to face, day after day.

The question that nags at me as I suspect it must at you is: What can we do to encourage and foster greater management attention to interpersonal communication? We know that we can't legislate it. We know that managers often fear such communication and the potential price of getting involved with their people. We also know that many managers will botch it up badly.

Then why do it?

My answer is that all of us who work in organizations owe it to one another. The pace of modern life is brutal. The tone of modern life similarly is also brutal. Here is one way to diminish the brutality and to say to people: "Look, you do matter. You have dignity, and I care enough about you to listen to you and to try to give meaning to your life in the workplace."

As communication professionals I believe that we can help create the kind of climate in our organizations where concern for people is seen as appropriate and necessary. The organizational culture of rugged individualism is passing. It has to, in our interconnected and fast-changing organizations. To accomplish the kind of work most people are called upon to do in the postindustrial society, we need teamwork and information sharing, not individuals going it alone.

We in this business, by virtue of the stories we publish, the programs we implement, and most importantly the senior managers we influence, can portray this sort of interpersonal communication as desirable and as necessary. You don't need me to tell you how to do that; you already know.

Through the stories we publish and the subjects we highlight we can provide models of candid communication. We can say subtly and not so subtly to managers in our organizations that it's okay to talk about the tough issues. We can highlight successful communicators in management and tell the world why and how they do it. We can help put on the shelf the old notions of the cowboy capitalist and the machismo manager who stop at nothing to win.

In brief, we can help make it intellectually respectable and even admirable for a manager to behave this way, just as we have made it respectable and admirable over the years for a manager to be seen as a tough-minded, hard-nosed, unsentimental type whose survival depended solely on the bottom line.

And, of course, we can encourage the trainers and even counsel them in the whole process of communication training for our managers. That takes us still further away from the security of print, but I don't see how any communication professional can be worth very much to his or her organization today without understanding the science of organization development and the management process in general.

Facilitating effective communication in this way will not solve all of the problems of the organization. But it will make communication with employees one of the most valuable and honorable of the communication specialties, because it will be helping to establish and reinforce the connection between people's humanity and their work lives.

I believe that the salvation of business both with its own employees and with the public at large rests with our willingness to care and to be honest, ethical, and responsive. I also believe that our obsession with *only* the bottom line of our various businesses is evil. I don't choose that word lightly. That obsession can, and often has, become the end that justifies just about any means.

You and I—by virtue of the kind of jobs and influence we have and the kind of values we share—can help see that the organization is more sensitive to and more responsive to human values than it historically has been. I submit to you that we should argue for those values for their own sake as well as for the well-being of our organizations. That probably means admitting at last that formalized communication alone won't motivate anyone; that it won't make anyone more productive; that it won't increase their loyalty. And that it won't make them one damned bit happier.

From all of this I would conclude that our traditional preoccupation with print and with technique has been a mistake. It has not been just our mistake alone, but it is a mistake nonetheless. The business of communication is really the business of human relationships. That is a tougher business than journalism, and it's not hard to understand why many of us have chosen the simpler, more mundane role of company editor.

In closing I want to remind you of an epitaph which Kurt Vonnegut dedicated to the hero of this book *Mother Night*. He calls him "a man who served evil too openly and good too secretly, the crime of his times."

I continue to believe that Vonnegut's epitaph is also our great occupational hazard.

SUMMARY

In this chapter, we presented an overview of the types of jobs held by organizational communication professionals in the variety of organizations in which they are employed. We discussed in detail the specific skills employed by these professionals as they perform their daily duties. Lists of job descriptions and job advertisements were presented to give further insight into the job of organizational communicator. Details about the course work and educational training needed to secure many of these positions were given. Information about cover letters, résumés, and interview guides was presented along with advice on how to confront the search firm. The steps involved in successful career pathing were outlined and a series of exercises to help gain insight into the motivations, needs, and accomplishments in your work was presented. The chapter concluded with a look at the future of the employee communication function.

EXERCISES

1. Study the job advertisements in the *New York Times, The Wall Street Journal,* and a local paper. Cut out the ones that either directly or indirectly call for organizational communication skills. Bring the advertisements to class and discuss the specific skills required for each job.
2. Select the job that you believe you are most qualified for (or will be qualified for when you graduate). Construct a cover letter to apply for the job.
3. What is the purpose of the cover letter?
4. List the characteristics of a good cover letter.
5. What is the purpose of the résumé?
6. Prepare your résumé. Attach the cover letter to it and mail these documents either to the organization whose job you are applying for or to a search firm that will help you find a job. Discuss your response.
7. Write to an organization to ask for its annual report. Look up this organization's financial history in *Standard and Poor's Register of Corporations* or *Dun and Bradstreet's Book of Corporation Management.* Also, check the indexes of the *New York Times* and *The Wall Street Journal* for additional information about this organization.
8. Based upon this information, construct an interview guide to use when you apply for a position in organizational communication.

9. Register with your placement center. Select at least three people who know you and are familiar with your competence, career goals, and personality, and ask each to write a letter of reference. File the letters with your placement center. Arrange for an interview with an organization that you are only mildly interested in. This interview can help you get firsthand practice in preparation for later interviews that interest you more. Prior to the interview, research the company (see exercise 7) and prepare a list of questions that you think could be useful in making your decision. Conduct the interview. What did you do well? do poorly? Share the results with the class.
10. List the characteristics of a good résumé.

BIBLIOGRAPHY AND REFERENCES

Business First of Buffalo, 12 September 1987.

D'Aprix, R. "Beyond Print: The Unfolding Role of Employee Communication." Keynote Address given at a meeting of the Industrial Communication Council, San Francisco, 1977.

Downs, C., and M. Larimer. "The Status of Organizational Communication in Speech Departments." Paper presented at a meeting of the International Communication Association, New Orleans, 1974.

Downs, C., and J. Tanner. "The Study of Decision Making in Selection Interviews." Unpublished manuscript, University of Kansas, 1982.

Foltz, R. "Communicating with Top Management." Paper presented at a meeting of the International Association of Business Communication, Denver, 1976.

Goldhaber, G. "Organizational Communication: Research and Curricular Perspectives." Speech given at the University of South Florida, Tampa, 1975.

IABC Profile 87, San Francisco, Ca.: IABC.

Leaper, Norman, G. "The Changing Role of the Professional Communicator." Speech presented at the XII Encuentro de Communicacion Organizacional AMCO. Ciudad de Mexico, D.F., Mexico. September 11, 1987.

Marshall Consultants. "Reverse Trend Seen in Communications Job Market." *ICC Newsletter* (December 1975):2–3.

O'Connell, S. "Career Options in Organizational Communication." *ACA Bulletin* 18 (October 1976).

Petrie, C., E. Thompson, D. Rogers, and G. Goldhaber. "Report of the Ad Hoc Committee on Manpower Resources." Report prepared for a meeting of Division IV of the International Communication Association, Chicago, April 1975.

PHOTO CREDITS

NAME INDEX

SUBJECT INDEX

Formal behavior, in network
communication, 21
Formal communication, 151
Formal network relationships,
152
Formal organization, 32
Scott's definition, 38
Formal role relationships, 152
Formal small-group activities,
241
Formal structure, 40
Fortune, 304, 434
Functional division of labor, 38,
39
Functional principle, 159
Functional roles, and group
variables, 241–243
Functionalist, 15–16
Fundamental interpersonal
relations orientation. *See*
FIRO theory
Furniture, and nonverbal
communication, 195–198

Gatekeeper, 377–378
Gay Liberation, 292
General counsels, *4*
General Electric Company, 288,
294
General interest, 36
General model of instruction. *See*
GMI
General Motors, 32, *45,* 109,
154, 261, 264–265, 291
General Services Administration,
38
General systems theory, 47
General training model. *See*
GTM
Gestures, and posture, 181
GeVa Theatre, 143
GMI, 389
Goals, organizational, and
measurement of
effectiveness, 51
Gobbledygook exercise, 133
Goodwrench, Mr., 291
Grace Commission, *8–9*
Grapevine, 161–163
Graphic Controls Corporation,
251
Graphics Control, 306
Great Britain, 261
and communication studies,
191
and factors of public
organizational
communication, 284
Greenbaum conceptual structure,
347–354

Group
ecology, and networks, 244–247
interaction analysis, Bale's, 259
level, and organizational
restructure, 57
in message networks, 147
variables, key, 241–258
Group Dynamics Center, 87
Groups, types of, in
organizations, 240–241
Groupthink, 105
GTM, 387, 389–390
Gunning-Fog Index, 370

Haney's Uncritical Test, 410
Hard diffusion methods, 153
Hard S's, 106
Hardware
and messages, 20
methods, 137
uses, 397
Harris Poll, 98
Harvard Business Review, 45
Harvard University, 77
Haskins and Sells, 306
Hawthorne studies, 43, 45, 77,
78, 80, 81, 87, 197, 255,
367
Hay Management Consultants,
67
Hay's ethical classification
system, 339
Hero, and charisma, 101
Herzberg's motivation-hygiene
model, 90
Hewlett-Packard, 5, 72, 75, 193
Hierarchal rules, 130
Hierarchy of needs, Maslow's,
78–81, 82
High Performance Goals, in
communication climate, 68
High-status personnel, and
nonverbal communication,
186–187
Hired hands, 92
Homophily studies, 346
Honesty, in organizational
relationships, introduced,
211
Honeywell, 261
Hong Kong
Job Titles, 420–421
Hooker Chemical Company, 306
Horizontal communication, 22,
23, 159–160
Human messages, 20, 144–145
Human needs, and Maslow,
78–81
Human relations
and human resources, 45
model, compared to human
resources model, 78

in participative leadership, 79
school, or organizational
theory, 43–46
Human resources
approach, to leadership and
management, 77–80
and human relations, 45
Japanese models of, 104–110
key, and leadership theories,
78–93
model, compared to human
relations model, 78
and motivation research,
introduced, 94
movement, key propositions,
92–93
in participative leadership, 79
Hyatt Hotel, 159

IABC, 326, 420, 425
address, 436
Communication World, 425
IBM, 74, 83, 252, 287, 294
ICA, 7, 338, 354–355, 375, 380
address, 436
communication audit, 354
Illustrators, 177
I Love New York, 292
Image making, and industrial
positioning, 291–294
Imagery, and charisma, 102
I'm Only Trying To Help You.
See ITHY
Implicit norms, 252
Inclusion, in small groups, 239
Individual communication
behavior, 143
Individual interest, 36
Individual level, and
organizational restructure,
56–57
Individual rules, 129
Industrial Communication
Council, address, 436
Industrial positioning, and image
making, 291–294
Industry, use of public
communication, 303–307
Informal
behavior, in network
communication, 21
communication, 152
network relationships, 161–165
organization, 45
role relationships, 152
small-group activities, 241
space, 190
Informational boundary-spanning
model, 280–281
Informational objectives, *13*

454   SUBJECT INDEX

Information
  control, and power, *5*
  processing, 139–140
  retrieval, 140
  sharing, 160
  shock, *4*
  transfer, 140–141
Information Systems Group. *See* ISG
Initiating structure, 87
Initiative, 37
Inner circle, 92
Innovative messages, 20, 147
Input
  in open system, 50
  procedural, 334
  theoretical, 334
Institute for Social Research, 84
Integration, 93–94
Intended receivers, 20
Interaction
  and room design, 196
  modeling modules, 404–406
Interactive computers, 141
Interdependence
  in organizational communication, 16, 23
Intergroup conflict, 256–257
Internal activities
  And public organizational communication, 288–289
  of public organizations, 294
Internal communication activities, 144
Internal Communication Association. *See* ICA
Internal contingencies, 96
Internal resources, in organizational development, 320–321
Internal Revenue Service. *See* IRS
Internal use of messages, 20
International Association of Business Communicators. *See* IABC
Interpersonal communication, 25
Interpretive paradigm, 17
Interracial communication problems, 182, 185
Intervention
  activities, in organizational development, 331–335
  practical problems of, 335–336
Interview
  in communication audit, 358
  for job, 430, 434–436
  questionnaire-, techniques, in communication audit, 368–370
Intimate distance, 190

Intragroup conflict, 257
Intrinsic conflict, 257
IRS, 37
ISG, 425, 426
Isolates, in message networks, introduced, 148

Japan
  and communication studies, 193
  government, and Lockheed Aircraft, 286
  models, of human resources, 104–110
  organizations, traditional and emerging, 107–108
  and quality circles, 260
J.C. Penney Co., 277
JET, 224
Job
  aids, 436
  applying for, 427–436
  and career paths, 419–426
  expectation technique. *See* Jet
  satisfaction, 142, 217
    and communication climate, 68–70
  tenure, and communication contingencies, 96
  titles in Australia, 420–421
  titles in Canada, 420–421
  titles in Hong Kong, 420–421
  titles in United Kingdom, 420–421
  titles in United States, 420–421
Jobholders meeting, *5*
Junk-communication phenomenon, *5*
Junk-food industry, *8*

Kansas State University, 298
Kick in the Ass, 90
Kinesics, 177–178
KITA, 90
KLM Royal Dutch Airlines, 123
K-mart, 164

Labor, division of, 38, 39
Labor-management committees. *See* LMC
Labor unions
  use of public communication, 294–296
Language modality, 19
Leader Behavior Description Questionnaire, 87
Leadership
  charisma factor in, 99–104
  contingency, 94–97

grid, 87, 88
  and group variables, 243–244
  human resources approaches to, 77–80
  participative, two models of, 79
  Tannenbaum's continuum, 244
  theories, and key human resources, 78–93
Learning, in communication training, 408–409
Lecture, 395–397
Legal factors, and public organizational communication, 285–286
Liaisons, in message networks, introduced, 149
Likert's systems, 84–85, 86, 87
Line organization, 39
Listening improvement programs, 396–397
Listening techniques, and dyadic relationships, 222–223
LMC, 86
Lockheed Aircraft, 286
Los Angeles Times, 98, 109
Love, in organizational relationships, introduced, 211
Lucasfilms, *5*

McDonald's Corp., 164
McGregor's Theory X and Theory Y, 81–84, 374, 396
Maintenance messages, 19, 145
Management
  of attention through vision, 95
  and communication problems, *9*
  Fayol's principles of, 36–37
  goals of, 94
  human resources approaches to, 77–80
  in intervention problems, 335
  of meaning through communication, 95
  by objectives. *See* MBO
  scientific, 36
  of self, 95
  of trust through constancy, 95
  value differentiation, 98–110
  walk-around, 63
Managers
  Peter-Principled, 23
  scientific, 77
  two-boss, 54, 55, 56
Managing up, 227–228
Manifest behavior, 220
Manipulation, 45
Marketing executives, *4*
Marshall Consultants, 420
Maslow's hierarchy, 80, 92, 238
Matrix organizations, 54–56